Planning Canadian Communities

An Introduction to the Principles, Practice, and Participants

Sixth Edition

Planning Canadian Communities

An Introduction to the Principles, Practice, and Participants

Sixth Edition

Gerald Hodge

David L.A. Gordon
School of Urban and Regional Planning
Queen's University

NELSON / EDUCATION

NELSON / EDUCATION

Planning Canadian Communities: An Introduction to the Principles, Practice, and Participants, Sixth Edition

by Gerald Hodge and David L.A. Gordon

Vice President, Editorial Higher Education:
Anne Williams

Publisher:
Paul Fam

Executive Editor:
Jackie Wood

Marketing Manager:
Leanne Newell

Developmental Editor:
Rebecca Ryoji

Photo Researcher:
Natalie Barrington

Permissions Coordinator:
Natalie Barrington

Content Production Manager:
Hedy Sellers

Production Service:
Cenveo Publisher Services

Copy Editor:
Maria Jelinek

Proofreader:
GanesanRamalingam

Indexer:
BIM Indexing Services

Manufacturing Manager:
Joanne McNeil

Design Director:
Ken Phipps

Managing Designer:
Franca Amore

Interior Design:
Trinh Truong

Cover Design:
Trinh Truong

Cover Image:
Top left: © Bill Brooks/Alamy; top right: © Robert Fried/Alamy; bottom left: Dave Reede/Getty Images; bottom right: Albert Normandin/Masterfile.

Compositor:
Cenveo Publisher Services

Library and Archives Canada Cataloguing in Publication Data

Hodge, Gerald Planning Canadian communities : an introduction to the principles, practice, and participants / Gerald Hodge, David L.A. Gordon. — 6th ed.

Includes bibliographical references and index.
ISBN 978-0-17-650982-8

1. City planning—Canada—Textbooks. I. Gordon, David L. A., 1954– II. Title.

HT169.C2H62 2013
307.1'20971   C2013-900842-X

ISBN-13: 978-0-17-650982-8
ISBN-10: 0-17-650982-8

To our students past, present and future - in many ways our teachers.

Contents

part two

Chapter 6

Chapter 7

Chapter 8

Chapter 9

Chapter 10

part three

part four

part five

Chapter 16

Chapter 17

Epilogue

Appendix   **446**

Index   **449**

List of Figures

Preface

With this edition, *Planning Canadian Communities* begins its 27th year of analysis of the public endeavour of community planning in the cities, towns, and regions of Canada. The past two and a half decades have been a time of immense learning, both for the field of community planning and for the authors. The task of community planning has become broader and more complex, as has the task reflecting upon it between these covers. One constant in this edition, as with its predecessors, is that it remains a personal view of how community planning started, how it works today, and who participates in it, albeit of two authors. Within this perspective, we occasionally offer our views of its shortcomings and its potential for further development.

Another constant is our belief that the *community plan* is an essential component in Canadian planning practice. A plan cannot, of course, be realistically attained and maintained without the use of effective and fully participatory processes; but processes without a plan to achieve are little more than political self-indulgence. Successful community planning is, therefore, a blend of both *plan* and *process*. Another constant is our view that there is a *Canadian* mode of community planning. In the hybrid tradition of this country, British, French, and American planning approaches have combined with our own needs and cultures to produce a distinctive and often-envied style and approach. A primary aim of this book is, thus, to examine community planning in diverse settings across this country and to reveal its *Canadian-ness*. In pursuit of this goal, we try to make the often bewildering array of activities and institutions that occur under the rubric of community planning more understandable to students of planning, practising professionals, and, not least, citizens.

We are aware that it is a tall order to facilitate a dialogue about the best way to build ecologically, economically, physically, and socially sound, as well as sustainable communities. And it is a task that has become no less easy in the 27 years since this book was first published (and promises not to become any easier in the future). However, presenting these topics through the structure comprising community planning's *principles, practice,* and *participants* still seems viable. And to aid in this, the sixth edition has three new chapters on neighbourhood plans, infrastructure, and planning for diverse and healthy communities. The other chapters have been extensively revised, so the entire book has been extensively renovated since the fourth edition to reflect the state of Canadian community planning practice at the beginning of the 21st century.

The introductory chapters dealing with the history and background of community planning were updated to include new scholarship on Canadian planning history from the 19th and 20th centuries. The chapters dealing with planning practice have been revised and extended to better reflect current perspectives in the field including those of planning for small, rural, and Aboriginal communities. A new section has been added that gathers the three new chapters on planning for people and places within the community.

Likewise, the chapters dealing with planning's participants have been broadened to reflect not only the diversity of people in our communities but also the most recent thinking regarding this key component. References to the literature have more than doubled to reflect the burgeoning Canadian writing on community planning, and a new set of "case studies," Planning Issues, which depict how current planning problems are being dealt with in communities across Canada, are integrated with the revised and updated text. We have more than doubled the number of illustrations in the book, featuring images from plans that won national awards from the Canadian Institute of Planners. An updated selection of relevant websites enhances the scope of each chapter, and a website devoted to the book includes additional online links, colour illustrations, and a comprehensive bibliography: www.planningcanadiancommunities.ca

In the end, community planning cannot be done from a book or a website. But it is our hope that these pages may foster a greater appreciation of the need for visions—plans—of what Canadian communities can become, plans that engage and involve the community in their preparation and implementation.

Acknowledgments

A substantial revision of a book, such as occurred for this sixth edition, reveals again how much depends upon the contributions of others. They helped us, as in the past, to build on the strong foundations created by the five previous editors, in order: Peter Milroy, Dave Ward, Avivah Wargon, Karina Hope, and Heather Parker. The team at Nelson for this edition were not only patient with the authors' schedules but in the face of knotty problems were also helpful and creative in solving them. We would like to thank especially Jackie Wood, Rebecca Ryoji, Maria Jelinek, Hedy Sellers, and Natalie Barrington. Thanks also to Serena Howett for last-minute proofing. Numerous other readers, reviewers, students, and colleagues also contributed along the way, not the least being the late Kent Gerecke. To all of them we offer our thanks for their support and thoughtful comments, and apologize for not being able to mention each one.

Many of Andrew Milos's original graphics remain, with others by Kelly McNicol and Xian Zhang following the same format. Our appreciation extends expressly to the Canadian Institute of Planners, who made their collection of award-winning plans available, and to Wayne Caldwell (Guelph), Patrick Condon (UBC), Cleo Corbett (Vernon), Andres Duany (Miami), Avi Friedman (McGill), John Guenther (Revelstoke), and Catherine Gryba (Saskatoon), who provided additional images. Throughout, Jo-Anne Rudachuk responded with forbearance and good humour when faced with yet another draft manuscript to process. Our research assistants deserve special thanks for timely and thoughtful contributions, especially Morgan Alger and Simona Rasanu who advised us from China and Guyana, after they left campus for international internships. Saharsadat Aghabozorgafjeh, Josh Berry, Golsa Kheirmoghadam, and Isaac Shirokoff provided last-minute assistance from Kingston. And, while in Cold Lake, Alberta, Tasha Elliott revised the table on planning legislation. Lastly, Raktim Mitra's original website for the book provided a good foundation to build upon.

Other Canadian planners advised us on provincial planning legislation, practice, and terminology, for which we are indebted, especially to Michèle Bertol (Iqaluit), Neil Craik (UNB), Steven Croft (Halifax), Howard Epstein (Dalhousie), Jane Glenn (McGill), Jill Grant (Dalhousie), Felix Hoehn (U. of Saskatchewan), Steven Horn (Yukon), Barb Jeffrey (York Region), Eran Kaplinsky (U. of Toronto), Andrea Law (Vancouver), Clarissa Lo (Iqaluit), Byron Miller (U. of Calgary), Elaine Mitchell (St. John's), Nalini Naidoo (Yellowknife), Ken O'Brien (St. John's), J.F. Schommer (Regina), Joy St. John (Concordia), Shelley Steel (Calgary), and George Stetkiewicz (Yukon). Not least, our thanks to the librarians at the Hornby Island Branch of the Vancouver Island Regional Library for facilitating many interlibrary loans and to John Meligrana for bringing the Queen's University Library to the West Coast.

The Social Sciences and Humanities Research Council of Canada and a Fulbright Fellowship supported David Gordon's suburbs and planning history research, which also benefited from comments by Eugenie Birch (Penn), Raphael Fischler (McGill), and Larry Vale (MIT). Our colleagues at Queen's University, Ajay Agarwal, Hok-Lin Leung, John Meligrana, Mohammad Qadeer, and Leela Viswanathan, provided new insights on infrastructure, feminist approaches, diversity, planning theory, and multiculturalism, and were always generous in their support. Other colleagues provided valuable suggestions in the course of preparing this edition, including David Amborski (Ryerson), Chris Fullerton (Brock), Penny Gurstein (UBC), Marcus Moos (Waterloo), Leonie Sandercock (UBC), Ryan Walker (Saskatchewan), Gerda Wekerle (York), and anonymous reviewers from seven other institutions. To the latter, we may not have written exactly the book you wanted, but your suggestions strongly influenced our revisions. And, as any teacher will attest, our students are a constant source of new insights and ideas—it is a rare week without another suggestion from another student or alumnus for the next edition of the book. We can only apologize that it sometimes takes a few years to answer some of the best questions from the classroom. Of course, no one named above is responsible for the book's contents or its stance; that responsibility remains with us.

Finally, as every author knows, there are not sufficient words or ways to acknowledge the companionship, patience, and support of one's partner when so much attention turns toward a book. To ours, Sharron Milstein and Katherine Rudder, very special thanks.

Gerald Hodge
Hornby Island, British Columbia

David L.A. Gordon
Kingston, Ontario

January 2013

About the Authors

Gerald Hodge is one of Canada's foremost community and regional planners. Dr. Hodge has been involved in planning, education, and research for more than 50 years. From 1973 to 1986, he was Director of the School of Urban and Regional Planning at Queen's University and has also taught planning at the Universities of Toronto, Calgary, and Hawaii, the Western Australian Institute of Technology, and UBC. Among his many publications are *Planning Canadian Regions* (with I.M. Robinson) and *Towns and Villages in Canada* (with M.A. Qadeer). Now retired to Hornby Island, B.C., he continues to write on planning matters, especially those concerned with Canada's aging population resulting in his recent book, *The Geography of Aging: Preparing Communities for the Surge in Seniors.* He remains involved in local planning issues such as the Age-Friendly Communities project for his home island. In 2008, he received the CIP President's Award for his contributions. He holds a Ph.D. from MIT, an M.C.P. from the University of California at Berkeley, and a B.A. from UBC.

David Gordon is Professor and Director of the School of Urban and Regional Planning at Queen's University. Prior to returning to Queen's, he practised in the public and private sector for 15 years, twice sharing the Canadian Institute of Planners' National Award of Distinction. His publications on planning history and urban redevelopment include *Planning Twentieth Century Capital Cities* and *Battery Park City: Politics and Planning on the New York Waterfront.* David has also taught urban design and development at Harvard, Pennsylvania, Ryerson, and University of Toronto. He holds a D.Des. from Harvard and an M.Pl. and B.Sc. from Queen's.

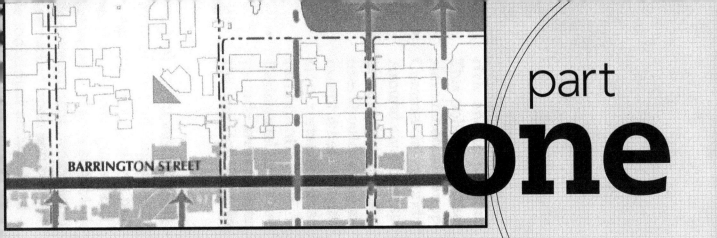

part one

The Foundations of Canadian Community Planning

Introduction

Our communities and the methods we use for planning them are a legacy of the past. Community planning did not grow independently of real urban problems in real cities and towns; nor did the approaches taken toward their solutions. Rather, it evolved alongside changing urban problems and perceptions of them by people, professionals, and governments. Over time, the experience of city building and rebuilding spawned various principles that came to be embodied in today's community planning. They include long-standing ideals, ideas, and premises regarding the physical form of communities and the natural environments that they share, along with the social needs of residents and the institutional means of planning. Our contemporary views of community planning are an amalgam of both past and present practice. The following chapters describe the unfolding of Canadian community planning to the present day.

The image above is from the project Halifax Waterfront Open Space and Development Plan, Halifax, Nova Scotia, which received the Canadian Institute of Planners' Award for Planning Excellence, Category of Overall Presentation, 2002.

Source: © Waterfront Development, Halifax.

1

Chapter One
The Need for Community Planning

Cities do not grow—all of them are planned.

Thomas Adams, 1922

Consider this: Canadian communities as diverse and widespread as Iqaluit in Nunavut, Ucluelet on the B.C. coast, Truro in Nova Scotia, Yellowknife, Winnipeg, Sudbury, and St. John's have, in the past decade, each framed plans to better their community! This is a testament to the value these cities and towns, and many dozens of others large and small, place on having a means to shape their growth and development. Clearly, community planning and plan-making, now well into its second one hundred years, is held in strong regard in Canada. Even in contentious situations such as the building of new shopping centres, high-rise apartments, and highways, or the demolition of historic buildings and the failure to conserve open space, the debates that surround them are not about the need for planning, but for *better* planning—not *whether* but *how* it should be done.

In every province and territory there exists some form of legislation that both sanctions the practice of planning and specifies the format of plans for that region's communities.[1] From coast-to-coast-to-coast it is considered a normal and necessary public function. However, even what has become a plethora of governmental and legislative means to facilitate community planning does not explain *why* a community needs planning. The sets of planning procedures and legalistic steps—zoning, subdivision control, height limits, and so forth—may sometimes seem overwhelming, but they are not in themselves community planning. They are the means to accomplishing it, not its ends.

The real need for planning arises when people in a community, its citizens, realize a desire to improve their community's built and natural environment. This need was not always so widely accepted, as we shall see in the following chapters. Slum conditions, unsanitary water and waste situations, and shabby townscapes were common well into the last century. That they are much less so today speaks for the growing influence of planning ideals and ideas to better community living spaces. Just as contemporary concerns raised by communities differ from those of the past, the resolution of future concerns will require innovations that we may barely imagine now. The planners for today's cities and towns work within community contexts in which populations have grown larger, aged, and become more culturally diverse. Additionally, citizens have become engaged by ideas that their communities can be environmentally sound and walkable and, not least, insistent on being part of the community-planning process. This makes for a more demanding climate for today's planners, and requires more sharply focusing on two questions that pervade much of the practice of community planning and all the chapters of this book:

- *What is community planning essentially about?*
- *How is the complexity and diversity of a community best planned for?*

The Essential Need for Community Planning

In order to appreciate the *raison d'être* for the planning that abounds in most communities, let us begin by focusing on the sorts of actions a few Canadian communities have taken.[2] This will provide a basis for deriving some guiding principles about the essential need for community planning.

- *Iqaluit*, the capital of Nunavut, won an international award for its Core Area and Capital District Plan, which aims to define the city in a way that is sensitive to the arctic environment and respects Inuit culture.
- Downtown plans for *Vernon*, B.C., and *Sudbury*, Ontario, have recently been on those communities' agendas with both seeking better street connections, walkability, and beauty in their historic central areas, and both being the outcome of extensive participation of their citizens.
- The *Flying Dust First Nation* of Meadow Lake, Saskatchewan, created, designed, and built their

Environmental Research Pavilion, as intended by their community plan, with the aim to help community members understand, protect, enhance, and monitor the environment. *Thunder Bay*, Ontario, celebrated its Aboriginal heritage with its new Spirit Park on the shore of Lake Superior (see Figure 1.5).

- The channel of the Little River in *Windsor*, Ontario, used to be a tire-filled wasteland; now it is rehabilitated and part of the city's plan for a connected greenway for the whole city.
- Distressed public housing projects, such as *Montréal's Benny Farm* and *Toronto's Regent Park* (Figure 1.1), are being redeveloped as green, mixed-income communities that incorporate social housing.
- *Abbotsford*, a metropolitan area suburb on Vancouver's eastern fringe, has a new neighbourhood, Auguston, which follows the design principles of the New Urbanism, with mixed housing types, garages in back lanes, front porches, and walks from the local commercial area. In *Calgary*, the Garrison Woods neighbourhood follows these same principles.
- The *City of Red Deer* and *Red Deer County* in Alberta have a concept plan for their river valley, which includes 136 kilometres of trails and 13 park nodes because its citizens place a high value on outdoor activities.
- In 2010, the Town of *Truro* in Nova Scotia adopted its Community Sustainability Plan in fulfillment of its own Sustainability Charter with its three broad aims: stewardship of the natural environment, pursuit of a thriving economy, and building a just and vibrant community.
- *Burnaby*, B.C., an old inner suburb on Vancouver's eastern edge, has had in place since 2011 a Social Sustainability Strategy to meet its challenges of increasing cultural diversity, high levels of poverty, and limited municipal resources. It envisions a community that is inclusive, livable, and resilient.
- *Fermont*, a resource town of 5,000 in Québec's sub-arctic region, has a unique weatherproof downtown core, while in *Tumbler Ridge*, B.C., *Leaf Rapids*, Manitoba, and *Fort McMurray*, Alberta, the planners also paid attention to the climate and the need to keep land uses compact for easy access in all seasons.

What do all these planning initiatives—the New Urbanism neighbourhood in Calgary; a refurbished downtown in Vernon; the Environmental Research Pavilion in Meadow Lake; and the restoration and conservation of riverbanks in Windsor—have in common? For one, each of these planning efforts deals with various elements of a community's built and natural environment.

Each community also undertook to make a plan for the purpose of achieving a goal desired by its citizens. In short, the answer to our question is: **community planning is about citizens aspiring to a *preferred* future for their built and natural environment**.

More specifically, the community preferences we see expressed in these examples arise from either, or both, of two basic needs. The situation of Fermont is helpful, for in providing a sheltering downtown core there is less need for its citizens to be exposed to extreme winter weather. Or, as at Thunder Bay's Spirit Park (Figure 1.5) Aboriginal and non-Aboriginal citizens alike can recapture some of their heritage. A look at the other examples will shows that either problems or aspirations, or both, regarding a community's built and natural environments guided the planning activity. Thus, there are two principal reasons that a community is stimulated to make their community plan, or renew it:

1. **A community may wish to *solve problems* associated with its present development and avoid related problems in the future;** and/or

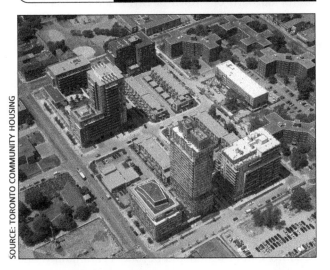

Figure 1.1	Redevelopment of Regent Park in Toronto

This troubled 1950s public housing project was a product of the urban renewal era. After extensive consultation with the residents, a plan was developed to replace every social housing unit while adding new condominium apartments, townhouses, shops, and community facilities. New streets, parks, and community services should improve the quality of life for the residents. The plan won the 2003 National Planning Award from the Canadian Institute of Planners and may take 20 years to implement.

2. **A community may aspire to *improve* the form, functioning, or fairness of its built and natural environment for all who live there.**

These two needs are often intertwined. For example, a community faced with the need to solve a particular development problem (e.g., the cleanup of a river course, as with Windsor) may decide to reassess its overall plan for parks and greenways. Likewise, plans that aim for preferred forms, functioning, or fairness almost always encounter latent development problems that need a solution.

The Need to Solve Present (and Avoid Future) Development Problems

Of the two basic reasons noted above, a community's need to solve present or prevent future problems in its built and natural environment, is probably the one most people think of first. The problematic situations that spark planning action reflect the concerns and conditions of the time. In the late-1990s and into the new millennium, for example, actual and potential deterioration of the natural environment were prominent planning concerns, and sustainable development projects like Simon Fraser University's UniverCity were highly praised (Figure 1.2). In the 1980s, growth management and affordable housing occupied much of planners' attention. And in the 1970s, the concerns were very often about the effects that new, large-scale projects might have on existing residential and public areas—e.g., apartment complexes, expressways, second airports, and shopping centres. The 1960s began with major concerns over physical deterioration in communities; urban renewal became the hoped-for solution, until the "bulldozer approach" used to achieve it was called into question. Canadian urban communities in the two decades after World War II were concerned with how to accommodate burgeoning populations—how to provide them with housing, public utilities, schools, and parks, as well as how to cope with their infatuation with the automobile. The problem of housing for the urban poor concerned communities in the 1950s (and 50 years before that), and still does today, but we now call it homelessness.

Because cities and towns are always changing, every decade has its characteristic problems, as well as new versions of past problems. Communities may grow in population numbers and the area they occupy or decline

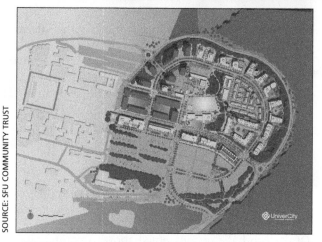

SOURCE: SFU COMMUNITY TRUST

The new neighbourhood adjacent to Simon Fraser University has been designed to the highest environmental standards, incorporating best practices for buildings, infrastructure, and public spaces. UniverCity has won environmental planning awards from the CIP and the American Planning Association.

in their economic well-being. Or their populations may diversify in cultural makeup and then demand to be heard in regard to their neighbourhood and its equitable treatment. Or women in the community may insist on being included in planning safer public transit. Thus, even when there is no quantitative growth, there will be changes in the population, buildings, and infrastructure that go on continually. The contemporary trend of dramatic population aging and the new needs it portends for housing, neighbourhood walkability, etc. is just a sample (see Chapter 13). The development of the built and natural environment of a community, new or old, can be overtaken by new trends in the economy, technology, attitudes, new activities, and populations. Whatever the source of change, each community will have to confront or plan to avoid development problems at one time or another. These will include traffic congestion, housing affordability, deteriorating natural environments, and neighbourhood stability, to name just a few.

Growth and Development Problems

Although the content of the "agenda" for planning may differ among communities, a common feature of all is the need for planning to deal with problems associated with growth and its consequent development.

The Vancouver Metropolitan Area is currently adding population at about 40 000 persons per year or 20 000 new households each year, for example. At the same time, many smaller communities in rural regions of B.C. and elsewhere are stable or declining in population numbers. Other places face a growth in the number of automobiles in their downtown areas while still others lose jobs as factories close. Each of these instances of **quantitative change**, either positive or negative, in turn, triggers other changes: more people usually means the need for more housing and traffic capacity; fewer elderly people may have the opposite effect. Sometimes, both negative and positive change may occur at the same time with mixed results. Thus, when we talk about "growth" in a community, it refers to either increases or decreases in the size of the population, the number of structures, the traffic, the space required for the community, and so on, that is **quantitative change.**

"Development," by contrast, refers generally to **qualitative change** in the community, such as the buildup of new areas, the replacement of one land use with another, a shift in the cultural mix of the population, or the emergence of new modes of building and doing business. A typical development situation these days is found in the growth of "big-box" retailing on the outskirts of a town or city; this often has major implications for a community's established downtown area and for its road network. An analogy from early in the 20th century would be the cities and towns that were trying to accommodate an influx of new population while trying to cope with the spread of disease and extensive fires (see Chapter 4). Housing was then in short supply and often inadequate, as were water and sewage systems, where they existed at all. Both examples indicate that growth and development may generate problems that affect the whole community. Further, both situations not only posed threats to parts of the established community but also caused uncertainty about the future form and condition of the overall community.

Both growth and development arise from a variety of sources, both within and beyond a community, and are always occurring. So, *is planning needed just because there is growth and development?* The answer to this is that the need for planning depends upon whether the growth and development give rise to actual or anticipated problems *for* the community and/or curtail the achievement of desired future conditions. In other words, the answer is yes, if planning will protect the interests of its citizenry.

The Public Interest

It was stated above that planning is concerned with a community attaining preferred future conditions regarding its built and natural environments. The *community's* preferences are thus the prime consideration when seeking a solution to growth and development problems, that is, in making a plan. Indeed, it is the "sum" of these community preferences that validates any proposed plan for they are considered to reflect the "public good," that is, to be in the "**public interest**." In other words, community planning aims to promote the interest of the entire public—of all citizens—and thereby gives social legitimacy to plans that are adopted.

As reasonable as this principle sounds, obtaining community agreement about what constitutes the public interest is not a simple matter. In 19th century Canada, decades passed before the public health and safety problems that plagued its cities were recognized and acted upon (see Chapter 3). If this seems incredible to us today, we need only consider that it is more than five decades since Rachel Carson, in her book *Silent Spring*, alerted us to the dangers of environmental degradation and pollution, problems that continue to plague us. In part, the task of identifying the public interest is made more complex by the fact that our communities are composites of privately owned properties, structures, and services—not to mention vehicles—and publicly provided facilities, programs, and means of travel and communication. All the diverse interests implied by this are involved in maintaining and developing communities, and their preferences do not always coincide. Much of community planning, therefore, involves trying to reconcile private and public preferences into acceptable community preferences to solve problems caused by growth and development. This is not always accomplished smoothly or quickly, and there is probably no reason to expect that either agreement or equanimity will always prevail in planning issues.

On the private side of the community, those whose interests lie in maintaining a stable, tranquil setting of a neighbourhood, for example, may clash with those who wish to pursue long-held development objectives and rights to change their properties and structures. Or there may be clashes between private interests and the public good such as proposals for development in what the community considers inappropriate locations. Halifax's concern that new development might block historic views is a typical case (Planning Issue 2.1, page 30), and so is the concern in many communities over allowing housing developments in flood-prone areas.

Sometimes clashes arise over proposals by public bodies to accommodate growth or new technologies, such as building an expressway, a subway, or a wind farm. Not infrequently, there are clashes between different public bodies and their interests and aspirations, as in where to locate dump sites for toxic wastes. Ironically, in such clashes each side tends to advocate *its* position as being for the common good, in the public interest.

How can this be? And how can planners "sum" the various preferences, especially with our communities accommodating more and more diverse interests? It is coming to be seen more and more that the "public interest" is not monolithic and neutral. Our cities and towns are made up of "multiple publics," each with a potentially different view of the public good.[3] The one-time scenario of a single, solid cornerstone of the public interest, which planners tended and interpreted in the realm of physical development, is shifting in the face of the increasing diversity of people and interests in today's cities and towns. The public interest is coming to be seen as something that *becomes known* through processes of consensus-building and collaborative planning.[4] The planner's task, then, is to ensure that these processes are as inclusive as possible and that all perspectives on what constitutes the public good are aired, including the views held by the planners.[5] In this way, something more appropriately termed the **common interest** can emerge and sanction planning actions. (The changing definition and role of the public interest in planning is discussed more fully in Chapters 6 and 18.)

External Effects

It is fair to say that most of the problems of growth and development that planning deals with arise from what are known as **external effects**. This term derives from the simple effect of, say, constructing a building upon other facets of the built and natural environment. Redevelopment of an old commercial strip will disrupt local shopping patterns. Even a single new house on a vacant lot can change neighbourhood dynamics. Such external effects as these, often called "overspill effects" or "externalities," may be localized or affect the entire community and even beyond. For example, traffic congestion results from traffic destined for (or leaving) one or a set of land uses (e.g., a stadium or a downtown area) exceeding the capacity of the means of moving the traffic, and the effects (e.g., noise, gridlock, pollution) then spill over into adjacent areas. Problems can arise from the development of a new professional office building or supermarket near a low-density residential area: it may generate traffic and parking needs that can be met only on adjacent streets. A school board's decision to close a neighbourhood school can have external effects when parents have to worry that their children will have to walk farther to school and perhaps cross dangerous streets as well. Or the design of a new subdivision's storm-drainage system will need to be checked to make sure that it doesn't cause pollution in a nearby stream that feeds into the community's water supply. Just as important, if more difficult to anticipate, are impacts that physical development has on the lives of citizens. For example, many women increasingly cite public transit systems as unsafe.

The idea of anticipating externalities accompanying development proposals and projects has come to be a central part of community-planning practice. Partly owing to greater understanding about how the various parts of a community function and relate to one another, community planning now takes into consideration the **potential** effects of a development project on a neighbourhood, the community as a whole, or even its region. Planners will examine plans for a proposed highway linking the city centre and the suburbs for its effects on the property values, traffic patterns, and air quality of the areas it passes through, for example. A good deal of community planning, therefore, is as much about trying to grasp the potential external effects of development as it is about responding to its direct and immediate effects.

The need to grasp potential problems arising from development proposals has brought two other considerations into planning. The first is the recognition that external effects may not be known from our previous experience—they may have to be estimated or possibly just guessed at. Moreover, we are beginning to realize that many effects of development may not even be known until well into the future, as has been the case with many pollution problems. A second consideration is the role of scientific and technical knowledge in understanding the complexity of a community's growth and change. The formulation of new means to analyze ecosystems, thereby more accurately grasping carrying capacities of local water bodies and wetlands, is one instance of this. The result is to make the professional planner's task increasingly demanding (some say "nigh impossible."[6])

The need to predict any problems associated with development proposals and other changes in the community has, for example, introduced into the planner's milieu the need to consider several sophisticated notions. One has to do with the *costs and benefits* associated with proposed developments, sometimes phrased as "who benefits and who pays"? For almost all development projects have external effects beyond the subject property. Another is the "precautionary principle" whereby the external effects of a project could possibly be harmful, but cannot be fully established. Yet another is the notion of making a "risk assessment" of a project's external effects becoming manifest. These and other planning analyses are discussed more fully in Chapters 6 and 17. The unintended consequences on people's lives and places in their community they hold dear and necessary are discussed in Chapter 13.

To recapitulate, community planning deals not just with solving problems but also with solving them so that the community turns out to be as good as, or better than, it was expected to be. Even in the solving of problems, a community tries through its planning to achieve some of its ideals. In this concern for ideals we see a connection with the other major reason for community planning—the desire to achieve improvement in the form, functioning, and fairness of the community.

GUIDING VALUES OF THE CANADIAN INSTITUTE OF PLANNERS/INSTITUT CANADIEN DES URBANISTS

1. To respect and integrate the needs of future generations. CIP members recognize that their work has cumulative and long-term implications. When addressing short-term needs, CIP members acknowledge the future needs of people, other species and their environments, and avoid committing resources that are irretrievable or irreplaceable.

2. To overcome or compensate for jurisdictional limitations. CIP members understand that their work can affect many jurisdictions and interests. Therefore they practise in a holistic manner, recognizing the need to overcome the limitations of administrative boundaries.

3. To value the natural and cultural environment. CIP members believe that both natural and cultural environments must be valued. They assume roles as stewards of

these environments, balancing preservation with sustainable development.

4. To recognize and react positively to uncertainty. CIP members believe that the long-term future is unpredictable and develop adaptable and flexible responses to deal positively with this uncertainty.

5. To respect diversity. CIP members respect and protect diversity in values, cultures, economies, ecosystems, built environments, and distinct places.

6. To balance the needs of communities and individuals. CIP members seek to balance the interests of communities with the interests of individuals, and recognize that communities include both geographic communities and communities of interest.

7. To foster public participation. CIP members believe in meaningful public participation by all individuals and groups and seek to articulate the needs of those whose interests have not been represented.

8. To articulate and communicate these values. CIP members believe in applying these values explicitly in their work and communicating their importance to clients, employers, colleagues, and the public.

Source: Canadian Institute of Planners, http://www.cip-icu.ca/web/la/en/pa/D1A0C3168CB244E4BA8A9BBBF94F3BEA/template.asp

The Need to Achieve Aspirations for the Built and Natural Environment

Community planning is concerned with more than solving the problems posed by current development. Goals, ideals, values, and aims are important as well. There is a tradition of idealism that influences much of what is done in the name of community planning. It is evident in the Canadian Institute of Planners' statement of values set out above. And it is central to probably the most quoted aphorism in planning by Daniel Burnham—"make no little plans":

> Make no little plans; they have no magic to stir men's blood and probably themselves will not be realized. Make big plans: aim high in hope and work, remembering that a noble, logical diagram, once recorded, will never die, but long after we are gone will be a living thing, asserting itself with ever growing insistency.

Burnham was the coauthor of the path-breaking 1909 plan for Chicago and its region. Others, like Jane Jacobs, have come along since to suggest that *small* plans such as better, walkable, and more just neighbourhoods are also worthy ideals.[7] Suffice to say that the *boldness* should be part of community plans at whatever scale.

An intrinsic part of most community-planning efforts involves the consideration of ideal situations and aspirations of people for their community. It is a tradition with deep roots in the history of city-building. The plans for ancient cities in Greece, Rome, China, the Middle East, and the Americas reveal a concern for the proper location of various functions of the city. The sites of religious buildings and public areas, and even the geographical orientation of the streets, often were considered symbolic and thus important. Cities themselves were seen as symbols of a society's aspiration to achieve progress and human betterment. As Aristotle noted, "A Citie is a perfect and absolute assembly or communion of many townes or streets in one."[8] Through succeeding eras, the city as a reflection of human aspirations continued to be a major theme in philosophy and culture, although the images changed from the religious to the secular as societies changed.

This tradition is still a powerful one in community planning. The sentiments expressed by Burnham and Jacobs encourage not just boldness but also *the community* to express its hopes and ideals in its plans, rather than merely deal with solutions to temporary problems or "choose among lesser evils," as David Riesman stated.[9] Indeed, Gordon Stephenson, a British planner who worked and taught in Canada in the 1950s, unequivocally observes: "I do not believe we can make worthy plans without having ideal conceptions...."[10] And there are many examples in Canada where the ideals of the plan-makers for human betterment are central to the community plan.

Nowhere is this more striking than on our resource frontier. Kapuskasing, Ontario, and Temiskaming, Québec (see Figure 4.16, page 81), both planned by

Chapter 1 The Need for Community Planning   9

Thomas Adams, and both spatial descendants of the 19th century tradition of planning model industrial towns with improved living conditions for workers (see Chapter 2), are two such places. Kitimat, British Columbia (Figure 11.17, page 270), which was largely designed by the acclaimed American planner Clarence Stein in the 1950s, follows in the same tradition of planning to achieve ideal living conditions for an entire community. Both these planners were well acquainted with the efforts of Ebenezer Howard in England to promote, and eventually build, self-contained Garden Cities (see Chapter 3). The latter concept of an ideal community became an extremely powerful model for those concerned with planning and building suburban communities in Canada, from Strathcona Park near Edmonton to Ajax near Toronto. A modern-day scenario is unfolding for the planners of Fort McMurray, who are considering a complete makeover of the boomtown of the oil sands (see Planning Issue 1.1).

Other Canadian community plans, while equally idealistic in concept, have striven to improve the environment on a less sweeping scale. One of the most notable is the 1915 plan for Ottawa, which aimed to achieve a monumental quality for the nation's capital.[11] Of the same genre is the Wascana Centre area around the legislative buildings in Regina. More recently, the planning of Toronto's central waterfront and False Creek in Vancouver reflects the aspirations of these communities to create a new but lasting image in their environments. In these examples, something new is designed and built. Rooted in this same theme are the historical conservation programs undertaken by some communities, such as Niagara-on-the-Lake, Ontario, and St. Andrews, New Brunswick, where the desire is to preserve surroundings of special value for future generations. Thus, whether the planning involves the design for some special new environment or the refurbishing of highly valued older environments, the thrust is essentially the same: creating an image, or vision, of a possible community environment. At its most dramatic, this facet of planning in modern times has produced plans that have resulted in completely new communities, for example, the capital cities of Brasilia in Brazil (Figure 5.4, page 112) and Chandigarh in India. Brasilia is even more successful than its planners hoped and now houses more than two million people, compared to the half million originally envisioned.[12]

But planning goes beyond defining uplifting physical forms for a community; it may also be framed around social ideals and fairness. One example is Ville de Montréal's 2002 declaration to make itself a city that is safe for women;[13] another is the Health and Healing Strategy by the people of the Kaska First Nation and the Town of Watson Lake, B.C., to address alcohol and drug addiction (which won a CIP award).[14] So, even in planning situations that strive for improved human conditions, there is a utopian element, an ideal. One such ideal is that of the "just city," that is, a city that is more than a physical structure or a place for economic activity and is one that allows opportunities for *all* citizens.[15] This ideal that has always lingered on the edges of planning is increasingly being given voice as planners encounter "diversity" in its *full* form—all the human groups that comprise a community, not least women and girls, youth, the poor, the multicultural, and the homeless—and offer them full *use* of the city and its resources, making them active *citizens* (see Chapter 13).

The most common planning experience today is not the heady one of a new town but the rebuilding, and refurbishing, and revitalizing of an already-developed community. Further, the motivation for an improved community environment nowadays is often less in terms of the appearance of a city or town and more in its "livability," "sustainability," and "equity." It is often about neighbourhoods and the inclusion of residents in defining a plan's criteria. The widespread adoption of visioning exercises as the starting point of community plan-making is a latter-day example of citizens expressing ideals for their community (see Chapter 15).[16] Increasingly, direct contact with citizens in meetings and group discussions is supplemented with a variety of other media for public engagement including social media, as exemplified in the City of Saskatoon's vast visioning project.[17] Today's planning milieu involves a wider array of participants and, as would be expected, a tug-and-pull of views notably when communities wish to deal with what is frequently referred to as the "diversity" in their populations. There are plans emerging that set a broad community framework for "social sustainability" within which, say, individual neighbourhood planning debates can be mediated.[18] This is not to say that these social goals, or others aimed at improving the built and natural environment, are achieved easily. For the reality in community plan-making is one of competing goals and objectives; this will be evident throughout the remainder of the book. Yet, as the old adage says: "A planner is someone with her/his head in the clouds and her/his feet planted firmly on the ground."

Putting the "Community" into Canadian Planning

The term "community planning," used throughout this book, requires some explanation. Although one

The Globe and Mail
October 24, 2011

Fort McMurray: The Heart of the Oil Patch Seeks Its Soul

Nathan Vanderklippe

It has country's highest household income, and no downtown. The city is trying to change that.

When Jennifer Keesmaat began thinking about how to transform the boomtown heart of the oil sands into a thriving centre, she grew slightly despondent.

"When we started in Fort McMurray, the very first thing we said is, 'This is the twilight zone. No rules that apply anywhere else apply here,'" said Ms. Keesmaat, an urban planner with Toronto-based Dialog, which has been hired to help fix the city. But she returned from an initial visit to the area this spring questioning how to do it.

"I came back and held my head in my hands and thought, 'Oh my, finally I've met my match. This nut is too big to crack.'"

But as Fort McMurray faces a future of explosive growth, it is nonetheless trying to do exactly that. It has employed a network of consultants, and petitioned its own people, in an attempt to figure out how to remake a modern-day hinterland gold rush town into an entertaining, vibrant city.

It's not just a municipal issue. Industry today spends tens of thousands a year on each worker it flies in and out of northern Alberta. That has created significant incentives to convince people to move nearer the oil sands.

With an average household income of $177,000—the highest in the country—Fort McMurray is awash in cash. But the town, and the Municipality of Wood Buffalo it sits in, have struggled to tread water amid the deluge of new arrivals. Planning for the future has been tough. Asked what's wrong with Fort McMurray's

downtown today, Toronto real estate executive Ron Taylor says simply: "There is none."

Josh Coles, a leader in the CEP union, which represents thousands of oil sands workers, has a different answer.

"Never have you seen so much money fly around a place where so many people are unhappy," he said. "We certainly support Fort McMurray becoming a proper city—if you can use that term without sounding derogatory."

Fort McMurray is cold. It's remote. It's pricey: Food is 73 per cent more expensive than the Alberta average, while shelter commands an 88 per cent premium. It's a town built on work. Its definition of play has tended to include more drinking and more drugs than other places. Its downtown is, in places, uncomfortably seedy. Its trucks seem to outnumbers its pedestrians.

Yet it's a city with ambitions to become something different. The municipality has spent $535,000 hiring a cadre of consultants and urban designers, including Ms. Keesmaat and Mr. Taylor, in hopes of shaping it into something great.

Taken individually, their ideas are hardly breathtaking: a network of river parks and paths. Wider sidewalks and better transit. An Ottawa-like outdoor skating area on the Snye, an arm of the Clearwater River. A downtown civic centre. A public square surrounded by restaurants. An arena fit for a WHL team. A stadium fit for a professional baseball team. An outdoor performance centre.

Taken together, though, those ideas point to a place that might sound, to many, attractive.

"This is not a radical transformation," Ms. Keesmaat said. "But it's a radically different way of envisioning the city."

And that, of course, is the goal—not only to build a home for oil sands workers, but also to grow a surrounding body of professionals,

CONTINUED

from lawyers to accountants to information technology experts.

"What if Fort McMurray had a great downtown environment with funky spaces, great cafés, with a real night life and places to gather? Would it be desirable for those office workers currently located in Edmonton to be located in Fort McMurray? Absolutely," Ms. Keesmaat added.

A PricewaterhouseCoopers report commissioned by the municipality suggests what's possible. Today, some 8,000 people work in downtown Fort McMurray. About 12,000 people live there, in roughly 3,000 units. By 2030, PwC suggests, downtown could be home to 45,000 workers, with 52,000 to 68,000 people living in 19,000 to 27,000 units—the wide range owing to uncertainty over how many families and spouses would move north.

"I didn't think I'd see in my career another project like this," Mr. Taylor said. "The changes that are going to transpire in Fort McMurray are the most significant, certainly, in our country. And they're starting to get the same attention from the U.S. and beyond."

Fort McMurray's mayor, Melissa Blake, suggests her home can compete with other global places that have used oil wealth to build remarkable cities.

"Look at what society has been able to create in Dubai. Why would we as Canadians look at our opportunities any differently?" she asked.

"We need to give ourselves more credit in this province."

Still, the obstacles are substantial. Will the pickup-truck crowd want to cram into 500-square-foot apartments and condos? Will new arrivals forsake sweeping new subdivisions for dense downtown living? Will six-figure households be content to take transit, or walk in –30 degree Celsius?

It will take time and perseverance to find out.

But outsiders say Fort McMurray has one major advantage: few other places seeking urban transformation can boast of similar growth. The town doubled in population over the past decade, to 77,000 people. It expects to add another 120,000 by 2030, which would make it Alberta's third-largest city.

In other words: Fort McMurray doesn't have to make over an existing set of people. It can reshape its future on fresh faces, who aren't resistant to change.

"You have a market where things can respond to your ideas," said Larry Beasley, who helped lead city planning in Vancouver before doing similar work around the world.

"That means you potentially can make something happen ... And boy, there's a lot of potential there if they just decide they want to do something."

does not encounter the term as often nowadays, it is peculiarly Canadian and especially appropriate to describe the activity of planning living environments in our variously sized settlements. "Community planning" entered the Canadian lexicon not long after World War II, when the Community Planning Association of Canada (CPAC) was formed. In the United States, the comparable term is "city planning," which has been in use since shortly after 1900. The British have used the term "town planning" since the late 19th century. In the academic world in Canada and the United States, "urban planning" has been the accepted term since 1960. There is no record available to explain why the Community Planning Association chose "community planning"

for use in Canada; the term "town planning" was in widespread use from the turn of the century. Provinces had their town-planning acts, cities their town-planning commissions, and the professional planners had their town-planning institute. The first significant use of the term "community planning" appeared in a report to the Canadian government by a committee giving advice on the problems the country would face when World War II ended. The 1944 Advisory Committee on Reconstruction prepared a report entitled *Housing and Community Planning*[19]—which came to be known as the "Curtis Report" after its principal author, Professor C.H. Curtis of Queen's University. It argued that town planning had two distinct but complementary meanings. Town planning, they felt, should encompass not only the "rational physical organization" of a city but also the concept of "better community living."[20] Perhaps this was the stimulus to adopt the term "community planning" when CPAC met two years later, for many of the founding members of Canada's first (and only) nationwide citizen organization in planning had also been members of the Curtis committee. One of the founders of UBC's School of Community and Regional Planning was Leonard Marsh, a principal author of the Curtis Report. It is not surprising that B.C. comprehensive land use plans are called Official Community Plans (Figure 1.3).

It is worth noting that, prior to World War II, Thomas Adams urged Canadians to use the term "town planning" in preference to the American term "city planning."[21] He contended that the American term gave too much emphasis to the physical side of city-building and did not seem to acknowledge the human side of city life. He felt that the British term "town planning" was more encompassing of the social, built, and natural environmental qualities of human settlements. His preference is understandable, as he had begun his career in planning with the founders of the English Garden City movement, who advocated building new towns that integrated human and physical factors. This latter dichotomy has for a considerable time been a source of debate among the professional planners and others involved in planning for our communities. The physical factors are the facets of a community that can be planned, regulated, and shaped most easily, so the practice of community planning quite naturally gravitates in this direction. Every so often, planners are accused of emphasizing physical factors at the expense of human factors in their planning solutions. While the emphasis ebbs and flows between the human and the physical factors, our planning efforts seldom comprise only one. Thus, community planning has merit in that it brings the human or community aspects clearly into the picture.

"Community planning" is an appropriate term for two other reasons. First, in the Canadian setting, a town is usually seen as a small-size settlement and a city, by contrast, a large one. However, Canadian settlements of all sizes are involved in planning, as are many rural areas that are not clusters of populations. But all may rightfully be called communities. Second, "community planning" conveys the idea that modern planning is an activity undertaken by the community and involving all who live in it. The terms "city planning" and "town planning" both suggest a technical activity dominated by professional planners. Humphrey Carver, one of the founders of CPAC, says that one of the main aims in establishing the association was to create "a framework of discussion in which laymen, professionals, and politicians could meet on equal terms to talk about their aspirations for Canadian cities."[22] The polite phrase "a framework for discussion" evolved into the more vigorous one of "citizen participation" as a way to describe the involvement of more than just planners and politicians in planning activity. Even though the involvement of community members is not uniformly practised, the question is not whether it should happen, but how and when. "Community" planning signifies the importance of the aspiration that the community should be doing the community planning, as seen in Burnaby, B.C. (Figure 1.4).

Planning Challenges for a New Generation

Community planning is a task that evolves as society evolves. Community planners therefore need to be aware of changes occurring in their communities and/or in the larger society that redound on them. With each instance of change or set of changes come challenges for

| Figure 1.3 | Cover of the North Vancouver Official Community Plan, 2002 |

SOURCE: CITY OF NORTH VANCOUVER

| Figure 1.4 | Burnaby Social Sustainability Strategy |

SOURCE: AVRIL ORLOFF/ AVRILORLOFF.COM

The public consultation process for the draft Strategy included mall displays in each geographic quadrant of Burnaby, B.C. The plan won the CIP 2012 Social Planning Award.

the planner. Some of the challenges that planners face today are new and others have only recently emerged; yet each must be faced (or faced again). To set the stage for the chapters ahead, it will be helpful to review briefly the major types of challenges already on Canadian planners' thresholds.

For a decade or more, since about the mid-1990s, the array of both planning issues and planning solutions being propounded has burgeoned. Some of these stem from the never-quite-achieved aim of full citizen participation. Others stem from the long-accepted but seldom-realized goal of environmental protection. Still others are relatively recent and derive from the accelerating cultural diversity of communities large and small. The emergence of globalization and its influences provide another challenge for planners, as do the needs of First Nations' communities. But it is not just problems that are being highlighted; solutions are too. There continues to be a need for more effective collaboration and cooperation among planning stakeholders as well as for physical designs for neighbourhoods that are both satisfying and equitable.

This is a vibrant period for community planning. The challenges listed below could be seen as obstacles, but they also constitute opportunities for all who are engaged in community planning to expand the scope and enrich the substance of this vital public activity:

- *Citizen Participation* in deciding planning issues would seem to be in accord with the basic value of democracy that planners have espoused since the beginning. Yet, despite considerable progress, the practice in Canadian community planning varies

noticeably.[23] Participants are sometimes overlooked; however participation is maturing with social media and other new forms being used to engage citizens (see Chapters 14 and 15).[24]

- *Ecological Planning*, or planning for the natural environment, should be incorporated into our community planning along with the built environment. This apparent goal, despite major strides over the past few decades, remains elusive in many communities. Moreover, it is vital that commitment to this aim be strong and enduring (see Chapters 7 and 12).[25]
- *Redeeming Place*, or planning communities in which the inhabitants' communitarian, ecological, and aesthetic needs are integral to the final outcome, by recreating neighbourhoods and stopping "mindless sprawl," is central to the urging of both New Urbanism and bioregionalism advocates (see Chapters 11–13).[26]
- *Cultural Diversity*, where planning meets multiculturalism, has risen high on the planning agendas of many communities, especially the "gateway" cities like Vancouver, Montréal, and Toronto, and challenges planners to move beyond simple awareness and sensitivity in their planning (see Chapter 13).[27]
- *Population Aging*, already a prominent feature of community life, will dramatically increase in all types of communities in all parts of the country

| Figure 1.5 | Spirit Garden, Thunder Bay waterfront |

SOURCE: FIRM: BROOK MCILROY, PHOTOGRAPHER DAVID WHITTAKER

An open space on the Thunder Bay waterfront celebrating Aboriginal values and heritage in the community. (CIP 2012 Aboriginal Community Planning and Development award)

and demand awareness of plan-makers to enable seniors and other older adults to maintain their independence in carrying out their daily activities in and around the community (see Chapter 13).[28]

- *Safety and Security* in communities both in terms of crime and the needs of people with disabilities, women, children, and the elderly, as basic as it seems, are not something to which plan-makers have been particularly attentive. Without them in place, citizens may justly feel excluded from their communities (see Chapter 13).[29]
- *Globalization* is already having impacts on planning methods, research, and practice and is bound to have more with the increasing interconnectedness of people, places, institutions, and economies, with implications for sustainable development, communications, and immigration, among others.[30]

Structure and Resources of This Book

The basic premise of this book is that community planning in Canada, or elsewhere for that matter, is best understood by looking at, first, why and what is being pursued in community planning; second, how community planning is done in communities large and small; third, which elements are planned to give social and physical form to the community; fourth, who gets involved in community plan-making, and fifth, how plans are implemented. These facets of community planning—the principles, practice, and participants—provide the focus for this book. They unfold through five major sections:

The Foundations of Canadian Community Planning

The remaining chapters in **Part One** examine the evolution of Canadian planning from earliest settlement to the present time. Community planning in Canada has roots in long-standing ideals, ideas, and principles about how a community should develop and how it should promote the common interest in the process of development. These four chapters consider the legacies of the **physical forms** we find in Canadian communities today. Chapter 2 looks at how cities began and what influenced the forms planners gave them up through the 18th century. The foundations that began to be laid down in the 19th century for Canadian communities, especially regarding concerns over their appearance, living conditions, functioning, and natural

environments, are introduced in Chapter 3. The 20th century saw the emergence of new planning concepts and the development professional practice in Canada in pursuit of these latter concerns; the period 1900–1950 is the focus of Chapter 4. The planning concepts and processes that emerged, and the challenges communities came to face in the second half of the 20th century, and up to the present, are the subject of Chapter 5.

Community Plan-Making in Canada

Part Two describes the practice of community plan-making in Canada at the present time. When community planning goes beyond ideal concepts and social concerns, a mode of practice develops to deal with elements of the environment being planned and to provide the organizational arrangements to conduct public planning. Contemporary community planning in Canada has well-developed modes of practice such that planning activities differ little from one part of the country to the other.

The five chapters in this part describe the approaches taken in planning for urban communities, regional and metropolitan communities, and small towns in Canada. The **making of a community plan** initiates the discussion (Chapter 6) with an overview of prevailing theory and the components and general flow of plan-making. The **built and natural environment**—the basic platform for community planning—and the way planners and others view it follows in Chapter 7. The focus then shifts to consider **scope and role of a community plan**, the centrepiece of planning practice, in three spatial settings: first, in large communities, **metropolitan areas** and non-urban regions (Chapter 8); second, in **urban communities** (Chapter 9); and third, in quite small ones, such as **towns and villages** in rural and northern regions, including Aboriginal communities (Chapter 10).

Planning for People and Places in the Community

At the heart of a community are the *people* who live there—its citizens—and the myriad *places* they are associated with, where they reside, work, shop, worship, or relax. The community plan, which embraces the entire community, all its residents and all its space, seldom does more than allude to the spatial and human nuances within it. **Part Three** addresses these more familiar parts of a community, its neighbourhoods and their residents, its distinctive districts, and the foundation of physical and natural infrastructure that gird it. Chapter 11 discusses the planning of neighbourhoods and special districts. Planning for the various infrastructures, physical and natural, that facilitate community functioning is described in Chapter 12. Chapter 13 comprises planning for diverse population groups and their needs—comfort, safety, equity, and the overall need for a healthy community.

Participants and Participation in Community Plan-Making

Part Four identifies the participants involved in making a community plan. Community planning obliges us to use collective decision-making processes because of the wide array of individuals and groups who have an interest in the future of the community. Procedures are usually conducted within a governmental framework and may be both formal and informal in nature. They, in turn, define who may participate in planning decisions and how and when decisions need to be made. Two chapters describe the texture and process of community planning decision-making: Chapter 14 provides an overview of the **sequence of decisions** that arise in response to the initiative of a local governing body to make or amend a plan including the main actors, both public and private. Chapter 15 provides an in-depth view of **the main participants**—planners, politicians, developers, and citizens—and the dynamics of their interaction along with the mediums of engagement currently being used.

Implementing the Community Plan and the Tools Used

Most planners would argue that it is essential to prepare a plan but that is only the beginning of a long-term process of bringing it to fruition, of implementing it. It is equally important to design and apply appropriate **tools** for guiding the decisions of participants so that the plan will be achieved. The chapters in **Part Five** examine the tools and approaches used in implementing a community plan. These follow two trajectories: the first, described in Chapter 16, are those involved in regulating land uses in a community such as zoning and other land use controls that guide the decisions of private landowners and other public agencies. The second are those initiatives that can be taken by the public policymakers of the community in budgeting for public facilities, building regulations, and other development incentives as examined in Chapter 17.

Anticipating the Future in Community Plans

Community planning is a task that evolves as society evolves. Cities and towns continue to develop, informed by both their past and their future. New problems arise along with new versions of old problems. Thus, the true progress of community planning is as much a measure of how it deals with existing problems as how well it anticipates future conditions. The final chapter discusses a number of salient issues that will challenge Canadian community plan-makers in the future including issues still in need of resolution, such as citizen participation and environmental protection, as well as issues that will become more central in the years ahead, such as the population's aging and its increasingly multicultural character, as well as the future of the suburbs.

Learning Resources

In addition to the main text, supplementary resources are provided with each chapter to expand the scope of learning about community planning. They proceed increasingly outward, from guiding questions within the text to stand-alone cases of contemporary planning issues in Canadian communities and to planning resources available on the Internet.

Guiding Questions

As one proceeds through the book, two sets of leading questions are provided in each chapter. The first, at the outset of the chapter, points the general direction in which the chapter will unfold, while the second, at the chapter's end, reflects on the foregoing discussion and its relation to material to come in the next and succeeding chapters.

Planning Issues

Community planning should always be seen as a part of the human dynamic. It does not take place in books but in council chambers, neighbourhood halls, and sometimes in the streets. It is intimately involved with the politics of the community. Some of the drama associated with community planning is introduced here by a series of case studies called Planning Issues, which depict contemporary planning stories from across Canada. Although these are necessarily "snapshots" at a particular point in time, and some may now be resolved, they are indicative of the planning issues that communities like yours and ours encounter.

Internet Resources

The Internet is already rich in resources that can be used for further study in community planning as well as in actual community-planning practice. Each chapter thus concludes with a selection of websites relevant to the subject of the chapter. Web addresses are current as of the year of publication.

Highlights of Canadian Community Planning

The evolution of community planning in Canada may be quickly grasped in the chronological listing of important events and achievements from the 1890s to the present time provided in the Appendix.

* * * * *

To reiterate, community planning, essentially, is about providing an appropriate physical foundation for community life. This is where our discussion begins in the next chapter. As you proceed, keep in mind the following questions:

- *What community needs have planners found, time and again, they must provide for in the built and natural environments of cities and towns?*

- *What factors will demand the planner's attention in the coming decade?*

Reference Notes

1. David L.A. Gordon and Tasha Elliott, "Lost in Translation: A Brief Comparison of Canadian Land Use Planning Terminology," *Plan Canada* 47:1 (Spring 2007), 28–31.
2. The awards for planning excellence given each year by the Canadian Institute of Planners and available at www.cip-icu.ca is the main source of this list. An older, but still useful source of Canadian community planning initiatives (and the one that originally suggested this list) is by the Canadian National Committee for Habitat, *The Canadian Settlements Sampler* (Ottawa: Community Planning Press, 1976), especially pp.14–43.
3. This is well argued in, among others, Leonie Sandercock, *Toward Cosmopolis: Planning for Multicultural Cities* (London: John Wiley & Sons, 1997).
4. Judith E. Innes, "Planning through Consensus Building," *Journal of the American Planning Association* 62:4 (Autumn 1996), 460–472.
5. Jill Grant, "Rethinking the Public Interest as a Planning Concept," *Plan Canada* 45:2 (2005), 48–50.
6. Sandercock, *Cosmopolis*.
7. Cf. Jane Jacobs, comments at the 1980 Great Cities Conference in Boston, www.theatlanticcities.com/arts-and-lifestyle/2011/11/jane-jacobs-and-power-women-planners/502/
8. From Aristotle's *Politics*, in a 1598 translation, as cited in Helen Rosenau, *The Ideal City* (London: Studio Vista, 1974), 12.
9. David Riesman, "Some Observations on Community Plans and Utopia," *Yale Law Journal* 57 (December 1947).
10. Gordon Stephenson, "Some Thoughts on the Planning of Metropolitan Regions," *Papers of the Regional Science Association* 4 (1958), 27–38.
11. The story of this remarkable plan is set out in David L.A. Gordon, "A City Beautiful Plan for Canada's Capital: Edward Bennett and the 1915 Plan for Ottawa and Hull," *Planning Perspectives* 13 (1998), 275–300. It and its antecedents are elaborated in David Gordon, ed., *Planning Twentieth-Century Capital Cities* (London: Routledge, 2006).
12. Joachim Domingo Roriz, "Brasilia: A National Project for Development and Integration," *Plan Canada* 40:3 (April–May 2000), 16–17; and Sylvia Ficher et al., "Brasilia: A Capital in the Hinterland" in Gordon, *Planning Twentieth-Century Capital Cities*, 164–181.
13. Ville de Montréal, *The Montréal Declaration on Women's Safety, 2002*, www.villemontréal.qc.ca and www.femmesetvilles.org
14. Liard First Nation, *Regional Treatment Strategy* (Watson Lake YT, 2010).
15. Penny Gurstein and Sylvia Vilches, "The Just City for Whom? Re-conceiving Active Citizenship for Lone Mothers in Canada," *Gender Place and Culture* 17:4 (August 2010), 421–436.
16. Robert Shipley, "Visioning in Planning: Is the Practice Based on Sound Theory?" *Environment and Planning A* 34:1 (2002), 7–22.
17. City of Saskatoon, *Community Vision: Saskatoon Speaks* (Saskatoon, June 2011); and Lynn Mandarano, Mahbubur Meenar, and Christopher Steins, "Building Social Capital in the Age of Civic Engagement," *Journal of Planning Literature* 25:2 (November 2010), 123–135.
18. City of Burnaby, Social Sustainability Strategy, June 2011, http://www.burnaby.ca/Assets/city+services/planning/Social+Sustainability+Strategy.pdf
19. Canada, Advisory Committee on Reconstruction, *Housing and Community Planning* 4 (Ottawa: King's Printer, March 1944), Report of the Subcommittee.
20. Canada, Advisory Committee on Reconstruction, *Housing and Community Planning*, 178.
21. Thomas Adams, "What Town Planning Really Means," *The Canadian Municipal Journal* 10 (July 1914).
22. Humphrey Carver, *Compassionate Landscape* (Toronto: University of Toronto Press, 1975), 90.
23. Among recent Canadian articles on citizen participation are: Laura Mannell and Heather Turnoway, "The Need to Do More: Advancing Planning with First Nations Communities," *Plan Canada* 48:2 (Summer 2008), 21–23; Noel Keough, "Calgary's Citizen-Led Community Sustainability Indicators Project," *Plan Canada* 43:1 (January–March 2003), 35–36; John Blakney, "Citizen Bane," *Plan Canada* 37:3 (May 1997), 12–17; and Beth Sanders, "View From The Forks: Coming to Terms with Perceptions of Public Participation," *Plan Canada* 38:2 (March 1998), 30–32.
24. Kathryn S. Quick and Martha S. Feldman, "Distinguishing Participation and Inclusion," *Journal of Planning Education and Research* 31:3 (2011), 272–290; and Penelope Gurstein, "Gender Sensitive Community Planning: A Case Study of the Planning Ourselves In Project," *Canadian Journal of Urban Research* 5:2 (December 1996), 199–219.
25. John Newton, "Exploring Linkages between Community Planning and Natural Hazard Mitigation in Ontario," *Plan Canada* 44:1 (January–March 2004), 22–24; Mary-Ellen Tyler, "Ecological Planning in an Age of Myth-Information," *Plan Canada* 40:1 (December 1999–January 2000), 20–21; and Dan Perlmann and Jeffry Milder, *Practical Ecology: For Planners, Developers and Citizens* (Washington, DC: Island Press, 2005).
26. Kirsty MacDonald, "Turning Alleys into Assets," *Plan Canada* 44:2 (April–June 2004), 48–51; and Andrea Gabor and Frank Lewinberg, "New Urbanism," *Plan Canada* 37:4 (July 1997), 12–17.
27. M.A. Qadeer and S.K. Agrawal, "The Practice of Multicultural Planning in American and Canadian Cities," *Canadian Journal of Urban Research* 20:1 (2011),

Reference Notes (continued)

132–156; Mohammad Qadeer, "Dealing with Ethnic Enclaves Demands Sensitivity and Pragmatism," *Ontario Planning Journal*, 20:1 (2005), 10–11; and Sandeep Kumar and Bonica Leung, "Formation of an Ethnic Enclave: Process and Motivations, *Plan Canada* 45:2 (Summer 2005), 43–45.

28. Gerald Hodge, *The Seniors' Surge: The Geography of Aging in Canada: Preparing Communities for the Surge in Seniors* (Montréal: McGill-Queen's University Press, 2008); and Mary Catherine Mehak, "New Urbanism and Aging in Place," *Plan Canada* 42:1 (January–March 2002), 21–23.

29. Gerda Wekerle, "From Eyes on the Street to Safe Cities," *Places* 13:1 (Winter 2000), 44–49; Rob Imrie, "Barriered and Bounded Places and the Spatialities of Disability,"

Urban Studies 38:2 (February 2001), 231–237; and Hester Parr and Ruth Butler, "New Geographies of Illness, Impairment and Disability," in H. Parr and R. Butler, eds., *Mind and Body Spaces* (London: Routledge, 1999), 1–24.

30. Manuel Castells, "Planning in the Information Age," *Plan Canada* 40:1 (December 1999–January 2000), 18–19; and Farokh Afshar and Keith Pezzoli, "Integrating Globalization and Planning," *Journal of Planning Education and Research* 20 (Spring 2001), 277–280, Editors' Introduction.

Internet Resources

There are several websites that are important in themselves for planning and also act as gateway sites for community planners to an array of links to other relevant sites. The list begins with Canadian sites and continues with those in the United States.

Chapter-Relevant Sites

Canadian Institute of Planners
www.cip-icu.ca

Canada Mortgage and Housing Corporation
www.cmhc-schl.gc.ca

Muniscope: Intergovernmental Committee on Urban and Regional Research
www.icurr.org

University of British Columbia Planning Library
http://guides.library.ubc.ca/planning

United Nations Habitat
www.unhabitat.org

American Planning Association
www.planning.org

Planetizen
www.planetizen.com

Cyburbia Resource Directory
www.cyburbia.org

University of California at Berkeley Environmental Design Library
http://www.lib.berkeley.edu/ENVI/planning_links.html

Chapter Two
The Beginnings of Today's Cities

Such is the tenacity of these simple geometric forms, the circle, the straight line, and the right angle. They survive because of their adaptability.

Hans Blumenfeld, 1943

The communities we know today are part of a heritage of city- and town-building knowledge stretching back several millennia. From Mesopotamia and the Nile Valley to China, India, Greece, Rome, and Renaissance Europe, there is vast experience in community planning available. Our geographic and historic circumstances may differ, but we can learn from the achievements and problems of past planners and the form and function of the communities they designed. These European precedents can be found in the form of the 17th and 18th century Canadian communities, while our 19th century cities began to benefit from planning concepts aimed at righting the ills of the emerging industrial city. In short, those involved in planning a Canadian community today are heirs of planning decisions and planning ideas of the past. Drawing from this repertoire of planning thought and action, consider the following questions:

- *What are the major physical development issues in community building that planners of the past faced and planners today still face?*
- *What lessons do we learn from early planners that planners today should not repeat?*

Perennial Planning Issues

Over the 7000 years since humankind began designing communities, six important issues have recurred for planners. These issues need to be addressed either when building a wholly new community or expanding an existing one.[1] They are fundamental to much of what this book is about and need to be reviewed now. The queries that accompany each are key ones for planners to consider, but there will always be others, depending upon the community and the era:

1. **The selection of the site.** Will it be a hilltop or valley, an island or cape, a harbour, or some other transportation advantage? How will it fit with its natural environment?
2. **The function (or purpose) of the community.** What needs is the settlement intended to satisfy? Is it to provide protection, facilitate commerce, act as a political or religious focal point?
3. **The form of the community.** What are the aspirations of the populace, the aesthetic considerations of the culture, the functional needs to be served?
4. **The allocation of land uses.** Where will the people live, do business, govern, worship, congregate for public activities?
5. **The need for connection.** How will people and goods circulate and be exchanged among various land uses?
6. **Accommodating growth and change.** Should the community be more intensively developed within its present confines or be extended on the periphery if it needs to grow?

Although planners must acknowledge all six of these issues, the importance they accord to each will vary depending upon a number of things: the community's values, the human needs, the nature of the site, the technology available (especially for building and circulation), and the economic and other functions. Once decisions are made and carried out in any of these issue areas, the physical shape and arrangement of the community will be influenced through all succeeding periods. Consider these points in regard to the various historical cases of city building and planning described throughout the remainder of this chapter and in those that follow.

Cities of the Ancient World

Our best archeological research about the beginnings of cities shows that substantial settlements were being built about 5000 BCE. There were village settlements long before this, and villages still abound, but these simple groupings of more or less equal social units are not cities. As eminent Canadian planner Hans Blumenfeld has noted, "Only where the plurality of social units of a villages is combined with the social and functional differentiation found in the castle can we talk of a city."[2] Thus, cities emerge when a society begins to distinguish such social needs as defence, promotion of worship, or symbolizing political control in a region, and then combines these functions with the need to house a large population nearby. The effort to combine these functions at a particular location constitutes the earliest community planning.

The archeological record identifies five major clusters of ancient cities:

- Mesopotamia from ca. 5000 BCE to perhaps 1800 BCE
- The Nile Valley from ca. 4500 BCE to perhaps 2100 BCE
- The Indus Valley from ca. 2300 BCE to 1800 BCE
- China from ca. 2500 BCE to today
- Central and South America from ca. 1000 BCE to 1500 CE

While the archeological research is fairly clear about the location and age of these ancient cities, there is no consensus about *why* the villages evolved into these early urban civilizations. The conventional view is that more efficient agricultural methods allowed some settlements to support activities other than subsistence farming through their surplus production.[3] And all of these civilizations did have substantial agricultural production, from Mesopotamian wheat to Aztec corn. But this "agriculture-first" view of urban civilization has been challenged by new theories suggesting the importance of economic creativity in urban development.[4] We will encounter these ideas again in later chapters that discuss planning post-industrial Canadian cities.

Cities of Mesopotamia

The cities of the Tigris and Euphrates Valleys, especially Babylon, provide good examples of planning in ancient times. Babylon (see Figure 2.1) was located in the Euphrates Valley (about 80 kilometres south of present-day Baghdad, Iraq). Its location was a "cape" in the river, which probably provided a good site for defence, transportation, and water supply. The river bisected the city and a wall encircled both sides enclosing an area of about 2 square kilometres. Powerful emperors lived in Babylon, and during their tenure the city was embellished in many ways. The most famous emperor, Nebuchadnezzar (625–551 BCE), as well as building the renowned Hanging Gardens, was said by the Greek writer Herodotus to have paved the great processional avenue with "limestone flags."[5]

Figure 2.1 | Babylon, 6th Century BCE

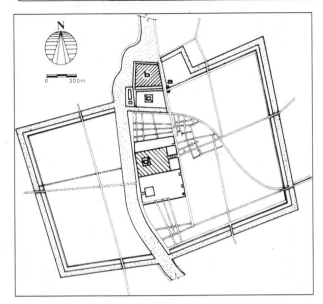

In the time of Nebuchadnezzar, Babylon spanned the Euphrates River, and its walls and moat encompassed an area of about 3 square kilometres. Its population was around 10 000. Key: (a) main gate, (b) fort, (c) Hanging Gardens, (d) temple.

Of the dwellings of common folk (the population of Babylon is reputed to have reached close to 10 000 at this time), little can be said. They would have occupied the bulk of the land in the city, but the residential areas seem not to have had any regular layout. Dwellings were arranged within blocks of land perhaps a hectare in size. The housing blocks were not regular in size or shape, and thus the spaces between them, which served as streets, were irregular.

Two factors account for the amorphous form of the interior of these cities. The first is that people moved around mostly on foot (wagons or carts were an exception). The second factor is that the commerce and manufacturing, and even a good deal of the agriculture, were conducted within the dwellings or land in the housing blocks. Streets were not required to provide easy connections throughout the city for the exchange of goods or for people to get to jobs. This general pattern of cities, comprising dominant public areas, a few major roads leading to monuments and gates, and rather undifferentiated residential areas all within a city wall, persisted until the Middle Ages in Europe.

The Nile Valley

Ancient Egyptian cities were quite different from the walled Mesopotamian fortresses. The Nile Valley was dotted with cities constructed as monuments to the Pharaohs; the desert, mountains, and Egyptian army were the defences against invaders. Although a temple city such as Memphis was settled for 1500 years, some royal capitals, such as Akhetatan (1369–1354 BCE), might be occupied for only 15 years while the Pharaoh's monuments were built. These cities had the semi-formal planning of a long-term construction camp, although some of the workers' villages were laid out in a tight grid pattern. These disappeared after the death of the Pharaoh, leaving the monuments to be maintained by priests.[6]

The Indus Valley

Urban civilization on the Indian subcontinent appears to have emerged in the Indus River basin almost 4200 years ago. Cities such as Harappa and Mohenjo Daro were laid out with their important streets in a basic grid, aligned in a north–south orientation (see Figure 2.2).

Figure 2.2 | Mohenjo Daro, India, ca. 2000 BCE

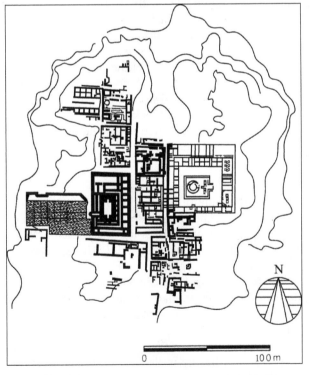

The regular geometric layout and orientation of the ancient cities of the Indus Valley are probably the earliest examples of deliberate urban planning for an entire community. Both the citadel, shown here, and the lower town were based on a grid of streets aligned north–south, probably for religious reasons.

Almost all housing was in the form of narrow, attached dwellings; detached houses were quite rare in ancient cities around the world. These cities held up to 30 000 people at their peak, but were mysteriously abandoned after about 500 years. But ancient Indian architectural manuals continued to promote strong geometric forms, based on Mandala, which influenced the plans of future cities.[7]

China

Ancient Chinese community planning dates back as far as the Mesopotamian period. Danish planner Steen Eiler Rasmussen tells us that when Emperor Kublai Khan built his capital in 1268, he chose a location where "five different towns had existed, one after the other, over a period of thousands of years; each one perfectly rectangular and each one oriented exactly north–south and east–west."[8] This precise orientation follows the ancient philosophical principle of *feng shui*, "wind and water," which promotes harmony between various pairs of physical factors within a geographic framework related to the sun. Early Chinese cities had fortified walls with a main gate on the south side. There was usually a great processional road leading from the gate directly north to the entrance of the ruler's palace or to a temple. Gates and main streets often led in the other three directions. The interior of the city was subdivided into square blocks of land with great families often segregated into special city districts with their own walls.[9] Lanes between housing blocks were narrow and not arranged in a uniform pattern. Housing blocks tended to be square (see Figure 2.3).

The Americas

On the other side of the world, the Aztecs, Mayans, and Incas were building elaborate cities in Central and South America, in places like the Yucatan, Central Mexico, Andean Bolivia, and Peru. The approach of the Incas to planning their communities is best seen in Cuzco, Peru. As American planner Francis Violich describes it, the Incan plan for Cuzco was divided into four sections, with a main plaza at the junction of the four main roads, each of which led to the four great regions of the Empire. Minor plazas were located elsewhere within the city walls and "each city block was an allotment for one city family; its distance from the centre of the city depended upon the degree of relationship to the Inca ruler."[10] Some of the more remote Incan cities, like Machu Picchu, occupied mountainous sites, quite different from the fertile valleys of the Asian

Figure 2.3   Khara-Khoto, Early Chinese Colony

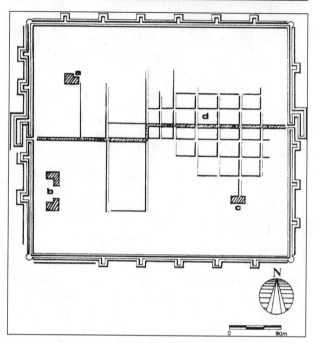

This "planted town" in Central Asia employs the rectangular grid geometry used in ancient cities in China, with walls and roads oriented precisely north–south and east–west. Roads from the gates are offset to prevent evil spirits from passing through. The town walls enclosed about 0.2 square kilometres and held a population of 4000 to 5000. Key: (a) tomb, (b) temple, (c) palace, (d) residential compounds.

civilizations. But the Aztec, Mayan, and Incan cities were largely destroyed during the Spanish conquest of the 16th century, so these ancient urban forms had little influence upon North American urban planning following European settlement.

Greek and Roman City Planning

European city development was extensively influenced by the urban civilizations of ancient Greece and Rome. Sir Peter Hall credits the golden age of Athens (500–400 BCE) with establishing the philosophic, scientific, and artistic foundations of Western culture.[11] The ancient Greeks were systematic planners of new communities and the Romans were extraordinary engineers, pioneering urban infrastructure techniques that would allow their imperial capital to grow to the largest city the world had ever known.[12]

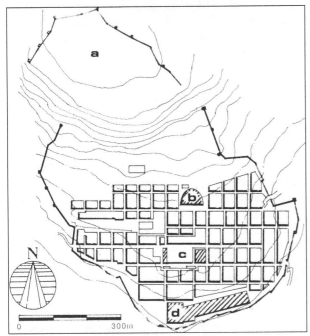

The gridiron pattern of Hippodamus is followed in this city of nearly 10 000. It provides for all dwelling blocks to be oriented to the southerly sun and main functional buildings and spaces to be within easy access. Key: (a) Acropolis, (b) theatre, (c) agora or marketplace, (d) stadium.

SOURCE: DAVID GORDON.

The north–south streets in Priene were stairways and the east–west streets cut across the contours to allow carts.

The Greek Planning Tradition

The experience of the ancient Greeks is important in the history of city development and planning. Greek architects and builders, especially Hippodamus, are usually credited with originating the **gridiron** street pattern, although this is not entirely accurate, as we saw in India and China above. However, Greek architects and builders probably should be credited with the first comprehensive community plans.

In the Greek community plan, the allocation of land to the individual dwelling was the common denominator. Rectangular blocks of land were arranged to allow the dwellings within them to be oriented to the southerly sun, a necessity for houses lacking central heating in the more northerly areas occupied by the Greeks. The location of public buildings and spaces determined the location of major streets. The *agora,* or marketplace, was usually built on one side of a main street, although not necessarily in the geographical centre of the city. Main streets also served the temple, the *pnyx,* an open-air podium where citizens met to consider affairs of state, the theatre, and the stadium.[13]

It should be noted that main streets were often only 7 to 9 metres wide and local streets were the 3- to 5-metre spaces left between the blocks of housing. Thus, the impression of gridiron street plans for Greek cities is only partly true; the rectangular blocks of land given over to housing, rather than the streets, determined the geometric pattern. Most towns were surrounded by protective walls.

The "classic city" of the Greeks, as these plans are often called, was built by the score around the shores of the eastern Mediterranean, into Asia Minor, and on the north coast of Africa. When the Greek colonizers sought sites for their new cities, defence and access to the sea were important; thus, they chose such sites as craggy headlands on the ocean. This meant superimposing the geometrical Hippodamian street pattern on rugged sites, with the result that numerous streets were so steep as to be built only as steps (see Figure 2.5). The pattern of streets may resemble today's gridiron, but it is worth remembering that most were not thoroughfares for vehicles. The plan for the town of Priene (see Figure 2.4) is a good example of classic Greek city building.

Towns and Cities of the Romans

From the 2nd century BCE, Rome succeeded Greece as the dominant European power. Over the next 500 years, the Romans extended their control from Britain to Algiers, and from Constantinople to the Danube Valley. In this period, they made two contributions to the development of community planning. The first was plans for towns in their colonies. The second was in the planning for the large cities that developed on the Italian peninsula.

In order to sustain power in distant lands, garrison towns were established and connected with roads to facilitate movement of the Roman legions. Thus, the old saying "All roads lead to Rome" aptly captures the extent of Roman domination. Hundreds of today's towns and cities of Western Europe owe their location to the sites the Romans chose for their garrisons. The Roman term *castrum*, meaning a military encampment, is found as "chester" in English town names; all such places originated from Roman camps.

The Roman garrison towns (or *coloniae*) were frequently used to deploy discharged soldiers from the huge armies of the time; all followed a similar pattern. Often rectangular in shape, they were surrounded by walls and bisected by two main streets that met at or near the centre. At this location was the forum. House blocks, or *insulae*, of 0.5 to 1.5 hectares, either square or oblong, were fairly uniform throughout the area enclosed by the walls. The two main streets were usually oriented so that one ran north–south and the other east–west; it has been conjectured that the latter street pointed toward the spot on the horizon where the sun rose on an important ceremonial day for the town. Although size varied among such towns, they were usually less than 2.6 square kilometres in size and often less than 20 hectares. The population of the larger garrison towns seldom exceeded 10 000 (see Figure 2.6).

Such home cities of the Romans as Naples, Pompeii, and Rome grew from early villages without benefit of the deliberate, overall plan used in building their colonial towns. These domestic Roman cities also represent the earliest known examples of planning and managing the development of cities of considerable size (see Figure 2.7). Pompeii, a small city, reached a population of 20 000 by 79 CE; Ostia, the port of Rome, had a population estimated to be 50 000 by the 3rd century CE; and Rome itself reached upward of 1.5 million about the same time. To be able to house populations of this size requires methods of distributing large amounts of water, providing for drainage and sewage, and moving people and goods, as well as taking into account shopping and cultural needs.

The Romans solved the technical problems created by their growing cities in unprecedented, and often dramatic, ways. Large aqueducts were built to supply water; Rome needed 14 aqueducts. Underground sewers were constructed that are still considered feats of engineering, and the 29 main highways leading to other parts of the Empire were, in most cases, paved.[14] Canadian planner Robert McCabe's studies show that the Romans provided for the shopping needs of citizens in what corresponds to our present-day shopping centres. In conjunction with a city's forum, a macellum was constructed, a structure for many shops, often on two or more levels. In Rome, the shopping centre portion of the main forum of the city had about 170 shops and covered almost 18 600 square metres.[15] Such a centre compares to the shopping centres built in many Canadian communities. Smaller planned shopping centres were also built in the various regions (districts) of Rome to provide for "neighbourhood" shopping needs.

The large Roman cities were, undoubtedly, complex communities, in many ways rivalling modern cities. This can be grasped by comparing the population densities. Pompeii occupied about 85 hectares and

| **Figure 2.6** | Ancient Roman Garrison: Silchester, England |

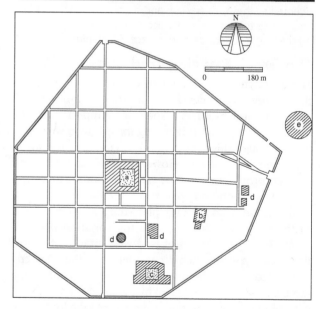

Roman garrison towns were usually dissected by two main streets, the *cardo* running north–south and the *decumanus* running east–west; the forum, with its shops, temples, and public buildings, was near their intersection. The population probably did not exceed 5000. Key: (a) forum, (b) baths, (c) inn, (d) temple, (e) amphitheatre.

| Figure 2.7 | The Forum in Pompeii |

SOURCE: GERALD HODGE.

Pompeii is perhaps the most well-preserved Roman city. This forum was a place of assembly and a shopping centre.

had 20 000 residents; Rome occupied about 26 square kilometres and had, possibly, 1.5 million residents. These represent densities of around 50 000 persons per square kilometre. Toronto has densities in its central area under 8000 persons per square kilometre, and densities of less than half that in its suburbs.

Ancient Cities in Summary

Cities in the ancient empires were established much like the "new towns" of modern times; they were often built where no previous settlement had been, or perhaps only a very small one. To quote Rasmussen again:

> [When] faced with the necessity of creating a new town in a strange place they must build it according to a preconceived plan or it will end in chaos. And that plan must, of necessity, be a very simple one, easily laid out, so that everyone with the least possible trouble can quickly discover what he has to do.[16]

The resulting physical form of cities until the 14th century shows two fundamental characteristics. First, land uses were arranged according to a "block plan," to employ Blumenfeld's term; that is, **blocks** of land devoted to public and residential uses, rather than streets, dictated the form.[17] Second, a surrounding wall often limited the community's growth and sometimes created a radial pattern to main streets providing access to gates, temples, and markets. This is the first evidence of the **radial-concentric** physical form. It is probably more accurate to describe ancient cities by these two characteristics than to compare them with later cities, where streets and traffic are much more crucial elements.

Origins of the Modern European City

It is important not to see these examples of city-building in the past as static concepts, or simply as maps. They were functioning communities that existed over long periods of time, and changed significantly during their history: shifting the allocations of land, adding new buildings, making new road connections, even expanding in many cases. They were "continuing" cities, to use the key word from the title of Vance's book.[18] The evolution that occurs in city form and composition should become even more evident as we proceed to describe more modern instances in this section. It is a necessary perspective when one considers not only where a city has come from but also what it might become, for you can be sure it will continue to change in the future.

From the Dark Ages to the Middle Ages

The several hundred years after the fall of Rome in the 5th century, the period called the Dark Ages, were characterized by a general social formlessness and a lack of large settlements in Europe. The political stability and protection provided by the empires of the Greeks and Romans ceased, and large cities could not be maintained; neither their supply of food nor their trade and other basic needs could be assured. The settlement pattern of Europe reverted to one of villages.

As strong kings, princes, and bishops emerged to provide security over larger regions, from the 9th century onward, European town life greatly expanded. Many towns and cities began from modest roots in the feudal countryside where, often, some dwellings and a market had been established at the gate of a castle or monastery, leading to the extension of the castle walls. Many new towns were also established in this period.

The urban historian A.E.J. Morris classifies the towns resulting from the urban expansion of the Middle Ages as being either **organic growth towns or new towns**.[19] The former were those places that grew on the sites of old Roman towns, on the sites of fortified feudal villages, or on the sites of agricultural villages. London, Cologne, and Paris grew from such roots and greatly expanded in this period. The physical form of organic growth towns is partly conveyed by the name—that is, they generally lack any overall pattern. Except for a few main roads, the streets meander, and blocks of land are irregular in shape, as the plan of Carcassonne shows (see Figure 2.8). One still finds a residue of this amorphous medieval development at the centre of many large European cities

Figure 2.8	13th Century Carcassonne, France

A typical "organic growth" town of the Middle Ages: the few main streets connect the gates, castle (a), church (c), and market (b) as needed, and the overall pattern is irregular.

Figure 2.9	Florence, Italy

SOURCE: GERALD HODGE.

Florence is a classic example of a major city that grew organically, and its medieval form can still be experienced today in its central areas, despite the invasion of cars.

(see Figure 2.9); there are even a few examples in North America, such as the "Lower Town" in Québec City.

Morris subdivides the new towns of the Middle Ages into two types: **bastides** and **planted towns**. Both were used to consolidate territorial control by a king or ruling house. Bastides, as the name suggests, were bastions, fortified towns built to a predetermined plan. They employed a clear pattern for streets and blocks of land within rectangular or circular walls. Bastides were built mostly in the 13th century, in France, Wales, and England by Edward I, and by other rulers in Germany and Bohemia. Planted towns were new towns developed to promote trade as well as protect territory; New Brandenburg (see Figure 2.10) is an example of one such town. Cities such as Londonderry in Ireland and Berne in Switzerland owe their existence to this new form of town development.

Moreover, bastides and planted towns would prove to be models for cities in the New World a century or so later. When bastides were first built, there was a need to attract settlers to these regions, and this was done in part by providing the newcomers with plots of land inside and outside the walls. Land use allocation was much more egalitarian in the bastides than in earlier settlements. Their general gridiron pattern facilitated this, and the English, in particular, would come to use this model in their North American colonies.[20]

Whether new towns or those developed from earlier settlements, medieval towns were alike in many respects. The component parts were the wall and its gates, the marketplace, often with a market hall and commercial buildings, the church, and, sometimes, the castle. Main streets connected the main buildings and the market with the gates, and joined main areas

Figure 2.10 | Fortified German Town: New Brandenburg, 1248

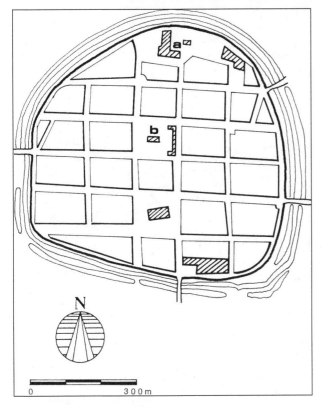

Towns such as this one were "planted" for territorial control in the late Middle Ages. They employed a fairly regular gridiron street pattern. Key: (a) church, (b) market square.

together. The rest of the land within the wall was allocated in blocks for residences and gardens. When land was needed for, say, a market or church square, either a block of land was left vacant or a street was widened at that point. Most streets were narrow, for movement was largely on foot.

During the town-building of the Middle Ages, material well-being also improved. Tradesmen, artisans, and merchants in many towns became prosperous and powerful enough to challenge the local rulers and gain citizenship. Especially in northern Europe, they often built guildhalls and a town hall adjacent to the market area of the town to signify the importance of the "burghers," or citizens of the "burg." In the long run of history, these steps to allocate the space of the city among king, church, and citizens were decisive to the development of a modern, segmented, urban way of life.

Renaissance and Baroque Cities: The Importance of Design

The period from 1400 to 1800, which encompasses the Renaissance and Baroque eras, is an influential one in regard to the form of cities today, for this is the period when the compact settlements of medieval Europe were dramatically extended, refined, and restructured. The city became an object of design, a means to express the aesthetic and functional aims of the period. These aims, in short, were a desire for order and discipline and a desire to impress. They can be seen in the designs of the painting and architecture of the time. In turn, they led to the designs for such special features as the gardens of Versailles, the grand boulevards of Paris, the avenues and piazzas of Rome (Figure 2.11), and the Georgian squares of London. The colonial cities that Europeans took to the Americas and Asia show the imprint of Renaissance/Baroque city design, as we see below.

Figure 2.11 | Giambattista Nolli's Map of Rome, 1748

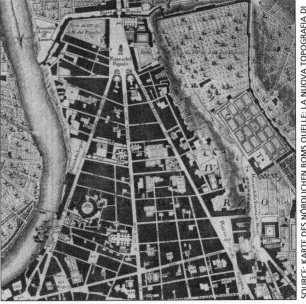

SOURCE: KARTE DES NÖRDLICHEN ROMS QUELLE: LA NUOVA TOPOGRAFIA DI ROMA COMASCO VON GIAMBATTISTA NOLLI, CA. 1692–1756.

Rome had collapsed from a city of over a million people at the height of its empire to under 20 000 in the Middle Ages. Pope Sixtus V (1520–90) cut several straight avenues from the gates through the organic street network and marked the intersections with obelisks in the piazzas. These interventions improved navigation for the many pilgrims visiting Rome and made the layout of the city clear to visitors, a feature that is still appreciated by modern tourists. The city's public space improvements influenced future city designers.

The major achievements in city-building in this period came after 1600. They were stimulated by the confluence of five factors: (1) the aesthetic theory and concepts coming from a revival of interest in the classical art forms of Rome and Greece; (2) the invention of printing and improvements in the production of paper; (3) the growth of wheeled traffic as a result of replacing the solid wheel with a lighter one made of a separate rim, spokes, and hub; (4) the invention of gunpowder, which rendered medieval fortifications obsolete; and (5) the accumulation of immense, autocratic powers by the heads of some nation-states and city-states.

The cumulative effect of these five factors was that cities were literally opened up by new avenues, public squares, and new residential districts. Moreover, the planning was a self-conscious undertaking, with certain design principles at the forefront: symmetry, coherence, perspective, and monumentality. The informal and somewhat ad hoc arrangements of the medieval town gave way to a "preoccupation," as Morris calls it, "with making a balanced composition" when making a city plan.[21]

Most of the planning activity was devoted to restructuring existing cities. The planners, who were mainly architects and engineers, employed three design components:[22] the main straight avenue, the gridiron pattern for local streets in new districts, and enclosed spaces. As Lewis Mumford says:

> The avenue is the most important symbol and the main fact about the baroque city. Not always was it possible to design a whole new city in the baroque mode; but in the layout of half a dozen new avenues, or in a new quarter, its character could be re-defined.[23]

The main avenue, often radiating from a monument or public square, was a functional necessity as much as a Renaissance/Baroque design concept (see Figure 2.12), for in this period the volume of wheeled traffic increased tremendously. There was resistance to this new mode of travel, as there would be later to railroads and urban expressways in cities, but the advantages were obvious for the flow of goods, people, and military equipment. The advent of the straight street for moving traffic, both on the main avenues and in new districts, marks the beginning of what Blumenfeld describes as the "street plan" for cities.

The public square was just as important in Renaissance/Baroque city design as the straight street. Squares were also conceived on an axial basis,

Figure 2.12 — 18th Century Karlsruhe, Germany

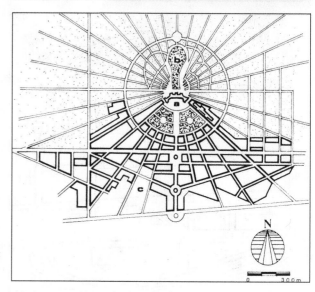

Figure 2.12 — 18th Century Karlsruhe, Germany

This is an example of the Renaissance city as an object of design, using straight and diagonal boulevards leading to focal points, in this case, the palace (a) and the royal gardens (b). The remainder of the town (c) had a modified gridiron street pattern.

sometimes provided by a main avenue leading to the square. In addition, squares were enclosed spaces; that is, they were designed as three-dimensional spaces to be surrounded by buildings or other landscape features providing an architectural harmony. Even main streets with their uniform façades took on this same sense of enclosure. This quality of architectural coherence, so often lauded by visitors to Europe's cities, probably best epitomizes the notion of urbanity in a city, a quality still sought in the building of present-day civic centres.

The cities of the 1400–1800 period still needed to be bastions of defence, but owing to the perfection of gunpowder and the cannon new means of fortification had to be found. Countless attempts were made to create an ideally defensible and livable city through the design of intricate systems of bastions and citadels. Plans for fortified towns, often based on the concepts of French military engineer Sebastian Vauban, were printed and widely available throughout Europe. Fortified cities influenced the modifications made to existing cities and the plans for several entirely new ones that have since become major cities: St. Petersburg in Russia, Mannheim in Germany, and Gothenburg in Sweden.

The Imprint of the Renaissance in the Americas

It was during the Renaissance, often called the Age of Discovery, that the systematic exploration and settlement of the Americas began. The initial European settlements were cast in the mould of city forms conceived in the home countries of the explorers and settlers. Defence of territorial claims was paramount at first, and the earliest settlements adopted the patterns of fortified towns in Europe, with a wall and citadel or main battery. Within the walls one finds the Renaissance street patterns and public squares. The plan for Louisbourg, Nova Scotia, provides an excellent illustration of the early French conception of new town-building in the New World. New Amsterdam, the original Dutch settlement at New York, was also built on similar principles.

The Spanish, the first and most assiduous colonizers, approached the planning of towns according to a set of written rules entitled The Laws of the Indies (sometimes called "America's first planning legislation"),[24] which covered everything from the selection of sites, the building of ramparts, and the specifications for the main plaza, to the location of principal streets and important buildings, and the size of lots.

The gridiron arrangement chosen by the French for Montréal, which faces on and parallels the St. Lawrence River, followed the bastide model; it is believed to have influenced such other French outposts in the Mississippi Valley as St. Louis, Mobile, and New Orleans.[25] The influence of Renaissance planning ideas through English settlement in North America is best seen in the towns established from New York to Georgia. These towns employed the gridiron layout of streets combined with public squares, following the pattern set by the new, fashionable residential districts of English cities in the mid-17th century.[26]

Two important examples are the plans for Philadelphia (see Figure 2.13) in 1682 and Savannah (Figure 2.14) in 1735, which carry forth the concept for an entire city. The plan William Penn chose for Philadelphia was a gridiron designed by surveyor Thomas Holme. The two major streets crossed near the centre and formed a public square, and each quadrant had its own square. James Oglethorpe's plan for Savannah made more refined use of the Georgian square by providing one in each ward of 40 houses; the wards were bounded by roads of the main gridiron and can be likened in concept to the "superblocks" used in 20th century planning.

The last direct Renaissance influence on North American cities came from the plan Major Pierre Charles L'Enfant prepared for Washington in 1791 (see Figure 2.15). L'Enfant was a French émigré engineer

Figure 2.13 — Philadelphia: Thomas Holme's Plan of 1682

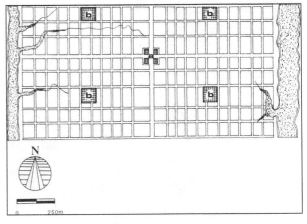

Governor William Penn chose a plan prepared by Thomas Holme reflecting English Renaissance city design, using the regular grid block and squares similar to those from London's Georgian era (a, b). The main cross streets were 30 metres (100 feet) wide, and stretched about 3 kilometres (2 miles) east and west and 1.5 kilometres (one mile) north and south. The central square (a) was 4 hectares (10 acres) in size.

Figure 2.14 — Savannah, Georgia: Oglethorpe's 1734 Plan

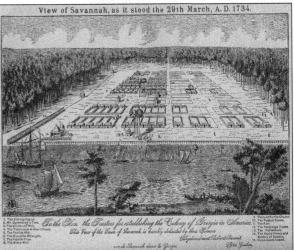

SOURCE: SAVANNAH 1734 BIRD'S EYE VIEW, PETER GORDON (1876). US LIBRARY OF CONGRESS/97683565.

James Oglethorpe's plan for Savannah was the basis for the expansion of the city for over a century. Its squares form the structure of the city's charming downtown neighbourhoods.

Figure 2.15 L'Enfant's Plan for Washington, 1791

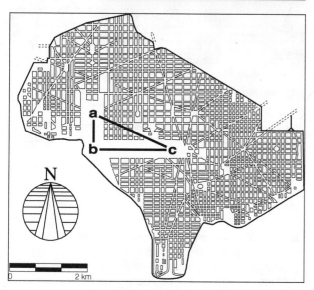

Pierre L'Enfant adopted the French Renaissance traditions for his grand plan for the government buildings and monuments of Washington. A system of radial streets focuses on important points and is superimposed on a gridiron. His "federal triangle" links (a) the President's (White) House, (b) the Washington Monument, and (c) the Congressional (Capitol) Building.

and artist who served under George Washington, and who had grown up at the court of Versailles. In remarkably short order, estimated at less than six months, he developed an adaptation of Baroque monumental vistas, city squares, and diagonal streets superimposed on a grid of local streets. Despite such mundane impediments as awkward intersections and building lots (caused by the radial avenues crossing the local grid), the plan is noteworthy for its grand scale and its assiduous application of Baroque concepts to an entire city. Plans for several other cities employing a similar radial-grid pattern—Detroit, Buffalo, and Indianapolis—followed shortly thereafter, but only small parts of them were ever completed.

The L'Enfant plan nearly did not come to fruition. Its implementation depended on the sale of private building lots to pay the costs of the new public buildings, avenues, and squares. Washington went through a long and fitful period when land either did not sell, or was not built upon, or, when built upon, encroached on public areas. Construction even took place on the Mall linking the Capitol and the Washington Monument, and a railway was authorized to cross it as well. For much of the 19th century, Washington was referred to as "a plan without a city."[27]

In contrast to city development in Baroque Europe, the communities of North America were promoted as places where colonists would have a large measure of freedom to develop their own land. Thus, the control

Planning Issue 2.1 In Halifax, Battle Lines Drawn in Controversy Over Views and Vistas

The Globe and Mail
April 17, 2012

In Halifax, Battle Lines Drawn in Controversy Over Views and Vistas

Jane Taber and Anna Mehler Paperny

City grappling with how to make itself more vibrant and modern while protecting heritage character

For nearly 40 years, the views of downtown Halifax from the city's historic Citadel Hill have been held sacred, with Haligonians protecting sweeping vistas of their harbour and the peninsula with a series of strict rules.

But significant change is in the wind. For the first time since the so-called "viewplane" legislation came into effect in 1974, the city is about to amend the law because of the absurd situation in which one Halifax developer has found himself.

Joe Metlege has had to put on hold his $150-million redevelopment project of Fenwick Tower, originally built in 1969. Last month, permits in hand and work about to begin, he discovered the corners on one side of the 12th floor of the 34-storey apartment building would protrude 3.5 feet into the viewplane from Citadel Hill to the harbour.

He alerted the city.

The encroachment, caused by a new glass skin that was to be put on tower's exterior, is indiscernible to the naked eye from Citadel Hill, which is about a kilometre away. It has been described by Robert Stapells, the former city councillor who helped created the viewplane rules, as the "equivalent of attaching a sewing needle to the building."

And so on Tuesday, council voted to start the public consultation process to adjust the viewplane boundaries to accommodate the technicality. The process will take at least five months – a delay that will cost Mr. Metlege and his company, Templeton Properties Ltd., about $1 million.

Halifax, like other big Canadian cities, is grappling with how to make its downtown core more vibrant and modern to attract business and people while at the same time protect the city's character. Part of that character involves iconic views, which cities such as Vancouver (with its North Shore mountains) and Toronto (with its landmark Queen's Park) have struggled to protect from high-rise condominiums and other new buildings.

Says Toronto's acting chief planner Gregg Lintern: "It's more than a luxury … People consider views to be a part of the city's landscape and part of the city's image."

In Halifax, defenders of the city's historical legacy feel that projects such as Fenwick are a threat to Halifax's very essence.

"The difficulty is that if council starts entertaining requests to allow viewplanes to be narrowed, it's a very slippery slope," says Phil Pacey, the chair of the Halifax Regional Municipality committee of the Heritage Trust of Nova Scotia.

"We know that there are sketches of people up on Citadel Hill for recreation as early as 1759 … so people have been enjoying the view … since 1759. That's 253 years," says Mr. Pacey. "We don't want to see the view whittled away by 3.5 feet at a time. It is a non-renewable resource. It is a finite resource and any blockage just takes away from that."

Mr. Pacey was not pleased by council's decision to proceed – but Sue Uteck, the councillor for the area, argues that redevelopment of the Fenwick Tower is not an "assault on the viewplane legislation."

Rather, this is an engineering issue. "Is Tom the Tourist going to be offended that we went into the viewplane by a foot? I don't think so."

And Fred Morley, vice-president of the Greater Halifax Partnership, an economic development group in the city, says a plan is merely a guideline. It is not cast in stone.

"We need to interpret these rules with a degree of common sense," he says, "and recognize there are people out there that don't want growth of any kind, that want to see some kind of freeze-dried Brigadoon. That's their vision for Halifax and that's not reality."

Reality or not, it is a view that has become entrenched as Halifax, whose identity is very much rooted in its history as a British redoubt. It has a very defined sense of itself and its heritage.

For Mr. Metlege, however, the rules are prohibitive. Just 29 years old, he is of a younger generation of Haligonians, who want their city to be vibrant and world-class.

That isn't happening, he argues, because of these viewplane restrictions, which he says have taken on an "almost sacred title."

He believes, they have compromised the "architectural integrity" of the city.

"No wonder you have no architecturally intriguing buildings in Halifax," he argues, suggesting that is why the downtown core is full of square, squat office buildings.

"I am not advocating getting rid of the viewplanes," he says. "I am advocating having a conversation about it. . . . What is the economic impact [of the rules] on the city?"

Councillor Uteck, meanwhile, shakes her head, adding: "Welcome to Halifax, where any building over five storeys is a controversy."

CONTINUED

Chapter 2 The Beginnings of Today's Cities

Three Canadian Cities and Their Battles to Protect the Views

Anna Mehler Paperny

Vancouver

It's a very Vancouverite kind of quandary: What do you do when a park full of trees is messing with your view of the mountains?

In 2008, the city took it upon itself to remove about 70 trees in Queen Elizabeth Park, and prune another eight. The park, the city's highest point, is one of more than 30 "view cones" designated as vistas to be protected. The trees, like any other view-obstructing new development, were not welcome.

Sound crazy? Not here.

"You're constantly interacting with the skyline," says assistant planning director Kevin McNaney. "It's not some abstract thing you see."

Toronto

The condo-crazy city has an often conflicted relationship with building in and around its most famous vistas and historic sites. Last year, the Ontario Municipal Board found the city's existing sightline rules didn't mean it could restrict a tall development that planners said would obscure sightlines leading to Queen's Park, Ontario's legislature. Now the city is making specific sightline rules for Queen's Park, City Hall and the courthouse at Old City Hall.

"This recent direction … is trying to be a bit more proactive," said acting chief planner Gregg Lintern. "The downtown area is generally a place where growth is encouraged. So you want to strike that balance."

Montreal

For a city built on an island, Montreal doesn't often give you an intimation of waterfront proximity.

"Often you don't even have the sense you're on an island: You don't see the shore, you don't see the water," says Suzanne Corbeil, a municipal lawyer who just won a legal planning victory for the Montreal borough of Pierrefonds-Roxboro. Quebec's Superior Court found officials acted fairly in enacting height restrictions that effectively blocked the construction of an eight-storey condominium on a riverside cul-de-sac.

Montreal's urban plan designates protected sightlines of both the waterfront and Mount Royal.

"The city considers that certain views are really part of our patrimonial heritage – our wealth," Ms. Corbeil said. "So they try to preserve that."

that rulers of European states were able to impose over civic structures in their home cities did not exist to the same degree in their colonies. Renaissance designs could be brought to North America, but could not always be achieved. However, the idea of creating views and vistas of prominent buildings and landscapes became an important component of planning in future Canadian cities.

Contributions of 19th Century Idealist Planners

Even as designs for cities in Europe were elaborated, these cities began to expand precipitously as the Industrial Revolution came into its own. The burden of this expansion was felt in inadequate housing, water supply, and sewage disposal; in short, in massive slums. The congestion, squalor, and filth made the lives of the lower class unbearable and threatened the quality of life for other sections of society. The Industrial Revolution also broke down the centuries-old connection between the town and countryside. The persistence of these conditions led to many proposals to create new urban environments. Philanthropic efforts from the ruling class, political initiatives from radicals and socialists, and ideas from utopian thinkers all combined to suggest ways to intervene in the deplorable physical conditions. Importantly, they all carried their own ideals and values about the conduct of community life as well. Many of these ideals remain firmly embedded in approaches to community planning today.

Robert Owen and the Utopians

One such idealistic scheme was that of **Robert Owen**, a rich English industrialist, who presented a plan for a cooperative community combining industry and agriculture in 1816. His proposal for New Lanark was for a settlement of 1200 people covering about 480 hectares of agricultural land. Dwellings were grouped around a large open square, three sides of which would be taken up by residence blocks for couples and children of less than three years of age; the fourth side would contain the young people's dormitories, the infirmary, and guest accommodation. The central area would have such public buildings as schools, a library, a communal restaurant, and clubs, along with other areas for recreation. Around the perimeter would be gardens, farm buildings, and industrial units. To complement his physical plan, Owen proposed a cooperative community structure with much emphasis on education and on blending work in the factory with study and leisure.

Owen did not succeed in gaining support from authorities to build a prototype of his new town in Britain. He tried to develop a similar community in the United States in 1825—New Harmony, Indiana—but had to give that up in a few years (Figure 2.16). Despite these disappointments, Owen's ideas were very influential. His **parallelogram system**, named for the rectangular form of the town he propounded, came to be widely known, much cited, and imitated.

Figure 2.16	Proposed Model Community of New Harmony, Indiana, by Robert Owen, 1825

New Harmony was a new town built in the wilderness. It pioneered innovative social concepts such as a free public library and a public school system for both women and men. This image was Robert Owen's promotional drawing for a larger town that was never built, after the economic base of the community collapsed.

Figure 2.17	Proposed Phalanstery Model Community by Charles Fourier, 1832

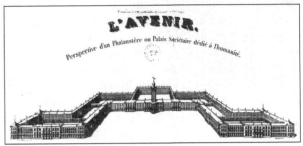

This illustration was reprinted in the title page of Fourier's influential 1832 booklet.

Charles Fourier, a French utopian writer of the same era, proposed a community of about 1600 people carefully chosen according to their ages, who would be housed in a single building, the Phalanstery, surrounded by over 2 square kilometres of land (Figure 2.17). All accommodation would be communal to concentrate human relationships and achieve the "universal harmony" he propounded. Between 1830 and 1850, there were at least 50 attempts to create Phalanstery in different countries. The connection with the pastoral landscape is also important, as planning historian Leonardo Benevolo notes about Fourier's plan:

> The land shall be provided with a fine stream of water, it shall be intersected by hills and adapted to varied cultivation; it should be contiguous with a forest and not far removed from a large city, but sufficiently so to escape intruders.[28]

Godin, a French admirer of Fourier's ideas, adapted the idea to the city and industrial production. His proposals for Familistery promoted the family unit, which would be housed in its own apartment, but with communal amenities; a workers' cooperative would control the housing and the factory. **Cabet**, another source of French utopian thought, proposed a city, called Icaria, of metropolitan scale. Cabet conceived of a physical form that would separate traffic from pedestrian walkways, put factories on the outskirts, and have two circumferential boulevards. A prototype of Icaria was begun in Illinois in 1849 by Cabet and several hundred followers, but never grew very large.

Two British ideal town plans of the mid-19th century sought to bring order to chaotic city environments through the design of the physical form alone and did not attempt to restructure social relations. Hygeia, planned by **Benjamin Richardson**, and Victoria, by **John Buckingham**, both insisted on the need for fresh air, light, and water, and on a regular and uniform design to bring order to the lives of city dwellers. Buckingham's plan is the best known, with its series of concentric squares, each containing rows of buildings for houses, workshops, and so forth. Public buildings were at the centre, as were the houses for the wealthiest inhabitants; factories and other industrial activities were located away from the centre. It was in many ways a plan to help achieve efficient production for factories and provide full employment and amicable surroundings for workers.

Although most of these ideal towns were never built, the efforts of the idealists were important in the development of planning concepts in two ways: (1) they were the first attempts at community planning that considered the sources of employment *and* the social structure of the inhabitants; and (2) they represented the beginning of the development of technical and geometric skills applied to community planning. The widespread enthusiasm garnered by these proposals indicated the increasing willingness of people to accept technical professional advice in improving communities.

Model Industrial Towns

The proposals of the Utopians, in stressing the connection between improved living conditions for industrial workers and social harmony, stimulated many industrial owners in the second half of the 19th century to build "model" communities. The aims were more paternalistic than philanthropic, concerned as they were with enhancing workers' efficiency. Nevertheless, the plans for model communities provided further evidence of the ability to conceive of technical solutions to some of the urban problems of the time. In 1846, building of the industrial village of Bessbrook began for linen mill workers near Newry, Ireland. In 1853, Titus Salt started building Saltaire, a model town for the 3000 workers at his textile mill near Bradford in England. Similar communities were built in France, Belgium, Holland, and Italy. The Krupp family of industrialists built four workers' settlements around Essen in Germany between 1863 and 1875.

Several new British industrial towns built toward the end of the 19th century are also worthy of note. Bournville, near Birmingham, was built by chocolate manufacturer George Cadbury in 1879; the "Bournville" has been a popular chocolate bar for decades. Residential areas were broken into groups through the use of intervening parks and playgrounds. The land on which the town was built was deeded to the community and has remained under town ownership to this day, while Cadbury remains one of the town's largest employers (see Figure 2.18).

Cocoa manufacturer Joseph Rowntree built Earswick near York in 1905; it too was made a community trust. The architects Barry Parker and Raymond Unwin planned Earswick as they had Port Sunlight for Lever Brothers in 1886. In these towns, Parker and Unwin began to design housing areas in large blocks with their own interior gardens and play spaces. These design features were key components of Unwin and Parker's plans for early 20th century garden cities and garden suburbs. Their garden suburb crescents and culs-de-sac are mirrored in post–World War II subdivisions across Canada.

Reflections

The ideas for new physical forms for communities and for alterations to existing forms, as traced above, represent technical design solutions to meet the needs of a community. Underlying these solutions is the aim of meeting the social needs of a community so that the daily activities of people, businesses, institutions, and governments can be conducted with relative ease. There must be adequate shelter, potable water, and means of disposing of waste; provisions for safety and security; ways of getting around; and venues for social occasions. From the time of the earliest city-builders, these needs were recognized and met with varying degrees of

Figure 2.18	Bournville Village Green, ca. 1929

This illustration of the Bournville Village Green was reprinted in a 1931 promotional booklet. The generous public spaces and landscape had matured into a model town.

SOURCE: SCIENCE PHOTO LIBRARY.

| Figure 2.19 | Patrick Geddes, ca. 1886 |

One of the most important 19th century contributors to planning ideas that are still cogent today is Patrick Geddes (Figure 2.19). Born in 1854, Geddes trained as a botanist with Thomas Huxley and thereby gained his enduring interest in ecological principles. His concern over the abysmal living conditions in British cities led him to try to apply these principles to the organization of cities. His means for doing this were pragmatic, intellectual, and professional. In the 1880s, he moved into one of Edinburgh's filthiest slum tenements and proceeded to help renovate it as a way of guiding the inhabitants to see how they could improve their own living quarters. In 1892, he established his Outlook Tower in Edinburgh, which allowed people to view the city and to view an exhibition of Geddes's ideas about the interrelationships of social, economic, and physical features of a city (see Figure 8.2).

As one biographer has said, "Geddes cannot be limited to a single discipline or profession, he must be described in a hyphenated manner, as a planner-teacher-sociologist-political economist-botanist-activist."[29] Because of these prodigious interests, Geddes brought a new approach to the task of community planning. He appreciated that human life and its individual and collective environments, both natural and manufactured, are all intertwined, and that improving cities means understanding them and planning for that reality rather than substituting another urban form. Geddes was a practical idealist:

> Eutopia, then, lies in the city around us: and it must be planned and realised, here or nowhere, by us as its citizens—each a citizen of both the actual and the ideal city seen increasingly as one.[30]

Geddes pioneered his ideas through various forms—exhibitions, lectures, writing—and through planning practices. In the early part of the 20th century, Geddes practised planning in Britain and in India. He saw community planning, in many ways, as a learning experience, both for the community and the planner. Geddes is often credited with the dictum "No plan before survey." He stressed the importance of knowing a town's geography, history, economy, social conditions, and means of transportation and communication. Not only was he the first planner to specify what should be in the "town survey" but he also advocated that its results—maps, charts, photographs, and so on—be put on public

CONTINUED

display. Canadian planner Kent Gerecke cites Geddes's "integrative linking" as perhaps the contribution most missing from today's planning.[31]

Geddes was among the first to give thoughtful consideration to what came to be called "urban renewal" in the 1950s. He saw no merit in bulldozing slum areas to the ground because the displaced people would simply be forced to relocate. His concept of **conservative surgery** required that efforts be made to remove as few buildings as possible and to repair and modify existing structures. Human disruption would thus be **minimized**, and the physical fabric of the city maintained. Geddes was also the first to recognize that as cities spread out they often grew together into a "conurbation." He cautioned against the effects on the natural landscape, agricultural resources, and rural communities that would result from simply letting cities grow outward. Patrick Geddes is truly the first regional planner (see also Chapter 8).

---

success. With the advent of the Industrial Revolution, communities began growing very quickly in both population size and industrial activity. Not only did it become difficult to meet these basic needs; they were also often overlooked or disregarded. The idealist planners were stimulated by these situations. They made a lasting contribution by clearly stating that community planning had *social* components and that planners could and should address them.

By the middle of the 19th century, the broad strokes of the future community-planning profession were becoming clear. For one, planning would need to go beyond a community's physical form and provide for **living areas**, **working areas** (for industry, shopping, business), **transportation**, and **public facilities** within the overall design. For another, it would need to recognize the natural environment as integral to a community's well-being. And, not least, it would need to devise the means by which a pluralist society could carry out such planning. The next three chapters trace the evolution of planners' and communities' sometimes fitful responses to this challenge over the ensuing century and a half, bringing us to the current community planning ethos and practice in Canada. In every endeavour, the past remains important because it is a road map to both the present and the future. Thus, questions to keep in mind regarding this and the next few chapters are:

- *How can we use the planning lessons of the past to better serve today's needs of a community's residents?*
- *What three contributions of 19th century idealist planners might be used today?*

Reference Notes

1. An excellent background on the issues surrounding city-building throughout history is found in James W. Vance, *The Continuing City* (Baltimore: Johns Hopkins University Press, 1990), 24ff. Perhaps the best chronological account of the physical planning of cities is A.E.J. Morris, *History of Urban Form* (New York: John Wiley, 1979). Spiro Kostof's *The City Shaped: City Patterns and Meanings Through History* (Boston: Little Brown, 1991) and *The City Assembled: Elements of Urban Form Through History* (Boston: Little Brown, 1992) address selected urban form issues in greater depth.

2. Hans Blumenfeld, "Form and Function in Urban Communities," in Hans Blumenfeld, *The Modern Metropolis*, edited by Paul D. Spreiregen (Montréal: Harvest House, 1967), 4.

3. Adam Smith, *The Wealth of Nations,* 1775; and Lewis Mumford, *The City in History* (New York: Harcourt Brace and World, 1961).

4. Jane Jacobs, *The Economy of Cities* (New York: Random House, 1969) and *Cities and the Wealth of Nations* (New York: Random House, 1984); also Peter Hall, *Cities and Civilization* (London: Weidenfeld and Nicolson, 1998).

5. F. Haverfield, *Ancient Town Planning* (Oxford: Clarendon Press, 1913), 25.

6. H.W. Fairman, "Town Planning in Pharaonic Egypt," *Town Planning Review* (April 1949); Mumford, *City in History*, Ch. 7; and Morris, *History of Urban Form*, 12–14.

7. Morris, *History of Urban Form*, 14–16, 255.

8. Steen Eiler Rasmussen, *Towns and Buildings* (Cambridge, MA: MIT Press, 1949), 8.

9. Thomas Adams, *Outline of Town and City Planning* (New York: Russell Sage Foundation, 1935), 47.

10. Francis Violich, *Cities of Latin America* (New York: Reinhold Publishing, 1944), 22ff.

11. Hall, *Cities and Civilization*, Ch. 2.

12. Hall, Ch. 22.

13. R.E. Wycherly, *How the Greeks Built Cities* (London: Macmillan, 1962).

14. Robert W. McCabe, "Shops and Shopping in Ancient Rome," *Plan Canada* 19 (September–December 1979), 183–199; and Hall, *Cities and Civilization*, Ch. 22.

15. McCabe, "Shops and Shopping."

16. Rasmussen, *Towns and Buildings*, 8.

17. Blumenfeld, "Form and Function," 24.

18. Vance, *Continuing City*.
19. Morris, *History of Urban Form*, 66.
20. Vance, *Continuing City*, 200ff.
21. Morris, *History of Urban Form*, 125.
22. Ibid., 125ff.
23. Mumford, *City in History*, 367.
24. John Reps, *Town Planning in Frontier America* (Princeton, NJ: Princeton University Press, 1969), 41; for Spanish colonial towns, see Reps, *The Making of Urban America* (Princeton, NJ: Princeton University Press, 1965), 26–55.
25. Reps, *Town Planning*, 82.
26. Vance, *Continuing City*, 234ff.
27. Frederick Gutheim and Antoinette Lee, *Worthy of the Nation: Washington, DC, from L'Enfant to the National Capital Planning Commission*, 2nd ed. (Baltimore: Johns Hopkins University Press, 2006).
28. As quoted in Leonardo Benevolo, *The Origins of Modern Town Planning* (London: Routledge & Kegan Paul, 1967), 59.
29. Marshall Stalley, ed., *Patrick Geddes: Spokesman for Man and the Environment* (New Brunswick, NJ: Rutgers University Press, 1972), xii; and Helen Meller, *Patrick Geddes: Social Evolutionist and City Planner* (London: Routledge, 1990).
30. Stalley, *Patrick Geddes*, 112.
31. Kent Gerecke, "Patrick Geddes, a Message for Today!" *City Magazine* 10:3 (Winter 1988), 27–35.

Internet Resources

Chapter-Relevant Sites

Planning Canadian Communities
www.planningcanadiancommunities.ca

Mohenjo-Daro: Indus Valley civilization
www.mohenjodaro.org

Mesopotamia
www.mesopotamia.co.uk

Greek and Roman architecture in the classical tradition
http://act.art.queensu.ca

City water resources in Rome, 800 BCE–2000 CE
www.iath.virginia.edu/waters

Interactive Nolli map of Rome
http://nolli.uoregon.edu/

Robert Owen and New Lanark: Urban planning 1794–1918, compiled by John Reps
www.library.cornell.edu/Reps/DOCS

Chapter Three

19th Century Foundations of Canadian Communities

The development of [Canadian] towns has been chaotic, and tens of thousands of so-called houses have been thrown together, which must, sooner or later, be condemned for sanitary reasons. As for town planning, there has been none.

Dr. Charles A. Hodgetts, 1912

The foundations of Canadian communities and their planning are emerged from an array of experiences and ideas of the late 19th century and even prior to that time. European settlers used physical forms familiar to them to start many of our cities and towns, often locating them where Aboriginal settlements had been for centuries before. Economic and population growth along with changes in technology led, in turn, to problems of ugly streetscapes, squalid living conditions, lack of open spaces, and inadequate public utilities. Each of these concerns generated community outcry and active movements urging that they be dealt with. Not infrequently, these were in competition with one another for public backing. Such backing was often not forthcoming from local governments, which were themselves underdeveloped.

Community planning emerged because of these concerns and also within the throes of their solutions. Indeed, it evolved alongside changing urban problems and community perceptions of them. The period just before and after 1900 was a vital and formative period for community planning and merits reflection on the following questions:

- *How was contemporary community planning shaped by factors prominent in 19th century Canada?*
- *What were the basic differences in the lay-outs of early French and British settlements?*

Aboriginal Settlements

The location and design of the Aboriginal communities in Canada had little influence upon European settlement in the 18th and 19th centuries when compared to Mexico, whose capital city is located on the site of the ancient Aztec city of Tenochtitlán. Across vast stretches of the western and northern parts of Canada, the Aboriginal peoples were nomadic hunter–gatherers, rather than city-builders. Their shelters were often portable tents or huts and domed snow houses that were renewed each season.[1]

Two regions that had more permanent Aboriginal communities were the southern Ontario lowlands, extending to Montréal, and along the Pacific coast. The Huron and Iroquois peoples were successful farmers, raising corn and living in rectangular, barrel-roofed houses (longhouses) in small villages. Most settlements were fortified with log palisades, due to continuing warfare, and the villages were often destroyed or moved (see Figure 3.1, top). In comparison, the well-built log-and-plank longhouses in the unfortified fishing villages of the Pacific coast might last for decades. Some of the villages of the Salish, Bella Coola, Haida, Kwakiutl, and Nootka peoples were still intact on their coastal sites in the late 19th century (see Figure 3.1, bottom).

If the early European settlers were clever, they paid close attention to the location of Aboriginal camps that offered clean water, shelter from winds, and access to river transportation and wildlife. Almost every settlement by European settlers prior to the railroad was sited near an Aboriginal camp for these environmental reasons, including Toronto and Kingston. Further, many place names have Aboriginal roots: Canada, Québec, Toronto, and Ottawa (indeed, Toronto meant "meeting place" to First Nations people of the area). But the design and construction of European settlements were little informed by Aboriginal practices. The expansion of farms and towns across the southern half of the country displaced entire Aboriginal communities onto reserves, often with disastrous social consequences.[2] Current planning for First Nations settlements is discussed in Chapter 10.

SOURCE: (TOP) ARTIST'S RENDITION OF THE DRAPER SITE, BY IVAN KOCSIS, COPYRIGHT MUSEUM OF ONTARIO ARCHAEOLOGY, LONDON; (BOTTOM) GEORGE M. DAWSON/LIBRARY AND ARCHIVES CANADA/PA-037756.

Figure 3.1	Aboriginal Settlements in Central and Western North America

Iroquois villages (top) consisted of a palisade of logs surrounding a collection of longhouses (ca. 14th century). Skidegate Village (bottom) of the Haida Nation in the Haida Gwaii (Queen Charlotte Islands), 1878.

Plans for Frontier Communities

The locations and the layouts used in the fortresses, trading posts, and railway towns from European settlement are still prominent features in their present city forms. Moreover, all but a few of the places that have become cities were developed initially on the basis of a simple site plan. From the towns of the French regime along the St. Lawrence and the British in the Maritimes, to those established later in Ontario, British Columbia, and the Prairie provinces, plans were usually made before or at the time of building of a community. A brief survey will help show the forms that characterized the early community plans as each region came to be settled.

French Canada

The earliest planned communities in Canada were those established by the French in the early 17th century. Three on the St. Lawrence River have become major cities today: Ville de Québec (1608), Trois-Rivières (1634), and Montréal (1642). Ville de Québec and Montréal are the most distinctive. Québec's Old City (Figure 3.2) has the character of a medieval organic growth town (see Figure 2.8, Carcassonne, page 26). The form of Montréal (Figure 3.3) is more like that of a planted town, or bastide, such as those developed for settling new territories in France and other parts of Europe in the Middle Ages (see Figure 2.10, Brandenburg, page 27).[3]

Ville de Québec's Lower Town, built by Champlain on a narrow river terrace, assumed a generally rectilinear pattern of narrow streets in which one block was left open for a public square, Place Royale, onto which fronted the town's church. The Upper Town developed outward from the fort and the cathedral. The *place d'armes* in front of the governor's fort gave an orientation to one set of rectangular housing blocks, while the *grande place* in front of the cathedral provided a different orientation

SOURCE: AUTHORS' COLLECTION.

Figure 3.3 | Old Montréal Plan, 1758

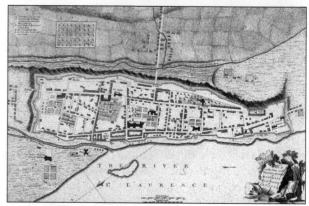

to another set of housing blocks. Housing development and fortifications expanded hand in hand as the Upper Town grew, with the walls, in the 1720s, reaching the extent we see today. In the late 18th century, in an attempt to give some overall order, two parallel streets were run through the town, each to a main gate in the wall.[4]

Montréal's Old City was laid out in a more regular form than Ville de Québec's. It is shaped, as a visitor in 1721 remarked, like a "long rectangle."[5] It extends for about 1 kilometre along the face of a ridge that slopes down to the St. Lawrence River. Walls eventually enclosed the town, but these are now gone. In 1672, two major streets that ran the length of the settlement were surveyed. Other streets, running up the hill between the two main streets, were not regularly spaced. The resulting pattern is an irregular, but now picturesque, gridiron, with many of the original public squares still remaining. Recently discovered manuscripts suggest that Montréal's original plan also may have derived from Champlain.[6]

The most interesting of the early French community plans, and among the few truly original Canadian plans, are those for three villages 10 kilometres northwest of Ville de Québec that were laid out by Jean Talon in 1667. In an effort to settle the rural population in villages (as in France) rather than in long, narrow lots strung out along the St. Lawrence River, Talon developed three villages: Charlesbourg, Bourg Royal, and L'Auvergne. The village design is based on the idea of farm lots radiating out from a central square surrounded by a road, on the outside of which would be located the village church, flour mill, shops, and so forth. Each village was about 2.5 kilometres on a side, and the central square, called the *traite-quarre*, about

Figure 3.2 | Ville de Québec Plan, 1764

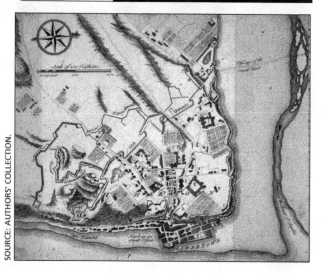

SOURCE: AUTHORS' COLLECTION.

275 metres on a side.[7] A main road was projected to bisect the area in each direction to link up with the other towns. There were 10 farms of 35 *arpents* (about 14 hectares) in each quadrant. Charlesbourg is now part of the urbanized area of metropolitan Québec, but its radial pattern can still be discerned. Figure 3.4 shows two of these villages.

Louisbourg, the imposing fortress town on Cape Breton Island, is another major example of French community design, but here the form and concept are completely "imported." French military engineer Jean-Francois de Verville constructed a fortified city in the tradition of Sebastian Vauban (see Figure 3.5). There were 4 major bastions, 5 kilometres of ramparts, many demi-bastions, and outworks surrounding the town. It was meant for 4000 persons and was laid out as a regular gridiron. The town lasted a scant 40 years; the British demolished its fortifications in 1760.[8] The restoration of Louisbourg according to its original plan, when complete, will provide the best example of a late-Renaissance fortified town outside Europe.

Atlantic Canada

St. John's, Newfoundland, is the oldest community in Canada. In 1583, Sir Humphrey Gilbert formally established the British claim to the area. No plan exists

---

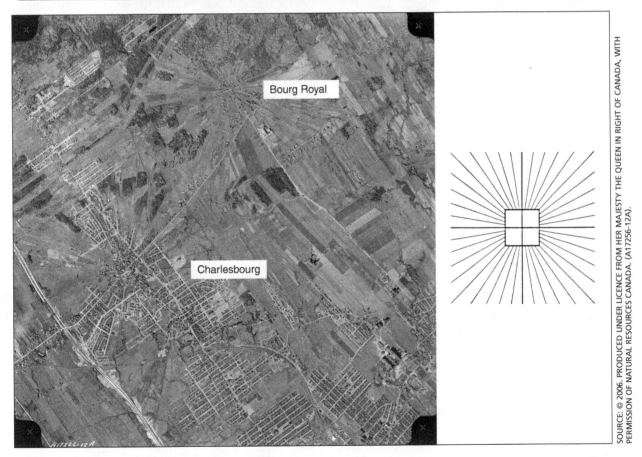

Jean Talon's radial plan for two villages north of Ville de Québec: Charlesbourg and Bourg Royal. A central square at the intersection of roads to neighbouring villages was reserved for a church, cemetery, and flour mill. Settlers' houses were arranged around the square on each of the 40 triangular farms. Each village was about 6 square kilometres. The 1960s aerial photo clearly shows the original radial pattern in these two towns. Both are now part of the Québec Urban Community.

Louisbourg, Cape Breton Island, 1720

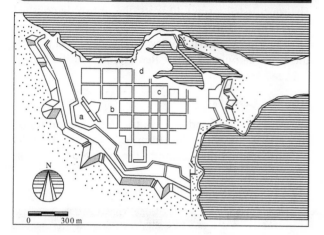

This French fortress town for 4000 combined the Renaissance gridiron street pattern and the fortification designed for the era of cannon and gunpowder. It is slowly being restored by Parks Canada. Key: (a) main bastion, (b) square, (c) hospital, (d) market.

for the founding of St. John's; it seems rather to have evolved from a fishing village oriented to the shoreline. The pattern that emerged gradually for the town, and that still dominates the city's central area, was of two streets that parallel the irregular curve of the shore. One, near the water's edge and called Lower Path, is now the main business street, Water Street; the other, further up the slope and called Upper Path originally, is also a major street today.

When the British began to establish permanent settlement in other parts of the Atlantic region, in the mid-18th century, communities were developed according to plans. These were almost invariably a regular gridiron, rectangular in shape, and carefully surveyed. Typically, British colonial towns of this period were laid out relative to a survey baseline along the harbour but sufficiently inland to provide an uninterrupted street on which other street lines could be established. This was the fashion in the original town sites for Charlottetown (1768) (see Figure 3.6), Saint John (1783), and even on the steep hillsides of Lunenburg (1753) and Halifax. These plans allowed space for a church, a governor's residence, barracks and parade ground, cemetery, and warehouses, and were usually surrounded by a palisade. In the 1749 plan for Halifax, Britain's primary North Atlantic naval station, five forts were located on the perimeter of the town. The

central fort remains today on Citadel Hill, overlooking downtown and the harbour.

Although the early plans for towns in this region generally follow the simplest of surveyor's layouts, they were based on the notion of providing a pool of relatively equal building sites. This was aimed at attracting settlers from Europe, many of whom would not normally be able to have their own land. The gridiron pattern of streets and lots fills this function most effectively and would come to be the most widely used city form as Canada spread westward in the 18th and 19th centuries.

One other plan merits attention. In 1785, the Governor of Cape Breton, a well-known cartographer, Colonel des Barres, prepared a plan for Sydney that is undoubtedly derived from the forms of Georgian England.[9] It is also similar to the plan for Annapolis, Maryland, with circular plazas and axial streets. Actually, the des Barres plan was a regional plan in that five satellite communities were envisioned outside Sydney, linked by boulevards radiating from the central circular plaza.

Charlottetown, 1771, by Thomas Wright

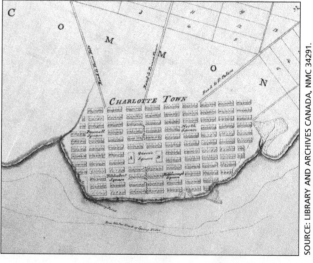

The first British colonial towns in Canada featured a regular gridiron of blocks divided into individual building lots for settlers. The grid typically started from a survey baseline along the harbour. The small blocks in Charlottetown's original waterfront grid have retained their historic ambience and charm. In this early map, note the central square and four neighbourhood squares, similar to the Philadelphia plan. The original town site was surrounded by commonland, which provided room for future expansion and defense works.

Upper Canada

Settlement of what is now Ontario began in the years following the American Revolutionary War. The Governor-General, Lord Dorchester, had ambitious plans for the development of this unsettled area, which included a system of townships each averaging 100 square miles (260 square kilometres) and each containing a town site (see Figure 3.7). The towns were to be a mile square (2.6 square kilometres) divided into one-acre (0.4-hectare) "town lots" and were to include space for streets, church, market, and defence works.[10] A large military reserve of land surrounded the town, which was surrounded, in turn, by a grid of 10-hectare "park lots" and 80-hectare "farm lots." Although the concept of "mile square" towns was contemplated on

| Figure 3.7 | Lord Dorchester's Model Township Plan, 1789 |

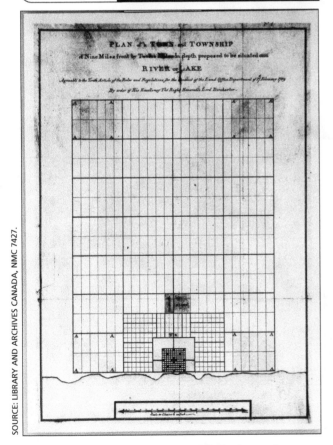

This demonstration plan for a town situated on a river or lake incorporated Canada's first town planning regulations. The ring of empty space surrounding the town was to be a military reserve, and the large lots immediately beyond were "park lots" for the country estates of favoured settlers.

| Figure 3.8 | Original Plan for Toronto, 1788 |

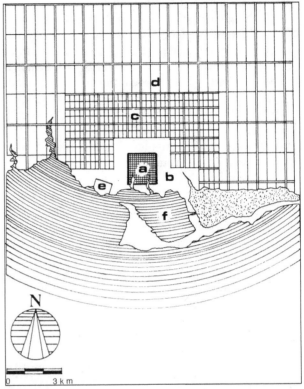

Called the "mile square" plan for the central town grid (a), which was one mile (1.6 kilometres) on each side, it designated five public squares and a wide surrounding common (b). This part of the plan was never implemented, but the subdivision of medium-sized "park lots" (c) and the larger farms (d) did materialize. The old Garrison Reserve (e) to the west of the town became Canada's first public park in 1848. A less ambitious town grew up beside the well-protected harbour (f).

maps prepared in Britain, such as the original plan for Toronto (see Figure 3.8), none of the five major towns that were first developed—Kingston, Toronto, London, Hamilton, and Ottawa—followed this design.[11]

Kingston was first surveyed for a town adjacent to the small military garrison in 1784 and followed the gridiron pattern being used in towns in the Maritimes at about the same time. Its gridiron was "bent" to follow the shoreline of Lake Ontario. The triangular space between the two grids was reserved for public uses: a market, church, jail, and battery. Other land was reserved for gardens, a hospital, and a school, while large parcels on the outskirts were granted to the clergy, members of government, and other prominent people.

This approach to town layout is the same as that of other major places developed around 1800 in Ontario. The original survey lines, moreover, continue to provide the basis for expansion. Today's arterial streets in Toronto were the original road allowances that bounded groups of six 80-hectare farm lots in Simcoe's 1793 survey.

The early Ontario gridiron town plans had no aesthetic pretensions. Their aims were primarily functional: to provide for fast, orderly development, the equitable distribution of land, and basic public land needs at the lowest possible cost of surveying the lots. Since most of the lots were to be given away, there was no revenue to offset the costs of more complex plans that might provide public amenities. Two community plans broke with this colonial tradition: Guelph in 1827 (see Figure 3.9a) and Goderich in 1829 (see Figure 3.9b). These two towns were to anchor the development of the 400 000 hectares of land, the Huron Tract, in western Ontario. The private developer of these towns, the Canada Company, had an incentive to create attractive plans, since they wished to sell town lots. Plans for both of these places, usually credited to John Galt, adopted the idea of a radial pattern of streets converging on a town market.

Guelph was arranged in a fan shape, outward from a market beside a river; Goderich was arranged around an octagonal central market square. As in Renaissance designs, a gridiron was used for local streets. John Galt is known to have been influenced by the town-planning approaches used by the Holland Company, which acquired rights to develop upper New York state.[12] The latter development was supervised by Joseph Ellicott, whose brother had succeeded L'Enfant as the planner for Washington. Thus, the plans for Guelph and Goderich are descended more from the L'Enfant concept than from Georgian England.[13] Other towns developed in the Huron Tract reverted to a common gridiron.

Western Canada

The growth of cities and towns in western Canada is, by and large, a product of national expansion rather than colonial development from Europe.[14] There were, of course, some pre-Confederation antecedents. Many places owe their choice of site to an early fur trading post, such as Edmonton, Winnipeg, and Victoria. And British Army engineers around 1860 laid out gridiron town sites for several communities in British Columbia, including

| Figures 3.9a and 3.9b | Canada Company Town Plans |

a) Guelph, Ontario, 1827

b) Goderich, Ontario, 1829

These two towns were planned by John Galt for the Canada Company to encourage settlement in western Ontario. Guelph shows the influence of the radial street pattern used in the plan for Washington, D.C.; note the central church and wedge-shaped market. The courthouse now occupies the octagonal central market square in Goderich.

New Westminster and Vancouver, while that region was still a British colony. However, it was the establishment of railway links with eastern Canada, especially in the 1880s, that gave the stimulus to widespread town development throughout western Canada (see Figure 3.10).

In barely 20 years, from 1871 to 1891, almost all the places that have become major cities and towns of the region were laid out in conjunction with the advance of the transcontinental railroad and its branches. Very often laid out by railway engineers, the plans followed a common gridiron, whether for small communities or large and regardless of the topography of the site. These were plans for the sale and distribution of land. To draw again from Blumenfeld: "The right angle and straight line, convenient for the division of land, are equally convenient for the erection of buildings, [and] for the laying of pipes and rails."[15] The gridiron also suited the ebullient and egalitarian spirit that characterized the settlement of western Canada: ample land, equal parcels, and similarity of sites.

The gridiron does not depend on the location of an important church, a fort, or marketplace for its beginnings. But it does depend on the ownership of land in the grid and, crucial to western Canada's communities, on where the railway station and freight yards are situated. Since the railway companies were granted land as an incentive to build in the West, they chose much of their land where they planned to build railway stations and could benefit from the sale of town lots. The initial town sites for Saskatoon, Regina, Calgary, and Vancouver did not coincide with the railway terminus. But it was the railroad's gridiron town site that became the dominant commercial centre and the location for public buildings.

In Edmonton, the presence of a 1200-hectare tract of land granted to the Hudson's Bay Company immediately west of the original town site influenced the development of its central district. Winnipeg's pattern owes much to the routes followed by fur traders north and south along the Red River and west along the Assiniboine, and to the long, narrow Métis farm lots that fronted on the rivers. Nevertheless, in western communities, regardless of rivers or rival town sites, the overall gridiron gradually reconciled many differences, and often the original survey lines still govern the direction of land development.

Early Problems of Urban Growth in Canada

The genesis of Canadian community planning began early in the 19th century, when problems associated with urban growth first became a concern. Canadian towns began to grow into cities as a result of the general industrial and commercial vigour of the 19th century. Canada was able to share in the supply of raw materials demanded by the burgeoning industrial structure of Europe, especially Britain. This meant economic expansion, population growth, and physical development for Canadian communities. The population in British North America between 1815 and 1865 grew from 0.5 million to 3.5 million people. Although most people still lived in the countryside, the major towns started to grow into cities in this period: Toronto from little more than 1000 people to about 50 000; Kingston from 6000 to 17 000; Montréal from 15 000 to 110 000; and Halifax from 15 000 to 25 000.

| Figure 3.10 | New Chaplin, Saskatchewan, 1907 |

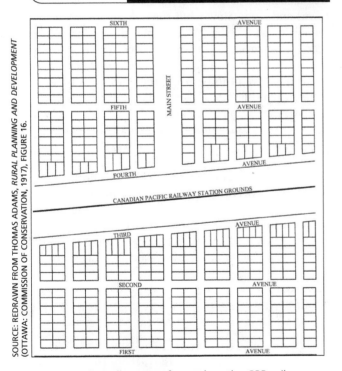

SOURCE: REDRAWN FROM THOMAS ADAMS, *RURAL PLANNING AND DEVELOPMENT* (OTTAWA: COMMISSION OF CONSERVATION, 1917), FIGURE 16.

A western Canadian town focused on the CPR railway station. These town sites were laid out according to standard rules for land surveyors. Thomas Adams criticized them: "The rectangular plans, with their unnecessarily wide main streets and lanes, have not led to good results.... The chief advantage of the rectangular plan is, unfortunately, that its uniform lot sizes and dimensions assist speculation in land."

But sharing in the benefits of the Industrial Revolution also brought a share of the burdens. In particular, the problems of rapid urbanization that began to afflict British communities in conjunction with the Industrial Revolution soon materialized in Canada's towns and cities. Here are descriptions of two urban situations in the first half of the 19th century. The first describes conditions in the new colonial town of York in 1832 (which would be renamed Toronto two years later) while the second, which differs little, describes Glasgow, Scotland, in 1840.

> York: Stagnant pools of water, green as leek, and emitting deadly exhalations, are to be met with in every corner of the town—yards and cellars send forth a stench from rotten vegetables sufficient almost of itself to produce a plague and the state of the bay, from which a large proportion of inhabitants are supplied with water, is horrible.[16]

> Glasgow: In many houses there is scarcely any ventilation; dunghills lie in the vicinity of the dwellings; and from the extremely defective sewerage, filth of every kind accumulates.[17]

Disease

Sanitary deficiencies were common in towns and cities of the time on both sides of the Atlantic. Moreover, those problems defied easy solution throughout most of the 19th century. There was inadequate technical understanding about the construction of a public sewer system. It was also not understood how subsoil conditions could allow outdoor privies to contaminate wells for drinking water, and it was considered normal that individual houses and businesses should provide their own water supply and waste disposal. Combine these factors with both the lack of public resources to construct sanitary and water supply systems and the lack of authority to compel private property owners to connect to such systems, and one has the setting for tragedy.

Virulent disease often spread within and between communities. Cholera, carried by immigrants from the British Isles, spread in 1832 from near Ville de Québec all the way to London, Ontario, and up the Ottawa Valley in a matter of two months, for example. Typhus hit many cities, including Ottawa and Kingston, in 1847; this epidemic helped spur on public health measures by provincial governments.

Although the public and governmental concern was there, the knowledge about the origin and spread of disease was not. Until the 1870s, when microbes were first isolated as the cause of many diseases, the prevailing wisdom (sometimes referred to as the "filth theory") attributed disease to the accumulation of wastes, human and otherwise; it was commonly believed that the air was poisonous in the vicinity of accumulated wastes. Impure water was also thought to cause disease, but it was not understood until near the end of the century that waterborne microbes might contaminate a community's water supply.

Water Supply

Efforts to bring piped water to all buildings and then to secure sources of pure water were very protracted in many communities. It took Winnipeg from 1882, when a public water and sewer system was started, until 1906 to pass a bylaw requiring all buildings to be connected.[18] Ottawa began a public water system in 1872, after debating it from 1855, but it was 1915 before a pure supply was obtained.[19] Deadly typhoid outbreaks in both these cities pushed their governments to solve the problem of water and sewer services.

The immediacy of the problems of disease and pollution was associated in people's minds with the growth of towns and cities. Slowly but surely it became clear that the solutions to these problems required community-wide action. So compelling became this concern that, well into the 20th century, obtaining "healthful conditions" was a prime objective of those who propounded community-planning remedies for towns and cities. And the importance of pure water supplies continues today, as the tragedy in 2000 in Walkerton, Ontario, and other centres show.

Fire

Another cornerstone for community planning came out of the concern over public safety from fire. Large fires were all too common in Canadian communities throughout the 19th century (see Figure 3.11). The extent of this menace can be seen in the following list of major conflagrations in large Canadian cities:[20]

Halifax	1750, 1861
Saint John	1837, 1841, 1845, 1877
Fredericton	1825
Ville de Québec	1815, 1834, 1845, 1862, 1865, 1866, 1876
Montréal	1765, 1768, 1803, 1849, 1852, 1901
Kingston	1847, 1854, 1857, 1890
Toronto	1849, 1890, 1895, 1904
Ottawa	1874, 1900, 1903
Vancouver	1888
New Westminster	1898

Figure 3.11	Fires in Early Cities: Ottawa, 1900

Frequent major fires occurred in Canadian cities in the early years of the 20th century before the introduction of adequate public water supply systems and firefighting equipment. These residents fled a fire that destroyed half of Hull and jumped the river to burn 14 percent of Ottawa.

The control of fire in towns and cities, however, was difficult for two reasons. First, the technology of firefighting was still rudimentary, lacking the necessary vehicles, hoses, and so forth, and fire hydrants had yet to be invented. Second, and even after equipment for firefighting was available, most Canadian communities lacked ample supplies of water. There are many reports of fires raging out of control because of either insufficient water or inadequate water pressure. Thus, the public's concerns over both health and fire losses were centred to a large degree on the supply of water.

The frequent loss of buildings in fires also caused fire insurance rates to climb dramatically in this period. Local businesses became increasingly worried over the waste and the cost of fires, which, in turn, prompted concern over the ways in which cities and towns were being built and maintained. The quality of building construction came in for scrutiny: Were buildings safe for their occupants? Would they deter the spread of fire to other buildings? These questions, considered straightforward today, were in the past not deemed appropriate: the construction of buildings was the private business of the builder or owner. As late as 1920, no province had a uniform building code and municipal building-inspection practices were also relatively new. The threat of fire is no longer the concern in city-building that it once was, but the issue of civic safety is no less present. Natural disasters such as floods and earthquakes are ever-present dangers to communities, as the floods in the Saguenay region of Québec, Manitoba in the mid-1990s, and New Orleans in 2005 attest. These latter kinds of concerns have spawned a sub-discipline within community planning called "disaster planning."[21]

Slums

As Canadian cities grew more populous in the latter part of the 19th century, attention turned increasingly to the quality of housing. The new populations in cities came almost entirely from Europe, and most of these were poor people. It was known that cholera epidemics were attributable to newly arrived immigrants. It was also observed that many immigrant workers lived in crowded, unsanitary, rudimentary dwellings (Figure 3.12). Tenuous and often unfair assumptions were made that the poor and their neighbourhoods were the prime sources of disease and fire (not to speak of moral turpitude). As one writer notes, "Bad plumbing and crowded housing were more easily fixed on as the culprit in the spread of disease and crime than the complete framework of poverty."[22]

There were extensive slums in Canadian cities of this period. A penetrating study by Herbert Ames of a working-class district in Montréal in 1896 provides details of housing conditions.[23] In an area of 2 or 3 square kilometres just to the east of Windsor Station, 37 000 people lived in 8300 tenement-type apartments. These densities of, respectively, 14 300 persons per square kilometre and 33 dwelling units per hectare, do not seem extremely high by the standards of today's high-density, high-rise housing projects. However, these conditions were for an entire district, not just a housing project, and most of the buildings were only two and three storeys high! Along with the narrow streets and almost no open public space, the result was very high density by any standards. Furthermore, half of the dwellings had outdoor privies. Ames noted that some other wards in Montréal had densities two and three times higher than the area he studied.

Figure 3.12 — Canadian Slum Housing, 1912

Wooden tenements in an eastern Canadian city, showing crowded rear lots, a narrow entrance from the street, and flimsy construction. Rear lots were seldom served by water and sewerage.

Figure 3.13 — Diamond Court, Montréal, ca. 1895

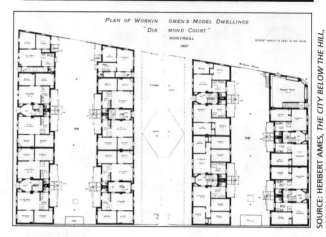

Montréal philanthropist and social reformer Herbert Ames built this apartment complex as a demonstration of better housing standards for the working poor.

Other Canadian communities suffered similar problems. In Winnipeg, for example, in 1884 the overall density of population in the built-up area was close to 4000 per square kilometre.[24] By 1900, about half of Winnipeg's houses still had outdoor privies; add to this the widespread use of horses for transportation and the need to dispose of animal wastes. The density of development just after mid-century (1860) in Toronto had already reached over 4800 persons per square kilometre.[25] There was concern over Toronto slums from as early as 1873, and, in 1884, the Toronto Tenement Building Association was established to build houses and apartments with "modern conveniences and sanitary appliances" for working-class populations. These overall density figures are for the entire city, but the poor usually lived in neighbourhoods at two and three times the average density. The consequent crowding often led to illness and social tension. By the end of the century, efforts were under way in many cities to deal with slum conditions through public health measures, improved building practices and codes, and even new housing built specifically for workers (see Chapter 4). Herbert Ames built Diamond Court in Montréal as a model apartment complex (Figure 3.13).

Railways, Streetcars, and Urban Form

Canadian cities, both western and eastern, were significantly affected by the introduction of railways.

The location of the passenger station was important to communities, but more important over the long run was the location of the marshalling yards and freight terminals, for they consumed large amounts of space. The freight yards and terminals were usually adjacent to the passenger station and, hence, next to the downtown area. In addition, the coming of railways to Canadian communities coincided with extensive industrialization in the country. Industrial firms were encouraged to locate near the freight terminals or along rail lines.

Railroad development, undoubtedly a boon to the economic development of communities, strongly affected the pattern of their growth. Typically, the railway passenger station "anchored" one side of the downtown commercial area, and on the other were the freight yards and industrial area and, frequently, the port. Housing development spread out from this core, but not evenly, for the freight yards proved to be both a physical and psychological barrier to residential growth.

Housing for the more affluent population was located away from the rail lines and industrial areas. Housing for poorer segments of the population was left to the land adjacent to industry and railways. The large, generally linear area occupied by freight yards and industries was also difficult for city development to cross without expensive underpasses or bridges. In inland cities, when development did succeed in leapfrogging the railway, it often resulted in the establishment of lower-income residential districts on, so to speak, "the other side of the tracks." In cities with harbours, the railway–related industrial development usually spread along the waterfront, creating a barrier between the community and its natural marine asset (see Figure 3.14).

The street railway was also introduced to Canadian communities in the late 19th century. This form of rail transport, especially after electrification, dramatically influenced the pattern of residential development. Prior to street railways, both the dependence on foot travel and poor roads tended to limit development to within 1.6 kilometres of the central area. In the 1870s the horse-drawn trolley permitted development to occur up to 5 kilometres from downtown and the jobs of the central industrial area. The electrification of streetcars around 1890 saw the extension of lines 10 kilometres

and more from downtown stores and jobs. This new mobility allowed families to live year-round in former cottage communities such as Toronto's Beaches and Ottawa's Britannia.[26] The norm was usually a half-hour trip—a norm that is only slightly longer today in North American communities.

The streetcar lines followed streets that radiated outward from the central area of the community and were a great stimulus for land development adjacent to those routes. As a result, the overall pattern of the city assumed a finger-like shape along transit routes. The oldest housing outside the central area is often found in communities served earliest by streetcar lines. A strip of retail and commercial establishments often served these extended new neighbourhoods, which are now popular sites for intensification and gentrification, such as Ottawa's Westboro. Almost always the gridiron formed

| Figure 3.14 | Impact of Railways on the Centre of the City: Toronto, 1870 |

SOURCE: TORONTO PUBLIC LIBRARY, T31103.

The advent of railways was associated with manufacturing and commercial developments, which were in the centre of most cities by the late 19th century. The marshalling yards for freight trains consumed large amounts of city space and, in port cities like Toronto and Vancouver, they cut off the harbour from the rest of the city and hampered its use by citizens.

Chapter 3 19th Century Foundations of Canadian Communities

the base of development; it was simply extended as the streetcar lines were built (see Figure 3.15).

| Figure 3.15 | Effect of Transportation Modes on the Form of the City: Toronto |

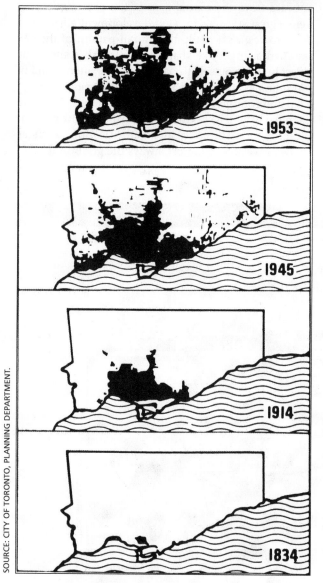

SOURCE: CITY OF TORONTO, PLANNING DEPARTMENT.

Toronto's form of growth relates to the dominant mode of transportation prevailing at the time. The city of 1914 with electrified streetcars not only is 20 times larger than in horse-and-foot-traffic times but also shows the growth adjacent to the radial streetcar routes, which is even more exaggerated by 1945. However, within less than a decade, the proliferation of the private automobile made for a much more dispersed form.

Emergence of Modern Planning Concepts

The rapid industrialization occurring in the 19th century (beginning around 1800 in Britain, 1840 in the U.S., and 1880 in Canada) centred on cities and brought with it new people, new wealth, and new problems. Toronto's population grew from just over 56 000 in 1871 to nearly 522 000 only 50 years later. At first, no cities on either side of the Atlantic were able to cope with the demand for housing, the need for transportation, and the provision of basic water supply and sewage-disposal services. Later, when technology and social conscience caught up with these needs, the result was cities that might best be described as "cluttered": smoky industrial districts, unpaved roads, mean and crowded working-class housing, half-finished suburbs, and a plethora of new electric poles and overhead cables.

During the late 19th and early 20th centuries, in most large Canadian communities the emerging physical patterns of cities prompted concerns not unlike those receiving attention in Britain and the United States at the same time.[27] In response to these concerns, a coterie of professionals emerged who gradually codified their ideas and experience about the best physical form for communities. The Canadian planning profession developed at this time and, with its British and American counterparts, generated a rich array of planning concepts, which continue to be drawn upon.

The planning concerns for the burgeoning cities just over one hundred years ago were rooted in at least four different perceptions of city problems. One viewed the major problem as the **shabby appearance of cities**; another viewed it as the **deterioration of living conditions**; others were concerned over the **loss of the natural environment**, or **inefficiency and waste**. From each sprang different planning concepts that might produce better communities. Out of the concern over the appearance of cities came the notion of the City Beautiful and the redesign of major streets and public areas in existing cities. Out of the concern over living conditions came the notion of Garden Cities, wholly new communities designed to allow new patterns of living in less congested surroundings. Concern over the natural environment led to the Parks Movement and resulted in public open spaces and preserved natural areas. Concerns about city efficiency led to proposals for infrastructure systems such as electric streetcars, sewers, and paved roads. Adherents of each approach often became part of competing planning movements, whose Canadian origins are discussed below (see Figure 3.16).

| Figure 3.16 | Evolution of Community-Planning Ideas, 1890–1900 |

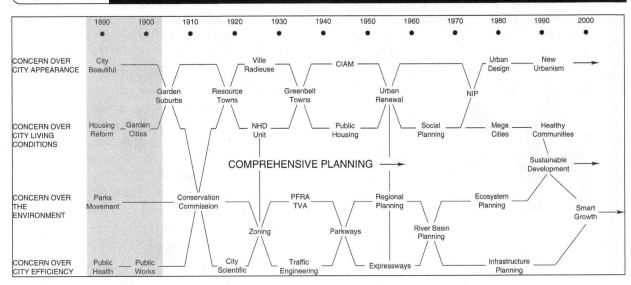

Modern community planning grew out of four basic concerns that emerged in the final decades of the 19th century. Each of these was initially articulated around broad social movements: city appearance (City Beautiful), city living (Garden Cities), the environment (Parks), and city efficiency (Public Works).

The imprint of each approach is to be found in Canadian community planning of the first half of the 20th century, as described in detail in Chapter 4. During this period, each approach evolved into more refined planning ideas that included garden suburbs, the neighbourhood unit, and greenbelt towns. The late 20th century legacy of each approach is examined in Chapter 5; we also see that current planning ideas such as Smart Growth, sustainable development, healthy communities, and New Urbanism have roots that can be traced back to the late 19th and early 20th centuries.

| Planning Issue 3.1 | For Healthy People, Build a Healthy City |

The Globe and Mail
November 27, 2011

For Healthy People, Build a Healthy City
David Ebner

How we build and manage our cities directly affects the health of the populace. With the population aging and health-care costs rising, urban planners are beginning to act on that simple idea

Trevor Hancock has always been ahead of the curve.

A doctor and long-time public health expert, he was also the first leader of the Green Party of Canada in 1984, when he ran federally (finishing fourth) in Toronto's Beaches neighbourhood.

But his day job, in public health, turned out to have far more impact than his brief political career. Beginning as one of a small international cadre that promoted ideas about urban planning's key role in human health, he is now watching his work over the past quarter-century start to explode into the mainstream.

It's a paradigm shift in the way urban planners and municipal leaders see the world:

CONTINUED

how we build and manage our cities directly affects the health of the populace. And with mounting research showing that cities where people walk more and drive less are healthier cities, the automobile is losing out to the pedestrian as the main focus of city-building.

In Vancouver, already ranked as Canada's healthiest city, they are nonetheless acting.

"These kind of seismic changes in our understanding take a long time to work into the system," said Dr. Hancock, who serves as a professor and senior scholar at the new School of Public Health and Social Policy at the University of Victoria, while working as a public health and planning consultant. "It takes a generation for the old guard to die or retire, and a new way of thinking to take its place."

Urban planning, in its modern sense, started in the mid-19th century.

Imagine animal carcasses and vegetables rotting in the streets, cramped housing and rampant spread of disease, belching smokestacks blackening the midday sky. These urban conditions in England moved civic planners to consider the health of the populace in the design of cities.

Smarter design equalled healthier citizens. But the connection between health and planning unravelled not long after. The idea of separating neighbourhoods from industrial and commercial activities took hold and, with the rise of the automobile, urban planners divided cities up into zones for living and zones for working, with roads between them.

The result is modern cities that make people sick. New research has found that cities designed for cars also foster obesity and diabetes. In studies from Atlanta to Vancouver, evidence shows that people who live in neighbourhoods that require cars to get around are fatter and less healthy than people who live near shops and grocers.

A quarter of Canadians are obese, which imposes added burdens on the nation's health-care system. Yet the solution to problems in health care is always more money for health care – even though research indicates that three-quarters of the factors that influence human health happen outside the health-care system.

Wilbert Keon, the renowned heart surgeon and retired senator, estimates that the "obesity epidemic," particularly among children, could cost billions in added medical expenses. "Diabetes, hypertension, organ failure, heart disease, you name it. It's abhorrent," said Dr. Keon. "It's one big chunk of money that could be pulled right out of health care if we could just build healthy communities."

Dr. Keon believes momentum is building in favour of healthier cities, even though a report on a "healthy, productive Canada" he led in 2009 failed to garner much notice, or action.

The challenges include co-ordinated action among different levels of government. Municipalities decide on zoning, allowing developers to build cul-de-sac suburbs kilometres from the nearest grocery store. Higher levels of government administer health-care dollars but have little say on what cities do with their road-building budgets.

Because of such disconnects, efforts have been piecemeal. Atlanta created a program to vet and fund projects that make the city healthier. Bogota built one of the world's best bike path networks. In Canada, Vancouver has taken the lead.

Vancouver has seen old left-right political divisions over urban planning break down, with a consensus emerging on what constitutes a desirable city.

On the right, Suzanne Anton was a Crown prosecutor and a soccer mom when she pushed a decade ago for more playing fields, work that led her to politics and a seat on Vancouver's parks board. Ms. Anton this month lost her bid for mayor to Gregor Robertson, a greener incumbent. But as a city councillor, she was an important force behind the city's adoption of "EcoDensity" – the promotion of greater housing density among the many single-family homes in the city, to combat sprawl.

"Dense urban environments are good for human health, because people walk," said Ms. Anton.

In Vancouver's ambitious goal to become the "world's greenest city" by 2020, "improved health" is one of the top results expected from a more intelligently designed urban landscape.

Ms. Anton describes herself as a "land use geek," arguing that zoning is the crucial lever to create a healthy city. One practical application is how to make neighbourhoods better suited to older residents as the number of seniors is set to double by 2025.

Health care, Ms. Anton said, starts at home. Using her own south Vancouver neighbourhood, Kerrisdale, a typical single-family home community, she points to the importance of "seniors housing" that is functional and within walking distance of real street life.

"An 80-year-old lady, she goes down the elevator, walks to buy bread, buy milk, sees her friends, walks home," said Ms. Anton. "That creates health for her."

CANADA'S HEALTHIEST CITIES
1. Vancouver
2. Victoria
3. Calgary
4. Edmonton
5. Ottawa

BY THE NUMBERS
- **25 per cent** of Canadian adults are obese
- This costs Canada **$12-billion** annually, to treat chronic diseases connected with obesity
- It costs the health care system **$1,500** more, each year, to treat obese Americans compared with people of normal weight
- **75 per cent** of factors that influence health occur outside the health care system
- Each grocery store within **1-kilometre** of a person's home reduces the likelihood of being overweight by 11 per cent

- Transit users are **3 times** more likely to meet daily minimum of recommended physical activity
- A walkable neighbourhood with shops and grocers near homes slashes the probability of obesity by **35 per cent**
- Improving a neighbourhood's "walkability" by just **5 per cent** gets people 32.1 per cent more active in their travel
- A typical white male who lives near shops weighs **10 pounds** less than the same man in a suburb of culs-de-sacs
- Young teenagers are **2.5 times** more likely to walk if there is a recreation destination within 1-kilometre of their home
- Women are about **20 per cent** less likely to be obese, or suffer from diabetes, if they live in a nice neighbourhood with services compared with a poor neighbourhood

Compiled by David Ebner; Sources: Lawrence Frank/University of British Columbia; SMARTRAQ; Government of Canada, U.S. Department of Housing; Trust for Public Land; Best Health Magazine

Concern over City Appearance: The City Beautiful Movement

In 1893 Chicago hosted the World's Columbian Exposition (see Figure 3.17). The design of the grounds and buildings of this fair is credited with stimulating a surge of concern for the design of cities in North America over the ensuing 40 years. The site on the shores of Lake Michigan was selected and laid out by Boston landscape architect Frederick Law Olmsted. A strong team of American designers, led by Chicago architect Daniel Burnham, conceived of a setting of buildings, avenues, statues, canals, and lagoons in true Baroque fashion. Planning historian Mel Scott calls it a "temporary wonderland of grand perspectives and cross axes … shimmering lagoons and monumental palaces … an enthralling amalgam of classic Greece, imperial Rome, and Bourbon Paris."[28]

Figure 3.17	Chicago World's Columbian Exposition, 1893, Court of Honour at entrance

Figure 3.18	Chicago 1908 Plan

This was the first view for visitors to the Chicago World's Fair. It left many visitors from the rather raw nineteenth-century Canadian cities slack-jawed. Many returned home with images from souvenir booklets like this one, convinced that their cities, towns, and villages could be improved and made more beautiful.

The need for the beautification of cities had been stirring in the United States for at least two decades before the Chicago World's Fair. It showed up in municipal art societies, civic improvement commissions, and in the attention given to both private and public landscape architecture, notably in the development of public parks and civic centres.[29] The Chicago fair strengthened this aesthetic effort by providing design principles that could (and subsequently did) govern the design of city halls, public libraries, banks, railroad stations, civic centres, boulevards, and university campuses. Burnham was involved with refurbishing L'Enfant's plan for Washington in 1902. His 1908 plan for Chicago (prepared with Edward H. Bennett; see Figure 3.18) is considered the benchmark of City Beautiful plans, containing schemes for new diagonal avenues, civic plazas, public buildings, and a series of parks along the lakeshore, and proposals for a network of highways for the entire metropolitan region of some 10 000 square kilometres and a chain of forest preserves and parkways on the periphery.[30] The plan was commissioned by the Commercial Club, representing the city's industrial elite, and an independent planning commission championed its implementation for a quarter-century.

The *Plan of Chicago* was unveiled in 1908 as an exhibition at the Art Institute of Chicago, and then published as a beautifully bound book in 1909 and as a paperback high school civics textbook in 1910. It included far-reaching proposals such as the waterfront parks, harbour, and railway relocation shown in this plan. Most of the railway and waterfront improvements were completed in the early 20th century, but the civic centre proposed at the intersection of the diagonal avenues at the top of the plan was never built. The last section of this waterfront open space became Chicago's Millennium Park, a century after planning for the area began.

Figure 3.19 Daniel Burnham

SOURCE: DANIEL H. BURNHAM, (1910). RYERSON AND BURNHAM ARCHIVES, COURTESY OF THE ART INSTITUTE OF CHICAGO.

Figure 3.20 Edward Bennett

SOURCE: EDWARD H. BENNETT, RYERSON AND BURNHAM ARCHIVES, COURTESY OF THE ART INSTITUTE OF CHICAGO.

Daniel H. Burnham (1846–1912; see Figure 3.19) was a leading American architect in the late 19th century. He rose to prominence as Director of Works for the 1893 World's Colombian Exposition, when he chaired a national committee of architects and artists, which produced a powerful classical design that had a profound effect on American architectural taste for the next twenty years. Burnham received much credit when the exposition became a runaway success, and he was later requested to reprise his WCE role with the 1902 McMillan Commission plan for Washington, D.C. Burnham's firm was the first prototype of the national architectural firm, and was expert at complex, high-cost downtown projects like office buildings (Flatiron Building, N.Y.), train stations (Washington, D.C.), banks, and department stores.

Burnham's many downtown building projects connected him with civic improvement advocates, and, late in his career, he took a leading role in proposals for a Cleveland civic centre (1903), a comprehensive plan for San Francisco (1905), and the Chicago plan (1908). Burnham was one of the early pioneers of the American planning movement, coining the oft-repeated phrase: *"Make no little plans."*[31]

Edward H. Bennett (1874–1954; see Figure 3.20) was co-author, with Burnham, of the *Plan for San Francisco* and *Plan of Chicago*. Burnham recruited him after his graduation from Paris' Ecole des Beaux Arts, but although Bennett was educated as an architect, he designed few buildings. His consulting practice ranged from the preparation of comprehensive plans for major cities (Minneapolis, Brooklyn, Portland, Ottawa) to the design of civic centres (Denver, Detroit, Pasadena), building ensembles (Washington's Federal Triangle), open spaces, infrastructure, and memorials. Bennett was extensively engaged in the implementation of the Chicago plan for over 20 years, designing bridges, parks, and road improvements. He was one of the first American urban designers, and was the leading City Beautiful planning consultant when retained in 1914 by the Federal Plan Commission for Ottawa and Hull.[32]

The impact of the Chicago exposition and plan were not lost on Canadian architects, engineers, and surveyors (who would soon make up the fledgling planning profession). They too were active in campaigning against the squalor and the ugly environments that were developing in Canadian communities in the period of rapid urbanization prior to World War I. Montréal architect A.T. Taylor complained (in 1893) after viewing the Fair:

> The average modern city is not planned—like topsy, it just grows, and we are only allowed to touch with the finger of beauty a spot here and there. One longs for the days of Pericles or Caesar, or even those of the First Empire, when cities were laid out with beauty and effect, and were exquisite settings for noble gems of architecture.[33]

The Renaissance design principles of symmetry, coherence, and monumentality were revived by the Chicago Fair and plan, and Canadian "planning advocates" promoted them widely with governments, chambers of commerce, and corporations. Beautification proposals often arose from local groups such as civic improvement societies or business organizations, aided by the local architects' association.[34] In Vancouver leadership came from the Vancouver Beautiful Association;[35] in Montréal and Calgary, railway companies were closely involved. These organizations initially drew membership from city elites, but debate on beautification efforts often drew in citizen activists, business people, and then, later, the new professional engineers, architects, and planners joined them.[36]

Concern over Housing and Living Conditions: Garden Cities and Settlement Houses

The Garden City concept emerged from concerns about terrible living conditions in late 19th century British industrial cities, documented by reformers such as Charles Booth and revolutionaries such as Friedrich Engels.[37] But Britain was just the leading edge of the Industrial Revolution, and the overcrowding, disease, and poverty of London and Manchester had arrived in North America by the late 19th century. Early reactions to poor living conditions included the utopian communities and settlements built by industrial philanthropists such as Lever's Port Sunlight and Cadbury's Bourneville, described

in Chapter 2. The university settlement houses led by Jane Addams in Chicago and Henrietta Barnett in London were early attempts to improve social conditions in inner-city neighbourhoods. The Garden City concept, espoused by Ebenezer Howard (see sidebar), proposed, however, to deal with poor city living conditions at both the local and metropolitan scales (see also Chapter 9).

In today's terminology, the Garden City would be called either a "satellite town" or "new town." Like its modern versions, the Garden City concept aimed at affecting the physical form of communities in two ways: first, it would disperse the population and industry of a large city into smaller concentrations, and, second, it would create community living environments in the periphery of large cities that were more amenable than those of the city.

The main dimensions of Howard's Garden City were:

1. A population of about 30 000;
2. A built-up town of 1000 acres (400 hectares);
3. An agricultural greenbelt of 5000 acres (2000 hectares) surrounding the town;
4. Provision of land for industry and commerce to supply employment to the residents:
5. An arrangement of land uses to promote convenience and reduce conflict; and
6. A means of rapid transportation between the central city and the Garden City.

An important feature of the Garden City's development was that all the land, including the greenbelt, would be owned by a single limited-dividend corporation and held in trust for both investors and the residents. The corporation would build infrastructure, homes, and industrial parks, leasing houses to residents and land to employers.

In the Garden City that Howard visualized, each house would have its own garden; each neighbourhood, its own area for schools, playgrounds, gardens, and churches; and the whole town its surrounding "garden," or agricultural estate, as Howard termed it. There would be a strong town centre with a town hall, concert and lecture hall, theatre, library, museum, and hospital, as well as a large public garden and ample room for shops. Each neighbourhood ("ward") would be bounded by major avenues and would house about one-sixth of the population, or about 5000 people, in individual or group housing and be only about 1.5

square kilometres in greatest extent. An innovative, but often overlooked, part of Howard's concept was for an internal "belt of green" 130 metres wide, a Grand Avenue (three times wider than University Avenue in Toronto), to separate the area for factories, warehouses, and so on from the residential area (Figure 3.21).

Howard's ideas were turned into reality with the building of two Garden Cities north of London. The first was Letchworth, about 56 kilometres north of London, which was designed by Barry Parker and Raymond Unwin and started in 1903. It has now reached close to its intended population.[38] Thomas Adams was associated with the building of Letchworth as secretary of the group of investors who initiated the first Garden City. A decade later, Adams came to Canada as the Town Planning Advisor to the Canadian Commission of Conservation (see Chapter 4). The significance of the Garden City concept is to demonstrate, as Adams remarked 30 years after Letchworth, "the advantage of planning communities in all their features from the beginning."[39] The second Garden City, Welwyn, was started by Howard in

Figure 3.22 Welwyn Garden City Plan, 1922

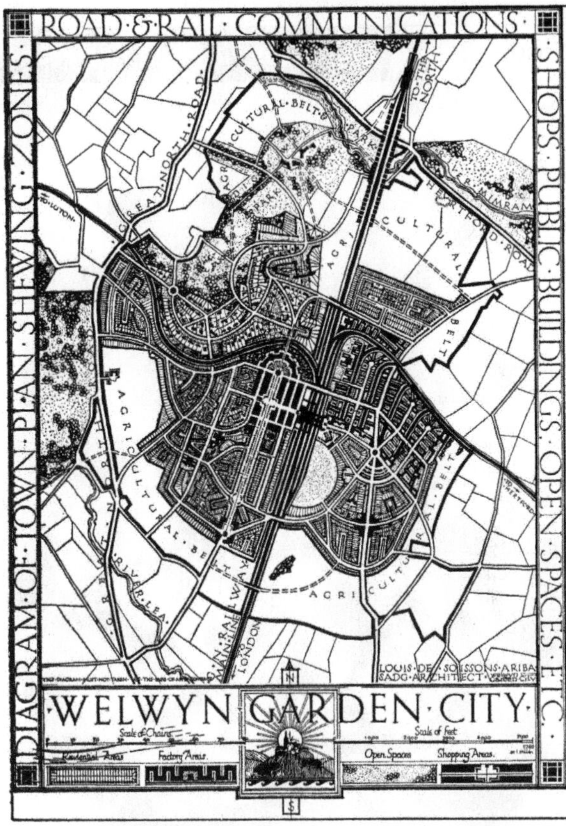

This plan by Montréal native Louis de Soissons formed the basis for development of the second Garden City at Welwyn. De Soissions was educated at Paris's Ecole de Beaux Arts, so the plan shows more classical geometry than the organic style of Parker & Unwin at Letchworth. The town's architecture is Georgian, rather than the Arts and Crafts style made famous at Hampstead Garden Suburb.

Figure 3.21 Garden City Diagram

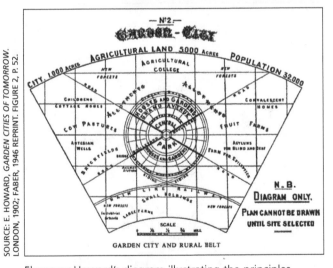

Ebenezer Howard's diagram illustrating the principles of Garden City design. A small constellation of these satellite cities was to be established at a distance from the central city, separated by a green belt. Howard was not an architect—he made these drawings with a pencil and compass to illustrate the general principles behind his ideas.

1919 about 27 kilometres from London. Canadian architect Louis de Soissions designed the plan for Welwyn Garden City (Figure 3.22) and supervised its development for its first quarter-century.[40] Garden City ideas influenced city plans around the world over well into the next century. By 1950, greenbelts and satellite towns were important components of plans for metropolitan Moscow (1935), London (1946), and Stockholm (1950).[41]

| Figure 3.23 | Ebenezer Howard Portrait |

SOURCE: ©MARY EVANS PICTURE LIBRARY/THE IMAGE WORKS.

Sir Ebenezer Howard (1850–1928; see Figure 3.23), the British originator of the Garden City idea, was not an architect or surveyor but a legal stenographer and, as one biographer emphasizes, an inventor. He was born in London and lived in Chicago for several years as a young man, before returning to his native city to work as a Parliamentary reporter. Howard was deeply concerned by London's poor housing conditions and active in Fabian social reform societies in the late 19th century.[42] In 1898, he published his utopian community ideas in *Tomorrow: A Peaceful Path to Real Reform*, which was edited and reissued as *Garden Cities of Tomorrow* in 1903.[43]

Howard presented his ideas for new towns as general diagrams rather than as plans for a particular community and location. Garden City principles were explained by his famous "Three Magnets" diagram (Figure 3.24), which contrasted the problems and opportunities of "Town" and "Country," concluding that the combination of "Town–Country" offered an ideal living environment. Millions of suburban dwellers might agree. Howard promoted his ideas constantly and used his social connections to start the limited-dividend corporations that developed Letchworth and Welwyn Garden City. He ended his years in Welwyn, having seen his ideas spread around the world through his Garden Cities and Town Planning Association—now the International Federation for Housing and Planning.

| Figure 3.24 | The Three Magnets |

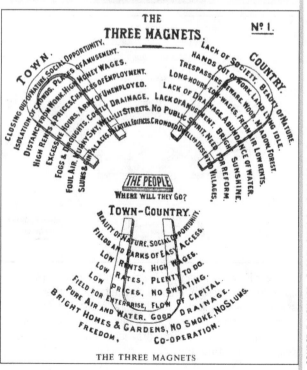

SOURCE: E. HOWARD, *GARDEN CITIES OF TOMORROW*. LONDON, 1902; FABER, 1946 REPRINT, FIGURE 1.

Settlement houses were another urban social reform movement that began in the late 19th century. The houses were established in impoverished neighbourhoods, starting with Toynbee Hall, founded by Samuel and Henrietta Barnett (Figure 3.25a) in the East End of London in 1884. The most prominent American settlement was Chicago's Hull House, established by Jane Addams (Figure 3.25b) in 1889. Volunteer middle-class settlement workers lived in the houses, undertook social planning studies, engaged in community organizing, and advocated for improved living conditions. The settlement workers were often university students or recent graduates, such as future Canadian prime minister William Lyon Mackenzie King, who lived at Hull House while studying for his master's degree at the University of Chicago, and volunteered at Toynbee Hall during his doctoral research in London. Church groups in Montréal and Toronto set up the first Canadian settlement houses, but secular institutions such as Toronto's University Settlement and Central Neighbourhood House were established in 1911 and continue to this day.

Background   Nineteenth-Century Social Planners

Figure 3.25a   Henrietta Barnett

SOURCE: SAMUEL AND HENRIETTA BARNETT BY H. VON HERKOMER (TOYNBEE HALL).

Figure 3.25b   Jane Addams

SOURCE: PHOTO BY FOTOSEARCH/GETTY IMAGES.

Dame Henrietta Barnett (1851–1936), the daughter of a wealthy businessman, married Samuel Barnett, a clergyman with strong social convictions. They founded the first university settlement, Toynbee Hall, and Henrietta went on to establish many other community institutions in London's impoverished Whitechapel district. She was also active in the Garden City movement, founding Hampstead Garden Suburb in 1904. Henrietta worked directly with architects Raymond Unwin and Sir Edwin Lutyens on the distinctive planning and Arts and Crafts design of Hampstead.[44]

Jane Addams (1860–1935) founded Hull House with her college friend Ellen Gates Starr in 1887, after visiting Toynbee Hall on a European tour. Addams's prodigious energy and networking ability soon made Hull House the centre of its immigrant neighbourhood in Chicago's Near West Side. Its community of resident university students provided social and educational opportunities for its working-class neighbours, focusing on children, families, public health, and adult education. Addams made strong contacts with the University of Chicago's school of sociology, which adopted the systematic methods of social surveys and mapping that Hull House pioneered. She used these surveys to build political support for improved social conditions, first in Chicago and later across the United States, becoming one of the leading reformers of the Progressive era. Her work as a peace advocate and social reformer was recognized when she was awarded the Nobel Prize in 1931.[45]

Concern over the Environment: Beginnings of the Parks Movement

Many of today's major public parks in Canadian cities came into existence in the late 19th century. Most were not part of the initial planning of our communities. The first plans for communities in eastern Canada provided for market squares, church squares, and military parade squares, but not public recreation areas; plans for communities in western Canada usually provided for neither squares nor parks. Indeed, the idea of space being set aside for public recreation only began to take hold in Britain in the 1840s.

Some of the earliest Canadian landscaped open spaces emerged from a serious public health problem—where to bury the dead. The early pioneers were usually buried in the yards of their original places of worship, but these soon filled up. The typhus and cholera epidemics of the mid-19th century filled every available open space in the affected towns with mass graves. The solution to this problem in several cities was the construction of a shared, non-denominational cemetery on rural lands,

some distance from the edge of the built-up area. It was a surprising example of ecumenical cooperation during a period when religious rivalries were strong.

The idea followed precedents from Père Lachaise cemetery in Paris (1804) and, especially, Mt. Auburn Cemetery (1831) just outside Boston. Rural cemeteries were built outside Kingston (Cataraqui, 1850), Montréal (Mount Royal, 1852), Ottawa (Beechwood, 1873), and Toronto (Mount Pleasant, 1876). The grounds of the cemeteries were beautifully landscaped according to plans designed by gardeners or civil engineers, since the landscape architecture profession had not yet emerged. Regular visits to the graves of family members became a social activity, rather like a picnic. The next step was to provide a public park for similar recreation, without requiring a trip to a rural cemetery.[46]

Canada's first public parks to be supported by municipal funding were established less than a decade after those in Britain and around the same time as those in U.S. cities.[47] A major stimulus was the transfer of land reserves held by the British central government, usually for military purposes, to the local government. The Garrison Reserve (now Exhibition Park) in

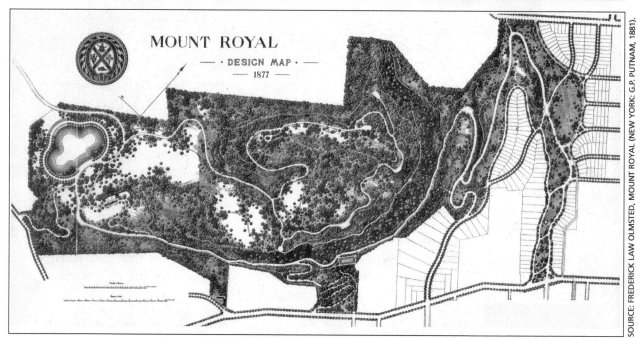

Figure 3.26 Mount Royal Park, Montréal, 1877, design by Frederick Law Olmsted

SOURCE: FREDERICK LAW OLMSTED, MOUNT ROYAL (NEW YORK: G.P. PUTNAM, 1881).

Frederick Law Olmsted's design for Mount Royal Park is perhaps the most important Canadian plan from the Parks Movement era. Olmsted's work is now cherished and recent repairs to the park have attempted to maintain his original vision.

Toronto came into existence this way in 1848, as did Kingston's City Park in 1852, Hamilton's Gore Park in the same year, Halifax's Point Pleasant Park in 1866, the Toronto Islands in 1867, London's Victoria Park in 1869, Montréal's Île Sainte-Hélène (the site of Expo '67) in 1874, and Vancouver's Stanley Park in 1886. All of these park areas were on the periphery of their respective communities at the time. There was no concept of neighbourhood parks until around the turn of the century, when various provinces introduced legislation to promote local parks.

As Toronto's parks chairman said in 1859, public parks offered "breathing spaces where citizens might stroll, drive, or sit to enjoy the open air."[48] The outlook reflected a desire to create a natural setting, often along with an appreciation of horticulture. The Public Garden in Halifax is an example of the latter; Mount Royal Park in Montréal, an example of the former. Mount Royal Park, purchased by the city in 1872, is also significant among Canadian urban parks because its basic layout (see Figure 3.26) was done by Frederick Law Olmsted (Figure 3.27), who had designed Central Park in New York City. He urged Montréal to "bring out the latent loveliness of [the] mountain beauty" and retain the "wilderness and sense of seclusion."[49] Olmsted's firm went on to prepare plans for parks at Niagara Falls, for Stanley Park in Vancouver, and for Rockwood Park in Saint John.

Background — Frederick Law Olmsted, Social Reformer and Landscape Architect

Figure 3.27 — Frederick Law Olmsted

Many of North America's most beautiful public parks were designed by the Olmsted family

firm, which was in practice for a century from 1857 to 1957. Frederick Law Olmsted (1822–1903) tried many careers as a young man—he was a clerk, a sailor in the China trade, a "scientific farmer," and a journalist who was a leading advocate for the abolition of slavery. During the American Civil War, he headed the U.S. Sanitary Commission, which was the forerunner of the American Red Cross. Olmsted began his most famous career almost by accident, when he joined with architect Calvert Vaux to enter the design competition for New York's Central Park in 1858. Olmsted's ideas on social reform combined with Vaux's design skills were a winning combination. Olmsted was appointed Superintendent of Central Park, having never designed a park in his life, but he defended the project from political corruption and saw that its magnificent plan was implemented. Olmsted and Vaux later designed Prospect Park in Brooklyn (1865); the Chicago suburb Riverside (1869), and parks systems for Buffalo and Milwaukee. After they split up in 1883, Vaux designed the grounds for Ottawa's Parliament Hill. Frederick Law Olmsted became more interested in large-scale environmental conservation, working to establish metropolitan parks systems and preserve scenic landscapes

CONTINUED

such as Yosemite National Park and Niagara Falls. He established the first landscape architecture firm, consulting on projects across North America from his office in the Boston suburb of Brookline.[50]

Frederick Law Olmsted retired in 1895, but his sons John Charles and Frederick Jr. expanded the practice and carried on for another 60 years. John Charles Olmsted master-planned many residential communities across the western United States and Canada, including Victoria's Uplands. Frederick Law Olmsted Jr. (1870–1957) deserves to be known as a planning pioneer in his own right. He apprenticed with his father on the 1893 World's Columbian Exposition in Chicago, and then took an important role as a member of Washington's 1901 Senate Park Commission, designing a regional open space system and the formal spaces in the Mall. Later, he designed residential communities, such as New York's Forest Hills Gardens, and prepared master plans for cities and universities. Olmsted Jr. became a leader in the new professions of landscape architecture and urban planning and founded both American professional associations and established the first university schools in both subjects at Harvard in 1900 and 1929 respectively.[51]

Concern over City Functioning: The City Efficient/Scientific

Fire, disease, and transportation problems of the 19th century city were slowly addressed by retrofitting the urban areas with physical infrastructure, and regulating the use of property and construction of buildings. The need for infrastructure became apparent when the private provision of services began to fail in more crowded cities. Water of dubious quality was delivered in barrels (Figure 3.28) to those who could afford it; human waste was thrown in pits on the streets; firefighting teams would watch your house burn if you had not insured with their company; city roads were almost impassable during the muddy seasons (see Figure 3.29); and the horse-drawn streetcars were often stuck.

As urban areas grew in overall size and density, politicians gradually acknowledged the need for city-wide systems of infrastructure. Planning for these systems fell into the hands of a new profession—civil engineering—that emerged at that time.[52] Roman innovations such as aqueducts, gravity sewers, and streets paved with stone blocks were revived in Paris, New York, London, and Boston after conditions became intolerable. In the mid-19th century, most Canadian cities were only a few decades removed from the frontier, and had few municipal services. New technical innovations quickly

| Figure 3.28 | Water Delivery in Ottawa, 1870s |

These horse-drawn barrels were barely adequate for hauling drinking water and almost useless for firefighting. The customers hoped that the pedlars filled up with the cleaner water from the river rather than from the open trenches in town. In the early days of settlement, it was probably safer to drink the beer at one of Bytown's many taverns.

followed in the late 19th century: piped water supply delivered by steam power, coal gas for light and heat, electric streetcars (see Figure 3.30), and streetlights.

But the pace of technical innovation greatly outstripped the ability of the cities to implement them. Most new utilities were "natural monopolies": the most efficient water system was a single supplier of piped water under pressure for both drinking and firefighting, for example. And the part-time, volunteer local governments originally set up for rural settlement often lacked the sophistication and financial resources to develop or maintain these systems, or even manage private companies who offered to install the system if granted a monopoly contract. They tried to address building problems with a patchwork quilt of regulations. A disastrous fire might lead to regulations prohibiting thatched roofs, requiring masonry for new construction, and limiting building height to the tallest ladder of the engine company. Dreadful smells from animal-rendering factories or coal-gas plants might lead

| Figure 3.29 | Horse-Car Stuck in the Mud in Ottawa's Sparks Street, ca. 1877 |

SOURCE: CITY OF OTTAWA ARCHIVES CA-1504.

Horse-drawn streetcars were no match for the morass of mud in the streets of 19th century Canadian cities. Transit companies attached wagon wheels to their horse-cars in the spring while the rails were repaired.

| Figure 3.30 | Inaugural Run of Ottawa's Electric Streetcar, 1891 |

SOURCE: CITY OF OTTAWA ARCHIVES CA-1510.

Ottawa pioneered this technology in the 19th century, led by local electrical entrepreneur Thomas Ahern. The first streetcars on steel rails were a technological breakthrough—fast, smooth, quiet, and odour-free. Ironically, Ottawa fell behind other Canadian cities in reintroducing light rail in the 21st century.

to bylaws controlling their use or location. But each city's or town's regulations were different, and all were constrained by a local government system designed for rural communities.

So, advocates for planning the efficient growth of a city using the latest scientific and engineering advances were often involved in attempts to reform local government or establish special purpose agencies, such as the Montréal Harbour Commission.[53] The great technical successes of the engineers in the early 20th century often had to wait for the institutional innovations of the legislators and lawyers.

Establishing a Local Government System

Local governments were not established in Canada until well after the original colonial town sites were surveyed and settled. In many cases this took over a hundred years and the process was often arduous. The colonial governments of Britain and France were usually loath to give up their control, especially to the local population. After the establishment of Upper and Lower Canada, progress began to be made toward local self-government. There was, however, little experience in doing so and no nationwide system to guide it. With Confederation in 1867, each province began to establish its own arrangements for local government, frequently learning from one another as their settlement patterns warranted it. As Plunkett and Betts conclude, "By the beginning of the 20th century, all ten provinces in Canada had established essentially similar systems of local government."[54]

The achievement of local government on a broad basis in Canada marks an important threshold for community planning. This institutional foundation was essential for community planning to become established and effective. To appreciate better this vital nexus, it is helpful to review the process of establishing local government in this country.

Precursors of Local Government

For the first 225 years of European settlement in what is now Canada, until the 1830s, few communities had anything resembling local government. This institution literally had to be invented. But why was it sought? The answer to that question is that any clustering of people to form a community will generate needs that are common to the setting, and some way must be found to satisfy these needs. In the early period of settlement, the needs are usually quite rudimentary. Roads and streets, a quay or dock may be needed, as well as a school and the means to fight fires. Some of these needs require construction, some require organization, and some continue to evolve into the indefinite future. All require resources—money, time, labour.

Deciding upon the needs of a community is relatively easy. Deciding upon how to mobilize the necessary resources is more difficult because it involves reconciling viewpoints on how best to provide for community needs. Much of the history of local government institutions in Canada is concerned with determining the best way to structure the decision-making process: Who should be involved? How much power should they have?

The earliest settlements were under French or British colonial rule, and the power to govern them did not lie in community hands. However, there are many instances in which the early settlers felt that neither the governments in Europe nor the colonial administrators adequately perceived the needs of their communities. Efforts to promote local self-rule began in Québec communities in the mid-1600s. Citizens elected a few representatives to discuss with the French governor the needs of the communities. These efforts were short-lived because the central government disapproved, and it was not until the early 1800s that further steps were taken to allow municipal institutions in Québec. The settlers of the Maritime provinces and Upper Canada (Ontario) were mainly from the newly independent United States.

They brought experience of local government with them, and soon sought a voice in their community's affairs; but there was little response from the British colonial government, with one notable exception. Saint John's 5000 Loyalist settlers from New England obtained a municipal charter in 1785, the first in Canada. It was 47 years before the second was issued.

Some communities in the British colonies had local government in the form of the courts of quarter session. This ancient institution consisted essentially of "magistrates" appointed by the colony's governor who attended court in each district four times a year for both judicial and legislative purposes. They were responsible for maintaining order and settling minor lawsuits, but they could also establish regulations for moving animals, license various businesses, and appoint minor officials to maintain roads.[55] Counties were delineated at this time, and a large centre within each served as the seat of the courts of quarter session. These occasional and centrally controlled mechanisms were not acclaimed by all settlers. Many, especially in Ontario, wanted locally elected councils empowered to deal with community needs. In 1812, the citizens of Kingston agitated for a charter that would allow a municipal council to pass its own bylaws and regulations.[56]

Various changes were made to meet these challenges. Local magistrates were appointed to administer "police towns," but this proved no more satisfactory than quarter sessions. The Public School Act in Ontario in 1816—the first such act in Canada—proved to be a breakthrough, however, as it allowed a community to erect a school, hire a teacher, and elect school trustees to raise taxes and administer the school. Not only did this confer the right of local election, but it also established the still-prevailing separation of education from other local functions in a community. In the 1830s and 1840s, local efforts to form municipalities began to succeed. Brockville was the first in Ontario in 1832, followed by York (Toronto), Kingston, and Hamilton; in Québec, Montréal and Ville de Québec obtained charters in 1832; and in the Maritimes, Halifax was incorporated in 1841, Fredericton in 1848.

The Emergence of Local Government

During the 1840s considerable effort was made to develop a sound system of local government in both Upper and Lower Canada. Ontario's Municipal Act of 1849, often referred to as the Baldwin Act after its originator, proved to be workable and enduring. Its format was for two classes of local government: (1) cities, towns, and villages for urban communities and townships for rural communities; and (2) counties that comprised the local municipalities. Sources of tax revenue were specified, as were the form of elections and the composition of local councils and their duties. With the exception of new local government arrangements designed for metropolitan areas (see Chapter 9), local government forms are not substantially different today than those specified in the early acts.

Two important contextual elements in the development of local government in Canada concern the provincial government's role. The first derives from the fact that, except for the Prairie provinces and northern territories, all the others began as colonies governed from abroad. The tendency of British colonial administration was for strong central control. If municipal institutions were allowed, the central government would ultimately be responsible, a model still found in Britain. Thus, as the Canadian provinces were emerging, there was only grudging acceptance of local self-rule. Self-rule was, and continues to be, hemmed in by various provincial audits, mandatory approvals, and supervision of local affairs. Witness, for example, the provincial hegemony regarding local governments in the Ontario government's imposed amalgamations in Toronto, Ottawa, Hamilton, and Kingston in the late 1990s, or similar actions in Québec and British Columbia.[57]

The second element concerns the constitutional setting for local government that was established in the British North America Act (BNA Act) of 1867. That original constitution did not provide communities with the right to a local government, but only specified that the responsibility for establishing municipal institutions lay with the provincial governments. Section 92 of the BNA Act defines this prerogative. (The 1982 Canadian Constitution carries forward the same section.) It is common to find municipalities referred to as "creatures" of the provincial government. While this superior role of the province is true in other federal states, such as the United States and Australia, what is significant in Canada is the alacrity with which provincial governments perform their role. The development both of local government and, subsequently, of community-planning institutions, bears this stamp of provincial paternalism.[58]

The local government systems that were created by the provinces in the latter half of the 19th century were limited in their roles and in their sources of revenue. Local governments were conceived primarily in terms of providing such services as roads, water, and fire protection to residences and places of business. This is often described as "providing services to property."

Early local government controls on built form emerged from property regulations and by-laws.[59] In turn, local governments were restricted to taxes applied to private property for their revenue. It is not too difficult to appreciate how this constraint has forced municipalities to emphasize property ownership in their bylaws and regulations, as well as how it colours their outlook on the community. As a consequence, property owners and those who desired to develop property came to feel that their demands on the local government were deserving of attention. They, after all, were the primary source of municipal revenues. Lastly, municipalities were limited in their ability to provide social services. Education, health, and welfare services were prerogatives retained by the province, to be delegated—if at all—to such special agencies at the local level as school boards.

The Reform Epidemic

The beginning decades of local government were not auspicious. Inexperience with locally run institutions, combined with a bias toward property ownership and owners, was responsible for many cases of inefficiency, uneconomic practices, and even corruption. By 1900, and the dramatic upsurge in urban development, many local governments appeared unable to cope with the new demands. They were faced with responsibilities for traffic control, parks, housing, and community planning, the extent of which had not been contemplated by those who framed the various municipal acts. Inter-municipal problems arose in transportation, water supply, and protective services, because residences spread into suburbs. And financial resources were often strained to the limit when large bond issues were needed to finance public works projects.

A municipal-reform movement arose primarily from within business and professional circles, since this would likely benefit their interests. They contended that a local government's main task was to provide services efficiently and economically. City growth translated for them into technical problems in engineering and fiscal management. Goldwin Smith, prominent among those involved in the reform movement in Toronto at the turn of the century, stated: "A city is simply a densely populated district in need of a specially skilled administration."[60] Good government for a municipality was thus cast in terms of a business management model. This became a powerful viewpoint, and one that persists today in many communities.

The reformers were also generally suspicious of popularly elected local governments (even though, until recent decades, only property owners could vote in most civic elections). They argued for boards and commissions with specific functions to perform and with an appointed membership. Ostensibly, the intention was, as Vancouver's Mayor Bethune said at the time, to attract "the services of bright able men who have not the time to serve on Council."[61] Thus, across the country many such agencies were formed, with elected representatives often excluded from serving. Montréal acquired a Park Commission; Vancouver, a Water Works Commission; and Fort William-Port Arthur (Thunder Bay), a Public Utilities Commission. These joined school boards, library boards, and police commissions in a plethora of quasi-autonomous bodies, most of which had independent budgets and their own technical and professional staff. Community planning and planners would have to vie for their own position within these organizational arrangements as Canada entered the 20th century.

Reflections

It seems paradoxical in some ways that this turbulent period in urban development and civic affairs was the milieu in which community planning emerged. Yet without this struggle to solve urban problems, debate the merits of various approaches, and strengthen local government, community planning appeared as not much more than idealistic rhetoric. This was no longer the time when kings and colonial masters decided on the form of cities and towns and on how they were governed. The Industrial Revolution broke those bonds, first in Europe and then in North America, where the ethos of pluralist society and local self-government was prominent. (The latter was fostered in considerable

measure by the colonial model of making land available under individual ownership to settlers.) Thus, as the various problems of city growth and development arose, there was the desire for broad debate about solutions.

Community planning, to this day, does not grow and develop independently of real urban problems or their solutions as perceived by citizens, professionals, and governments. So, in the arduous period of wrestling with how to attain urban betterment of the 19th century, those who championed comprehensive community planning were being informed, were learning, of the perceptions of the time. These views would, in turn, need to be thrashed out by a pluralist society (however defined at the time) and be implemented. But this required effective local institutions that had, literally, to be invented in many instances. Therefore, this was a period of enormous social learning, not least for the advocates of community planning.

By the beginning of the 20th century, community planning had achieved a sufficiently stable footing to start making a difference in the form, living conditions, and functioning of Canadian cities and towns, as we shall see in Chapters 4 and 5. But note that this unfolding future was not without its own urban problems and competing views of their solution. Thus, keep in mind these questions:

- *What parallels are there for community planning in the 20th century to the experience of the previous century?*

- *Look at the aerial photographs in a program such as Google Maps and consider: how have early settlement plans like Charlesbourg and Bourg Royal affected the modern landscape in the suburbs of Ville de Québec?*

Reference Notes

1. Marc Denhez, *The Canadian Home: From Cave to Electronic Cocoon* (Toronto: Dundurn Press, 1994).
2. R. Cole Harris, *The Resettlement of British Columbia: Essays on Colonialism and Geographical Change* (Vancouver, BC: UBC Press, 1997).
3. James W. Vance, *The Continuing City* (Baltimore: Johns Hopkins University Press, 1990), 200ff.
4. Peter Moogk, *Building a House in New France* (Toronto: McClelland and Stewart, 1971), 14.
5. As quoted in ibid. This is in reference to the settlement that evolved to the north of the original French village of Ville Marie.
6. John Reps, *Town Planning in Frontier America* (Princeton, NJ: Princeton University Press, 1969), 82; Phyllis Lambert and Alan Stewart, *Opening the Gates of Eighteenth-Century Montréal* (Montréal: Canadian Centre for Architecture, 1992); and Jean-Claude Marsan, *Montreal in Evolution: Historical Analysis*

of the Development of Montreal's Architecture and Urban Environment (Montréal: McGill-Queen's University Press, 1990).
7. E. Deville, "Radial Hamlet Settlement Schemes," *Plan Canada* 15 (March 1975), 44 (reprinted from *Conservation of Life*, April 1918).
8. A.J.B. Johnston, "From Port de Pêche to Ville Fortifiée: The Evolution of Urban Louisbourg 1713–1858," in *Aspects of Louisbourg* (Sydney, NS: The University College of Cape Breton Press, 1995), 3–18.
9. Michael Hugo-Brunt, "The Origin of Colonial Settlements in the Maritimes," in L.O. Gertler, ed., *Planning the Canadian Environment* (Montréal: Harvest House, 1968), 42–83.
10. J. Williams, *Rules and Regulations for the Conduct of the Land Office Department* (Québec: Province of Québec Land Office Department, February 17, 1789).
11. R.L. Gentilcore, ed., *Ontario's History in Maps* (Toronto: University of Toronto Press, 1984).

12. Clarence Karr, *The Canada Land Company: The Early Years*, Research Publication No. 3 (Ottawa: Ontario Historical Society, 1974), 24ff. Also Gilbert Stelter, "Guelph and the Early Canadian Town Planning Tradition," *Ontario History* 77 (June 1985), 83–106.

13. John Reps, *Town Planning*, 350, makes a similar point regarding the origins of the radial pattern of Buffalo, New York, which was laid out for the Holland Company by Ellicott.

14. Larry D. McCann and Peter J. Smith, "Canada Becomes Urban: Cities and Urbanization in Historical Perspective," in Trudi Bunting and Pierre Filion, eds., *Canadian Cities in Transition* (Toronto: Oxford University Press, 1991), 69–99.

15. Hans Blumenfeld, *The Modern Metropolis* (Montréal: Harvest House, 1967), 27.

16. As quoted in Charles M. Godfrey, *The Cholera Epidemics in Upper Canada 1832–1866* (Toronto: Secombe House, 1968), 20.

17. As quoted in William Ashworth, *The Genesis of Modern British Town Planning* (London: Routledge and Kegan Paul, 1954), 49.

18. Alan Artibise, *Winnipeg, A Social History of Urban Growth, 1874–1914* (Montréal: McGill-Queen's University Press, 1975), 232ff.

19. John H. Taylor, "Fire, Disease and Water in Ottawa," *Urban History Review* 8 (June 1979), 7–37.

20. J. Grove Smith, *Fire Waste in Canada* (Ottawa: Commission of Conservation, 1918), 277–289.

21. John Whittow, "Disaster Impact and the Built Environment," *Built Environment* 21: 2/3 (1996), 81–88; and Lawrence J. Vale and Thomas J. Campanella, eds., *The Resilient City: How Modern Cities Recover from Disaster* (New York: Oxford University Press, 2005).

22. Shirley Spragge, "A Confluence of Interests: Housing and Reform in Toronto, 1900–1920," in A. Artibise and G. Stelter, eds., *The Usable Urban Past* (Toronto: Carleton Library, 1979), 247–267.

23. Herbert B. Ames, *The City Below the Hill* (Montréal: Bishop Engraving, 1897), 27–47.

24. Artibise, *Winnipeg*, 150ff.

25. Peter G. Goheen, *Victorian Toronto 1850 to 1900* (Chicago: University of Chicago, Department of Geography, 1970), Research Paper 127, 84.

26. Nik Luka, "From Summer Cottage Colony to Metropolitan Suburb: Toronto's Beach District," *Urban History Review* 35:1 (Fall 2006), 18–46.

27. For an example of the breadth of concerns, see Paul Rutherford, ed., *Saving the Canadian City: The First Phase, 1880–1920* (Toronto: University of Toronto Press, 1974).

28. Mel Scott, *American City Planning since 1890* (Berkeley: University of California Press, 1969), 33.

29. William H. Wilson, *The City Beautiful Movement* (Baltimore: Johns Hopkins University Press, 1989).

30. Daniel H. Burnham and Edward H. Bennett, *Plan of Chicago* (Chicago: Commercial Club, 1909).

31. Thomas Hines, *Burnham of Chicago, Architect and Planner* (New York: Oxford University Press, 1974).

32. David Gordon, "The *Other* Author of the 1908 Chicago Plan: Edward H. Bennett," *Planning Perspectives* 25:2 (2010), 229–241.

33. As quoted in Walter Van Nus, "The Fate of City Beautiful Thought in Canada, 1893–1930," in G.A. Stelter and A. Artibise, eds., *The Canadian City: Essays in Urban History* (Toronto: Macmillan, 1979), 162–185.

34. For the role of architects, see Harold Kalman, *A History of Canadian Architecture* 2 (Toronto: Oxford University Press, 1994), 649–659.

35. Lance Berelowitz, *Dream City: Vancouver and the Global Imagination* (Vancouver, BC: Douglas & McIntyre, 2005), Ch. 5.

36. Gilbert Stelter, "Rethinking the Significance of the City Beautiful Idea," in Robert Freestone, ed., *Urban Planning in a Changing World: The Twentieth Century Experience* (London: Spon, 2000), 98–117.

37. See Peter Hall, *Cities of Tomorrow* (London: Basil Blackwell, 2002), Ch. 1; and Friedrich Engels, *The Condition of the Working Class in England in 1844*, W.O. Henderson and Witt Challoner, trans. (London: Blackwell, 1958/1845).

38. Mervyn Miller, *Letchworth: The First Garden City* (Chichester, UK: Phillimore, 2002).

39. Thomas Adams, *Outline of Town and City Planning* (New York: Russell Sage Foundation, 1935), 275.

40. Maurice De Soissons, *Welwyn Garden City: A Town Designed for Healthy Living* (Cambridge, UK: Publications for Companies, 1988).

41. See Stephen Ward, ed., *The Garden City: Past, Present and Future* (London: Spon, 1992); and Stephen Ward, *Planning the Twentieth-Century City: The Advanced Capitalist World* (New York: Wiley, 2002).

42. F.J. Osborn makes the point in his Preface to Ebenezer Howard, *Garden Cities of Tomorrow* (London: Faber and Faber, 1946). See also Peter Hall and Colin Ward, *Sociable Cities: The Legacy of Ebenezer Howard* (Chichester, UK: Wiley, 1998).

43. Ebenezer Howard, *Tomorrow: A Peaceful Path to Real Reform* (London: Swan Sonnenschein, 1898); and *Garden Cities of Tomorrow* (London: Swan Sonnenschein, 1902); Howard's original 1898 work has been reprinted as *Tomorrow: A Peaceful Path to Real Reform* (London: Routledge, 2003) with useful commentary by Peter Hall, Dennis Hardy, and Colin Ward.

44. Mervyn Miller, *Hampstead Garden Suburb: Arts and Crafts Utopia?* (Chichester, UK: Phillimore, 2006).

45. Jane Addams, ed., *Hull-House Maps and Papers: A Presentation of Nationalities and Wages in a Congested District of Chicago, Together with Comments and Essays on Problems Growing Out of the Social Conditions* (Boston: Thomas Crowell, 1896); and *Twenty Years at Hull-House: With Autobiographical Notes* (New York: Macmillan, 1910).

46. David Schuyler, *The New Urban Landscape: The Redefinition of City Form in Nineteenth-Century America* (Baltimore: Johns Hopkins University Press, 1986); J.R. Wright, *Urban Parks in Ontario, Part I: Origins to 1860* (Toronto: Ontario Ministry of Tourism And Recreation, 1984); and Jennifer McKendry, "The Role of Cataraqui Cemetery in the Rural Cemetery Movement," *Historic Kingston* 44 (1996), 3–9, 52.

47. J.R. Wright, *Urban Parks in Ontario, Part II: The Public Park Movement, 1860–1914* (Toronto: Ontario Ministry of Tourism And Recreation, 1984). The author provided the original stimulus for this section.

48. As quoted in Elsie Marie McFarland, *The Development of Public Recreation in Canada* (Toronto: Canadian Parks/Recreation Association, 1974), 14.

49. Frederick Law Olmsted, *Mount Royal* (New York: G.P. Putnam's Sons, 1881), 64.

50. Frederick Law Olmsted, *Civilizing American Cities: A Selection of Frederick Law Olmsted's Writings of City Landscapes* (Cambridge, MA: MIT Press, 1971); Charles Beveridge and P. Rocheleau, *Frederick Law Olmsted: Designing the American Landscape* (New York: Universe, 1998); Witold Rybczynski, *A Clearing in the Distance: Frederick Law Olmsted and America in the Nineteenth Century* (New York: Scribner, 1999); and Nancy Pollock-Ellwand, "The Olmsted Firm in Canada: A Correction of the Record," *Planning Perspectives* 21 (2006), 277–310.

51. Jon Peterson, "Frederick Law Olmsted, Sr. and Frederick Law Olmsted, Jr.: The Visionary and the Professional," in Mary Corbin Sies and Christopher Silver, eds., *Planning the Twentieth-Century American City* (Baltimore: Johns Hopkins UP, 1996), 37–54.

52. Richard White, "Professionals before Professionalization: The Pre-Confederation Civil Engineers," *Scientia Canadensis: Canadian Journal of the History of Science, Technology and Medicine* 24 (2000), 73–95.

53. Richard White, "The Engineers' Engineer: Sir John Kennedy and the Port of Montreal," *Scientia Canadensis: Canadian Journal of the History of Science, Technology and Medicine* 27 (2003), 5–26.

54. T.J. Plunkett and G.M. Betts, *The Management of Canadian Urban Government* (Kingston: Queen's University Institute of Local Government, 1978), 58.

55. Plunkett and Betts., 48.

56. Plunkett and Betts., 50.

57. John Meligrana, ed., *Redrawing Local Government Boundaries: An International Study of Politics, Procedures and Decisions* (Vancouver, BC: UBC Press, 2004).

58. Meligrana.

59. Raphaël Fischler, "Development Control in Toronto in the Nineteenth Century," *Urban History Review* 36:1 (Fall 2007), 16–31.

60. As quoted in Weaver, *Shaping the Canadian City*, 72.

61. Weaver., 70.

Internet Resources

Chapter-Relevant Sites

Planning Canadian Communities
www.planningcanadiancommunities.ca

Canadian urban history
http://scale.cs.uoguelph.ca/history/urban/sitemap.html

The City Beautiful Movement
http://xroads.virginia.edu/~CAP/CITYBEAUTIFUL/city.html

The Plan of Chicago
www.encyclopedia.chicagohistory.org/pages/10537.html

Garden Cities of To-Morrow
www.library.cornell.edu/Reps/DOCS/howard.htm

Frederick Law Olmsted
http://www.fredericklawolmsted.com

National Association for Olmsted Parks
www.olmsted.org

The City Scientific
www.library.cornell.edu/Reps/DOCS/ford_13.htm

Chapter Four

Pioneering Community Planning in Canada, 1900–1945

You may ask, is it reasonable … to make plans for generations in the distant future? We have only to study the history of older cities, and note at what enormous cost they have overcome the lack of provision for their growth, to realize that the future prosperity and beauty of the city depends … upon the ability to look ahead.

Frederick Todd, 1903

It is widely accepted today that community planning aims to improve the quality of daily life in our cities, towns, and regions. But any such public activity does not come into being either quickly or independently of its context. There has to be acknowledged, first, that one or more problems is affecting community well-being, and then a desire to find a solution to it. The latter, importantly, depends on a sufficient body of people being convinced that the activity can contribute significantly to the welfare and prosperity of city and town dwellers. As the 20th century opened, a succession of major problems affected Canadian cities and towns, from their disparate appearance to their inefficient functioning and their unsanitary housing. Each of these sought a response in the new activity of community planning and, in turn, influenced its development through the first half of the century.

The period 1900–1945 saw the pioneering of the ideas and practice of community planning in Canada. It consisted of communities taking some halting steps to assume responsibility for their planning problems and to draw upon technical and professional assistance in this regard. It was also a tumultuous period, with further dramatic growth of cities and advances in transportation, both of which brought new problems. Nevertheless, this period is among the most important in the evolution of community planning. Within it we see the development of the first locally sponsored plans in Kitchener and Toronto, the path-breaking work of the Commission of Conservation, the emergence of provincial planning legislation, and the emergence of a planning profession. In this context key questions to consider are:

- *How and why did we come to use the planning tools and institutions to which we are so accustomed today?*
- *How do the political philosophies behind Garden City, City Beautiful, and City Scientific planning differ?*

The Impact of 20th Century Urban Problems

The 20th century presented new problems for Canadian cities and towns. The first dozen years of the century constituted a period of unparalleled prosperity, from the wheat fields of Saskatchewan to the wharves of Vancouver and Saint John. Immigrants poured into Canada ostensibly "to open up the West," but most of them ended up in the nation's cities. Urban-based industries thrived on the new inexpensive labour supply. In addition, technological solutions provided cities with infrastructure, both below ground (water and sewerage) and above ground (electric lines, paved roads), fairly rapidly and inexpensively. Probably most important in this period, however, was the advent of powered urban rail transportation—the electric streetcar and the commuter railroad—and slightly later, the self-propelled bus.

Problems of Excessive Subdivision

Urban growth was so highly valued by communities that it was pursued through aggressive "boosterism." Ample supplies of land were deemed essential to accommodate the hoped-for growth. No thorough study has ever been made of the amount of land that was subdivided in anticipation of urban growth in the decade or so before World War I (Figure 4.1). However, it is possible to infer its extent in several cities from concerned accounts of the problems raised by over-subdivision. Here are a few examples comparing the actual population just prior to

Figure 4.1	Excess Rural Subdivision Creating Bad Suburban Conditions in Ottawa, ca. 1914

Thomas Adams described this image as "unhealthy conditions in a rural district outside Ottawa where there are hundreds of acres of fertile land lying fallow because of injurious speculation."[1]

1914 with the population that could be accommodated on the already subdivided land:

Calgary	50 000/770 000
Ottawa-Hull	123 000/1 600 000
Edmonton	40 000/500 000
Saskatoon	12 000/750 000
Vancouver	115 000/750 000

Abetting this surge in land speculation were dramatic increases in the coverage of street railways. Figures for Toronto and Vancouver convey something of the picture that was occurring in other cities. In 1880, Toronto had 30 kilometres of street railways, and only ten years later had 110 kilometres, while Vancouver went from 26 kilometres in 1900 to 165 kilometres by 1914. The impact of such expansion can be appreciated from the fact that each linear kilometre of streetcar line could serve about two square kilometres of residential land or, in pre-1914 densities, potentially 10 000 persons. Not until the automobile freeways of the 1950s would Canadian cities again witness such an impact on this scale.[2]

And, like the freeways later, the streetcar lines brought potential development but, frequently, not actual building. Land was surveyed by the hundreds of hectares, and subdivision plans were registered in land titles offices. There were, of course, not enough people heading for Canada's cities to come close, in most cases, to absorbing the amount of new building lots (Figure 4.2). Severe problems arose for cities in the short run because of the premature subdivision. As Walter Van Nus notes:

> A developer's desire to extract the maximum number of lots … often led him to ignore the location and/or width of projected or existing streets nearby, if by doing so he could squeeze more lots out of the property.[3]

This lack of simple coordination of the extensions to cities often required, at a later time, expensive road relocation by the municipalities. In addition, the subdivision development was usually scattered, and this meant extra costs in providing municipal services such as water and sewer lines, roads, sidewalks, and street lighting. Because intervening undeveloped land did not pay its share of the servicing costs, the taxes had to be raised from the new building lots. And, frequently, the land that came into actual development was unsuitable for building—topographically too steep, many rock outcroppings, or poorly drained—and this not only led to immediate problems for communities but often was also a source of problems that many decades later would be termed "urban sprawl."

Cities that espoused growth found themselves on the horns of a dilemma. First were the enormous costs of servicing the new suburbs. Those that demurred in making these expenditures might find the building going to an adjacent municipality. Second, people seeking a building lot were finding land values and taxes much higher along streetcar routes and accordingly sought land beyond the end of the streetcar line. This tended to spread the costs further afield, but not necessarily the benefits. Third, most cities were faced with large housing shortages, which the mere subdivision of land on the fringe did little to alleviate. Land prices and rents rose sharply in Canadian cities in the several years before World War I, especially in and around downtown areas. Poor people and manufacturing firms traditionally located near the centre suffered most. Many firms moved to suburban locations, not infrequently followed by the shacktowns of their workers.

During this period of crises in city-building, a crucial ideological issue had to be resolved. The boom reflected the ethos of economic progress for many, while bringing debilitating circumstances for most others. In whose interest should reforms be made? The view that came to prevail, to quote historian John Weaver, was that "civic resources should assist the endeavours of those who do most for the material growth of the community, namely business and real estate interests."[5]

New Dimensions to Urban Problems

These new urban problems had several significant impacts for the fledgling planning profession.[6] They created an awareness of the importance of land subdivision, the developers who undertook it, and the problems of efficiency often associated with it.

Land Subdivision The unprecedented scale of pre-1914 subdivision brought home the unintended consequences of this process. When subdividing a larger property into house lots or other small parcels of land, the new pieces of property acquire independent status, and the community is obliged to honour this whenever they should be built upon. A community's future development pattern and its quality are thereby constrained. On the one hand, there are such technical aspects such as road alignment, drainage, lot size, and ease of providing water and sewer lines in which the community has a rightful interest. On the other hand, there is the issue of the degree to which a community should intervene in the development of privately owned property.

The Land Developer The act of subdividing land in a speculative way involved a relatively new actor in the planning and development of communities—the land developer. The surge of growth created a demand for city land so

Figure 4.2	Excess Rural Subdivision along Streetcar Lines in Ottawa, 1915

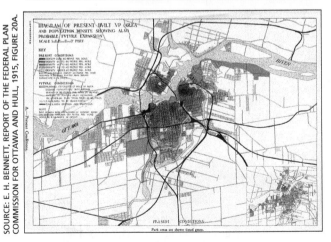

Many of the isolated subdivisions in this map were not occupied for 40 years. Thomas Adams used this drawing to highlight the problem in his 1917 book.[4]

large that it attracted many more people and groups to seek profit in providing space for newcomers. They joined such old land grantees as the Canadian Pacific Railway, the British American Land Company, and the Hudson's Bay Company; the latter frequently influenced the location of new municipal development by their decisions. On a smaller scale, but equally pervasive, were a coterie of individual landowners (large and small), their agents, and brokers, all anxious to share in the potential profit of the new growth. This was the period for the beginning of a real estate industry. The views of land development interests, the real estate industry, and homeowners all focused upon the primacy of private property. Their concerns held sway in most municipal councils at that time, much as they tend to do today.

Efficiency The unfettered land development in the early 20th century led to unconnected streets and poorly drained sites, among other inefficiencies. Faced with this large-scale, rapid land development, the tendency of planners to prepare physical designs for new development seemed often to be out of tune with the vigorous, widely supported process of land speculation. Planners thus began to promote planning as a means of obtaining efficiency in city development.

Planning Responses to Early Urban Problems

As communities tackled the problems of disease, pure water supplies, fire, sanitation, slums, and excessive subdivision, their experience gave rise to two important realizations. First, it became evident that these problems resulted from the pace of growth and development of cities. Second, and more slowly, came the realization that the solutions to these problems lay in better coordination, regulation, and physical arrangement of the overall development of cities. The issues of public health, fire safety, and adequate housing became the first social goals of community planning. These issues would be found, time and again, enshrined in the preambles of planning legislation proclaiming that the bylaw or plan was aimed at "improving the health, safety, and public welfare" of the community.

Further, five areas of public concern about city and town development had gathered considerable momentum as the 19th century came to an end. Four of these grew out of substantive issues that have already been identified (see Figure 4.3). The fifth grew out of a widespread dismay over the capability of local

| Figure 4.3 | Evolution of Community Planning Ideas, 1900–1945 |

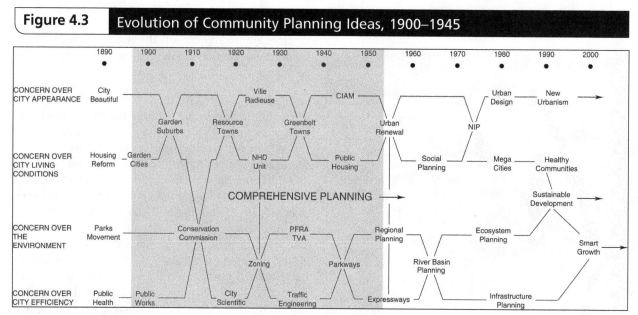

The first half of the 20th century saw the initial planning concerns of the late 1800s put into practice and refined, blended with others, and professionalized. Architects, for example, are often involved in plans concerned with city appearance; social workers and housing advocates are key allies when addressing city living conditions; landscape architects and ecologists help address environmental concerns; and engineers, public health advocates, and lawyers are involved in plans to improve city efficiency. The foundations of contemporary planning approaches were laid in this period.

government officials to deal adequately with the needs of a community:

1. the city's appearance
2. urban living conditions and housing
3. the state of the natural environment
4. concern over efficient city functioning
5. reform of local government

An active movement developed around each of these concerns among members of the public, various professions, newspapers, and many public officials who lobbied for the mitigation of urban problems, the beginnings of which were described in Chapter 3. Often the concern focused on a special-interest organization. There was, of course, overlap in the interests of each; indeed, as can happen in a small country, many of the same people were involved in two or more of these crusades for improvement in Canadian city life.

The community (town) planning movement came out of the confluence of these five streams of concern during the first dozen years of the 20th century. The proponents of each shared many objectives, but they also brought with them differences in values, professional outlook, skills, and jurisdictional focus.

Concern over City Appearance

The burgeoning City Beautiful movement, so profoundly influenced by the 1893 Chicago World's Fair, lent considerable momentum to addressing concerns over the appearance of Canadian cities in the early 20th century. But beautification as an objective began to falter after World War I as new concerns over city efficiency, the environment, and living conditions gained prominence, and the Beaux Arts basis for City Beautiful aesthetics was attacked by the Modern Design movement of the 1920s and 1930s. By the Depression of the 1930s, any proposal to make cities more attractive seemed like a waste of scarce public resources.

The Peak of the City Beautiful, 1900–1915

In 1906, the first citywide planning proposal in Canada to emanate from City Beautiful approaches was undertaken for Toronto by the Ontario Association of Architects and the Toronto Guild of Civic Art. It contained plans for a series of diagonal streets and a system of parks connected by parkways. Similar principles guided the plans made for Berlin (now Kitchener) by Charles Leavitt Jr. in 1914 (see Figure 4.4), and the 1915 plan for Ottawa and Hull

(Figure 4.5) jointly prepared by Edward Bennett, Daniel Burnham's associate on the 1908 Chicago plan, and Canadian Arthur Bunnell, whose name would recur in connection with planning in Canada through the next several decades.[7]

Plans prepared in the City Beautiful style also influenced the development of some provincial capitals, especially Regina. English landscape architect Thomas Mawson's 1914 plan for the lands surrounding the new Saskatchewan legislative building influenced all future designs for the Wascana Centre, although the new City Hall was not built until 1978.[8]

The achievement of civic grandeur was an aim of City Beautiful planning.[9] This was often expressed in plans of civic centres, with monumental public

| Figure 4.4 | City Plan for Greater Berlin (Kitchener-Waterloo, Ontario), 1914 |

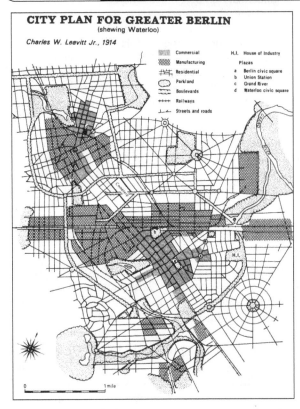

This plan by American planner Charles Leavitt Jr. employs all the City Beautiful design devices: diagonal avenues leading to city squares, circular streets, and parkways. Kitchener was named Berlin prior to World War I.

Figure 4.5	City Beautiful Plan for Canada's Capital, 1915

Proposed plan for an Ottawa municipal plaza and railway station by Edward Bennett, Daniel Burnham's partner on the influential *Plan of Chicago*. The City Beautiful style was perhaps most appropriate for a capital city, where a little grandeur might be appropriate. Bennett wisely kept the Beaux Arts urban design to this civic centre, leaving the wonderful Gothic revival building group on Parliament Hill to be viewed on a diagonal axis, maximizing the picturesque effect of its architecture and siting on the riverside bluff.

buildings grouped around a public square and a broad tree-lined avenue leading to it as in the one proposed for Edmonton (Figure 4.8). Others were proposed (but never built) for Calgary (Figure 4.6) by British landscape architect Thomas Mawson in 1914[11] and for Vancouver by American planner Harland Bartholomew in 1929.[12] Canadian Horace Seymour collaborated on the latter plan and also included City Beautiful elements in other plans he made at the time.[13] In 1921, another respected Canadian planner, Noulan Cauchon, prepared a plan for Hamilton's civic centre in the same tradition (Figure 4.7) and the monumental quality we now see in Toronto's University Avenue, which leads to the provincial legislative buildings, was cast in a 1929 redevelopment plan for that city.[14] One might add to this list of City Beautiful projects the former city of Maisonneuve and the many railway stations built in a grand manner in Canadian cities in this period.[15]

The **City Beautiful** movement was later commonly described in condescending terms—as "mere adornment,"

Figure 4.6	Thomas Mawson's Calgary Civic Centre Plan, 1914

Paris comes to the Prairies, to glorify the Canadian Pacific Railway and the Hudson's Bay Company. None of this was built, and the impracticality of some of its transportation proposals gave City Beautiful planning a bad name.

Figure 4.7	Noulan Cauchon's Hamilton Civic Centre Plan, 1917

The City Beautiful is more suited to a war memorial, such as this proposal for Hamilton.

as having failed to address the "real problems" of city housing and sanitation, as extravagant.[16] A number of important factors are missed in these debates. First, the classic mode that characterized many of the architecture and design concepts was the design style of the time, and it was a style that favoured adornment

SOURCE: GLENBOW ARCHIVES NC-6-161.

A typical proposal for a grandiose civic centre by Morell and Nichols, similar to those in other Canadian cities in this period, when Edmonton had barely 40 000 people. The Minneapolis landscape architects prepared similar proposals for Saskatoon. The aim of such City Beautiful designs was municipal boosterism—to bring a sense of civic grandeur to otherwise mundane cities and to indicate to potential investors that they had a bright future.

of buildings and public places. Second, the design style was rooted in powerful aesthetic principles that had endured from Renaissance times: symmetry, coherence, perspective, and monumentality. Even those not professing City Beautiful tenets used design elements that drew upon these principles. Ebenezer Howard had his Grand Avenue and radial streets leading to the town centre; Thomas Adams's plan for several resource towns

employed a central tree-lined boulevard around which to organize the community. As recently as 1979, the plan for a new civic centre in Calgary was criticized on the same grounds as Mawson's City Beautiful centre half a century earlier. Third, regardless of design style, City Beautiful planners had correctly identified most of the main elements of a community's physical form with which a planner needed to work: the street pattern, the public buildings, and the parks—the elements under public control.[17]

The Rise of Modernism and Le Corbusier

The Beaux Arts roots of City Beautiful were attacked in the clamorous times following World War I. The Modernist movement in literature, art, and architecture declared "the end of history," and models of Greek and Roman buildings were consigned to the basement storerooms of architectural academies. At the influential Bauhaus School of Weimar, Germany, students in art, architecture, and city planning started with common studios that focused on the design possibilities of modern materials, rather than the historic precedents from the past. Planners were given a clean slate—*tabula rasa*—and asked to imagine the perfect modern city.

The results were often shocking, sometimes brilliant, and a striking departure from the classical compositions of the City Beautiful or the small-scale arts and crafts humanism of Garden City projects. Perhaps the most influential ideas for cities came from the Swiss-born architect Le Corbusier (see sidebar) in the 1920s, who declared that a house is a "machine for living." Instead of small clusters of mostly single-family homes, each with its neighbourhood park, Le Corbusier envisioned the city as a huge park where 60-storey office towers and 10-storey apartment buildings were woven in zigzag form across landscaped space in his Contemporary City (Ville Contemporaine) concept (see Figure 4.10). Hardly more than 5 percent of the ground would be covered, and many buildings constructed on stilts would allow the park space to flow underneath. Le Corbusier promoted skyscrapers and the possibilities they gave for "concentrating" the population without "congesting" it.[18] His concept had people living within a park at very high densities—3000 persons per hectare—but also promised to save them considerable time in horizontal travel compared to a low-density, spread-out city.

Figure 4.9   Le Corbusier

SOURCE: AP PHOTO.

Charles-Édouard Jeanneret (1887–1965) was an architect, designer, painter, urbanist, and writer. He was born in Switzerland, adopted the pseudonym Le Corbusier in the 1920s, and became a French citizen in 1930. Le Corbusier started his career designing villas in the Parisien suburbs in the 1920s and ended it with building entire precincts in Chandigarh, the capital of the new Indian states of Punjab and Haryana. His buildings such as the Villa Savoye (1928) and Ronchamp chapel (1954) are widely admired for their proportions, sculptural form, and use of concrete.[19]

Le Corbusier was a founder of the Congrès International d'Architecture Moderne (CIAM) and believed that Modern Design principles should be followed not just in architecture but also in all elements of life, including urban planning, landscape architecture, interior design, painting, and industrial design. Le Corbusier was a principal author of the CIAM's urban planning manifesto, the Athens Charter, and used it as the basis for his plan for Chandigarh.[20] He built prototypes of the big apartment blocks advocated in his plans (Unité d'Habitation) in Marseilles, Nantes, and Berlin, but these were not widely adopted. Although the large-scale demolition and urban reconstruction shown in Le Corbusier's Plan Voisin (Figure 4.11) was not permitted in central Paris, it became the basis for many destructive post-war urban renewal schemes in Europe and North America.

Le Corbusier's architecture and furniture designs are much praised and he is regarded as perhaps the most influential architect of the 20th century.[21] However, his urban planning ideas were denounced as dangerous and thoroughly discredited by cultural and design critics such as Lewis Mumford, Jane Jacobs, and Colin Rowe.[22] Although new variations of Modern architecture remain avant-garde in the early 21st century, urban renewal and Modern urbanism have been replaced by other ideas.

Although the Contemporary City was designed as the ideal solution for building a modern city for three million people on a "green field" site, Le Corbusier also believed that his principles should be applied in the reconstruction of existing European cities such as Paris, his adopted home. In his 1925 Plan Voisin, he proposed demolition of most of the historic centre of Paris, north of the Seine, to build a modern city centre with high-rise office buildings, avenues for fast-moving traffic, and apartment blocks (see Figure 4.11). Since Paris was considered the epitome of urban sophistication and beauty at the time, the Plan Voisin was greeted

Figure 4.10	Le Corbusier's View of the Contemporary City, 1922

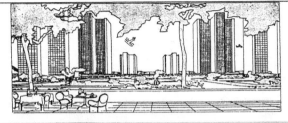

In Le Corbusier's eyes, modern technology allowed cities to avoid congestion and to enjoy open space at their very centres. Tall towers are arranged within a park-like setting, with very little of the ground area covered by buildings (top). His concepts were still quite influential into the mid-20th century as shown by the towers of Montréal's 1961 urban renewal project, Habitations Jeanne Mance (bottom).

with consternation, but the uproar made Le Corbusier famous.

The CIAM and the Athens Charter

By the mid-1920s, Le Corbusier made links with the leaders of the German design schools and other European architects and planners. He became a central figure in the CIAM (Congrès International d'Architecture Moderne), which discussed the new theories for building and planning.[23] Although Le Corbusier was not successful in building his early plans, other CIAM members built demonstration projects in Frankfurt, Amsterdam, and Vienna.

The CIAM continued to refine its planning theories during the economic depression of the 1930s, when little building took place in Europe or North America.

Figure 4.11	Le Corbusier's Plan Voisin for Central Paris, 1925

Le Corbusier's proposal was to demolish the streets and buildings in central Paris, leaving only the Louvre. The vacant land was to be rebuilt with the elements of the Ville Contemporaine—tall office blocks, mid-rise apartments, and expressways. Paris rejected this plan, but a surprising number of cities followed the formula during the 1950s and 1960s.

Some Modern architects and planners tried their hand in the Soviet Union, while others prepared a framework for planning, named after the 1933 CIAM Athens conference. The Athens Charter recommended that urban planning be divided into four functions: dwelling, work, recreation, and transportation. It also recommended rigorous separation of land uses and their connection by high-speed transportation, making use of automobiles on exclusive roadways, electric railroads in subways, and aircraft.[24] The Modern planners regarded the historical city as inefficient and obsolete, and were ready with a well-elaborated theory for planning a new kind of city in the reconstruction after World War II.

Concern over Housing and Living Conditions

In the early 20th century, the concern over urban living conditions continued, and the first steps were made in housing reform to provide inexpensive homes for working-class families. Some Garden City principles were incorporated into garden suburbs and planned resource towns in the Canadian north. And a new set of residential planning principles—the neighbourhood unit—was tested in the Radburn and Greenbelt "new towns" in the United States.

Figure 4.12 Housing Project for Workers: Toronto, 1913

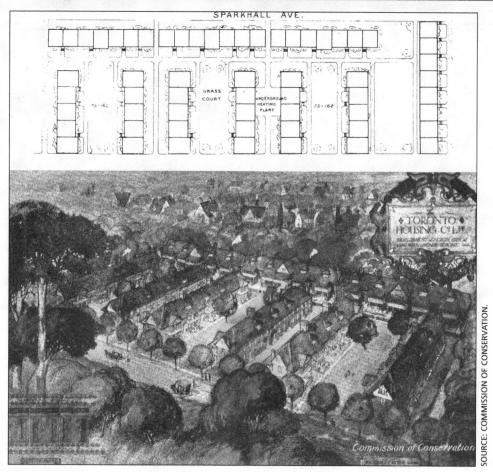

SOURCE: COMMISSION OF CONSERVATION.

Plan and sketch view of a housing development for working-class families. There were 204 "cottage flats" (one- to four-bedroom row houses). The Toronto Housing Company (a limited-dividend corporation) built the project, which is still in use as a downtown non-profit housing cooperative.

The Housing Reform Movement

Those involved with public health matters were among the first to try to arouse public concern over housing conditions, especially for the poor. They urged sanitary improvements and reductions in density. The initial arguments were humanitarian in nature, and, as broader support was sought, they were augmented later with the plea that poor housing promoted disease and caused major costs for the nation's businesses. Industrialists and businessmen had joined the debate over housing in the late 1890s. From their perspective, poor housing, which facilitated disease among workers, also led to absenteeism and lowered productivity. Moreover, much of the poor housing occupied by workers was expensive, and high rents usually meant pressure for more wages, the industrialists unabashedly stated.[25]

But obtaining better housing for workers was difficult. With the dramatic growth of Canadian cities in the early part of the 20th century, the cost of suburban land was pushed up and inner-city land prices stayed high as downtown areas burgeoned. Municipally provided (public) housing was considered but did not receive much support until the 1920s. Tenant cooperatives were also proposed following the urgings of Henry Vivian, a British MP who toured Canada in 1910 to promote the idea of a partnership of tenants subscribing the capital for a housing development. The most notable such project was Cité Jardin in Rosemont.[26] In Montréal, industrialist Herbert Ames built a model tenement project called Diamond Court to demonstrate how low-income housing could be improved (Figure 3.13, page 48).

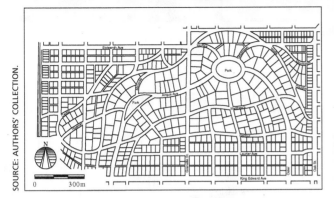

The planners of the first Garden City, Unwin and Parker, popularized this form of street layout in planning new suburbs. It was used in the design of such districts for wealthy Canadian homeowners as Mount Royal in Calgary, Leaside in Toronto, and the Town of Mont-Royal (TMR) in Montréal, as well as this one in Vancouver. Frederick Todd discarded the gridiron in favour of curving streets, which respected the hilly topography. The photo shows The Crescent—the gracious tree-lined circular street surrounding the park in the northeast quadrant.

Limited-dividend housing (providing a fixed rate of return on the investment) built with private capital was favoured mostly by affluent members of the community. It tapped their philanthropic spirit and reduced any "socialist" tendencies to have the municipality provide housing. A popular phrase of the time was Thomas Roden's "philanthropy and five percent," which referred to the dividend that investors would receive in building worker housing, similar to the British proposals for the Garden City corporations. In 1907, Roden helped form the Toronto Housing Company, which eventually built several hundred dwellings. This experience is important in several ways. First, there was local government involvement in the projects, for although private investors started the company, its bonds were guaranteed up to 85 percent by the city government. Ontario passed legislation allowing this in 1913, following the lead of Nova Scotia, which included the option in its 1912 Town Planning Act (the second in the country). Second, the projects were designed as row houses surrounding ample courtyards in the tradition of Hampstead Garden Suburb housing (see Figure 4.12). In this way, both high density and amenity were achieved, and to this day, the projects retain a distinctive, pleasing character. And, third, organizers of the company, most notably G. Frank Beer and Sir Edmund Osler, were also prominent in arguing for community-wide planning. They campaigned widely to provide playgrounds and better transportation, as well as to reduce the congestion of the population. Beer, in his remarks to the 1914 conference of the Commission of Conservation in Ottawa, linked "city planning" to conservation: "The conservation of life and desirable living conditions … are inseparable."[27]

The Garden Suburb

A hybrid of Garden City and City Beautiful approaches was the Garden Suburb, so called because it employed the generous residential environment of the newly developed Letchworth Garden City, and was usually located just beyond the built-up urban area. Further, as with City Beautiful ideas, it broke with the standard gridiron pattern of streets, often termed at the time the "monotonous grid."

The forerunner of the Garden Suburb approach is Hampstead Garden Suburb in London, England, which was designed by Raymond Unwin, co-designer of Letchworth. Its curving streets fitted to the topography, and its parks and open space gave the inspiration for dozens of such residential areas across North America as well as Europe.[28] The most important Garden Suburb experiment in the U.S. was Forest Hills Gardens in New York City, planned by Frederick Law Olmsted Jr. and developed by the Russell Sage Foundation.[29] The notable Garden Suburb projects in Canada are Oak Bay in Victoria,[30] Shaughnessy Heights in Vancouver (see Figure 4.13), Mount Royal in Calgary,[31] Tuxedo

Park in Winnipeg, Leaside and Forest Hill in Toronto, and Lindenlea in Ottawa.[32] The Town of Mont-Royal in Montréal was declared a National Historic Site in 2008 for its planning and design.[33] All of these were begun before 1920 and many of them were built on land owned by a railway company. The Garden Suburb designers were usually major landscape architecture firms such as the Olmsteds' or Frederick Todd.

Thomas Adams's 1917 plan for the rebuilding of the Richmond District in Halifax is a notable Garden Suburb design and an early example of disaster recovery and resilience planning. Halifax was devastated by an enormous munitions ship explosion that was the world's largest detonation before nuclear weapons. Much of the North End, was subsequently destroyed by fires; this created an interest in fireproof construction for the redevelopment of the area.

The Richmond district originally had a common gridiron pattern, even though it was on a steep hillside. Adams's proposed curving streets (see Figure 4.14) conformed to the topography, and his plan was largely applied in the reconstruction.[34] Adams' adjacent Hydrostone neighbourhood provided affordable housing made of fireproof concrete block ("Hydrostone"). Adams's simple and inexpensive design alternated service alleys and residential streets with wide central boulevards. The alleys hide the service poles and garages, while leaving an attractive streetscape. The tree-lined central boulevards provide a small park for every block. The Hydrostone neighbourhood has had enduring appeal, and was the first area designated as a National Historic Site for its planning principles (see Figure 4.15).

Most Canadian Garden Suburbs were developed by the railway companies to serve upper middle class families and were never intended to provide housing for the mass of people in the community. Their generous—even by today's standards—design features meant high prices were attached to the building lots. Yet the high design standards have proved a crucial factor in the persistence of such areas as Shaughnessy Heights and the Town of Mont-Royal as favoured residential districts for three-quarters of a century while some adjacent areas have deteriorated. The site planning of affordable Garden Suburbs, such as Lindenlea and Hydrostone, was excellent, and their modest homes now command a premium in their neighbourhoods. Finally, the Garden Suburb approach provided the stimulus to later community designers of resource towns and metropolitan suburbs alike in Canada.

<table>
<tr><td>**Figure 4.14
and
Figure 4.15**</td><td>A Garden Suburb with
Affordable Housing: The
Richmond District and
Hydrostone Project, Halifax</td></tr>
</table>

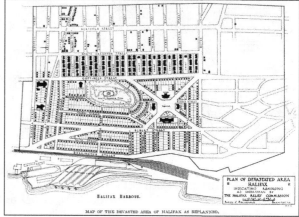

SOURCES: "PLAN OF DEVASTATED AREA HALIFAX INDICATING REHOUSING AS UNDERTAKEN BY THE HALIFAX RELIEF COMMISSION." ROSS & MACDONALD, ARCHITECTS, IN CONSTRUCTION, VOL. XII, NO. 10 (TORONTO, OCTOBER 1919), P. 295; NSARM, HALIFAX RELIEF COMMISSION, MG 26, SERIES R, NO. 1717.29; PHOTO BY DAVID GORDON.

Thomas Adams's 1917 plan for schools at the central square, and a memorial on top of the hill at the central park. The Hydrostone neighbourhood is the regular grid of short blocks, north of the park. Each block has a wide central boulevard that serves as a park, and rear lanes, which accommodate utilities and servicing while leaving an attractive streetscape. The photo is a recent view of Hydrostone townhouses, where the architects executed the Arts and Crafts style from Hampstead and Letchworth using fireproof concrete block, which current residents have stuccoed over to good effect.

Planned Communities for Resource Development

The development of dozens of new towns on the Canadian resource frontier paralleled the expansion of cities in the early part of the 20th century. The planning of these resource settlements ranged in sophistication from a simple grid survey appended to the site for the mine, mill, or smelter, to conscious attempts to create attractive, healthful communities. Possibly the first such planned resource town was Nanaimo, British Columbia, with an interesting "cobweb" street design (dating from about 1880) of radials and circumferentials. In 1904, a plan of grandiose proportions was prepared for Prince Rupert, also in British Columbia, by prominent U.S. landscape architects. Its two main avenues and its circles, crescents, and public sites were meant to be the centre of a city of 100 000 people, rivalling Vancouver for Pacific trade.[35] Although this dream was not realized, the original planned layout is still evident in the present community. On a more modest scale were the plans for three pulp and paper mill towns: Iroquois Falls (1915) and Kapuskasing (1921) in Ontario, and Temiskaming (1917) in Québec.

The plan for Temiskaming (see Figure 4.16) is noteworthy both because it was designed by Thomas Adams and because it shows the influence of Garden City planning principles. The resource frontier town, of course, gave the opportunity of planning for an entire community from the ground up and employing such ideas as the greenbelt, the separation of conflicting uses, street patterns fitting the contour of the land, and ample land for housing. These towns could demonstrate the importance of careful, overall planning that planning efforts in already built-up cities couldn't achieve. Thomas Adams said, in reference to his plan for Temiskaming:

> The object of such plans should be to provide healthy conditions for the workers in the factories and the mills, together with convenience of arrangement to secure the most efficient methods of carrying on the industry, and not merely blind conformity to meaningless division of lines of a rectangular (gridiron) division.[36]

That Adams could prepare and have such plans accepted clearly indicates how readily planning ideas were accepted by the corporations for whom the towns were being built. Some companies actually sent representatives to Britain and other parts of Europe to study model towns that various industrialists had built in order to obtain for their employees housing more desirable than that available in the congested industrial revolution cities.[37] These intellectual connections have continued in the planning of dozens of resource

SOURCE: THOMAS ADAMS, *RURAL PLANNING AND DEVELOPMENT*, COMMISSION OF CONSERVATION, 1917, FIGURE 19.

Figure 4.16 — A Garden City in the North: Temiskaming, Québec, 1917

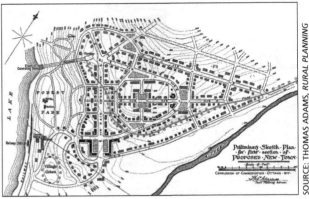

Resource producers in Canadian frontier areas have often sought to build livable communities to attract and hold their labour force. Thomas Adams was commissioned in 1917 to design this town where pulp and paper was (and still is) produced. He employed Garden City planning notions in the arrangement of streets, shops, public buildings, and parks.

development towns, mostly in the Canadian north, right up to modern resource communities as Leaf Rapids, Manitoba, and Arvida and Fermont, Québec.[38]

The Neighbourhood Unit

Around 1920, with better living conditions now their prime objective, community planners began to search for a workable unit of human scale around which housing and community services could be organized and designed. This search culminated in 1929 with the ideas of sociologist Clarence Perry for a neighbourhood unit.[39] Against a backdrop of increasing automobile usage—and auto-related deaths and injuries—Perry proposed a way both to insulate residential areas from traffic and to link the social needs of families to their environment. His concept was for residential areas to be organized in units of about 64 hectares, or sufficiently large to "house enough people to require one elementary school." The exact shape was not specified, but it was expected to provide an area within which young children had only about 400 metres walking distance to the neighbourhood school at the centre. Main streets would bound the area, not pass through it. Total population would be 5000 to 6000 people, or about 1500 families (see Figure 4.17).

Figure 4.17 — The Neighbourhood Unit Concept, 1929

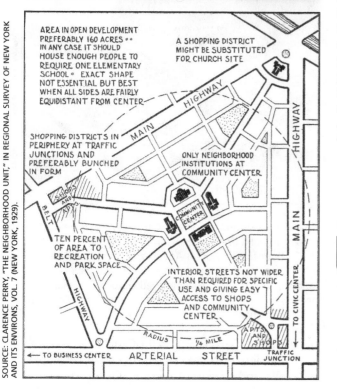

Clarence Perry's 1929 proposals, showing the central school and park, with sites for two places of worship. Shops and apartments are at the corners, and everything is within a radius of a 10-minute walk.

Despite arguments that spatial units could not actually encompass, much less promote, a cohesive social environment, Perry's plan has been widely used. Community plans in Canada, the United States, and Europe have repeatedly used the neighbourhood unit notion in a variety of formats to structure the residential portion of the city. Suggested populations for units have ranged from 3000 to 12 000, but the essential characteristics of a school-oriented, traffic-insulated area have persisted. The neighbourhood unit became probably one of the strongest physical organizing principles in modern community plans. Its outcome is readily seen when one flies over almost any Canadian city (see Figure 4.19).

Radburn and the Greenbelt Towns

Another major planning concept during the period between the world wars was expressed in the "new town" plans of U.S. planners Henry Wright and Clarence Stein. Heavily influenced by the Garden City approach, they persuaded a private corporation to undertake such a venture on the undeveloped edge of New York City, in New Jersey. The first town was called Radburn and was, according to Stein, "not a Garden City as Howard saw it," but rather one planned for a society entering "the Motor Age."[40] Begun in 1928 and planned to grow to a population of 25 000, Radburn pioneered new design relations between houses, roads, paths, gardens, parks, blocks, and neighbourhoods (see Figure 4.18). It was one of the first practical applications of Perry's neighbourhood unit.

The main elements of the Radburn plan were:

1. the superblock, an area of 12 to 20 hectares with major roads on the perimeter so that through traffic would not intrude into housing groups;
2. specialized roads that would allow different traffic needs, from service vehicles for houses to through

Figure 4.18 — Radburn, N.J., Clarence Stein and Henry Wright, 1928

One neighbourhood unit was completed before the project collapsed in the Great Depression. All the culs-de-sac back onto a park and every child can walk to the central school without crossing a street, thanks to a pedestrian underpass below the central collector road.

truck traffic, to proceed efficiently and with minimum impact on the community;

3. extensive use of culs-de-sac following Unwin and Parker's designs for Letchworth and Hampstead Garden Suburb;[41]

4. separation of pedestrians and automobiles by a system of walkways in different places and roads at different levels where they cross;

5. parks as the backbone of the neighbourhood, with open space left in the centre of superblocks and joined from one to the other in a continuous park; and

6. houses turned around facing gardens and parks instead of streets, with the latter becoming mainly service lanes for clusters of houses.[42]

In the Depression period of the 1930s, the U.S. government sponsored several more towns of the Radburn type. They were called Greenbelt Towns, and three of the four planned were built. These towns combined Garden City ideals, the neighbourhood unit, and Modern architecture advocated by Le Corbusier and other European designers. Although these federally sponsored towns were widely publicized, their impact on American suburban planning was not as influential as that of the 1932 President's Conference on Home Building. The research reports for this conference, prepared by Robert Whitten and Thomas Adams, featured the neighbourhood unit and Radburn-style culs-de-sac and crescents as the preferred alternatives to the inflexible gridiron pattern of subdivision used by most suburban builders. The model subdivision guides and mortgage insurance regulations that emerged from this era helped promote the neighbourhood unit and Stein and Wright's Radburn plan in the post-war expansion.[43]

Clarence Stein also left his mark in Canada in his 1951 plan for the aluminum smelting town of Kitimat, British Columbia (see Figure 4.19). Wildwood (1947) in Winnipeg and Cité Jardin (1948) in Montréal closely followed the Radburn cul-de-sac design. And there is hardly a metropolitan suburb planned since the end of World War II, from Fraserview in Vancouver to Churchill Park in St. John's, that does not embody the neighbourhood unit principles pioneered by Perry, Wright, and Stein to some degree.

Concern over the Environment

The turn of the century saw increased concern about public health in Canadian cities and the rise of the conservation movement and its concern over the

| Figure 4.19 | Kitimat, B.C., Designed by Clarence Stein |

First phase of a new Canadian community, Kitimat, B.C., seen in 1957. Clarence Stein retained many elements of his Radburn plan, but Kitimat featured short loop streets instead of culs-de-sac.

SOURCE: REPRINTED WITH THE PERMISSION OF ALCAN INC.

natural environment. The 19th century parks movement expanded from municipal parks to national parks in wilderness areas.

The Conservation Movement

The turn of the century gave rise to the recognition among the industrialized countries that industrial processes were consuming natural resources at an alarming rate, often leaving in their wake waste and pollution. The persistence of these problems in city and country alike led to strong national initiatives in the field of conservation of resources. This was the era in which the wilderness lands of the Rocky Mountains were secured for national parks (in both Canada and the U.S.).

In 1909, following the lead of the United States but going even further, Canada established a Commission for the Conservation of Natural Resources. Winnipeg lawyer and federal Cabinet minister Clifford Sifton was made chairman of the Commission of Conservation, as it came to be called. The Commission concerned itself with many resource questions: lands, forests, minerals, fisheries, game and fur-bearing animals, waters and waterpower. Somewhat unique was the Commission's commitment, from the outset, to human resources. Dr. Charles Hodgetts was one of the first to be appointed to the permanent staff as the Advisor on Public Health.

Figure 4.20   Thomas Adams

The person who did the most to establish the substance and credibility of the Canadian planning profession in the first quarter of the 20th century was, of course, Thomas Adams (1871–1940). Born in Edinburgh, Adams began by studying law but is referred to variously as a journalist, as a surveyor, and, in the initial roster of the Town Planning Institute of Canada (TPIC), as a landscape architect. This may well be a measure of his several talents and interests. In any case, he was acquainted with Patrick Geddes and the latter's work in Edinburgh, and also with Ebenezer Howard and the Garden City movement. For six years,

Adams was secretary of the company that undertook to build the first Garden City at Letchworth. He was instrumental in promoting passage of the benchmark 1909 Housing and Town Planning Act in Britain, and was subsequently selected to organize the Local Government Board, which was to oversee municipal compliance with the new act. He was a founder and the first president of the British Town Planning Institute in 1914; half a dozen years later he became the first president of the Town Planning Institute of Canada. As one of his biographers, planner Alan Armstrong, notes, "On his arrival here he was already well-known as an eloquent author and speaker on the Garden City movement, on agricultural land use and on housing and town planning aspects of local government."[44]

Thomas Adams was enticed to Canada by Clifford Sifton to assume the high-profile post of Town Planning Advisor to the Conservation Commission of Canada. This post allowed Adams access to the highest government circles in Ottawa and in the provinces, since senior provincial ministers sat on the commission. It allowed him flexibility for travel, of which he never seemed to tire, in order to address groups in government and in business and the public-at-large in communities from coast to coast to persuade them of the virtues of planning. It also offered him a platform as a writer for the Commission's excellent journal, *Conservation of Life*, and for numerous other magazines.[45] Thomas Adams stayed with the Commission until it was summarily abolished by the government of Arthur Meighen in 1921. He continued as a consultant in Canada until 1923 and then was appointed to a new trend-setting planning venture as Director of the Regional Plan of New York and Environs. Adams finished his career with a British consulting practice and taught planning at Harvard and MIT.[46]

In his years with the commission, he would often echo the maxim "Population is our most valuable national resource."[47]

Hodgetts, in his report to the commission in 1912, showed that he was fully aware of the scope of planning for an entire community. He set down the "essentials of town planning" in very sophisticated terms:

> The questions involved are more numerous and complicated than the mere building of a house. The various constituent parts of a modern town have to be considered and arranged in such a manner that they will form an harmonious whole.... [A] plan for town extension contemplates and provides for the development of the whole of every urban, suburban, and rural area that may be built on within from thirty to fifty years.[48]

By the beginning of World War I, the commission's involvement with community planning had become very extensive. First, the commission drafted a model "Town Planning Act for Canada," which it hoped each province might adopt in order to promote local planning. Second, it hosted the National City Planning Conference at its sixth convention in Toronto in 1914. These annual meetings were already well-established gatherings at which planners from North America and Europe exchanged ideas. Thomas Adams, a prominent British planner who had been associated with the Garden City movement, came to the attention of the commission at these conferences. Third, the commission hired Adams as its Town Planning Advisor in 1914 (see sidebar and Figure 4.20).

By promoting community planning, the commission provided a national forum sponsored by the federal government, which, undoubtedly, meant a quicker, wider dissemination of planning ideas than would have otherwise occurred in such a large and sparsely settled country. By giving Thomas Adams the central role in this endeavour, it highlighted the role of the professional in the planning of communities, and by linking community planning with the resources sector, it helped incorporate in planning the general economic values espoused by the commission. Clifford Sifton revealed these views at the 1914 convention:

> People must appreciate the idea that town planning is not born with the intent of spending money, it is simply not a new kind of extravagance, but is conceived with the idea of preventing extravagance and preventing waste and getting good value for the money which is expended.[49]

Parks Movement

The municipal parks movement continued to expand in the early 20th century. Canada's first resident landscape architect was Frederick Todd, who trained in the Olmsted office. Todd designed public open spaces and garden suburbs across the country in the early 20th century (see sidebar and Figure 4.21). These park projects often represented the first major efforts of these communities to shape and give character to their physical environment and humanize their development patterns.[50]

Todd's 1903 report to the Ottawa Improvement Commission is perhaps the most valuable contribution of the parks movement in this era.[51] This report recommends that the federal and local governments develop a system of parks that covers the entire national capital region. Todd proposed that natural reserves, suburban parks, and urban squares be linked by a system of riverside parkways to form an integrated network of open spaces, following the model of Boston's "Emerald Necklace." Although Todd only designed Macdonald Park in Ottawa, his regional open space system was the basis for the parks and parkways that grace Canada's capital today.[52]

Concern over City Efficiency: The City Scientific

The "City Efficient" began to replace the City Beautiful as the main focus of Canadian planning between 1910 and 1920.[53] While both notions contained compelling values, most of the pre–World War I beautification schemes sat on a shelf, unimplemented. Edward Bennett's 1915 comprehensive plan for Ottawa and Hull languished, despite the resources of the federal government. Only Confederation Square was built before 1945.[54] Meanwhile, public health advocates and engineer-planners such as Noulan Cauchon (see sidebar and Figure 4.22) influenced the Canadian planning movement with their practical proposals to immediately improve the quality of life in cities.

The Public Health Movement

Although most early 20th century cities in Canada did not suffer the alarming epidemics of half a century earlier, there were serious health problems. Many of these problems were attributable to the unsanitary housing conditions under which most new urban immigrants had to live. It was common, at the time, to attribute the cause to the customs of "foreigners," rather than to slum conditions. But since disease affected the wealthy as well as the poor, action was eventually taken. Public health

Figure 4.21   Frederick Todd

SOURCE: © MCCORD MUSEUM/II-175018

Frederick Gage Todd (1876–1948) became Canada's first resident landscape architect when he established an office in Montréal

in 1900. A native of Concord, N.H., Todd studied at the University of Massachusetts. From 1896 to1900, he worked in the famous Olmsted office in Brookline, M.A. Although Frederick Law Olmsted Sr. retired due to health problems in 1895, Todd was exposed to outstanding landscape architects during his apprenticeship, including John C. Olmsted, Charles Eliot, and Frederick Law Olmsted Jr. The office was then implementing the remarkable "Emerald Necklace" regional parks system for Boston and had ongoing work with Mount Royal Park in Montréal, first planned by Olmsted Sr. in 1871.[55]

When Todd opened the Montréal office, he started with a variety of local clients from the Olmsted firm, including Mount Royal Park, Montréal and Trinity College, Toronto. He designed parks across Canada in St. Johns (Bowring Park), Québec (Plains of Abraham), Montréal (St. Helen's Island), Stratford (Avon River), Winnipeg (Assiniboine Park), and Regina (Wascana). Todd was a founding member of the Town Planning Institute of Canada and designed attractive and popular garden suburbs, such as Montréal's Town of Mount Royal, Toronto's Leaside, and Shaughnessy Heights in Vancouver.[56]

laws were passed to try to ensure pure water supplies, to eliminate slum dwellings, and to provide for the purity of milk and other foods.

Public health advocates made slow progress in addressing disease and slum housing problems by direct municipal expenditures. By the late 19th century, they turned to regulatory structures rooted in statutes at the provincial and national levels. The first provincial Board of Health was set up in Ontario in 1883 and headed by Dr. Peter Bryce, a vigorous supporter of better health measures at the community level. He was also responsible for establishing better

systems for recording vital statistics, which could be used to substantiate the needs in public health. Several other provinces also passed public health acts in this same period.

Dr. Charles Hodgetts, who succeeded Bryce at the Ontario Health Board in 1904, mounted a strenuous campaign for the improvement of housing. Toward this end, he advocated the use of town-planning techniques he had witnessed in Europe. Toronto's Medical Officer of Health (MOH), Dr. Charles Hastings, argued equally vigorously for better building standards and sanitary and water systems in this same period, as did Winnipeg's MOH:

Figure 4.22   Noulan Cauchon

Joseph-Eusebe Noulan Cauchon (1872–1935) had an unusual background among the founders of the Canadian planning profession. He was born in ville de Québec, the son of an Irish mother and a French-Canadian politician, journalist, and entrepreneur, Joseph-Édouard Cauchon. Noulan's stepmother, Emma LeMoine, was part of a prominent Québec family with a French, English, and Scottish background.[57]

Cauchon received a classical French-Canadian education in Manitoba and Québec but pursued a non-traditional career as a railroad surveyor and engineer. He apprenticed with the Canadian Pacific Railroad, first as a surveyor, then draftsman, and finally as an assistant engineer. Noulan left the CPR after twenty years, establishing a consulting engineering practice that was his principal employment base for the next quarter-century. He prepared railway and infrastructure plans for Chicoutimi, Hamilton, London, Montréal, and St. Catherines, and might have enjoyed a quiet professional career as a consulting engineer except that he developed an interest in town planning during the early years of his new firm.

Cauchon was a member of the organizing committee and a founding member of both the Civic Improvement League of Canada (CIL) and the Town Planning Institute of Canada (TPIC). He was the chairman of the Ottawa Town Planning Commission (OTPC) from its inception in 1921 to 1935,[58] and was twice elected president of the TPIC (1924–26). It was a rare month in the 1920s when Cauchon's opinion on planning issues could not be found in the local or national press. While his role on the OTPC was focused on small-scale local issues, his national work included unusual proposals for more esoteric issues such as new canals, hexagonal planning, and resettlement of veterans. Although he passed away at the nadir of Canadian planning, Cauchon's City Scientific ideas influenced the early evolution of the profession in Canada and the redevelopment of the national capital after 1945.[59]

[We must] ensure that every place occupied as a dwelling unit within the City—no matter how humble it may be—is perfectly sanitary and a fit and proper place in which to bring up Winnipeg's most valuable asset—her children.[60]

This strong role of the local MOH in city development continues to the present time in most provinces.

The Medical Officer of Health wielded considerable power, owing not only to the public health legislation but also to the status accorded medical practitioners. Other bureaucratic structures were established to enforce building codes and conduct inspections of food and water. Building inspectors were appointed and building departments were established in many communities. Frequently, the new "experts" were paternalistic and authoritarian in their approach. The thrust of many of the new prohibitive measures was not social reform but enhancement of those with an interest in continued growth and expansion. The 1909 Manitoba Tenement Act may well have been framed with the fear of contagious disease in mind but, as Weaver notes, it was enforced as if its prime concern were the protection of property values.[61]

Public Works

The engineer–planners of the City Scientific era built impressive infrastructure systems while the City Beautiful's civic centres remained long-term dreams in most cities. City-wide systems for fresh water, sewerage, electricity, gas, paved streets, and electric streetcars had improved public health and the quality of life for most urban citizens in large cities such as Montréal.[62] And the new discipline of traffic engineering produced impressive

| Figure 4.23 | 1912 Toronto Harbour Commissioners' Plan |

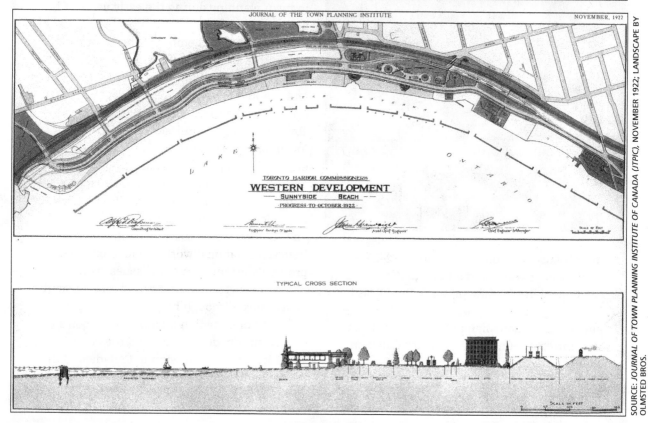

SOURCE: JOURNAL OF TOWN PLANNING INSTITUTE OF CANADA (JTPIC), NOVEMBER 1922; LANDSCAPE BY OLMSTED BROS.

The 1912 THC plan had parks designed by the Olmsted firm, but it clearly showed its City Scientific origins with plenty of infrastructure: new harbour quays, storm sewers, and Lake Shore Boulevard, which originally resembled an elegant boulevard before it was widened to six lanes and topped with the Gardiner Expressway in the 1950s. The plan also proposed that the Don River be put into a concrete ditch and its marsh filled into industrial land. This treatment is now regarded as a major error, and Waterfront Toronto is implementing a new plan to re-naturalize the mouth of the Don.

innovations to deal with the emerging technology of the automobile,[63] such as parking garages, traffic signals, and limited-access highways.

The public works projects of the early 20th century often addressed a variety of objectives simultaneously. For example, the 1912 waterfront plan prepared by the Toronto Harbour Commissioners (THC) not only provided for a new port but also for major new sewers, popular public parks along the western and eastern beaches, and a landscaped boulevard along the entire waterfront.[64] The project was under the direction of THC chief engineer E.L. Cousins and the public parks, beaches, and boulevards were built to the highest quality. They were designed by Boston's famous Olmsted landscape architecture firm (Figure 4.23).

By the mid-1920s, the functional approach to planning had become the official position of the Town Planning Institute of Canada. In a front-page editorial in the first volume of the *TPIC Journal*, the president, Thomas Adams, declared:

> Town Planning is a Science ... knowledge and art—and action on these possessions—constitute the foundation of social progress. The most important first step in creating a sound town planning policy in Canada, therefore, is to develop the science of town planning.[65]

The leading example of the City Scientific planning techniques is Vancouver's 1929 comprehensive plan, prepared by American engineer–planner Harland Bartholomew, with Canadian engineer Horace Seymour as the resident planner (see Figure 4.24).[66] Although it provided plans for a park system and a City Beautiful–style civic centre, it is filled with City Scientific analyses—population growth, and traffic, streetcar, and harbour use. Bartholomew and Seymour's comprehensive plan includes city-wide systems for roads, bridges, streetcars, and utilities that were a guide for public investment for several more decades. Its land use proposals were furthered by a sophisticated zoning bylaw that was adopted immediately by both the City of Vancouver and Point Grey municipality[67] and became a landmark in Canadian planning. Bartholomew's firm produced many similar plans for other American cities,[68] while Horace Seymour went on to become the chief provincial planner for Alberta; his daughter Marion was one of Canada's first female civil engineers and professional planners.[69]

The Civic Reform Movement

The final major influence on community planning was a widespread movement to improve the quality of local government. There were three fairly distinct areas of concern at various times: the social welfare of city dwellers, public ownership of basic utilities, and the efficiency of local government organizations. The issues ranged from procrastination of local councils to technical incompetence to municipal graft, and sometimes all three.

The earliest concerns had to do with such social problems as disease, poverty, crime, and poor housing. These efforts had gained considerable momentum in the 1880s, aided by new popular newspapers like *The Montreal Star*, *The Ottawa Journal*, and *The Vancouver News-Advertiser*, and by reform-minded clergymen such as Winnipeg's J.S. Woodsworth.[70] Their approaches, although motivated by a mixture of humanitarianism and professional and business self-interest, were characterized by the use of statistics, the advocacy of government regulation, and the promotion of the use of experts and professionals.

The second stream of civic reform concerned the provision of municipal utilities. The waterworks, street railways, and electric power and telephone systems had been developed largely by private interests on franchises offered by municipal councils on "extremely generous terms to the entrepreneurs."[71] However, as growth pressures mounted, the services were often found wanting, contracts were not being met, there were instances of influence peddling, and private utilities were often reluctant to expand into new suburban areas. Moreover, civic leaders, who were mostly drawn from the business community, wished to appear progressive and willing to have industry in their communities. As the Mayor of Medicine Hat said at the time, "Municipal ownership (of utilities) and industrial progress go hand in hand."[72]

Guelph purchased its gas works and electric power system in 1893; Edmonton had a publicly owned power system in 1902; and similar efforts can be cited from coast to coast. But the progressive-looking municipal utilities were, not infrequently, a mixed blessing: sprawl was increased when premature land development was served, operating surpluses were not always forthcoming, and inept administration was not uncommon. Despite these difficulties, the move to municipal ownership established, from then on, the rights and the responsibilities of communities to provide community-wide services.

The third target of the urban reformers was urban government itself. The scale and rapidity of urbanization in this period was unprecedented; as well, much of the technology was new and local government was relatively inexperienced. Reformers sought to reduce

| Figure 4.24 | Vancouver, B.C., Major Street Plan, 1929, by Harland Bartholomew & Assoc. |

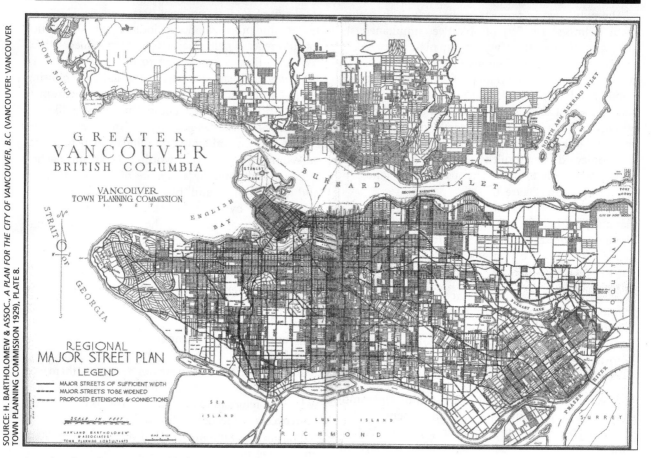

A regional roads system provided in the City Scientific style. Many of the street widenings were implemented, but the elaborate road network for the University Endowment lands at the extreme left was not.

the power of city councils and their committees and substitute special boards and commissions. These, it was contended, could administer the various functions that communities needed to handle their growth—waterworks, transportation, parks, planning, police, schools, libraries—more efficiently because they would not be subject to political pressures. The attempts to separate politics from the administration of public services did not always result in increased efficiency, and it had two long-term effects on the planning and governing of communities. First, it led to a proliferation of agencies, each responsible for a separate function while not having to coordinate their activities with those of either the city government or other bodies. Second, because the special bodies needed to develop special

skills, they fostered the use of experts in the solution of urban problems. The special boards and commissions tended to acquire considerable discretionary powers and vested these in professionals and administrators and thereby further increased their independence.

The various urban reform movements helped Canadian communities to cope more rationally with expansion, to ensure more stability in the provision of services, and to maintain a degree of humanitarian concern for the less fortunate of their citizens. But they also initiated much more complex means of local government, which necessitated the cooperation and coordination of many bodies. This situation remains a source of frustration for community plan-makers to this day in many urban areas.

Local Government: The Residue of Reform

Civic administration was transformed in the 1900–1920 period in both substance and structure. Local government was limited to a role of "providing services to property," while matters involving economic development and what we now call the "quality of life" were assigned to parallel local agencies. Municipal government was weakened by the reform epidemic. Not only was its competence questioned but it also failed to provide for broad public discussion on community issues. Municipal administration was favoured over municipal political debate; councillors often became preoccupied with administrative details, and administrators with policy-making. This rather introverted view of municipal government effectively excluded participation by the public while it gave special interests in business and the property industry, as well as administrators, the "right" to run the local government. The quality of municipal administration improved over the next 25 years (1920–1945), but, when the public came to demand a voice in the big new development decisions after World War II, local governments were generally unprepared.

Further, most provinces introduced various "overseer" methods for controlling municipal activities. These took two forms. On the one hand, provincial departments or ministries of municipal affairs were established to provide for consistency in the day-to-day operation of the municipalities the provinces had created. Guidelines and legislation covered financial affairs, administrative practices, and legal foundations, many of which required regular reports to a provincial ministry. On the other hand, many provinces also established quasi-judicial tribunals for the purpose of reviewing such municipal activities as borrowing capital. Examples are the Municipal Board in Manitoba, the Québec Municipal Commission, the Local Authorities Board in Alberta, and the Ontario Municipal Board. These boards dealt with individual municipalities on an issue-by-issue basis, frequently as a form of appeal body against decisions made by municipalities. In recent decades, such boards have handled appeals in community planning matters. The various supervisory methods used by the provinces with respect to their municipalities thus made for a master–servant relationship between the two.

Civic Improvement Associations and Private Groups

Another response to urban problems at the beginning of this century was the direct involvement of elite groups in the planning of cities, towns, and villages. This took two forms. Civic improvement associations sprang up in many places in the decade from 1900 to 1910. These appeared in communities of all sizes, from the biggest cities to the fictional Avonlea, P.E.I., where Anne of Green Gables led the Village Improvement Society, with amusing results.[73] (Later, these civic improvement associations were promoted by the Commission of Conservation in communities where they did not yet exist.) They often took upon themselves the task of preparing a city plan, as with the Toronto Guild of Civic Art, or of urging the city government to prepare one, as in the case of Kitchener.[74]

The other form of involvement was by such varied interest groups as boards of trade, chambers of commerce, the Canadian Club, and social and professional associations of architects and engineers. These groups sponsored lectures by prominent persons in planning and municipal government—Thomas Adams was a favourite speaker—and actively lobbied for civic improvements, especially visual enhancement of their city. The Commission of Conservation set up a speakers' bureau that provided scripts and glass lantern slides to allow local planning advocates to make compelling presentations in communities across Canada. In the era before television or even widespread cinema, an evening lecture with a "magic lantern show" was a high-tech method to reach a mass audience. It was used to great effect by designers like Edward Bennett, who launched a plan for Canada's capital with a 1914 speech to Ottawa's Canadian Club.[75]

There are two important facets of this private-sector interest in planning: (1) it clearly served the interests of property owners; and (2) it presumed a strong role for property and business interests in community planning and local government affairs. The advocacy by these groups of visual order, efficient transportation, and, later, municipal reform, was in the interest of protecting property values and promoting new opportunities for land development. What developed was a "proprietary interest," so to speak, in civic affairs that translated, over ensuing decades, into a seeming right to membership on planning boards, municipal councils, and other local boards and commissions that endures to this day.

Establishing Community Planning Institutions

Coincident with efforts to restructure local government was the pioneering of ideas about the aims of planning and the nature of its practice. This led to the emerging institutions of community planning being affected by the then-current reform outlook on local government and the constitutional setting established by the province. We deal below with each of these in turn.

The Social and Political Context

In many ways, community planning became a handmaiden to the interests promoting civic reform. Planning was seen to embody many of the same values reformers sought for local government—technical rationality, efficiency, and order. It became commonplace to champion planning either through existing organizations, such as boards of trade, or through new groups. Kitchener (then Berlin), Ontario, had its Civic Association, Calgary and Edmonton had the Alberta Housing and Town Planning Association, and Montréal had its City Improvement League. Some groups actually sponsored the preparation of a plan for the community and then urged its implementation on the municipal government. Another approach was to urge the city government to establish an independent planning committee for the purpose of preparing a plan. Notable instances of the latter approach were the Civic Improvement Committee, appointed by Toronto's city council in 1909, the Calgary City Planning Commission and the Winnipeg Town Planning Commission, both established in 1911, the Regina Town Planning Committee of 1913, and Vancouver's Town Planning Commission (Figure 4.25).[76]

The initial efforts to link action in community planning to the local government follow the model favoured by the civic reformers—that is, the establishment of a body outside the direct control of elected officials. This approach was propounded for U.S. communities in the same era of local planning. In contrast, British communities adopted the approach of appointing a planning committee from the membership of municipal councils. The rationale for the semi-independent planning committee in Canada was: (1) it would keep "politics" out of planning; and (2) community planning, being essentially a technical task, is better achieved by a small group devoted to it. Usually unstated was the reason that a special-purpose planning body would probably direct its efforts more narrowly to the development of private property.

The few semi-independent planning bodies for community planning that have survived to today in Canada usually were established at this time. In the West they tended to be called by the U.S. name, "planning commissions," while in the East they were more

Figure 4.25 The Vancouver Town Planning Commission, 1926

This planning commission from the Civic Reform era contained nine citizen representatives, drawn from the region's elite, including just one woman. Ex-officio members included the Vancouver mayor and the chairs of the Parks, Harbour, Sewage & Drainage, and School Boards. They were supported by Harland Bartholomew's town planning consultant team and Horace Seymour, Bartholomew's "Resident Engineer" in the City Scientific tradition.[77]

likely called "planning boards" or "advisory planning committees." Where necessary, the provinces passed legislation permitting such bodies to be established. The primary function of the new agencies for community planning was to prepare a plan, or "town planning scheme" as they were then called, for the community. In larger cities, the agency might have its own staff, but more likely it employed consultants, as in Kitchener and Vancouver. The plan would then be passed on to the municipal council to be implemented through regulations and public works expenditures.

Despite its supposed advantages, as with every institution there were costs to bear. In the first place, unlike other special-purpose bodies favoured at this time, such as harbour commissions, park boards, and transit authorities, the planning commissions did not operate any facilities. They could only advise the municipality. The municipal council alone had the powers necessary to intervene in the development of private property or to create streets or to build needed public infrastructure. A second dilemma was that the recommendations of an advisory planning agency would have little, if any, direct bearing on the actions of other operating agencies. A third issue concerned the element of participation by the public. Although the semi-independent planning agency represented a form of populism, it fell outside the community-wide forum of municipal council. The views expressed often reflected only limited interests in the community, such as those of downtown merchants, the real estate industry, or the residents of a well-to-do neighbourhood.

In other words, the institution of the special-purpose planning agency created tensions within the local government structure. While attempting to keep community planning at arm's length from the political arena, it heightened the connection between the two. As Milner was to reflect later:

> Planning boards do not exist to take planning out of politics. In a democracy, planning is a political activity…. A planning board gives advice—I hope honest advice. It should not be too concerned whether the council takes the advice or not. This is council's business.[78]

The Constitutional Setting and the First Planning Acts

Many of the powers necessary for a municipality to prepare a plan did not exist in the early period of planning. For a plan to have statutory power over all properties in a community, the sanction of the province was required. If public works expenditures were envisioned to secure the plan's objectives, or if land use regulations were considered desirable to achieve the plan, the legal authority would need to be obtained from the province. This is because there is a convention in Canada that a municipality may not do anything that its province has not empowered it to do.

A province must *enable* its municipal governments to carry out such functions. The need for provincial planning legislation was recognized early in the 20th century. In a period of less than 12 months, starting in the spring of 1912, four provinces passed planning legislation that would enable a municipality to prepare and/or carry out a plan. New Brunswick was first in April 1912, followed by Nova Scotia, Ontario, and Alberta. Within about a decade, four other provinces enacted similar legislation. It is especially interesting since, except for Ontario, most provinces had few cities, and these were not large in any case.

A number of factors probably influenced the provinces to enact planning legislation. For one, there was considerable subdivision of land in suburban areas and often chaotic development accompanying it. For another, the Commission of Conservation strongly promoted such legislation, especially through the efforts of, first, Charles Hodgetts and then, Thomas Adams; the premiers of both New Brunswick and Alberta sat on the

commission. (Indeed, Premier Arthur Sifton of Alberta was the older brother of the commission's chairman.)[79] In Nova Scotia, local planning advocates led by the Halifax Civic Improvement League pushed the provincial government to enact legislation.[80] Other likely influences were the planning efforts in Great Britain and the United States, which received extensive publicity, in particular the Housing and Town Planning Act in Britain in 1909. And probably as important as any factor was the desire of Canadian governments to appear progressive.

The British Housing and Town Planning Act of 1909 provided the model for provincial planning legislation. The early Canadian acts shared three things in common with the British act:

- planning was confined to land in suburban or fringe areas that had the prospect for development (built-up portions of cities were initially excluded);
- landowners could claim compensation if public plans adversely affected private property; and
- local planning would be subject to close scrutiny by central government authorities.

The first and second provisions are evidence of the great reluctance at the time to intervene in existing property development. The third provision, notably, is still a fundamental part of Canadian planning institutions: most planning actions by communities usually cannot take effect until approval by the province or its agencies. More than anything else, this feature distinguished planning practice in Canada from that in the United States. The early Canadian planning acts were not, however, simply duplicates of the British act.[81] Some variations were made to suit the Canadian approach, and several of these have endured to the present time. It will be helpful to elaborate on the five basic components of these 1912–13 planning acts.

1. The Scope of Planning

Three acts (in Nova Scotia, New Brunswick, and Alberta) permitted municipalities to prepare "town-planning schemes," and specified the aspects of the community that the plan should cover. To quote from the New Brunswick act,

> A town planning scheme may be prepared … with the general object of securing suitable provision for traffic, proper sanitary conditions, amenity and convenience in connection with the laying out of streets and the use of the land and of any neighbouring lands for building or other purposes.[82]

Plans were thus envisioned to encompass quite broad features of the built environment. However, they were to apply only to "land which is in the course of development, or is likely to be used for building purposes"—that is, to suburban extensions to communities. Provision was allowed for the province to authorize the inclusion of adjacent built-up land that might be affected by the plan. Nevertheless, this carefully limited the area covered by plans.

Municipalities were allowed considerable scope in carrying out plans. They could purchase, using powers of expropriation, properties needed to implement the plan, say for a park or a street extension. They could also make expenditures for such public works as water and sewer systems to put a plan into effect, but were required to specify in the plan how they planned to obtain these funds; we now call this a "capital-improvements budget." There was also provision for a municipality to remove any building that contravened a plan and to complete any work of a private developer that would delay the plan's coming into effect. The planning acts of New Brunswick, Nova Scotia, and Alberta also envisioned the province drawing up regulations for formulating and carrying out a plan. In particular, these regulations were expected to allow communities to control the density of development and the mixture of land uses—that is, to perform what came to be called **zoning**. However, no such land use regulations were forthcoming until later years.

The planning legislation enacted in Ontario in 1912 allowed much less scope. The Cities and Suburbs Plans Act was enacted simply to control the subdivision of suburban land by private interests. It applied only to those cities with a population of at least 50 000 and covered the area within 8 kilometres of the city. All plans for subdivision of land in such locales had to be submitted to a provincial government agency for approval. Consideration of plans was limited to the number and width of streets, the location of streets, and the size and form of lots. Minimum street widths were specified at one **chain** (66 feet or 20 metres).

2. The Role of the Province

All four planning acts included a strong role for the province in the planning process, although the form differed in each case. To quote Alberta's planning act, "A town-planning scheme prepared or adopted by a local authority shall not have effect unless approved by written order of the Minister."[83] This power of ministerial approval also included the power to amend a local plan to suit provincial government standards. In Nova Scotia and New Brunswick, the provincial authority in planning lay with the Cabinet (or the Lieutenant-Governor-in-Council, as provincial legislation usually refers to it). In Ontario, the approving body was the Ontario Railway and Municipal Board (now called the Ontario Municipal Board). In Alberta, it was the Minister of Municipal Affairs who approved local plans; Alberta was one of the first provinces to establish a provincial department to support and supervise its local governments. Such departments became common later in all provinces. Provincial planning legislation has only recently begun to be changed to reduce the central government's scrutiny of locally made plans.

3. The Local Planning Structure

In both the New Brunswick and Alberta planning acts, provision was made for municipalities to appoint a planning commission to undertake the local planning effort. To quote the New Brunswick act again, "For the purpose of preparing a town planning scheme and carrying the same into effect, a local authority ... may appoint a commission of not less than five or more than ten members."[84] Neither province's legislation required that the format of the semi-independent commission be used; it was one option. However, when the Nova Scotia act was revised in 1915, it required that a town-planning board be established in every municipality. It also specified the membership: the mayor, two other members of council, and at least two ratepayers.[85]

The creation of a separate board for making and carrying out a local plan was intensively discussed at the international meeting of planners held in Toronto in 1914. It seems clear, especially from the comments of Charles Hodgetts, that the reform mood permeating North America in regard to local government, as noted above, was the main reason for this feature in an otherwise British-style act. Hodgetts said:

> It is proposed to remove the important matters in connection with town planning out of the hands of our municipal councils.... I may say, after twenty-seven odd years of public experience, I am not impressed with the achievements or capabilities of "town councils."[86]

4. Effects on Private Property

In essence, provincial planning legislation involved delegating some provincial powers concerning property rights to a municipality. Given the strong belief in the sanctity of private property and individual enterprise, these were powers the provinces gave up reluctantly. The provisions that the province held for approval or rejection of local plans were one way of restraining municipalities from extending community rights over private interests. The acts also allowed a property owner to claim **compensation** "whose property is injuriously affected by the making of a town planning scheme," to quote the phrase in the Nova Scotia, New Brunswick, and Alberta acts.

There was also a counterpart to the compensation provision included in these early acts called **betterment**. It allowed a municipality to claim up to half of any increase in the value of a property beneficially affected by a plan. Planners had argued from the time of Ebenezer Howard and the first Garden Cities that proper planning could enhance the value of property. Thomas Adams was particularly forceful on this point, both before and after he came to Canada. He and others contended that this betterment of property was due to *public* efforts, and any rise in the value of a private property because of a public plan should thus be shared with the community. It is not clear whether any of the three provinces ever published the necessary regulations on the workings of compensation and betterment. In any case, these concepts proved difficult to define and do not appear in present-day planning acts.

The compensation/betterment notion cuts to the heart of the issue concerning the extent of public versus private property rights. While a private property owner may be able fairly easily to determine "injury" to his or her property, it is notoriously difficult to determine the extent to which a property's value may have increased due to a plan. A major difference is that the injury to a property is usually apparent when the plan is being implemented, whereas an increase in a property's value that is due to a plan may not materialize for many years. These early planning acts thus recognized some prior rights for municipalities by deeming that compensation could not be claimed if the provisions of the plan were for the purpose of "securing the amenity of the area." These included provisions that might "prescribe the space about buildings or limit the number of buildings to be erected, or prescribe the height or character of buildings."[87] This clause is the precursor for allowing zoning controls over height and lot coverage, although at the time (ca. 1912) the provisions could be applied only to specific areas for which plans were submitted.

5. Land for Parks

The Alberta Town Planning Act of 1913 took one further important step. It allowed the municipality to acquire up to 5 percent of a new subdivision area for park purposes at no cost to itself.[88] This is called **compulsory dedication** and is the same kind of requirement made of land developers to provide road access to the building lots they create and then deed the road allowance to the municipality. While it is clear that residences deserve road access as a matter of rights, how, in a new subdivision, is the simple amenity of a park to be provided except from the land that would normally be subdivided for houses? Further, there is the question of who should pay for the new park land. Alberta legislators took the approach that those benefiting from the park most directly should bear the cost—the developers who could offer a higher quality subdivision and the homebuyers whose property values would more likely be sustained. They may also have been influenced by the converse of this principle: that is, the community as a whole should not have to bear the cost of acquiring land later, the value of which could be much higher. Thus, the Alberta planning act was especially perceptive and its requirements were modest—the equivalent of only one building lot in every twenty. It took over three decades, however, before this groundbreaking step was followed in other provincial planning acts.

The Development of Planning Tools

The first planning acts established the formal milieu for community planning, but they did not assure the preparation of plans or their implementation. In large part, this was because support for the idea of planning advanced faster than the development of the tools to carry it out. There were very few professional planners available at the time. There was also relatively little experience anywhere in the world with carrying out local planning under government sanction. Thus, Canada cannot be said to have lagged in supporting planning: 1909 is the date both of the first British planning act and of the first North American planning conference in Boston; by 1912, three provincial planning acts had been passed in Canada, and in 1914, the sixth planning conference was held in Toronto. The first comprehensive zoning bylaw was that of New York City in 1916. Thus, the tools that Canada's planners would need to use were still being "invented" as the formal machinery of planning was being assembled.

The planning of cities and towns by the communities themselves under the aegis of their local governments was virtually untried until the last decade of the 19th century. The prototypes that existed, whether Garden Cities, model industrial villages, socialist utopias, or Garden Suburbs, were all conceived as having a single or collective ownership of the land and facilities. Planning tools had not yet been devised for communities with multiple property owners whose interests must be reconciled through self-governing institutions. Planners thus struggled to devise acceptable tools that would provide:

1. **Planning policy for the entire community.** Some way to define the quality and direction of development for the entire community for some future period, for existing built-up areas as well as for vacant areas, is desirable. It should include both public and private development efforts.
2. **A framework for guiding private development.** Since the bulk of the land in the community is privately owned and will be developed by private interests, some ways are needed to achieve development that will be consistent with the aims of overall policy. The approach for development on vacant land will likely differ from that for already built-up areas.
3. **A framework for public capital investment.** Since the community must provide support services for private development as well as public facilities, some means are required to allocate public funds that will achieve the aims of the overall policy.

Today, we would think of the above tasks, respectively, as (1) preparing the community plan, (2) formulating the land use and subdivision regulations, and (3) preparing the capital improvements program. But the meagre experience available to planners at the time made these formidable tasks. Let us examine the first two of these provisions briefly for the dilemmas they posed and their eventual resolution. (We deal with capital programming in Chapter 14.)

The Community Plan

The earliest planning acts empowered a municipality to prepare a town-planning scheme. However, such a scheme was not meant to be a plan for an entire town. It was more like what is now called a subdivision plan, showing the layout of streets, building lots, open spaces, and public utilities for a new residential suburb, similar to German town-extension schemes that were widely

admired at the time.[89] These are typically submitted by a private developer or public agency desiring to open up a parcel of vacant land. But how would a community's plan be structured to cover a multiplicity of such subdivision plans where, moreover, much of the land would not be developed until far into the future? And how would it integrate the new development with already built-up areas, with needed transportation links between all parts of the community, and with the infrastructure of services and facilities?

The 1912 Ontario City and Suburbs Plans Act refers to communities having a "general plan into which a town-planning scheme might fit." This concept is repeated in the much-expanded Planning and Development Act, which Ontario passed in 1917. It gives the following definition:

> Such a plan shall show all existing highways and widening, extension or relocation of the same which may be deemed advisable, and also all proposed highways, parkways, boulevards, parks, play grounds and other public grounds or public improvements, and shall be certified by an Ontario land surveyor.[90]

Although this definition still emphasizes the rationalization of road patterns, the act represents a major departure—it distinguishes the *general* plan from the *detailed* subdivision plan.

The most notable early Canadian plan of this general type appeared in 1915. It was prepared by Edward Bennett for the report of the Federal Plan Commission, which was charged with preparing a plan for Ottawa and Hull.[91] Indeed, the authors called it a general plan and presented proposals in map form for various land use districts, for future population expansion, and for streets, parks, and waterways (Figure 4.26). Accompanying this plan were analyses of population density, land use, industrial employment, and public transit. This plan was very modern in its approach and not too dissimilar to those that would be common by the 1960s.[92] A second notable example is the 1923 plan prepared for the adjacent cities of Kitchener and Waterloo, Ontario, by Thomas Adams and Horace Seymour. It is also supported by extensive analyses of traffic, land use, and population, and included a "skeleton plan" for the region.[93] However, Vancouver's 1929 plan was the best community plan of the inter-war years, with detailed analysis and comprehensive proposals for improving the fast-growing city. Bartholomew and Seymour's plan had a major effect on shaping the growth of the city until the mid-1950s.[94]

SOURCE: REPORT OF THE FEDERAL PLAN COMMISSION ON A GENERAL PLAN FOR THE CITIES OF OTTAWA AND HULL (1915); DRAWING NO. 19B: "DIAGRAMS OF BUSINESS, MANUFACTURING AND RESIDENCE AREAS—CONDITIONS CONTROLLED BY DISTRICTS."

Figure 4.26	Early Zoning Proposal: Edward Bennett's "Land Use Districts" for Ottawa and Hull, 1915

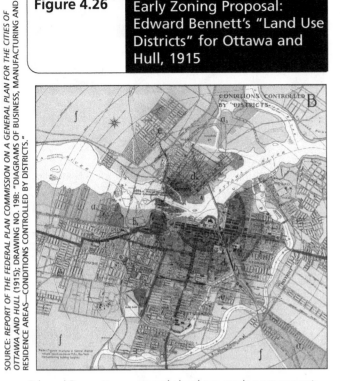

Edward Bennett was an early land use zoning proponent, which he called "districting," in the German tradition. This map from the 1915 Federal Plan Commission report for Ottawa and Hull proposed different intensities of land use in concentric rings from Parliament Hill. The local governments did not adopt the proposal, and it would be decades before comprehensive zoning was approved for the local governments in the national capital region.

An examination of both the Ottawa and Kitchener plans, however, reveals a dilemma that affected the development of planning tools. Whereas nowadays the acknowledged approach is first to prepare an overall community plan and then to devise the regulations, bylaws, and other instruments to attain the goals of the plan, the reverse seems to be proposed in both of these historic documents: that is, the community plan's role was seen as providing support for land use regulations. Two provincial planning acts of the 1920s, the 1925 act for British Columbia and the 1929 act for Alberta, made significant departures in regard to this situation. First, they clearly distinguished the roles of the community plan and the zoning bylaw. Second, they permitted them to be used independently.

However, because the early provincial legislation permitted municipalities to engage in the planning activities they preferred, and because local governments wanted to handle development problems directly, rather than simply provide guidelines for others, this led to the widespread adoption of zoning bylaws without corresponding community plans. Thus, in the 1930s in Alberta, 26 municipalities used the new planning act and passed zoning bylaws, and a further 31 followed suit in the 1940s, but most had never adopted a community plan.[95] In Ontario, as late as 1971, it was found that 544 municipalities had enacted a zoning bylaw, while only 356 had adopted a community plan. The requirement that a municipality adopt a community plan before adopting a zoning bylaw did not appear in provincial planning legislation until well after World War II.

Land Use Regulation

It became clear to public authorities in this period that they could not ensure that private land, which made up the largest part of their cities and towns, would be developed to high standards. It was further realized that private land development fell into two general categories: that occurring on tracts of vacant land and that occurring on individual parcels of land within built-up areas. These two needs spawned their own land use controls—subdivision control and zoning, respectively. In general, there is a sequence to these two controls: land is first subdivided and then it is zoned. They are discussed below in that order.

Subdivision Control

The subdivision of a tract of land transfers ownership and thus requires that all new owners be given the institutional protection of their land titles. The need for subdivision control became insistent in the decade preceding World War I. The relatively simple tasks in earlier times of transferring ownership and registering deeds for individual parcels of land were complicated by the land boom of the time. As well, the long-term consequences for the entire community of the individual new subdivisions were recognized and made obvious the need to assure compliance by the new landowners with various planning and development standards.

Further, the process of dividing up the land may not be connected with immediate building upon, or even sale of, the land. Frequently, subdivision precedes actual urban development by a considerable period of time. From its perspective, the community must know the obligations it might face to service the new parcels of land as well as the consistency of the new layout with adjacent tracts. Also important is the time at which development is expected to occur. The main concerns were for street layouts, open space provisions, drainage, and the size and shape of building lots. Early community planning advocates railed against the monotony and inefficiency of laying out a grid street plan over undulating topography, such as Ottawa's Lindenlea[96] (Figure 4.27).

The requirement that plans for new subdivisions be submitted for approval established the right of the community (and the province) to review plans for development on private land. In later land booms, especially during the late 1920s and the post–World War II periods, the administration of subdivisions became the central planning activity for many municipalities. The subdivision process is now usually accorded a separate section in provincial planning acts and elaborate systems of checking subdivision plans have been set up in provincial ministries. (See Chapter 16 for present-day practices of subdivision control.)

Zoning

The planning tool that deals with the use of land and the physical form of development on individual parcels of privately owned land is called districting or, more commonly, zoning. It deals, essentially, with (1) the use that may be made of a parcel of land, (2) the coverage of the parcel by structures, and (3) the height of buildings. Long before zoning, there were regulations dealing with these factors to assure public health, structural safety, and fire prevention.[97] However, what distinguishes zoning regulations is the application of use/coverage/height standards to districts or areas within a city. The outlook of early planners in Canada in regard to zoning is captured in the following extract from the recommendations for the 1915 plan for Ottawa and Hull:

> … that the authorities take steps to segregate industry into certain areas, to control the districts devoted to business and light industry, to control and protect the residential districts and to control the height of buildings.[98]

The first efforts at city-wide districting are credited to German cities in the 1890s.[99] They were based on the experience that similar land uses tended to congregate in common districts and also that dissimilar uses had a disturbing effect on one another when mixed together. The separation of nuisance uses was the prime aim of early zoning. Six different land use districts were envisioned in the plan for Ottawa and Hull. Prior to this, attempts had been made simply to separate residential from non-residential uses within cities.

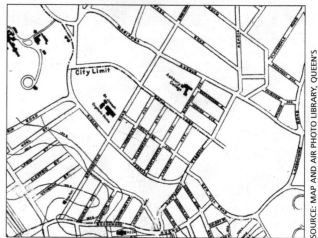

SOURCE: MAP AND AIR PHOTO LIBRARY, QUEEN'S UNIVERSITY, CLASSIFICATION NO. 613.959 GNBD-1913.

Figure 4.27 Lindenlea Grid vs. Garden Suburb Subdivision Design

SOURCE: JOURNAL OF TOWN PLANNING INSTITUTE OF CANADA (JTPIC), VOLUME 1(3), APRIL 1921.

The original street and block plan for the Lindenlea area (top) placed an extension of the Ottawa street grid over the site, which included a small ridge that had precluded development for many years. Thomas Adams's 1919 Garden Suburb subdivision design had better street grades and used the topography to create interesting open spaces. Although this was a low-cost, subsidized housing project, its good site planning gave the area lasting value.

The earliest Canadian bylaw was enacted in 1903 in London, Ontario. The City of Toronto's 1904 bylaw to control "the location, erection, and use of buildings for laundries, butcher shops, stores and manufactories" in effect excluded them from residential districts. Through Ontario legislation enacted in 1912, the exclusion of "apartment and tenement houses" from residential districts was also allowed in large cities.

In Toronto, as in other cities, the various health, safety, and occupancy regulations were usually enacted on a district-by-district basis.[100] While this procedure commended itself for being flexible and responsive to the needs of individual districts, it was also complicated to administer and, not infrequently, subject to inequities between areas. Some areas were not regulated at all, or only partially, and these often turned out to be the areas where poor people lived as tenants. Planners began to urge comprehensive zoning bylaws that would provide not only greater uniformity of application of regulations but also a city-wide view of private development, consistent with the view of the community plan. As it turned out, this was no easy task.

The districting of a city according to specified land uses is a double-edged sword. Since zoning usually respects the kinds of uses and buildings already in a district, existing owners, or those with the desire to develop land in a like manner, will have their investments justified. But those with aspirations to build differently from existing uses, whether with real intentions or simply because they want to have free rein on the use of their property, will be restrained. Planners, seeking a position that would reconcile these two outlooks, chose the argument that zoning would stabilize and protect land values. That is, it would provide more certainty for landowners about what they could expect to be built in their areas and for municipal governments about what expenditures they would have to make for services, as well as the tax revenues they might receive. This was a strong argument, but it was usually grudgingly received, first, because there was little immediate experience in most places, and second, because it depended on the current prospects of the land market. If property prospects were not good or if they had been erratic, acceptance of zoning was usually facilitated. In buoyant situations, such as that of mid-1920s Kitchener (Figure 4.28) or Vancouver, it could take several years for all the interests to agree on the final version of a zoning ordinance.[101] Opposition from real estate interests killed the Ottawa Town Planning Commission's proposed 1926 zoning bylaw, and the City of Ottawa did not adopt a comprehensive zoning bylaw until almost 40 years later.[102]

| Figure 4.28 | Early Zoning Proposal: Thomas Adams and Horace Seymour's "Land Use Districts" for Kitchener, 1924 |

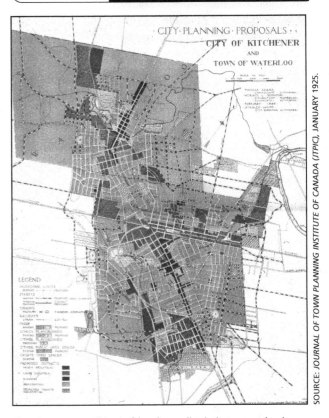

SOURCE: JOURNAL OF TOWN PLANNING INSTITUTE OF CANADA (JTPIC), JANUARY 1925.

The German tradition of land use districting may also have influenced the Kitchener (formerly Berlin) citizens, who lobbied the Ontario government for authority to enact the province's first comprehensive zoning bylaw. Adams and Seymour's zoning plan had five simple land use districts: Heavy Industrial, Light Industrial, Business, Residential, and Detached Private Residential.

Related to the reluctant response to early zoning is the criticism over the exclusionary approach that many zoning bylaws took. There were instances of zoning being used to exclude some classes of people from certain areas by excluding the commercial uses with which those classes were associated. Immigrant groups were often blatantly discriminated against in this way because, for example, they usually chose to live in the same building as their place of business.[103] The other, more common, form of exclusion was to separate types of dwelling units into different zones. Thus, two and three-family dwellings would be excluded from single-family zones, and apartment buildings (or tenements) in yet another zone, because renters were considered less stable than homeowners. And further discrimination might also have been made between low and high-income homeowners by requiring houses to be built on larger, and thus more costly, lots in areas where the well-to-do wished, as Milner noted, "to prevent intruders from spoiling an already established area."[104] In fairness, while zoning does involve separating incompatible land uses, its overzealous application is not inherent in this planning tool. Indeed, approaches to zoning change as planning experience accumulates so that, today, the mixing of different residential types with retail and commercial uses is now considered desirable.

There are two fundamental problems with zoning. The first is the dilemma between protecting existing land uses and promoting the planning of future land uses. Zoning bylaws often seek, in Levin's terms, "to create those elements in the physical environment which the community finds desirable where they do not exist."[105] In other words, zoning seeks to protect present as well as future land uses and values. This gives zoning a dynamic role, but one that it cannot easily play because it is a legislative tool that must be uniformly applied and not readily amended. A second problem has to do with the administration of zoning bylaws. Although the intent is that all the properties in a zone be treated equally under the bylaw, physical conditions affecting the land in a zone may make this impossible. The topography of an area may render some parcels of land difficult to build upon and still meet zoning requirements, for example. Or an old street pattern may have left an awkward shape of building lot. In such situations, the bylaw is generally regarded as causing an "undue hardship" on a property, and mechanisms have been devised to allow a property owner to seek a **variance** from the provisions of the bylaw. A locally appointed appeal body called a Zoning Board of Appeal or Committee of Adjustment hears these requests today. Such appeals are meant only for minor changes to the bylaw and not, say, to changes in the use of land. The latter requires an amendment to the bylaw by the planning board and council and only after scrutiny of the implications for the community plan.

A Planning Profession Emerges

A community vests the responsibility of identifying and advising on many solutions to its important problems in its professionals, such as doctors, lawyers, architects, and engineers. Increasingly, communities in the first few decades of the 20th century sought the advice and skills of town

planners. By the end of the World War I, over 100 people practised town planning in Canada and they formed, in January 1919, a Town Planning Club, preparatory to establishing a formal institute. In May of the same year, the Town Planning Institute of Canada (TPIC) was formed, with 117 members and branches in four cities: Ottawa, Toronto, Winnipeg, and Vancouver. The organization exists to this day under the name of the Canadian Institute of Planners and has several thousand members.

The TPIC received its charter in 1919. The efforts of Hodgetts, Adams, Cauchon, and a score of others had borne fruit. They could now promote the acceptance of planning ideas in Canada, and also identify Canadians possessing the necessary technical skills to carry out planning ideas. Indeed, by 1919 all but two of the provinces had passed substantial planning statutes, and Canadian planners had helped in drafting them. Cities across the country now sought the assistance of planners, from both Canada and abroad, in planning civic centres, suburban extensions, and parks. The skills of these hundred or so new "town planners" included those of several traditional professions. The constitution of the TPIC originally set out that membership was limited to architects, engineers, landscape architects, surveyors, sculptors, artists, and sociologists. Lawyers could seek associate membership. This array of professional skills reveals a good deal about how planners saw the task of planning: a concern for building design, physical layout, the natural environment, civic design, social factors, and legal and administrative processes. These professions and concerns were reflected in the TPIC's new crest (Figure 4.29), developed by TPIC vice president, Noulan Cauchon.[106]

The names of a few of these pioneer Canadian planners should be acknowledged because of their groundwork in the modern planning of many of our cities. Among them were architects Percy Nobbs of Montréal, J.M. Kitchen of Ottawa, and J.P. Hynes of Toronto; engineers James Ewing and R.S. Lea of Montréal, Noulan Cauchon and Horace Seymour of Ottawa, W.A. Webb of Regina, and A.G. Dalzell of Vancouver; landscape architects Frederick Todd of Montréal and Howard Dunnington-Grubb of Toronto; and E. Deville, the Surveyor-General of Canada.

Developing a Canadian Planning Outlook

Thomas Adams helped significantly to define an approach to planning Canadian communities. In philosophy, he espoused a utilitarian view similar to John Stuart Mill and Jeremy Bentham, who championed the notion that the aim of society should be *to produce the greatest good for the greatest number*. In planning

Figure 4.29 — Town Planning Institute of Canada Corporate Seal, Designed by Noulan Cauchon

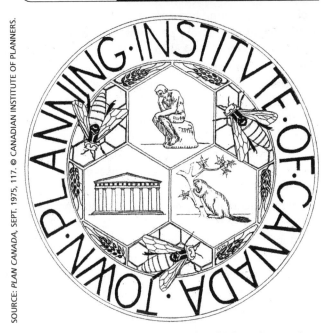

The planner is shown as Rodin's "The Thinker," integrating the work of the architect (the Greek temple) and the engineer (the beaver). They are surrounded by Canada's natural environment, represented by the wheat and honeybees. All the items are embedded in a hexagonal grid that represents a honeycomb but also reflects Cauchon's City Scientific fascination with hexagonal street grids, for which he was the principal proponent during the 1920s.[107] This crest is incorporated in the corporate seal of the TPIC and its successor, The Canadian Institute of Planners/ L'Institut canadien des urbanistes, so it has been placed on the certificate held by every Canadian professional planner.

terms, this might translate into a community not having to bear the burden of traffic congestion caused by faulty street layouts in private development projects. Or it might also justify a community providing adequate sanitary facilities for all inhabitants, so that the costs of disease and epidemics need not be borne by others.

The utilitarian ethic embodied a number of principles that affected planning outlooks profoundly:

1. The notion of *social progress*, carried out with public consensus;
2. The *application of reason* to determine solutions to social problems that will lead to progress; and
3. The acceptance of *government intervention* to achieve the public good.

The utilitarian outlook thus provided a rationalization of planners' views about the need to clear slum areas and to ensure proper suburban extensions to cities. It also provided the logical underpinning for the planning objectives of promoting *order and efficiency* in the development of communities. A Canadian planning historian characterizes the early 20th century planner's view as follows:

> By creating well-planned urban environments, happy and healthy homes would be made available to working families, constructive social intercourse would be facilitated, the economic and social efficiency of the nation would be enhanced, and the general happiness would be increased.[108]

One finds this view widely espoused by Adams and his planning colleagues in Canada in the 1920s, possibly most succinctly on the masthead of the *Journal of Town Planning Institute of Canada*:

> Town planning may be defined as the scientific and orderly disposition of land and buildings in use and development with a view to obviating congestion and securing economic and social efficiency, health and well-being in urban and rural communities.

There are three fundamental aspects to the outlook of the early Canadian planners that, although not much discussed today, are no less a part of the intellectual makeup of contemporary Canadian planners. Community planning is concerned with

1. the functioning of the city rather than with its beauty, and its approach is rational (i.e., "scientific").
2. the social well-being of the community as a whole, as exemplified in Adams's dictum that "town planning includes every aspect of civic life and civic growth."[109]
3. finding technical solutions to planning problems for which planners are equipped to supply.

The first two of these foundation stones distinguished Canadian planners from their U.S. and British counterparts. The broad social view of responsibility for community health and housing is derived from the British; the functional view of arranging streets, utilities, and the use of zoning is distinctively American. The Canadian planners shunned City Beautiful approaches, and possibly as a consequence did not develop concepts of overall community design. They did, however, succeed in building a legislative base for the planning of communities through provincial planning acts. Canadian planning professionals

Globe and Mail
February 25, 2011

Can We Reinvent the Suburbs?

Marcus Gee

A Toronto architect who specializes in 'greyfield' projects says it's already happening

When most people look at suburban intersections, they see malls, gas stations and parking lots. Cliff Korman sees potential.

The Toronto architect specializes in "greyfield" development. Greenfield developers build on farmland or other undeveloped space. Brownfield developers build on old industrial lands. Greyfield developers exploit the grey asphalt of suburbia. The aim is to unleash the value of underused suburban land, replacing parking lots, low-rise malls and sprawling warehouses with new apartment towers, office buildings and shopping streets.

Mr. Korman's firm, Kirkor architects, has its hand in 10 greyfield projects in the Toronto region. It's good for business at his company of just 62 employees, but it's even better for the city. By taking advantage of greyfields, he says, Toronto can reinvent its suburbs. His projects strive to bring urban vitality to barren suburban intersections by creating mixed-use "live, work, shop" development.

At Yonge and Sheppard, where a parking lot now stands, 45-storey and 37-storey towers mixing residential and office space will rise to create the new Hullmark Centre. Farther north near Steeles, another pair of glass-and-steel towers will go up at 7171 Yonge St., a mixed-use project incorporating two public parks.

Over at Don Mills and Steeles, Mr. Korman is hoping to replace a down-at-heel mall and big parking lot with a project that again mixes residential towers, parks and street-level shops. In an artist's conception, what is now

a bit of a dead-zone becomes a lively new mini-community where people walk and take transit instead of being slaves to the car.

He says there are dozens of similar underused intersections in suburban Toronto with nothing but "acres of grey and a little strip of plaza – there's just miles of it." In one site developers are considering for intensification, a warehouse with 60 employees covers seven acres, a gross waste of urban real estate.

If you concentrate development at suburban nodes, "think of how many less roads you build, how many less sewer lines you build, how many less fire hydrants you need, how much less police and fire trucks you use. This is ultimately sustainable. We're talking a more sustainable world."

That kind of thinking has been conventional wisdom in city planning departments for years. The problem is getting local residents to go along. Many fear more intense development will worsen traffic and hurt real estate values.

Not true, says Mr. Korman, a fast-talking dynamo who darts in and out of the room to fetch sketches and plans. His projects are designed to discourage car use. Many incorporate bike lockers and auto-share spaces.

As for property values, "Let's get rid of one huge urban myth: A mixed-use intensified project is going to devalue my property. Forget it! Total opposite. All we do is value-up the neighbourhood. We're the top end of the market."

Governments stand to gain, too. In one project, property taxes are expected to rise to $5-million from $200,000, a windfall for the municipality, which will also rake in big development fees.

Even so, Mr. Korman spends countless hours soothing community groups, preparing detailed submissions to the Ontario Municipal Board and negotiating with politicians. "Local councillors," he says, "are elected to protect the status quo."

In the project at Don Mills and Steeles, there have been no less than 22 ratepayers meetings on the supposed horrors of a modest development, already much scaled back in height and density from a developer's original proposal. The local councillor won election by loudly opposing it.

Despite such hurdles, Mr. Korman is optimistic. After years of planning and design work, many of his projects, and others like them,

are finally taking shape. Hundreds of thousands of immigrants are streaming into the city, many of them people who were accustomed to apartment living back home, who want to avoid the expense of a car and who like living where the action is – even if the action is at Dufferin and Sheppard instead of Queen and Spadina. "The city can absorb a million people, but you've got to have a plan," he says.

That plan has to include a remake of Toronto's neglected greyfields.

concentrated their approach on administrative and legislative processes, borrowing broad planning statutes from the British and local zoning laws from the United States.

Lastly, the acceptance of a planning profession in Canada meant that community planning was moving out of the phase of being a "cause" propounded by a "movement." It was beginning to be legitimized and institutionalized. It also put in planners' hands the opportunity to develop, evolve, and mould the social values of planning. Thereafter, the development of planning ideas became bound up with the outlook of the planning professionals. These people became important actors in the planning process, for they, in many ways, had invented it.

The Collapse of the Canadian Planning Movement

The gains of the planning movement in the 1920s were almost eliminated in the Great Depression of the 1930s and the war period that followed. With the onset of the Great Depression, community planning lost a great deal of momentum in Canada. Many promising efforts in planning were halted, such as the closing of Alberta's Provincial Planning Office. The *TPIC Journal* ceased publication in 1931, and the Institute itself collapsed in 1932 for lack of dues-paying members; national planning conferences ceased and local planning commissions often stopped meeting. (In the United States, by contrast, the concepts of public housing and regional planning became cornerstones in the Roosevelt New Deal programs for coping with the Depression, thereby nurturing planning ideas

and the planning profession.) By the end of World War II, only one city in Canada—Toronto—had a formal planning department and fewer than two dozen towns had zoning bylaws and plans (most of them outdated). Only the largest cities, Montréal and Toronto (Figure 4.30), had current plans in hand.[110] The state of Canadian community planning in 1945 was essentially comatose, and it would take a mighty push to revive it.

Reflections

By the end of World War II, a distinctively Canadian planning framework was in place. The provincial planning acts, the various institutional arrangements through which planning is accomplished and adjudicated, the planning tools, and the professional staffs could truthfully be said to be "made in Canada." There had, of course, been much borrowing of concepts (and personnel) from our two main influences, Great Britain and the United States, but they were gradually moulded to suit Canadian conditions, social outlook, and governance.

The legacy of the formative decades from 1900 to 1945 should not be forgotten; nor should it be forgotten that the institutions that emerged to promote and facilitate community planning were the product of human effort. That is, the elaborate sets of local and provincial planning institutions that screen, evaluate, and reconcile land use decisions, and shape our communities, grew out of and reflect the values and norms of the people who nurtured and built them. The planning problems of the past were responded

Figure 4.30   1943 Toronto Plan

SOURCE: EUGENE FALUDI, THE MASTER PLAN FOR THE CITY OF TORONTO AND ENVIRONS, TORONTO, 1943, CITY OF TORONTO PLANNING DEPARTMENT.

The City of Toronto Planning Board's 1943 plan was prepared by Eugene Faludi, an architect planner trained in Rome, who emigrated to Canada in 1940. Note the extensive "Super-Highway" network shown in the solid black lines, or black lines with dots, if the expressways were to have rapid transit in their medians.[111] This plan would require demolition of a vast swath of midtown Toronto for the Crosstown Expressway, just north of Bloor Street, which set off a famous citizen revolt in the late 1960s.

to with solutions that were acceptable to professional and political interests and to citizens at the time. Planning arrangements, tools, and processes, being social constructs, change with new social currents, new technology, and new generations. For example, broad citizen participation, which plan-makers today cannot avoid, was almost entirely the purview of the elite and property and business interests until the 1950s.[112] This legacy raises the following questions:

- *Compare and contrast the planning approaches of Thomas Adams, Edward Bennett, and Noulan Cauchon based on their illustrated public lectures available at www.PlanningCanadasCapital.ca*

- *What social situations do you anticipate will affect planning processes, tools, and institutions in the next two decades?*

Reference Notes

1. See Len Gertler's commentary on this issue in Wayne Caldwell, ed., *Rediscovering Thomas Adams: Rural Planning and Development* (Vancouver: UBC Press, 2011), 207–211.

2. Nik Luka, "From Summer Cottage Colony to Metropolitan Suburb: Toronto's Beach District," *Urban History Review* 35:1 (Fall 2006), 18–46.

3. Walter Van Nus, "The Fate of City Beautiful Thought in Canada, 1893–1930," in G. Stelter and A. Artibise, eds., *The Canadian City: Essays in Urban History* (Toronto: Macmillan, 1979), 162–185.

4. Thomas Adams, *Rural Planning and Development* (Ottawa: Commission of Conservation, 1917), Map 1.

5. John C. Weaver, *Shaping the Canadian City: Essays on Urban Politics and Policy, 1890–1920*, Monograph No. 1 (The Institute of Public Administration of Canada, 1977), 40.

6. Godfrey L. Spragge, "Canadian Planners' Goals: Deep Roots and Fuzzy Thinking," *Canadian Public Administration* (Summer 1975), 216–234.

7. Elizabeth Bloomfield, "Town Planning Efforts in Kitchener-Waterloo, 1912–1925," in A. Artibise and G. Stelter, eds., *Shaping the Urban Landscape* (Ottawa: Carleton University Press, 1982), 256–303; and David Gordon, "A City Beautiful Plan for Canada's Capital: Edward Bennett and the 1915 Plan for Ottawa and Hull," *Planning Perspectives* 13 (1998), 275–300.

8. J. William Brennan, "Visions of a 'City Beautiful': The Origin and Impact of The Mawson Plans for Regina," *Saskatchewan History* 46: 2 (Fall 1994), 19–33.

9. William H. Wilson, *The City Beautiful Movement* (Baltimore: Johns Hopkins University Press, 1989).

10. The entire text and illustrations of the plan are available in the 1915 Plan section of http://www.PlanningCanadasCapital.ca

11. Thomas H. Mawson, *Calgary: A Preliminary Scheme for Controlling the Economic Growth of the City* (London, T.H. Mawson & sons, city planning experts, 1914).

12. Harland Bartholomew & Assoc., *A Plan for the City of Vancouver, BC* (Vancouver: Vancouver Town Planning Commission, 1929); and William T. Perks, "Idealism, Orchestration and Science in Early Canadian Planning: Calgary and Vancouver Re-Visited, 1914/1928," *Environments* 17:2 (1985), 1–28.

13. Elizabeth Bloomfield, "Ubiquitous Town Planning Missionary: The Careers of Horace Seymour, 1882–1940," *Environments* 17: 2 (1985), 29–42.

14. Kenneth Greenberg, "Toronto: The Unknown Grand Tradition," *Trace* 1: 2 (1981), 37–46.

15. Paul-André Linteau, *The Promoter's City: Building the Industrial Town of Maisonneuve, 1883–1913* (Toronto: Lorimer, 1985).

16. Van Nus, "The Fate of City Beautiful."

17. Gilbert Stelter, "Rethinking the Significance of the City Beautiful Idea," in Robert Freestone, ed., *Urban Planning in a Changing World: The Twentieth Century Experience* (London: Spon, 2000), 98–117; and Harold Kalman, *A History of Canadian Architecture* 2 (Toronto: Oxford University Press, 1994).

18. Arthur B. Gallion, The Urban Pattern (New York: Van Nostrand, 1950), 376; and Le Corbusier, *The City of Tomorrow and Its Planning* (London: John Rooker, 1929).

19. William J.R Curtis, *Le Corbusier: Ideas and Forms* (London: Phaidon, 1994).

20. Eric Mumford, *The CIAM Discourse on Urbanism, 1928–1960* (Cambridge, MA: MIT Press, 2000); and Robert Fishman, *Urban Utopias in the Twentieth Century: Ebenezer Howard, Frank Lloyd Wright, and Le Corbusier* (Cambridge, MA: MIT Press, 1982).

21. Kenneth Frampton, *Le Corbusier* (London, Thames and Hudson, 2001).

22. Lewis Mumford, *The City in History* (New York: Harcourt Brace, 1961); Jane Jacobs, *The Death and Life of Great American Cities* (New York: Random House, 1961); and Fred Koetter and Colin Rowe, *Collage City* (Cambridge, MA: MIT Press, 1978).

23. Eric Mumford, *The CIAM Discourse on Urbanism.*

24. J.L. Sert, *Can Our Cities Survive?* (Cambridge, MA: Harvard University Press, 1943).

25. Cf. Thomas Roden, "The Housing of Workingmen," *Industrial Canada* 5: 7 (1907).

26. Marc H. Choko, *Une cité-jardin à Montréal* (Montréal : Meridien, 1988).

27. G. Frank Beer, "A Plea for City Planning Organization," in *Report of the Fifth Annual Meeting*, Commission of Conservation (1914), 108–116.

28. Mervyn Miller, *Letchworth: The First Garden City* (Chichester, UK: Phillimore, 2002); and Mervyn Miller and A.S. Gray, *Hampstead Garden Suburb: Arts and Crafts Utopia?* (Chichester, UK : Phillimore, 2006).

29. Susan Klaus, *A Modern Arcadia: Frederick Law Olmsted Jr. & The Plan for Forest Hills Gardens* (Amherst, MA: University of Massachusetts Press, 2002).

30. Larry McCann, "Suburbs of Desire: Shaping the Suburban Landscape of Canadian Cities, c. 1900–1950," in Richard Harris and Peter Larkham, eds., *Changing Suburbs—Foundation, Form and Function* (London: Routledge, 1999), 111–145.

31. Bev Sandalack and Andrei Nicolai, *The Calgary Project: Urban Form/Urban Life* (Calgary: University of Calgary Press, 2006).

32. Jill Delaney, "The Garden Suburb of Lindenlea, Ottawa: A Model Project for the First Federal Housing Policy, 1918–1924," *Urban History Review* 19 (February 1991), 151–165.

33. Larry McCann, "Planning and Building the Corporate Suburb of Mount Royal, 1910–1923," *Planning Perspectives*, 11(1996), 259–301.

34. John Weaver, "Reconstruction of the Richmond District in Halifax," *Plan Canada* 16 (March 1976), 36–47.

35. Nigel Richardson, "A Tale of Two Cities," in L.O. Gertler, ed., *Planning the Canadian Environment* (Montréal : Harvest House, 1968), 269–284.

36. Thomas Adams, *Rural Planning and Development* (Ottawa: Commission of Conservation, 1917), 66.

37. Institute of Local Government, Queen's University, *Single-Enterprise Communities in Canada*, A Report to Central Mortgage and Housing Corporation (Kingston: Queen's University, 1953), 24.

38. Alan Artibise and Gilbert Stelter, "Canadian Resource Towns in Historical Perspective," in A. Artibise and G. Stelter, eds., *Shaping the Urban Landscape* (Ottawa: Carleton University Press, 1982), 413–434; Iguarta Jose E., *Arvida au Saguenay: Naissance d'une ville industrielle* (Montréal: McGill-Queen's University Press, 1996); and Lucie K. Morisset, "Arvida, Cité industrielle made Real, *Architecture au Canada* 36:1 (2011), 3–40.

39. Clarence Perry, "The Neighborhood Unit," in *Regional Survey of New York and Its Environs* 7 (New York, 1929).

40. Clarence Stein, *Toward New Towns for America* (New York: Reinhold, 1957), 19.

41. K.C. Parsons, "British and American Community Design: Clarence Stein's Manhattan Transfer, 1924–74," *Planning Perspectives* 7 (1992), 191–210.

42. K.C. Parsons, 39ff.

43. Robert Whitten and Thomas Adams, *Neighbourhoods of Small Homes: Economic Density of Low-Cost Housing in America and England* (Cambridge, MA: Harvard University Press, 1931); and Eran Ben Joseph and David Gordon, "Hexagonal Planning In Theory and Practice," *Journal of Urban Design*, 5: 3 (December 2000), 237–265.

44. Alan H. Armstrong, "Thomas Adams," 28. See also David Lewis Stein, "Thomas Adams, 1871–1940," *Plan Canada*, Special Edition (July 1994), 14–15; and Michael Simpson, *Thomas Adams and the Modern Planning Movement: Britain, Canada and the United States, 1900–1940* (London: Alexandrine Press, 1985).

45. For a guide to Adams's articles on Canadian planning, see J.D. Hulchanski, "Thomas Adams: A Biographical and Bibliographic Guide," Papers on Planning and Design, no. 015 (Toronto: University of Toronto, 1978).

46. David Johnson, *Planning the Great Metropolis: The 1929 Regional Plan of New York and Its Environs* (New York: Spon, 1996); and Thomas Adams, *Outline of Town and City Planning: A Review of Past Efforts and Modern Aims* (New York: Russell Sage Foundation, 1935) for the basis of his American teaching; his British practice is summarized in *Recent Advances in Town Planning* (London: J. & A. Churchill, 1932).

47. As quoted in Alan H. Armstrong, "Thomas Adams and the Commission of Conservation," in L.O. Gertler, ed., *Planning the Canadian Environment* (Montréal : Harvest House, 1968), 17–35. See also Nigel H. Richardson, "Canada in the 20th Century: Planning for Conservation and the Environment," *Plan Canada*, Special Edition (July 1994), 52–69.

48. C.A. Hodgetts, "Housing and Town Planning," in *Report of the Third Annual Meeting*, Commission of Conservation (1912), 136.

49. Clifford Sifton, "National Conference on City Planning," in *Report of the Sixth Annual Meeting*, Commission of Conservation (1915), 243. See also David Lewis Stein, "The Commission of Conservation," *Plan Canada*, Special Edition (July 1994), 55; and Michel Girard, *L'ecologisme retrouve: Essor et declin de la Commission de la conservation du Canada.* (Ottawa: Les Presses de l'université d'Ottawa, 1994).

50. Peter Jacobs, "Frederick G. Todd and the Creation of Canada's Urban Landscape," *Association for Preservation Technology (APT) Bulletin.* 15: 4 (1983), 27–34.

51. Frederick G. Todd, *Preliminary Report to the Ottawa Improvement Commission* (Ottawa: OIC, 1903); and David Gordon, "Frederick G. Todd and the Origins of the Park System in Canada's Capital," *Journal of Planning History* 1: 1 (March 2002) 29–57; the entire text and illustrations of the plan are available in the 1903 OIC Report section of http://www.PlanningCanadasCapital.ca

52. David Gordon, "Frederick G. Todd," 43–50.

53. Walter Van Nus, "Toward the City Efficient: The Theory and Practice of Zoning, 1919–1939," in A. Artibise and G. Stelter, eds., *The Usable Urban Past* (Toronto: Macmillan, 1979), 226–246.

54. David Gordon and Brian Osborne, "Constructing National Identity: Confederation Square and the National War Memorial in Canada's Capital, 1900–2000" *Journal of Historical Geography* 30: 4 (October 2004), 618–642.

55. Peter Jacobs, "Frederick G. Todd"; and Cynthia Zaitzevsky, *Fredrick Law Olmsted and the Boston Park System* (Boston: Harvard/Belknap, 1982).

56. Jacobs, "Frederick G. Todd"; Gordon, "Frederick G. Todd"; McCann, "Planning and Building"; and Vincent Asselin, *Frederick G. Todd Architecte Paysagiste: Une Pratique de l'aménagement ancrée dans son époque 1900–1948* (Unpublished thesis presented at Université de Montréal, Faculté de l'aménagement, 1995).

57. Sally Coutts, "Science and Sentiment: The Planning Career of Noulan Cauchon," Master's thesis, Carleton University, Department of History, 1982.

58. Cauchon's 1918 illustrated lecture on planning and his proposal for a federal district in Ottawa and Hull is available in the 1922 Federal District section of http://www. PlanningCanadasCapital.ca

59. W. DeGrace, "Canada's Capital 1900–1950: Five Town Planning Visions," *Environments* 17: 2 (1985), 43–57; and K. Hillis, "A History of Commissions: Threads of An Ottawa Planning History," *Urban History Review* 21: 1 (1992), 46–60; and David L.A. Gordon, "'Agitating People's Brains: Noulan Cauchon and the City Scientific in Canada's Capital," *Planning Perspectives* 23: 3 (2008), 349–379.

60. Canada, Commission of Conservation, *Report of the Third Annual Meeting* (1912), 141.

61. Canada, Commission of Conservation, 32.

62. Robert Gagnon et Natasha Zwarich; "Les ingénieurs sanitaires à Montréal, 1870–1945 : Lieux de formation et exercice de la profession," *Urban History Review* 37: 1 (2008), 3–20.

63. Étienne Faugier, "Automobile, transports urbains et mutations : l'automobilisation urbaine de Québec, 1919–1939," *Urban History Review* 38: 1 (2010), 26–37.

64. James Lemon, *The Toronto Harbour Plan of 1912: Manufacturing Goals and Economic Realities*, Working Papers of the Canadian Waterfront Resource Centre, Royal Commission on the Future of the Toronto Waterfront (Toronto, 1990).

65. Thomas Adams, "Editorial: Town Planning is a Science," *Journal of the TPIC* 1: 3 (April 1921), 1–3.

66. H. Bartholomew & Assoc., *A Plan for the City of Vancouver, BC* (Vancouver: Vancouver Town Planning Commission, 1929).

67. William Perks, "Idealism, Orchestration and Science in Early Canadian Planning.":

68. Norman J. Johnston, "Harland Bartholomew: Precedent for the Profession," in Donald A. Krueckeberg, ed., *The American Planner: Biographies and Recollections* (New York: Taylor and Francis, 1983), 279–301.

69. Elizabeth Bloomfield, "Ubiquitous Town Planning Missionary"; Marion Seymour was a planner for the City of Ottawa in the 1950s and 1960s before becoming a consultant. She was Corporate Secretary of the TPIC in the 1960s and 1970s.

70. Kurt Korneski, "Reform and Empire: The Case of Winnipeg, Manitoba, 1870s–1910s," *Urban History Review* 37: 1 (2008), 48–62.

71. Paul Rutherford, "Tomorrow's Metropolis: The Urban Reform Movement in Canada, 1880–1920," in G. Stelter and A. Artibise, eds., *The Canadian City* (Toronto: Macmillan, 1979), 368–392.

72. As quoted in John C. Weaver, "Tomorrow's Metropolis Revisited: A Critical Assessment of Urban Reform in Canada, 1890–1920," in Stelter and Artibise, *Canadian City*, 393–418.

73. Lucy Maud Montgomery, *Anne of Avonlea* (Boston: Page, 1909), ch. 9.

74. Elizabeth Bloomfield, "Town Planning Efforts in Kitchener-Waterloo, 1912–1925," *Urban History Review* 9 (June 1980), 3–48.

75. For an example of Adams' lecture on "Town Planning Methods" given in Saint John, NB, ca. 1919, see Library and Archives of Canada, CIP Fonds, W.F. Burditt papers, MG-28.1275, Volume 16, File: Address on Town Planning, displayed in the Lindenlea section of http://www.PlanningCanadasCapital.ca; Bennett's speech is located in the 1915 Plan section of the same website; see also David Gordon, "Introducing a City Beautiful Plan for Canada's Capital: Edward Bennett's 1914

speech to the Canadian Club," *Planning History Studies* 12: 1–2 (December 1998), 13–51.

76. To compare Calgary and Vancouver's commissions from this era, see Perks "Idealism, Orchestration."

77. Bloomfield, "'Ubiquitous Town Planning Missionary': The Careers of Horace Seymour 1882–1940," *Environments* 17: 2 (1985), 29–42.

78. J.B. Milner, "The Statutory Role of the Planning Board," *Community Planning Review* 12: 3 (1962), 16–18.

79. P.J. Smith, "The Principle of Utility and the Origins of Planning Legislation in Alberta, 1912–1975," in A. Artibise and G. Stelter, eds., *The Usable Urban Past* (Toronto: Macmillan, 1979), 196–225. Carleton Library No. 119.

80. Jill L. Grant, Leifka Vissers, and James Haney, "Early Town Planning Legislation in Nova Scotia: The Roles of Local Reformers and International Experts," *Urban History Review* 40: 2 (2012), 3–14.

81. Grant et al., "Early Town Planning," Table 1.

82. New Brunswick, *An Act Relating to Town Planning*, Chap. 19, 2 Geo. V, 1912, Sect. 1(I).

83. Alberta, *An Act Relating to Town Planning*, Statutes of Alberta, Chap. 18, 1913, Sect. 1(6).

84. New Brunswick, *An Act Relating to Town Planning*, 2(2).

85. Nova Scotia, *Town Planning Act*, 1915, 2(3)

86. Canada, Commission of Conservation, *Report of the Sixth Annual Meeting* (1915), 271.

87. Cf. New Brunswick, *An Act Relating to Town Planning*, and Alberta, *An Act Relating to Town Planning*, 6(2).

88. Alberta, *An Act Relating to Town Planning*.

89. Stephen Ward, *Planning the Twentieth-Century City: The Advanced Capitalist World* (New York: Wiley, 2002), 26–31, 52–56.

90. For a full discussion of this act, see J. David Hulchanski, "The Evolution of Ontario's Early Urban Land Use Regulations, 1900–1920," a paper presented to the Canadian–American Comparative Urban History Conference, Guelph, 1982.

91. Canada, Federal Plan Commission, *Report of the Federal Plan Commission on a General Plan for the Cities of Ottawa and Hull* (1915); the plan and commentary can be found at http://www.PlanningCanadasCapital.ca

92. David Gordon, "A City Beautiful Plan."

93. Elizabeth Bloomfield, "Town Planning Efforts in Kitchener-Waterloo."

94. H. Bartholomew & Assoc., *A Plan for the City of Vancouver, BC.* and Lance Berelowitz, *Dream City: Vancouver and the Global Imagination* (Vancouver, BC: Douglas & McIntyre, 2005).

95. J. David Hulchanski, *The Origins of Urban Land Use Planning in Alberta, 1900–1945*, Research Paper 119 (University of Toronto, Centre for Urban and Community Studies, 1981).

96. Thomas Adams, *Report of the Planning And Development of the Lindenlea Estate*, Ottawa; City of Ottawa Archives, Ref no. RGI-3, File#1; *Journal of Town Planning Institute of Canada* (JTPIC) 1:3 (April 1921); the plans and reports can also be found in the Lindenlea section of http://www.PlanningCanadasCapital.ca

97. Raphael Fischler, "Development Control in Toronto in the Nineteenth Century," *Urban History Review* 36:1 (Fall 2007), 16–31.

98. Federal Plan Commission, *Report*, 46; see also the description of these zoning districts in David L.A. Gordon, "A City Beautiful Plan for Canada's Capital."

99. Thomas H. Logan, "The Americanization of German Zoning," *Journal of the American Institute of Planners* 42 (October 1976), 377–385.

100. Raphael Fischler, "Development Control."

101. E. Bloomfield, *City-Building Processes in Berlin/Kitchener and Waterloo, 1870–1930*, unpublished PhD thesis, University of Guelph, 1981, 432; Zoning bylaw of the City of Kitchener, *Journal of the Town Planning Institute of Canada* 4: 1 (January 1925), 4–8; John C. Weaver, "The Property Industry and Land Use Controls: The Vancouver Experience, 1910–1945," *Plan Canada* 19 (September–December 1979), 211–225.

102. "Where There Is No Zoning Bylaw: Ottawa," *Journal of the Town Planning Institute of Canada* 9: 1 (February 1930), 20; David Gordon, "'Agitating People's Brains': Noulan Cauchon," 361–363.

103. David Gordon, "'Agitating People's Brains': Noulan Cauchon," 361–363.

104. J.B. Milner, *Development Control* (Toronto: Ontario Law Reform Commission, 1969), 12.

105. Earl Levin, "Zoning in Canada," *Community Planning Review* 7 (June 1957), 85–87.

106. Library and Archives Canada, MG 28 I 275, Canadian Institute of Planning (CIP) fonds, files 1–8 & 11–16 and MG 30 C105, Noulan Cauchon fonds, vol. 9. File: Development of the Town Planning Institute Crest; "The Seal of the Institute," *Plan Canada*, 15: 2 (Sept. 1975), 117.

107. Noulan Cauchon, "Hexagonal Blocks for Residential Districts," *The American City* 17 (1925), 145–146; and Eran Ben-Joseph and David Gordon, "Hexagonal Planning in Theory and Practice," *Journal of Urban Design* 5, 3 (2000), 255–263.

108. P.J. Smith, "The Principle of Utility and the Origins of Planning Legislation in Alberta, 1912–1975," in A. Artibise and G. Stelter, *Usable Urban Past,* 196–225. See also

David Sherwood, "Canadian Institute of Planners," *Plan Canada*, Special Edition (July 1994), 20–21.

109. Thomas Adams, "What Town Planning Really Means," *The Canadian Municipal Journal* 10 (July 1914).

110. Stephen Bocking, "Constructing Urban Expertise: Professional and Political Authority in Toronto, 1940–1970," *Journal of Urban History* 33:2 (2006), 51–76.

111. City of Toronto Planning Board, *The Master Plan for the City of Toronto and Environs* (Toronto, 1943); John Sewell, *The Shape of the City: Toronto Struggles with Modern Planning* (Toronto: University of Toronto Press, 1993), 55–60; and *The Shape of the Suburbs: Understanding Toronto's Sprawl* (Toronto: University of Toronto Press, 2009), 30–35.

112. For an excellent review of the evolving context of Canadian community planning see Jeanne M. Wolfe, "Our Common Past: An Interpretation of Canadian Planning History," *Plan Canada*, Special Edition (July 1994), 12–34.

Internet Resources

Chapter-Relevant Sites

Planning Canadian Communities
www.planningcanadiancommunities.ca

Our Common Past: An Interpretation of Canadian Planning History—Part 1
www.cip-icu.ca/web/la/en/fi/
ce7ddb14f3144381a18ffe8268be8be5/get_file.asp

Canadian urban policy archive
www.urbancentre.utoronto.ca/policyarchive.html

Thomas Adams in Canada
www.cip-icu.ca/web/la/en/fi/1F1D5BAD155C41BFA97EDEFCCB1
0407C/get_file.asp

Hampstead Garden Suburb
www.hgs.org.uk

Canberra—an ideal city?
www.idealcity.org.au

Planning Canada's capital: six historic plans
www.PlanningCanadasCapital.ca

Canadian Council on Social Development
www.ccsd.ca

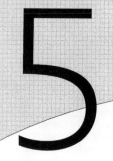

Chapter Five

The Growth of Canadian Community Planning, 1945–2010

[E]lbow room is a desirable characteristic.

Macklin Hancock, 1954

The second half of the 20th century posed as many challenges for community plan-makers as did the first half. It began with a pressing demand for housing and urban infrastructure that had been put aside because of the Great Depression and World War II, as well as a need to refurbish planning institutions. City populations that had swelled as people flocked in to fill wartime jobs continued to grow, and grow quickly. As the century continued, the baby boom, post-war economic expansion, and increased automobile use and home ownership further fuelled urban expansion into the suburbs and exurbs. The 21st century began with increasing efforts to deal with the impacts of mass suburbanization ("sprawl repair") and the decline in affordability within the cores of Canada's largest cities.

While the challenges were new, the same sets of concerns as had energized plan-ning approaches before and after the beginning of the century came again to the fore. The visual appearance of cities, and their living conditions, natural environments, and efficient functioning each vied for attention as the public's concerns about their com-munities waxed and waned. Communities became more diverse, with changing family structures, more women in the labour force, and massive immigration, especially to the largest cities. New concepts appeared, such as Smart Growth, New Urbanism, and Healthy Communities, as well as new technologies, such as Geographic Information Systems (GIS), and new modes of working, such as telecommuting using the Internet. Probably most noteworthy was the strong emphasis on protection of the natural envi-ronment and, more latterly, sustainability. In other words, the activity of community planning was called upon to modify its processes and its tools as it has always done with changing times. This chapter discusses the evolution of community planning in Canada from 1945 to 2010, the period that immediately underlies contemporary planning practice. With this perspective, keep the following question in mind:

- *In which ways do today's plans and plan-making processes reflect the concerns of planners in the latter half of the 20th century?*

Post-War Planning Challenges for a Suburban Nation

Canada changed from a rural to an urban nation in the first half of the twentieth century. Demographers point to 1931 as the first year in which the majority of Canadians lived in urban areas.[1] However, the strong urban development of the 1900–1930 period stalled during the Great Depression of the 1930s, and the rapid expansion of Canada's industrial facilities for the war effort created a housing crisis in many cities. Community planning institutions were also left to languish during the same period. After the war, the federal government pushed to revive these institutions, which would soon be sorely needed to guide the growth and development of Canadian cities and towns. As they struggled with these problems, citizens and planners developed some new methods and models that were widely admired in the last decades of the century.

Canada was not an urban nation for very long. The term "**exploding metropolis**"[2] aptly captures the state of urban affairs of the 1950s and of the decades that followed. Cities grew in population, expanded their boundaries, and increased in both density (with taller buildings at the centre) and area (with more houses and factories on the outskirts). By 2006, Canada was clearly a suburban nation, with two-thirds of its population living in suburban environments and only 10–15 percent of the national population living in active, walkable cores.[3]

Three forces combined to produce the suburban metropolitan environments we are familiar with today. First, there were demographic forces due to (a) the migration of people from rural areas to urban centres; (b) people emigrating to Canada from abroad, most of whom went to the larger cities; and (c) a dramatic increase in the natural growth of the population, known as the "baby boom."[4] Second, there were economic forces. The nation's economy continued to expand and produce jobs and rising incomes for the new and old

populations of cities. There was also a pent-up demand for housing and other urban accoutrements created by its suppression during 15 years of depression and war.[5] The third force, and in many ways the most momentous in its effect on the form of cities, was the vast expansion in automobile use. These three forces combined to reshape the metropolis, and Canadian community planning had to face a number of challenges whose resolution would establish foundations for its future.

Advent of the Baby Boom, 1946–1965

In addition to the surging city populations of the wartime period, communities across the country were soon to feel the impact of an unanticipated boom in population that would last 20 years—the baby boom. Family formation and birthrates in the 1946–65 period increased dramatically. To appreciate just how much, consider that the annual birth group size for the previous two decades (1926–45) had been approximately 250 000; it then boomed to 425 000 per year, an increase of 70 percent. In other words, an additional 3.5 million births occurred in the post-war period up to 1965.[6]

Although the birth groups of this period are often referred to as the "baby boom generation," they do not constitute a true generation, but rather two 10-year age cohorts. Their significance for community planning is that these cohorts spurred sudden increases in demand for housing, schools, playgrounds, and health and other social services. And, over ensuing decades, this led to a demand for more colleges and universities, and more housing and health and social services. This demographic bulge still continues to add new dimensions to community planning as it contributes to a surging seniors' population that will expand dramatically within the decade ahead.[7]

Mass Automobile Use

Although we now seem accustomed to large, spreading cities, the tenor of the 1950s regarding this change is caught in the following quotation:

> Of all the forces reshaping the American metropolis, the most powerful and insistent are those rooted in changing modes of transportation. The changes are so big and obvious that it is easy to forget how remarkable they are. The streetcar has all but disappeared, the bus is proving an inept substitute, commuter rail service deteriorates, subways get dirtier, and new expressways pour more and more automobiles into the centre of town.[8]

These writers might well have added that more and more automobiles were pouring into the outskirts of cities because that is where the growing populations could be housed most easily, and it is also where the old public transportation systems did not usually reach, or service well if they did. Mass automobile ownership and expressways gave Canadians a transportation alternative that was private, convenient, flexible, and fast (See Figure 5.1). Public transit ridership, concomitantly, declined from 13 percent to 5 percent of all trips between 1950 and 2000.[9]

Two more auto-oriented facilities shaped the post-war city: the shopping centre (Figure 5.2) and the industrial park. Both of these facilities signalled a reorientation of major community functions away from a single dominant centre. Major shopping facilities in pre-1950 cities were tied to downtown areas because most personal transportation focused on downtown, especially streetcars and buses. Industries were often tied to rail or harbour access. When the automobile's widespread availability favoured the development of suburbs beyond the reach of public transit, it meant that stores and businesses not only had a market but could also take advantage of easy truck transport of goods on

SOURCE: COURTESY OF THE NATIONAL FILM BOARD OF CANADA.

| Figure 5.1 | Impact of Expressways on the Metropolitan Landscape: Longueuil, Québec |

In an aerial photograph of any Canadian metropolitan area, the most prominent artificial feature will probably be an expressway. It was hoped that these massive modern facilities would relieve downtown congestion and facilitate movement among the new suburban housing and industrial areas. Building expressways significantly changed the physical structure of urban areas because they consumed lots of land and became barriers in the urban landscape.

| Figure 5.2 | Park Royal Shopping Centre, 1952 |

SOURCE: PHOTO: ART JONES, 1952/VANCOUVER PUBLIC LIBRARY, VPL81959.

Park Royal Shopping Centre in West Vancouver, B.C., was one of Canada's first suburban malls. These centres rapidly reduced the Central Business District's share of metropolitan retail trade.

suburban roads. Shopping centres and industrial parks subsequently became common elements in the fabric of Canadian communities and injected a new set of relationships into planning because they both needed considerable land and easy automobile access to a large area. These changes also had an impact on downtown cores, often leaving the older central stores wanting for business, and former industrial areas in decline.

Meeting Housing Needs

The change in housing options was driven by less visible but equally powerful preferences. A suburban single-detached home offered privacy, more space, personal control, green surroundings, and a long-term real estate investment that many families preferred over a rental unit in the city.[10] The federal government had tested the development of large-scale suburban housing projects at big wartime plants that needed worker accommodation. The federal agency Wartime Housing Ltd. built 32 000 rental homes for workers and returning veterans between 1941 and 1947.[11] These homes were sold, and mass home ownership for other middle-class and working-class families was made possible by changes in mortgage arrangements described below. The home ownership rate increased from 57 percent in 1941 to 65 percent in 1951 and has remained at approximately that level since.[12] In metropolitan areas, the housing stock increased between 10 percent and 20 percent from 1945 to 1950. In this period, 11 000 new dwellings were built in Winnipeg, 3000 in Halifax, 21 000 in Vancouver, and 31 000 in Montréal.[13]

Suburban development further accelerated in the 1950s and 1960s. The total effect was an extraordinary transformation—the country had changed from an urban to a suburban nation. Surprisingly, these momentous social and economic forces that reshaped Canadian communities were anticipated and somewhat encouraged by national planning efforts for the post-war period (as we shall see later in this chapter), as well as by early metropolitan planning in Winnipeg and Toronto, described in Chapter 9.

The Canadian love affair with the suburban home appears to be slowing early in the new century. Two key indicators demonstrate the change. From 2001 to 2011, single-family detached homes declined from 59 percent to 42 percent of all new housing starts; 2008 was the first year in memory that more multiple dwellings (row houses, apartments) were built than singles.[14] The large-scale extension of condominium tenure to row houses and apartments has allowed the residents of these housing types to obtain many of the benefits of home ownership that were previously reserved for single houses. Secondly, from 1996 to 2006, the active cores of metropolitan areas grew faster than the suburbs.[15] The suburbs are still the location of most housing growth, but demographic forces and regional planning restrictions on outward expansion of the largest metropolitan areas may finally be slowing growth rates for single-family houses.

The three great post-war challenges—population growth, the housing boom, and mass automobile use—all contained elements of the main themes of Canadian community planning from the late 19th century: city appearance, living conditions, the environment, and city efficiency (see Figure 5.3). The emphasis among the broader themes ebbed and flowed during the rapid metropolitan development over ensuing decades. City efficiency and appearance were major concerns in the construction boom of the 1950s and 1960s. Engineers and architect–planners were busy with vast infrastructure projects and major urban renewal schemes, and almost every Canadian community was engaged in comprehensive land use planning. By the late 1960s, the social and environmental impacts of these programs were being questioned, and sustainable development became a dominant issue in Canadian planning in the late 1980s. At the end of the century, community design and infrastructure issues re-emerged in Smart Growth, New Urbanism, and transit-oriented development. More sophisticated and complex planning approaches characterize the last few decades and mark the growing maturity of the Canadian planning movement.

Figure 5.3	Evolution of Canadian Planning Ideas, 1945–2010

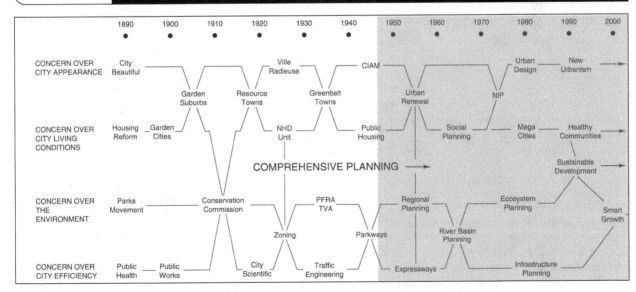

Today's planning themes of comprehensive planning, sustainable development, Smart Growth, New Urbanism, and Healthy Communities continue to echo the four basic planning concerns of more than a century ago.

Concern over City Appearance

The organizing and theoretical work regarding the form and functioning of cities done by the CIAM (Congrès Internationaux d'Architecture Moderne) in the 1930s paid off after World War II. Their message about the obsolescence of historic city centres and the need to rebuild them using Modern planning principles found a willing audience in the reconstruction of European and Japanese cities destroyed by war or in new towns and capital cities such as Brasilia (Figure 5.4). The CIAM principles from the Athens Charter entered North America through architecture and planning schools, which were usually combined in that era.[16] Most North American schools switched from Beaux Arts to CIAM approaches during the 1950s.

Figure 5.4	A Modern Plan for a New Capital City: Brasilia, 1957

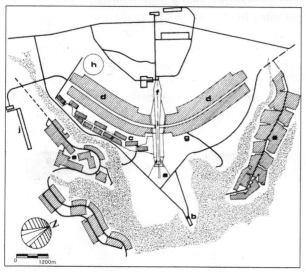

The idea for an inland capital for Brazil dated from its independence in 1822. A competition for a plan was held in 1956, and the curved cruciform plan of Lucio Costa was chosen. His plan for Brasilia closely followed the CIAM's principles from the Athens Charter, clearly separating land uses and transportation modes. The plan was entirely executed in Modernist architecture, mainly by Oscar Niemeyer, who had collaborated with Le Corbusier in Rio and on the UN headquarters in New York. The first phase of the highly symbolic city was completed in 1960 and became an important reference point for Modern urbanism. Key: (a) main square, (b) President's residence, (c) foreign embassies, (d, e) residential areas, (f) recreation area, (g) university, (h) cemetery, (i) main traffic interchange, (j) airport.

Rebuilding the Inner City

One of the consequences of this shift to Modern planning concepts was to focus professional attention on large-scale rebuilding of the inner city. This manifested itself in four overlapping programs—urban renewal, neighbourhood redevelopment, public–private partnerships, and private megaprojects—that unfolded over the next several decades (see Figure 5.5).

Urban Renewal

Urban renewal emerged in recognition of the fact that large portions of the buildings in Canadian communities were half a century or more old. The Central Mortgage and Housing Corporation (CMHC) reported in 1956 that almost 900 000 housing units were of this vintage and, moreover one-tenth of all housing was in need of major repairs.[17] "Blighted" conditions, as they were then called, could also be found among old factory and warehouse buildings, many of which were being abandoned for sites in suburban industrial parks. The central parts of many cities, which were also the oldest sections, suffered most from physical deterioration (Figure 3.12, page 48). Urban renewal was an effort to restore the commercial attractiveness of downtown areas and avoid the loss of investment they represented. Hoping to eliminate substandard housing, the federal government established a program for financing these "slum clearance" projects. Just as the name suggests, dilapidated housing would also be bulldozed. Residents of the area would be re-housed in public housing projects (a companion program to urban renewal), sometimes on the same site. Occasionally, the newly razed area was considered more valuable as a place for new commercial development, and the displaced residents were forced to move to public housing in another district, or to crowd in with friends or neighbours if they did not want to leave their neighbourhood.

The leaders of social reform, such as Catherine Bauer, Humphrey Carver, and Albert Rose, initially supported urban renewal. Planning for the first Canadian project, Toronto's Regent Park, had begun in the 1930s and had solid public support when it began development in 1948.[18] Many blocks of 19th century housing in poor condition were demolished to create a master-planned project with 2100 public housing units (Figure 5.6). Similar projects were begun in most North American cities, with Canadian practice in the 1950s guided by Gordon Stephenson, a British architect–planner who had studied with Le Corbusier and planned Stevenage, the first British New Town.[19] Stephenson was director of the University of Toronto's planning program in the late

Figure 5.5   Rebuilding the Inner City

	URBAN RENEWAL	NEIGHBOURHOOD DEVELOPMENT	PUBLIC/PRIVATE PARTNERSHIP	PRIVATE MEGA-PROJECTS
Time period	1950–1970	1965–1990s	1975 +	1990 +
Project type	Slum Clearance	New Precinct	Waterfront/CBD	Rail Yards
Typical projects	Jeanne-Mance [Montréal] Regent Park [Toronto] West End [Boston]	False Creek South [Vancouver] St. Lawrence [Toronto]	Harbourfront [Toronto] Quincy Market [Boston] Battery Park City [NYC] Docklands [London] Granville Island [Vancouver]	False Creek North [Vancouver] Railway Lands [Toronto] Mission Bay [San Francisco] Riverside South [NYC]
Land use change	Residential to Residential & Institutional	Industrial/Transport to Residential/ Mixed	Industrial/Transport/ Commercial to Mixed Use	Transport/Industrial to Mixed Use
Leadership	Housing Authority	Redevelopment Agency	Redevelopment Agency & Private Sector	Private Sector
Early capital	Public Sector	Public Sector	Public & Private	Private Sector
Change in ownership	Private to Public	Public to Public	Public to Private	Private to Private
Plan responsibility	Housing Authority & City	Redevelopment Agency	Redevelopment Agency & Developer	Developer & City
Planning mode	Master Plan	Site Plan & Urban Design Guidelines	Design Guidelines & Site Plan	Site Plan & Urban Design Guidelines
Key success factors	Public Grants Expropriation Power	Public Grants Expropriation Power	Private Investment Expropriation Power Public Borrowing	Land Ownership Private Investment Political Approval
Problems	Displacement No Market Response	Limited Public Funds	Uncoordinated Development Few Social Benefits	Loss of Public Control Few Social Benefits

Source: D. Gordon, "Phases of Redevelopment in North American Inner Cities" in M.H. Yeates, *The North American City*, 5th ed. (Longman, 1998), pp.401–403.

1950s and prepared urban renewal studies for Halifax, Kingston, London, and Ottawa in his summers.[20]

However, an avalanche of criticism from social scientists in the 1960s brought these programs to a halt.[21] Urban renewal became very unpopular because of the displacement of residents and destruction of close-knit communities such as Halifax's Africville, a community that had existed for over 100 years, which was razed in 1964, following Stephenson's plan.[22] Citizens were outraged by expropriation of their homes, and politicians were disappointed when some of the

bulldozed sites remained vacant due to lack of market response. The social and physical deterioration of high-density urban public housing projects magnified the perception that urban renewal was a planning disaster.[23]

The programs that replaced urban renewal were influenced by the ideas of noted urban critic Jane Jacobs.[24] Her advocacy for mixed uses, higher density, greater diversity, and retention of older buildings supported new programs for urban infill and rehabilitation. Although urban renewal was phased out in the late 1960s, it embodied some important

Figure 5.6	Regent Park North Plan, ca. 1950

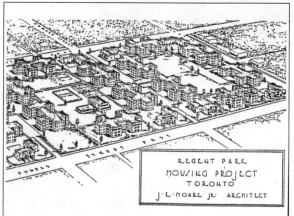

Regent Park North was Canada's first large-scale public housing project, built on a "superblock" created by expropriation in urban renewal. Architect J.E. Hoare designed the project as a series of three apartment buildings and townhouse blocks on a sea of grass, closely following other Modern urban renewal projects in the United States. Regent Park was a successful mixed-income community in its early years, but social conditions gradually deteriorated in the latter part of the century. It is now being redeveloped.

features for community planning. In the first place, its focus on the need to rebuild cities complemented the planning concerns with new development on the fringes. In the second place, it established the need for the involvement of senior levels of government to facilitate such action, especially in its financing. Urban renewal programs instituted the idea of "shared cost" approaches in community planning where, for example, the cost of a site designated for urban renewal would be shared 50 percent by the federal government, 25 percent by the provincial government, and 25 percent by the municipality. A third, and possibly most important, feature was the requirement that the municipality have a community plan that took into account the future use and role of redevelopment areas. One finds these principles in use today in various new programs for renewing communities.

Neighbourhood Development

Citizen protests over urban renewal and expressway projects in major Canadian cities were the impetus for the election of reform-oriented municipal councillors in the early 1970s in cities across the country. In a

Figure 5.7	St. Lawrence Neighbourhood Plan, Toronto

This early sketch of the spine of the St. Lawrence Neighbourhood, David Crombie Park, was directly inspired by Commonwealth Avenue in Boston's Back Bay. This use of historic precedents from well-planned neighbourhoods is an indication of the switch from Modern to post-Modern urbanism. The short blocks and extension of Toronto's street grid reflect Jane Jacob's planning principles.

Figure 5.8	False Creek South Model, ca. 1975

Christopher Alexander's urban design ideas for low-rise, high-density, organic urban form can be seen in this model, which was prominently displayed in CMHC's Ottawa head office in the 1970s.

burst of creativity, the reform councils sponsored inner-city development such as Toronto's St. Lawrence Neighbourhood (Figure 5.7) and Vancouver's False Creek South (Figure 5.8).[25] The planning principles that guided the St. Lawrence Neighbourhood were strongly influenced by Jane Jacobs, who had moved to Toronto in 1968 (see Figure 5.20).[26] The plans for the south side of False Creek were strongly influenced by Christopher Alexander's urban design ideas, particularly his pattern language.[27]

False Creek and St. Lawrence were postmodern urban projects that challenged the Modern planning principles embedded in the CIAM Athens Charter. Their mixed-use, mixed-income, mixed-tenure approach was judged a success and widely admired.[28] However, they relied on large federal and provincial grants for land expropriation, infrastructure, and housing subsidies. When these grants were cut back in the 1980s, it became difficult to start similar projects, and the cost of environmental remediation made redeveloping other former (brownfield) industrial sites too expensive.

Public–Private Partnerships for Urban Redevelopment

After the federal and provincial urban renewal funds disappeared, some North American cities turned to partnerships with private developers to implement urban redevelopment projects using the techniques discussed in Chapter 17. Many cities had underdeveloped land in the downtown and waterfront areas. Boston's Quincy Market, Baltimore's Inner Harbour, and New York's Battery Park City were early examples of public–private partnerships, where local governments attracted private developers to implement urban revitalization projects using well-located land, good urban design, and limited infrastructure funds to attract investment.[29] The Canadian response was to establish federal or provincial agencies for waterfront redevelopment in Vancouver, Winnipeg, Toronto, Montréal, Québec, and Halifax. The record on these initiatives is varied. Vancouver's Granville Island Trust used an innovative plan by Hotson Bakker Architects to transform a declining industrial site into a vibrant, mixed-use waterfront with a distinctive sense of place[30] (Figure 5.10). The Winnipeg, Montréal, and Halifax waterfront projects have proceeded slowly, but with generally positive results. Toronto's Harbourfront started out with great promise and some fine re-use of industrial buildings, but dissolved into an intense controversy over parks and building heights.[31] In the meantime, other public authorities, such as hospitals, airports, universities, utilities, and housing agencies, began to use the public–private partnership tools pioneered on the waterfront to attract private investment to their sites.

Private Megaprojects

Another type of inner-city project emerged in the 1990s, when very little public funding was available for urban redevelopment. Private corporations with ownership of large, well-located sites close to the central business district, such as old railway yards, began to negotiate with local governments for redevelopment plans. Although the railway companies often started the planning process for sites such as San Francisco's Mission Bay, Manhattan's Riverside South, Vancouver's False Creek North, and Toronto's Railway Lands, large-scale private developers eventually acquired most of the sites. The planning techniques for these megaprojects used the approach of site plan/urban design guidelines pioneered in new urban neighbourhoods (see Figure 5.4).

The municipalities had little bargaining power to extract public benefits during the megaproject approval process since they were not contributing land or capital to any significant extent. The railways bargained hard, and if they didn't like the deal, they could just wait, as happened in Montréal's Outremont. As a result, projects such as Vancouver's Concorde Pacific Place and Toronto's City Place have substantially lower proportions of social housing and open space than the adjacent False Creek South or Harbourfront projects. The Vancouver planners had some success on urban design issues by negotiating a commendable water's edge promenade (Figure 5.11) and pioneering a point tower and townhouse block hybrid-building type that combines high density with good streetscapes.[32]

Evolving Planning Perspectives
Emergence of Urban Design

The urban renewal debate gave large-scale master planning a bad name in the 1960s, and concern over city appearance almost disappeared in Canadian planning and Canadian planning schools over the next two decades.[33] Although Modern master-planning principles from Regent Park (see Figures 5.6 and 5.9) were discredited, it was eventually acknowledged that while physical design could not solve social problems on its own, it could help create a better built environment. Urban design emerged as a new interdisciplinary specialty addressing the craft of "designing cities without designing buildings," as Jonathan Barnett phrased it.[34] Urban design was influenced by postmodern planning ideas that avoided large-scale master planning by a single architect in favour of flexible site plans and guidelines to direct a variety of designers over the many years it takes to build a city.[35] Urban design guidelines became

Figure 5.9

Figure 5.9 Comparison of Planning and Urban Design for Urban Renewal Projects and New Urban Neighbourhoods

URBAN RENEWAL PROJECTS	NEW URBAN NEIGHBOURHOODS
Planning Factors:	*Planning Factors:*
• Single income group (low/moderate)	• Mix of income groups
• Single tenure (rental)	• Mix of tenures (co-op, condo, rental)
• Single developer	• Variety of developers
• Single management and owner	• Diversified management and owner
• Separation of land uses	• Mixed-use development
• High density	• High density
• Site clearance and redevelopment	• Preservation of existing buildings
• Master plan	• Site plan and urban design guidelines
Urban Design Factors:	*Urban Design Factors:*
• New precinct/separate	• Extension of the city fabric
• Superblock/ring road	• Extension of the street grid
• Separation of vehicles and pedestrians	• Street as focus of activity
• Project address	• Address from a street
• Large parcels, coarse grain	• Small parcels, fine grain
• High-rise buildings	• Low-/medium-rise buildings
• Family housing on internal pathways	• Family housing on local streets
• Single landscape treatment	• Many landscape treatments
• Single architect	• Many architects

Source: D. Gordon (ed.), *Directions for New Urban Neighbourhoods: Learning from St. Lawrence*, Toronto: Ryerson SURP, 1990, Table 4–1.

important parts of plans for downtown areas and redevelopment projects in the 1990s (see Chapter 11 for more details). As the 21st century began, most large and medium-sized Canadian cities had urban designers on staff and many consulting firms offered urban design services. The Council for Canadian Urbanism (CanU) was formed by architects, planners, and landscape architects in 2006 to advocate for better design.[36]

Historic Preservation

Heritage preservation was another area where the CIAM planning principles were rejected in the 1970s. A few of the more enlightened urban renewal plans, such as Philadelphia and Kingston, Ontario, incorporated some historic buildings into their new designs.[37] But the Modern *tabula rasa* approach had led to the destruction of many fine 19th century structures. Citizen opposition increased when important public buildings such as New York's Penn Station and Toronto's post office were razed and replaced with mediocre Modern structures. Heritage advocates first rallied public support to preserve threatened city halls and railway stations. Then developers were encouraged to incorporate historic buildings into their redevelopment projects, as happened with Montréal's Maison Alcan. Finally, planning agencies began to protect and enhance whole districts of historic buildings, starting with the National Capital Commission's Sussex Drive in the 1960s and extending to Vancouver's Gastown, Vieux Montréal, Ville de Québec's Lower Town, and Halifax's Historic Properties. Old Québec was honoured as North

Figure 5.10 — Granville Island, Vancouver

Buildings on Granville Island include a successful restaurant and farmers' market, right under the Granville Street Bridge. An art college in former industrial buildings adds to the lively activity on the island, which is attached to False Creek South. New York's Project for Public Places declared Granville Island to be North America's best public place in 2004.

America's first UNESCO World Heritage Site in 1985 (Figure 5.12). By the end of the century, many Canadian communities, from small towns to metropolitan centres, had planning policies in place to protect their built heritage (see Chapter 11 for more details).[38]

Figure 5.11 — False Creek North, Vancouver, 2006

The north side of False Creek was a former industrial brownfield that served as the site for Expo '86. It was cleaned up by the provincial government at great expense and sold to a private developer. The site has a much-higher-density built form than the southern shore. Note the thin "point block" towers designed to allow views to the mountains on the skyline. The Vancouver planners negotiated for high-quality public spaces and community amenities, including an elementary school and community centre.

Figure 5.12 — Old Québec UNESCO World Heritage Site

Old Québec was the first North American city to be designated as a World Heritage Site.

Redevelopment of Modern Projects

Many of the earliest Modern housing projects were reaching the end of their useful life by 2000, creating an interesting planning problem. The United States and Britain had begun large-scale programs to demolish their most distressed high-rise public housing, starting with St. Louis' Pruitt-Igoe project in 1972. Montréal's Benny Farm was the leader in this field, when a 1940s veterans' housing project was redeveloped by Canada Lands Company early in the new century after years of vigorous debate on the future of the site.[39] Social housing, condominium apartments, and new community facilities were added by infill and selective demolition (Figure 5.13). The latest "green building" techniques were pioneered (with some teething problems), and the project is regarded as a model of 21st century urban redevelopment. After an extensive public consultation process, Toronto decided to gradually demolish Regent Park, replacing it with a mixed-use, mixed-income, medium-rise neighbourhood modelled on the St. Lawrence neighbourhood (Figure 1.1, page 5).[40] The Woodward's project (Vancouver) is another interesting case that mixes a heritage department store, and social and market housing with public spaces.[41]

Conventional Suburban Development

While the urban renewal battles raged downtown, another, more profound, change in planning principles was happening in the suburbs, where smaller projects and self-building were the norm before 1950.[42] Modern planning principles such as the super-block, separation of

Figure 5.13	Benny Farm Master Plan, 2006

The existing small apartment blocks in Benny Farm were renovated and extended. New mid-rise veterans' housing and condominium apartments were built on the east edge of the site and new townhouses on the west edge. Benny Farm received the Holcim award for green building in 2006.

Figure 5.14	Cité Jardin, Montréal, 1947

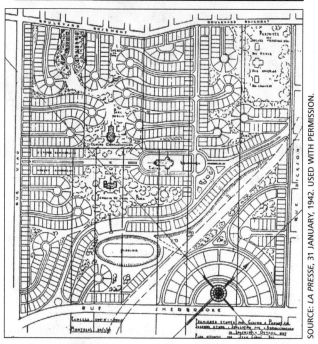

The project's name suggests that Cité Jardin might emulate a garden city such as Letchworth, but Samuel Gitterman's plan was the purest example of a Radburn plan Canada has seen. Note the culs-de-sac and the central landscaped open space. Cité Jardin was sponsored by the Catholic Church, so it is no surprise to find the local church and parish school at the centre of the neighbourhood, rather than Radburn's public school.

uses, and the neighbourhood unit had been demonstrated in Radburn, New Jersey (Figure 4.18, page 82), in the late 1920s and were well known in the immediate post-war period.[43] Canadian projects followed these examples, such as Cité Jardin (Figure 5.14) in Montréal (1947), designed by Samuel Gitterman,[44] and Wildwood in Winnipeg (1948), designed by Hubert Bird.[45]

A more important design precedent emerged in 1952 when industrialist E.P. Taylor assembled an 800-hectare parcel of rural land in North York. He financed, planned, and implemented Don Mills, Canada's first large-scale suburb produced by a private developer. Taylor created a model suburban project, perhaps because he took a chance and hired a young landscape architect, Macklin Hancock, to plan Don Mills. Hancock had studied at Harvard's Graduate School of Design (GSD) with Walter Gropius, the founder of the Bauhaus and a CIAM leader. He drew on the neighbourhood unit and Modern "new towns" near London and Stockholm as precedents to design a satellite community that was closer to a "new town" than a bedroom community.[46] Don Mills was considered a model suburban community using the Modern planning principles; its plan was exhibited and discussed at the GSD's 1959 Urban Design Conference, chaired by CIAM secretary Josep Lluis Sert.[47]

The Don Mills community (see Figure 5.15) would house 35 000 people and create jobs for 20 000. The core residential area comprised four neighbourhood units connected by a ring road. Each neighbourhood unit had an elementary school and places of worship at its centre, and an interconnected open-space system that allowed most children to walk to school without crossing a major street. The centre of the community included a shopping centre, apartment blocks, high school, and other community facilities; all were planned using the best Modern architectural design. Traffic was sorted by a firm hierarchy of streets, with loops and crescents at the local level, rather than Radburn's culs-de-sac. An equal amount of land was set aside for industrial parks and soon filled with factories and offices designed by Canada's best architects. Finally, the area's ecological features were protected, with the original drainage system and Don River Valley preserved. Many other companies followed Taylor's innovations and established large development corporations to buy up huge tracts of farmland, build infrastructure, and sell building lots. But few developers provided the mix of housing types, community facilities, good landscape design, and jobs–housing balance of the original Don Mills model.

By the late 1980s, low-density, automobile-oriented suburbs had changed from an interesting alternative to urban living to the dominant model for Canadian family life. Shopping followed the residents, first in shopping centres, and then in isolated big-box stores. Finally, jobs started flowing out to big office parks and manufacturing plants near freeway interchanges.[48] The result was a vast expanse of low-density separated land uses, which Melvin Webber christened the "non-place urban realm."[49] Some urban economists hailed suburban development as a pure expression of the people's preference for single-detached homes and automobile travel, citing Los Angeles as the new model for urban life.[50] Others called it **urban sprawl** and a new design movement arose to attack its worst features.

New Urbanism

By the late 1980s, the conventional suburban development model was degraded as amenities disappeared, lots grew narrower, and two to three-car garages popped out the front of homes that were often referred to as "snout houses" (see Figure 5.17). Some suburban streets began to resemble a wall of garage doors. By the early 1990s, postmodern urban design ideas began to affect Canadian suburban planning, perhaps first at Bois Franc in Montréal.[51] Calgary's McKenzie Towne and Markham's Cornell (Figure 5.16)

| Figure 5.15 | Don Mills Plan, 1954 |

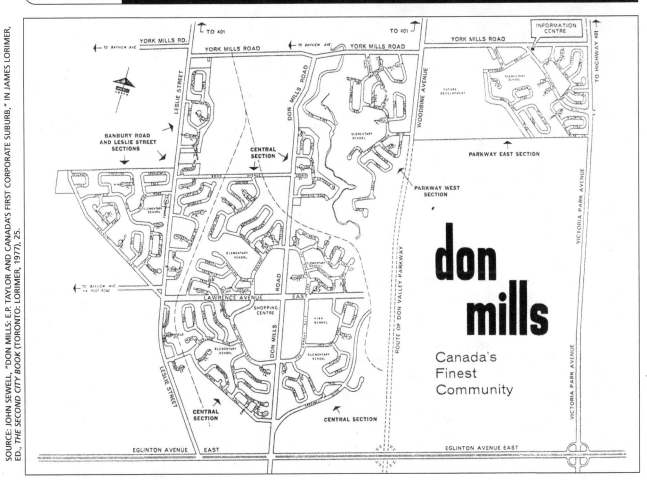

Macklin Hancock's 1954 plan for Don Mills, Toronto, started with four neighbourhood units, connected by the collector ring road in the centre of the diagram from this contemporary sales brochure. Employment areas ("industrial parks") were located to the north and south; the open space in the valley to the west was disrupted by construction of the Don Valley Parkway (dotted lines).

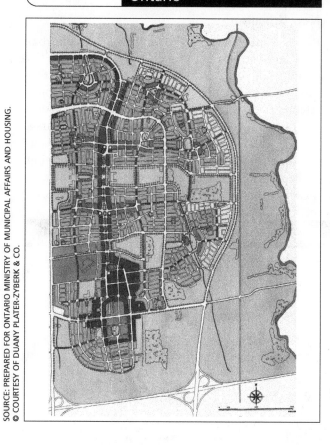

were designed by Andres Duany and Elizabeth Plater-Zyberk, both leaders of the Congress for the New Urbanism (CNU).[52] The CNU issued its own *Charter of the New Urbanism* to rival the CIAM's Athens Charter, but with quite different planning principles. New Urbanists call for a variety of planning approaches, depending on regional location (see Figure 7.10, page 181), and advocate mixed uses, mixed tenures, mixed building types, and a high standard of urban design for public places. In the United States, the CNU has been influential in establishing the Smart Growth Network, developing new form-based codes to replace zoning, renovating inner-city public housing projects (HOPE VI), and developing new street designs.[53] Most recently, the CNU has collaborated with the U.S. Green Building Council and the Natural Resources Defense Council to develop LEED-ND, an environmental planning evaluation system for neighbourhood development.[54]

The CNU charter recommends that street networks be an interconnected web that accommodates cars but is primarily designed to meet the needs of pedestrians, transit, and cyclists.[55] These design principles recall the best pre-Radburn neighbourhood unit designs, such as New York's Forest Hills Gardens and London's Hampstead Garden Suburb. But, more controversially, the New Urbanists suggest that the design of buildings in the neighbourhoods takes cues from local precedents. Seaside Florida, the first New Urbanist project, drew ideas from southern U.S. towns, while Cornell in Markham drew from the adjacent Victorian-era villages and Toronto neighbourhoods (see Figure 5.16). Many Modern architects decry this historicism, and some cheap knockoffs by developers have led some critics to dismiss the whole movement as "sprawl with porches."[56] More serious criticism is that most New Urbanist projects, built in the post-1995 social housing funding drought, have little affordable housing. This has contributed to a reduction in the social diversity they advocate; market forces and consumer preferences for socially homogenous housing also affected such projects.[57] Another serious concern arises regarding housing design and its appropriateness for the elderly.[58] For example, in striving for compact development, New Urbanist neighbourhoods tend to offer narrow, multi-level houses with several flights of stairs inside and steps to a porch outside. Designs such as these present substantial barriers to accessibility for many seniors—more barriers than in existing neighbourhoods.[59]

However, carefully planned projects, such as Calgary's Garrison Woods or Markham's New Urbanist neighbourhoods (Figure 5.18), appear to support much higher gross densities than the conventional suburban development of the 1980s, while accommodating good ecological planning.[60] A recent comparison of Canadian New Urbanist (NU) and similarly located conventional suburban developments found that the residents of the NU projects had more pedestrian routes, more housing choice, less land per housing unit, less car use for weekday urban travel, more walking and bike use, greater use of public transit, and more social interaction with neighbours.[61]

Gated Communities

While social critics are divided on the New Urbanism, most are quite critical of gated communities, the latest design trend to make its way north from the United States, where they make up a substantial proportion of new suburban construction.[62] Gated suburbs are appearing particularly in British Columbia and elsewhere in seniors' and lifestyle communities (Figure 5.19). Although the

| Figure 5.17 and Figure 5.18 | Conventional Suburban Development ("snout house") and New Urbanist Streetscapes in Markham, Ontario |

| Figure 5.19 | Swan Lake, a Gated Community in Markham, Ontario |

The gates at Swan Lake exclude anyone who is not a resident or a guest.

numbers are small at present, this trend raises important planning issues, such as private roads, control of the public realm, visual impacts of walls, and increased separation of the affluent from the rest of society, which have yet to be addressed by Canadian municipalities.[63] The advent of gated communities also turns attention back on long-standing concerns about city living conditions.

Greyfields and Sprawl Repair

The vast areas of first-generation post-war suburbs are now starting to show their age. Some suburban uses have become almost obsolete, such as medium-sized community shopping centres that have been put out of business by big-box retailers. These "greyfield" sites[64] are sometimes converted to "power centres" to the dismay of the surrounding neighbourhood, which may have seen their indoor shopping mall replaced with big boxes surrounding an outdoor parking lot. These environments are so awful for pedestrians that shoppers will often drive from store to store, since even a 100-metre walk in these conditions is unpleasant. If the neighbourhood has a good retail market, the old enclosed shopping centre from the 1970s may be replaced by a "Lifestyle Centre," a retail mall with more pleasant outdoor amenities for pedestrians that mimic a public street. The Don Mills Centre has recently undergone a similar transformation.

More sophisticated forms of suburban infill, known as "sprawl repair,"[65] see former malls turned into mixed-use centres, such as Markham's Olde Thornhill Village and the proposed transformation of Vancouver's Oakridge Mall following the opening of the Canada Line rapid transit station.[66] Other proposals call for redevelopment of strip malls, abandoned gas stations, used car lots, and other low-intensity automobile-related commercial sites. And Toronto has discovered that its older suburban apartment towers are an important supply of affordable rental housing that must be rejuvenated and made more walkable for their low-income residents.[67]

Concern over Housing and Living Conditions

After years of advocacy by social activists, Canada finally instituted a public housing program in 1949. Regent

Park in Toronto was followed by the Jeanne Mance (Montréal) and Mulgrave Park (Halifax) projects, each in the slum-clearance tradition. Municipal housing authorities later used federal and provincial funds to build low-income housing on undeveloped suburban sites, and over 250 000 public housing units were built from 1948 to 1986. But by 1961, urban renewal began to be criticized by astute observers of the urban environment.

Social Planning and the Attack on Urban Renewal

"This book is an attack on current city planning and rebuilding. It is also, and mostly, an attempt to introduce new principles of city planning and rebuilding, different and even opposite from those now taught in everything from schools of architecture and planning ..."

So begins one of the most influential books on city planning, Jane Jacobs's 1961 *Death and Life of Great American Cities*.[68] Jacobs (Figure 5.20) used detailed observations of her own neighbourhood in Manhattan's Greenwich Village to critique urban renewal and develop new principles for mixed uses, density, and conserving older buildings. Her critique focused attention on the social aspects of cities and away from aesthetic and functional planning issues.[69] A wave of public activism against urban renewal swept across Canada, from Strathcona in Vancouver, to Portage and Main in Winnipeg, to Milton Park in Montréal, and to Quinpool Road in Halifax. The opposition of citizens caused a series of policy reviews

Background   Jane Jacobs

Figure 5.20   Jane Jacobs, Urban Theorist

SOURCE: FRANK LENNON/GETSTOCK.COM

Jane Jacobs (1916–2006) was the most important writer and theorist on urban issues from the second half of the 20th century. She was born in Scranton, Pennsylvania, and moved to New York during the height of the Great Depression, earning a living as a writer and stenographer. She had two years of general studies at Columbia University, but she never completed a degree; she was entirely self-taught in her

fields. Perhaps this was why she could see new ideas and complex patterns in chaotic urban systems.

Jane married architect Robert Jacobs in 1944 and in 1952 began writing for the magazine *Architectural Forum*. Her stories on urban planning and urban renewal were based on close personal observation of downtown neighbourhoods. They challenged the conventional wisdom of the day as expressed in the Modernist doctrine of expressways, urban renewal, and large-scale public housing projects.

Jacobs' first book, *Death and Life of Great American Cities* (1961), has inspired two generations of planners and regularly tops lists of the most influential books on urban planning.[70] Ironically, shortly after it was published, her neighbourhood, West Greenwich Village, was scheduled for demolition for an expressway and an urban renewal program proposed by New York's "Master Builder" Robert Moses. Jacobs became a civic activist and leader in a famous fight to save the neighbourhood.[71] She succeeded, but grew disillusioned with life in New York.

Jane Jacobs and her family emigrated to Canada in 1968 and she lived over half her adult life in downtown Toronto. Here she published several other books on urban issues, including *The Economy of Cities* (1969), *Cities and the Wealth of Nations* (1984), *The Nature of Economies* (2000), and *Dark Age Ahead* (2004). Her ideas on urban economies have influenced the work of Richard Florida and Edward Glaeser.[72]

Shortly after Jacobs arrived in Toronto, her new neighbourhood, The Annex, was also targeted for demolition for the Spadina and Crosstown Expressways. Once again, she became a civic activist, rallying downtown residents to oppose the urban renewal programs. The 1975 cancellation of the Spadina Expressway was a watershed moment in Canadian urbanism. Along the way, Jacobs became an advisor to reform politicians; many became mayors, including David Crombie, John Sewell, Barbara Hall, and David Miller. Her planning ideas were directly implemented in Toronto's neighbourhood planning program, the design of the St. Lawrence neighbourhood and the removal of land use planning restrictions in the King-Parliament/King-Spadina districts, which led to their re-urbanization.

and a major change in Canadian urban renewal and housing policy in 1973 toward small-scale, more locally sensitive approaches.

The Neighbourhood Improvement Program (NIP) was one of the approaches that replaced slum clearance. Cities received small-scale grants to upgrade amenities and public infrastructure following Jane Jacobs's ideas. Public housing funding was phased out, and replaced by a range of programs for construction of cooperative and nonprofit housing. The Residential Rehabilitation Assistance Program (RRAP) upgraded existing housing. Municipalities combined these programs in innovative ways, leading to such projects as Vancouver's False Creek South and Winnipeg's Core Area Initiative.[73] These programs were driven by their social agenda for affordable housing, community control, and neighbourhood revitalization, and social planners were key members of the professional teams.

Many of the social housing and neighbourhood improvement programs were cancelled during the 1980s and early 1990s. A wave of conservative governments was elected at the federal and provincial levels, slashing housing, social services, and urban redevelopment programs to help reduce deficit spending. And what couldn't be cut was sometimes downloaded to other levels of government, until municipal budgets were near crisis. Eventually, the federal and some provincial governments began limited programs for housing in the most desperate situations after the numbers of homeless people sleeping in streets and public spaces of major cities became a national embarrassment.[74]

Social planners took up the safety issue, another of Jacobs's themes, starting in distressed public housing projects. While good aesthetics could not overcome poor social conditions, poor physical design could make a public housing project quite dangerous. Defensible space techniques were used to modify or redesign some projects, and identify others for demolition.[75] Feminist planners pushed safety higher up the planning agenda, and neighbourhoods, transit systems, and institutions were designed with Crime Prevention through Environmental Design (CPTED) techniques.[76] (See Chapter 15 for contemporary views on this topic.)

Healthy Communities

The last decade of the 20th century saw a revival of public health issues in community planning, starting with the Healthy Communities movement. The Canadian Institute of Planners, Canadian Public Health Association, and Federation of Canadian Municipalities vigorously adopted this program, which originated in the World Health Organization's (WHO) European office. The approach was different in each municipality, being guided by local priorities. Common themes included environmental clean-up, reduced pesticide use, emphasis on cycling and walking, and expanded community recreation programs.[77] But the local approach and social agenda of Healthy Communities were different from the public health crusades against epidemics led by doctors earlier in the century. The most recent connections between public health and community planning are more research-driven, as scholars investigate the effects of our "automobility"

The Globe and Mail
May 06, 2011

Jane Jacobs: Honoured in the Breach

Stephen Wickens

Jane Jacobs hated it when reporters called her an "urban guru." Once, when I made a mildly reverential comment about The Death and Life [*of Great American Cities*] she bristled, "Oh come on," and then unloaded: "Nice words from politicians, planners and columnists hardly matter when we continually repeat mistakes we made decades ago. It's like we made some progress, then hit a wall.

"Many places still have zoning laws on the books ensuring we repeat the mistakes. The bureaucratic machinery enforces bad planning and design, and nobody thinks to question a property-tax system that encourages sprawl and all its hidden costs."

She had no time for ideology - left, right or whatever - and felt that many who invoke her name "cherry-pick ideas to suit their purposes."

That urban planners had eventually come to accept the benefits of density was no consolation: "In the absence of a pedestrian scale, density can be big trouble." Few people, she felt, saw what she really meant.

Vancouver planning chief Brent Toderian, author James Howard Kunstler and former Toronto mayor John Sewell all sympathize with Ms. Jacobs's frustrations, but they seem more optimistic about her likely legacy.

"There isn't a person or book more influential in creating 'Vancouverism' than Jane and *The Death and Life*," says Mr. Toderian. "I know what she means about people misunderstanding density - that's why we emphasize density done well rather than density as a mathematical exercise. [But] people 'round the world praise Vancouver's livability, and she had a big hand in it."

Mr. Kunstler, known for the 1993 bestseller *The Geography of Nowhere*, says we still develop badly because politics inhibit "changing the predictable rules of a very profitable game." But he expects Ms. Jacobs's effect to increase as urban crises erupt in coming decades: "She might not be fully appreciated until 2061, but nobody threw a cocktail party for Galileo in his time."

Mr. Sewell says it's "tragic" that politicians merely pay her lip service: "In Ontario, I'm aware of no provincial policies and no official plans that reflect some of the key points she raised." But he sees hope in "the simplicity and applicability" of her approach.

"What she's saying is: Forget the theories. If you want to make really good cities, go out and look for yourself at good parts of cities, places that feel right. Figure out why they work, then replicate them."

Canadian-raised architect and author Witold Rybczynski, , complains that she had gaping holes in her historical knowledge, overestimated planners' influence and underestimated suburbia's lure. Still, he calls *The Death and Life* "the dominant book about planning of the second half of the 20th century, perhaps of the entire century."

About that buried thesis

There are more intertwined concepts in The Death and Life than any newspaper story can outline.

· But page 150, lists four conditions for any part of a city to generate "exuberant diversity": that districts have a mix of primary uses; that most blocks be short; that buildings be of various ages; and that the area have sufficient density. It was indispensable that these areas accommodate various levels of income and commercial rents.

But simply to list the factors without the examples and complicated dynamics found in the book is almost to miss the point.

"If you've read to the last chapter," she told me, "you know cities—their parks, transportation planning, development policy, density ratios ... are, like the life sciences, problems of organized complexity. It's no good wishing it were any other way."

Thus, when I asked Random House's Jason Epstein whether the 50th anniversary might occasion not only a new edition but something more 21st century—an interactive website or multimedia version—Ms. Jacobs' long-time editor said he feared it would be superficial.

"Jane's work is really a very subtle attempt to show how civilizations form, whether on the scale of neighbourhoods or eons. This would be hard to convey in a different format."

Hard, yes. But to ensure the afterlife of *The Death and Life*, someone will have to find a route to the "mixed use" of Ms. Jacobs's ideas. It's no good wishing it were any other way.

Source: © Stephen Wickens. Used with permission.

and suburban environments on air quality and obesity.[78] It is not yet clear whether our suburbs make us fat, but the connection between community design and public health may give additional traction to urban health issues. The effect of a small urban epidemic—the 2003 Toronto SARS outbreak—reinforced the public's understanding of the need for public health planning.[79] The Canadian planning profession then began to reach out to public health agencies and researchers to make Healthy Communities a major policy initiative (Figure 5.21). The first initiatives in many communities were efforts to improve the use of active transportation—walking and cycling. Public health units and planning departments made common cause to advocate for better pedestrian and cycling facilities.[80]

Social activism on housing and slum-clearance issues changed the nature and techniques of community planning during the 1970s. The planning schools filled with social scientists and design studios almost disappeared. In the municipal planning offices, social planners were hired and community organizers often replaced the architects and engineers who ran the urban renewal projects. Citizen participation and advocacy planning techniques were developed to engage the community in the planning process (see Chapters 14 and 15). By the end of the century, social planning had begun to reconsider the importance of the community design through safety and public health issues. And social activists made strong connections to environmental advocates through the concept of sustainable development.

| Figure 5.21 | OPPI Healthy Communities Policy Paper |

The Ontario Professional Planners Institute made Healthy and Sustainable Communities a major policy focus after 2006, linking with the Ontario government and the Heart and Stroke Foundation.

Concern over the Environment

The environment became a major Canadian planning focus again in the 1970s, more than a half-century after the demise of the Commission of Conservation. Although some river basin planning occurred in post-war Ontario and on the Saint John, South Saskatchewan, and Fraser Rivers, it took Rachel Carson's *Silent Spring* (in 1962), which warned of the dangers of pesticides and other chemical pollution of the natural environment, to revive the North American environmental conservation movement.[81]

Environmental Planning: Designing with Nature

Yet another path-breaking book, Ian McHarg's *Design with Nature* (Figure 5.22), established a method for environmental planning.[82] Taking a lead from Patrick Geddes's valley section (see Figure 8.1, page 187), McHarg drew transects through natural regions to analyze how ecological processes might interact with human activity. More importantly, he prepared maps of ecological, physiographic, and socioeconomic features that were overlaid to identify the areas of least environmental impact for urban expansion and highway projects. The evaluation factors were originally mapped on layers of clear plastic acetate; McHarg's method was later converted into computer use as an early version of Geographic Information Systems (GIS).

The federal and provincial governments, in the mid-1970s, all adopted environmental impact assessment (EIA) or environmental assessment (EA) processes. New provincially chartered regional planning agencies, such as the B.C. Agricultural Land Commission and the Niagara Escarpment Commission, protected large-scale agricultural and environmental features under stress from urbanization (see Chapter 8). A new cadre of environmental planners was trained to run the environmental agencies and manage the EIA and EA processes, often producing alternative development scenarios. The ecological basis for environmental planning improved steadily in the final two decades of the century. Landscape ecology developed more advanced techniques to design large regions for improved biodiversity,[83] and these techniques were applied to large urban regions such as Ottawa (Figure 5.23) and Hamilton, and smaller suburban areas such as Markham.[84]

Environmental planning came to entire metropolitan areas with the work of Michael Hough and his attention to the ecological values of urban open-space systems

Figure 5.22   Ian McHarg

SOURCE: BOB PETERSON/TIME LIFE PICTURES/GETTY IMAGES

Rachel Carson's *Silent Spring* (1962) started the widespread environmental conservation movement, but Ian McHarg's *Design with Nature* (1969) is perhaps the most influential environmental planning book of the 20th century. McHarg combined passionate advocacy for natural systems with a practical method for environmental planning, using map layers as shown above.

and incorporating natural processes into urban development. Good planning practice now protects environmentally sensitive areas such as wetlands, connects parks and river valleys with greenways, and incorporates stormwater ponds into neighbourhood open space. Degraded urban valleys such as Toronto's Don River are being rehabilitated and re-naturalized, and involve extensive citizen participation.[85] Hough also had a major influence on the Crombie Royal Commission on the Toronto waterfront, pushing it to expand its frame of reference to the entire Toronto bioregion (see Figure 8.4, page 193).[86]

SOURCE: NATURAL ENVIRONMENT SYSTEMS STRATEGY, REVIEW OF THE NATURAL ENVIRONMENT IN OTTAWA-CARLETON POSTER, REGIONAL MUNICIPALITY OF OTTAWA-CARLETON PLANNING AND PROPERTY DEPARTMENT, FEBRUARY 1995. CITY OF OTTAWA ARCHIVES/2008.0190.1/0013.11

Figure 5.23	Environmental Planning Process for the 1999 Ottawa-Carleton Regional Plan

ASSESS EXISTING INFORMATION

COMPLETE REGIONAL DATA BASE

FORESTS
SOILS
RARE SPECIES
STREAMS

WE ARE HERE

DEFINE A BASIS FOR ASSESSING IMPORTANCE THROUGH TECHNICAL REVIEW & PUBLIC DISCUSSION

DEVELOP INITIAL OPTIONS WITH IMPORTANT NATURAL AREAS & CONNECTIONS

NATURAL AREAS
CONNECTIONS
RARE SPECIES

REFINE THE INFORMATION BASE - FIELD WORK

DEVELOP A PROPOSED NATURAL ENVIRONMENT SYSTEM & RELATED POLICIES

POLICY

The environmental planning process for the 1999 Ottawa-Carleton regional plan was based on principles developed by Ian McHarg and Michael Hough. A sophisticated GIS allowed the regional planners to develop options that incorporated important natural areas and connections. The ecological planning was done first, and the natural environment system strategy formed the foundation for the regional land use planning.

Landscape Urbanism emerged as a new theme early in the new century, combining avant-garde urban design and landscape ecology. Its proponents argue that landscape, rather than architecture, is a better foundation for urban design. Landscape urbanists pushed for large-scale interventions at the regional level, such as river delta and coastline management for climate change. They also advocated urban open-space design with an ecological foundation, such as Toronto's Downsview Park and the natural features put into Manhattan's rehabilitated High Line Park on a former railway viaduct.[87]

Brownfield redevelopment is another theme in current environmental planning practice, focusing on the rehabilitation of former industrial sites that often contain contaminated lands. Most Canadian cities have brownfield sites, as a result of the migration of industries from old downtown and waterfront sites to new and larger sites served by expressways on the urban periphery. If the contamination issues can be addressed, brownfield sites often have the potential for new commercial and residential development that can take advantage of existing infrastructure and improve the context of adjacent downtown neighbourhoods.[88] Redevelopment of former industrial sites is not a new idea, but extensive and expensive remediation of contaminated lands is a characteristic of projects such as Victoria's Dockside Green, Ottawa's LeBreton Flats, Montréal's Angus Yards, and the Moncton Yards.[89] Innovative financial tools are slowly emerging to make these brownfield projects more competitive with new greenfield development.[90]

Sustainable Development

Environmental planning, social planning, and economic development came together in the 1990s as sustainable development. The 1987 Report of the World Commission on Environment and Development (often called the Brundtland report) defined sustainable development as "ensur[ing] that [development] meets the needs of the present without compromising the ability of future generations to meet their own needs."[91] This broad concept became a primary goal in many Canadian community plans at the end of the 20th century, pushed along by public concerns about global warming, climate change, and other future legacies. Individuals and communities were invited to reduce their "ecological footprint"—the size of the natural area required to sustain the impact of their lifestyle on the environment.[92] As the new century began, many cities were examining how their community plans might improve sustainability, and ecological planning became a standard component of Canadian planning practice, as we shall see in Chapter 7. The Greater Vancouver Regional District has cast most of its activities, including planning, under the umbrella of its Sustainable Region Initiative.[93] Ottawa's greenbelt has been re-planned as an ecological feature rather than merely an urban separator,[94] and the Oak Ridges moraine is being protected as the north boundary of the Greater Toronto Area.[95]

Although ecological planning has become standard practice, Canadian communities are still experimenting with planning policies that might address the long-term impacts of climate change.[96] The CIP has shown some leadership on this issue, sponsoring conferences and case studies such as Prince George, B.C.'s climate change adaptation strategy, Waterfront Toronto's carbon tool, and the Tantramar Dykelands infrastructure.[97]

Concern over City Efficiency

Physical infrastructure construction literally paved the way for the metropolitan expansion in the post–World War II era. Like the CIAM architects, the civil engineers had earlier developed new prototypes for urban growth but had little opportunity to deploy the expressways and regional utility networks during the period of depression and war. A new generation of engineers was taught the techniques of municipal utilities, traffic engineering, and transportation planning, and was given an opportunity to build infrastructure on a scale unrivalled since the railway boom a half-century before.

Infrastructure Planning

The utility work to support metropolitan expansion, in the 1950s and beyond, started with 19th century technology. Most Canadian cities were providing treated water for drinking and firefighting in pressurized pipes throughout most of the inner city. These areas often had combined sanitary and storm sewers that drained into the nearest water body, hopefully downstream of the water treatment plant. Meanwhile, adjacent rural townships usually could not afford piped services, so most of the scattered pre-war suburbs relied on wells, septic tanks, and privies. The Prairie cities had sewage treatment plants in place before the war, and other inland Canadian communities were forced to treat their sewage after 1945, when rapid metropolitan expansion put tremendous strain on adjacent water bodies. The Ottawa River was basically an open sewer downstream from the national capital in the 1950s, and the federal government contributed to intercepting sewers and a primary treatment plant as part of the National Capital Commission's program. Federal infrastructure assistance was extended nationally when CMHC made grants for water and sewer plants from 1960 to 1980. The provincial governments started to contribute, beginning with the Ontario Water Resources Commission, in 1956.[98]

Stormwater planning also saw a major change in the post-war period. Many of the new suburbs required separate storm sewers to collect rainfall and discharge it to local streams and rivers rather than mix it with the sanitary waste that was treated in the new plants. More sophisticated hydrological models allowed planners to predict the flow of rivers after a storm and identify areas prone to flooding. Municipal land use plans then prohibited future development in flood zones, or rebuilding in the worst areas after a disaster. Major floods gave special emphasis to disaster planning, with Edmonton and Toronto protecting their valleys, while a major floodway was built to bypass Winnipeg, where much of the city was occasionally endangered by the Red River (Figure 5.24).

Large-scale suburban development required reforms to local government organization and financing for trunk sewer and water infrastructure. At Don Mills, E.P. Taylor demonstrated that a large-scale developer could provide the local water mains and sewers that previously had been built by a municipality. He even contributed to a sewage treatment plant on the Don River. But some form of large-scale capital financing was needed for regional water-treatment plants, trunk mains, and major roads; the tax base of the rural townships in the region could not provide it. The regional metropolitan governments described in Chapter 9 were, in many respects, innovations for infrastructure construction. The regional governments could issue bonds to finance the big pipes and roads out of future revenues; the developers built the local roads and pipes to city standards and handed them over as part of the land subdivision process (see Chapter 13).

Transportation Planning for the Automobile

The metropolitan boom of the 1950s and 1960s was facilitated by a thoroughly planned expansion of road networks and parking to support automobile use. The transportation planners prepared detailed specifications for all elements of the vehicular network. Zoning bylaws required houses to have garages, and all commercial and institutional uses to have parking and loading spaces. Community and regional plans reserved land to widen existing roads and protected corridors for future arterials and expressways. New industrial parks were planned near suburban expressway interchanges, for easy truck access, with zoning requirements for employee parking. Downtown redevelopment plans showed large new parking facilities built at public expense. And most municipalities adopted infrastructure standards that required wide roads, high-quality pavements, and generously sized parking spaces to make driving fast, cheap, and convenient, especially compared to public transit. These plans were quite popular and had broad political support because, at first, they worked. A high-speed drive on an uncongested expressway through a major city could be an exhilarating experience in the early 1960s.[99]

Figure 5.24 | "Duff's Ditch"—The Manitoba Floodway

Most of Winnipeg is built within the flood plains of the Red and Assiniboine Rivers. The city was heavily damaged in the 1950 flood, and Manitoba premier Duff Roblin was ridiculed for spending millions of dollars to build a diversion channel east of the city. However, the floodway has saved the city from inundation several times. It narrowly contained flood flows in 1997, when an additional rise of half a metre would likely have overwhelmed Winnipeg's diking system and caused several billion dollars in damages. So the floodway was expanded over the past decade.

Toronto had a draft metropolitan expressway plan prepared in 1943 by Eugene Faludi, and other Canadian communities prepared transportation plans in the 1950s and 1960s using increasingly sophisticated computer models imported from the U.S. to analyze traffic flows associated with various land use scenarios. The recommendations typically called for a regional network of expressways supported by a grid of arterial roads. The

expressways allowed rapid travel throughout the urban area, and were built through suburban farmland, down valleys, and along corridors through under-utilized land along waterfronts and rail lines. But in the inner urban areas, the connecting links had to be built in trenches (Montréal's Decarie Expressway), on stilts (Toronto's Gardiner Expressway), or in corridors created by demolishing houses, using urban renewal as a pretext. Ottawa's proposed King Edward Expressway required expropriation and demolition of most of Lowertown East (Figure 5.25).

The urban renewal techniques caused citizens' revolts that stopped expressway construction before it began in Vancouver, in mid-flight in Toronto, and deflected two highways into Ottawa's greenbelt. Toronto's experience was perhaps the most dramatic, drawing strength from successful freeway revolts in San Francisco and Boston. The Stop Spadina movement defeated a proposal to extend an expressway into downtown Toronto through a ravine and a stable residential neighbourhood.[100] The elevated Scarborough Expressway was literally halted in mid-air just short of the Beach neighbourhood (see Figure 5.26). Canadian cities were left with significantly smaller expressway networks than their American counterparts.[101]

Figure 5.25 | Ottawa's Lowertown: Urban Renewal for an Expressway

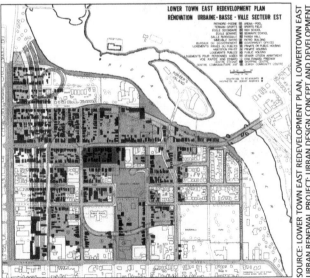

Ottawa Lowertown Urban Renewal Plan. The proposed King Edward Expressway is at left. The expressway was later cancelled, but the damage to the community was done, since many of the expropriated houses were demolished.

| Figure 5.26 | Public Art: Scarborough Expressway Pillars |

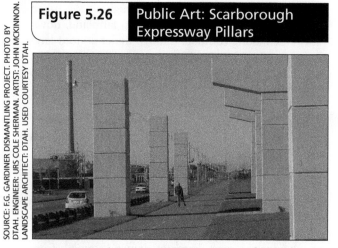

The end of the Scarborough Expressway. This elevated freeway was demolished in the late 1990s and replaced with a boulevard and bike path. Some of the expressway pillars were left as a monument to a previous era.

Transit Planning

In the late 1970s, transportation planning in larger Canadian communities placed more emphasis on public transit. The transit systems had never been completely abandoned in the major cities. Toronto retained its signature streetcars after the war, and started construction of North America's first new subway system in 1954. It also adjusted its land use policies to promote high-density re-redevelopment around stations such as Yonge–Eglinton, and development of transit-supported city centres in suburban Scarborough and North York. These measures helped keep Toronto's per capita transit ridership higher than any North American city until the 1990s.[102] Montréal built its subway for the 1967 World's Fair, and continued to expand it over the next two decades. The central business districts of both cities developed extensive networks of underground passages lined with shops, interconnecting the office buildings and subway stations.[103]

Edmonton (1978), Calgary (1981), and Vancouver (1986) each developed Light Rail Transit (LRT) systems, and, in 1983, Ottawa developed North America's most effective busway rapid transit system.[104] But the pace of construction of transit systems slowed during the public financial crisis toward the end of the century, and transit's share of work trips continues to decline. Moreover, Canadian cities have had little success in attracting transit-oriented development (TOD) around the suburban LRT stations as had been advocated (more on this in Chapter 12).[105]

Environmental Issues and Smart Growth

Infrastructure issues became more aligned with environmental issues in the last decades of the century. There was a brief burst of planning for energy efficiency after the 1973 oil crisis,[106] but it died away as prices stabilized. Declining air quality and increasing road congestion, however, dragged infrastructure issues back onto the public agenda. Increased automobile use is closely connected to urban air-quality issues; and as the 21st century began, urban Canadians began to hear about smog days and ozone alerts. Suburban road congestion proved to be a particularly intractable problem since there are usually few alternatives to driving for most trips in these areas.[107]

Infrastructure planning, sustainable development, and New Urbanism came together in the Smart Growth Network established in the mid-1990s by the U.S. Environmental Protection Agency and Congress for the New Urbanism. Smart Growth has proved to be politically appealing, advocating infill and brownfield development in inner cities, and compact suburban development and preservation of ecological systems ("green plans") in suburban areas.[108] The American approach, pioneered in Maryland and Portland, has been largely based on state and federal incentives, due to their weaker metropolitan and regional planning agencies. Smart Growth has also been a useful umbrella policy in British Columbia and Ontario for brownfield development, New Urbanism, transit-oriented development, and ecosystems planning, but with limited results.[109]

Reviving Canadian Planning Institutions after 1945

Community planning did not quite disappear in Canada during the Great Depression and World War II. A number of infrastructure projects and some rural planning initiatives were undertaken during the Depression years (see Chapters 4 and 9). More importantly, the economic crisis inspired some innovative thinking about social planning, most notably by the **League for Social Reconstruction** (LSR). The LSR comprised some of the country's leading intellectuals, including Humphrey Carver, King Gordon, Leonard Marsh, Frank Scott, and Frank Underhill. Their 1935 report, *Social Planning for Canada*,[110] was a comprehensive review of Canadian conditions that proposed much of the post-war social safety net—unemployment insurance, pensions, and health care. Community planning (although then called town planning) was also regarded as part of a progressive social planning agenda.[111]

The need to deal with slum housing conditions was actively pursued throughout the 1930s by a cadre of socially minded architects, social workers, planners, and citizens, led by Humphrey Carver.[112] In 1939, this group encouraged people from across Canada to hold a national housing conference on the problems of slum housing. Among the participants were George Mooney of the Canadian Federation of Mayors and Municipalities, planner Horace Seymour, Vancouver city councillor Grace MacInnis, Nova Scotian S.H. Prince, and Leonard Marsh, who would later be the principal author of the 1944 federal committee's report on housing and planning. This conference clearly demonstrated the wide support for what Carver called "social housing" or, simply, the concept that government should be responsible for the provision of adequate housing for all Canadians regardless of income.

In 1944, with the end of World War II in sight, the federal government began to consider the future, hoping to avoid another post-war recession as had occurred after World War I. The government established a powerful Advisory Committee on Post-War Reconstruction, which was chaired by McGill president Cyril James. It prepared an economic and social plan for the future, including what the authors called "community planning" (see Chapter 1). Many important elements of the post-war planning agenda were set out in its 1944 subcommittee report *Housing and Community Planning*, prepared by Queen's University economist Clifford Curtis and social planner Leonard Marsh. The Curtis subcommittee noted extensive "congestion, deterioration, misuse and blight" in Canadian communities.[113] It recommended broad-scale housing programs to accommodate the backlog of housing demands caused by the Depression and the war, new housing to meet projected population growth, and the renewal of over 100 000 dwellings in the older parts of cities. It also alerted governments at all levels to the need for comprehensive community planning, including the establishment of a federal Town Planning Bureau, a program of public education, and professional training programs for planners at universities. Out of the idea for a Town Planning Bureau came the **Central (now Canada) Mortgage and Housing Corporation** (CMHC), which subsequently fostered community and university planning education programs, as well as housing and planning research, and undertook the provision of housing for the poor and programs of urban renewal.

CMHC took an active role in reviving the planning profession in the post-war period. Graduate planning programs were funded at McGill (1947), Manitoba (1949), UBC (1950), and Toronto (1951), and student scholarships were provided for over 50 years. The agency helped revive the Town Planning Institute of Canada (TPIC) in 1952. CMHC also established its own planning branch, staffed it with many expatriate British planners, and produced many useful planning reports.[114] The agency also commissioned pure and applied research on community planning, a role that continued until 2011.

Developing a Role for Citizens

The Curtis subcommittee also strongly recommended involving citizens in the planning of their own communities. The approach they suggested would, today, be considered paternalistic: that is, "to struggle against public inertia . . . people will accept and support what they can understand." It was, however, a new initiative in Canadian community planning. There had been various citizen movements prior to this time to lobby for civic needs in public health, housing, local government organization, and beautification, and even groups of property owners (ratepayers) to protest planning measures. But they did not play a continuing role within the planning process. What was envisioned were citizen groups that could be "educated" and energized to support the proposals of the planners. For example, the Toronto Citizens' Housing and Planning Association, led by Harold Clark, which had been organized in 1944, was instrumental in securing the Regent Park slum-clearance project.

The recommendations of the Curtis Committee were embodied in the 1944 version of the National Housing Act and called upon CMHC to promote public interest in planning. The outcome of this was the formation of the **Community Planning Association of Canada** (CPAC) in 1946. It was a national organization, with provincial and local branches, that was largely underwritten by CMHC. For 30 years, CPAC provided a forum in which citizens, planners, and politicians could discuss the needs of Canadian communities. Although, as Carver notes, "CPAC did not evolve into an instrument of local activism" as did later citizen efforts,[115] it did provide a springboard for many good ideas, and for individuals to become knowledgeable about planning and to participate vigorously inside and outside CPAC. No little credit for this is due to Alan Armstrong, the association's director for the first decade and the editor of their influential journal, *Community Planning Review*. As well, CPAC was a more inclusive organization than the professional planners' institute, TPIC.

Susan Hendler's research has shown that women made up about 40 percent of CPAC's membership and some of its national council (Figure 5.27) during a period when there were few women members of the TPIC.[116] This "dammed-up reservoir of talent" sometimes had considerable influence over the direction of post-war Canadian planning at the national level as well as in the communities in which they lived.[117]

The Progress of Citizen Participation

For a variety of reasons, there was dissatisfaction over the outcome of much planning in the 1945–65 period. In coping with vast urban growth, the planning solutions were often large-scale and disruptive: expressways sliced through residential and park areas, old neighbourhoods were levelled for new office and apartment complexes or public-housing projects, and new shopping centres either displaced old commercial areas or dispersed the new populations, or both. Moreover, the solution to one planning problem not infrequently created other problems for which "more of the same" seemed to

| Figure 5.27 | CPAC Female Councillors, 1967 |

In 1967, the CPAC's female councillors included (left to right) Elsie Shepherd (B.C.), Barbara Lambert (Ottawa), and Lynn Elliott Good (Kingston). Lin Good would be the only woman elected President of CPAC.

many citizens to be the planners' prescription. Proposals by planners began to be questioned, often vociferously, by ordinary citizens and neighbourhood groups. Terms such as "citizen activism," "participatory democracy," "advocacy planning," and "NIMBY" were coined.

Throughout Canada, planning proposals became issues for public debate. Some protests were protracted and rancorous. Many of the disputes became nationally known and celebrated in books.[118] Their names were synonymous with the victory or defeat of planning ideas, depending upon which side one was on: the Pacific Centre in Vancouver, Sunnyside in Calgary, Trefann Court in Toronto, Lower Town in Ottawa, Concordia Village in Montréal, and Quinpool Road in Halifax, to cite some of the well-known ones. As citizen participation became more pervasive, it stimulated a number of significant changes in the conduct of community planning. Some were formal, such as new provisions that were written into provincial planning acts to ensure avenues for public comment and consultation. Many municipalities instituted new channels of communication with citizens' groups and, in general, made their planning processes more open with public meetings, newsletters, open houses, design charrettes, and so forth; none more so than Vancouver.

These latter moves increasingly involved citizens in the preparation of plans, of articulating objectives and proposing alternatives. They also opened up for debate the question of how to move citizens farther up the "ladder of citizen participation" Arnstein had proposed in 1968;[119] that is, the role for citizens in getting plans carried out rather than just offering advice. This, in turn, led to extensive discussion of new methods of participation, such as consensus-building, and the related issue of the inclusiveness of planning processes to involve women, the physically impaired, ethnic populations, the elderly, and so on. In other words, the traditional participants—the politicians, the planners, other bureaucrats, and politically well-connected groups—began to shift their positions in order to accommodate citizens at the plan-making table. (See also Chapter 12.)

Growth of the Planning Profession

When the TPIC was revived in 1952, there were fewer than 30 professional planners employed in public planning agencies in Canada, and it is likely that no more than twice that number comprised all the planners in the country, including private consultants.[120] The professional institute slowly rebuilt itself, with the assistance and encouragement of CMHC and CPAC. Local chapters were started in most provinces, the TPIC annual conference was revived, and in 1959 the institute launched an ambitious new journal, *Plan Canada*, which combined academic and professional articles on Canadian planning.[121] By 1961, the number of planners in Canada had grown to over 300, and to more than 600 by 1967. By the latter date, almost all municipalities with a population over 25 000 had their own professional planning staffs, nine provinces had planners on staff, and there were nearly 100 private firms of consulting planners.

This demand for trained planners was met in three ways. The first was to shift people who had been associated with planning and development as engineers, architects, surveyors, and landscape architects into full-time planning jobs. The second way was to recruit from other countries, primarily Great Britain; CMHC obtained many of its early staff members in this way, many of whom subsequently went on to private and other public agencies. The third way was to recruit from the new professional planning education programs in Canada. By 1972, there were 11 different programs, including undergraduate degrees from the University of Waterloo and Ryerson Polytechnic University. The Canadian university programs in community planning and closely associated fields were supplying almost all the staffing needs for professional planners by the beginning of the 1970s, as they do today.

Membership in the Canadian Institute of Planners in 2009 was reported at over 7000, and its gender composition had changed radically since the 1950s—women comprised 53 percent of the new CIP members and 40 percent overall.[122] More than half of these planners work for governments, mainly at the municipal and other local levels, and over a third work as consultants, developers, or advisors in private business. The latter figures show not only the growth of the profession generally but also its increasing presence in other public and semi-public agencies, bringing the latter the capacity to frame development proposals. Sometimes, as seen in Chapter 17, this new capacity competes with a city's own planning program. Thus, the institutional perspective for community planning is both an evolving situation and one that is becoming ever more complex.

As the Canadian planning profession matured and its institutional perspective grew more complex, the role of the professional planner in society became more complicated. In the 1980s, the CIP adopted a "Statement of Values" to reflect the core values of planning (Chapter 1), and several provincial affiliates adopted codes of ethics to guide professional practice.[123] The CIP has recently been tightening membership standards, school accreditation policies, and continuing education requirements to match the public interest requirements of other modern professions such as law, medicine, and engineering.

Finally, the scope and sophistication of Canadian community planning gradually widened from 1950 to 2010. In the immediate post-war period, Canadian planners were engaged in rolling out well-established American models of the suburban dream and inner-city urban renewal, all guided by Modern planning principles. Many Canadian planners were still engaged in traditional suburban land use planning practice at the turn of the century, but the profession had expanded to include many other topics. The CIP National Planning Awards program, established in 1983, soon had multiple categories that included urban design, social planning, environmental planning, and infrastructure, reflecting the four broad themes described in these last three chapters (concern over city appearance, living conditions, environment, and efficiency), while *Plan Canada* looked forward with new attention to healthy communities, multiculturalism, and climate change.[124] This expanded range of Canadian community planning concerns will be explored in the chapters ahead.

New Planning Tools

Several provinces refurbished their planning acts in the post-1945 period, the most notable being Ontario's Planning Act of 1946. This legislation did not so much invent new planning approaches as consolidate the concepts and experience gained previously, and establish a clear and workable framework for municipal land use planning. It also made the preparation of comprehensive land use plans a *required* activity for most cities, rather than a *permitted* one. The act's framework is still largely intact today and has been much copied by the other provinces. Its main features provide for:

1. the creation of planning units, usually one or more municipalities.;
2. preparing, adopting, and approving "official plans," as well as specifying the legal effect of these statutory plans;
3. a system of subdivision control;
4. the delegation of powers to municipalities to enact zoning bylaws;

5. a quasi-judicial appeal procedure with respect to municipal planning decisions;
6. a plan-making body composed of citizens—the planning board—to advise municipal council;
7. involvement and education of the public through public meetings at various points in the planning process.

A comparison of provincial planning parameters is found in Figure 9.8, page 230.

The spate of planning activity that took place in the two decades after World War II is amply illustrated by Ontario's experience. In 1946, only 36 municipalities had established themselves as planning areas, only one municipality had an official plan, and only one had a comprehensive zoning bylaw. Within a decade, 200 more communities were in planning areas, 57 had official plans, and 48 had zoning bylaws. By 1965, over half of the municipalities were in planning areas, and 75 percent of the province's population was covered by official plans in effect in municipalities. And in each of the decades from 1946 to 1955 and from 1956 to 1965, almost 10 000 subdivision plans were processed as nearly three million people were added to the Ontario population.[125]

An important addition to the planner's kit of tools during the 1950s was that of **development control**. Development control is an extension of the power that municipalities possess to undertake zoning and gives them the right to review proposed plans for new development in already built-up areas. Many other tools were added in the decades ahead. (See also Chapters 16 and 17.)

The post-war advocacy for community planning by the Curtis Report, CPAC, and CMHC was remarkably successful. By the end of the 20th century, every Canadian city and town had a comprehensive land use plan and zoning bylaw, and provincial legislation requires that the plans be kept up to date.[126] Community planning is a *mandatory* municipal activity in Canada, which is a major difference from the United States, where it is an *optional* activity in most states. For better or worse, the suburban nation that Canadians built after 1950 is largely a planned community.

Reflections

The planning practice we witness today is an amalgam of accumulated knowledge and experience, especially those of the second half of the 20th century. This most recent period showed both growth and maturity for community planning, its institutions, and its participants. What may

have appeared half a century ago, perhaps naively, as a means of "curing the ills" of the city had, toward the end of the century, become its own set of social, economic, and environmental realities to contend with. In the process, planning became an accepted, institutionalized part of community-building. There would not likely be much support today to discontinue planning activities. Further, planners are now much better equipped to know what does and doesn't work.

The legacy of these formative decades just past should not be forgotten, for it is the continuing foundation for today's practice of community planning. Nor should we forget that planning arrangements, tools, and processes are *normative*. Assumptions about the best way to proceed and who needs to be involved are built into them. And arriving at those assumptions, in the 1945–2010 period, involved a learning process for all participants to recognize better both the substantive aspects of how communities develop and the social relationships among participants. Wholesale urban renewal—bulldozing the slums—gave way to more incremental approaches to improve the built environment. Planners also came, somewhat grudgingly at times, to realize that citizens, even in their opposition, could make useful contributions to planning situations (as well as recognize their rights as citizens). Not least, the vital importance of caring for the natural environments of communities was accepted into the planning milieu. Community planning practice is different and richer today as a result of all these changes.

This was also a period in which the larger social dynamic shifted from a Modern to a post-modern view of the world. Big was not always better, and eclecticism became a norm in community-building as elsewhere. There will continue to be changes in community plan-making, but perhaps not as momentous as those experienced since 1945. Community planning will doubtless be called upon to respond to new issues, because it deals with values and norms, with new ideas and social forces. So, as one views contemporary community-planning practice, as presented in the next several chapters, it will be useful to consider two questions:

- *Do community planning tools, processes, and institutions reflect appropriately the needs of today's communities and their populations?*

- *How is a gated community like Figure 5.19 any different from an apartment building with a doorkeeper?*

Reference Notes

1. Leroy Stone, *Urban Development in Canada* (Ottawa: Dominion Bureau of Statistics, 1969), 39.
2. The Editors of Fortune, *The Exploding Metropolis* (New York: Doubleday, 1958).
3. David Gordon and Mark Janzen, "Suburban Nation? Estimating the Size of Canada's Suburban Population;" ACUPP/ Canadian Association of Geographers conference, Calgary, 2011; see also Trudi Bunting, Pierre Filion, and H. Priston, "Density Gradients in Canadian Metropolitan Regions, 1971–1996," *Urban Studies* 39:13 (2002), 2531–2552, Table 1 and Table 5.
4. David Foot and Daniel Stoffman, *Boom, Bust and Echo 2000* (Toronto: McFarlane, Walter & Ross, 2000).
5. Albert Rose, *Problems of Canadian City Growth* (Ottawa: CPAC, 1950).
6. Foot and Stoffman, *Boom, Bust and Echo.*
7. Gerald Hodge, *The Geography of Aging: Preparing Communities for the Surge in Seniors* (Montréal: McGill-Queen's University Press, 2008).
8. Editors of Fortune, *The Exploding Metropolis,* 53.
9. IBI Group and Richard Soberman, *National Vision for Urban Transit to 2020* (Ottawa: Transport Canada, 2001), Ex. 1.1.
10. Richard Harris, *Creeping Conformity: How Canada Became Suburban, 1900–1960* (Toronto: University of Toronto Press, 2004*).*
11. Jeanne Wolfe, "Our Common Past: An Interpretation of Canadian Planning History," *Plan Canada* 34:4 (July 1994), 23.
12. John Miron, *Housing in Postwar Canada: Demographic Change, Household Formation and Housing Demand* (Kingston & Montréal: McGill-Queen's University Press, 1988), Table 1 and p. 168.
13. Albert Rose, *Problems.*
14. Canada Mortgage and Housing Corporation, *Canadian Housing Observer* (2011), Table 2.
15. David Gordon and Mark Janzen, "Suburban Nation?"
16. Bauhaus directors Walther Gropius and Mies Van der Rohe relocated to Harvard and the Illinois Institute of Technology in the 1940s and CIAM secretary J.L. Sert became dean of the Harvard Graduate School of Design in the 1950s; see Eric Mumford, *The CIAM Discourse on Urbanism, 1928–1960* (Cambridge, MA: MIT Press, 2000).
17. Canada, Central Mortgage and Housing Corporation, *Housing and Urban Growth in Canada* (Ottawa, 1956), 9.
18. Albert Rose, *Regent Park: A Study in Slum Clearance* (Toronto, University of Toronto Press, 1958); and Peter Oberlander and Eva Newbrun, *Houser: The Life and Work of Catherine Bauer, 1905–1964* (Vancouver, BC: UBC Press, 1999).
19. Gordon Stephenson, in C. DeMarco, ed., *On a Human Scale: A Life in City Design* (Fremantle, WA: Fremantle Arts Centre Press, 1992); see also the special issue on Stephenson in *Town Planning Review* 83:3 (March 2012).
20. Gordon Stephenson, *A Redevelopment Study of Halifax, Nova Scotia* (Toronto: University of Toronto Press, 1957); George Muirhead, *A Planning Study of Kingston, Ontario* (City of Kingston, 1957); D. Guard, *Urban Renewal London, Ontario* (City of London, 1960); see also David Gordon and Michelle Nicolson, "Beyond the Tabula Rasa: Gordon Stephenson and Urban Renewal in Kingston, Ontario," *Town Planning Review* 83:3 (2012), 337–354.
21. Jane Jacobs, *The Death and Life of Great American Cities* (New York: Random House, 1961); and Herbert Gans, *The Urban Villagers: Group and Class in the Life of Italian-Americans* (New York: Free Press, 1962).
22. Magill, D.W., *Africville: The Life and Death of a Canadian Community* (Toronto: McClelland and Stewart, 1999), *3rd edn.*; see also Jill Grant and Marcus Paterson, "Scientific Cloak/Romantic Heart: Gordon Stephenson and the Redevelopment Study of Halifax, 1957," *Town Planning Review* 83:3 (2012), 319–336.
23. Alice Coleman, *Utopia on Trial: Vision and Reality in Planned Housing* (London: H. Shipman, 1990).
24. Jane Jacobs, *Death and Life.*
25. John Sewell, *The Shape of the City: Toronto Struggles with Modern Planning* (Toronto: University of Toronto Press, 1993); and Claire Hellman, *The Milton Park Affair: Canada's Largest Citizen-Developer Confrontation* (Montréal: Véhicule Press, 1987).
26. David Gordon and Steven Fong, "Planning St. Lawrence," in D. Gordon, ed., *Directions for New Urban Neighbourhoods: Learning from St. Lawrence* (Toronto: Ryerson SURP, 1990).
27. Thompson Berwick and Pratt and Partners, "Patterns," Part Three, *False Creek Proposals, Report 3* (City of Vancouver, False Creek Study Group, September 1971).
28. David Hulchanski, *St. Lawrence & False Creek: A Review of the Planning and Development of Two New Inner City Neighbourhoods* (Vancouver: UBC Planning Papers, no. 10, 1984); and Stephen Ward, *Planning the Twentieth Century City* (New York: Wiley, 2002), 219–224 and 288–294.
29. Bernard Frieden and Lynne Sagalyn, *Downtown Inc.* (Cambridge, MA: MIT Press, 1989); and David Gordon, *Battery Park City* (New York: Routledge, 1997).
30. John Punter, *The Vancouver Achievement: Urban Planning and Design* (Vancouver: UBC Press, 2003). In 2004, the New York–based Project for Public Spaces rated Granville Island first in a list of best North American public places. See "The 20 Best North American Districts, Downtowns, and Neighborhoods," *Making Places* (November 2004), www.pps.org/info/newsletter/november2004/november2004_neighborhoods
31. Royal Commission on the Future of the Toronto Waterfront, *Regeneration: Toronto's Waterfront and the Sustainable City, Final Report* (Toronto: Queen's Printer, 1992); and David Gordon, "Managing Change on the Urban Edge: Implementing Urban Waterfront Redevelopment in Toronto," in G. Halseth & H. Nicol, eds., *(Re)Development At The Urban Edge* (Waterloo, ON: University of Waterloo Press, 2000), 175–226.
32. Punter, *Vancouver Achievement,* Ch. 6; and Elizabeth Macdonald, "Street-Facing Dwelling Units and Livability: The Impacts of Emerging Building Types in Vancouver's New High-Density Residential Neighbourhoods," *Journal of Urban Design* 10:1 (February 2005), 13–38.
33. Herbert Gans, "Planning for People, Not Buildings," *Environment and Planning* 1:1 (1969), 33–46.
34. Jonathan Barnett, *An Introduction to Urban Design* (New York: Harper and Row, 1982).
35. Kevin Lynch, *The Image of the City* (Cambridge, MA: MIT Press, 1961); Christopher Alexander, *A Pattern Language: Towns, Buildings, Construction* (New York: Oxford University Press, 1977); and Gordon Cullen, *The Concise Townscape* (London: Butterworth, 1971).
36. www.canadianurbanism.ca
37. Edmund Bacon, *Design of Cities* (New York: Penguin, 1974); Gordon Stephenson and George Muirhead, *Kingston: A Planning Study*; and David Gordon and Michelle Nicholson, "Beyond the Tabula Rasa."
38. Mark Fram and John Weiler, eds., *Continuity with Change: Planning for the Conservation of Man-Made Heritage* (Toronto: Dundurn Press, 1984).
39. Saia Barbarese Topouzanov architectes, *Benny Farm Redevelopment Plan* (Montréal: Canada Lands Company, 2003).
40. Regent Park Collaborative Team, *Regent Park Revitalization Study* (Toronto: Toronto Community Housing Corporation, December 2002).
41. Helena Grdadolnik, "Woodwards Takes Shape: Nothing Like it in North America," *The Tyee* (May 11, 2006), www.Tyee.ca
42. Richard Harris, *Unplanned Suburbs: Toronto's American Tragedy, 1900 to 1950* (Baltimore, MD: Johns Hopkins University Press, 1996).
43. Kun-Hyuck Ahn and Chang-Moo Lee, "Is Kentlands Better Than Radburn? The American Garden City and New Urbanist Paradigms," *Journal of the American Planning Association* 69:1 (Winter 2003), 50–71; and Eugenie Birch, "Radburn and the American Planning Movement: The Persistence of An Idea," *Journal of the American Planning Association* 46:4 (October 1980), 424–431.
44. Marc Choko, *Une cité-jardin à Montréal. La cité-jardin du Tricentenaire, 1940–1947* (Montréal, Méridien, 1988).
45. Don Gillmor, "Wildwood Childhood," *Canadian Geographic* (July/August 2005), 54–64; and Michael Martin, "The Landscapes of Winnipeg's Wildwood Park," *Urban History Review* 30:2 (2001), 22–39.
46. Macklin Hancock, "Don Mills: A Paradigm of Community Design," *Plan Canada* (July 1994), 87–90.

47. Eric Mumford, *Defining Urban Design: CIAM Architects and the Formation of a Discipline, 1937–69* (New Haven, CT: Yale UP, 2009), 149.

48. Joel Garreau, *Edge City: Life on the New Frontier* (New York: Doubleday, 1991); and Richard Harris, *Creeping Conformity*.

49. Melvin Webber, "The Urban Place and the Nonplace Urban Realm," in M. Webber, ed., *Explorations into Urban Structure* (Philadelphia: University of Pennsylvania Press, 1964), 79–153.

50. Peter Gordon and Harry Richardson, "Are Compact Cities a Desirable Planning Goal?" *Journal of the American Planning Association* 63:1 (Winter 1997), 95–106; Reid Ewing, "Is Los Angeles-Style Sprawl Desirable?" *Journal of the American Planning Association* 63:1(Winter 1997), 107–126; and Larry Bourne, "Self-Fulfilling Prophecies? Decentralization, Inner City Decline, and the Quality of Urban Life," *Journal of the American Planning Association* 58 (1992), 509–513.

51. Louis Sauer, "Creating a 'Signature' Town: The Urban Design of Bois Franc," *Plan Canada,* 34:5 (September 1994), 22–27.

52. Andres Duany and Elizabeth Plater-Zyberk, "The Second Coming of the American Small Town," *Plan Canada* 32:3 (May 1992), 6–13; and Andres Duany, Elizabeth Plater-Zyberk, and Jeff Speck, *Suburban Nation: The Rise of Sprawl and the Decline of the American Dream* (New York: North Point Press, 2001).

53. http://contextsensitivesolutions.org/

54. *LEED 2009 Green Neighborhood Development Reference Guide* (Washington, DC: U.S. Green Building Council, 2009), www.usgbc.org/leed/nd/

55. Congress of the New Urbanism, *Charter of the New Urbanism* (New York: McGraw Hill, 2000).

56. Hok-Lin Leung, "A New Kind of Sprawl (New Urbanism)," *Plan Canada* 35:5 (September 1995), 4–5; and Todd Bressi, *The Seaside Debates: A Critique of the New Urbanism* (New York: Rizzoli, 2002).

57. Jill Grant, *Planning the Good Community: New Urbanism in Theory and Practice* (New York: Routledge, 2006); Andrejs Skaburskis, "New Urbanism and Sprawl: A Toronto Case Study," *Journal of Planning Education and Research* 25 (2006), 233–248; Jill Grant and Katherine Perrott, "Producing Diversity in a New Urbanism Community: Policy and Practice," *Town Planning Review* 80: 3 (2009), 267–289; and Jill Grant and Katherine Perrott, "Where is the Café? The Challenge of Making Retail Uses Viable in Mixed-Use Suburban Developments," *Urban Studies* 48:1 (January 2011), 177–195.

58. Gerald Hodge, *The Geography of Aging*

59. Mary Catherine Mehak, "New Urbanism and Aging in Place," *Plan Canada* 42:1 (2002), 21–23.

60. David Gordon and Shayne Vipond, "Gross Density and New Urbanism: Comparing Conventional and New Urbanist Suburbs in Markham, Ontario," *Journal of the American Planning Association* 71:2 (Winter 2005), 41–54; and David Gordon and Ken Tamminga, "Large-Scale Traditional Neighbourhood Development and Pre-emptive Ecosystem Planning: The Markham Experience, 1989–2001," *Journal of Urban Design* 7:2 (Winter 2002), 321–340.

61. Ray Tomalty and Murtaza Haider, *Comparing New Urbanist & Conventional Suburban Developments in Canada* (Ottawa: CMHC, 2010).

62. Edward Blakely and Jill Grant, "An American Effect: Contextualizing Gated Communities in Canadian Planning Practice," *Canadian Journal of Urban Research* 16:1 (2007), Supplement 1–19 and Mary Gail Snyder, *Fortress America: Gated Communities in the United States* (Washington, D.C.: Brookings Institution, 1997).

63. Jill Grant, K. Greene, and K. Maxwell, "The Planning and Policy Implications of Gated Communities," *Canadian Journal of Urban Research* 13:1 (Summer 2004), 70–88; Jill Grant and Leah Carson, "Privatizing the Fringe: Patterns of Private Streets in a Slow Growth Region," *Urban Design International* (2008), 253–262; and Jill Grant and Andrew Curran, "Privatized Suburbia: The Planning Implications of Private Roads," *Environment and Planning B: Planning and Design* 34 (2007), 740–754.

64. CMHC, *Greyfield Redevelopment for Housing in Canada—Case Studies* (Ottawa: CMHC, 2011).

65. Galina Tachieva, *Sprawl Repair Manual* (Washington, DC: Island Press, 2010).

66. Brian Morton, "Oakridge Centre Redevelopment Plan Sent for Public Comment: New Proposal for Retail Site Would Add Housing, Offices, Parks," *Vancouver Sun* (July 25, 2012).

67. Paul Hess and Jane Farrow, "Walkability in Toronto's High-Rise Neighbourhoods," University of Toronto Cities Centre (2010).

68. Jane Jacobs, *Death and Life.*

69. Herbert Gans, *Urban Villagers,* and "Planning for People."

70. Ken Greenberg was one of the planners inspired by her work; see his *Walking Home: The Life and Lessons of a City Builder* (Toronto: Random House, 2011); and Pierre Filion, Robert Shipley, et al., "Works Planners Read: Findings from a Canadian Survey," *Canadian Journal of Urban Research* 16:1 (Summer 2007).

71. Anthony Flint, *Wrestling with Moses* (New York, Random House, 2009); and Christopher Klemek, *The Transatlantic Collapse of Urban Renewal, Postwar Urbanism from New York to Berlin* (Chicago: University of Chicago Press, 2011).

72. Max Allen, ed., *Ideas that Matter: The Worlds of Jane Jacobs* (Toronto: Ginger Press, 1997).

73. Jim August, "Partnership for Renewal: Winnipeg's Core Area Initiative," *Plan Canada* 34:4 (July 1994), 80–81.

74. Jeanne Wolfe, "Reinventing Planning: Canada," *Progress in Planning* 57 (2002), 207–235.

75. Oscar Newman, *Defensible Space: Crime Prevention through Urban Design* (New York: Collier 1973); Coleman, *Utopia*; and Sewell, *Shape of the City,* Ch. 8.

76. Gerda Wekerle and Carolyn Whitzman, *Safe Cities: Guidelines for Planning, Design, and Management* (New York: Van Nostrand Reinhold, 1995).

77. Hugh Barton, C. Mitcham, and C. Tsourou, *Healthy Urban Planning in Practice: Experience of European Cities* (Copenhagen: World Health Organisation, 2003); and David Witty, "Healthy Communities: What Have We Learned?" *Plan Canada* 42:4 (2002), 9–10.

78. Lawrence Frank and H. Frumkin, *Urban Sprawl and Public Health: Designing, Planning, and Building for Healthy Communities* (Washington, DC: Island Press, 2004).

79. Richard A. Matthew and Bryan McDonald, "Cities under Siege: Urban Planning and the Threat of Infectious Disease," *Journal of the American Planning Association,* 72:1 (Winter 2006), 109–117; Lawrence Frank, James Sallis, et al., "Many Pathways from Land Use to Health: Associations between Neighborhood Walkability and Active Transportation, Body Mass Index, and Air Quality," *Journal of the American Planning Association* 72:1 (March 2006), 75–87; Lisa Wood, Lawrence Frank, and Billie Giles-Corti, "Sense of Community and Its Relationship with Walking and Neighborhood Design," *Social Science & Medicine* 70:9 (May 2010), 1381–1390; and Lawrence Frank, Michael Greenwald, Steve Winkelman, James Chapman, and Sarah Kavage, "Carbonless Footprints: Promoting Health and Climate Stabilization through Active Transportation," *Preventative Medicine* 50, Supplement (January 2010), S99–S105.

80. Ontario Professional Planners Institute, *Healthy Communities, Sustainable Communities: The 21st Century Planning Challenge* (Toronto: OPPI, November 2007); and CIP Healthy Communities Committee, "Our 21st Century Challenge: Healthier Communities," *Plan Canada* 52:1, 53–56.

81. Rachel Carson, *Silent Spring* (Boston, Houghton Mifflin, 1962).

82. Ian McHarg, *Design with Nature* (New York: Doubleday/Natural History Press, 1969).

83. Richard Forman, *Land Mosaics* (New York: Cambridge University Press, 1995); and W. Dramstad, J. Olson, and R. Forman, *Landscape Ecology Principles in Landscape Architecture and Land Use Planning* (Washington, DC: Island Press, 1996).

84. Charles Hostovsky, David Miller, and Cathy Keddy. "The Natural Environment Systems Strategy: Protecting Ottawa-Carleton's Ecological Areas," *Plan Canada* 35:6 (1995), 26–29; and Ken Tamminga, "Restoring Biodiversity in the Urbanizing Region: Towards Pre-emptive Ecosystems Planning," *Plan Canada* 36:4 (July 1996), 10–15.

85. Michael Hough, *Cities and Natural Process* (New York: Routledge, 2004); and "Toronto, The Task Force to Bring Back the Don," *Bringing Back the Don* (Toronto: City of Toronto, 1992).

86. Royal Commission, *Regeneration*; Gerda L. Wekerle, L. Anders Sandberg, Liette Gilbert, and Matthew Binstock, "Nature as a Cornerstone of Growth: Regional and Ecosystems Planning in the Greater Golden Horseshoe," *Canadian Journal of Urban Research* 16:1 (2007), 20–38.

87. Charles Waldheim, ed., *The Landscape Urbanism Reader* (New York: Princeton Architectural Press, 2006); Julia Czerniak, *CASE—Downsview Park Toronto* (Munich: Prestel, 2001); Nina-Marie Lister, "Insurgent Ecologies: (Re)Claiming Ground in Landscape and Urbanism," in M. Mostafavi with G. Doherty, eds., *Ecological Urbanism* (Zurich: Lars Muller Publishers, 2010), 524–535.

88. Chris De Sousa, "Brownfield Redevelopment in Toronto: An Examination of Past Trends and Future Prospects," *Land Use Policy* 19 (2002), 297–309; Pamela Welbourn, H. Cleghorn, J. Davis, S. Rose, *The Story of Brownfields & Smart Growth in Kingston, Ontario: From Contamination to Revitalization* (San Diego, CA: Classroom Complete Press, 2009).

89. CMHC *Brownfield Redevelopment for Housing: Case Studies* (Ottawa: CMHC, 2006).

90. Casey Brendon et al., "Urban Innovations: Financial Tools in Brownfield Revitalization," *Plan Canada* 44:4 (October–December 2004), 26–29.

91. World Commission on Environment and Development, *Our Common Future* (Oxford: Oxford University Press, 1987), 43; David Brown, "Back to Basics: The Influence of Sustainable Development on Urban Planning with Special Reference to Montréal," *Canadian Journal of Urban Research* 15:1 (2006), 99–117; and Patrick Condon, *Seven Rules for Sustainable Communities: Design Strategies for the Post-Carbon World* (Washington, Covelo, London: Island Press, 2008).

92. M. Wackernagel & W. Rees, *Our Ecological Footprint: Reducing Human Impact on the Earth* (Gabriola Island, BC: New Society Publishers, 1995); Fiona Akins and Joel Thibert, "L'empreint écologique comme critère de performance: Le cas du magasin MEC de Montréal," *Urbanité* (October 2007), 24–26; J. Wilson and J. L. Grant, "Calculating Ecological Footprints at the Municipal Level: What is a Reasonable Approach for Canada?" *Local Environment: The International Journal of Justice and Sustainability* 14:10 (2009), 963–979; and Beate Bowron and Gary Davidson, "Ecological Footprint and Land Use Scenarios: Calgary, Alberta," *Climate Change Planning: Case Studies from Canadian Communities* (Ottawa: Canadian Institute of Planners, March 2012).

93. A description is available at www.gvrd.bc.ca/sustainability/about.asp

94. Richard Scott, "Canada's Capital Greenbelt: Reinventing a 1950s Plan," *Plan Canada* 36:5 (Sept 1996), 19–21; David Gordon and Richard Scott, "Ottawa's Greenbelt Evolves from Urban Separator to Key Ecological Planning Component," in Marco Amati, ed., *Urban Greenbelts in the 21st Century* (London: Ashgate, 2008), 187–217.

95. Robert Lehman, "The 50 Year, 10 Million People Plan," *The Ontario Planning Journal* 19:6 (November 2004), 22–5; R. Christopher Edey, Mark Seasons, & Graham Whitelaw, "The Media, Planning and the Oak Ridges Moraine," *Planning, Practice & Research* 21:2 (May 2006), 147–161; Marco Amati and Laura Taylor, "From Green Belts to Green Infrastructure," *Planning Practice & Research* 25:2 (2010), 143–155; and Sara Macdonald and Roger Keil, "The Ontario Greenbelt: Shifting the Scales of the Sustainability Fix?" *The Professional Geographer* 64:1 (February 2012), 125–145.

96. Patrick Condon, "Planning for Climate Change," *Land Lines* (Lincoln Institute of Land Policy, January 2008), 1–7; and Nathalie Bleau, "Impacts des changements climatiques dans le golfe du Sainte-Laurent," *Urbanité* (Winter 2009), 12–14.

97. Beate Bowron and Gary Davidson, "Climate Change Adaptation Strategy: Prince George, British Columbia," "Waterfront Toronto's Carbon Tool," "Tantramar Dykelands Infrastructure at Risk," *Climate Change Planning: Case Studies from Canadian Communities* (Ottawa: Canadian Institute of Planners, March 2012).

98. Jamie Benedickson, *Water Supply and Sewage Infrastructure in Ontario, 1880–1990s*, The Walkerton Inquiry Commissioned Paper 1 (Toronto: Queen's Printer, 2002). By the 1990s, 69% of the Ontario population had tertiary treatment vs. 39% nationwide (p. 76). Several large Canadian cities (Victoria, Vancouver, Montréal, Québec, Saint John, Halifax, St. John) continue to send partially treated sewage into local water bodies.

99. Reyner Banham, *Los Angeles: The Architecture of Four Ecologies* (London: Allen Lane, 1971).

100. David Nowlan and Nadine Nowlan, *The Bad Trip: The Untold Story of the Spadina Expressway* (Toronto: New Press, 1970); and John Sewell, *Shape of the City*.

101. Michael Goldberg & John Mercer, *The Myth of the North American City* (Vancouver, BC: UBC Press, 1986).

102. Peter Newman, "Public Transit: The Key to Better Cities," *Sustainable Cities White Papers* (New York: Earth Pledge, 2000).

103. John Zacharias, "Pedestrian Behaviour and Perception in Urban Walking Environments," *Journal of Planning Literature* 16:1 (2001), 3–18.

104. Robert Cervero, *The Transit Metropolis: A Global Inquiry* (Washington, DC: Island Press, 1998). Ottawa also began to experiment with LRT in 2001.

105. Peter Calthorpe, *The Next American Metropolis* (New York: Princeton Architectural Press, 1993); Hank Dittmar & G. Ohland, eds., *The New Transit Town: Best Practices in Transit-Oriented Development* (Washington, DC: Island Press, 2004); and CMHC, *Transit Oriented Development: Case Studies* (Ottawa: CMHC, 2010).

106. Peter Boothroyd, "The Energy Crisis and Future Urban Form in Alberta," *Plan Canada* 16:3 (September 1976), 137–146; and Hans Blumenfeld, "Some Simple Thoughts on the 'Energy Crisis'," *Plan Canada* 20:3 (September 1980), 145–153.

107. Anthony Downs, *Still Stuck in Traffic: Coping with Peak-Hour Traffic Congestion* (Washington, DC: Brookings, 2004).

108. Anthony Downs and F. Costa, "Smart Growth: An Ambitious Movement and Its Prospects for Success," *Journal of the American Planning Association* 71:4 (Autumn 2005), 367–381; John Frece, "Preserving What's Best about Maryland," *Plan Canada* 41:4 (October 2001), 21–23; and Andres Duany, Jeff Speck, and Mike Lydon, *The Smart Growth Manual* (New York: McGraw Hill, 2009).

109. Ray Tomalty and Don Alexander, *Smart Growth in Canada: A Report Card* (Ottawa: CMHC, December 2005); Pierre Filion, "The Smart Growth and Creative Class Perspectives versus Enduring Urban Development Tendencies," *Plan Canada* 44:2 (April 2004), 28–32; Grant Moore, "Immigration: The Missing Issue in the Smart Growth Deliberations," *Plan Canada* 44:1 (January 2004), 32–35; Pierre Filion, "Towards Smart Growth: The Difficult Implementation of Alternatives to Urban Dispersion," *Canadian Journal of Urban Research* 12 (2003), 48–70; Pierre Filion, "The Mixed Success of Nodes as a Smart Growth Planning Policy," *Environment and Planning B: Planning and Design* 36 (2009), 505–521; Pierre Filion and Kathleen McSpurren, "Smart Growth and Development Reality: The Difficult Coordination of Land Use and Transport Objectives," *Urban Studies* 44:3 (March 2007), 501–523; and Pierre Filion, "Urban Change on the Horizon? Smart Growth in a Recessionary Context," *Plan Canada* (Spring 2010), 38–41.

110. League for Social Reconstruction (LSR), *Social Planning for Canada* (Toronto: Nelson, 1935).

111. LSR, *Social Planning*. Canadian Prime Minister William Lyon Mackenzie King also regarded planning and housing as part of a social agenda. See W.L.M. King, *Industry and Humanity* (New York: Houghton Mifflin, 1918); and David Gordon, "William Lyon Mackenzie King, Town Planning Advocate," *Planning Perspectives* 17:2 (2002), 97–122.

112. The group was established as "The Housing Centre" at the University of Toronto; the flavour of this period in Canadian housing and planning is superbly described in Humphrey Carver, *Compassionate Landscape* (Toronto: University of Toronto Press, 1975), especially 49–57.

113. Canada, Advisory Committee on Reconstruction, *IV Housing and Community Planning* (Ottawa: King's Printer, 1944), Report of the Subcommittee, 161.

114. For example, Harold Spence-Sales, *How to Subdivide for Housing Developments* (Ottawa: Community Planning Association of Canada, 1950).

115. Humphrey Carver, *Compassionate Landscape*, 90.

116. Susan Hendler, "A Dammed-Up Reservoir of Ability: Women on the National Council of the Community Planning Association of Canada," *Plan Canada* 45:3 (September 2005), 15–17.

117. Susan Hendler and Julia Markovich, *"I Was the Only Woman": Women and Planning in Canada* (Vancouver: UBC Press, forthcoming 2013).

118. Illustrative of this Canadian "participation literature" are the following: Graham Fraser, *Fighting Back: Urban Renewal in Trefann Court* (Toronto: Hakkert, 1972); Jack Granatstein, *Marlborough Marathon* (Toronto: James, Lewis and Samuel, 1971); Donald Gutstein, *Vancouver Ltd.* (Toronto: James Lorimer, 1972); Donald Keating, *The Power to Make It Happen,* (Toronto: Green Tree Publishing, 1975); and John Sewell, *Up Against City Hall* (Toronto: James, Lewis and Samuel, 1972); and, not least, *City Magazine*.

119. Sherry R. Arnstein, "A Ladder of Citizen Participation," *Journal of the American Institute of Planners*, 35:3 (July 1969), 216–224.

120. Gerald Hodge, *The Supply and Demand for Planners in Canada, 1961–1981* (Ottawa: CMHC, 1972), 17; and "Part of the Way It Was: Canadian Planners and Planning in 1967," *Plan Canada* 50:3 (Summer 2010), 24–25.

121. David Gordon, "Reviving a Professional Journal," *Plan Canada* 50:3 (Summer 2010), 12–14. The first issue was edited by Gerald Carrothers and contained a biography of Thomas Adams; subsequent issues were edited by Len Gertler, a founder of the York and Waterloo planning programs. Gerald Hodge, Mohammad Qadeer, and Godfrey Spragge from Queen's edited the journal from 1974 to 1978; see Hodge, "Six Years in the Life of Plan Canada," *Plan Canada* 50:3 (Summer 2010), 15–16.

122. Ian Skelton, "CIP and Affiliates by the Numbers: The Growth of Professional Planning Institutions in Canada since 1967," *Plan Canada* 50:3 (Summer 2010), 26–29. Also see Canadian Institute of Planners website, www.cip-icu.ca.

123. Susan Hendler, "Contemporary Issues in Planning Ethics," *Plan Canada* 42:2 (2002), 9–11; Jill Grant, "Understanding Ethics and Values," in Jill Grant, ed., *A Reader in Canadian Planning: Linking Theory and Practice* (Toronto: Thomson Nelson, 2008), 75–79.

124. Jill Grant, "Fads, Fancies and Form-Based Codes: 50 Years of Planning Issues"; David Gordon, "Retrospective: CIP National Planning Awards"; and Ian Skelton, "Retrospective: Plan Canada Feature Awards," *Plan Canada* 50:3 (Summer 2010), 17–23.

125. Ontario Economic Council, *Subject to Approval* (Toronto, 1973), 50.

126. Vancouver is the exception, since its City Charter *permits* it to prepare plans, but does not *require* it to keep a comprehensive plan up to date. Perhaps that is why there is no great hurry to complete all the elements of *CityPlan*, despite Vancouver's strong planning culture. See John Punter, *The Vancouver Achievement: Planning and Urban Design* (Vancouver: UBC Press, 2004).

Internet Resources

Chapter-Relevant Sites

Planning Canadian Communities
www.planningcanadiancommunities.ca

Our Common Past: An Interpretation of Canadian Planning History—Part 2
www.cip-icu.ca/English/plancanada/wolfe2.htm

Jane Jacobs: Ideas that matter
www.ideasthatmatter.com

St. Lawrence Neighbourhood Toronto
www.toronto.ca/planning/stlawrence_west.htm

Congress for the New Urbanism
www.cnu.org

Council for Canadian Urbanism
www.canadianurbanism.ca

The Centre for Sustainable Community Development
www.sustainablecommunities.fcm.ca

Urban renewal: Making the case for culture
www.creativecity.ca/resources/making-the-case/urban-renewal-3.html

Sustainable Community Planning: Case studies of brownfield, greyfield, infill, and TOD projects
www.cmhc-schl.gc.ca/en/inpr/su/sucopl/index.cfm

Healthy Cities
www.euro.who.int/healthy-cities

Smart Growth BC
www.smartgrowth.bc.ca

two

Community Plan-Making in Canada

Introduction

Broadly, a community's plan is a statement of what the community wants to become. This is true for this country's many communities from the largest to the smallest, from the metropolitan area to the small town in the North. Their plans focus on the community's built and natural environments and aim for efficacy in its functioning and equity in its social distribution of resources.

Plan-making of this scope is normative as well as technical; it is as much concerned about reconciling individual and community values regarding the use of land as it is about marshalling the necessary facts and information needed by plan-makers. And in the process of making the plan there is immense community learning by ordinary citizens, professional planners, elected officials, and others about community problems, aspirations, and prospects. Seen in this light, the community plan plays a distinctive role in *governing* a community. It's akin to the keystone in an archway on which many other aspects of a community's governance depend. This is true whether the "community" is a city, small town, or region.

The image above is from the Montréal Master Plan project, Montréal, Québec, which received the Canadian Institute of Planners' Award for Planning Excellence, Category of Community Planning, 2005.

Source: City of Montréal

6

Chapter Six
Components of Community Plan-Making

In order to be able to make a plan we must be able to predict; in order to be able to predict we must know; in order to know we must develop hypotheses or theories; in order to establish theories we must obtain and classify facts; we must observe.

John Dakin, 1960

When a community sets out to make a new plan, or to amend or renew its existing plan, it is embarking on the process of plan-making. The goals the community adopts for its future built and natural environments mark the beginning of this process. The plan it adopts from this process marks the culmination of plan-making. In other words, the activity of community plan-making comprises both a **plan** and a **process**, each of which, in its own way, are essential components.

Unlike other kinds of decision-making in a community that are aimed at finding solutions to specific problems such as widening a congested road, creating a neighbourhood park, or establishing setbacks from a watercourse, making a community plan involves the collective concerns and aspirations of the community. Plan-making of necessity combines technical analyses with human judgments arising out of differences in beliefs, attitudes, and expectations about the community's built and natural setting in the future. As such, it requires *deliberations* among diverse community interests, and these lead to community plan-making having a distinctive **normative** component. Filling out the process are **technical**, **design**, and **evaluative** components. Beyond this, all facets of plan-making are conducted and mediated within an institutional framework covering the community's government and its accompanying political milieu. This chapter discusses the components of plan-making and the resulting community learning that accompanies them. As that discussion proceeds two questions worthy of consideration are:

- *How do the essential components of community plan-making differ?*
- *What makes community plan-making primarily a normative process?*

Planning Theory: **Plans and Plan-Making**

"Planning" means the scientific, aesthetic, and orderly disposition of land, resources, facilities and services with a view to securing the physical, economic and social efficiency, health and well-being of urban and rural communities.[1]

This is how the Canadian Institute of Planners (CIP) currently defines the practice carried out by its members. Given the distinction made above that community plan-making comprises both a plan and a process, one might understandably wonder to which of these components does this definition refer, or is it to both? Resolving the dilemma posed by this particular definition is beyond the scope of this chapter. However, this provides a useful starting point to explore the difficulties of distinguishing plan and process encountered in discussions of planning theory over the past few decades, and which continue to this day.

The Rational Model of Plan-Making and Its Limitations For the first half-century or so of community planning's history there was little evidence of theoretical concern over what planners do and how they do it. Plans got made, zoning bylaws adopted, and parks systems developed. But interest in what constituted the core and the limits of planning increased in the 1950s as projects under the aegis of planning got larger and their spatial and social impacts more evident (e.g., freeway building, large housing projects, and urban renewal). The mid-1950s study of the Chicago Housing Authority's efforts to build new housing projects (by planner Martin Meyerson and political scientist Edward Banfield) was one of the first to consider how planners went about planning.[2] It was soon to become very influential for the systematic model or method it presented regarding planners making plans—the **rational–comprehensive** method. This method was itself to become very contentious as a valid theory of plan-making and will be discussed later.

Planners from the 1920s onward, as discussed in Chapter 4, put more and more emphasis on achieving efficiency in city-building. The "efficient" use of land in a city carried with it the assumption that the planner could "scientifically" demonstrate attainment of this aim; further, the idea of efficiency was a rational concept. The rational–comprehensive approach contended that a planner would be acting *rationally* by following three general steps: (1) considering all the possible alternative courses of action in making a plan; (2) identifying and evaluating all of the consequences following from the adoption of each alternative; and (3) selecting the alternative that would most likely achieve the community's most valued objectives. Canadian planner Ira Robinson adapted Meyerson and Banfield's formulation and came up with the following five steps:[3]

1. Identify the problem or problems to be solved, the needs to be met, the opportunities to be seized upon, and the goals of the community to be pursued, and translate the broad goals into measurable operational criteria.
2. Design alternative solutions or courses of action (plans, policies, programs) to solve the problems and/or fulfill the needs, opportunities, or goals, and predict the consequences and effectiveness of each alternative.
3. Compare and evaluate the alternatives with each other and with the predicted consequences of unplanned development and choose, or help the decision-maker or decision-making body to choose, that alternative whose probable consequences would be preferable.
4. Develop a plan of action for effectuating or implementing the alternative selected, including budgets, project schedules, regulatory measures, and the like.
5. Maintain the plan on a current and up-to-date basis, based on feedback and review of information to adjust steps 1 through 4 above.

This concept of a rational planning process was sometimes called *synoptic*, in that it attempted to provide for all the principal parts of the community, physical and social, to be brought into the picture. And it had the further virtue of linking planning goals to action. Such a view had venerable roots going back to the work of Patrick Geddes at the beginning of the 20th century. Geddes put great stress on being able to see, to know, and to appreciate all the basic facets of any community before making plans for it. His view always encompassed the people, the geography, and the economy of the community, and he advised planners "that survey and diagnosis must precede treatment."[4]

Despite its worthy roots the rational–comprehensive method of plan-making came to have its critics, especially around its claims of being both *rational* and *comprehensive*. Among the questions raised were: How can planners be truly rational in achieving diverse and often competing goals? Whose rationality is used in choosing which goals to maximize? How can planners know what is in the public interest?[5] How can planners fully comprehend land use and its many activities and purposes, which may vary by neighbourhood? A more recent observer commented that the rational–comprehensive method "… attributes vast cognitive powers to the human mind."[6]

Beyond this general failing, criticism of the rational planning model increased in the 1970s and 1980s around the contention that it does not describe adequately either how planners actually make decisions or the context in which this occurs. Critics pointed out that forecasting planning outcomes is difficult, goals are often fuzzy, and criteria for evaluating outcomes of alternatives may be conflicting. In addition, planning decisions are affected by the diversity of interests involved in them and the existing political context.[7] These criticisms led to a number of alternative models being proposed including Simon's notion that any rational approach is constrained and limited by available knowledge and the culture and values that prevail: such situations he termed as having limited or "bounded rationality."[8] Other theoretical alternatives were proposed including "contingency planning," "mixed scanning," and "critical pragmatism." As Baum noted, each of these alternative models "acknowledged that contexts matter in defining and limiting choices" that planners are able to select in plan-making.[9] Notably, these new models each maintained a form of rational thinking in their constructs.

Shifts in Plan-Making Theories The 1990s saw theorists focus primarily on two modes of plan-making. The first is the **critical pragmatic** approach flowing from Forester's work on the importance of the political context in which planners work and its effects on the direction(s) planners are able to pursue.[10] According to this perspective, the power differentials between local politicians and planning staff as well as between politicians and outside interests, such as the business sector, inevitably intrude on goal-setting and the viability of alternative courses of planning action. The term "critical" alludes to the planner being prepared to examine

critically the political context for plan-making that prevails. The appendage "pragmatism" refers to the pragmatist philosophy approach of working with existing relations that the planner encounters while also considering the potentialities for human betterment.[11] This approach further assumes that the planner, in whatever context he or she works, has a stake in the outcomes of plan-making and may need to find ways to support them. Friedmann refers to planning in this perspective becoming increasingly a *"political act."*[12]

The second theoretical perspective on plan-making developed during the 1990s was the **communicative** model, sometimes called the collaborative model. It differs from the critical model in that it looks at community plan-making as a set of deliberations with the community and its various interests.[13] It emphasizes the need for planners to mediate among stakeholders to arrive at an agreement on planning action(s) that will further their mutual interests, forging a consensus if possible. Often the term "pragmatism" is appended to indicate its roots in pragmatist philosophy of "acting in the world," of dealing with actual differences in viewpoints impinging on planning actions.[14] Like the critical model, it focuses on the role of the planner and asks what he or she should be doing to achieve more rational, or at least more defensible, outcomes in plan-making. Thus both models of this decade embrace the aspect of the rational model that eschews insensitive, selfish, and self-serving outcomes and continues to retain the link of knowledge to action.

The Plan and Its Substance The latter two perspectives that have come to dominate planning theory education[15] focus on planners being *critical* of the contexts in which they plan and/or maximizing *communication* among participants when they make plans. Not that these are undesirable traits to have in plan-making, but they offer little on what should be done about cities and regions. In other words they give little guidance on the spatial and social substance of a community **plan**. First, there are the buildings, roadways, watercourses, housing complexes, and playgrounds that give a city or town its physical presence. These non-human features, these physical objects, Beauregard calls the "things" planners deal with in their plans.[16] That is, he contends, when planners "communicate" with citizen groups, developers, politicians, and others, the talk is about such "things" as housing units, wetlands, shopping malls, schools, and office buildings, about how they look and function. This is an essential aspect of the substance of a community's intentions and aspirations that is represented in its plan.[17]

Chapter 6 Components of Community Plan-Making

The second aspect comprises the people of the community whose daily lives, economic well-being, environmental concerns, aesthetic values, and social inclusion are moulded by the built and natural environments that are given shape in a plan. Their spatial behaviour and personal dispositions are affected by plan-makers' decisions regarding a community's physical objects, spaces, and locations. Some theorists insist on going beyond the efficient functioning of a city or town's physical components and including social equity in the distribution of outcomes for its residents. Their aim is to arrive at the "good city" or "just city."[18]

Overview on Plans and Plan-Making The foregoing discussion of theoretical viewpoints establishes the need to incorporate several components in plan-making. First, the **plan** for a community should include both of the following substantive elements:

1. A representation of the spatial and locational disposition of the physical objects comprising the built and natural environments that are intended to achieve planning goals through verbal, graphical, and visual means; and
2. A commitment in verbal and other means of the intention to achieve specified social outcomes of both a spatial and distributional nature through the planning of physical objects that comprise the current and future community.

Second, **plan-making** should incorporate two constituent processes related to the community's social and political context within which plan-makers—planners—are inextricably involved:

3. Engagement of community members so that they are afforded the opportunity to deliberate the intentions and the substance of all aspects of the plan; and
4. Assessment of the socio-political context within which the planner works to assure a common commitment to the plan's intentions.

The theoretical deliberations of the past three decades have concentrated on the *way* planners do planning, on essential components in the process. Also, clarity has been added regarding the necessary *content* of a plan. However, as valuable as these contributions are, neither addresses *how* planners plan. They are mute on where the process of plan-making begins, when it ends, and the course of its flow. These important aspects of making a

community plan are identified in the following section and discussed more fully in Chapters 14 and 15.

The Flow of Community Plan-Making

The making of a community plan has a beginning and an end. Using as a guide the formal, legislative process required of most communities in Canada authorized to make such plans, its beginning is the adoption by the municipal council of an official motion to prepare a plan. It concludes when the council adopts, again by an official motion, the document comprising the plan and its components. This course of plan-making is true whether the plan is entirely new or is being amended and applies also to the making of supplementary plans such as for zoning, creating special districts, or protecting wetlands. The planning actions of extra-municipal public agencies (e.g., highways, waste disposal, and recreation) follow a similar course, although the initiating/adopting body may differ. Moreover, the formal record of a council's proceedings would confirm this delineation of plan-making for a community.

However, the planning process portrayed above raises two broad and substantive questions. First, what occurs between its beginning and its end? Literally, how does the plan become more than the intention to make a plan? Second, how is the intention to make a plan arrived at? Is there planning occurring prior to officially making a plan? Starting with the latter question, it is reasonable to assume that considerable discussion will occur in a community among a variety of interests regarding the need for a plan (see Chapter 1). That need could be based on the desire to ameliorate some substantial problems ranging across such issues as reinvigorating downtown, dealing with undue traffic conditions, and housing a fast-growing population. Or, as also discussed in Chapter 1, it could be the aspiration within the community to improve its livability, its connections with the natural environment, or any combination of initiatives aimed at bettering a community's quality. It is not uncommon for community plan-making to be generated by both kinds of need.

There seems little doubt that whatever initiative stimulates the official decision of a community to make a plan, it will have emanated from a wide variety of inputs. It may have originated from political interests, the bureaucracy, the development and real estate sectors, as well as from community groups advocating various needs. It may have derived from negotiations and

Figure 6.1

General Model of the Community Plan-Making Process

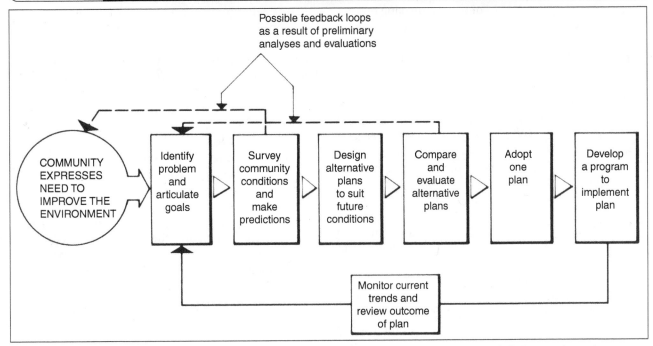

Possible feedback loops as a result of preliminary analyses and evaluations

COMMUNITY EXPRESSES NEED TO IMPROVE THE ENVIRONMENT

Identify problem and articulate goals

Survey community conditions and make predictions

Design alternative plans to suit future conditions

Compare and evaluate alternative plans

Adopt one plan

Develop a program to implement plan

Monitor current trends and review outcome of plan

Although the process is essentially linear, there is ample opportunity for review of decisions and choices at the various steps and for reiteration of all or part of the process.

bargaining, some of it possibly intense. This pre-planning phase has received little attention from planning theorists. It is, however, clearly an integral part of the social and political context of plan-making, which the critical–pragmatist proponents urge planners to understand.[19] This phase involves the critical examination of the planning topics being advocated for inclusion, both for and against, and by whom.

Returning to the first question: what consumes the time and energy of those engaged in plan-making from its official beginning to its end? Although this phase of planning, is subject to much critical analysis, its substance and flow are not well documented. However, two of its attributes may be safely assumed. For one, it comprises a set of interrelated subjects each having to undergo its own process of deliberation, debate, and resolution. A minimum set would include addressing the determination of community preferences, the articulation of goals and objectives, and the delineation of land use areas.

It can be further assumed that this stage of plan-making does not flow in a strict sequence of steps such as propounded by the rational–comprehensive paradigm. The main reason for this is that each of the subject areas that must be dealt with requires its own deliberative process. Further, being interrelated, the progress

achieved in developing each subject area depends upon the outcome in each of the other areas. New information such as revised forecasts of population or economic activity may need to be evaluated and further study may be required. The overall flow of plan-making could also be interrupted or delayed by significant contradictions between the outcomes of the sub-processes such as land use designations conflicting with the goals identified by citizens in a visioning process. Such "disconnects" as they are called often cannot be foreseen until a phase is virtually complete.[20] (Chapter 14 discusses more fully the phases of developing a plan's substance.)

Nonetheless, plan-making does move progressively from its beginning to its end. Problems are identified and aspirations acknowledged and transformed into stated intentions to resolve and achieve them and represented in the final plan through text, data, and graphic means. In practice, this substantive phase may not unfold or flow in a regular sequence; it seldom does and of course there is no need for it to do so. Portraying this erratic-seeming, yet entirely realistic, course of activities is only possible in a general sense. As has been shown, the outcome of one of the separate deliberative phases may affect a previous, or even later phase and interrupt the total flow. These potential disconnects are indicated as **feedback**

loops in the chart below. Only a few of the possibilities can be portrayed here, however. Thus, Figure 6.1 should be treated as a *general model* of the plan-making process, as indicative of the flow of community plan-making.

The Normative Side of Community Plan-Making

The actual process a community goes through in planning its land base approximates the general model described above but may deviate from the sequence or accord special weight to certain steps. The reason for this is that the land use patterns of communities stem from the outcomes of various social, economic, and political behaviours. Myriad decisions made by individuals, groups, businesses, institutions, and governments are involved in the use to which the parcels of land in a community are put. Each of these "actors" behaves in the context of individual and shared values. Since there is never a perfect match of individual and community values in land use, one might say that the process of community plan-making is concerned to a large degree with determining **norms** by which the various value orientations may be reconciled. Thus, it is a normative process: it both recognizes and intervenes in the value system of community members.

It follows that the place given to the identification and articulation of goals is bound to be prominent in actual community planning. Indeed, any steps in the process that invoke the need to define goals for the community plan or to evaluate whether the plan will attain stated goals will assume more importance and visibility the more intense the planning process and the more extensive the participation of the public in the plan-making. The technical aspects, the analyses, and the administrative requirements of the plan are less subject to community debate. Almost of necessity as a community plans, it should allow for many feedback loops in the process of refining goals and planning proposals. Let us examine briefly how the process is initiated and the arrangements that are made for its conduct in actual community settings.

The Determinants of Land Use

When a community initiates plan-making it is, so to speak, seeking to harmonize the various factors, forces, and interests that determine the disposition of land in its built and natural environments. The determinants of land use stem from four broad value orientations within the community—that is, those motivated primarily by economic values, those by social values, those by public interest values, and those related to the natural environment. Each of these is examined in the following sections; however, it should be noted that land use patterns seldom are the result of only one of these determinants. Not only do the individuals, businesses, government agencies, and other groups who participate combine *all* the basic values to some degree, but many land use decisions that affect each determinant also evolve concurrently.

Environmental Determinants

Inherent natural conditions may affect the use of land. The climate of a region will influence both ecological processes and human activity, becoming a more important constraint in northern Canada. The physiographic characteristics of the land (slope, drainage, bedrock conditions, bearing capacity, erosion) may constrain or even prevent construction of buildings, while floodplains or landslide zones may create hazards to human use. Prudent long-range planning usually prohibits development of these hazard lands to prevent the destruction of human life or property.

A second group of ecological conditions (soils, forest, wildlife) may require careful environmental assessment of whether development is appropriate. It may be physically possible to convert environmentally sensitive areas to urban and suburban uses, but the ecological damage may be too great or the natural resources may be too rare to replace.

Environmental determinants are best analyzed early in the land use planning process, since some constraints are absolute (hazard lands), while others can be prohibitively expensive to amend, such as protecting a settlement in a major flood plain.

Economic Determinants

The land use of a community is influenced by economic forces operating both outside the community and within its boundaries, either by external determinants or internal determinants, or both. **External** economic forces are the trends and conditions in the larger (provincial and/or national) economy in which the community exists. Primarily they act through the demand for the goods and services supplied by the community and may affect land use in several ways. One main way is through the investment in key establishments for manufacturing, commercial, or institutional use and, therefore, in the buildings they use and the land they occupy. This is most obvious in a community dominated by a major manufacturing plant, transportation facility, or public institution. These uses often require large amounts of land in strategic locations. Since the decisions regarding the future of these large establishments (e.g., whether to expand them or close them) are usually made outside the community, they may not always reflect the wishes of residents, and there may not be unanimity in the community about privileges that might be accorded these land users. Another significant way external economic forces may influence community land use is in the amount and rate of land development. If the larger economy is expanding, for example, this may call for more land to be developed for houses, stores, parks, and schools. Conversely, if the larger economy is stagnant or in a recessionary phase, local markets for a community's land and buildings may be affected and result in vacancies and foreclosures. Any of these situations affect, in turn, the choices available to plan-makers when planning the use of land.

In contrast to external forces that affect a community's economic composition and vitality, **internal** economic forces determine most of its land use arrangements and the physical character. This is done through the forces of supply and demand acting within the local land market. The land (or real estate) in a community may be looked upon as a commodity to be bought and sold and has a value because of its potential to produce income through some future sale or development. The actual market value of land varies between parcels in the same area and between different areas in the community. Each parcel of land is unique in its location, size, shape, form of building space, tenure, and other features. Thus, certain locations and districts come to be valued for one kind of use or another depending upon the perceptions and preferences of potential owners and tenants. When it comes to housing, some may be preferred for residential neighbourhoods and, as John Hitchcock notes, households differ (e.g., by size, composition, income, and culture) and make different demands for housing.[21] Housing is also strongly affected in its value and usability by the activities carried out on other parcels of land, especially those in the same vicinity.

In any event, land is usually owned by a large number of different persons or organizations and developed by still others, all with their own personal aims, resources, and concerns. Take, for example, the process of creating housing in a community, the largest use of urban land. It involves landowners, the home-building industry, brokers and facilitators, and homebuyers and renters. When the land is in private ownership and the new housing is to be built on raw land, the interrelations among these actors could resemble those shown in Figure 6.2. Most of the same actors are also involved in converting already built-up land to other uses. Depending upon the planning proposals, some part of the array of values represented by these actors will enter into the planning process and, it goes without saying, they frequently do not coincide with one another. Thus, a critical aspect of the normative planning process is to find a balance for the diverse economic interests in community land development.

Finding such a balance is often difficult when the economic stakes are high. This occurs when there is strong competition for a certain site or location. For example, when householders feel threatened by an unwanted neighbourhood development and avidly defend their residential property values. Or, say, when a big-box retailer seeks a rezoning against the wishes of local businesses. Imbalances may also occur when there are substantial differences in viewpoints about whether the development of land should be directed by the private or the public sector. The neoliberal tendency strongly favouring private-sector initiatives that currently prevails can affect the realization of social goals. Numerous communities seeking to create low-income housing have experienced economic pressure to favour private developers. Others planning public facilities for uses such as waste disposal or transportation may be pressed to include private involvement in their development in the form of a public–private partnership (PPP). Finding a resolution for such economically contentious situations has become a major task for planners in many communities, as discussed in Chapters 14 and 15.

Figure 6.2	Steps in the Conversion of Land to Residential Use

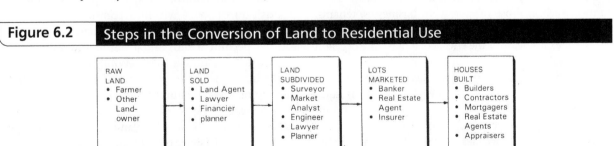

Many persons and groups have an economic interest in the process by which raw land is converted to use for housing.

Chapter 6 Components of Community Plan-Making

Social Determinants

Although it often seems that all land use decisions in a community are stated in dollar terms, many are influenced primarily by social factors. There are two main ways in which social factors influence land uses: one is the social "ecology" of the patterns of residence; the other is the social response to proposed changes in the community. People have strong feelings about the way their community or neighbourhood is arranged and functions. These feelings are rooted in values that, not infrequently, oppose values of economy and efficiency, as citizen protests against planning proposals frequently show.

Among the aggregation of people who constitute a community, one frequently finds clusters of household units that reflect income, ethnic, cultural, and/or age compatibility of residents. And they, in turn, may choose to live apart from commercial or manufacturing areas. Of course, the reverse may also happen. It is important to note that the segregation of uses and districts is a continuous process of sorting the community into physically and geographically distinct parts according to values, attitudes, income, and social interests. Thus, some people like to live in mixed-use neighbourhoods while others prefer not to. Still others may not possess the economic resources to make housing choices in more affluent districts; those who rent their dwellings often find themselves in similar circumstances. And yet others, because of social mores, may find themselves limited to housing choices in particular districts.

The prestige (and/or economic power) of some groups of people or firms leads, accordingly, to a hierarchy of areas in the community. Some residential areas come to enjoy more prestige than others, and some commercial areas are more favourably located than others. The results of this sorting are not always beneficial for the living conditions and economic prospects of all residents or firms. The tensions thus created become part of the milieu of social values with which planners must frequently contend and that may cause difficulties in plan-making of reconciling community goals. Further, interest groups may be formed, such as those of ratepayers, businesses, tenants, or residents of particular districts wishing to express concerns, for example, over the effects of a planning decision on land values and rents. But, just as often, they voice concerns over maintaining social cohesion in the areas in which they live or do business as well as about the equitable distribution of public services and housing opportunities that may be affected in plan-making.

Over the past two decades, there has been a noticeable increase in the number of social values that community planners must take into account. This has happened, notably, with respect to four issues:

- The quality of the natural environment;
- The importance of historical features of the community;
- The needs and concerns of women; and
- The increasing ethnic and cultural diversity of the population.

These issues are often advocated vigorously in various land use decision-making arenas by individual citizens and groups who may have no direct interest in the affected lands through ownership, tenancy, or proximity of residence. Each of these issues thus introduces additional values about the substance and form of communities into plan-making. Not infrequently during such deliberations, flaws are revealed in the planning process itself. Canadian women planners have noted, for example, that women and other groups tend to be excluded from involvement in the planning process because of the time of day meetings are scheduled or the lack of transportation or the unavailability of child care and/or language constraints.[22] The process of community plan-making is hereby being challenged to reconcile not only economic and social values but also differences in social values. With the increasing diversity of community populations, the latter challenge is certain to increase.

Public Interest Determinants

Community planning not only mediates between private land interests; it is also active in determining the patterns of development in the built and natural environments of communities on behalf of the public interest. Out of the values, institutions, and practice of community planning have arisen principles and standards for the location of both public and private facilities, the design of public spaces, and the protection of the natural environment. The provision of water and sewer systems, the design and alignment of roads, and the allocation of park space are ways in which public-interest factors control, or at least pre-condition, the disposition of space within a community. As public concern has risen regarding environmental matters, this too has become a substantial public interest factor. It has led to measures for conserving natural attributes, regulating effluents, and delineating the siting of development relative to natural features.

Whereas the private economic and social interests who participate in the community plan-making generally advocate on behalf of a single piece of land or a single issue (such as the environment), it is up to the community's planners to prepare plans that ensure sound, amenable development in the interest of the community *as a whole*. The public interest, perhaps not surprisingly, is not based on a single entity or set of values. Although the local government of the community is usually the most important entity in this realm, other jurisdictions may also be involved. For example, the local or regional school board, the housing authority, the public utilities commission, and the provincial ministries of highways and environment are some of the other public bodies one encounters. Each has its own mandate to interpret what is in the public interest in matters of the built and natural environments within the community. Usually, the views of these other bodies are mediated through the local government and its planning structure—the mayor, council, planning board, and planning staff. They become the focal point for implementing public-interest matters in land and building matters.

The Importance of Goals

Framing a community plan is, in large measure, a process concerned with sorting out the values and attitudes in the spheres of each of the main determinants—economic, social, natural environment, and public interest. What is put in place, the community plan, amounts to a public commitment regarding the future disposition of land and buildings that will encourage these interests to act in harmony. In other words, it is a statement of *intentions* to establish a context within which its future physical form would evolve. Its centrepiece is a statement of goals that articulate these intentions.

A pivotal notion of modern community planning is that the identification of goals is an integral component. Other public city-building activities, such as engineering, architecture, transportation, and recreation, tend to begin with a limited number of goals already given. A community's planning goals, however, must be derived from its citizens through their expressions of the need to correct and improve the built and natural environments.[23] For example, the perceived shortage of downtown parking space might suggest a goal of maintaining the vitality of the downtown area. The expressed desire to provide adequate park space for each neighbourhood could suggest a goal to designate specific areas for parks. Thus, goals may justify proposed solutions to problems as well as stimulate a solution. In practice the focus alternates from one to the other as objectives, designs, and project ideas are refined.[24] Indeed, one planner sees plan-making as a progressive refinement of goals into projects.[25]

As important as they are, planning goals are not produced by the professional planners; they should derive from the community's citizens, should represent their concerns and aspirations. In current planning practice it is common to derive the goals from a broad-scale engagement of the public, often in the form of a visioning exercise. The citizenry at large and significant sub-groups (e.g., business, seniors, indigenous people, youth) are invited to describe or state their preferences for the future built and natural environment. A complete process of this sort will result in planners refining these preferences into a set of goal statements; following that, citizens are requested to review them and signify their approval and/or the need to reformulate the draft goals. (See Chapter 15 for further discussion of visioning and goal formulation in community plan-making.)

Goals, Objectives, and Policies

Before broaching other important areas of the normative process, it will be helpful to sort out a few semantic difficulties. The term "goal" is used in a variety of ways in planning, along with a variety of such synonyms as aims, ends, purposes, objectives, and policies. However, distinctions need to be made, in particular, between goals, objectives, and policies, because each reflects a different facet of plan-making:

- A "**goal**" refers to an ideal, a condition, or a quality to be sought in the community's built and natural environments. It might be to provide, for instance, maximum access to the waterfront for all members of the community. Thus, a goal in community planning expresses a desire for the community's development to move in a particular direction.
- An "**objective**" is, by contrast, something that the community seeks to attain; it is like a target that can be acted upon, measured, and reached (and thereby monitored). The term "actionable objectives" is preferred nowadays. While the nature of a goal is general, that of an objective tends to be specific or concrete. The waterfront access example above could become an objective to provide a public walkway at the water's edge.
- A "**policy**" may be defined as the preferred course of action to be followed in achieving an objective or a goal. At its root, policy is about choices made by or on behalf of people; it is the course of action the local government thinks will be most acceptable to the diverse interests of the community. Thus, in regard to its waterfront, a community's policy may be to purchase a strip of land along the waterfront for the purpose of constructing a public walkway. This example illustrates not only how goals,

objectives, and policies form a sort of hierarchy of community intent, but also how they represent the progressive translation of general ideas into operational targets and then into actual, physical projects.

A good example of the use of planning goals and objectives is found in the 40-year visioning document, *Vision 2051*, for the Regional Municipality of York. *Vision 2051* contains eight goals and associated objectives for the Region's future, creating a blueprint for the community the Region will work towards creating:[26]

1. A Place Where Everyone Can Thrive
2. Livable Cities and Complete Communities
3. A Resilient Natural Environment and Agricultural System
4. Appropriate Housing for All Ages and Stages
5. An Innovation Economy
6. Interconnected Systems for Mobility
7. Living Sustainably
8. Open and Responsive Governance

Each of these goals is, in turn, complemented by a number of "action areas" (i.e., objectives), examples of which are given here (and their links to the goals above):

• Safe and Secure Communities (Goal 1)
• Complete Communities (Goal 2)
• A Protected, Connected, and Enhanced Regional Greenlands System (Goal 3)
• Housing Choices That Match Our Needs (Goal 4)
• Infrastructure and Resources Supporting a Knowledge Economy (Goal 5)
• A System That Prioritizes People and Reduces the Need for Travel (Goal 6)
• Adapting to a New Climate, Mitigating the Change (Goal 7)
• Open Government (Goal 8)

These goals and objectives will be integrated into the decisions made by the Region's Council, and reflected in the work performed by Regional staff. *Vision 2051* will be monitored and evaluated for its success; this phase of plan-making is discussed later in the chapter.

Tensions in the Planning Process

Community planning, as with other public policy-making, moves with difficulty from goals to objectives, programs, and projects. That is, having identified *which* needs are to be served, it is necessary to translate those into *whose* needs are to be served. If, for example, a new expressway is deemed necessary to serve the entire

community, its actual location will impinge on some neighbourhoods and some groups of people in the community more than on others (see Figure 6.3). Here we encounter one of the most fundamental tensions in community planning—between facts and values. Difficult value-based judgments must be made if the planning process is to progress toward implementing community goals. Technical analyses, by providing relevant facts and information, help bring plan-makers to this threshold, but do not carry them over it. This is because beyond facts lie preferences, and, to this point, the scientific approaches to sorting out personal and group preferences are likely to be of little use to community planners. An Environics poll approach, for instance, will not work well within a community with diverse values.

There are several inherent tensions that frequently emerge during plan-making; they are a reality of the process and should not be denied. The most significant of these derive from the following dichotomies that are encountered when making community plans:

1. **Neighbourhood/City.** The final outcome of planning (the actual projects) occurs at the neighbourhood level of a community; thus, judgments arise regarding the status of the values of people in local areas against those of the entire community. This tension often triggers the "not-in-my-backyard" (NIMBY) syndrome (see especially Chapter 15).

| Figure 6.3 | Citizens Protest New Hog Plant, Winnipeg |

SOURCE: KEN GIGLIOTTI/WINNIPEG FREE PRESS, 30 JUNE 2006, REPRINTED WITH PERMISSION.

Inherent tensions in the planning process are exposed when neighbourhood residents dispute the decisions of planning bodies.

2. **Natural/Built Environment.** Protecting and enhancing natural features and ecologically sensitive sites may create two tensions: it may remove land considered valuable for physical development and/or it may convey value to developable land.

3. **Long Range/Short Range.** As the time frame of planned change increases, the degree of accuracy of predictions decreases while the commitment of the community to projects well into the future will increasingly compete with the desire to solve immediate problems.

4. **Ameliorative/Developmental.** The nature and pace of change in a community may either be forced on a community by external circumstances or it may be sought in order to achieve desirable environmental qualities. Whichever the source of change, each is a normal source of debate.

5. **Fact/Value.** Establishing the facts of trends, conditions, and impacts relevant to planning actions is different from establishing a community's social perspectives of what might be accomplished through plan-making.

Integral to public decisions about the built and natural environment of a community is the notion of **intervention**. With regard to both private profit-making and social interests and to other agencies with public-interest mandates, the means of intervention to be used must be developed to resolve the tensions on behalf of the community as a whole. Such a resolution takes place within the "political climate" that characterizes the community. In other words, the content of the plan and the means of intervention will reflect what is acceptable to those individuals, firms, and groups in the community who wield influence. The underlying tension in the normative side of plan-making involves the need to bring together the various interests sharing a concern, not least those that wield little or no economic or political influence. The judgments made about any of the inherent tensions should reflect a community consensus, something that may not be easily achieved if the plan invokes fundamental value cleavages.[27] However, once this consensus is achieved, the plan should become a matter of public record of what was agreed upon, as well as the basis for decisions. As one U.S. planner has put it, "If we could all remember what we did and why we did it, we could do very well without a plan."[28]

The Technical Side of Community Plan-Making

Community plan-making is underpinned by studies and analyses of, for example, population, land use, the economy, traffic, and the natural environment. The community's planner or consultant is usually responsible for these technical tasks. In turn, they complement the normative side by providing information for those involved in plan-making to enable them to understand the problems and the policy implications flowing from the various analyses. Two broad areas of analysis are usually undertaken in plan-making: diagnosis of problem situations and prediction of ongoing factors. In this section, these are briefly outlined and placed within the context of plan-making.[29] They are discussed more fully in Chapters 9 and 17. A further technical area, evaluation of outcomes, follows.

Diagnostic Studies

Planning studies at this stage are essentially descriptive. Using problem situations such as downtown traffic congestion and housing shortages will help demonstrate the diagnostic approach. In the case of traffic congestion, the planner would seek data on current conditions: the volume of traffic on affected streets, evidence of delays at certain points and times, the degree of use of parking facilities, and possible associated problems, such as businesses affected or the effect on pedestrian flows. In the case of housing shortages, the planner would seek data on household size and composition of the current housing stock, its condition, and vacancy rate. In both of these types of planning problems, the planner would also seek data on past conditions in order to examine trends over time, map the current trends, as well as seek data regarding comparable situations in other communities.

Two key studies undertaken in the diagnostic phase concern the natural and built environments. For example, ecosystems planning must be done *before* planning for urban expansion. This is called a "**pre-emptive environmental study.**"[30] The community planner would look at an inventory of flood plains, environmentally sensitive areas, and ecological links before proceeding with plans for the built environment.[31] The City of Ottawa provides such a regional inventory and environmental strategy for its constituent communities to follow.[32] For the built environment there are two basic planning diagnoses: the first has to do with the area being planned (e.g., population, economy). The second has to do with whether current conditions in a problem situation are stable or changing and its spatial context.[33] Survey research (e.g., questionnaires) is often used to provide more penetrating observations.[34] And with Geographic Information Systems (GIS) planners are enabled to make more accurate and complete analyses and maps of environmental, physical, and social patterns to inform the planning process.[35] However, its use carries with it cautions regarding the use and interpretation of data inputs and outputs.[36]

Predictive Studies

For this technical phase, the planner moves from description to prediction. Forecasting the population is often the first of such studies with graphical and/or mathematical extrapolations. For special population groups such as the elderly or visible minorities, more extensive data and more elaborate methods will be used.[37] Economic forecasting is also important because of its connection with the need for housing, public utilities, and transportation. For example, through the prediction of employment, the planner has a way of linking the economy of a place to the size and needs of the population.[38] Methods for predicting environmental and land use changes are less well developed. Environmental planners and civil engineers may predict changes in flood plains due to increased stormwater flow after urbanization of watersheds. One useful land use model can predict the impact of a new shopping centre on established businesses.[39] (See also Chapters 9, 12, and 17.)

Evaluation in Community Plan-Making

Plan evaluation is a crucial step in plan-making. Not only is it an opportunity to review a plan before its implementation but it is also the phase where an appreciation of the completeness of the plan, or any of its stages, is best obtained. Plan evaluation may occur at different stages in the process of plan-making,[40] for example, (a) before the plan is fully formulated to assess it for consistency; (b) after the plan (and alternative plans) have been formulated to test for unintended consequences; and (c) following adoption of the plan, the so-called post hoc, or ex post, stage. The planner assists plan-makers by providing means by which the relative merits of plans can be evaluated. When a community plans, it anticipates and prepares for change. Thus, the plan that is chosen will have consequences, and the planner's evaluation studies aim to determine the nature of those consequences beforehand. Much

needs to be done both to clarify the need for plan evaluation and to develop the methods for accomplishing it.[41] Nonetheless, some tools are available to point out the direction that plan-makers need to pursue.[42]

Plan Assessment

Community plan-making should be considered as a process of learning about future possibilities. For this there are few certainties; it requires a process of embracing errors when they are revealed. Thus, opportunities for evaluation should be sought from the beginning to the end of the process. In the early stages, the various components of the plan need to be assessed for consistency of goals, objectives, policies, background data and projections, etc. with one another. A salient aspect that needs to be examined is the consistency of language that is employed throughout the plan. Goals should clearly reflect the intentions of plan-makers, and statements of objectives and policy should, in turn, clearly reflect the goals. One means for such an evaluation is "content analysis."[43] As shown in Figure 6.1, the findings of even such preliminary evaluation may evoke the need for a feedback loop to obtain, say, a better diagnosis of problems.

Articulating Goals One of the main starting points in plan-making is to identify the goals and objectives community members wish to achieve with the plan. A community's goals will tend to reflect a number of different facets for which change and/or improvement are sought (e.g., the economy, rate of population growth, appearance of the community, natural environment). The example of York Region in Ontario cited earlier showed eight goals. Since goals are the foundation of a community's plan, it is important that they each contribute to its outcome. It is, therefore, valuable to assess whether a plan's goals are consistent.

Not surprisingly, any community's (or region's) goals are related. The issue for the planner, almost at the outset of plan-making, is whether all of the goals can be achieved and to what degree. Behind this issue is the realization that each goal derives from the same social and economic milieu and, if achieved, will draw from the same pool of community resources. In essence, the plan's goals are implicitly in competition with one another for, among other things, capital and land resources, and attention. The desire for a new airport may vie with the desire to conserve land for agriculture, for instance. It is also true that some goals may complement other goals, as when an improved rapid transit system aids both economic development and residents' needs.

A method available to identify the effect of achieving each goal on each of the other goals is called **cross-impact analysis**. It involves the use of a square matrix with rows and columns for all goals.[44] This method was used by the Greater Vancouver Regional District in its *Livable Regional Plan* and employed a simple rating approach in which each cell in the matrix is filled in by asking: does achievement of the specified goal enhance (+), reduce (−), or have no effect (0) on each of the other goals?[45] In this way, plan-makers can check the efficacy of goals prior to plan formulation and thereby improve both their research and implementation strategies.

Assessing Environmental Impact Impact studies have become familiar, especially regarding the effect of new development on the natural environment. Environmental impact-assessment procedures are now in widespread use, although they are not required as a matter of course in community planning in Canada as they are in the United States. Such provincial government agencies as departments of highways undertake them; many large projects, such as energy projects, require them, both in southern Canada and in the Far North. The scope of environmental concerns in local planning is increasing. For example, the British Columbia government now has legislation requiring local plans to take into account impacts on fish stocks and fish-spawning streams, and the Ontario government has adopted an Environmental Bill of Rights.

The **environmental-impact statement** (as it is often called) attempts to forecast the consequences of a project for its surrounding natural environment, including plant life, wildlife, soils, water, and air conditions. The natural interrelations and interdependencies of phenomena in the environment require that impact assessment capture the ecological interactions. The actual complexity of natural systems as understood by biologists, botanists, and zoologists has, however, defied the development of precise means of environmental-impact assessment. The most common approach uses a checklist of potential effects in order to ensure that impacts are not overlooked and that those identified may be pursued in depth. More elaborate are matrix techniques that identify the interactions that occur when a project disturbs one part of the environment. The magnitude of each effect may be included in the matrix, either in absolute terms or on the basis of a rating of the expected impact.[46]

The concerns of environmentalists have also led to efforts to extend the same ecological concepts into other realms of planning practice. **Social-impact assessment** methods help determine the effects on people's lives, community functioning, and social and cultural traditions of possible changed conditions resulting from large projects. Such assessments are required prior to the initiation of large projects in the Far North; as well, they are becoming a more common part of the planning scene in other parts of Canada.[47] Indeed, the Environmental Assessment Act in Ontario requires impacts on social, cultural, and historical, as well as economic, "environments" to be assessed, and the federal government has a specific process for projects coming under federal jurisdiction to study and report on their environmental impacts administered by the Federal Environmental Review Office.

Plan Testing

As plan-making progresses, various alternatives emerge often with different consequences for resource use and support for basic goals. An important evaluation step is to understand the consequences of each alternative plan that may be put forward as a possible final plan. This phase has been called "pre-adoption evaluation." Two evaluation methods are available for use in this phase: one for testing economic impacts, and the other for achieving goals. It needs to be noted that the main responsibility for this testing falls on the community's planners.

Testing for Costs and Benefits A form of economic impact analysis with strong roots in planning is **cost–benefit analysis**. Developed originally in the 1930s for use in river-basin planning, it is now widely used in other planning endeavours. The term "cost–benefit" has become something of a generic phrase in planning to show an awareness that proposed projects carry with them costs as well as benefits. Further, there is recognition that often neither all the costs nor all the benefits of a project can be quantified in dollar terms. In water-resource projects, for example, it was recognized that the costs of displacing people from their homes were intangible (i.e., not measurable in dollars), just as there might also be intangible benefits from the improvements in recreation. It is not difficult to imagine analogous tangible and intangible costs and benefits from expressway-building, urban renewal, and airport development projects.

It is also not difficult to imagine that as the multitude of factors that the planner tries to take into a cost–benefit reckoning expands to include intangible (but still very real and pertinent) items, the more difficult the summation of costs and benefits becomes. Several variants of the approach have arisen, for example, limiting the reckoning to costs and revenues that can be rendered in dollar terms or broadening it to include an evaluation of effectiveness in achieving specified goals. Planning-programming-budgeting systems (PPBS) are a form of the latter, but the most pertinent for planners is the Planning Balance Sheet developed by Lichfield.[48] It mixes both "hard" and "soft" data about the plan in an effort to include measurements of all its effects. Weights are not assigned to the various impacts; rather, that type of judgment is left where it properly belongs—with the plan-makers.

Testing for Achievement of Goals Economic efficiency is the essential criterion of cost–benefit approaches, but planners have never regarded this as the only or main measure of a plan's worth. The goals and objectives decided on by the community are considered the paramount criteria for evaluation by many planners. In other words, if a plan is to help achieve a community's goals, then the worth of the plan must be looked at in terms of whether it represents progress toward those goals. In response, planners have developed "goals–achievement" evaluation and other similar methods. These methods allow plan-makers to compare complete plans without the necessity of disaggregating them, as in the Planning Balance Sheet described above.

The best known of these techniques, the **goals–achievement matrix**, was framed by planner Morris Hill[49] and emulated by many others. The goals–achievement matrix is a way of summarizing overall performance with respect to each goal of each alternative plan. In its simplest form, the columns of the matrix represent the alternative plans or policies being considered; the rows represent the goals and objectives the community has set. Since not all goals are usually considered of equal importance, this method allows each to be weighted to reflect its importance to the community. Further, if some goals have several facets, as is often the case, then each row may be elaborated into several to capture the range of aims. The most thorough approach is to define quantitative measures, or scores, that reflect degrees of success in achieving each goal that could, in turn, be "summed." These may turn out to be only ranked scores, but this still provides a strong base of comparison.[50]

Post Hoc Evaluation

"Does planning work?" is a cogent question for planners and other plan-makers and one not easily answered.[51] It makes sense that, after adopting and implementing plans, plan-makers want to know if their efforts were successful in bringing about the desired changes. However,

such *post hoc* evaluation poses a number of challenges, as Canadian planner Mark Seasons notes, including the following that are key:

- The kinds of planning outcomes that are to be evaluated;
- The appropriate period of time to measure outcomes; and
- The methods by which to measure them.[52]

Planning outcomes may be looked at in terms of either the links between plans and actual development, called **conformance-based evaluation**, or whether the plan is used in decision-making processes, which is known as **performance-based evaluation**.[53] Evaluating the conformity of actual development to planned development is one of the most common approaches, especially in the area of environmental concerns. For example, evaluations have been made by assessing whether development permits for subdivisions achieved desired the protection of wetlands.[54] Ontario's regional municipalities tend to use quantitative measures such as numbers of housing units built, growth of population, level of water quality, and numbers of jobs created.[55] Still others combine quantitative and qualitative measures in their evaluations.

Timing, or frequency, of evaluations also vary, and the choice is likely to depend upon the amount of time required for results to show; environmental improvement may take longer to become evident than improvements in transportation, for example. The 2012 Official Plan of Ontario's Regional Municipality of York, which was referred to above, calls for its planners to assess success every three years of the next fifteen using a set of performance-type indicators (see Figure 6.4). A U.S. project to maintain riparian health utilizes citizens who are given training to monitor its watersheds every year, which proves both cost-effective and succeeds in raising public awareness.[56] The Canada Lands Company has adopted "triple bottom line" reporting to address the environmental, social, and economic objectives included in sustainable development.[57] These few examples indicate the increasing interest in monitoring outcomes of plans and evaluating them. More and more planning agencies are coming to realize the importance of not only displaying success to their councils and citizens but also being more aware of planning processes, not least when shortfalls are revealed. However, much remains to be done to strengthen this part of plan-making, such as in better linking of goals and outcomes, choosing indicators, and giving the task due priority in the planning agency.[58]

Figure 6.4	Official Plan (2010) Targets to be Monitored in York Region, Ontario

Policy 8.2.3: [It is the policy of Council] to develop, in co-operation with local municipalities, common measuring and reporting tools to monitor progress towards targets established in this Plan, including

a. a minimum of 40% of all residential development will occur within the built-up area as defined by the Province's Built Boundary in *Places to Grow: Growth Plan for the Greater Golden Horseshoe*, by 2015 and each year thereafter;

b. an average minimum density that is not less than 50 residents and jobs per hectare in the developable area within the York Region *designated greenfield area*;

c. a minimum 25% new *affordable* housing units across the Region;

d. a minimum density of 2.5 *floor space index* per development block in the Regional Centres;

e. a minimum density of 3.5 floor space index per development block at, and adjacent to, the Vaughan Metropolitan Centre Station on the Spadina Subway Extension, and the Langstaff/Longbridge and Richmond Hill Centre Stations on the Yonge Subway Extension;

f. energy and water efficiency standards and other sustainable building policies in this Plan; and,

g. a minimum woodland cover of 25% of the Region's total land area.

Official Plans can establish targets that indicate the desired conditions in a community's future. Municipalities must monitor these targets to ensure that a plan is succeeding in meeting its goals.

The Design Side of Community Plan-Making

Beyond numerical analyses there is the need to weave houses, stores, streets, parks, etc. into a physical, visual community. That task falls into the realm of land use design and it involves aesthetics and, as Canadian planner Hok-Lin Leung has stated, "Modern city planning is rather blind to aesthetics."[59] The concern that citizens often voice about new high-rise buildings or the removal of old trees is as much about aesthetics as anything else. Other observers have also noted that today's planners are, with rare exceptions, oblivious to visual and three-dimensional elements of city form and texture.[60] It usually devolves upon the planner to draw upon knowledge gained from experience with urban development and growth to conceive and present possible future physical designs for the community or parts of it.

The design task in planning a community's built environment is one of combining the right physical elements into a unified whole. And what is "right" for the design is informed by (a) the goals and objectives that have been agreed upon, and (b) the results of analyses that have been undertaken. It is a process of *synthesis* that is very important to the successful acceptance of the plan. European planner Andreas Faludi notes that for a plan to be viable it must incorporate a graphic organizing principle that conveys the way in which the planning area is to be arranged.[61] A striking Canadian example is the "greenbelt" in Gréber's 1950 plan for the Ottawa region (Figure 6.5); its recent counterpart for the Toronto region (Figure 8.11, page 204) may have the same effect. Further, the design task demands capacities in the planner to "see problems in new ways, to break out of conventional boundaries of thought, to use analogy and metaphor."[62] Proponents of the New Urbanism, for example, advocate injecting design metaphors drawn from small towns and garden suburbs into city designs.[63] Their aim is to improve community living situations through design solutions that recast the patterns of typical suburban development (or "mindless sprawl," as it is often called) with "mixed-use, walkable, transit-served districts and neighbourhoods."[64] Although this discussion focuses on the spatial design of the environment, it is important to mention that the design of policies, programs, and regulations for managing community-building, say, a program for future housing needs, will also involve the planner in imagining future possibilities.

Figure 6.5   Ottawa Greenbelt Sketch

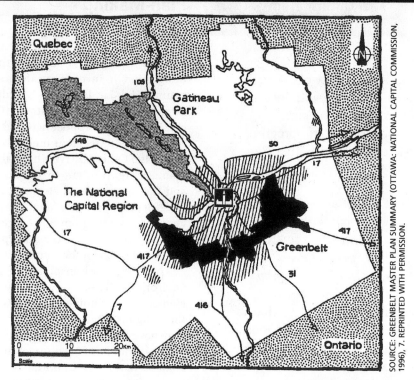

The 1950 Ottawa Greenbelt plan was an example of a simple graphic organizing principle for a plan. In this case, the idea was to have a belt of open space to control sprawl, but it didn't work because the population grew much faster than forecast, due to the baby boom and post-war expansion of the federal government. The greenbelt was later re-purposed as an ecological corridor and urban agriculture resource and remains useful today.

Design Development

Design is an elusive process to describe, whether for planning, architecture, engineering, or the arts. Prominent U.S. planner Kevin Lynch provides some helpful touchstones for our purposes. He notes that most environmental designs are adaptations of previously used solutions.[65] Many urban forms are now applied customarily in community design: for example, the neighbourhood concept for residential areas, or the layouts for local shopping plazas. Most are mere imitations of these stereotypes, but more imaginative solutions may also emerge by improving upon earlier designs. The converse of this adaptive approach is to seek optimum, or "ideal," design solutions that best satisfy the objectives of the community or the project, such as the proposals for the 1948 "Finger Plan" for Copenhagen (Figures 6.6 and 6.7). The design of entire new towns, such as Fermont, Québec, or of innovative housing, such as Habitat '67 in Montréal, are usually approached in this spirit. Another approach to design may be generated out of a neigh-

bourhood SWOC collaborative analysis of Strengths, Weaknesses, Opportunities, and Constraints for specific locations. This approach focuses on the present reality and is appropriate where the planned changes will "intrude" on an existing situation, as, for example, in the location of new arterial roads or expressways in built-up neighbourhoods. There are a number of variations on these approaches, and the planner will likely gravitate to one or another for the planning problem at hand on the basis of both professional experience and personal preference, for all designing entails a high degree of personal involvement.

In the design phase of planning, there remains the question of how to introduce possible designs into the planning process. This question arises mainly for two reasons: first, there are always numerous possible design solutions to planning problems; and, second, both planning boards and citizens will make choices among designs. The planner may employ one of two general strategies: (1) generate a limited set of alternatives that

SOURCE: GREENBELT MASTER PLAN SUMMARY (OTTAWA: NATIONAL CAPITAL COMMISSION, 1996), 7. REPRINTED WITH PERMISSION.

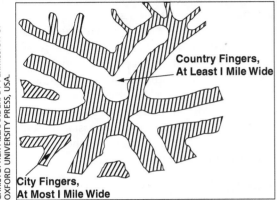

SOURCE: A PATTERN LANGUAGE BY CHRISTOPHER ALEXANDER (1977) ILLUSTRATION P. 25 © 1977 BY CHRISTOPHER ALEXANDER. BY PERMISSION OF OXFORD UNIVERSITY PRESS, USA.

Urban theorist Christopher Alexander documented hundreds of ideal urban patterns for community building, ranging in scale from regional form (such as this suggestion for city–country fingers) to house design. Each pattern was illustrated with a simple, easily understood sketch or photograph and a brief text, which makes the patterns quite useful for illustrating design alternatives. This presentation technique has been adapted for *The Smart Growth Manual*.[66]

reflect the likely range of possibilities; or (2) develop one reasonable possibility and refine it on the basis of verbal deliberations. The first of these strategies may be time-consuming and expensive. Sometimes the planner may have one preferred design; this may save money in the design phase if the selection is good, or incur waste if it is not. In actual design, some compromise is often made between these two strategies by first identifying the range of basic alternatives and then choosing one for full development.

A third approach is to subject proposed designs (from architects, developers, and staff planners) to assessment by a Design Review Panel.[67] Many Canadian cities use this method, including Ottawa, Toronto, Niagara Falls, Calgary, and Vancouver; they appoint a group of external reviewers, often comprising architects, engineers, and builders, to advise on the appropriateness of the design of development proposals. Design review is most effective when proposed projects are introduced early, panel members are politically independent, urban design guidelines are already in place,[68] and the review process is open to the public. In regard to the latter point, open discussion broadens community learning about planning realities.

Collaborative Design

The community's planners play a key role in structuring the design process for other plan-makers, either through providing alternative designs or through encouraging collaborative processes involving community members in actually making designs. The latter mode is used more and more in cities large and small in processes generally

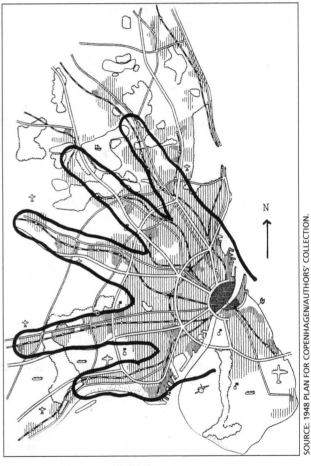

SOURCE: 1948 PLAN FOR COPENHAGEN/AUTHORS' COLLECTION.

The 1948 plan for Copenhagen called for urban development to be concentrated in corridors in the valleys outside the city, separated by "green wedges" of open space along the higher ground, similar to Alexander's theoretical pattern above. Rail and road facilities were improved in the valleys, leading to urban form in the shape of fingers leading from the historic core. This basic form was memorably illustrated by a simple sketch of a hand overlaid on the growth plan.

called **visioning**.[69] The notion is a simple one of developing a description of what the community should "look like" in the future through citizen-produced maps, drawings, and text. One of the most ambitious, and successful, uses of visioning is that employed by planners in the City of Vancouver, which started in 1997 to link neighbourhood planning to its citywide *CityPlan*.[70] Its community vision process* operated in the following way for each of the city's neighbourhoods:

- A 15-month, four-step process including extensive outreach; the identification of community needs, ideas, issues, and opportunities on all the *CityPlan* topics; the creation of Vision options and directions; broad community voting on preferred options and directions; and Council endorsation of the final Vision. Subsequently, the community worked on setting priorities for Vision implementation.
- Each step provided a variety of ways for people in the community to be involved in creating, reviewing, and deciding on their Vision—including meetings, workshops, and discussion groups, community events and festivals, brochures and surveys.
- The process provided for an ongoing Community Liaison Group (CLG) made up of people from the community.
- Communities were asked to look 30 years ahead. They were given information to help them consider both the short-term and the 30-year future.

This process produced design ideas for the city's plan-makers but also aided in community learning and building public consensus regarding the plan's outcome. A variation on visioning is the design charette that brings together people with diverse expertise to create design solutions for planning projects.[71] The idea is also "to give visual form to ideas and policies." However, the charettes are designed to be used by smaller groups of people rather than a whole community (often including a variety of specialists) and are to be concluded in a short period of time, say, from three to four days. Further, they tend to work best when focused on a given site, often one that is contentious, to develop options that would integrate with broader community planning. An extension of the community-design charettes to an entire urban region, using a 100-year planning horizon, was conducted in 2004 for the Greater Vancouver Regional District with considerable success in an international competition.[72] Other forms of visioning are described in Chapter 15.

Influencing the design of the physical form of the community prior to development or redevelopment has become of increasing interest in planning in recent decades. It has led communities to publish **design guides** that promote the community's viewpoint on what constitutes the desired standard of quality for its physical environment.[73] They provide guidelines on street layouts, building patterns, public spaces, and lot layouts, among other physical design attributes, and are made available to builders and land developers as well as to the public. In the case of the small city of Collingwood, Ontario, their *Urban Design Manual* was published in 2010 and also made accessible online, and in this way allows both citizens and those proposing development to know what to expect.[74]

Plan-Making and Community Learning

Not infrequently, situations arise in community plan-making (and implementation) that illuminate the differences between, for example, plan-makers and neighbourhood residents as to how each group views the plan's aims and outcomes. To better understand such differences, it is appropriate to characterize the community plan-making as a **learning process**, both for plan-makers and for neighbourhood residents; that is, one in which plan-makers and citizens learn from each other. In this way it can be seen that the difficulties over plan proposals arise out of differences in how each learns—not only differences in the amount of time each has to spend learning but also differences in perception of the substance of a proposal, in prevailing values, and in the source of knowledge. The professional planners, for example, have technical expertise grounding their views, while citizens bring their personal knowledge of an area into their viewpoint. Further, not everyone, including official plan-makers, enters the process either at the same time or with the same background and the same propensity to learn what is needed to make a decision.

This realization has led to a call that a "more active relationship should be developed between planners and their clients."[75] Increased interaction, deliberation as it's presently called, particularly through verbal communication, is aimed at mutual learning for both planners and clients.[76] Mutual learning generally leads both to broader participation and to a less bureaucratic style of planning. It helps all participants to appreciate better the respective positions of others in the plan-making process. This includes the interactions of planners with developers, as well as with private citizens. Hok-Lin Leung describes

---

*Reprinted with permission from the City of Vancouver Planning Department.

an excellent example of mutual learning in practice in a Toronto suburb, Scarborough, Ontario. Their planning department undertook to negotiate with developers over its planning criteria for an office and commercial development. The municipal planners learned that they could "soften" their criteria for such stipulations as Floor Area Ratios and density and still attain their planning objectives. The developers learned about the "logic of land use designation ... [and] came to appreciate the need to go beyond market demand and jobs and argue their case on planning grounds as well."[77] Not least, mutual learning in this case helped to streamline the negotiation process and also made a case for seeking "accommodation" in seemingly contentious situations.

Community learning involves all plan-makers, including professional planners, in a process that accepts that it is natural for citizens and developers to want to be involved in planning their community. Further, it requires that citizens and others outside the formal plan-making process also be accorded the status of "clients" of the plan-makers, along with those who have plan-approval powers. As Friedmann has noted, much of a community's planning is a "sequence of interpersonal relations," that is, of planners and clients "communicating valid meanings to each other," or at least trying to. He saw the planning process as a set of "transactions" that lead to mutual learning.[78] Several instances of how this can occur in actual planning processes have been cited above, including design charettes, citizen monitoring of watersheds, and Vancouver's visioning exercises. The small British Columbia city of Vernon exemplified community learning when it challenged citizens who had participated in its visioning project: "Did we get it right?"[79] These are among the recent efforts where the emphasis in the planning process is on interaction and communication, on "collaborative planning" (or sometimes "communicative planning"), as it is now called.[80]

Community learning, intended or otherwise, can also occur in conjunction with other facets of plan-making. The use of surveys to obtain citizen ideas and attitudes aid in making planning approaches open to broader public understanding, especially if the results are made available to citizens. The same applies with the use, increasingly, of online surveys and planning websites. The use of design guides also broadens the community's base of understanding even to the extent of fostering citizen dissent. Where employed, design review panels help planners, architects, and builders "see opportunities and shed light" on proposed projects, observes Canadian urban designer Ken Greenberg.[81]

Not least, an integral part of plan evaluation in whatever form involves learning by all parties—if they are open to it—and should not be overlooked. It cannot be assumed, as Mark Seasons notes in his review of Ontario planning departments, that individual planners or their organizations will embrace learning from evaluation outcomes.[82] Whether there is support for evaluation among staff, managers, and politicians may differ with the culture of the particular organization. Other reasons may lie with the availability of staff resources, time, and funding as well as the political understanding and support that prevail. Where evaluation and monitoring of planning activities are encouraged, this process is the result of having a "learning organization" which thereby enhances its plan-making.

Reflections

Describing how a community plan evolves only in words, as this chapter attempts to do, has a number of limitations due to its very nature. Not least is its complexity involving many persons and groups, each with their own understanding of the factors that need to be engaged in developing this instrument into a viable representation of a community's intentions for its future built and natural environments. Add to this the increasing insistence that these considerations be conducted in a deliberative, communicative manner with all the human foibles that reveals. The latter viewpoint also points out the distance travelled from the rational–comprehensive model of the 1950s, which lent itself more easily to verbal description. Yet one needs to ask: did the basic components of plan-making really change in the intervening decades? Probably not. There has always been a plan and a process. Likewise, there has always been a normative side to the making of plans for a human community. Since Geddes's time, the technical needs have been incorporated, and Howard set a high standard for the design side of community plan-making.

What then characterizes community plan-making in the second decade of this century in contrast to the past? There has been a broadening of each of the components and allowance for the process to be non-linear, more open to the citizenry, and receptive to evaluation and critical analysis. And, fortunately, it has also returned to an appreciation of the physical form of communities; unfortunately, the same appreciation regarding the social equity outcomes of plan-making still seems to be elusive. More hopeful, when the focus moves away from planning theory, is that actual practice seems more ready to accommodate itself to ongoing problems and learn from their resolution without fearing the loss of basic planning precepts. This is evident through both greater collaboration and a willingness to prescribe, as with design guides, desired outcomes.

It is now worth considering the following questions regarding the plan-making process described in this chapter:

- *Where in the plan-making process do opportunities for community learning occur?*
- *What distinguishes the planner's role during the different components of plan-making?*

Reference Notes

1. Notably, this definition differs hardly at all from its 1920's version, www.cip-icu.ca/web/la/en/pa/3FC2AFA69

2. Martin Meyerson and Edward C. Banfield, *Politics, Planning and the Public Interest* (Glencoe, ILl.: The Free Press, 1955), esp. 312–322.

3. Ira M. Robinson, ed., *Decision-Making in Urban Planning* (Beverly Hills: Sage Publications, 1972), 27–28.

4. Patrick Geddes, *Cities in Evolution*, 3rd ed. (London: Ernest Benn, 1968), 286. See also Artur Glikson, Regional Planning and Development (Leiden: A.W. Sijthoff, 1955), 73ff.

5. This is still an issue of debate in community planning; for example, see, Jill Grant, "Rethinking the Public Interest as a Planning Concept," *Plan Canada*, 45:2 (2005), 48–50.

6. Niraj Verma, "Pragmatic Rationality and Planning Theory," *Journal of Planning Education and Research* 16:5 (September 1996), 5–14.

7. Cf. John Forester, "Power, Politics, and Ethics: Abiding Problems for the Future of Planning," *Plan Canada* 26:9 (December 1986), 224–227.

8. As discussed in Herbert Simon, *Administrative Behavior* (New York: Free Press, 1965).

9. Howell S. Baum, "Why the Rational Paradigm Persists: Tales from the Field," *Journal of Planning Education and Research* 15:2 (January 1996), 127–135.

10. John Forester, *Planning in the Face of Power* (Berkeley: University of California Press, 1989).

11. Patsy Healey, "The Pragmatic Tradition in Planning Thought," *Journal of Planning Education and Research* 28:3 (March 2009), 277–292.

12. John Friedmann, "The Uses of Planning Theory," *Journal of Planning Education and Research* 28:2 (Winter 2008), 247–257.

13. Judith E. Innes, "Planning Theory's Emerging Paradigm: Communicative Action and Interactive Practice," *Journal of Planning Education and Research* 14:3 (April 1995), 183–189.

14. Patsy Healey, "The Pragmatic Tradition in Planning Thought."

15. Richard E. Klosterman, "Planning Theory Education: A Thirty-Year Review," *Journal of Planning Education and Research* 31:3 (September 2011), 319–331.

16. Richard A. Beauregard, "Planning with Things," *Journal of Planning Education and Research* 32:2 (June 2012), 182–190.

17. Charles Hoch, "Making Plans: Representation and Intention," *Planning Theory* 6:1 (March 2007), 1–35.

18. Susan S. Fainstein, *The Just City* (Ithaca, NY: Cornell University Press, 2010); and Susan S. Fainstein, "New Directions in Planning Theory," *Urban Affairs Review* 35:4 (March 2000), 451–478.

19. Cf. Bent Flyvberg, *Rationality and Power: Democracy in Practice* (Chicago: University of Chicago Press, 1998).

20. Carolyn G. Loh, "Four Potential Disconnects in the Community Planning Process," *Journal of Planning Education and Research*, 32:1 (March 2012), 33–47.

21. M.A. Qadeer, "The Nature of Urban Land," *The American Journal of Economics and Sociology* 40 (April 1981), 165–182. See also John R. Hitchcock, "The Management of Urban Canada," *Plan Canada* 25:4 (December 1985), 129–136, for an excellent discussion of supply and demand for housing.

22. Penelope Gurstein, "Gender Sensitive Community Planning: A Case Study of the Planning Ourselves In Project," *Canadian Journal of Urban Research* 5:2 (December 1996), 199–219.

23. One of the earliest and best discussions of planning goals is Robert C. Young, "Goals and Goal-Setting," *Journal of the American Institute of Planners* 32 (March 1966), 76–85; also helpful in this regard is Robinson, *Decision-Making in Urban Planning*, 33–41.

24. This idea is expressed well in Ian Bracken, *Urban Planning Methods* (London: Methuen, 1981), 11–35.

25. John Friedmann, "Planning as a Vocation," *Plan Canada* 6 (April 1966), 99–124.

26. Regional Municipality of York, *Vision 2051*, 2012. Reprinted with permission.

27. Judith E. Innes, "Planning through Consensus Building," *Journal of the American Planning Association* 62:4 (Autumn 1996), 460–472.

28. W.G. Roeseler, *Successful American Urban Plans* (Lexington, MA: DC Heath, 1982), xvii.

29. Useful books on planning analysis include Philip Berke, Edward Kaiser, David Godschalk, Edward Kaiser, and F. Stuart Chapin Jr., *Urban Land Use Planning*, 5th ed. (Urbana, IL: University of Illinois Press, 1995/2006); and Richard E. Klosterman, *Community Analysis and Planning Techniques* (Savage, MD: Rowman and Littlefield, 1990).

30. Ken Tamminga, "Restoring Biodiversity in the Urbanizing Region: Towards Pre-emptive Ecosystems Planning," *Plan Canada* 36:4 (July 1996), 10–15.

31. David L.A. Gordon and Ken Tamminga, "Large-Scale Traditional Neighbourhood Development and Pre-emptive Ecosystems Planning: The Markham Experience, 1989–2001," *Journal of Urban Design* 7:3 (2002), 321–340.

32. City of Ottawa, *Ottawa 2020: Environmental Strategy (2003)*; for background on this strategy see Chuck Hostovsky, David Miller, and Cathy Keddy, "The Natural Environment Systems Strategy: Protecting Ottawa–Carleton's Ecological Areas," *Plan Canada*, 35 (November 1995), 26–29.

33. For example, see Vanmap at http://www.city.vancouver.bc.ca/vanmap/setup/index.htm

34. Nancy Nishikawa, "Survey Methods for Planners," in Hemalata Dandekar, ed., *The Planner's Use of Information* (Chicago: APA Planners Press, 2003), 49–78.

35. Britton Harris and Michael Batty, "Locational Models, Geographic Information and Planning Support Systems," *Journal of Planning Education and Research* 12:3 (1993), 184–198.

36. Robert E. Kent and Richard. E. Klosterman, "GIS and Mapping: Pitfalls for Planning," *Journal of the American Planning Association* 66:2 (Spring 2000), 189–198.

37. H. Craig Davis, *Demographic Projection Techniques for Regions and Smaller Areas* (Vancouver: UBC Press, 1995).

38. For a Canadian example, see Craig Davis, "Assessing the Impact of a Firm on a Small-Scale Regional Economy," *Plan Canada* 16 (1976),17, 1–176.

39. Robert W. McCabe, *Planning Applications of Retail Models* (Toronto: Ontario Ministry of Treasury, Economics and Intergovernmental Affairs, 1974).

40. William C. Baer, "General Plan Evaluation Criteria: An Approach to Making Better Plans," *Journal of the American Planning Association* 63:3 (Summer 1997), 329–344.

41. Cf. Emily Talen, "Do Plans Get Implemented? A Review of Evaluation in Planning," *Journal of Planning Literature* 10:3 (1997), 248–-259.

42. An excellent overview and history of plan evaluation is found in Vitor Oliveira and Paulo Pinho, "Evaluation in Urban Planning: Advances and Prospects," *Journal of Planning Literature* 25:4 (June 2010), 343–361.

43. Richard K. Norton, "Using Content Analysis to Evaluate Local Master Plans and Zoning Codes," *Land Use Policy* 25:3 (July 2008), 432–454.

44. Cross-impact analysis has much more sophisticated mathematical antecedents that employ statistical probabilities in the cells. Cf. Norman C, Dalkey, "An Elementary Cross-Impact Model," in Murray Turoff and Harold A. Linstone, eds., *The Delphi

Technique: Techniques and Applications (Newark, NJ: New Jersey Institute of Technology, 2002), 317–329.

45. Robert W. Burchell et al., *Development Impact Assessment Handbook* (Washington: Urban Land Institute, 1994).

46. Peter Boothroyd, "Issues in Social Impact Assessment," *Plan Canada* 18 (June 1978), 118–134.

47. Edward Kaiser, David Godschalk, and F. Stuart Chapin Jr, *Urban Land Use Planning* (Urbana, IL: University of Illinois Press, 1995).

48. Nathaniel Lichfield, *Community Impact Evaluation* (London: UCL Press, 1996). An earlier book is Nathaniel Lichfield et al., *Evaluation in the Planning Process* (Oxford: Pergamon Press, 1975); on cost-benefit analysis, a valuable text is E.J. Mishan, *Cost-Benefit Analysis*, 2nd ed. (London: G. Allen, 1971).

49. Morris Hill, "A Goals-Achievement Matrix for Evaluating Alternative Plans," *Journal of the American Institute of Planners* 34 (1968), 19–29; this is also reproduced in Robinson, *Decision-Making.*

50. Cf. John C. Holmes, "An Ordinal Method of Evaluation," *Urban Studies* 9 (1972), 179–191.

51. Samuel D. Brody and Wesley E. Highfield, "Does Planning Work? Testing the Implementation of Local Environmental Planning in Florida," *Journal of the American Planning Association* 71:2 (Spring 2005), 159–175.

52. Mark Seasons, "Monitoring and Evaluation in Municipal Planning: Considering the Realities," *Journal of the American Planning Association* 69:4 (Autumn 2003), 430–440.

53. Lucie Laurian, Maxine Day, et al., "Evaluating Plan Implementation: A Conformance-Based Methodology," *Journal of the American Planning Association* 70:4 (Autumn 2004), 471–480.

54. Brody and Highfield, "Does Planning Work?"

55. Seasons, "Monitoring and Evaluation in Municipal Planning."

56. Bill Fleming and David Henkel, "Community-Based Ecological Monitoring: A Rapid Appraisal Technique," *Journal of the American Planning Association* 67:4 (Autumn 2001), 456–465.

57. http://www.clc.ca

58. Seasons, "Monitoring and Evaluation."

59. Hok-Lin Leung, *Land Use Planning Made Plain*, 2nd ed. (Toronto: University of Toronto Press, 2003), 129.

60. Jean Trottier, "Putting Design Back into City Planning," *Plan Canada* 47:4 (Winter 2007), 34–36; and Allan B. Jacobs, *Looking at Cities* (Cambridge, MA: Harvard University Press, 1985).

61. Andreas Faludi, "European Planning Doctrine: A Bridge Too Far?" *Journal of Planning Education and Research* 16:1(1996), 41–50.

62. Michael Teitz, "Urban Planning Analysis: Methods and Models," *Journal of the American Institute of Planners* 43 (July 1977), 314–317.

63. James Howard Kunstler, *Home from Nowhere* (New York: Simon and Schuster, 1996).

64. Ellen Dunham-Jones, "New Urbanism as a Counter-Project to Post-Industrialism," *Places* 13:2 (Spring 2000), 26–31.

65. Kevin Lynch, *Site Planning*, 2nd ed. (Cambridge, MA.: MIT Press, 1971), chapter 12, 270–288, provides all the references used in the accompanying discussion.

66. Andres Duany, Jeff Speck, and Mike Lydon, *The Smart Growth Manual* (New York: McGraw Hill, 2009).

67. Sandeep Kumar Agrawal and Emma Landouceur, "Design Review Lessons for Toronto," *Plan Canada* 47:1 (Spring 2007), 32–35.

68. Agrawal and Landouceur, "Design Review Lessons."

69. Amy Helling, "Collaborative Visioning: Proceed with Caution," *Journal of the American Planning Association* 64:3 (Summer 1998), 335–349; and Norman Walzer, ed., *Community Strategic Visioning Programs* (Westport, CT: Praeger, 1996). See also Robert Shipley, Robert Feick, Brent Hall, and Robert Earley, "Evaluating Municipal Visioning," *Planning Practice and Research* 19:2 (May 2004), 195–210.

70. The visioning process employed in Vancouver is described at www.city.vancouver.bc.ca/commsvcs/planning/cityplan/Visions/

71. Canada Mortgage and Housing Corporation, *Sustainable Community Planning and Development: Design Charette Planning Guide* (Ottawa: CMHC, 2002).

72. Canada Mortgage and Housing Corporation, *Tools for Planning Long-Term Urban Sustainability: The CitiesPLUS Design Charettes* (Ottawa: CMHC, 2004).

73. Oliveira and Pinho, "Evaluation in Urban Planning."

74. City of Collingwood, ON, *Urban Design Manual*, www.town.collingwood.on.ca.node/3354

75. Anne Westhues, "Toward a Positive Theory of Planning," *Plan Canada* 25:3 (September 1985), 97–103.

76. Judith E. Innes, "Planning Theory's Emerging Paradigm."

77. Hok-Lin Leung, "Mutual Learning in Development Control," *Plan Canada* 27:2 (April 1987), 44–55.

78. John Friedmann, *Retracking America* (New York: Anchor/Doubleday, 1973), 171–193.

79. City of Vernon, *City Centre Neighbourhood Plan* (September 2011), 4–5.

80. Patsy Healey, *Collaborative Planning: Shaping Places in Fragmented Society* (Vancouver: UBC Press, 1997); and Judith Innes, "Consensus Building and Complex Adaptive Systems: A Framework for Evaluating Collaborative Planning," *Journal of the American Planning Association* 65:4 (Autumn 1999), 412–423.

81. Ken Greenberg, *Walking Home: The Life and Lessons of a City Builder* (Toronto: Random House Canada, 2011), 310.

82. Seasons, "Monitoring and Evaluation."

Internet Resources

Chapter-Relevant Sites

Planning Canadian Communities

www.planningcanadiancommunities.ca

Canada Land Company

www.clc.ca

City of Vancouver Visioning

www.city.vancouver.bc.ca/commsvcs/planning/cityplan/Visions/

York Region Official Plan

www.york.ca/Departments/Planning+and+Development/Long+Range+Planning/ROP.htm

City of Calgary Design Review Panel

www.calgary.ca/PDA/LUPP/Pages/Current-studies-and-ongoing-activities/Urban-design-services.aspx

Visualizing Density

www.lincolninst.edu/subcenters/visualizing-density

Chapter Seven

Focus on Natural and Built Environments

Planners ... when driven to the wall to define their special field of competence tend to fall back on land use planning.

Hans Blumenfeld, 1962

What is it that community planners plan? The many demands made on planners in the last few decades give the impression of a diverse range of concerns, interests, and focus of their practice: policy planning, impact analysis, growth management, the natural environment, social planning, economic development, and more. The diffusion of planners' practice is, however, more illusory than real. The focus is, and always has been, on the built and natural environments of cities and towns. As the Alberta ministry responsible for community planning stated in 1978, the concern is with "the forces [that] influence the physical shape of communities."[1]

At first glance, this seems straightforward enough and, indeed, every Canadian city has a plan. Then we realize that professional planners usually talk in terms of **land use planning**. This is a type of planning for the natural and built environments that provides the focus to the endeavour we call community planning. It is in the nature of a social institution (of which community planning has become) to distinguish its activities and the responsibilities of its practitioners from those of other institutions. Thus, planning is not architecture, or engineering, or the practice of law, even though the professionals in these fields also help shape the community environment in their practice. Moreover, a good deal of the defining of planning is done by the planning practitioners in the field as they carry forward the aims they and the community have for the activity. This chapter identifies the basic dimensions of the community environment with which community planning is concerned. This will allow us to see how community planning's view of the built and natural environment is circumscribed and how other interests in the community view and participate in it. The key questions to focus on in order to grasp community planning practice are:

- *In which ways does the community planner view the natural and built environment and how is this reflected in plans for a community?*
- *What are the main functional areas of a community that planners use to describe the built environment?*

How Planners View the Natural Environment

The best long-term community planning starts with considering the natural environment in which human settlement is found. Ecological planning is especially important in Canada because, although most of the nation's population lives in cities and suburbs, these settlements are scattered across an enormous continent and a diverse range of natural environments.

Planners analyze this range of environments in a variety of ways. The most basic is Patrick Geddes's regional view of the *valley section*. Ian McHarg gave us a more complex view by considering the natural landscape in *layers* in *Design with Nature*. Michael Hough and Anne Whiston Spirn showed the importance of understanding the connections between city form and natural *processes*. Finally, ecologists such as Richard Forman have shown how these processes interact with the *landscape* in both natural and built environments.

Each of these viewpoints will be briefly considered below.

Patrick Geddes's Regional View: The Cross-Section

Geddes taught us to consider human settlements from a regional perspective, using a cross-section though a valley (Figure 8.1, page 187). Different locations in the valley section were suited to different types of human activity—mining and quarrying in the mountains, forestry on the slopes, farming in the valley, and fishing at the water's edge.[2] Geddes demonstrated how to review the natural environment in *cross-sections*, sometimes called transects. His contribution to regional planning is discussed in more detail in Chapter 8.

Ian McHarg's Layers

Ian McHarg used Geddes's transects to analyze some natural environments, such as a coastal dune or a river valley. McHarg combined these sections with maps in multiple *layers* (Figure 5.22, page 125) that analyzed natural and human environments. For natural environments, typical layers included:

- Slope
- Surface drainage
- Soil
- Bedrock
- Soil foundation
- Susceptibility to erosion
- Flooding
- Forest
- Wildlife

These layers were combined to produce a composite of environmental constraints.[3] This analysis is typically done with computers combining the layers in a Geographic Information System (GIS).

Environmental planning agencies now create GIS layers (Figure 7.1) by combining maps and satellite images from a variety of sources:

| Figure 7.1 | Landscape Analysis Layers |

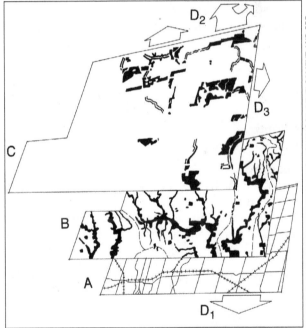

Composite layers from the 1996 Markham Natural Features Study:

(A) Cultural landscape—the roads, railways, and buildings;
(B) Environmental protection areas (EPAs)—flood plains, sensitive areas;
(C) Ecological restoration areas (ERAs)—new connections to make a better landscape matrix;
(D1) Connections to the Lower Rouge Park;
(D2) Connections to the Oak Ridges Moraine;
(D3) Connections to Trans-municipal and inter-watershed linkages.

- Agricultural land capability might come from the Canada Land Inventory.
- Forest resources may come from a provincial department.
- Flood plains are mapped by regional agencies such as conservation authorities.
- Birds and wildlife inventories may come from local field naturalist societies.

The lands with environmentally sensitive characteristics are typically expressed as constraints maps to prohibit development or steer it away.

City Form and Natural Process

More advanced environmental planning considers how natural processes can be incorporated in human settlement planning. Anne Whiston Spirn introduced this topic in an urban environment in her book, *The Granite Garden*.[4] Canadian environmental planner Michael Hough considered natural systems at a wider metropolitan scale in *Cities and Natural Process*.[5] He suggests that planners consider urban ecology as a basis for community design, using the following major categories:

- Climate
- Energy
- Water
- Wildlife
- Plants
- Urban agriculture

Hough was an early and prominent advocate of city farming. Traditional agriculture at the industrial scale of most North American farms is a process that causes great damage to the natural environment, replacing many species of plants and animals with one or two crops. Spirn and Hough argued that small-scale allotment gardens and city farming would increase biodiversity in the urban setting, add to local food supplies, and reconnect people to their local environment.

Landscape Ecology

The layering process began by *Design with Nature* produced simple constraints maps that were useful for obvious problems like flood plains and agricultural land. However, interpreting the composite maps for more complex natural processes required a sophisticated and experienced eye, such as Ian McHarg.

Some of the craft of environmental planning has been supplemented over the past 40 years by extensive biological research using scientific methods. The research from landscape ecology is particularly useful for environmental planners. Landscape ecologists perform scientific research on the interaction of plant and animal systems with diverse landscapes, including the edges of metropolitan regions. Richard Forman has developed a "patch-corridor-matrix" model that is useful for regional environmental planning.[6] *Patches* (Figure 7.2a) are habitats from plant and animal species—the larger and more complex patches (marshes, forests) support more species. *Corridors* (Figure 7.2b) are linear features such as streams and hedgerows that allow movement and migration of plant and animal species. Patches and migration corridors are combined into a landscape *matrix* that supports natural life. The more interconnected the matrix, the more robust its protection of species. Landscape ecologists have a fairly simple decision rule: if a landscape change increases biodiversity, it is useful; if it decreases biodiversity, it is harmful.

Environmental planners can use these landscape ecology tools to increase biodiversity, even as agricultural land on the edge of the metropolitan area is converted for human settlement. If patch sizes (wood lots, marshes) and corridors (streams, greenways) are widened and interconnected and natural systems are enhanced (Figure 7.2c), then the switch from cornfields to suburban habitat may actually increase biodiversity.[7] Figure 7.2d shows how fuzzy, complex edges add value to a patch.

Effective environmental planning should be done at a regional scale, decades ahead of metropolitan expansion. A "greenprint" and "blueprint" are needed to protect patches and corridors while land prices for forests, marshes, and lakes are at rural values. It becomes much more difficult, and expensive, to organize good environmental reconstruction once the typical speculators have acquired the land on the urban edges.[8]

Land Use and the Built Environment

One can distinguish the built environment of communities from that of, for example, an agricultural area by the prevalence of structures and other forms of development of the ground space (or land) for activities of people. In everyday terms, it comprises the houses, parks, industrial plants, institutions, stores and offices, streets and highways, and other transportation facilities. All of these elements, directly or indirectly, involve the existing and prospective use of land by both public and private interests.

Figure 7.2 | Patches, Corridors, and the Landscape Matrix

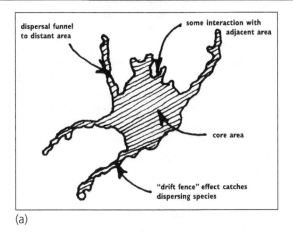

(a)

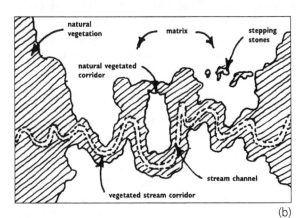

(b)

A good patch, like this wetland (a), has a large core and extensions that reach out to other areas to act as "drift fences" to catch dispersing species.

Good corridors, like this vegetated stream corridor (b), connect patches to make a landscape matrix.

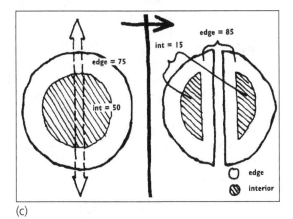

(c)

A road that splits a patch (c) will reduce the valuable interior habitat that supports multiple species. The interior habitat has decreased 50 percent to 15 percent in this example; it would be better to route the road around the patch.

Fuzzy, complex edges are better for patches and corridors than straight lines (d). Trimming the edge of a woodlot and clearing its understory reduces the value of a patch.

SOURCE: FROM LANDSCAPE ECOLOGY PRINCIPLES IN LANDSCAPE ARCHITECTURE AND LAND USE PLANNING BY WENCHE E. DRAMSTAD, JAMES D. OLSEN, AND RICHARD T.T. FOREMAN. COPYRIGHT © 1996 PRESIDENT AND FELLOWS OF HARVARD COLLEGE. REPRODUCED BY PERMISSION OF ISLAND PRESS, WASHINGTON, DC.

One of the main tasks of community planning is to develop an understanding of how a community's physical elements function, the amount of land they require, and their relations with one another. Planners thus seek to identify typical patterns and trends in the use of the land of the community. In order to do this, they must understand how to organize their observations of these elements. Community land use can best

be understood by separating it into three basic—and interrelated—components: (1) *physical facilities* that require space; (2) *activities* of people that use space; and (3) the *functions* that the land serves. These, in turn, are mediated in terms of three main dimensions that determine a community's land use patterns and the trends in patterns: **location**, **intensity**, and **amount** of land required. The understanding thus obtained makes it possible to predict the land use patterns that may be expected when proposals are made for new development or redevelopment of the ground space of a community. But before discussing planning proposals, we must establish more precisely the nature of the three main components of the built environment of communities.

Components of Community Land Use

One of the important characteristics of a city, Jane Jacobs reminds us, is its diversity, and nowhere is this more apparent than on a city's streets.[9] Here we see that there are many uses of the land, even on a sedate residential street: houses of various kinds, possibly some with separate garages; sidewalks, maybe with children walking on their way to school; the road, probably with some cars parked at the side and other cars or bicycles passing along it; delivery trucks, street trees, and possibly even a neighbourhood park.

In this commonplace scene, we encounter instances of each of the three components of community land use. There are physical *facilities* and features (houses, garages, sidewalks, street trees, the road, a park). There are *activities* that are both in view (the children walking to school, the delivery of goods, people moving on bicycles and in cars) and those carried on inside structures (people residing in houses, cars being stored in garages). And the physical features we see have one or more purposes or *functions* (the houses function as residences, the sidewalks provide a path for walking, and the roads provide a path for wheeled vehicles and space to store vehicles).

Figure 7.3 pictures the six basic uses of land in communities: that used for residences, commercial establishments, employment, transportation, institutions, and open space. It must be noted that each of these categories exhibits many physically different forms (i.e., facilities) and performs various functions in the contemporary community. For example, land used for commercial activities may take the form of a shopping street, local plaza, shopping mall, big-box outlet, corner store, or office building. And while all are commercial in nature of their activities, each performs a different function. The same is true of the physical forms and functions in other types of land use.

Planners have devised ways, despite this diversity, of classifying the observations they make about land uses. The most highly regarded methods use three components—facilities, activities, and functions—and permit rigorous measurements to be made in each category.[10] These measurements would usually be done for each parcel of land in the community. The accumulation of such data allows the planner to determine, as Guttenberg points out, "how much space and what kind of facilities a community will need for activities in order to perform its functions at a certain level."[11] These components can be defined in more formal terms as follows:

1. **Facilities**: a description of the physical alterations made to parcels of land and public rights-of-way, especially buildings and other structural features. The type of building (e.g., detached house, office building) needs to be noted because this will indicate the form and quantity of indoor space available to users. Non-building constructions (e.g., pavement, power poles, and recreation equipment) may also need to be recorded.

2. **Activities**: a description of what actually takes place on parcels of land and in public spaces. This involves observing the various users and the form their use takes, usually focusing on the relationships of people obtaining goods and services and the mode of transportation involved. Thus, a house is normally for residential activities, a fire hall for protection activities, a parking lot for vehicle-storage activities.

3. **Functions**: a description of the basic purpose of an enterprise or establishment located on a parcel of land. Individuals, families, firms, and institutions use a specific location for places of residence, business, government, or assembly, and it is these latter purposes that need to be noted.

Planners have not always been assiduous in the classification of land uses in communities. It is not uncommon to find a set of categories such as the following:

Residential	Industrial	Roads	Commercial	Public
• single-detached	• light	• local	• retail	• schools
• semi-detached	• medium	• collector	• auto	• recreation
• townhouse	• heavy	• arterial	• offices	• greenbelt

Figure 7.3 Basic Land Uses in Communities

(a)

(b)

(c)

(d)

(e)

(f)

SOURCE: GERALD HODGE AND DAVID GORDON

Six land uses occupy most of the land in a typical community: (a) residences; (b) employment; (c) commerce or business; (d) institutions; (e) open space, and (f) the streets and roads that connect them all. As we see here, the land uses can take a variety of physical forms.

There are several inconsistencies in such a list: the categories "residential," "commercial," and "industrial" specify the function of a piece of land while "public" denotes ownership and "roads" refers to a facility. And within categories there are references both to facilities (such as "school" and "offices") and to functions (such as "retail" and "recreation"). The residential category refers to building types, while the industrial category, on the other hand, distinguishes intensity of activities between firms. Finally, the residential, industrial, and roads categories are hierarchies, while the commercial and public categories are merely lists. Our ability to understand the built environment of communities is limited, if not flawed, by such inadequate land use classifications.

There are several other characteristics that enter into the description of land use in a community, although they are normally secondary to those above. Such physical characteristics as **slope**, **drainage**, **bearing capacity**, and **view** may play a part in determining the use for the land. In considering the stock of land in a community, we need also to distinguish property that is **developed** from that which is **undeveloped**. The latter category provides an indication of space that could be available for future development. Also often included in land use analyses are the **performance characteristics** of the activities on the land. Some activities generate a lot of traffic, some are carried on mostly in the daytime, others are nighttime activities or have peaks of activity at certain hours, and some may generate noise or odour. These characteristics are important because, although initiated by the land use on one parcel of land, they may spill over onto adjoining parcels or even affect a whole neighbourhood, causing *external effects* (as pointed out in Chapter 1). Activity characteristics often dominate the issues cited by both proponents and opponents when planning proposals are brought forth.

Performance characteristics of land uses are important to note because they enter into planning decisions regarding **mixed-use** development that Canadian planners are increasingly favouring.[12] Mixing of land uses at greater densities and diversity, often following the "traditional neighbourhood design" (TND) concept of the New Urbanism movement, aims at providing greater choice of housing and greater accessibility to other uses in contrast to the highly separated patterns of current suburbs.[13] The essential issue plan-makers face in mixed-use situations is the compatibility of different land uses (each with their particular activity characteristics) when located adjacent to or nearby one another.

Land Use at Different Scales

As suggested above, land use also occurs at different scales or spatial levels. These start from (1) **the individual parcel of land** or **"lot"** and progress outwards to (2) the **block**, (3) the neighbourhood or **district**, (4) **the community**, and (5) **the metropolitan area** or **region.** It can be seen that these are logically connected: parcels make up blocks, which make up neighbourhoods, which make up communities, and so on. The importance of making these distinctions is that the planner will emphasize different facets of land use at each different spatial level. For example, at the level of the single parcel of land, the land use is described in detail (e.g., building types), whereas at the district level, the dominant land use is usually the basis of the description (e.g., retail shopping). When we view an entire community, the land use is usually described by groupings of districts or groupings of uses (e.g., residential areas, local commercial areas). At the regional level, the description of land use will distinguish between urban areas, agricultural areas, open spaces, and their ecosystem components. Further, there is a progression of concern with the three land use components (i.e., facilities, activities, functions) as one moves from the individual parcel level to the block, community, or city, level, as the examples below show.

Parcel Level When the subject is development or redevelopment of a single parcel, the planning issues tend to centre on the physical facility or improvements to be placed on the site: What type of building? How big will it be? What will it look like? There will also be concerns over the activities on the site and in the immediate vicinity of the parcel in question: Will there be a lot of traffic? Noise? Will the building block the sun?

Block Level Within a block, there are often context questions: Will the buildings next door be similar types? How about across the street, or behind our backyard? What sorts of streetscape elements are present—trees, sidewalks, on-street parking? Rear lanes or driveways?

District Level As one moves to district-level planning, there is less concern with structures and physical appearance and more with patterns of activity. Of special interest are the patterns associated with pedestrian movements and auto traffic, as well as those associated with such district-wide facilities as schools, playgrounds, and shopping areas.

Community-Wide Level At the community-wide level, the land use component dealing with the function or purpose of a facility becomes most important because this will affect the other facilities and areas in the community to which it is linked and its need for transportation connections.

Metropolitan/Region Level At this scale the concern is usually with broad land use purposes, such as those of a special district like the downtown, and with facilities that serve the entire area, such as an airport, regional park, or bridge.

An important parallel for community planners to the above land use perspective exists also for the **natural environment**. It, too, is concerned with ecosystems at all scales from, for example, the neighbourhood stream to the regional watershed, and their interdependencies. Similarly, the road and transit corridors that connect urban neighbourhoods perform a comparable role to the natural corridors that connect patches in ecosystem planning.

Relations among Land Uses

The built environment of a community involves a complex set of relationships with many potential conflicts. Planners must be able to understand land use relations, for example, to assess and plan for the impact of changes that may result from new development. The photographs in Figure 7.3 (page 167) show two of these relationships: first, how the land use components (facilities, activities, functions) are related to one another at any single location and, second, how land uses at different locations are related and linked to each other, especially by streets and roadways. A third set of relations is associated with the distribution of particular land uses. Each is discussed below.

Locality Interaction Each parcel of land in a community is linked directly or indirectly to every other parcel. Take, for example, the common situation of a parcel of residential land with a single-family house on it. The road (a facility) provides for the access to the lot and house (another facility), while the sidewalk (a facility) provides space for children to walk and to play (an activity). Analogous relationships can be seen in any shopping plaza between the store buildings, the parking lot, the walkways, shoppers, and drivers. Now suppose that the owner of a house on a large corner lot of a quiet residential street decides to demolish it and build a small shopping plaza. The adjacent homeowners will likely be concerned about the impacts of traffic in their local street, a parking lot next to their front lawn, dumpsters and delivery trucks next to their backyards, and so forth.

These latter land uses may not be acceptable without some form of buffer or separation.

Another important aspect that should be noted is the many activities and/or functions that physical facilities are required to accommodate. The road in front of a store may provide for customer access, for parking customers' and employees' cars, and for facilitating deliveries to the store. The store building may, at different times, house different establishments: a store, office, repair shop, even a residence. Thus, not only are the land use components interrelated, but also the relationships may change. Through all this, the facilities may change little, if at all. Physical facilities have a high degree of permanence among the various land use components, a fact that planners must keep in mind. Many planning issues centre on whether present facilities should be changed to accommodate new activities and functions: Should roads be widened? Old buildings demolished?

Community Interaction The second important aspect involves how land uses in one part of a community are linked to and affect land uses in other parts. Households need to make purchases of food and other goods, and thus create the need for access to stores. If that access is in the form of automobiles, the stores, which depend upon customers, may provide a parking lot. The workers at factories, offices, and stores tend to come from households located in many different parts of the city or town. And the factories, offices, and stores will likely receive their supplies from warehouses and producers in yet other locations. The various facilities associated with transportation in our communities—roads, sidewalks, streetcar lines, rapid transit, bus stops—are the visible evidence of these necessary connections. Under the ground are utility lines, which also allow different facilities and activities to take place at a wide variety of locations and, in Toronto and Montréal, subways for transporting people among locations of activity. While these interactions are necessary for urban life, they may make impacts upon adjacent land. A shopping centre's owners may be delighted that a rapid transit station is proposed for the corner of their property, since it will bring more customers to their stores. But the residents of a collector street may not want a bus stop adjacent to their house, or buses travelling on their street.

Regional Distribution A third set of relational considerations in community land use results from the fact that various facilities are distributed differently across an urban region. Houses, stores selling daily needs, and elementary schools are usually widely distributed, whereas factories, department stores, hospitals, airports, and audi- toriums are not. The latter often tend to be concentrated in one or a few areas. Yet facilities (e.g., transit, roads, and expressways) must be provided for their intercon- nection. Also, care must be taken over whether a change in one level of land use will affect changes in another at a different location, as, for example, in the case of shutting down a neighbourhood elementary school. If a com- munity is experiencing growth, a major planning issue is where the new concentrations of stores, factories, or offices should go—or if they should simply be added to previous concentrations. Poor planning decisions for the regional distribution of land use may show up in wider inefficiencies rather than local conflicts. For example, local objections to shopping or employment uses may lead to a jobs–housing imbalance and possible single- use "bedroom communities" elsewhere in the region that, in turn, cause heavy traffic peaks on adjacent roads.

In conclusion, the built environment must accommo- date a great variety of facilities, activities, and functions. Some have very localized impacts and others might affect an entire region. Moreover, the structures and sur- face improvements have a great deal of permanence. The latter tend to be either adapted or extended over time as new development needs to be accommodated, but are seldom removed. There are, therefore, many areas of potential conflict among the components of land use at any level of the community, as well as between levels. A good deal of the effort put into community planning involves trying to foresee conflicts between land uses, or incompatibilities, as they are often called.

How Planners View the Built Environment

It is the job of the professional planner to understand the workings of built environments of communities, for, as noted, a great deal of planning centres around two issues:

1. The **spatial impact** of proposals for new develop- ment on the built environment; and
2. The **spatial coordination** of the various functions and activities that comprise the built environment.

In facing these two issues, the planner must contend with the built environment's complexity. To do this the planner must find ways to "measure" the important features and relationships in that environment. The three basic components devised to classify land uses— facilities, activities, and functions—constitute one such measuring tool. To achieve a more complete picture of the community environment, five additional dimen- sions and concepts are required.

Dimensions of the Community Environment

The planner is primarily involved with planning for neighbourhoods, districts, or the entire community. This requires that the planner obtain measurements of the built environment larger than that of a single parcel. Since the larger scales are an aggregation of the land use on single parcels of land, the planner will need to combine the observations and also make comparisons between single land uses. Five dimensions provide the planner with most of the information needed about the community environment. These are type, amount, intensity, spatial distribution, and location.

1. Type

With this dimension, the planner considers the funda- mental question of "What is it?" In ecological planning, the concern may be what sort of habitat is involved: Is the land occupied by a forest, a marsh, or a meadow? In land use planning, the land may be occupied by resi- dential, commercial, industrial, or institutional uses. In urban development, land could be occupied by a single- detached, semi-detached row, or tower type of building. In urban design, public space could be a square, a green, or a park.[14] Typological questions are usually analyzed by a classification scheme, which often allows for hybrids, or mixture of types—retail uses in the ground floor of an office building, or a row of townhouses attached to a point-block tower, like the new districts of downtown Vancouver (see Figure 7.8h).

2. Amount

With this dimension, the fundamental question of "How much?" may be broached: How much land is involved, how many dwelling units, how much traffic, how much commercial space, how much school population? It can be seen from these representative questions that the planner may be interested in land, dwelling units, traffic, people, spaces, or floor area. Whether one or several of these variables are involved will depend upon the size of the area and how comprehensive the planning is to be.

3. Intensity

With this dimension, the fundamental question of "How does this compare?" may be applied to a devel- opment proposal. The answer will determine differences between the proposal and either some development one is already familiar with or some planning standards. In general, the measures used are in the form of ratios: persons per hectare, persons per dwelling unit, dwelling units per hectare, floor space per lot area, employees per hectare, and autos per household. This dimension is associated with the common notion of "density," which is discussed later in this chapter.

4. Spatial Distribution

With this dimension, the distribution of facilities, people, and activities may be reckoned. On the one hand, the goal may be making facilities (parks, schools) and services (shopping plazas) available to people more or less equitably. On the other hand, the goal may be avoiding over-concentration of facilities (apartment buildings, stores, public buildings), which could lead to various public utilities and transportation modes being overtaxed. The planner often talks about accessibility and congestion in relation to this dimension.

5. Location

With this dimension, the planner is concerned primarily with the "relative" location of facilities, especially those of community-wide or district-wide interest; that is, how facilities relate to each other—homes to local schools and parks, major shopping areas to the road network, industrial plants to shipping facilities, and so on.

Patterns in the Community Environment

Planners have observed, measured, and analyzed the land uses in many different community situations and have thereby discerned certain patterns and relationships. Many of these, such as the amount of land commonly devoted to roads or the spatial distribution of elementary schools, provide ready guidelines in understanding the layout of the community. Observations about the intensity of various land uses, such as those related to different **building types**, provide the basis for the important concepts of **density and bulk**. Functional relations, or "linkages," between major land uses and districts have generated the concept of **accessibility** as well as the notion of **traffic conflicts**. Many of these patterns are so well established as to be used by planners as principles and standards in planning communities. These are part of the *lingua franca* of professional planners, and it is essential to have a grasp of them. The patterns are sometimes organized into hierarchies of use (e.g., elementary/junior/high schools) or of function (e.g., local/collector/arterial streets). New Urbanist planners have assembled these

patterns into a broader synthesis called **transect planning**, which is described below. A simple Geographic Information System (GIS) can be used to map these various patterns for community design purposes.[15]

Land Use Requirements

When the land in urban communities is tabulated according to seven major urban functions, it is typically found to be distributed in the proportions shown in Figure 7.4. These land use shares are derived from communities in the Vancouver Metropolitan Area, but are typical of other Canadian communities. When communities differ in land use, the difference usually appears in the increase of land required for institutions (e.g., Kingston, Ontario), or in the generous provision of parks (e.g., Edmonton), or in the large amount of industry (e.g., Trois-Rivières).

The type of terrain in a community can also affect the amount of space required by different types of land uses. For example, one that is hilly will probably have few industries and a greater share of residences, while a community that is a transportation terminal will probably attract a greater than average share of industry, commerce, and transport land uses. Communities may also vary in the quality of residences constituting the residential sector, depending upon the income bracket to which their housing market caters. And where two communities are adjacent, one may contain the bulk of the living areas while the other contains the working areas, because of old municipal boundaries.

Two further facets of the data in Figure 7.4 should be noted. The first is that the three land uses that are normally held in private ownership—residential,

Figure 7.4	Typical Land Use Shares of Major Urban Functions

URBAN FUNCTION	PERCENTAGE OF URBAN AREA
Residential	51.0
Commercial	2.5
Industrial	8.0
Institutional	8.0
Transportation/Utilities	4.5
Recreation/Open space	5.5
Streets	20.5
Total urban uses	**100.0**

The Globe and Mail
Thursday, November 17, 2011

Between a House and a High-Rise

Marcus Gee

The thickets of condominium towers growing up in Toronto are changing the face of the city at an astonishing pace. Less remarked on, but potentially as important, is the proliferation of mid-rise buildings on the city's main streets.

It has been the dream of city planners for at least two decades to build up the "avenues" - streets like Queen, Dundas, Bloor and Eglinton. Outside the downtown core, they have traditionally been lined with two- or three-storey buildings with shops on the ground floor and apartments or offices upstairs. That urban form has remained much the same for decades.

If developers could be persuaded to build up those avenues, replacing old buildings and empty lots with structures of five, six, 10 or 11 storeys, it would do wonders for the city. Toronto is expected to grow by 500,000 people over the next 20 years, reaching a population of more than three million. If the city is to remain livable, planners want as many as possible to live on or near key main streets, close to transit and community services.

A recent report said that the main streets have about 200 kilometres of frontage that could be filled with new mid-rise buildings. Those buildings could house around 250,000 people, half of the city's projected population growth.

For a long time, the avenues plan was just pie in the sky. Mid-rise buildings were not worth the hassle of assembling land and clearing hurdles at city hall. Developers much preferred to bang up a 40-storey glass tower on the site of an old parking lot. As a result, Toronto is a city of soaring towers and squat houses, with little in between.

Now, at last, that has begun to change. With the rise in real-estate values and the growing lure of downtown living, developers are flocking to build mid-rise buildings on the avenues that offer an alternative to high-rise condo living and single-family-home ownership.

City planner Lorna Day says the city has been "pleasantly surprised" to find that about a quarter of growth over the past few years has been on the main streets. "We've seen tremendous interest from every scale of developer," she says.

Consider what just one small architecture firm, RAW Design, is doing. On College Street in Little Italy, it designed Cube Lofts, a 21-unit, six-storey block that looks from the front like stacked glass cubes.

A few blocks away, its 1245 Dundas St. will replace an old garage with an eight-storey block marked by jutting overhangs. The eight-storey, 43-unit project plays on the rapid gentrification on Dundas, luring those who "who want to live in an intimate and integrated downtown neighbourhood." Across town in the Beach, the Bellefair condominium overlooking Kew Beach Park will take shape from the shell of an old church.

Projects like these draw people who want to enjoy the active street life of the avenues, but don't want to live up in the sky and don't want the expense or trouble of a house in a popular neighbourhood. "They're not blockbusters," says architect Roland Rom Colthoff, who teamed up with Richard Witt to form RAW in 2007. "By definition they have to fit into the neighbourhood."

The trouble is red tape. Despite all the earnest talk about intensifying the avenues — a goal set out in the city's official plan — city hall still places all sorts of obstacles in the way of developers who want to go mid-rise. Often they have to spend months or even years fighting for a zoning change. Once they get approval, they have to cope with restrictive, often nonsensical rules. One requires them to put a big electrical-transformer vault in the building, gobbling valuable space; another to build an "amenity space" like a gym or party room, often redundant in a busy neighbourhood with amenities all around.

"Their plan says they want to develop the avenues," says Mr. Rom Colthoff, "but they have an old set of rules that presents a big delay in bringing these projects to market."

If the city really wants to build up its avenues, it should learn when to get out of the way.

commercial, and industrial—constitute nearly two-thirds of the area of the community. The second is that one-fifth of the community's space is required for streets and roads. The latter, when combined with parks and some institutional uses of land, constitutes the public space of the community over which the local government has direct control; that is, only about 30 percent of the total community area.

Functional Arrangements

In order to plan comprehensively for a community, whether for the entire community or only a portion of it, it is necessary to have an integrated view of it. This means moving beyond simple land use composition and obtaining a picture of how the community functions. The knowledge that has accumulated about cities and towns allows the planner to utilize basic tendencies about how communities function in structuring the community's planning needs, as, for example, with the tendencies in community composition and the hierarchy of facilities in a community.

Functional Composition Almost every community may be seen as comprising a number of major functional areas that reflect basic human activities. At its most fundamental level a community consists of **living areas, working areas**, and **community facilities**, all linked together by a **circulation system.** This simple concept of the functioning parts of the community contains the essential elements with which the planner is concerned—that is, people must have places to live and to work. The circulation system will provide for the necessary interconnections between living areas and working areas and also for access to community facilities. The latter are necessary adjuncts for the social, economic, and governing facets of a community. The category of working areas may be elaborated to distinguish between those providing goods and services to

residents—commercial areas—and those involved in the processing and distribution of goods—industrial areas. These four functional elements become a focus of virtually every community plan.

Functional Reach of Facilities It is easy to see in a community that some facilities are provided for the use of the community as a whole, such as a civic auditorium or a general hospital, while others serve only small parts, such as a local park or an elementary school. The same is true for commercial facilities and also for streets and highways. In other words, key public and private facilities each have a particular **functional reach** out into the community by virtue of the roles they play. Planners utilize this principle when proposing accessibility standards (Figure 7.5) and the distribution of various public and commercial facilities, and in the designation of

Figure 7.5	Standards of Accessibility from Home to Selected Urban Land Uses and Facilities

DESTINATION	TIME/DISTANCE
Place of work	20 to 30 min
Central business district	30 to 45 min
Local shopping centre	0.8 km or 10 min
Elementary school	0.8 km
High school	1.6 km or 20 min
Playgrounds and local parks	0.8 km
Major park or conservation area	30 to 45 min
Commercial deliveries	30 to 60 min

Source: F. Stuart Chapin Jr., *Urban Land Use Planning*, 2nd ed. (Champaign-Urbana: University of Illinois Press, 1964, 376.) Reprinted with permission from the author.

streets in a community plan. Further, there is ample justification for this from two points of view. First, it streamlines services and makes the best use of funds for public investments. Second, it allows districts—residential, commercial, or industrial—to serve their primary purposes as living, working, or shopping areas most effectively. There have been notable refinements in recent years in the locational arrangements of retail and educational facilities, for example, with big-box stores, cinemas, and specialty schools that modify traditional facility hierarchies.[16]

Density and Space Needs

One of the greatest concerns about city-building in the late 19th and early 20th centuries was congestion: too many people, too little space between buildings, too much traffic. The consequences for health and safety had been amply demonstrated (see Chapters 3 and 4), and much of the effort in community planning since then has been devoted to avoiding congestion in its various forms. Intensity of land use is, as we noted earlier, one of the main dimensions planners employ in measuring the adequacy of planning proposals. Since congestion is simply the too-intense use of a community's ground space, planners seek indicators that show when land uses would be approaching congested conditions, in order to avoid them. The most widely used indicators are those relating to density. **Density,** as planners define it, means the number of land uses or land users on a specified unit of ground space in the community. It is a ratio with a *numerator* (e.g., number of persons) and a *denominator* (e.g., an area of land, usually in hectares).[17] Most commonly, density indicators are used in regard to residential development: the number of persons per hectare or the number of dwelling units per hectare. There are analogous density measures for industrial and commercial areas, such as the number of employees per hectare. The appeal of the density measure is that it readily links the available land, structures, and activities that need space. Thus, by knowing the type of development that is proposed—for example, the construction of a certain number of single-family detached houses—the amount of land that will be required can be calculated by knowing the density at which such housing is normally built. Or, if a certain number of apartment units were proposed on a site, it could be ascertained whether this would result in an acceptable density. Equally important, it is a measure that is comparable to other development sites (when the same numerators and denominators are being used). Two variants of the density measure deserve attention:

- **Net density**, when used in regard to residential areas, refers to the number of dwelling units, households, or persons being accommodated on specified parcels of land (Figure 7.6a). It does not include public roads, lanes or sidewalks, or other community land uses. It is sometimes called parcel density or net site density.
- **Gross density**, when used in regard to residential areas, also refers to the number of dwelling units, households, or persons but this time includes the specified parcels of land **and** the public roads, lanes or sidewalks, and other community land uses such as parks, schools, and churches considered *relevant* to the residential area (Figure 7.6b). It is also referred to as neighbourhood density.

It can be seen in the case of gross density that the denominator can vary depending upon which features of the community are included in the land measure. Indeed, gross density ratios may be sought for a variety of areas, such as for one or several neighbourhoods or even for an entire community, using the municipal boundary as the land measure. Although a very useful measure, it is important when comparing gross densities that land areas be defined the same way.

Typically, planners measure residential density in terms of dwelling units per hectare because this has a direct connection to the built environment. When applied this way it carries with it the professional's knowledge of the type and intensity of such dwellings under average circumstances. It also carries with it, implicitly, some norm of acceptable and/or desirable density for the type of dwelling. Indeed, there is now widespread agreement among builders and planners about the density of dwellings that will contribute to an amenable community environment. The chart in Figure 7.7 describes the densities that typically result when different types of housing are built.

Comparing net densities using dwelling units per hectare assumes that the variation in the size of dwelling units is not important. This assumption may be adequate in suburban areas, but often is not appropriate in downtown areas, where the bulk of apartment buildings is a planning issue. The wide range in urban apartment unit sizes, from 50-square-metre bachelor units to 250-square-metre penthouses means that Floor Area Ratio (discussed on page 176) is a more appropriate net density measure.

| Figure 7.6 | Net and Gross Density |

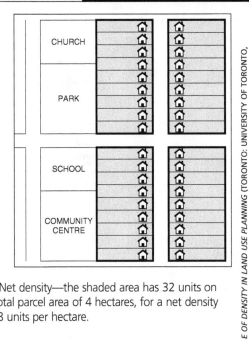

SOURCE: ADAPTED FROM HITCHCOCK, JOHN, *A PRIMER ON THE USE OF DENSITY IN LAND USE PLANNING* (TORONTO: UNIVERSITY OF TORONTO, PROGRAM IN PLANNING, DEPARTMENT OF GEOGRAPHY, 1994), PAPER NO. 41.

(a) Net density—the shaded area has 32 units on a total parcel area of 4 hectares, for a net density of 8 units per hectare.

Total area of residential parcels: 4 hectares
Total area of public streets (rights-of-way): 2 hectares
Total area of residentially related uses: 2 hectares
Gross Residential Area (shaded): 8 hectares
Number of residential units: 32
Gross Residential Area Density: 4 units/hectare
(1.6 units/acre)

(b) Gross density—the shaded area now also includes 2 hectares of roads and 2 hectares of community facilities. So the gross density is 32 units divided by 8 hectares, or 4 units per hectare. Note that failing to specify whether a density is calculated upon a *gross* or *net* basis means that a planner could be incorrect by a factor of 50–100 percent.

Dwelling unit densities start, of course, from population densities: each dwelling unit is accommodation for a household. The number of people in households and the composition of household populations differ within a community. This generates the need for different kinds of accommodation. In Figure 7.7, household sizes that are typical of different types of housing have been applied to arrive at the net density ranges. For example, families with young children tend to prefer housing that has direct ground access and are most often found in low-density housing or row housing. The average household size of these families is commonly found to average 3.0–3.5 persons. By the same token, families with children tend not to seek high-density housing.[18] The latter housing usually accommodates an older population: young adults, couples, families with teenagers, elderly couples, and single-person households, both young and old. In these accommodations, the household size tends to average 2.0–2.5 persons or less. The planner can, thus, estimate the various kinds of housing needs for a community by knowing the composition of the population and, following from there, the types of services and facilities that will be needed in the various housing areas. Hence, low-density areas with children need schools and playgrounds within easy access, while high-density areas that generate more traffic need easy access to major roads, and so on. Examples of the physical outcome of housing at different densities are shown in Figure 7.7.

As alluded to above, a measure of population density is often sought for an entire municipality, where the latter is the denominator. Among its uses is to estimate the amount of land that might be consumed by a new municipality or the amount of land needed when an increase in population is anticipated.[19] (Gross municipal area density figures are provided for municipalities and all other census-reporting units by Statistics Canada in their "Community Profiles.")[20] Canadian municipalities tend to have gross densities of 1000 to 7000 persons per square kilometre, depending upon the age and size of community. Newer and smaller communities usually have lower densities, with the converse being true for older and larger communities. This raises a second issue about differences in density. There are differences not only because of the size and age of a community, but also because of the style of building that is acceptable in the community. For example, 125 dwelling units per hectare is considered high density in Kingston, Ontario, and is the maximum normally allowed, whereas densities several times higher are considered acceptable in other cities.

	Figure 7.7	Typical Densities (Net) of Different Forms of Housing		

DENSITY	HOUSING TYPE	BUILDING HEIGHT IN STOREYS	DWELLINGS PER NET HECTARE	PERSONS PER NET HECTARE
Low	One-family detached	1–2	12–17	43–48
	Two-family	1–2	19–29	48–84
Medium	Row house, garden apartment	2–3	24–48	72–144
	Walk-up apartment	3–4	48–96	120–192
High	Multi-family	5–10	96–192	192–360
	Multi-family	10–16	192–240	360–480
	Multi-family	over 16	240–960	480–1680

The density indicator is thus used not only in determining housing and land requirements, but also in assessing the compatibility of proposed development with the existing physical form of the community (Figure 7.8).

Bulk of Buildings

Closely associated with the idea of density is the concept of **bulk.** The density on a site may increase by increasing the height of a building, covering a larger portion of the site with a building, or both. In general, the larger the area of a site that a building covers, the bulkier it will be, not only in actuality but also in our visual impression of the building. Bulk is thus a measure of the actual **volume** of a building (its height times its basic footprint or area of ground covered). Building bulk needs to be considered in three different ways by the planner: its aesthetic aspects, its land use implications, and its economic viability, as discussed below.

Aesthetic Considerations The standards of taste and appearance by which members of a community assess the bulkiness of buildings have to be taken into account. A community that has no very tall buildings, such as Saint John, New Brunswick may want to limit the height of new buildings; a community that has lots of open space, such as Saskatoon, may want to limit the coverage of buildings on a site. In Vancouver, where the mountain vista is treasured by most citizens, the bulk of downtown buildings is a frequent subject of planning debate. Tall, thin towers may allow better views than short, wide slabs. Thus, zoning bylaws often contain the aesthetic concerns of citizens in their bulk regulations. As well, some communities include Design Guidelines in their plans and still others publish (and make available online) Design Guides to indicate preferred bulk of new structures.

Land Use Considerations The bulk of a building also has land use implications. The bulkier the building, in general, the greater the number of activities associated with it—that is, more dwelling units, commercial establishments, and so forth, will be located there. The planner is aware that more intense use of a site may put pressure on public services and facilities, such as sewer lines, roads, and schools. In addition, the bulk of the building will affect the amount of ground space that might be needed on the site for access, for parking, and simply for open space for the occupants of the building. Bulky buildings may affect the light and air available both to occupants and to people on adjacent properties. Tall buildings may shade lower buildings and nearby properties from the sun, an issue that has become important to the installation of solar-energy units.

Economic Considerations The economics of building are directly associated with the matter of building bulk. The value of the land, the economical size of the establishment, and the costs of building all enter into the original proposal made by those wishing to develop a site. Take a simple case: apartment buildings more than 3–4 storeys tall usually require the installation of an elevator and extra fire exits, but it is normally not economical to build at less than 6–8 storeys in order to recover the extra costs. Thus, the taller building imposes the need for the land to accommodate twice the number of apartment units. How can this extra bulk be accommodated? For what else could the site be used? There are similar versions of this trade-off argument for all types of structures built for commercial purposes in a city or town. An analogous issue pertaining to residential structures arose in the late 1980s with the advent of "mega-houses" (popularly called "McMansions") in the new-house market (see also Chapter 16).

Figure 7.8

Figure 7.8   Types of Housing Comprising Different Densities

SOURCE: GERALD HODGE AND DAVID GORDON.

(a) The **single-family detached** house dominates many low-density districts; (b) a **semi-detached** unit is divided by a wall; (c) townhouses arrange units in a row, with individual entrances; (d) **stacked townhouses** like these Montréal "plexes" provide 2–3 units with separate access to grade; (e) **garden apartments** provide housing at medium density and human scale; and taller apartment buildings can provide high-density living in either (f) **slab blocks**, (g) **perimeter blocks**, or (h) **point towers**. These point towers have townhouses defining the edges of their blocks, which has proved to be a successful inner-city urban design concept for Vancouver.

Indexes of Bulk In order to deal with the issue of building bulk, planners have devised an index of building bulk called the **Floor Area Ratio** (FAR) in order to respond to the various aesthetic, planning, and economic interests in these matters. Sometimes, it is called the Floor Space Ratio (FSR) or Floor Space Index (FSI). The FAR relates the floor area of a building to the area of the site. A FAR of 1.0 is the equivalent of a one-storey building covering the entire lot. A one-storey building may not suit the owner, who may wish, for example, to provide parking, so a 1.0 FAR might be translated into a two-storey building covering only half the site, or a three-storey building covering one-third of the site, and so on. At some point, the builder may find it economically unfeasible to add height, or the community may find only certain heights of buildings acceptable. On the latter point, there appear to be community norms on downtown building bulk. For example, in Toronto a FAR of 12.0 is acceptable, but in Vancouver an FAR of 6.0 is considered high. Smaller cities seem to prefer a FAR of 3.0.

The Floor Area Ratio is used to determine more than just the acceptable levels of building bulk. There may be setback requirements from the front, back, and side lot lines, parking space requirements, and, in some cases, requirements to provide recreation space and landscaping. Each of these will reduce the amount of the lot that can be built upon at ground level, thereby forcing the building to be made taller. The FAR may also be used to obtain more open space at ground level than is normally required. In parts of cities where land costs are very high (as in many downtown areas and at key intersections) and where the economics of development demand the intense use of a site, a higher than normal FAR may be offered as a bonus in return for providing extra open space at ground level. The widespread appearance beginning in the 1950s of plazas and sitting spaces in areas with tall office buildings and hotels is evidence of this incentive system being applied.

Often overlooked is that the height of a building is not necessarily related to its density. Many citizen conflicts over increased density are actually a concern about changes in the type of building in their neighbourhood. Since it is possible to have many different types of buildings at the same density, it is often more important to ensure compatible building types. Most low-density, low-rise, urban neighbourhoods would find the 30-storey tower in Figure 7.9 below to be an unacceptable change in scale. Yet the four-storey stacked townhouses have exactly the same net density, expressed in Floor Area Ratio, and are built with little complaint in many urban and suburban areas. It would be better to prohibit high-rise towers than to reduce the permitted density.

Linkages and Accessibility

In the planner's view, the community environment is a set of living and working areas, each occupying a specific part of the ground space, and community facilities distributed at various locations. Implicit in this view is the notion that interaction must be facilitated among them. Essentially, this means there must be a means of circulation available, so that individuals, households, firms, and institutions that are separated from one another may be in contact. In this view of the built environment, the planner focuses on the patterns of interaction between people, firms, and institutions. Although there is a great deal of individuality and complexity in these interactions, important patterns can be discerned in the fairly repetitive routines that people or organizations follow when engaging in activities in the community.

Some activities are regularly patterned, such as the daily journey to work or regular food shopping; some are casual or infrequent, as in partaking of entertainment activities and visits for medical care. Commercial firms and public institutions have comparable patterns: they receive supplies, make deliveries, and are the destination for employees and clients. A commonplace example is the daily pattern of children, teachers, and other staff travelling to their local school. The planner thinks of these interactions in terms of **linkages** and seeks to accommodate them, both by arranging a suitable pattern of land uses and by providing an appropriate transportation network. Perry's classic Neighbourhood Unit was, for example, based on facilitating children's walking journeys to school (see Chapter 4).

An early step in community planning for land use is the consideration of which activities need to be linked and how close this access ought to be. Another consideration is the various means of transportation that are likely to be used. Accumulated experience in these matters indicates that closeness of access is more appropriately measured in terms of time and cost rather than pure distance, especially if the linkage must be made by automobile or public transit. Where access is usually achieved on foot, such as to local schools, parks, and shopping areas, distance is the limiting factor. The table in Figure 7.5 shows the time and distance standards that planners have found will provide a high level

| Figure 7.9 | Density and Built Form |

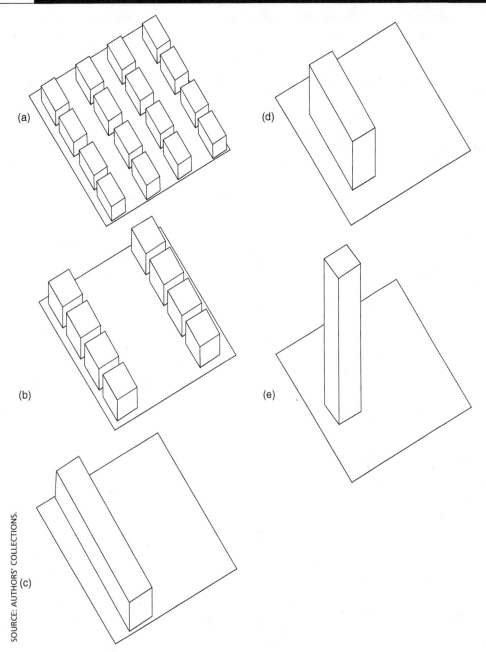

SOURCE: AUTHORS' COLLECTIONS.

The density of development is only partially related to built form. In all five of the examples above, **the density is exactly the same**. They all have a Floor Area Ratio (FAR) of 1.0, which can be achieved by (a) two-storey townhouses covering 50 percent of the site; (b) four-storey townhouses covering 25 percent of the site; (c) six-storey deck access apartments covering 16 percent of the site; (d) a ten-storey slab apartment building covering 10 percent of the site; or (e) a thirty-storey point tower covering 3 percent of the site. Most arguments about densification revolve around **building type**, not **density**, since the townhouses might be acceptable to many neighbours in single detached houses, but the point tower would not.

Chapter 7 Focus on Natural and Built Environments

of convenience for most residents (probably 85 percent or more) in most urban communities.[21] Interestingly, these parameters, although derived in the 1960s, have remained relatively constant to the present day.

Every linkage is, of course, accomplished by some form of transportation, and the planner must be cognizant of the modes of travel that might be used for different linkages. For some time now, perhaps since the planning of the model industrial villages well over a century ago, planners have recognized the incompatibility of wheeled and foot traffic in many situations. The response has been to try and find ways to separate modes of travel: most simply, sidewalks are provided as well as roadways, or exclusive footpaths may be used, as in the designs for the greenbelt towns. Nowadays, bikeways and entire pedestrian shopping precincts may be set aside. Another facet of planning for traffic separation was recognized when automobiles came into widespread use in the 1920s. The car could not only travel much faster than all other modes; it could also cover greater distances. Yet the car holds no advantage unless it is allowed to move expeditiously. Areas not originally designed for such traffic may thus suffer through having to accommodate it. A perennial planning problem is to find ways of providing auto and truck access to living and working areas while also providing the means for large volumes of motorized traffic to move freely.

Transect Planning

Transect (cross-section) planning, a relatively new approach, is based on the notion of a continuum of environments, ranging from rural to urban, each with their appropriate composition.[22] It derives from a cross-section that one might draw from the core of a city to the outer (rural) edge of the city's region as can be seen in Figure 7.10. (It is a variant of Patrick Geddes's "valley section," as discussed earlier.) These sets of environments vary in their degree of urban character. Further, transect planning draws heavily on ecological principles, dividing its continuum into six "ecozones," and seeks to find the "proper balance between natural and human-made environments."

In practice, transect planning involves allocating urban elements spatially along the transect to the location at which they are deemed appropriate; that is, situating the urban elements where they best fit with other elements of the natural and built environments. In making such spatial allocations, attention is paid not only to land use but also to building types and frontages, streetscapes, roads, and open space. This leads, in turn,

to a mixing of land uses in districts rather than single-use districts as with much conventional zoning. Transect planning thus complements the New Urbanism principles embodied in traditional neighbourhood design (TND).[23]

Planners' Principles of Community Land Use

Planners have developed a number of principles to use when arranging land uses in a community, which have grown out of a century of planning thought, analysis, and practical experience. These principles (or "should" statements), which are usually implicit in advice that planners offer rather than stated outright, have been accepted as desirable goals by builders, architects, engineers, and the general public. Although not heralded, their importance in the actions that give form to the community environment should not be underestimated. The basic ones are listed here:

1. The community's built environment and its natural ecosystem should be planned jointly so that they may function harmoniously.
2. Land uses should be located such that their activity characteristics do not conflict with one another and each is allowed to function effectively.
3. The pattern of land uses should provide for the integration of all functions and areas.
4. The circulation system should support the land use pattern.
5. Social cohesion should be promoted by providing the opportunity for the proximity of home, employment centres, shopping opportunities, recreation areas, and schools.
6. Residential areas should be safe, attractive, and well drained, and have variety in their design.
7. Housing should be provided in a range of types to suit the income structure of the community and allow for a range of choice for residents.
8. Commercial and service areas should be located so as to be convenient and safe for clients and efficient for businesses.
9. Traffic with different movement, speed, and volume characteristics should be separated from one another.
10. The downtown area should be considered the social and business heart of the community.

This list of planning principles may be added to or modified as conditions and tastes change in a community. Two tendencies are often at work to modify these

Figure 7.10 | The Rural–Urban Transect

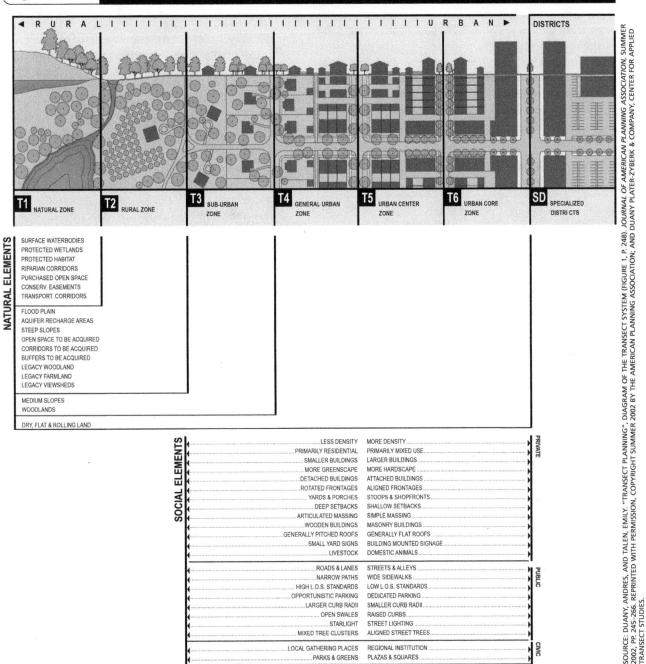

SOURCE: DUANY, ANDRES, AND TALEN, EMILY. "TRANSECT PLANNING". DIAGRAM OF THE TRANSECT SYSTEM (FIGURE 1, P. 248). JOURNAL OF AMERICAN PLANNING ASSOCIATION. SUMMER 2002, PP. 245–266. REPRINTED WITH PERMISSION, COPYRIGHT SUMMER 2002 BY THE AMERICAN PLANNING ASSOCIATION; AND DUANY PLATER-ZYBERK & COMPANY, CENTER FOR APPLIED TRANSECT STUDIES.

New Urbanist community planners recommend different types of urban design and built form for each zone in this rural–urban transect. Standards for housing types, streets, and parks should be different for suburban and urban districts. This idea may seem obvious, but many municipalities have only a single set of development standards that mirror the mature urban area.

basic principles. The first is the realization that many of these principles emanate from earlier planning concepts that may now be considered too rigid, such as the separation of uses or traffic.[24] The second tendency is the desire to establish new planning principles as new issues arise, such as for waterfront planning, environmental pollution, energy conservation, aging of the population, or affordable housing. Indeed, the first principle in the list above is a relatively recent addition to Canadian planners' set of principles.

Other Views of the Built and Natural Environments

The land use perspective that planners bring to the task of community plan-making comprises several dimensions and, as well, is subject to ongoing social and cultural refinement. In other words, land use and the built environment can be, and is, viewed in different ways at different times by other professionals who become involved in community planning. Other professions, for example, are involved in assisting a community shape its physical form, some as colleagues of planners within local government, some as consultants to developers, and some as advocates for the community. Further, how land is used in a community is a reflection of its citizens' values and, as we saw in preceding chapters, the aspects of land use considered important to plan for and regulate tend to change both over time and among communities. Thus, the planner's aim to strive for comprehensiveness in a community's plan must be able to accommodate diverse professional and cultural views of the meaning of land use that comprises the built environment.

As Seen by Other Professions

While the planner has the central professional role in planning the built environment of a community, views other than those of the planner also enter into such deliberations. Especially significant are the perspectives of several other professions. Lawyers, architects, engineers, landscape architects, environmental planners, and social workers all play substantial roles in the planning and development of communities. They bring their special concerns into community plan-making and, in so doing, add their distinctive views of the built environment to those of the planner. Below, we briefly examine the views of these professional areas regarding a community's built environment. Each of these affect the focus as well as the nature of the physical plans that

are prepared, but, at the same time, they help to better reflect the complex physical milieu of the built environment within which planners work.

1. The **lawyer** views the community environment as, essentially, a configuration of parcels of land, each of which has a legal description and carries a certain set of property rights. The lawyer thus seeks great precision in regard to plans affecting the parcels of land that constitute the community. Because planning proposals may have the effect of redefining property rights—limiting uses, heights, and placement of buildings—lawyers have a natural concern that planning processes be conducted properly and that prior property rights not be arbitrarily taken away. The two types of physical plans that most closely reflect the built environment for the lawyer are the subdivision plan and the site plan because of the precision accorded to property lines. And, of course, the written land use regulations and planning policies that have legal stature are of great importance to the lawyer involved with community planning matters (see Chapter 16).

2. The **architect's**, **landscape architect's,** and **urban designer's** view of the community environment is mostly a three-dimensional one—that is, the architect is concerned with what can be built on the ground space of the community and what the resulting construction will look like. This concern extends from the design of individual buildings and other structures to groupings of buildings (e.g., an apartment complex), to streetscapes and the design of open spaces in the community. Architects and landscape architects may design subdivisions to achieve certain groupings of buildings and other features, and they usually prepare the site plan for a project. Except with respect to special district plans and the height regulations for buildings, many community plans have little to say explicitly about the visual outcome of land development. Comprehensive plans may state a policy of wishing "to preserve the character" of, say, an historic area, but it usually remains the prerogative of the designer to bring in the third dimension. As building and site aesthetics are often the subject of vigorous debate in a community, it is easy to see that visual qualities are very important in planning. They are, however, not easily resolved, impinging as they do on people's values about aesthetics, the extent of land use control, and the nature of growth and change

in the community. The landscape architect may also become involved in environmental issues regarding a site (see below).

3. The **engineer's** view of the community environment is primarily functional. Thus, the engineer is concerned with how well the various physical elements function in the community—the street system and other forms of transportation, the water supply and sewerage system, the electricity and communications systems—both individually and in conjunction with one another. The engineer's view is both comprehensive and detailed in regard to the community environment, but tends to be limited to providing a framework of services and streets within which land development can take place. A special concern of the engineer is the way in which natural drainage patterns may be affected by land development. It is the duty of the municipality to try to ensure that, when the surface of the land is modified in any land development, nearby properties are not affected adversely in regard to drainage. The engineer's concern is, indeed, among the traditional concerns of community planning that were addressed in the first planning acts in Canada: the alignment of streets, the efficient extension of public utilities, and drainage conditions. Subdivision plans and site plans that are required to address these matters directly often involve an engineer in their preparation and review.

4. The **environmental planner** and, not least, **environmental interest groups** have brought into sharp focus concerns over the effect of planning decisions on the natural environment of a community. Their view encompasses the land, water, and air of the community and the quality of each. The most pressing concerns are with the effluents generated by various land uses: sewage, other liquid effluents, smoke and fumes, noise, and solid wastes. Belatedly, it seems, we have come to know that these effluents, if they are not planned for and managed properly, can be dangerous to the health and safety not only of people on neighbouring properties but of the entire community. There are also related concerns with more passive elements of the environment, such as the disturbance of areas of natural vegetation (e.g., marshes and woods) and the preservation of views. Community plans increasingly respect these factors, and planners scrutinize

development proposals regarding their environmental impact, usually with the assistance of environmental planners and landscape architects. Nonetheless, environmental issues are still in many ways very technical, complex, incompletely understood, and often controversial.[25]

5. The **social worker's** view of the built environment is, primarily from the perspective of housing. This involves issues of affordability and adequacy of housing, as well as the more recent issues of homelessness and housing for the burgeoning immigrant population.[26] Given that the largest use of community land is for housing, these are substantial issues that need to be addressed. A complementary role is that of the **social planner** in the few communities that provide such a governmental focal point.

Emergent Views

Just as we saw the physical planning perspective in previous generations evolving as new issues and ideals emerged (see especially Chapters 4 and 5), so, too, are views of the built environment being extended nowadays, sometimes quite dramatically. New planning specialities for diverse and healthy communities are emerging in current practice. Specialized planning programs for seniors, women, youth, immigrants, and Aboriginal peoples can be found in many Canadian communities, while meeting the needs of the frail and physically-challenged has become a mandate from several provinces. Finally, a strong public health perspective regarding the built environment has returned, re-connecting community planning to one of its founding disciplines. All these emergent planning views are discussed in Chapter 13.

Many different types of plans will be discussed in the chapters ahead. Large-scale regional metropolitan plans are introduced next in Chapter 8; then urban community plans in Chapter 9, followed by plans from small towns and northern areas in Chapter 10. The many types of neighbourhood and district plans are described in Chapter 11, followed by plans for infrastructure systems in Chapter 12.

Reflections

The set of land uses that comprise the built environment of a city, town, or rural community is the realm of the planner, and the practice of community planning influences the development of these land uses toward a desired physical shape for the community.[27] To this end, planners devise means for systematically describing land uses regarding their space needs, functional relations, and linkages to one another. Through the experience of past practice, an array of plans has evolved to deal with different aggregates of land use. The outcome has been a nested set of land use plans, with the comprehensive community plan encompassing all the land uses in the community and subsidiary plans covering districts, specific land use functions, and individual sites, as well as developed or undeveloped land.

Understandably, this system for analyzing and portraying land uses, which evolved in the practice of planning communities over 65 years, reflected a particular perspective on land use—the professional planner's perspective. Although that perspective has been shaped and refined by the ideas and approaches to land use of associated professions, it is relatively recent that citizen from outside the professional spectrum have insisted on having their views incorporated into community plans. These initiatives and others are challenging long-held assumptions that land use planning is only about land, physical facilities, and natural features, and not about the people who use the land or the natural setting for land use.

Traditional planning practices have begun to acknowledge these emerging needs and concerns and incorporate them into the comprehensive community plan. That these viewpoints are all contending for recognition and a role in the community plan indicates the importance of this planning tool, but it also means that the community plan (and its subsidiary plans) will have to continue to change, possibly more profoundly than in the past. The thrust is for comprehensive community plans to become more truly comprehensive, to integrate the physical, social, and natural elements of a community. In light of this goal, consider the following questions:

- *Why is it necessary to differentiate between net and gross density in assessing residential projects?*
- *How can community plans better integrate physical, social, economic, and natural environmental components of a community?*

Reference Notes

1. Alberta, Department of Municipal Affairs, *Planning in Alberta: A Guide and Directory* (Edmonton, 1978), 1.
2. Geddes, Patrick, *Cities in Evolution*, 3rd ed. (London: Ernest Benn, 1968).
3. Ian McHarg, *Design with Nature* (New York: Doubleday, 1969) 36–41.
4. Anne Whiston Spirn, *The Granite Garden: Urban Nature and Human Design* (New York: Basic Books, 1984).
5. Michael Hough, *Cities and Natural Process: A Basis for Sustainability* (New York: Routledge, 2004).
6. Richard Forman, *Land Mosaics: The Ecology of Landscapes and Regions* (New York: Cambridge University Press,1995); and *Urban Regions: Ecology and Planning beyond the City* (New York: Cambridge University Press, 2008).
7. Dan Perlmann and Jeffry Milder, *Practical Ecology: For Planners, Developers and Citizens* (Washington, DC: Island Press, 2005); Ken Tamminga, "Restoring Biodiversity in the Urbanizing Region: Towards Pre-emptive Ecosystems Planning," *Plan Canada* 36:4 (July 1996), 10–15; and David Waltner-Toews, James Kay, and Nina-Marie Lister, *The Ecosystem Approach: Complexity, Uncertainty, and Managing for Sustainability* (New York: Columbia University Press, 2008).
8. David Gordon and Ken Tamminga, "Large-Scale Traditional Neighbourhood Development and Pre-emptive Ecosystem Planning: The Markham Experience, 1989–2001," *Journal of Urban Design* 7:3 (2002), 321–340.
9. Jane Jacobs, *The Death and Life of Great American Cities* (New York: Random House, 1961).
10. Cf. Albert Z. Guttenberg, "A Multiple Land Use Classification System," *Journal of the American Institute of Planners* (August 1959), 143–150; and Gerald Hodge and Robert McCabe, eds., "Land Use Classification and Coding in Canada: An Appraisal," *Plan Canada* 8:2 (June 1968), 1–28.
11. Guttenberg, "A Multiple Land Use Classification System."
12. Jill Grant, "Mixed Use in Theory and Practice: Canadian Experience with Implementing a Planning Principle," *Journal of the American Planning Association* 68:1 (Winter 2002), 71–84.
13. Congress for the New Urbanism, *Charter of the New Urbanism* (New York, NY: McGraw-Hill, 1999).
14. Nathan Cherry, with K. Nagle, *Grid/Street/Place: Elements of Sustainable Urban Districts* (Chicago: APA Planners Press, 2009).
15. Emily Talen, *Urban Design Reclaimed: Tools, Techniques and Strategies for Planners* (Chicago: APA Planners Press, 2009).
16. Cf. Ken Jones and M. Doucet, "Big-Box Retailing and the Urban Retail Structure: The Case of the Toronto Area," *Journal of Retailing and Consumer Services* 7:4 (October 2000), 233–247.
17. John Hitchcock, *A Primer on the Use of Density in Land Use Planning* (Toronto: University of Toronto, Program in Planning, 1994), Paper No. 41 thoroughly discusses this important measurement tool.
18. Martin Laplante, "A Simple Model of Urban Density," *Plan Canada* 45:1 (Spring 2005), 23–26.
19. Martin Laplante, 8.
20. www.statcan.ca
21. F. Stuart Chapin Jr., *Urban Land Use Planning*, 2nd ed. (Champaign-Urbana: University of Illinois Press, 1964), 376ff. More recent editions continue to confirm these parameters.
22. Andres Duany and Emily Talen, "Transect Planning," *Journal of the American Planning Association* 68:3 (Summer) 2002, 245–266.
23. Congress for the New Urbanism, *Charter*.
24. Jill Grant, "Mixed Use in Theory and Practice."
25. Mary-Ellen Tyler, "Ecological Plumbing in the Twenty-First Century," *Plan Canada* 34:4 (July 1994), (Special Issue) 169–176.
26. J. David Hulchanski, *Housing Policy for Tomorrow's Cities* (Ottawa: Canadian Policy Research Networks, 2002), Discussion Paper F27.
27. Richard A. Beauregard, "Planning with Things," *Journal of Planning Education and Research* 32:2 (June 2012), 182–190.

Internet Resources

Chapter-Relevant Sites

Planning Canadian Communities
www.planningcanadiancommunities.ca

Visualizing Density
www.lincolninst.edu/subcenters/visualizing-density

The Land Centre
www.landcentre.ca/index.cfm

Urban Land Institute
www.uli.org

Smart Growth/Urban Sprawl—Ontario Nature
www.ontarionature.org/discover/resources/PDFs/misc/urban_
sprawl.pdf

International Initiative for a Sustainable Built Environment
www.iisbe.org/

Canada Green Building Council (CaGBC)
www.cagbc.org

Project for Public Spaces
www.pps.org

Transect planning
www.transect.org/transect.html

Chapter Eight

Planning Regional and Metropolitan Communities

Planning has to be at a scale which is large enough to work out a strategy for growth within a setting as broad as the entire urban-centered region.

Leonard Gertler, 1966

Many planning problems have effects on areas well beyond their source. The drainage of stormwater from a subdivision into a watercourse has the potential of causing pollution to areas downstream, for example; or a major sports facility in one community may generate large amounts of traffic flowing through normally quiet residential areas in another. Probably the classic example is **suburbanization**, when those who work in an older central city choose to reside in a newer, lower-density community on the edge of the city and shop in yet another locale. Indeed, planning problems and/or their solutions are seldom confined within the borders of an individual community. The reasons stem from the interrelationships of various economic and social activities in a community, and the ways in which the effects of development are transmitted through space by transportation, water flow, air currents, and economic transactions, among other factors. Thus, it is often necessary and even preferable to plan for areas larger than one community, areas large enough to encompass the major effects of development.

Planners have traditionally proposed the regional approach for two kinds of planning problems: one, involving the growth and spread of cities into the countryside; the other, the development and conservation of natural resources in rural and non-urban settings. Both concerns have generated distinctive forms of regional planning, and there are many examples of each in Canada. This chapter reviews the nature of planning for large areas and describes the Canadian experiences with this facet of planning called regional planning. Two key questions to keep at the forefront when exploring this chapter's material are:

- *How does the scope of regional planning differ from that of community planning in terms of both the space being planned for and the content of plans?*
- *What are the main elements of a metropolitan plan?*

The Regional Planning Perspective

Planning for the built and natural environment is commonly talked about on two levels—city or urban (community) planning and regional planning. Although the two are obviously complementary, each has developed in its own distinctive way. This fact stems partly from basic differences in the planning issues and objectives addressed by each, and partly from differences in jurisdictional arrangements. Regional planning is concerned with many facets of the built environment, the natural environment, and the social and economic activities occurring in large areas that may include cities and towns. As well, such planning takes place in spatial situations that, in most instances, do not have well-defined political boundaries. Indeed, starting from its roots, regional planning has developed a different outlook from that of community planning.

The Roots of Regional Planning

Regional planning is a product of the intellectual and social ferment of Europe and North America in the mid and late 19th century. It parallels in many ways the responses of the proponents of utopian communities of that period, which were discussed in Chapter 2. Many observers of the growth and spread of cities of that time believed that the natural environment and agrarian activities were being threatened by the demands of modern, capitalist, and urban society. Among the most prominent were Frédéric Le Play in France and, later, Patrick Geddes in Britain. They turned their attention to promoting ways to make the earth more habitable and, especially, to achieving a balance between human and natural factors.

Patrick Geddes was the first among latter-day planners to sense the need for larger area planning. He observed the spread of urban development in 19th century England and coined the term "conurbation" to capture the interdependent quality of linked cities. Geddes tried many ways to demonstrate his notions; his hypothetical geographical unit "The Valley Section" (Figure 8.1) is

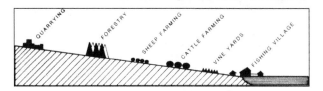

Geddes used the example of activities at different levels in a valley to emphasize the need to plan for them together. This integrated view of planning, dating from 1892, is the forerunner of modern ecosystems planning.

one example. The Valley Section presented the spatial relations of a set of settlements, each with distinctive geographical and human values in the form of a transect from wilderness to urban use. He propounded the need to plan together *all* the features of a river basin (e.g., the land and natural features, as they are affected by agriculture or industry or water control) and the needs of a population for land for recreation and residences. Within this seemingly simple diagram are embodied two essential principles of regional planning: (1) the need to take a synoptic approach to regional problems in order to encompass the interrelationships of areas; and (2) the planning of each area in coordination with adjoining areas. Thus, the planner sees in a given region that the different factors interact such that change in one leads to changes in others. Of course, the use of a river basin to illustrate these principles made very good sense, for much of human settlement has taken place in such regions, and the parts of river basins are clearly linked to each other. The concept of the river basin as a natural region of high order proved to be a powerful one in planning, as discussed below.

Geddes was noting how areas are unified by either the problems of their development or by their resource base, and often by both. He called for the planning of regions as well as for their constituent communities. Geddes also propounded in his famous trinity that three intrinsic factors of any region always be taken into account in its planning (see Figure 8.2). He called them *Folk* (the people of the region), *Work* (the economy of the region), and *Place* (the geographical and natural environmental dimensions of the region).[1] The trinity flowed from the work of French social geographer Frédéric Le Play in the mid 19th century whose phrase was "lieu, travail, famille."[2] An essential aspect of this concept is the interrelatedness of each of the factors. Artur Glikson later added a crucial fourth factor,

Figure 8.2	The Trinity of Factors Intrinsic to Regional Planning	

Place–Folk • Community • Neighbourhoods	**Work–Folk** • Labour Force • Economic Base	**FOLK** **(The Population)**
Place–Work • Downtown • Airport	**WORK** **(The Economy)**	**Folk–Work** • Income Distribution • Transport System
PLACE **(The Geography)**	**Work–Place** • Industrial Area • Mining District	**Folk–Place** • Heritage District • Recreation Areas

Geddes's schematic diagram of the three main factors present in every region, including their interrelationship, that must be taken into account in surveying and planning a region.

Circulation (transportation).[3] The interrelations among these four factors signify the integrity of any region and suggest a basic checklist for regional planners when making a plan.

A contemporary connection to the Valley Section is found in the New Urbanism concept of transect planning.[4] Instead of a cross-section through a river valley, the modern concept features a cross-section through an urbanized region from urban core to rural fringe (see Figure 7.10, page 181). Like its Geddesian forbear, the urban–rural transect sees the urban and rural environments (and those in between) as being deeply connected and displaying basic ecological principles such as a sequence of habitats, interrelatedness of habitats, and internal diversity.

The River-Basin Planning Region

There have been many efforts in river-basin planning throughout the world: in the United States, Colombia, Russia, India, and even in Canada. A dramatic and successful example began in the 1930s for the Tennessee River basin, a major tributary of the Mississippi River, in the southeastern United States. This region of several thousand square kilometres was for many decades subject to major floods, owing to inordinate cutting of its forests and debilitating agricultural practices that rendered its soils largely incapable of holding water. Since the basin spread over several states, the U.S. federal government established a special agency, the **Tennessee Valley Authority** (TVA), with

the power to plan and economically develop the region. The mandate of the TVA was to rehabilitate the region for the benefit of its inhabitants. This was carried out through the construction of dams, the generation of electric power, reforestation, the promotion of improved agricultural methods and irrigation, and the building of new towns. This broad mandate was based on the same principles of the interdependence of the parts of the region that Geddes espoused. Urban historian Lewis Mumford commented as follows about the TVA:

> The Tennessee Valley project, with its fundamental policy of conservation of power resources, land, forest, soil, and stream, in the public interest, is an indication of a new approach to the problems of regional development.... The river valley has the advantage of bringing into a common regional frame a diversified unit: this is essential to an effective civic and social life.[5]

There is more than a hint in Mumford's remarks of a strongly held philosophy about planning for human communities. For him and others who witnessed the growth and spread of large cities in the 1920s and 1930s, and the consequent debilitation of resources and the environment, the region was a special place created by people interacting with their environment. The natural region could be a bulwark against massive urbanization and the standardization of culture. This regionalism—a belief in the profound connection between humankind and the territory it inhabits—has re-emerged in Canada and elsewhere in recent years under the name **bioregionalism**. Many of the same sentiments have always pervaded regional planning and may be detected in, for example, the 1969 plan for the Mactaquac River Valley in New Brunswick.[6] There are also echoes of regionalism in New Urbanist planning.[7] This humanistic view, it must be noted, has not always been easy to reconcile with the rigidities of political boundaries, bureaucratic jurisdictions, and economic determinism, which are characteristic of the history of regional planning in Canada.

Characteristics of Regional Planning

In general, regional planning is rooted in the importance of using natural resources wisely. From this resource perspective emerged four venues for regional planning in Canada:[8]

- **Planning for watersheds.** In the tradition of the TVA, the planning is for the control and use of water resources to prevent floods, to provide irrigation to agricultural lands, to generate electricity, and to create recreational opportunities, or some combination of these. The conservation authorities that were established for a score of river basins in southern Ontario in the late 1940s epitomize this type of regional planning in Canada.

- **Planning for rural land resources.** There are two venues for rural region planning. One is in the vicinity of large, expanding cities with efforts to achieve a harmonious balance between urban and rural land needs. The other is in planning for "completely rural" regions—those regions with broad areas of resource use and land occupancy by resource producers and with many small settlements.[9]

- **Planning economic development in resource regions.** These regions depend heavily on the economic performance of their natural-resource sectors. In many of these regions, the resources have become obsolete (as with coal) or depleted (as with minerals and timber), or the technology for exploiting them has become outdated (as with farming and fisheries).

- **Planning for large urban regions.** Canada is a leader in the planning of growing and expanding metropolitan areas. (This form of regional planning is examined in the final sections of this chapter.)

Even though the substantive concerns of each of these approaches of regional planning differ, all the approaches have certain characteristics in common:

1. **Regional Planning Deals with Large Areas.** "Supra-urban space" is the criterion used by John Friedmann[10] to describe the spatial scope of regional planning. Regional planning efforts encompass areas larger than a single city, from metropolitan regions of a few thousand square kilometres to large resource regions of several hundred thousand.

2. **Regional Planning Is Concerned with the Location of Activities and Resource Development.** Since large areas are being planned, it is vital to know where activities and/or resource development occur (or might occur) in a region, so that their spatial relations (i.e., transportation, communications) with each other and with other regions can be planned for effectiveness and efficiency, both socially and economically.

3. **The Scope of Regional Planning Includes Social, Economic, and Environmental Factors.** Regional planning is intimately tied up with social and economic questions, more so than city planning,

and also with natural environment issues, through its connection to natural resources. Indeed, it has a special concern with the relationship between human use and the natural landscape and environment; the need to achieve "man/land harmony" (or balance, as we call it today), was often cited in the earliest regional planning literature.

4. **Planning Regions Have No Constitutional Basis.** Regions for regional planning are not part of Canada's governing structure. Thus, planning regions literally have to be invented each time we want to conduct regional-planning activities. The power to define a planning region lies with the province and is usually superimposed on existing local governing units (municipalities, special functional districts, etc.). British Columbia is a major exception to this situation by having established a system of two dozen regional districts covering almost all the province, each of which may undertake regional planning. In almost all cases, regional planning is involved with more than one governmental jurisdiction, and very often with more than two governmental levels.

Although regional planning is a public, governmental activity, it does not always take the form of

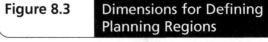

Figure 8.3 | **Dimensions for Defining Planning Regions**

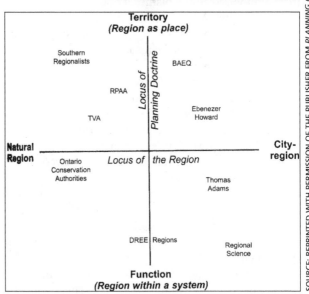

The essential dimensions for defining appropriate planning regions and the locus of precursors' work in the field.

direct government action. Many times, regional planning is only an *advisory* activity. This reflects the need to blend the governing powers of all the public units that are involved. Regional planning in Canada, therefore, has been undertaken under a variety of formats. In some cases, an agency has the authority to make and carry out plans; in others, the agency only has advisory powers on the implementation of plans. The former category includes the James Bay Development Corporation, which was established by the province of Québec to plan and develop the hydroelectric resources of an immense area in the northern part of the province. The latter category includes regional-planning commissions such as those in New Brunswick, which have the authority to make plans for their regions but wield almost no powers of implementation. In between are a variety of other arrangements for regional planning as, for example, the use of Regional Growth Strategies in regional districts in British Columbia, which require constituent municipalities to commit to achieving regional growth objectives.[11] Other devices include establishing development corporations with limited powers, interdepartmental committees, and federal–provincial planning agreements.

The Problem of Regional Boundaries

Often, "regional planning" seems a nebulous term. This arises from the fact that what constitutes a region from one point of view may not constitute a region from another. Regional planning boundaries cannot be drawn with precision because of the variety of concerns involved. Even the boundaries of a watershed, which define the extent of water resources of a region, may not encompass the human interactions of commuting to work or the shipment of goods in and out of the same region. Moreover, since regional planning is a public effort to bring improvement to a region, that public effort will need to be expressed within the appropriate governmental jurisdictions: that is, regional-planning boundaries must reflect the boundaries of the governments involved. This recognition often involves compromise between government units to determine an acceptable planning region. Moreover, governmental boundaries seldom follow the patterns of natural regions. As an example, when a river is used as a boundary between government units, the natural region is split.

The issue of regional boundaries for planning purposes can never be finally resolved. There may be a unique set of river-basin regions, but human activities cannot be defined so neatly and, significantly,

their spatial configurations change over time. Political boundaries, meanwhile, tend to remain fixed over long periods of time. This ambiguity must be tolerated in regional planning. Rather than pursue the elusive ideal boundary for a planning region, it is more productive to plan explicitly for the boundary areas in conjunction with the adjacent region. It is wise to remember that wherever the region's boundaries are drawn, there is another region on the other side.

Planning for Rural and Non-Metropolitan Regions

Regional planning began in Canada in the decade just prior to World War II. Those early efforts concentrated, as they did in several other countries, on the problems being experienced in largely rural regions and only later did attention shift to the planning needs of large urban and metropolitan regions.[12] The latter planning experience is discussed later in the chapter.

Canadian Experience in Planning Rural and Non-metropolitan Regions

Planning for rural and non-metropolitan regions is diverse, in response to the sheer size of Canada's territory (about 10 million square kilometres) and the variety of regional situations within it. Three broad streams of regional planning have characterized efforts of planners to grasp this diversity: (1) planning aimed at rural resource conservation; (2) planning for settlements in low-density rural regions; and (3) planning for rural region economies. Each is described briefly below before attention is turned to contemporary rural regional planning.

Planning for Resources Conservation

The history of regional planning in Canada could be said to have begun with the concern over the deterioration of natural resource regions as the 20th century began. Indeed, it was one of the main stimuli for the creation of the federal Commission on Conservation in 1909 (see Chapter 4) and for the work of Thomas Adams on rural planning and development in the decade or so following.[13] However, it was during the 1930s under the influence of the unified approach to planning river basins, such as the TVA in the United States, that Canadian rural region planning efforts emerged in this country. Although they were not as grandiose as the TVA, their imprint can be seen in the establishment of the Prairie Farm Rehabilitation Administration (PFRA) and the Maritime Marshland Rehabilitation Administration (MMRA). The PFRA sought to develop various measures for soil and water conservation in the then drought-stricken Prairie region, and MMRA's later mandate was to reverse incipient saltwater intrusion into coastal agricultural lands in the Maritimes.

Something close to the "classic" form of river-basin planning appeared in Canada in 1946 when Ontario proclaimed a new Conservation Authorities Act. It established regional conservation authorities to conduct multipurpose planning for a dozen or more river basins in the province. The fruits of this planning are still enjoyed today in terms of flood control measures, wetlands conservation, and water-based recreation. Conservation authority boundaries were also the basis of the exemplary work of the 1990 Crombie Royal Commission on the Future of the Toronto Waterfront.[14] The underlying doctrine of the connection between humankind and the territory it inhabits is also found in regional planning in the 1960s and 1970s, as for example in the planning for the Mactaquac River Valley of New Brunswick,[15] for the impacts of the Diefenbaker Dam in Saskatchewan, for the Cumberland Sound region in the Northwest Territories, and for the Niagara Escarpment plan in Ontario. The same foundation can be seen in the federal-provincial-local-First Nations initiative to plan for the Fraser River Basin in British Columbia in the 1990s.[16]

Planning for Settlements in Low-Density Rural Regions

Among the most successful and long-lived regional planning experiences in Canada is the planning for settlements in low-density rural regions. Regional planning commissions in Alberta and New Brunswick, county planning in Nova Scotia and Ontario, and regional–district planning in British Columbia are forms that provinces have devised to respond to the planning needs of low-density settled regions. The oldest of these agencies are five non-metropolitan regional-planning commissions in Alberta created in the 1950s.[17] The reasons for their establishment in Alberta, and later elsewhere, are obscure, but it was probably a response to urban-type problems in rural areas, including spillover from growing towns and the consequences of subdivisions and ribbon development along countryside roads. However, they seem not to have been formed to deal with the lack of growth in towns, loss of land used for crop production, and population decline. Nevertheless, it was recognized that their regions did not need conventional urban physical planning.[18] Each town or township needed solutions to its specific problems, such as the provision of basic utilities, disposing of trash, refurbishing Main Street, or reducing residential scatter (see Chapter 10 for a full description of small-town planning problems and approaches). Several provinces also established agencies to provide planning services to small communities, such as Prince Edward Island's Land Use Services Centre and Manitoba's and Newfoundland's field planning offices.

Worth special mention are the efforts of two provinces, British Columbia and Québec, to conserve agricultural lands. In 1973, British Columbia set up the Agricultural Land Commission, which, in turn, established Agricultural Land Reserves (ALRs) to restrict urban development on areas with soil types that could support agricultural production (usually soil types 1, 2, and 3). The Land Commission continues to this day and has control over the subdivision of land in ALRs inside and outside municipal boundaries. Its worth has been proven in protecting agricultural land in the Vancouver metropolitan area.[19] A similar step, taken in Québec in 1978 with Bill 90, An Act to Protect Agricultural Land, established a commission to protect agricultural land in "protected zones."[20] Both provinces have had considerable success in preventing non-agricultural uses in protected areas.[21]

Planning for Rural Region Economies

Toward the end of the 1950s, Canada's economy entered a new spatial phase with metropolitan regions replacing rural-resource regions in economic importance. In the process, many of the country's agricultural, fishing, mining, and forestry regions were exhibiting signs of economic underdevelopment. Poverty, illiteracy, poor housing and infrastructure, inefficient technology, obsolete resources, and out-migration were in evidence. The awareness of unequal development among regions of the country captured the attention of people and politicians at both the provincial and federal levels. "Regional disparities" became a familiar phrase, and the concerns led to considerable amounts of mostly federal funds (some have estimated $15 billion) being devoted to trying to mitigate regional economic differences. This, it should be noted, was not a new phenomenon in Canada, as the Rowell-Sirois Royal Commission had pointed out in 1940: "[T]he income of the country is concentrated in a few specially favoured areas."[22] They were referring, in particular, to the urban–industrial corridor from Windsor to Ville de Québec that Canadian geographer Maurice Yeates would later call "Main Street."[23]

The first major effort at countering regional disparities came in 1961, with the passage of the federal Agricultural Rehabilitation and Development Act (ARDA). Under ARDA, low-income agricultural regions were targeted for programs to enlarge farms, establish community pastures, and improve farm market roads. Over the next few years, 40 regional planning efforts were undertaken, three of which deserve special mention, to show both the scope and difficulties surrounding ARDA regional planning. One was the truly grassroots redevelopment program in the Gaspé, the Bureau d'Amanagement de l'est du Québec (BAEQ), involving all sectors of the community, citizens as well as agencies, in what nowadays would be called "collaborative planning" of the region's future. A second was the "top-down" Newfoundland Outport Resettlement Program, which succeeded in relocating 300 outports of the 600 that were targeted, but caused numerous splits in families and communities that are still evident today. A third was the multi-faceted Interlake Region program in Manitoba, which might be considered ARDA's success story.[24]

A host of other alphabetic agencies joined ARDA during the 1960s: ADA, the Area Development Agency; ADB, the Atlantic Development Board; and FRED, the Fund for Rural Economic Development. They were all gathered under the umbrella of DREE, the Department of Regional Economic Expansion, in 1969.[25] DREE's approach was generally comprehensive in regard to a region's needs and included housing, municipal infrastructure, transportation, and education, along with job creation. Throughout this period, the regional-planning efforts involved both federal and provincial levels of government, for although the necessary funds were available at the federal level, the responsibility for regional resources lay with the provinces. This was, as Gertler notes, "a period of experimentation" in regional planning, owing, as much as anything, to the need to evolve an approach to joint planning between two levels of government.[26] This vigorous 25-year period in Canadian regional planning is hard to characterize: there were seldom permanent planning staffs in DREE-designated regions, and there was seldom a published regional plan. Not least, it was regional planning from *outside* the region that could be extremely upsetting to local councils and planners, as witness B.C. Hydro's plans to flood Arrow Lakes' communities[27] and the mega-industrial projects along the Canso Strait in Nova Scotia.[28] These "experiments" Gertler spoke of are far behind us, but most of the same rural regions continue to contend with lack of population growth and desultory economic prospects. This is bringing forth calls for new regional planning strategies to tackle these seemingly perennial issues of rural regions, and they are discussed later below.

Planning for Bioregions and the Environment

Brief mention should be made of several other approaches to regional planning. One concerns the planning for regional transportation systems, especially expressway planning. Almost all the large metropolitan areas have had such plans prepared. Québec took a major step regarding regional planning in 1980 when its Regional and City Planning Act established a new regional-planning framework.[29] It provided for the creation of 94 Regional County Municipalities (Municipalités regionales de comte, or MRCs), and one of their main tasks was to prepare a regional plan. The act defined very specifically the contents of such a plan. Briefly, the plan had to include proposals for land use; delimitation of areas to become urban; identification of environmentally sensitive, historical, and cultural areas; and the location of inter-municipal facilities and public utilities.[30] With this legislation, Québec took the most comprehensive step in province-wide regional planning of any province because, significantly, it linked regional plan preparation to governmental powers of implementation.

Bioregional approaches have been widely used in Canadian regional planning, one of the first being in planning for the Kitimat-Stikine Regional District in northwest British Columbia in the late 1980s.[31] This and other initiatives drew upon the emerging field of bioregionalism, which is not a specific planning paradigm so much as an "action-oriented movement based on ecological principles."[32] It is holistic in its outlook, in that a bioregion is a system comprising three sub-systems: a "biophysical" sub-system (the natural environment); an "inhabiting" sub-system (communities, agriculture, transportation); and a "network" sub-system (the economic and political systems). Bioregionalism rejects existing political units in favour of "contiguous, mappable geographic regions" based on similarities of topography, plant and animal life, culture, and economy, such as watersheds.[33] What appears in Canadian regional planning is not full-blown bioregionalism but rather the application of some of its principles. The Crombie Commission on the Toronto waterfront utilized the watershed bioregion notion as its organizing principle (see Figure 8.4). As well, the large municipality

Figure 8.4   Greater Toronto Bioregion

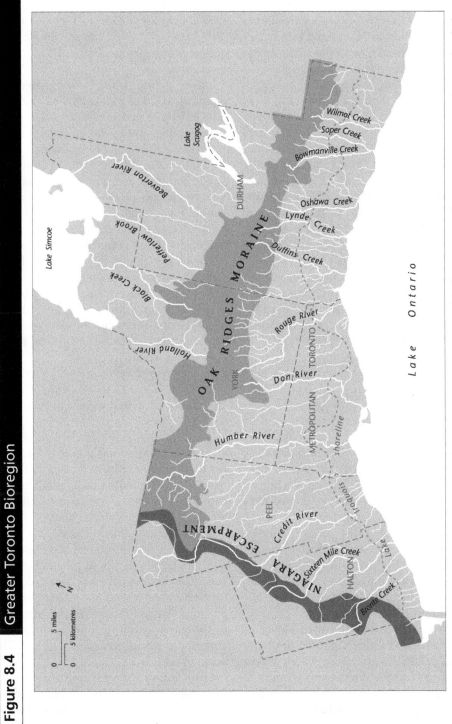

Conventional planning tends to treat a region's economy and built forms as separable from nature. The ecosystem approach to regional planning starts with a context in which all elements are considered in an integrated way.

SOURCE: GERALD HODGE AND IRA M. ROBINSON, *PLANNING CANADIAN REGIONS* (VANCOUVER: UBC PRESS, 2001), FIGURE 15, 223. REPRINTED WITH THE PERMISSION OF THE PUBLISHER. © UBC PRESS. CARTOGRAPHY BY ERIC LEINBERGER.

of Markham northeast of Toronto has conducted a comprehensive environmental-planning study emphasizing not only environmental protection but also restoration of ecological diversity and the integration of these with cultural patterns in the area.[34] A similar approach is taken in the updated plan for the greenbelt surrounding Ottawa, which propounds a "connected ecological system" and employs nodes, buffers, and links, as the bioregionalists call the landscape components.[35]

Bioregional concepts and values are increasingly influencing both regional and local planning with important implications for planning practice. For example, the bioregional approach links ecology and community and puts them at the centre of planning, rather than, say, land use and economic development.[36] Not least will be the need to negotiate new regional boundaries and implementation powers. In the meantime, one of the key components of life—water, and its regional situation—has been receiving considerable attention by planners. In the Calgary region, the stewardship of a number of watersheds is sparking interest in inter-municipal[37] planning while "integrated water management" is receiving attention by Québec's planners to avoid over-exploitation of water and harmful impacts of conflicting water uses, and to plan for natural regeneration of regional water resources.[38]

Planning Rural and Peripheral Regions: Persistent Issues

Canada's development pattern has from the time of permanent European settlement been one of dispersed clusters on ocean coasts, along valleys, at transportation nodes, and on resource frontiers. They comprised, from early on, hamlets which sometimes became towns and then cities over time. The settlements were coupled with extensive adjacent rural areas (regions) being exploited for their natural resources, be it fish, forest, minerals, and/or agricultural soils. The most noticeable change in this overall pattern has been the vast expansion of its urban component, especially over the past 125 years and even more so over the past 60 years. We now talk about some urban clusters as "super regions."

However, the sustained existence of the rural component in our national development pattern has been noticed only occasionally. And on those few occasions where notice has been taken of these vast and diverse regions it has stemmed from a concern that they are not exhibiting "growth" either in economic terms or in their population. It was loss of population in rural regions

in the 1911 Census that caught Thomas Adams's attention and that of others.[39] Adams, however, considered healthy rural regions as essential as towns and cities in overall national development. In his time, nearly a century ago, older rural regions in eastern Canada were losing population as their resource development stabilized or declined and the development of western regions was yet to burgeon. In 1961, when national concern about rural regions again arose, it was over "disparities" in the economic development levels of rural regions and led to regional planning efforts as discussed above. Similar concerns have arisen in Ontario in the past decade, again with population decline at their centre. It has been accompanied by a change in terminology that refers now to settlements being "at risk"[40] and "peripheral regions" as being in jeopardy.[41]

Two aspects of these periodic assessments of the conditions in rural Canada, every 50 or so years, merit scrutiny. One is the perspective from which these assessments emerged; the other is the understanding of rural regions and their development on which they are based. Adams's assessment aside, the mid-century assessment that begot ARDA and DREE saw "disparities" between rural regions and other regions, notably urban regions. More recent assessments compare population growth in rural regions with those of growing regions in Canada (i.e., urban regions). However, it is fair to ask: are such comparisons viable? That, in turn, raises another question: what is our understanding of the development characteristics of rural regions as compared to non-rural regions?

Both of these questions need to be answered before embarking on any new regional planning approaches for rural regions. Most pressing is the need to grasp that what are broadly called "rural" regions are diverse within themselves as well as different from urbanized regions. To begin with it is necessary to distinguish *rural* regions and *peripheral* regions. The latter comprise the northern portions of most provinces and the three northern territories (more than half of Canada's area), and their development has occurred as a general scatteration of settlements, each based on the exploitation of a local natural resource and/or on trade. It is fair also to call them remote regions. Examples are Northern Ontario, north of Lakes Superior and Huron, Alberta north of Edmonton, Québec's mining region, Northern British Columbia, north of Kamloops, and the entire Northwest Territories. The remaining non-urban regions to the south, and the non-urban portions of the Atlantic Provinces, encompass Canada's rural regions. Their development patterns are characterized by spatially extensive resource use and more regularly spaced settlements providing services. For rural regions think of the Prairies, the active forestry region of New Brunswick, Québec's Eastern Townships, and the farming areas that neighbour southern Ontario's cities.

Population decline or very slow growth is common among the settlements of both peripheral and rural regions. This is not a new condition or problem as the census returns have shown for many decades past. However, another facet of change among settlements, particularly in peripheral regions, is the sharp spikes in growth found in selected resource frontier communities such as currently with Fort McMurray (see Planning Issue 1.1, page 11). These changes are most often caused by intensive capital investment in a currently profitable natural resource and tend to be highly localized. They continue a generations-old viewpoint of seeing peripheral regions simply as "resource banks" from which resources are withdrawn as required by urban industrial regions.[42] Such focused corporate and public investment leads to differentiation among settlements and not to integrated and sustained development on a regional scale.

Thus, differences in degrees of change in settlement population and economic levels are unexceptional, both in growth and decline. They are part of the ongoing picture of rural and peripheral regions and not necessarily the basis for judging their developability. This returns us to the questions raised above regarding one's position for viewing rural and peripheral regions; for example, the stance taken in Ontario as portrayed in Figure 8.5 is clearly that of one from the metropolis. Consider, however, that these same regions now seen in "jeopardy"[43] have existed for a century (or much more in Aboriginal reckoning) as distinctive groupings of peoples, settlements, and cultures. They are "places" in their own right, places that are diverse and resilient, places with economic potential beyond being resources' handmaidens to urban Canada. A strong case is currently being made for economic renewal in northern British Columbia, which seems equally applicable to other Canadian peripheral rural regions.[44] It begins with according these regions a rightful place among the regions of a province when

---

| Figure 8.5 | Typology of Small, Rural, and Remote Communities (Ontario) |

SOURCE: ENID SLACK, LARRY S. BOURNE, AND MERIC S. GERTLER, "SMALL, RURAL, AND REMOTE COMMUNITIES: THE ANATOMY OF RISK," PAPER PREPARED FOR THE PANEL ON THE ROLE OF GOVERNMENT, TORONTO, AUGUST 2003, TABLE 3, P. 12. USED WITH PERMISSION OF THE AUTHOR.

Settlement Size	Degree of Remoteness/Isolation/Accessibility			
	Within Metro Region	Adjacent to Metro Region	Not Adjacent but Near Metro Region	Isolated
Rural <1,000 <400 p/km²	King Twp Scugog	Haldimand	Grey County	Most of Northern, Eastern Ontario
Small towns <10,000	Beamsville Caledon East Tottenham	Ingersoll Smith Falls Tweed	Bancroft Mount Forest Walkerton	Dryden Hearst Wawa
Small City >10,000 <30,000	Dundas Orangeville Uxbridge	Midland Leamington Lindsay Port Hope	Elliot Lake Owen Sound Pembroke	Kenora Kirkland Lake
Large City >30,000 <100,000	Newmarket Clarington Welland	Belleville Brantford Chatham Peterborough	Brockville Cornwall Sarnia	North Bay Sault Ste. Marie Timmins

Notes: 1) Metro region: Defined as all CMAs (census metropolitan areas) with populations over 100,000 in 2001.

2) Isolated places defined as those in which commuting to work (or for services) to a metropolitan area is impractical or impossible because of long distances and high transportation costs.

An example from Ontario of the differences among settlements in rural and peripheral regions according to their degree of remoteness/accessibility to metropolitan centres.

considering policies for overall social and economic development. It follows with the need for investment in social and physical infrastructure in these regions based, one would hope, on the principle of territorial equity (fairness for all citizens regardless of where they live).[45] And, crucially, it is *inclusive* of all peoples and cultures, Aboriginal and non-Aboriginal, in the planning of the region. There are no ready templates for planning rural and peripheral regions. However, some principles for planning these regions can be distilled from the failings of past efforts, the few successes, and current calls for renewal.

1. **Be attuned at the outset to the individual spatial, economic, and social attributes of the region.** Planners will encounter settlements that differ in size, economic base, demography, and cultural composition, including Aboriginal communities.[46]
2. **Avoid planning strategies aimed primarily at economic and population growth of one or a few centres.** Rather, policies should recognize the diverse tendencies among the region's settlements and even be prepared to accommodate decline for some.[47]
3. **Employ a collaborative planning approach to cultivate a common commitment among diverse communities, interests, and governments.**[48]

Planning for Metropolitan and City-Regions in Canada

Canada is a leader in metropolitan planning in the western Hemisphere. Almost all of the country's 27 metropolitan areas—the regions of our largest cities—have active planning agencies. This experience is now seven decades old, having started with Winnipeg in 1943 and Toronto a few years later. In this section are described some of the highlights of Canadian metropolitan planning, with the aim of identifying the forms it has taken, the problems it has tackled, its accomplishments, its relationship to local community planning, and its new challenges as metropolitan areas have begun to expand into super regions. But before doing this, it will be helpful to examine the backdrop for metropolitan planning.

Nature and Origins

While the planning of cities goes back two millennia, thinking about planning for large metropolitan cities is barely a century old. Ebenezer Howard, instigator of the Garden City movement, was concerned with not only planning single new towns but went beyond to also determining how best to organize the territory around large cities. That is, how to concentrate populations and provide open space between towns rather than let cities sprawl. Figure 8.6 illustrates Howard's regional ideal for the new towns and how they would be connected to the large city by railways. Howard's 1898 diagrammatic concept for satellite Garden Cities has been far-reaching. A greenbelt of farms and forests would separate all communities, but major transport routes would interconnect them. Metropolitan plans for Ottawa, London, and Washington owe much to this model. As well, some planners, nowadays, tout Howard's model as a prototype for *sustainable* development of metropolitan regions.[49]

Metropolitan planning is, thus, a special form of regional planning. It not only deals with a large area, but it also deals explicitly with the growth and expansion of a major city on which the larger region is usually focused. Further, its planning normally is conducted in an institutional setting involving several municipalities. Broadly speaking, metropolitan planning is concerned with the allocation of land uses; the location of major

| Figure 8.6 | Ebenezer Howard's Concept of the Metropolitan Region |

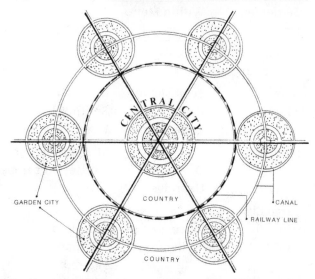

Howard's 1898 diagrammatic concept for satellite Garden Cities has been far-reaching. A greenbelt of farms and forests would separate all communities, but major transport routes would interconnect them. Metropolitan plans for Ottawa, Vancouver, Washington, D.C., and London (Ontario) owe much to this model.

public works throughout the region of a metropolis; movement in, out, and within the region; and, more recently, with protecting the natural environment.[50] In many ways, metropolitan planning is community planning "writ large."

Three factors about metropolitan planning should be grasped at the outset. The first is the *scale of the area* involved. Metropolitan planning areas are usually defined to encompass the potential spread of urban development, and this often means 1000 square kilometres or more. Moreover, the area will be developed at different densities and interspersed with agricultural areas and open spaces for recreation. The second concerns the *size of population*. Planning for large aggregates of population requires recognition of the increasing division of the metropolitan community into separate areas for work, residence, shopping, and leisure. Metropolitan planning must try to accommodate, as Hans Blumenfeld says, a number of "contradictory requirements," such as providing a "minimum need for commuting but maximum possibility for commuting."[51] The third factor is the *inter-municipal setting* for planning. Given the autonomy accorded to local governments in Canada, the planning for several of them simultaneously must seek ways to blend competing aims for development in the interest of all the citizens of the metropolitan community. Achieving this planning blend requires special organizational arrangements, and these have taken a number of forms, as will be seen later.

The emergence of metropolitan planning in Canada coincides with the end of World War II, when cities all over the world began to have dramatic surges of population growth and commercial and manufacturing development. For example, in 1941 Canada had 15 metropolitan areas, which comprised about 40 percent of the total population. By 1961, five more cities had been added to the metropolitan class, and metropolitan populations had become 51 percent of the total. Even more dramatic is the fact that in this 20-year period, 5 million more people crowded into Canada's largest cities, more than doubling the population living there. In 2011, the population of the current 33 metropolitan areas comprised nearly 23.1 million people, or 69 percent of Canada's total.[52]

This vast growth of cities after 1950 created a host of problems for both the central cities and their surrounding regions in which the new suburbs were being built. For the central city, the problems were a combination of an aging physical environment and a lack of vacant land for new development. There was deterioration of physical infrastructure and of some older residential and industrial areas as populations and factories moved to the outskirts, thus leading to the need for rehabilitation and redevelopment. (In modern planning parlance, the latter are known as "brownfields.") The new suburbs, at the same time, faced problems in providing services such as water, sewerage, garbage disposal, police and fire protection, roads, and schools. Their problems stemmed from the size of the new suburban growth and the meagre financial resources available to previously small municipalities. In addition, with the rapidly growing population and the vast areas being settled came the need for new facilities to serve the entire metropolitan area—among them hospitals, expressways, parks, airports, new sources for water supplies, and sewage-treatment plants.[53]

Metropolitan planning originated in this complex, large-scale urban development. It grew out of the realization that no single municipality in a metropolitan area could deal with an array of problems as intertwined as these, with the need to balance growth and to provide metropolitan-wide facilities. For example, the location of a large subdivision or a shopping centre in one part of the area may generate the need for improved highway access, new schools, or new trunk sewers in other areas. Conversely, local desires for development could depend upon the availability of metropolitan facilities and services. Achieving coordination in the land use planning of diverse communities is thus a major aim of metropolitan planning. Manitoba, British Columbia, and Alberta were the first three provinces to establish metropolitan planning agencies, followed closely by Ontario.

Organizational Approaches

The first formal metropolitan-planning agency established in Canada (indeed in North America) was that created by the Manitoba government in 1943—the Metropolitan Planning Commission of Greater Winnipeg. The dozen or so municipalities that then constituted the metropolitan area were members of the commission and contributed financially to its operation, as did the provincial government. It had a small and energetic staff, headed by Eric Thrift, and produced (by itself and with the help of consultants) an impressive series of reports on traffic, parking, the central business district, and parks. Municipalities could choose whether to participate and the plans that were made by the Commission were not binding on any municipality. This same cooperative, advisory form of metropolitan planning was adopted later in Vancouver (1949), Edmonton (1950), and Calgary (1950).

It became evident that metropolitan planning without a commensurate level of government authorized to implement planning policies could achieve only limited results. This was especially true in regard to decisions about the location and financing of facilities to serve the entire metropolitan area. It was also true for local land use regulations and capital investments that could thwart the intent of the metropolitan plan. This division of authority among local units of government was, of course, the product of the long-standing primacy accorded municipalities by the provinces. Ontario was the first to intervene in this tradition and form a metropolitan government.

Metropolitan Toronto

Origins and Context In 1953, the Ontario government established the Municipality of Metropolitan Toronto, the first metropolitan government in either Canada or the United States. It followed the form of a **federation** of the 13 local municipalities that made up the metropolitan area at the time. (The alternative form, an **amalgamation** of municipalities into a single unit for the entire metropolitan area, was debated and rejected at the time.) Within the federation, each municipality retained responsibility for its own local planning and land use regulation, and its own local public works. The metropolitan government, "Metro Toronto" as it came to be called, assumed responsibility for major regional services and such facilities as public transportation, water supply, and expressways. Metro Toronto also had the power to raise funds for capital-works projects. It was also provided with an Advisory Planning Board like those of other municipalities in the province. The major difference, however, was that the Metro Toronto Planning Board had jurisdiction in planning over a surrounding area that was twice as large again as Metro. The planning area covered a total of 1970 square kilometres, of which 620 square kilometres comprised the 13 metropolitan municipalities, while the remaining area comprised 13 fringe-area local governments.

The Metropolitan Toronto Planning Board was charged with preparing an Official Plan to which municipalities both inside and outside of Metro were required to conform in their planning and public works projects. Within Metro, the zoning of local municipalities had to conform to Metro's Official Plan and Metro had to approve local subdivision plans. It should be noted that the Official Plan of Metro was only advisory and could not bind the local municipalities, but it was a strong persuasive force. An important reason for this, as Blumenfeld notes (he was Deputy Commissioner of Planning for Metro for many years), is that each municipality sent representatives to Metro Council, where they had a voice in adopting the Official Plan.[54]

Later Changes Fifteen years after it's founding, in 1968, pressure on the City of Toronto to consolidate all 13 municipalities into one single city resulted in a review of Metro's organization and functioning. The government structure was altered; the 13 local governments were reduced to 6. In 1971, the province began instituting a program to establish regional governments, somewhat modelled on Metro, for all major urban areas in Ontario as well as for the urbanizing area surrounding Metro. The Regional Municipality of York was established to the north, Peel Region was instituted on the west, and Durham Region on the east. The significant change was the elimination of the fringe portion of Metro's planning area, thereby reducing it to the size of the metropolitan area. The evolution of the structure of Metropolitan Toronto region continued again in 1997 with the amalgamation of the six constituent municipalities into one metropolitan unit, the new City of Toronto. The debate was at times rancorous, often centring on the loss of democratic rights in the way the decision was made and the loss of presumably more responsive local government entities.[55] Similar amalgamations were also instituted for other urban areas including Ottawa, Hamilton, London, and Kingston. Ottawa and Hamilton became single-tier governing arrangements rather than the two-tier federated models previously used; two-tier arrangements remained in the regional municipalities surrounding Toronto. Curiously, the province's proposal barely touched on the impact that amalgamation would have on the content and process of planning for what has become an even larger "super region."[56] A plan for this enhanced region was adopted in 2006 to cover the urban agglomeration stretching east and west of Toronto, which is now being called the Greater Golden Horseshoe; it is discussed later.[57]

Metropolitan Winnipeg

Metropolitan planning in Winnipeg was given governmental backing in 1960 when the province created the Metropolitan Corporation of Greater Winnipeg, the second metropolitan government in Canada. The corporation was given responsibility for water supply, sewage disposal, transportation, and planning.

Winnipeg chose a two-tier system of government, with the local municipalities remaining along with the new metropolitan corporation, yet it was not a federation as in Toronto. Metropolitan councillors were elected directly rather than drawn from local governments. This created tension between the two levels of government. Further, the metropolitan corporation had no control over the capital spending of the local-level governments. These two conditions frequently resulted in a failure to implement metropolitan plans.[58] In 1971, Manitoba restructured the metropolitan government, this time in the form of a single tier arrangement, they called Unicity and included the City of Winnipeg, and all other local governments.

Other Metropolitan Areas

In **Vancouver** and **Victoria**, the approach of cooperative, advisory, inter-municipal planning remained in practice until 1966. At that time, Regional District governments were formed across the province and these two-tier boards were assigned the planning function. Both the Capital Region District (Victoria) and the Greater Vancouver Regional District prepared metropolitan-area plans. The Vancouver plan, The Greater Vancouver Livable Region of 1976 under the direction of Harry Lash, was the first of a progression of plans. The latest (2011) is now called a Regional Growth Strategy and its land use proposal is shown in Figure 8.7.

| Figure 8.7 | Metro Vancouver Regional Growth Strategy |

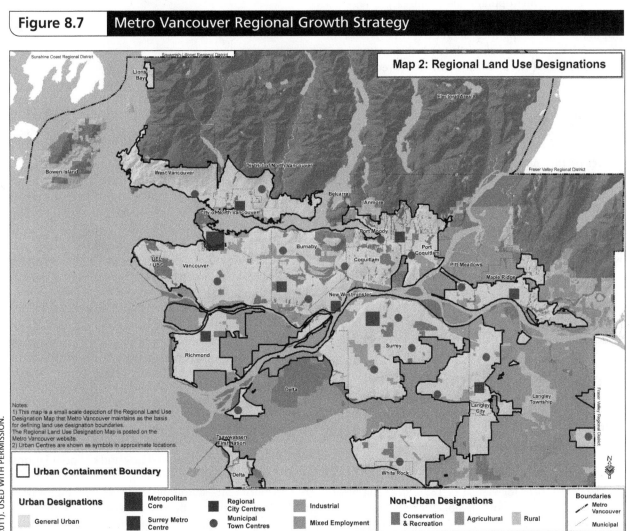

SOURCE: METRO VANCOUVER 2040: SHAPING OUR FUTURE, MAP 7 (VANCOUVER: GREATER VANCOUVER REGIONAL DISTRICT, 2011). USED WITH PERMISSION.

Chapter 8 Planning Regional and Metropolitan Communities

Two other early metropolitan planning efforts, in **Edmonton** and **Calgary**, did not evolve into metropolitan governments. In both cases, the regional planning commissions were continued, but with increased powers. For example, not only were these commissions empowered to prepare a regional plan, but they were also the designated authority for approving subdivision plans for all parts of their respective metropolitan areas outside the central cities. As well, all cities in Alberta had planning authority over an additional 5-kilometre zone outside their boundaries. Calgary was a special case: the city annexed large areas on its fringes in the 1960s to bring the potential urban area under a single jurisdiction. Alberta withdrew its regional planning legislation in the early 1990s. Planning for the **Montréal** region is the responsibility of the Montreal Metropolitan Community (Communauté métroplitaine de Montréal), a regional level of government. It comprises five zones: (1) densely populated municipalities including the Island of Montréal, Laval, and Longueil; (2) low-density municipalities located north of the Mille-Îles River; (3) low-density municipalities south of the St. Lawrence River; (4) low-density suburbs on the Vaudreuil-Soulanges Peninsula; and (5) the eastern suburbs of Longueil (see Figure 8.8). A recent Metropolitan Land Use and Development Plan (2012) covers the 3838 square kilometres of this region's land use, transportation, and environment (Plan de métropolitaine de émenagement et de développement, PMAD).[59] A comparable regional planning arrangement exists for **Québec City**.

The four main municipalities in the **Halifax** urban area (Halifax, Dartmouth, Bedford, and Halifax County) were amalgamated in 1996. The Halifax Regional Municipality (HRM), a single-tier government, now provides planning service for the entire 5577-square-kilometre region and its nearly 400 000 residents (2011). Its Regional Municipal Planning Strategy of 2006 is undergoing a five-year review.[60]

Planning the Form of the Metropolis

As much as metropolitan-area planning seems like a peculiarly contemporary challenge, European, especially German, planners and architects were broaching it more than a century ago.[61] Otto Wagner presented his modular *Grosstadt* plan for Vienna in 1893, not long before Ebenezer Howard put forth his plan for satellite Garden Cities (Figure 8.6). Other satellite models appeared in Germany in 1909 and 1911. A decade later, Corbusier

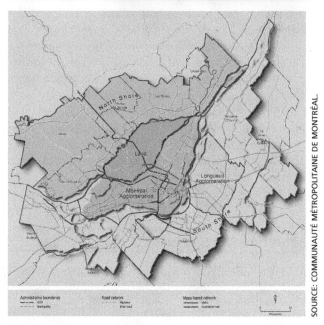

SOURCE: COMMUNAUTÉ MÉTROPOLITAINE DE MONTRÉAL.

Figure 8.8 Metropolitan Community of Montréal

The metropolitan planning region for Montréal has five constituent areas. The regional plan is noted for its "blue plan" (river edges) and its "green plan" (natural systems). It received the CIP 2012 Urban and Regional Planning Award.

contemplated the "city of three million" (see Chapter 4) and Thomas Adams soon after would present his Plan for New York and Environs. The advent of the widespread use of the automobile, and its impact on land use, is one of two defining characteristics of the latter-day metropolis that Canadian planners have had to confront. Canada's metropolitan areas did not grow as large or as early as had those in Europe and the United States, and the first challenge was the auto-oriented "exploding metropolis."[62] The other defining characteristic now confronting planners is the protection of the natural ecosystems of the metropolitan region. Each is discussed below.

Taming the Exploding Metropolis

The vast metropolitan growth that characterized the 1950s and 1960s (and since) did not bring forth compact cities. Rather, it dispersed new and old populations, businesses, and factories over large areas. Modern means of transportation—automobiles, trucks, and highways—and better communication systems came into their own in this period, enabling people and firms to seek an ever-widening array of locations. More and more people sought the new suburbs, with country on one side and city on the other, only to find, as Blumenfeld notes, "as more and more people move out into ever widening rings of suburbs, they move farther and farther away from the city and country moves farther and farther away from them."[63] This perception led planners of that time to propose patterns of urban development that would be consonant with the new, large scale of cities, the need to blend the amenities of both city and country, and the necessity to provide a maximum of accessibility among all parts of the metropolitan area. In short, there was much seeking after urban forms that would give coherence and cohesion—a sense of community—to the "exploding" metropolis. Planning models were brought back from the past, adapted and reinvigorated, and/or borrowed from other jurisdictions.

Four patterns gained early prominence among planners: the "concentric" city; the "central city with satellites"; the "star-shaped" or "finger-plan" city; and the "linear" or "ribbon" city (see Figure 8.9). They are, of course, ideal types, and in practice they must be modified to fit the geography of the area and the past history of development. Nevertheless, each has had an influence at one time in metropolitan plans that have been drawn up in Canada.

The **concentric plan** is based mainly on sustaining the primary business centre by ordering new residential development and other activities more or less at equal distance around the centre. The aim is to keep travel distances to the centre for work or business at a minimum for all sectors of the community. The main means for accomplishing this is by favouring transportation investments that concentrate travel movements in the centre, as with the subway investments in Toronto and Montréal and the light rapid transit (LRT) systems in Edmonton, Calgary, and Vancouver. In such large cities, the growth of suburbs gradually reaches limits where travel to the centre for all major activities becomes inefficient. At this stage, planners call for major sub-centres of business, or "new towns in-town," as they are sometimes called. The 1976 plan for Metropolitan Toronto followed this latter concept, creating three new "town centres"—Scarborough, North York, and Etobicoke—each roughly 16 kilometres from downtown Toronto.[64]

The **central city with satellites** derives from Ebenezer Howard's idea of Garden Cities surrounding a major city, described earlier in this chapter (Figure 8.6). This metropolitan concept became a reality with Patrick Abercrombie's plan London, England, after World War II.[65] A greenbelt

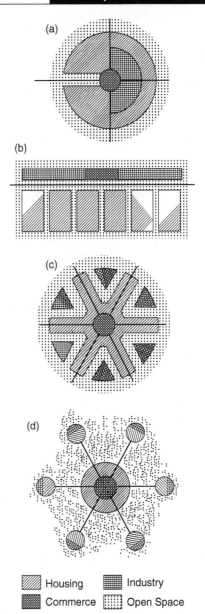

Figure 8.9 Four Forms of Metropolitan Development

(a)

(b)

(c)

(d)

Housing Industry
Commerce Open Space

Four concepts were often adapted to plan metropolitan expansion: (a) the concentric city; (b) the linear city; (c) the star-shaped city or finger plan; and (d) the city with satellites. Each has been used as a model in planning Canadian metropolitan regions, suitably transformed to fit the prevailing topography. Each diagram is drawn to the same scale, illustrating the typical transportation axes, open space pattern, and area required for similar land uses.

of parks, agriculture, and exurban development was established to limit the physical expansion of the central city about 16 kilometres from the centre. Beyond the greenbelt, outwards about 30 to 40 kilometres, a dozen or more new satellite towns were planned to surround London and absorb its new growth, as well as to decant some industrial development from the central city. The new towns were planned to connect with the centre by high-speed transportation, but were also expected to be relatively self-sufficient. The towns would not be large, from 30 000 to 60 000 in population, and would afford residents quick access to the countryside.

The 1996 Livable Region Strategic Plan for the Vancouver metropolitan area proposed a satellite scheme with eight "regional town centres" east and southeast of Vancouver, all connected to the central city by a rapid-transit system. Residential development was focused on the town centres with the aim of creating "complete communities" with a "better balance" in the availability of jobs, housing, public services, and transportation.[66] There is no formal greenbelt in the Vancouver plan, although an extensive network of "Green Zones" are used to establish a "long-term boundary for urban growth." These can be seen in the most recent Regional Growth Strategy (Figure 8.7).

The 1947 Copenhagen plan is the best-known example of the **star-shaped** or **finger plan**. (Figure 6.7, page 157). The essential feature of this concept is that development is confined to radial corridors emanating from the business centre, with green areas between each corridor. Major highway and rail transit routes serving the central city follow the corridors. This interpenetration of green space and urban development increases the distance to the city centre over that of the concentric plan, but also maximizes the access of city dwellers to the countryside. The unimplemented 1974 plan for the National Capital Region of Ottawa–Hull proposed the finger-plan concept, along with a greenbelt. The plan called for a continuous open space system with "the penetration of rural wedges" into the urban area.[67]

The **linear** or **ribbon city plan** proposes urban growth in modules along major transportation routes. A greenbelt would separate the major uses of industry, residences, and transport from one another in this concept. A variation on this type was used in one alternative plan considered for the Toronto metropolitan region in a major transportation planning report in 1967.[68] The concept was for a spine of transportation running east and west from the city, along which would be arrayed, to the north and south of the spine, a series of communities separated from each other by greenbelts.

The Green Metropolis

In the closing decade or so of the 20th century, Canadian planners of communities large and small began to embrace the notion that the natural environment, and its protection, must become an integral part of decisions regarding the future physical form of the place. One is unlikely to find a metropolitan area plan, nowadays, that does not put its natural environment to the forefront. For example, the 2005 Halifax Regional Municipal Planning Strategy has "Environment" as its first substantive chapter and it begins:[69] "Protection of water, land and air is a cornerstone of the Regional MPS." Another example is found in one of the major objectives in the 2004 Montréal Master Plan:[70] "Preserve and enhance the natural heritage." Calgary's special environmental feature of numerous, fragmented wetlands led the City to prepare the *Calgary Wetland Conservation Plan* in 2004 to regulate land use in their vicinity. A recent review of this policy showed that while it reduced wetland loss the reduction was less than hoped for. Developers tended most often to pay compensation for wetland sites rather than restore them or seek non-wetland locations.[71] Canadian metropolitan planners have embraced greenbelts in their plans and a few deserve discussion.

Ottawa and Its Greenbelt

In 1915, the Federal Plan Commission prepared a plan for Ottawa and its environs that proposed many of the projects that have since come to pass—for example, the relocation of railways out of the downtown area and the creation of the Gatineau Park greensward to the north.[72] Following World War II, French planner Jacques Gréber was commissioned to prepare a plan that encompassed a region on both sides of the Ottawa River, including the City of Hull in Québec. This plan, submitted in 1950, proved to be very influential in creating the present physical environment of the capital region[73] including the development of a greenbelt around Ottawa, the expansion of Gatineau Park north of Hull, and various urban parks and parkways. The greenbelt covers about 20 000 hectares, about eight kilometres from Parliament Hill, and varies in width from two to eight kilometres (see Figure 8.10).

The federal government first attempted to implement the greenbelt using local land use regulations, without success, because the rural townships preferred to permit low-density suburban development. In 1959, the federal government created the National Capital Commission (NCC) and hired Winnipeg's metropolitan planner, Eric Thrift, to manage the agency. As the NCC said in its

Figure 8.10   The Greenbelt in the National Capital Region

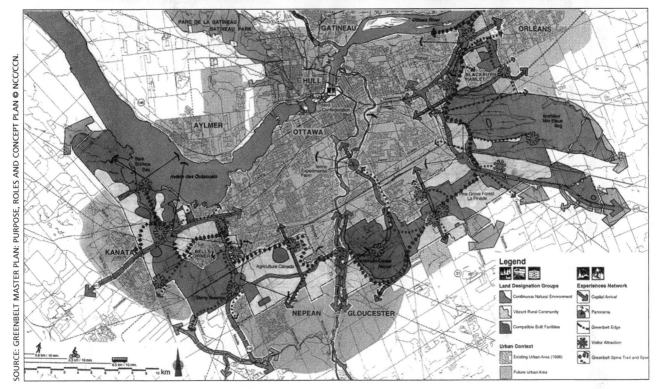

SOURCE: GREENBELT MASTER PLAN: PURPOSE, ROLES AND CONCEPT PLAN © NCC/CCN.

1974 plan for the region, "in implementing the Gréber plan ... the NCC used as its basic planning and development tool the ownership of land."[74] Expropriating the greenbelt lands was controversial but a crucial factor in securing it in perpetuity. In 1996, the NCC adopted a new plan for the greenbelt, which added to its extent and made it much more ecologically oriented (Figure 8.10). A primary component became its continuous natural environment, which included several core natural areas (i.e., large, sensitive, natural environments), natural-area buffers that surround the core areas, and natural-area links for maintaining continuity of plant life and facilitating animal movement within and beyond the greenbelt.[75] This new orientation adds an important dimension to what was initially just a way of shaping the urban form of Canada's capital. In planning for the newly enlarged City of Ottawa, the greenbelt is linked to an even broader environmental strategy for the entire urban region within eastern Ontario.[76]

Toronto's Greenbelt

A major initiative regarding metropolitan Toronto took place in 2005 with the establishment of an extensive greenbelt surrounding the total urbanized region. The province instituted a greenbelt of nearly 7300 square kilometres north and west of the area, from Hamilton to Oshawa, a region in which over six million people reside (see Figure 8.11). The purposes of the greenbelt are stated as follows:[77]

- Protects against the loss and fragmentation of the agricultural land base and supports agriculture as the predominant land use;
- Gives permanent protection to the natural heritage and water-resource systems that sustain ecological and human health and that form the environmental framework around which major urbanization in south-central Ontario will be organized; and
- Provides for a diverse range of economic and social activities associated with rural communities, agriculture, tourism, recreation, and resource uses.

The new greenbelt enhances the protective measures of the Oak Ridges Moraine of 2001 and the Niagara Escarpment of 1990. Further, the greenbelt more than doubles the protected area. Overall, the Toronto greenbelt has two goals: to contain sprawl in the urbanized area, and to permanently protect green space and rural areas that surround the urban area. Thus, while it

Figure 8.11 | South-Central Ontario's Greenbelt Plan

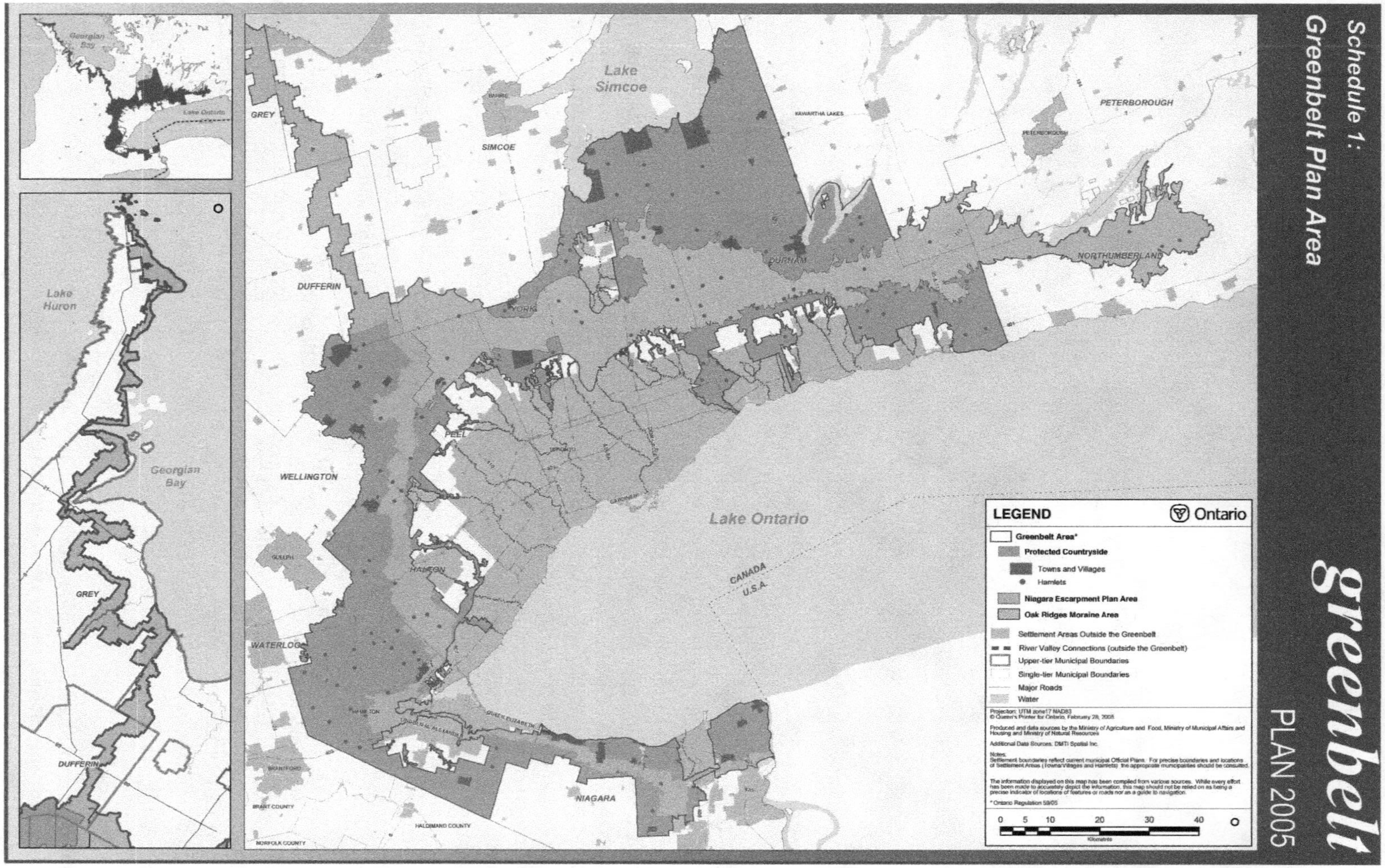

Schedule 1:
Greenbelt Plan Area

greenbelt
PLAN 2005

Ontario's provincial government prepared this plan in 2005 to preserve natural features and shape urban growth for Canada's largest urban region. The plan received the 2007 CIP Environmental Planning Award.

SOURCE: © QUEEN'S PRINTER FOR ONTARIO, 2005. REPRODUCED WITH PERMISSION.

is effectively an "urban growth boundary," it is not a fixed demarcation line as advocated in conjunction with Smart Growth initiatives. The greenbelt's boundaries are partly based upon ecological features that are more amorphous. Further, the greenbelt area is, essentially, an extensive non-urban zone with environmental and rural imperatives to achieve boundaries with which development must comply. Although its status is not guaranteed by public ownership, as in the Ottawa situation, Toronto's greenbelt is backed by substantial provincial legislation and complementary regulations, which can override local planning policies.

Vancouver's Green Strategy

Rather than a greenbelt, the approach taken in the Vancouver metropolitan region to emphasize the importance of the natural environment employs a combination of measures "to protect and enhance natural features and their connectivity."[78] These comprise the natural mountain buffer to the north; protected agricultural lands in provincial Agricultural Land Reserves to the south and east; and other ecologically important lands, major parks, and recreation areas. Together, along with a fixed Urban Containment Boundary and Greenways that connect recreation areas, they define the limits to urban expansion. Protecting the Green Zones is the first of the four listed "fundamental strategies" of the metropolitan plan. In 2002, the Greater Vancouver Regional District (GVRD) adopted a Sustainable Region Initiative (SRI) to reinforce its commitment to protecting the environment.[79] It applies, first, to all programs and activities of the GVRD and, second, to other governmental and public agencies with which it works. Sustainability measures include upgrading water reservoirs, transforming old gravel pits into parks, and integrating greenways and utility corridors.

Planning and the Super Region

The explosive development of Canadian metropolitan areas in the second half of the 20th century foreshadowed a new spatial form, the city–region. It is larger, more complex, more diverse, and more extensive than the metropolitan areas of the past and is already evident in the country's three largest urban regions, most notably in and around Toronto, leading to it now being called a super region.[80] The region being referred to stretches from St. Catharines in the southwest to Peterborough in the northeast and Barrie in the north and encompasses 32 000 square kilometres,110 municipalities, and a population of 8.1 million (2006), a population

that is headed toward 11.5 million by 2031. These are the basic parameters of Ontario's Greater Golden Horseshoe (GGH) and for which the province prepared an influential Growth Plan in 2006 (see Figure 8.12). It is a 25-year plan with the following goals:[81]

- Revitalize downtowns to become vibrant and convenient centres.
- Create complete communities that offer more options for living, working, learning, shopping, and playing.
- Provide housing options to meet the needs of people at any age.
- Curb sprawl and protect farmland and green spaces.
- Reduce traffic gridlock by improving access to a greater range of transportation options.

The plan promotes intensification of development by requiring that 40 percent of new residential development occur within existing built-up areas through infill and/or redevelopment. Each regional municipality and county will have an intensification target, and these will be monitored and building permit and assessment data tracked by a GIS-coded system. In addition, growth will be promoted in 25 centres within existing large and mid-sized cities as well as in proposed new centres. All local plans must also conform to the overall GGH Plan. A critical element in implementing the plan is through coordination of capital investments for infrastructure, especially in public transit.[82]

Reflections

Regional planning always confronts planners with a dilemma: what is the appropriate area for which we should be planning? It's a dilemma because of the interconnectedness of social and economic activities, not to mention the connections we have with the natural environment and it with us. We know that whatever spatial extent we choose for planning—municipality, county, census metropolitan area, river basin, soil region, urban agglomeration—its boundaries will never be sufficient to encompass all relationships. Yet the regional planning that has taken place in Canada, at its best, has mostly taken this dilemma in its stride—it has recognized that human activities and natural phenomena may have correlates on the other side of the region's boundary, and has recognized the need to deal with the planning problems within the region.

Out of this dilemma have come two important realizations about planning in general: the first is how human and natural facets of our world are interconnected in spatial terms; the second is that, despite the need to plan

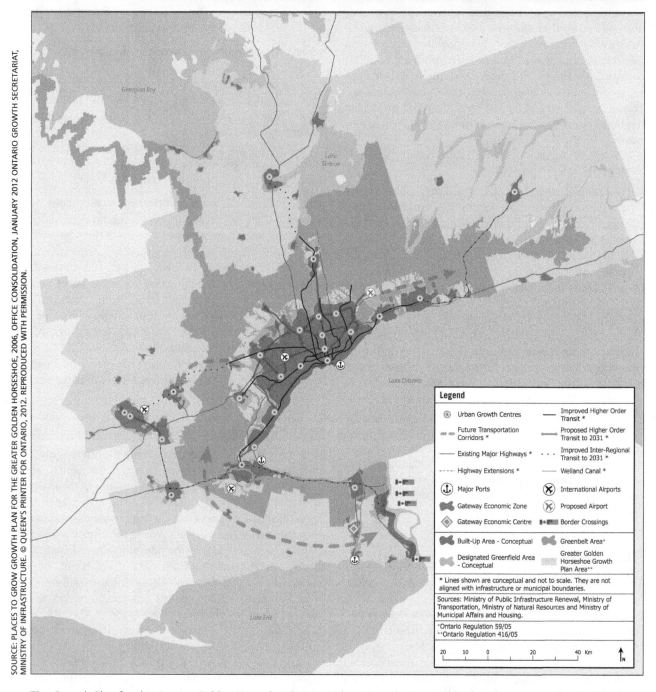

Legend

⊚ Urban Growth Centres	—— Improved Higher Order Transit *
Future Transportation Corridors *	Proposed Higher Order Transit to 2031 *
—— Existing Major Highways *	· · · Improved Inter-Regional Transit to 2031 *
- - - - Highway Extensions *	—— Welland Canal *
⚓ Major Ports	✈ International Airports
Gateway Economic Zone	✈ Proposed Airport
◈ Gateway Economic Centre	Border Crossings
Built-Up Area - Conceptual	Greenbelt Area⁺
Designated Greenfield Area - Conceptual	Greater Golden Horseshoe Growth Plan Area⁺⁺

* Lines shown are conceptual and not to scale. They are not aligned with infrastructure or municipal boundaries.

Sources: Ministry of Public Infrastructure Renewal, Ministry of Transportation, Ministry of Natural Resources and Ministry of Municipal Affairs and Housing.

⁺Ontario Regulation 59/05
⁺⁺Ontario Regulation 416/05

20   10   0   20   40 Km

The Growth Plan for the Greater Golden Horseshoe locates Urban Growth Centres (dots) and transportation facilities in south-central Ontario with the 2005 Greenbelt Plan (Figure 8.11) as its natural systems framework.

The plan received the 2007 CIP Award for Reurbanisation and the American Planning Association's 2007 Daniel Burnham Award for a Comprehensive Plan.

with predetermined spatial units, it is often necessary to consider the *interface* with other spatial units, adjacent and otherwise, to deal fully with the problems planners are confronting. Thus, we are always going to need to do regional planning; there is an "irrepressible imperative" to use the region as a platform for public-policy efforts, as British planner Urlan Wannop has said.[83] At the same time, both our planning regions and the content of their planning will vary as the need arises. We should not expect uniformity, or even seek it, in our regional planning; it is one of its strengths that it can respond in different forms. There is, however, a crucial element in this perspective, and that is the dependence upon the province to recognize and act to create, support, and, where necessary, revise both the boundaries of planning regions and the resources given to regional planners, for no regional planning can take place

without the approval of the province. Managed growth of this scope will require leadership and extensive collaboration among all levels of government and across agencies. While some planning problems often seem to demand a larger area for their comprehension, just as often other planning problems are limited to a specific area. In the next chapter, the spatial focus shifts to that of the planning needs of individual small towns that occur in most regions. Thus, in consideration of this scale change, guiding questions should be:

- *How should the boundaries for metropolitan planning reflect the presence of small towns in the region?*
- *What is the appropriate role for small towns in a metropolitan region in the planning of that region?*

Reference Notes

1. Patrick Geddes, "Civics as Concrete and Applied Sociology, Part II," a presentation to the Sociological Society, London, January 23, 1905, 70ff.
2. Geddes, "Civics as Concrete and Applied Sociology," 70.
3. Artur Glikson, *Regional Planning and Development* (Leiden: A.W. Sijthoff, 1955), 70–85.
4. Andres Duany and Emily Talen, "Transect Planning," *Journal of the American Planning Association* 68:3 (Summer 2002), 245–266.
5. Lewis Mumford, *The Culture of Cities* (New York: Harcourt, Brace, 1938).
6. Cf. L.O. Gertler, "Regional Planning in Canada," *Plan Canada*. 45:3 (Autumn 2005), 22–24.
7. Andres Duany and Emily Talen, "Transect Planning"; Peter Calthorpe and W. Fulton, *The Regional City* (Washington, DC: Island Press, 2001); and Michael Leccese and Kathleen McCormick, eds., *Charter of the New Urbanism* (New York: McGraw-Hill, 1999), especially Section 1, "The Region: Metropolis, City and Town."
8. Gerald Hodge and Ira M. Robinson, *Planning Canadian Regions* (Vancouver: UBC Press, 2001), 6–12.
9. Hodge and Robinson, *Planning Canadian Regions*, 141.
10. John Friedmann, "Regional Planning as a Field of Study," *Journal of the American Institute of Planners* 29:3 (August 1963), 168–178.
11. Sharon Fletcher and Christina Thomas, "Coping with Growth in the Regional Districts of BC," *Plan Canada* 41:4 (Winter 2001), 16–18.
12. Hodge and Robinson, *Planning Canadian Regions*, 12–15, provides the basis for this section.
13. Thomas Adams, *Rural Planning and Development* (Ottawa: Commission of Conservation, 1917). See also Wayne J. Caldwell, ed., *Rediscovering Thomas Adams: Rural Planning and Development in Canada* (Vancouver: UBC Press, 2011).
14. Canada, Royal Commission on the Future of the Toronto Waterfront, *Watershed*, 2nd Interim Report (Ottawa: Ministry of Supply and Services, 1990).
15. L.O. Gertler, *Regional Planning in Canada* (Montréal: Harvest House, 1972), 86–96.
16. Fraser Basin Management Program, *2nd Anniversary Report*, Vancouver, 1994.
17. Alberta, Department of Municipal Affairs, *Planning in Alberta* (Edmonton, 1978), 77.
18. A good review of the history of Canadian rural planning is found in Wayne J. Caldwell, "Rural Planning in Canada," *Plan Canada* 45:3 (Autumn 2005), 25–28;

his *Rediscovering Thomas Adams: Rural Planning and Development* (UBC Press, 2011) contains commentary on Adams's foundational text by leading Canadian planners.
19. Barry E. Smith and Susan Hald, "The Rural–Urban Connection: Growing Together in Greater Vancouver," *Plan Canada* 44:1 (Spring 2004), 36–39.
20. Evelyne Power Reid and Maurice Yeates, "Bill 90—An Act to Protect Agricultural Land: An Assessment of Its Success in Laprairie County, Quebec," *Urban Geography* 12:4 (1991), 295–309.
21. Wayne J. Caldwell and Claire Dodds-Weir, "Canadian Approaches to the Preservation of Farmland, *Plan Canada* 49:2 (Summer 2009), 17–20.
22. Canada, Royal Commission on Dominion–Provincial Relations, *Recommendations*, Book II (Ottawa: King's Printer, 1940), 75.
23. Maurice Yeates, *Main Street: Windsor to Quebec City* (Toronto: Macmillan, 1975).
24. Helpful references for this period are T.N. Brewis, *Regional Economic Policies in Canada* (Toronto: Macmillan, 1969); Helen Buckley and Eva Tihanyi, *Canadian Policies for Rural Adjustment* (Saskatoon: Canadian Centre for Community Studies, 1966); and Economic Council of Canada, *The Challenge of Growth and Change*, 5th Annual Review (Ottawa: Queen's Printer, 1968).
25. Cf. John Perry, *Inventory of Regional Planning Administration in Canada* (Toronto: Intergovernmental Committee on Urban and Regional Research, 1974).
26. Gertler, *Regional Planning in* Canada, 71–85.
27. James W. Wilson, *People in the Way* (Toronto: University of Toronto Press, 1973).
28. A. Paul Pross, *Planning and Development: A Case Study of Two Nova Scotia Communities* (Halifax: Dalhousie University Institute of Public Affairs, 1975).
29. Gouvernement du Québec, *Guide explicatif de la loi sur l'amanagement et l'urbanisme* (Québec: Ministère des Affaires municipales, 1980).
30. Jean Cermakian, "Geographic Research and the Regional Planning Process in Quebec: A New Challenge," *Proceedings of the New England St. Lawrence Valley Geographical Society*, 1984.
31. For a Canadian statement on bioregionalism see Mike Carr, *Bioregionalism and Civil Society* (Vancouver: UBC Press, 2004); and Doug Aberley, *Boundaries of Home: Mapping for Local Empowerment* (Gabriola Island, BC: New Society Publishers, 1993); the seminal work in bioregionalism is Kirkpatrick Sale, *Dwellers in the Land: The Bioregional Vision* (Philadelphia: New Society Publishers, 1985).
32. W. Donald McTaggart, "Bioregionalism and Regional Geography: Place, People, and Networks," *The Canadian Geographer* 37:4 (1993), 307–319.

33. Stephen Frankel, "Old Theories in New Places? Environmental Determinism and Bioregionalism," *Professional Geographer* 46:3 (1994), 289–295.

34. David L.A. Gordon and Ken Tamminga, "Large-Scale Traditional Neighbourhood Development and Pre-emptive Ecosystems Planning: The Markham Experience, 1989–2001," *Journal of Urban Design* 7:3 (2002), 321–340.

35. Richard Scott, "Canada's Capital Greenbelt: Reinventing a 1950s Plan," *Plan Canada* 36:5 (September 1996), 19–21.

36. Ian Wight, "Framing the New Urbanism with a New Eco-regionalism," *Plan Canada* 36:1 (January 1996), 21–23.

37. Stan Schwartzenberger, "A Region of Watersheds," *Plan Canada* 40:5 (November/December 2000), 23.

38. Michel Dupras, "The Necessity of Integrated Water Management in Quebec," *Plan Canada* 40:5 (November/December 2000), 24–25.

39. Michael Troughton, "Commentary," in Wayne J. Caldwell, ed., *Rediscovering Thomas Adams: Rural Planning and Development in Canada* (Vancouver: UBC Press 2011), 57–61.

40. Enid Slack, Larry S. Bourne, and Meric S. Gertler, "Small, Rural, and Remote Communities: The Anatomy of Risk," paper prepared for the Panel on the Role of Government, Toronto, August 2003.

41. Richard Sheamur and Mario Polese, "Development in Peripheral Canada: Oxymoron or Reasonable Policy?" *Plan Canada* 47:2 (Summer 2007), 32–37.

42. Sean Markey, Greg Halseth, and Don Manson, *Investing in Place: Economic Renewal in Northern British Columbia* (Vancouver, UBC Press, 2012), 15ff.

43. Richard Sheamur and Mario Polese, "Development in Peripheral Canada."

44. Sean Markey, Greg Halseth, and Don Manson, *Investing in Place*, 267–288.

45. Abdul Khakee and Nicholas Low, "Central-Local Relations in Sweden and Australia: Power, Responsibility and Territorial Equity in Comparative Perspective," *International Planning Studies 1:3* (1996) 331–356.

46. Heather M. Hall, "Northern Ontario Growth Plan," *Plan Canada* (Winter 2008) 48:4, 15–18.

47. Slack, Bourne, and Gertler, "Small, Rural, and Remote Communities."

48. Anthony Kittel, "Creating a Regional Growth Strategy: A Recipe for Successful Collaborative Planning, *Plan Canada* (Spring 2012) 52:1, 19–24.

49. Stephen M. Wheeler, "Planning for Metropolitan Sustainability," *Journal of Planning Education and Research* 20:2 (December 2000), 133–145.

50. Cf. Charles Hotovsky et al., "The Natural Environment Systems Strategy: Protecting Ottawa–Carleton's Ecological Areas," *Plan Canada* 35:6 (November 1995), 26–29.

51. Hans Blumenfeld, "Metropolitan Area Planning," in Paul D. Spreiregen, ed., *The Modern Metropolis* (Montréal: Harvest House, 1967), 79–83.

52. Year 2001–2011 data from Statistics Canada, www.statcan.ca

53. A good description of metropolitan conditions just after World War II is found in Albert Rose, *Problems of Canadian City Growth* (Ottawa: Community Planning Association of Canada, 1950).

54. Hans Blumenfeld, "Some Lessons for Regional Planning from the Experience of the Metropolitan Toronto Planning Board," in *Modern Metropolis*, 88–92.

55. See, for example, Anne Golden, "The Agony and the Ecstasy," *Plan Canada* 38:6 (1998), 22–25; and John Sewell, "Thanks, Tories, for City Chaos," *NOW*, May 8–14, 1997.

56. Melanie Hare, "Super Regions: The Regional Planning Challenge of the 21st Century," *Plan Canada* 47:3 (Autumn 2007), 51–55.

57. Ontario Growth Secretariat, "Implementing a New Vision for Growth in Canada's Largest City Region," *Plan Canada* 47:3 (Autumn 2007), 28–32.

58. George Nader, *The Cities of Canada* 2 (Toronto: Macmillan, 1976), 293.

59. Montreal Metropolitan Community, www.cmm.qc.ca

60. Austin French and Hugh Millward, "The 2006 Halifax Regional Plan: Process and Overview," *Plan Canada* 47:1 (Spring 2007), 40–43, www.halifax.ca/regionalplanning/FinalRegPlan.html#RegPlanDoc

61. Renate Banik-Schweitzer, "The City as Form and Idea," in Eve Blau and Moniker Platzer, eds., *Shaping the Great City: Modern Architecture in Central Europe* (Munich: Prestel Verlag, 1999), esp. 78–86.

62. William H. Whyte Jr., ed., *The Exploding Metropolis* (New York: Doubleday, 1958).

63. Blumenfeld, "Metropolitan Area Planning," 82.

64. Municipality of Metropolitan Toronto, *Metroplan Concepts and Objectives* (Toronto, 1976), 2.

65. Patrick Abercrombie, *Greater London Plan 1944* (London: HMO, 1945).

66. Greater Vancouver Regional District, *Livable Region Strategic Plan* (Vancouver, 1996), 2ff.

67. Canada, National Capital Commission, *Tomorrow's Capital* (Ottawa, 1974), 27ff.

68. Ontario, Department of Municipal Affairs, *Choices for a Growing Region*, a report of the Metropolitan Toronto and Region Transportation Study (Toronto, 1967).

69. The 2005 draft regional plan for the Halifax Regional Municipality is found at www.halifax.ca/regionalplanning/RegionalPlanDraft1.html

70. The 2004 Master Plan for Montréal is found at www.ville.montreal.qc.ca/plan-urbanisme/en/index.shtm

71. Steven Snell and Chris Manderson, "Calgary's Wetland Conservation Plan: Lessons Learned and Unintended Consequences," *Plan Canada* 52:1 (Spring 2012), 26–28.

72. Francois Lapointe and Pierre Dubé, "A Century of Urban Planning and Building in Canada's Capital Region," *Plan Canada* 40:3 (April/May 2000), 18–19.

73. David Gordon, "Weaving a Modern Plan for Canada's Capital: Jacques Greber and the 1950 Plan for the National Capital Region," *Urban History Review* 29:2 (March 2001), 43–61.

74. Ottawa, National Capital Commission, *Greenbelt Master Plan Summary* (Ottawa, 1996), 19.

75. Ottawa, National Capital Commission, *Greenbelt Master Plan Summary* (Ottawa, 1996), 19; see also Scott, "Canada's Capital Greenbelt," and David Gordon and Richard Scott, "Ottawa's Greenbelt Evolves from Urban Separator to Key Ecological Planning Component," in Marco Amati, ed., *Urban Greenbelts in the 21st Century* (London: Ashgate, 2008), 187–217.

76. City of Ottawa, *Ottawa 20/20: Environmental Strategy,* October 2003.

77. Ontario Ministry of Municipal Affairs and Housing, *Greenbelt Plan 2005* (Toronto: OMMAH, 2005), www.mah.gov.on.ca/userfiles/HTML/nts_1_16289_1.html

78. Greater Vancouver Regional District, *Metro Vancouver 2040: Shaping Our Future*, July 2011, 33ff, http://public.metrovancouver.org/planning/development/strategy/

79. Greater Vancouver Regional District, *Building a Sustainable Region* (Vancouver 2002).

80. Melanie Hare, "Super Regions: The Regional Planning Challenge of the 21st Century."

81. Ontario, *Growth Plan for the Greater Golden Horseshoe, 2006*, Toronto, https://www.placestogrow.ca/index.php?option=com_content&task=view&id=9&Itemid=14

82. Ontario Growth Secretariat, "Implementing a New Vision for Growth in Canada's Largest City Region," *Plan Canada* 47:3 (Autumn 2007), 28–32.

83. Urlan Wannop, The Regional Imperative: Regional Planning and Governance in Britain, Europe and the United States (London: Jessica Kingsley, 1995), 364.

Internet Resources

Chapter-Relevant Sites

Planning Canadian Communities
www.planningcanadiancommunities.ca

Halifax Regional Plan (2006)
www.halifax.ca/regionalplanning/FinalRegPlan.html#RegPlanDoc

Montréal Metropolitan Community Plan (2012)
www.cmm.qc.ca

MetroVancouver, Regional Growth Strategy (2011)
www.metrovancouver.org/planning

Saskatoon, Meewasin Valley Authority
www.meewasin.com

Manitoba Capital Region
www.gov.mb.ca/ia/capreg/index.html

Ontario Places to Grow plans
www.placestogrow.ca

Ottawa, National Capital Commission
www.capcan.ca

Nova Scotia, Association of Regional Development Authorities
www.nsarda.ca

New Brunswick, Regional Development Corporation
www2.gnb.ca/content/gnb/en/departments/regional_development.html

Chapter Nine

The Urban Community Plan: Its Characteristics and Role

The Master Plan is not an end but a directive. It cannot be definitive and inflexible, but must be constantly adapted to changing conditions. Such adaptations ... are to be made only with the whole scheme in mind.

Jean-Claude LaHaye, 1961

The activity of community planning has many facets. It comprises several types of plans and a variety of processes, but it is not a random set of plans and processes. It has a coherence that is provided by the comprehensive community plan. Like the keystone in an archway, the community plan (master plan, general plan, municipal plan, official community plan) is the fundamental component in planning for communities large and small (see Figure 9.6). It is the component that provides both the context and the *raison d'être* for detailed plans and regulations. It is the criterion for judging private development proposals and public investment decisions, and for making regulations with regard to land use. Indeed, the latter, which include zoning bylaws and capital budgets, are often referred to as "tools" for implementing the community plan, thus indicating their dependence on the overall plan.

Seen in this light, the community plan is more than a design for improvement of the built environment, more than a statement of what the community wants to become. The community plan plays a distinctive role in *governing* a community, whether it is an urban area, small town, or region. In this chapter, the focus is on the plan for urban communities, on its scope and content, on whom it serves, and on its relation to other planning tools. The scope and content of plans for larger (regions) and smaller (towns) entities have their own rationale. Discussion of them is found in Chapters 8 (regions/ metro) and 10 (small towns). Nonetheless, consider two questions that are pertinent regardless of size of community:

- *What is the role of the community-wide plan in the overall activity of community governance?*
- *Why should a community plan be amend-able and by which criteria?*

The Scope of the Urban Community Plan

To describe the scope of a community plan is not a simple task, because it is not a simple device. A community plan spans several important dichotomies in the life and development of a community. First, there are *future* aims versus *immediate* needs; then, there is one concerned with the *ideal* view versus the *pragmatic* view; and, of course, there is the *citywide* view versus the *local* view. Implicit in each of these is the basic dichotomy that a community plan tries to address: the *planning* of land use versus the *control* of the physical development. This brings the community plan to a consideration of the basic values and objectives that inform the decisions of the governing body. In order to sharpen our perspective on the inherent complexity of the community plan, we should look first at the general concerns that a plan addresses.[1]

Concerns of the Community Plan

The concerns addressed by a community plan were described in the preceding two chapters. The plan focuses on the built and natural environments, it frames a planning viewpoint, and ultimately it acts as a policy instrument. These concerns are reviewed briefly here.

1. Importance of the Built Environment

From the time of the first planning acts in Canada, the focus of community planning has clearly been the built environment. These acts very often carried a statement of general aims—namely, to allow a community "to plan and regulate the use and development of land for all building purposes." In other words, the focus has been on the "built" environment, both in terms of what already existed in the way of houses, stores, factories, parks, schools, institutions, roads, and so forth, and in terms of the prospects for built development on vacant land. Concern for the health and maintenance of the natural environment in which the community exists was added to this focus in the late 20th century.

Coinciding with the growth and refinement of professional planning practice, it became apparent that planning for the built environment required taking into account the natural environment along with the social, economic, and financial aspects of the community. For instance, the type of people in the community, their level of affluence, and their values, as well as the kind of economic development, all affect the kind of built community that exists or will exist. More recently, the impact on energy use of different forms and patterns of urban development is being included in the focus of community planning. This expanded perspective asked of plan-makers does not mean that the community plan is a plan *for* the social, economic, natural, and energy dimensions of a community as well as for the built environment. Most of these other dimensions are outside the direct control of local councils, so it is vital to grasp the constancy and importance of the built environment in promoting community well-being. Two pragmatic issues are central here: first, almost everything that gets built has a long lifespan, and second, the public investments needed for support and service involve large capital outlays and must be financed over a long period of time. The primacy of the built environment in preparing a community plan has been reiterated in new planning legislation in several provinces. This sharp focus does not, however, preclude consideration of other dimensions of the community. Indeed, since the community's physical plan is usually the only overall plan it has, it can (and has come to) serve as the focal point for planning social, economic, and natural environmental factors in a coherent manner. This is especially evident in recent planning endeavours in larger urban areas such as Vancouver, Edmonton, and Ottawa.

2. Patterns and Processes of Land Development

A community's built environment develops on a land base that is mostly privately owned, some of which is built on and some of which is vacant. Furthermore, the built environment is ever-changing, either through the natural aging of buildings and facilities or in response to change through population and economic growth, new technology, and new values and goals. A good deal of the thrust of any community plan is to promote ways in which the land base should be developed in order to respond to anticipated change in the community. The solution is usually not self-evident because the land base is owned by a large number of different persons, groups, and organizations, each with their own vision of the future of their own land as well as their own aims for the community as a whole. A progression of typical questions that plan-makers must ask will help illustrate the range of concerns:

- Will change (e.g., growth) require additional land?
- Is new development best on the fringe of the community or located within already developed sections?
- Where is vacant land available and for sale?
- Are there built-up areas that might be appropriate for redevelopment instead rather than new development?
- Will redevelopment increase densities and place pressure on adjacent stable areas?
- What will be the cost to the community to provide public utilities and roads to vacant undeveloped land?
- Will growth in one section of the community lead to decline in other sections (as with a new shopping centre and the old downtown)?
- In sections of the community where stability and continuity of land use are sought, how can these sections be protected and also encouraged to renew themselves?
- Which kind of new development, internally or on the fringe, will have the least negative impact on the natural environment?
- Which should have precedence: maintenance of the health of local ecosystems or new physical development?

The above types of concerns mean that a community plan must be able to take into account the dynamics of land and building development. Further, it must provide an interface between the ideals and goals of the community and the need to manage land development activity. Land development is a vital and dynamic process often in need of control. While the community plan does not directly regulate land use, it does provide the criteria—the terms of reference—for regulatory efforts. The community plan thus acts to mediate such difficult questions as: Which land is to be developed? Where would development best be located? When? And whose land is to be developed?

3. Establishing Good Planning Principles

Experience in planning and building cities has shown that certain ways of structuring the built environment work best. Out of this have developed planning principles (such as we referred to in Chapter 6) that guide or motivate plan-makers. They tend to reflect, in turn, the basic values of planning: health, safety, welfare, efficiency, and amenity. Planning principles are thus like obligations for plan-makers. The community plan "ought to" promote their achievement because this will help ensure a "good" community environment.

Four important planning principles have come to direct planning behaviour in a consistent way in modern communities:

1. **Environmental integrity.** The land, water, and air of the community comprise a vital base upon which, and within which, land uses and development activities take place, and the impacts on this natural environment should be mitigated or minimized.
2. **Appropriate land use assignment.** Each land use usually has distinctive locational and activity characteristics. Land uses should be spatially located where they will function most effectively and not conflict with other uses (e.g., separating heavy industry from residences, locating shops next to transit routes).
3. **Integration of activities.** Since the activities associated with various land uses need to be linked to one another, systems for moving people and goods should be provided that are convenient, economical, and safe (e.g., between homes and jobs, between industry and transportation terminals).
4. **Neighbourhood integrity.** Residential areas should be clearly defined, large enough to maintain their own character and values, fully protected from the hazards of major traffic routes, and have parks, schools, and stores within easy reach by walking.

It will be readily noticed that the fourth principle follows closely the "neighbourhood unit" concept propounded by Perry in the 1920s. Further, it parallels contemporary ideas about the neighbourhood planning advanced by the advocates of the New Urbanism.[2] This illustrates how deeply such physical planning design notions have penetrated community-planning thinking. Also, the idea of respecting the integrity of residential districts is carried over into the design principles for other districts—shopping precincts, industrial parks, historic districts, waterfront areas—so that their distinctiveness and effectiveness can be promoted. And respecting the integrity of the natural environment is rooted deeply in the conservation ethic that guided much early planning.

Planning principles for the built environment are, in many ways, at the heart of a community plan. They determine the actual physical conditions under which people will live, work, shop, and play in the community. They may or may not be made explicit in a community plan, but they are, nevertheless, embedded in it and in the implementing tools.

4. Coordination

There is probably no closer synonym in most people's minds for the idea of "planning" than "coordination." A good deal of the original justification for community planning was the chaos of traffic and slums in the centre of cities, and the helter-skelter subdivision of land on the fringes of cities. The wisdom of developing cities in an orderly fashion—aligning the street patterns of adjacent subdivisions, providing utility and transport lines at the time they are needed, providing schools and parks in residential areas—did not escape the notice of citizens. The coordination of city-building activities gave people confidence in the government's use of tax resources, added to their sense of physical well-being, and contributed to their aesthetic sense of a pleasant and smoothly functioning community.

Given the diversity of bodies that make decisions, in both the public and private sectors, regarding the future built environment, it is clear that there must be a means of coordination. Further, the coordination must be intentional and provide a focus of responsibility. Those plan-makers primarily involved in establishing an overview of community needs—the local council, its planning board, and planners—are not themselves the agencies that actually develop and redevelop the community. Their overall plan provides a focus: for example, the parks department or transit authority might use the plan as a guide in designing their services; or builders, land developers, and business firms can know of the community's intentions and be guided by the plan. In municipalities with sophisticated corporate planning strategies, the urban community plan may be one component in a suite of coordinated plans to meet the overall goals of the local government (see Figure 9.1).

5. The Need for Policy

Physical development (planning) matters occupy perhaps half the agenda of the average municipal council at its regular meetings. This attests to the important position that planning matters occupy in community government. But it is also important to realize that by the time planning matters arrive on the city hall agenda, councillors are caught up in the press of other day-to-day issues and must make decisions. The existence of agreed upon policies for the physical development of the community enables councillors to judge development problems and proposals in light of ideas about the kind

| Figure 9.1 | Functional Plans within the Ottawa 2020 Strategic Plan |

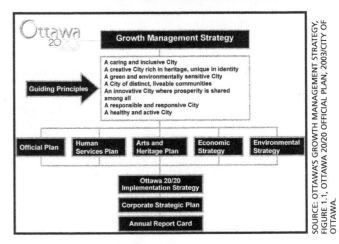

The City of Ottawa has a suite of coordinated functional plans. The comprehensive land use plan for this community is called the "Official Plan" in the Ontario context.

of community they and their citizens want, rather than on grounds of expediency.

In order to deal with the array of planning concerns discussed above, it is necessary to do more than just identify them: yes, it is sensible to have a certain arrangement of land uses; yes, we should apply the best planning principles; yes, it is wise to have coordination of investment actions. But in order to provide some assurance that these concerns can be met, a commitment must be made to the community's objectives for its built and natural environments—that is, there must be a **public policy**. The community plan is an expression of this policy, in effect stating, "In these kinds of situations, we will act in this way for these reasons." It states the community's position in advance and requires a persuasive argument before any deviation can be considered. Serious community planning demands that we go beyond speculation and idealization and make a commitment to strive for goals. Effective community planning requires a plan that embodies firm commitments.

Key Features of the Community Plan

In general, a community plan's main characteristics may be derived from the above set of concerns. In one sentence: *the community plan is a long-range, comprehensive, general policy guide for future physical development.* These are the four essential features of the

Globe and Mail
May 16, 2011

Winnipeg Rethinks Suburban Sprawl with Downtown Reinvention

Siri Agrell

Fighting back against the rush to the suburbs that began in the 1970s, the city is moving to realign itself, coaxing life back to its centre as it looks to the future

It's 5 p.m. on Portage Avenue and a parade of cars, buses and pedestrians is making its way out of the downtown as quickly as possible, speeding past shuttered storefronts and lonely side streets. But for the first time in years, the daily commuter rush is passing something new: construction.

An unprecedented level of development is under way in the Manitoba capital, as Winnipeg attempts to reverse decades of movement out to the suburbs.

"We want to have a situation where you don't have a massive population downtown between nine and five and then all of a sudden it's six o'clock and it's empty," says Mayor Sam Katz. "But what people don't realize is that you can't correct the mistakes of the past in just a year or two."

Around the world there is a growing understanding that suburban sprawl is unsustainable, and that, for cities to survive, they must shrink back in on themselves, tightening up, promoting density and pushing their growing population into space already served by existing infrastructure and social services.

For Winnipeg, the need for change is especially pressing. The city's population in 2006 was 633,451, but of those, only 13,470 lived downtown. A rush to the suburbs in the 1970s gutted the inner city and crippled downtown retail. Heritage buildings that would be hot commodities elsewhere have sat unoccupied for years, and parking lots seem to occasionally outnumber the cars that use them.

Now, the city is desperately trying to realign itself, drawing life back to its centre as a way to sustain its economic core.

And it is not alone.

Most planning experts agree that sprawl is creating a looming bubble, and that governments will soon be forced to contend with the hidden costs of a thinly spreadout population and how it uses everything from health care to energy.

In Ontario, the provincial strategy known as Places to Grow is designed to increase density in key locations, especially close to major transit routes.

And Calgary Mayor Naheed Nenshi took office having promised to put distance between municipal politicians and the developers pushing for more housing on the city's outskirts. He is an advocate of Plan It Calgary, which aims to cultivate downtown walking, cycling and transit and focus on sustainable land use as the city welcomes an estimated 1.3-million more people over the next 60 years.

On the other end of the spectrum, Detroit, Mich., has offered the world an apocalyptic vision of the urban future, having recently begun razing huge swaths of its abandoned inner city.

Ken Greenberg, a Toronto-based architect and urban planner, says cities around the world are realizing that promoting population density is no longer negotiable.

"Whether you like it or not, what's going to drive the change between city and suburb is the cost of energy," he said. "This is a crisis. It's not even worth debating whether it's worthwhile making these changes, the trick is to get ahead of the curve as much as possible."

This means getting people to live inside cities rather than on their periphery, as sprawl requires new infrastructure and support services, which municipal governments do not have the money or the time to adequately provide.

In Winnipeg, Mr. Katz hopes to bring about at least 3,000 people into the downtown core over the next few years.

It may not sound like a lot, but it requires a change of mindset as well as changing laws.

Winnipeg's hollow centre is largely the result of an archaic municipal bylaw, first introduced in 1919, which enforced a strict separation of land use. Some streets were for commercial buildings, others for housing, and the distinction stalled downtown residential development.

According to Mr. Katz, this bylaw prevented the building of mixed-use developments, like the condos that have become ubiquitous in other city centres.

"You go to any other major downtown, Chicago, Boston, you will see retail on the main floors and then mixed-use residential above. For whatever the reason, it wasn't allowed here," Mr. Katz said.

When city council wanted to start pushing mixed use in 1988, they discovered that the bylaw was still on the books and set about changing it. But it was only in 2004 that new zoning bylaw 100-2004 was introduced, allowing mixed-use development and truly accommodating private-sector investment in downtown living.

Now it's just a matter of convincing people to actually live there.

Programs like the city's arms-length Centre Venture Development Corp. and the Portage Avenue Action Strategy were created to promote a new downtown vibe.

The idea is to build up communities around existing draws like the MTS Centre, an indoor arena that hosts acts like Roger Daltry and is home to the American Hockey League team, the Manitoba Moose. New hotels, condos and retail projects are planned for the historic Exchange District and The Forks, a popular market destination at the confluence of Red and Assiniboine Rivers that will be home to the $310-million Canadian Museum for Human Rights, slated to open in 2013.

In March of 2010, the city and province teamed up to offer $20-million in development grants and tax incentives for the construction of downtown residential units, and the money was snatched up within 10 months. Another $20-million in funding was announced earlier this year.

The city is also hoping to develop some of the 154 surface parking lots spread across Winnipeg – valuable real estate that sits empty outside of business hours – and has offered a tax credit to homeowners who buy new infill-housing in established residential neighbourhoods.

So far, it seems to be working. Next year, construction will begin on a $45-million residential high-rise called Heritage Landing, the first private-sector project of its kind in more than 20 years. The riverfront property will include 19 townhouses, a 25-storey tower and three floors of commercial space.

Near City Hall, the historic Avenue Building and Union Bank Tower are both undergoing dramatic conversions that will introduce residential units and student housing to Portage Avenue.

And the municipal government is not acting alone. Some of Winnipeg's biggest names have thrown themselves into the effort.

Lloyd Axworthy, former minister of foreign affairs and now president of the University of Winnipeg, has been tapping into the city's business community as part of his

CONTINUED

development of the school's downtown real estate holdings.

After his appointment in 2004, he created an arms-length renewal corporation with the flexibility to negotiate loans and acquire property on the school's behalf, and seems to have set about buying much of the western end of Portage. He hopes to help rebuild his city around an education hub, and envisions the school's expansion spawning downtown student housing, retail, restaurants and even pubs, although he admits the latter would make the city's Mennonite forbearers shudder.

Already, the faculties of business and continuing education have moved into the John and Bonnie Buhler Centre on Portage Avenue, which opened last August with the help of a $4-million gift from the philanthropist couple. Just a few blocks away, past a row of abandoned store fronts and empty bridal outlets, Ray McFeetors of Great West Life has given his money and his name to a new student residence and day care. And this fall, the $40-million Richardson College for the Environment and Science will open at the corner of Portage and Langside Street, the recipient of a $3.5-million donation from the city's Richardson family and a glittering sign of modernity in a desolate part of the city.

"I think it's starting to buzz now," Mr. Axworthy says of Portage. "I think a lot more people feel secure now in the downtown. And they are excited."

Jino Distasio, director of the Institute of Urban Studies at the University of Winnipeg, says the city is just beginning to recover from the suburban rush of the 1970s when the downtown and its surrounding inner city neighbourhoods witnessed population losses as high as 50 per cent.

"We're still fighting the culture of Winnipeg that downtown is a negative," he said. "Downtowns have changed and they need to reinvent themselves."

The city was dealt another blow by the big-box store explosion of the 1990s, which fuelled further migration to the suburbs while gutting downtown retail environments.

But for good or bad, he believes Winnipeg has perfected the "urban intervention model," leveraging government dollars to invest in the right kinds of revitalization projects before it's too late.

Whether the city is truly able to change, he notes, will depend on whether other groups take up the cause.

"The public investment can take us only so far," he said. "We have to make sure that, privately, people want to come into the downtown core because they can make a profit and they'll be successful. And, more than anything, people have to want to live here."

plans prepared for urban communities, regardless of the name conferred on them by their respective provincial planning acts (official plans, general municipal plans, etc.). There are, in addition, several other features that provide a linking function to such aspects as the background analyses, staging of the plan, and capital investment needs.

The first planning acts offered planners the opportunity to prepare detailed "town-planning schemes," but experience seemed to show that a broad, policy-oriented plan must precede and give direction beyond immediate development problems. In recent years, there have been suggestions for financial plans, social plans, energy plans, and environmental plans, but all these turn out to depend upon the general community plan. To reiterate, the four key features of a community plan are:

1. **Focused upon the natural and built environments.** The plan should encompass the entire land (and water) base of the community and take into account both man-made and natural features of the environment. The plan should deal

explicitly with five basic physical elements of the community (see also Chapter 7):

1. Natural environment—the local and regional ecosystem and its biodiversity;
2. Living areas—the areas comprising the residences of citizens;
3. Working areas—the areas comprising industries, places of commerce, and other forms of economic development;
4. Community facilities—the location and character of public and private facilities that provide community services for both the neighbourhood and the overall area; and
5. Circulation—the systems and facilities needed to enable people and goods to move between living areas, working areas, and community facilities, as well as between the community and its region.

2. **Long-range and forward-looking in direction.** The time scale of the plan is determined by factors relevant to the particular community, such as population and economic growth, the condition of structures, and the need for utilities and amenities. Modifying the existing government, building new facilities, and paying for the public infrastructure all take considerable time. A common time horizon for plans is 20 years, as in Ottawa's 20/20 plan; York Region, on the other hand, uses a 15-year horizon (see Figure 6.4, page 155). Intermediate targets may be set for specific projects included in the plan, such as a new expressway or urban renewal project.

3. **Comprehensive in viewpoint.** The plan should comprehend, or take into account, "all significant factors physical and non-physical, local and regional, that affect the physical growth and development of the community"[3] That is, the plan should deal with the basic physical elements, as indicated above, as well as any other significant physical areas or features that are distinctive to the community. The viewpoint must also be broad enough to take into account conditions and trends in the larger geographical setting of the community.

4. **General and broad-based in perspective.** To be effective as a comprehensive instrument and as a policy guide, the plan should focus on the main concerns and issues of the community and the broad design components for its physical development. The plan is not a blueprint and should not include any details that detract from

overall physical-design proposals and policies. Its primary purpose is to define the general location, character, and extent of desirable future development, and to be a guide against which detailed proposals may be evaluated. It may be necessary to provide some specific details in order to clarify the intent of policies or to provide physical images to which the community can relate.

Other Important Features of the Plan

In addition to the four key features of a community plan described above, there are several other important features that are included in many plans. Some plan-makers assign them an individual place within the plan report because of their importance in linking the general physical design with the policy role of the plan, as well as with related policy areas. These additional features are:

1. Linked to social and economic objectives Even though a community plan focuses on the built environment, it is in many respects a vehicle for achieving social and economic objectives, at least in part. Indeed, a physical development plan that is not harmonized with these objectives may be less than successful. The two most obvious subject areas where we find strong interactions between physical and socioeconomic objectives are in housing[4] as well as in the provision of space for industry and commerce. It is vital that the process of community planning take into account social and economic factors. In addition, the plan must clearly state social and economic objectives that can be furthered by the physical development proposals. In this way, the community plan serves to focus attention on non-physical planning goals and to point out the need for coordination in their attainment in other functional plans of the community (see Figure 9.1).

2. Based on planning analyses The analyses of current conditions and the forecasts of future conditions in the community combine to form one of the two cornerstones of the plan, the other being the community objectives. The analyses of population, economic base, land use, circulation, and the natural environment define the range of possibilities for the plan-maker. It is important that at least the main findings and the rationale behind the analyses be reported within the plan. Moreover, many of the analyses pertain to non-physical factors (e.g., population age, income, culture, employment), and this will assist in clarifying the relationships between the physical plan and social and economic factors in the community, as we shall see below.

3. *Implemented by stages* In contrast to older community plans, which presented a single long-range concept, it is now common for the progression of development to be stated. This is important because not all new development areas are likely to be opened up at the same time; if development is left to disperse, it could result in costly extensions to roads and utilities in the municipality; sprawling development can be inefficient for commuters as well as for those providing commercial services. The inclusion of a staging plan clearly signals the community's intentions to land developers, homeowners, business firms, institutions, and other public bodies. Additionally, the staging plan is often backed up nowadays with fixed limits to the areal extent of new building. They are called Urban Containment Boundaries by some and Urban Growth Boundaries by others.[5]

4. *A guide for capital improvement* An overall plan is intended to help predict and anticipate the demands for public works and other capital investments. Most plans provide only a very general indication about needed investments, as, for example, when a new area is opened up for residential development and roads, utilities, parks, and schools are planned. A greater degree of specificity is, however, more helpful to the local council for scheduling capital projects. To this end, many communities prepare a Capital Improvements Program (CIP) in conjunction with their overall plan (see Chapter 17). The CIP is often structured to relate to the annual budgeting process of the community and also to project several years into the future as anticipated by the community plan. Thus, it makes the stages for development proposed in the plan more realistic.

5. *A basis for community design* An ever-present value of planners and an expectation of citizens is that of visual beauty for the community. The community plan's proposed pattern of land uses is the base upon which the three-dimensional environment of buildings and open spaces is designed and constructed. Although community plans result in a particular community form, in recent years the design element has been notably absent from many community plans.[6] A design component of an overall place can be vital in communicating to citizens and developers the key built and natural features and special districts that have a particular significance for the community. It "lets them see" what the plan proposes.[7] (This issue is discussed in Chapter 6 and later in this chapter.)

Most provincial planning acts provide only a broad hint of the plan's scope, much less its content and characteristics. The above points thus attempt a synthesis of concepts and experience that reflects planning practice in Canada. It is perhaps unwise to seek a more precise definition, for every community plan will need to respond to the aspirations and problems of its particular community setting. The community plan must ultimately persuade citizens that it reflects their best interests as well as those of future citizens. In this task of human communication, community plans take a variety of forms. There are those that convey their message in a colourful booklet, those that use a newspaper tabloid format, those that are bound in ponderous tomes, and those that are laid out as a one-page poster. But, regardless of plan format or community size, the most effective community plans have the scope indicated above (see Figure 9.2).

Technical Foundations of a Community Plan

Preparing a community plan is a craft that combines both science and art. The development of design alternatives for a community is an art that requires good skills in urban design, landscape architecture, and physical planning, as we saw in Chapter 6. Urban design and site planning skills are especially important for small-scale plans. The large-scale technical analysis for community plans may require some design skills at the landscape scale, but will rely more on analysis of environmental, population, employment, land use, and transportation data.

The planner draws upon methods of analysis capable of distinguishing the factors involved in the planning problem. On the substantive side, the population, economy, and land uses need to be taken into account to predict their outcome should conditions change in the future. The complexity associated with any one of the major factors is obvious; even more complex are the relationships among them.

The methods developed to cope with this complexity draw upon the concept of systems analysis. In this view, the various parts of a problem are perceived to be linked, forming a functioning whole, or **system**. A system's overall character affects the way in which the separate parts work, so that the parts cannot be adequately understood without understanding the whole. Thus,

Figure 9.2 Community Plans for All Sizes of Communities

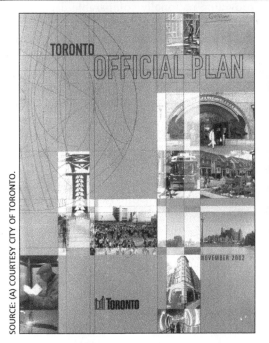

SOURCE: (A) COURTESY CITY OF TORONTO.

SOURCE: (B) COURTESY CITY OF SAINT JOHN.

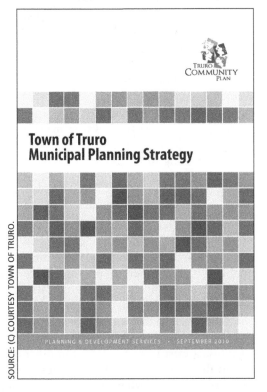

SOURCE: (C) COURTESY TOWN OF TRURO.

SOURCE: (D) COURTESY CITY OF IQALUIT.

for example, a neighbourhood may be thought of as a system (more properly, a sub-system of the city system) in which the age composition of the population is linked to the need for housing, the use of schools and parks, and traffic and safety considerations. A particular neighbourhood will also have a distinctive character, in terms of tradition, location, status of residents, and so on, which affects the functioning of the various elements within it. Other parts of the city may be similarly perceived. While this approach is persuasive, it must be acknowledged that analytical methods cannot offer us a complete view of the complexity of a city system. However, partial views are available through analytical **models** (the analyst's way of replicating a system) of the economy, population growth, and the housing market, to name the main ones. The planner's tendency to think in terms of interrelationships and interdependencies allows the gaps between partial models to be identified, even if not fully understood.

Data Sources

Data for the inventory and analysis of the natural and built environment is usually obtained in the form of satellite images, aerial photography, or maps from other public agencies. Regional environmental planners must be skilled in interpreting data from all three sources, while urban planners may rely more upon local maps and aerial photographs. A municipal or regional planning agency in a fast-growing area might arrange to have aerial photography of their jurisdiction updated every two years, and some municipalities put their spatial information online for public access.[8]

A common source of data for many other diagnostic studies is the Census of Canada, especially the sections dealing with population, housing, and labour force. Every 10 years, the census provides a complete set of data for each incorporated city and town; every 5 years, it provides a limited set of population data. The value of the census lies in its accuracy, complete coverage, continuity, and consistency. This provides a community planner with an objective baseline of information at any time, and also with the data to trace trends in information over fairly long periods. It also allows easy comparison among communities throughout the country. One can obtain data for small areas (census tracts) within a city as well.

As useful as the census is to planners, it has relatively large time spans between publications of its findings. This can be a problem when a community is experiencing high population movements in and out or changes

in its economy, each of which may happen between censuses. Moreover, since the census is geared toward providing nationally comparable data, it cannot cover distinctive local conditions. The planner, therefore, may need to seek other secondary data sources or to develop primary data sources within and for the community. Another source of data is the property assessment data that is collected in most parts of Canada by provincial agencies. These data are highly detailed, based as they are on individual properties. Also helpful to the planner are data gathered by other local agencies—for example, neighbouring planning departments, public utility departments, and school boards.

However, there is hardly any planning problem for which diagnoses or other analyses can be completed on the basis of secondary sources. Each community has unique features, as does each neighbourhood and district. To get a complete picture of a place, it is necessary to gather first-hand information and even to gain first-hand experience. The planner obtains this through field visits, observing the continuous activities and functioning of an area, perhaps at different times of the day or week or year, and speaking informally with its users. Some planners may claim that this is not objective data; however, there is simply no substitute for the personal understanding, or local knowledge, obtained "on the spot."

The formal, objective approach to such knowledge employs questionnaires and other formal surveys that record observations about an area. These may take the form of personal interviews with users of an area or facility, such as householders who may be affected by a school closing or shoppers who may have to deal with reduced parking in a business area. Or they may take the form of inventories of, for example, an area's traffic, building conditions, or lot coverage. Survey research can yield high-quality information when the research instruments (e.g., questionnaires) are constructed thoughtfully and with scientific objectivity. The design of the research instrument is, therefore, important in enabling the planner to provide more penetrating observations, as through the use of statistical analyses. There are established methods for survey research that should be used in this regard.[9]

It has always been evident to planners that much useful data exist in maps or files in other departments within the same city, in adjacent cities, and in special-purpose agencies. Where these can be consolidated and combined, more broad-based information systems can make diagnostic studies more complete.

Metropolitan and regional planning agencies often play this role. There are still difficulties in combining data from some sources, owing to differences in format and dates of collection. Since most planning analyses are for small portions of the entire community, these difficulties are not insuperable and good case-by-case databases for analysis are also possible. These should, of course be conducted in a consistent manner so that they can become part of a larger database.

The advent of **Geographic Information Systems** (GIS) and their continued refinement has enabled planners to make more accurate and complete analyses and maps.[10] Some of the typical planning applications include environmental impact assessment, land use inventories, recording and enforcement of zoning maps and regulations, and mapping traffic congestion. The novelty and ease of use of GIS technology, however, carries with it problems of misuse and misinterpretation of data inputs and outputs, which planners must keep in mind.[11]

Natural Systems Analysis Natural systems planning must be done long in advance of urban development to be effective. Regional environmental planning described in Chapter 8 above may provide a large-scale policy framework for an urban community plan. At the metropolitan scale, environmental analysis using techniques from landscape ecology can provide a natural systems framework for the expansion of an urban community, as discussed in Chapter 7.[12] This analysis is usually conducted by an environmental planning agency, using a GIS. The results can include a "greenprint" (a system of interconnected patches) and a "blueprint" (plans for rivers, lakes and waterfronts). The results will indicate the best areas for urban expansion, environmentally sensitive areas that must be protected, and environmental restoration areas that should be set aside in the development process to strengthen natural systems (see Figure 7.1, page 163).[13]

Population Forecasting Because of the importance of population growth and change in a community, there is hardly a planning study anywhere that does not begin with this factor. Of a variety of methods for forecasting population, the simplest extrapolates data on past population levels into the future using graphical and/or mathematical means. This often provides the planner with a satisfactory overview of population tendencies. However, the planner may need to understand the role of births, deaths, migration, birth rates, age, income, or ethnicity in regard to a population

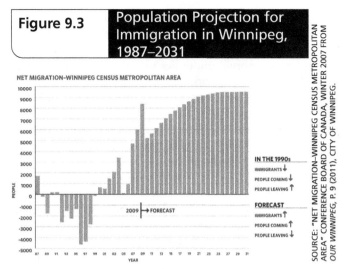

Figure 9.3 Population Projection for Immigration in Winnipeg, 1987–2031

SOURCE: "NET MIGRATION–WINNIPEG CENSUS METROPOLITAN AREA" CONFERENCE BOARD OF CANADA, WINTER 2007 FROM *OUR WINNIPEG*, P. 9 (2011), CITY OF WINNIPEG.

Immigration is an important component of a cohort-survival population projection in many Canadian communities because the birth rate has declined. Almost all population growth is a result of immigration in many cities.

change to plan for a particular client group, such as the elderly or visible minorities (Figure 9.3). The much anticipated surge of the baby boom bulge in the population to become seniors began in 2011 for communities large and small.[14] For analyzing such changes in population cohorts, the planner will need to use more extensive data and more elaborate methods.[15] Among the most useful of these tools is the **cohort-survival method**, which allows each age cohort for either sex to be forecast independently.

Economic Forecasting The future of the local economy is important because of its connection with the need for housing, public utilities, and transportation. Economic studies at the city or town level attempt to determine employment opportunities, rather than volume of business. They use techniques drawn from the theory of urban land markets.[16] Through the prediction of employment, the planner has a way of linking the economy of a place to the size and needs of the population. Probably the most common type of question raised in regard to a local economy would be one such as, "If we were to get that new factory with its 500 jobs, what effect would it have on the local economy?" The answer to such a question is usually approached through a **community economic base model**, or one of its variations. The foundation of these methods is to estimate the impact of the additional income brought to the community by firms that export their products to other communities and regions (which is the case with most factories). The community economic base model uses the notion of an economic multiplier to estimate the portion of the exporting factory's income that will accrue to the community and thus generate other jobs in the local economy.[17]

Of course, it is not just factories that may be considered "export industries." All forms of activities catering to tourists are almost wholly export-oriented, because they serve people from other communities. The same is true for firms in the business districts and shopping centres of cities and towns: a substantial part of their business volume is due to purchases made by people from the countryside and other communities. There are other more elaborate economic models that may be used in understanding and predicting economic impacts on communities (especially for larger cities and metropolitan areas), such as **input–output** and **industrial–complex** analyses. Indeed, the tools available for economic analysis are often the best developed among those the planner has available. A general note of caution is appropriate at this point, for one frequently hears dramatic multiplier effects claimed by community boosters, such as "every job in the tourism industry generates five other jobs in the community." It is extremely rare for new export industries to generate more than one additional job each in the community, and the ratio is often much less.

Analysis for community economic development has been influenced by the works of Michael Porter, Jane Jacobs, and Richard Florida. Porter's analysis of the role of economic clusters in the competitiveness of city regions has been used to develop strategies to strengthen technology clusters in the Ottawa Valley and Kitchener-Waterloo regions.[18] Jane Jacobs alerted planners to the importance of the service sector to the economies of cities. Richard Florida extended Jacobs's work to demonstrate the importance of arts and culture, of the creative class, to the economy of city-regions. As a result, many Canadian cities are focusing less on attracting new steel mills and more on growing their creative economy and cultural industries.[19] Cirque du Soleil may be as important as Bombardier Aerospace to the global reach of the Montréal economy.[20]

Land Use Forecasting Methods for predicting **land use changes** are less well developed. This is especially so at the detailed level of individual properties because here the reasons for land use decisions and the responses to the decisions of others are affected by the personal views and values of those involved. Analytical approaches to land use thus favour a broader view of the community, such as predicting the amount of residential land that would be needed in light of population growth or economic expansion or the opening up of a new highway.[21] There are also useful models in existence for predicting the impact of a new shopping centre on established businesses.[22] But, all in all, this area of analysis remains relatively underdeveloped.

Before leaving this discussion of predictive studies, it should be noted again that the planner's view of a community is of a *linked set of factors*. Therefore, by knowing about the changes in one factor, the planner can estimate the changes in another. For example, when the future population of a community is known, the proportion of the population that will be in the labour force or the number of households that compose that population can be deduced. In this way, sometimes known as a **step-down analysis**, estimates can be made of future job levels in the economy and land use needs for business and industry. Or, stepping down from population to households, estimates can be made of residential land use needs and even housing types. Since these relations tend to be transitive, it is also possible to employ a **step-up analysis** to estimate population from knowledge of the number of jobs expected in the community (see Figure 9.4). Or, in a parallel way, to estimate housing and facilities for seniors from trends in the elderly population. The results of such analyses are, of course, limited by the assumptions one makes about the connections between the factors

Transportation Forecasting The distribution and interaction of the population, employment, and other land uses create demand for mobility within the community. Transportation planners have developed sophisticated models for forecasting the trips generated by various land uses and distributing these trips through the transportation network.[23] Some of the models require very large surveys of travel behaviour on specific days about once a decade. Regional transportation agencies also count vehicular traffic on key routes on an annual basis for planning purposes.

These models were initially designed by traffic engineers to forecast the need for improvements to the road and transit networks. A journey by foot or bicycle did not count as a "trip" in some of the earlier models. These planning tools are now being adapted for use with all types of transportation, after many communities have adopted policies to increase the share of walking, biking, and transit to meet economic, environmental,

Figure 9.4 Chains of Reasoning Employed in Predictive Studies

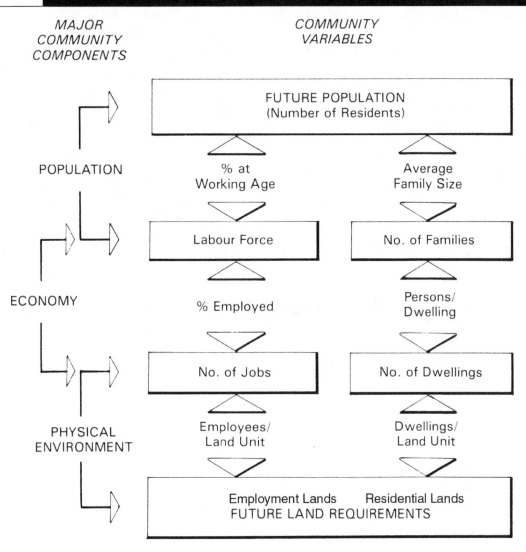

Planners use the functional relationships between people, jobs, and housing to make predictions about the future population, labour force, number of dwellings, and the land required for various community uses.

and public health objectives.[24] Transportation planning is discussed in more detail in Chapters 11 and 12.

Built Environment Analytical Dimensions

There are two basic sets of dimensions of planning diagnoses for the built environment. The first set has to do with substantive information about the community, district, or neighbourhood that is being planned. This could be called the "what" of the diagnostic study. The second has to do with the procedural perspective by which the planner is approaching the diagnosis, or what could be called the "how" of the study.

Substantive dimensions are of three main types: population, the physical environment, and the economy. All three recur throughout the various analytical phases of the planning process. In the diagnostic phase, the planner is mainly concerned with identifying who or what is involved and at what scale. The data are, thus, mostly numerical counts: the number of people, building types, dwelling units, automobiles, jobs. Alternately, the average values of such data may be sought: average income, years of schooling, age of dwelling. At this level of analysis, interrelationships between characteristics may also be helpful, such as persons per dwelling unit, automobiles per employee, persons per unit of land (density). Figure 9.5 indicates typical diagnostic information for a neighbourhood planning situation. If the planning focused on a commercial area or an industrial area, the information would reflect the characteristics of such areas.

Procedural dimensions reflect how a planner thinks about a planning problem and its analysis. Specifically, integral to the planner's view is the twofold notion of the problem and its larger context, that any specific problem area is part of the surrounding community and may be affected by it, or vice versa. Even if there is no

direct connection between the two, knowledge of comparable conditions in other parts of the community can aid in understanding the local situation. The planner also will want to know whether current conditions in a problem situation are stable or changing. For example, the housing in a neighbourhood may change little, but, as families age, the use of such facilities as schools and parks may change. Data on past conditions are often as important as those that portray the present in diagnosing whether conditions are improving or worsening.

The Policy Roles of the Community Plan

A community plan is foremost a **policy statement** about the future built and natural environments. The content and scope that we have defined provide the necessary direction for its use in planning the community. But it

| Figure 9.5 | Types of Information Used in Neighbourhood-Planning Analyses |

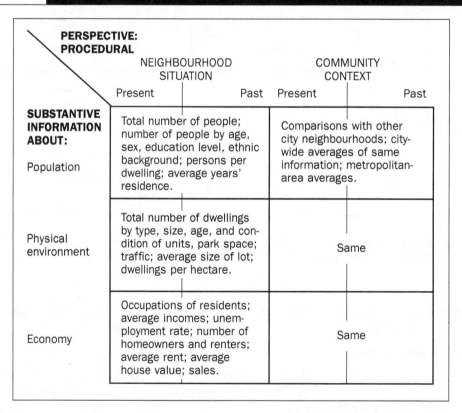

The planner seeks information about the population, the economic milieu, and the physical features of a neighbourhood. Data showing present conditions and past tendencies allow forecasts to be made. Information about other neighbourhoods is used to compare present conditions and future prospects.

is a document—an instrument—to be used in the realm of community governance. Thus, the community plan plays a number of roles, according to its uses in policy determination and implementation by the local council, planning board, and planning staff, as well as by citizens and developers. These roles call for the plan to have other more functional characteristics so that it may effectively achieve what the community wants for its future built and natural environment. The community plan must be a vehicle for both policy determination and policy implementation.

The Plan in Policy Determination

The community plan's role in policy determination is a progressive one. It begins with the preparation and initial adoption of the plan and continues through its regular review and evaluation as day-to-day physical development matters are considered. The community plan is an ultimate base of policy in its own right. It is also the basis for formulating secondary policies for, say, transportation, housing, and parks.

The efforts that go into the initial adoption of the plan are the most important, for when the plan is adopted it will represent the culmination of thorough deliberation about major alternatives by many sectors of the community, as well as by the planning board and local council. Ultimately, it is the council that adopts the plan, but the deliberations that lead up to that point are vital. Usually a draft plan is made available to community members to communicate the basic ideas and alternatives. The reactions, both positive and negative, are part of a process of educating the community and the council about the major issues in physical development. If this period of public learning and debate is effective, it will normally mean that the council is not surprised later by unresolved issues. There are three important policy characteristics of a community plan that can assist in the initial deliberations, as well as throughout the life of the plan:[25]

1. The plan should be in a form suitable for public debate.
2. The plan should be available to the community.
3. The plan should clearly communicate its proposals to the public.

The council's adoption of the plan is in effect a declaration of the policies that it intends to apply to future physical development proposals. This allows private interests (citizens as well as developers) to anticipate the probable reaction to proposals for

development. The impact of the plan as a statement of policy is as important inside the local government framework as outside of it. Coordination of the actions of public officials in various city departments as well as in semi-independent commissions and boards is facilitated. Lastly, the plan's policies are an important guide for judicial bodies in appeals against land use regulations.

While it is important that community plan policies be firm and be applicable over a long period of time, a plan should not be considered immutable. Conditions in a community do not remain static and, not infrequently, new problems arise that were not anticipated when the plan was adopted. For example, trends may change in population growth or job creation, or new information may become available that affects land use decisions, as with new knowledge about ecological systems or the aging of the population. Moreover, some policies may prove unworkable or unrealistic. The council should thus be willing and able to amend the community plan if the situation or conditions warrant it. Proposals for large new projects—a new airport, sports arena, or big-box store, for instance—may trigger the need to review the compatibility of the project with the plan. Or a new transportation study may show how the road network could be refined. It is important that the plan be able to accommodate review and renewed debate. In short, plan-makers can never know all the things that will happen during the course of the plan's life. Thus, we should add a fourth characteristic to facilitate policy roles of the plan:

4. The plan should be amendable.

Although the plan should be amendable, it should not be subject to trivial challenges that would threaten its role as a continuous statement of policy. Moreover, frequent amendment probably indicates a lack of agreement and commitment on basic policies. If not abused, amendability of the plan is important, for it means that basic development policy can be debated and refined and the extent of community agreement broadened in the process. This also means that the plan is being consulted in regard to decisions that need to be taken. For all these reasons, there is in most provincial planning acts provision for the community plan to be reviewed on a regular basis. The Planning Act of Ontario requires a maximum of five years between regular reviews of the plan by the council. Some planners try to have their planning boards review the plan annually.

There is also a host of current topics brought before council that impinge on plan policies. These cover such matters as parking regulations, use of public parks for non-recreational activities, or the use of advertising signs in public thoroughfares. Usually, specific concerns such as these are not part of the community-plan policies. However, cumulatively, as part of the day-to-day actions of a council, they may affect the community environment. The plan's effectiveness may be impaired if the decisions are not consistent with its policies and/or the plan is amended too frequently. Nonetheless, council's actions may reveal its perception of changed conditions or outlooks, and thus the need to reconsider policies set forth in the plan. It is in the best interests of plan-makers to create a community plan that becomes an explicit part of the backdrop against which the local government and its officials make their decisions—that is, a community plan that becomes a "working plan." In this way, its policies are being used and frequently tested. This day-to-day use of the plan means its policy-determination role overlaps with its policy-implementation role.

The Plan in Policy Implementation

The means for bringing a community plan into effect are increasingly specified in provincial planning acts and provincial policy statements. Local councils are thus required to take a number of formal steps that give legislative effect to the policies of the community plan. If land use is to be regulated by zoning, provincial planning acts require that the local council pass a zoning bylaw. It is now normal to require that the community have an overall plan in place before enacting zoning regulations and, moreover, that the zoning bylaw be consistent with the community plan. Provincial planning acts tend to include, in addition to zoning, such other important measures for implementing the plan as subdivision control, urban redevelopment, and site-plan control, and to specify council's role in enacting, approving, or amending proposals in these areas.

In general, there are two levels of action that councils take in regard to plan implementation. At the first level, the matters are legislative in nature; that is, the passing of local bylaws based on the principles and policies of the plan. The two most common are for the control of land use on already developed or developable land—**zoning**—and for the arrangement of new properties for development on vacant land—**subdivision control**. Some provinces provide for councils to pass **development control** bylaws that allow the community to review proposals for development on a property-by-property basis rather than on a district basis, as in zoning, and to take

aesthetic considerations into account in their decisions. And in some places, the public **program for capital improvements** in the community is required to conform to the community plan. There are, in addition, detailed plans for development that a council is occasionally called upon to approve. These may include plans for downtown revitalization, street and highway improvements, and parkland acquisition and development. (Chapters 16 and 17 elaborate on the role of these tools and others in implementing the community plan.)

At the second level, there are many routine council decisions that arise in conjunction with implementing the bylaws that council has passed. Councils are usually required to approve proposed plans of subdivision, development-control agreements, and applications for rezoning, as well as public works expenditures, under the capital improvement program. Other routine council decisions that may affect the plan's policies are requests for street closings, traffic regulation, transit routes, and the locations of fire halls, libraries, and schools.

Policy Perspective for the Community Plan

The perspective that has been described above for the use of the community plan is, essentially, hierarchical. The plan may be considered the keystone in an arch of planning activities, as in Figure 9.6. One can see the hierarchy of control measures, and the distinction

Figure 9.6	Key Role of the Community Plan in Land Use Control

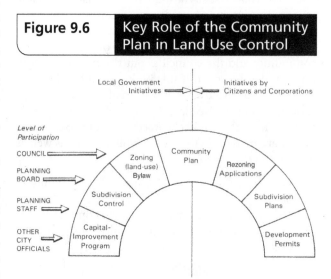

The community plan has the same position as that of a keystone in an arch. Initiatives of both the local government and the citizens and corporations depend upon its integrity.

between those that operate in the public and the private sectors, as well as the roles of various participants.

On the left side of the diagram are the initiatives that are taken by city officials and boards in support of the overall plan. These may be required under the planning act in some provinces. It can also be seen that, as one moves away from the locus of the community plan, they deal progressively with *specific* parts of the built environment. The zoning bylaw usually deals with the entire community; subdivision control is applied to specific areas within the community; and the capital-improvements program specifies individual projects. Further, as the general concerns shift toward the specific, the involvement in decision-making shifts to a wider array of participants. The planning board and staff have roles in formulating the zoning bylaws and subdivision controls, and additional members of the municipal staff become involved in formulating the program for capital improvements. Council is thus dependent upon the advice and actions of several levels of participants within local government circles in preparing the plan and in providing the supporting legislative framework. Note also that the initial stages of plan preparation—basic forecasts, background studies, identifying alternatives, initial designs—are usually allocated to an advisory committee or board and to professional staff. Although the board and staff are advisors to council, theirs is not a passive role. Indeed, they function more as joint participants and can influence council on the progress of planning more than any other participants, if they choose.

Referring again to the arch diagram, the right-hand side comprises those initiatives normally taken by individual property owners and other development interests and agencies. In other words, any person or corporation that wishes to develop or redevelop land in the community must apply to the municipality. Each application to, for example, rezone a property to allow a different use or to construct new buildings on vacant land, represents a potential step in shaping the built environment. The review and approval of such applications are important steps in carrying out the policies of the plan. In general, these applications ultimately have to be approved by the council, which can determine their consistency with the plan's policies. However, planning staff and other officials (such as building inspectors) play crucial roles in receiving the applications and judging their acceptability at the outset. The relationship between the municipal plan and development regulations and other policy instruments in Edmonton shown in Figure 9.7

demonstrates the vital role of the community plan in this set of linkages.

In summary, once a community plan is adopted, it sets in motion efforts by various participants to implement its policies and proposals. There are, basically, two policy streams. One is used by the council to secure *compliance* (through bylaws, budgets, and regulations) with the policies it has approved in adopting the plan. The other is used to *communicate* to others (officials, citizens, and developers) the aims and policies as well as the hopes and expectations of council regarding the future built and natural environment. Both streams frequently converge as, for example, when experience shows the nature of applications from the private sector differing from forecast trends, or when budget constraints affect capital spending. As a result the plan may need to be amended. An effective community plan is one that is put to use in the continuing development of the community. A plan that is used to evaluate proposals for development may need its own policies re-evaluated and, if necessary, its sights reset.

The Plan in the Context of Public Planning

Community planning, as we observed right from the opening chapters, is a widely accepted public activity in Canada. In this country, community planning is accomplished in a setting with its own statutory foundations, formal processes of plan-making, and structures for appeals. It is important to grasp this institutional setting, for Canadian community planning is characterized, as perhaps is the case in few other countries, by a highly structured legalistic/bureaucratic format that operates in conjunction with a rather open land market of multiple owners. It offers many opportunities for public initiatives to shape the outcome of community planning efforts that do not exist in the United States for example. Or, looked at from the point of view of constraints, the formal setting establishes the boundaries of planning action by both public and private actors.

Statutory Foundations

Since the 1920s, nine of the ten Canadian provinces have had substantial planning legislation in effect. (All the provinces and territories now have such statutes.) These planning acts, as we call them generically, are the foundations for land use planning and implementation

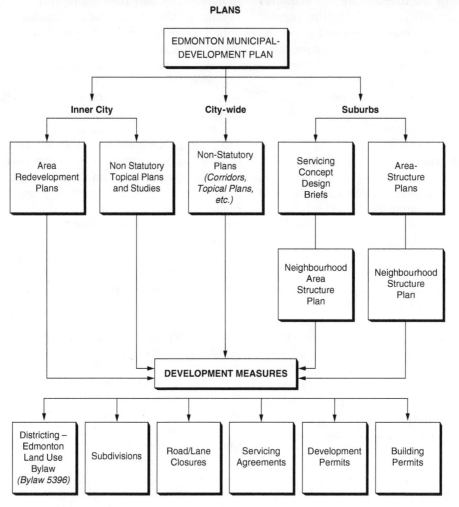

PLANS

A community plan, once adopted, articulates and coordinates a host of planning, regulatory, and development efforts by public and private participants, as we see here with Plan Edmonton, the City's Municipal Development Plan.

at the local government level. Planning acts are the type of statute often referred to as **enabling legislation** because they enable, or allow, a municipality to carry on a specified governing activity. Such legislation is necessary for local planning so that the powers over private property and land use residing with the province are available to the municipality; that is, are delegated to the municipality. Planning acts in some provinces are *permissive* in their provisions; they do not require municipalities to make plans and land use regulations.

(Some provinces are not fully permissive in their planning legislation in allowing municipalities to decide to make a plan. Alberta requires that municipalities over 3500 in population prepare a Municipal Development Plan and encourages those with fewer people to do so.[26]) In any case, when a community prepares a plan the act prescribes the planning content and the procedures to be followed. Then, any local plans and planning bylaws take on much of the force of the planning act; they too are statutes. This is the basis for describing Canadian community planning as *statutory*: it is empowered by statute, and its output (which falls within the terms of the act) has the power of a statute.

This statutory feature, which has characterized Canadian community planning for nearly a century, generates a high degree of dependence on the province by local planners. All provinces and territories strongly encourage community planning. Provincial grants are often available to assist new or small municipalities to prepare their first plans. And provincial or federal funding for infrastructure and housing programs are often conditional on the municipality having an approved and up-to-date community plan that directs the work. The province, until recently, has also been the final arbiter of community plans in all provinces and of local land use regulations in most. Provincial planning establishments oversee local planning efforts and refine the process of planning for land development by formulating guidelines for special situations and applying the planning act.

Provinces usually refresh their planning acts every 20 years or so. Starting around the mid-1970s, eight provinces undertook extensive revisions of their planning acts and there was another round of revisions in the mid-1990s. These efforts sought to refine (or "streamline") the elaborate planning legislation and its supporting bureaucratic structures. Thus, local planning in Canada operates within a provincially generated framework making it seem, not infrequently, as if the province were the ultimate client and the planning act an incontestable authority.

The planning act (or the applicable legislation in the province) specifies *who* may plan, *what* they may plan, and *how* they may plan for community planning to be statutorily correct. There are differences among provinces in the methods and the styles that are used, but the general thrust remains the same. Planning acts normally deal with the following five matters:

1. The creation of planning units;
2. The establishment of organizational machinery for planning;
3. The content, preparation, and adoption of statutory plans;
4. The format for enacting zoning, building, and housing bylaws; and
5. The system for subdividing land.

The pervasiveness of community planning in Canada has, in many respects, led to a new level of maturity among communities regarding planning. The provinces continue to revise their planning acts to devolve their responsibility for approving plans and bylaws onto regional municipalities and local governments. It is now generally assumed that municipalities and their consultants know how to prepare a proper community plan; the province will generally limit itself to a review to make sure that provincial interests are protected.[27] Not a little of the initiative for this devolution comes, of course, from budget cutting and consequent reductions in the size of provincial planning staff. Nevertheless, it points the way to a less paternalistic process.

To give a better sense of the statutory structures for planning that exist across Canada, Figure 9.8 lists the various legislative tools available in each province and territory. It will be noted that there are few instances where planning tools are not provided at all levels. The names may differ, but the pervasiveness of community planning potential is clear.

Before leaving this discussion of statutory foundations for planning, it must be noted that all provinces have other pieces of major legislation that affect the substance and organization for planning. Almost all provinces now have some form of legislation for environmental assessment and protection. Nearly as common are statutes covering the establishment of condominiums, the designation of historic buildings, the location of pits and quarries, transportation, water quality, and the use of natural resources. In British Columbia, for example, municipalities may have to deal with the provincial Agricultural Land Commission in regard to the zoning and subdivision of land. And, recently, the province passed legislation requiring that the care and quality of fish-spawning streams be taken into account in local official community plans. The administration of these statutes is most often in the hands of officials from ministries other than that containing the provincial planners. As with most provincial legislation, these statutes can provide opportunities for planning as well as constraints. Therefore, it is wise to be aware of the range of the provincial statutory foundations that could affect the outcome of a particular planning effort.

Formal Steps in Plan-Making

The last chapter discussed the process of plan-making in a normative context—that is, the refinement of community goals through a more or less rational set of steps comprising both technical studies and community participation. But how does this general planning process translate in terms of the statutory planning framework described in the preceding section?

Figure 9.8 | Comparative Provincial Planning Terminology

LEVEL OF DETAIL	BRITISH COLUMBIA	ALBERTA	SASKATCHEWAN	MANITOBA	ONTARIO
Provincial planning legislation	Local Government Act / Vancouver Charter	Municipal Government Act	Planning and Development Act,	Planning Act	Planning Act
Plan/Zoning Appeal body		Subdivision & Development Appeal Boards (local) / Municipal Government Board (provincial)	Development Appeals Board (local) & Saskatchewan Municipal Board	Manitoba Municipal Board or Council	Ontario Municipal Board
Regional plan	Regional Growth Strategy	Regional Land Use Plans / Metropolitan Plans (Calgary, Edmonton) / Inter-municipal Development Plan	District Official Community Plan	Regional Strategy / Special Planning Area	Growth plan (GGH & North) / Upper Tier Plan / Joint Planning Areas
Municipal land use plan	Official Community Plan	Municipal Development Plan	Official Community Plan	Development Plan	Official Plan
District plan	Area Development Plan; Comprehensive Development District (Vancouver)	Area Structure Plan/Area Redevelopment Plan	Local Area Plan/ Concept Plan/Sector Plan	Secondary Plan / Redevelopment Plan	Secondary Plan
Street & block layout	Neighbourhood Plan	Neighbourhood & Industrial Structure Plans/Conceptual Scheme/Outline Plan	Plans of Survey (Descriptive Plan Type I & II)	Secondary Plan	Tertiary Plan
Land subdivision	Preliminary Proposal/ Plan of Subdivision	Proposed Plan/Plan of Subdivision	Proposed Plan/Plan of Proposed Subdivision/ Plans of Survey	Proposed/ Registered Plan of Subdivision	Draft/ Registered Plan of Subdivision
Zoning	Zoning bylaw	Land Use Bylaw/Zoning Bylaw	Zoning bylaw	Zoning by-law	Zoning by-law
Site plan review	Development Permit	Development Permit/ Architectural Controls	Development Standards/ Architectural Controls/ Contract Zoning/ Development Permit	Development Permit	Site Plan Control / Development Permit

Source: Based on research by Tasha Elliot, Greg Newman, and David Gordon.

QUÉBEC	NEW BRUNSWICK	PRINCE EDWARD ISLAND	NOVA SCOTIA	NEWFOUNDLAND & LABRADOR	YUKON	NORTHWEST TERRITORIES	NUNAVUT
An Act Respecting Land Use Planning & Development, (Loi sur l'aménagement et l'urbanisme)	Community Planning Act	Planning Act	Municipal Government Act	Urban and Rural Planning Act	Municipal Act, Area Development Act, Subdivision Act	Planning Act; Cities, Towns and Villages Act	Planning Act; Nunavut Land Use Plan (draft)
Commission municipale du Québec	Assessment and Planning Appeal Board	Regulatory and Appeals Commission	Nova Scotia Utility and Review Board	Four regional appeal boards	Yukon Municipal Board	Development Appeal Boards (local)	Development Appeal Boards (local)
Land Use Planning and Development Plan (Schéma d'aménagement et de développement)	Regional Plan	Regional Plan	Intermunicipal Planning Strategy	Regional Plan/Joint Municipal Plan	Regional Structures or Joint Development Plan	Land Use Plan	
Planning Programme (Plan d'urbanisme)	Municipal Development Plan	Official Plan	Municipal Planning Strategy	Municipal Plan	Official Community Plan/Local Area Plan/Planning Study	General Plan	Community Plan/General Plan
Special Planning Programme (Programme particulier d'urbanisme)	Development Scheme s. 32 of the Act		Secondary Planning Strategy	Development Scheme/Comprehensive Development Area Plan	Area Development Scheme/Planning Study	Development Scheme	Development Scheme
Special Planning Programme (Programme particulier d'urbanisme)	Tentative Plan/Subdivision Plan	Proposed Subdivision	Subdivision Regulations		Proposed Subdivision/Concept Plan	Plan of Subdivision	Plan of Subdivision
Subdivision By-Law (Règlement de lotissement)	Tentative/Subdivision Plan	Preliminary/Final Subdivision Plan	Tentative/Final Subdivision Plan	Subdivision Regulations	Preliminary Plan/Proposed Subdivision	Plan of Subdivision/Plan of Survey	Plan of Subdivision; Plan of Survey
Zoning by-law (Règlement de zonage)	Zoning by-law	Municipal Planning Bylaws	Land Use/Zoning by-law	Land Use Zoning Regulations	Zoning Bylaw/Area Development Regulations	Zoning bylaw	Zoning bylaw
Site Planning and Architectural Integration Programme (Plan d implantation et d'intégration archtecturale)	Building Permit Final Subdivision Plan	Approved Subdivision Development Permit	Site Plan Approval/Development Permit	Development Permit	Development Permit/Development Review Committee	Development Permit	Development Permit

Planning acts, as noted, not only specify *who* may plan but also prescribe *how* they may plan. A minimum series of steps that must satisfy the statutory requirements of the act is set forth. These formal steps parallel many of the steps in the normative process. The differences lie in various technical and participatory steps undertaken in the real community setting to accommodate the social, economic, environmental, and physical conditions unique to that community. Thus, when a Canadian community plans, its normative process is articulated by the requirements of the provincial act that permits planning; in short, the community's planning actions are punctuated by several required steps. Figure 6.1, page 145 shows the general steps required to bring a community plan into effect. These steps are much the same as those required for making amendments to a plan and for enacting and amending a zoning bylaw. But, as we noted above, some provinces are eliminating the final step, that of provincial approval, thereby shortening the process and leaving responsibility with the community.

One feature of the normal process of plan-making is that planning decisions are the product of several bodies, not just the local council and its advisory committees. In some provinces, such as Saskatchewan, the outcome of a community plan or zoning bylaw or subdivision plan may be the result of modifications made at three levels: the community, the ministry, and the appeal board. Within the first two levels, a large number of other, non-planning agencies may also be involved in the outcome. Within the municipality, provision is usually made to have planning proposals reviewed by all technical departments and public utility companies. At the provincial level, there is also widespread distribution of municipal planning proposals to various ministries and Crown corporations. Somewhat in contrast is the rather limited role for citizens—the general public—in the formal process. It seems, therefore, that in light of the efforts taken to preserve the statutory basis of the plan, and of the inherent paternalism of the provinces, one would be justified in speculating on *whose plan* is represented in the final output. Among the provinces, Alberta, Ontario, British Columbia and Newfoundland have evolved the formal plan-making system that most respects the integrity of locally made planning decisions.

Structures for Appeals

The statutory nature of Canadian community planning imparts a legalistic bias to many of its activities, but especially to the structures for appeals of planning decisions. Most provinces have established some form of quasi-judicial body to hear appeals from people or agencies that object to an official plan, zoning bylaw, or subdivision plan. The Ontario Municipal Board (OMB) has been the model for some planning-appeal bodies.[28] Its proceedings are conducted much like those of a courtroom (through the adversarial process), and its decisions have the force of law. Objectors (including citizens and citizen groups) and proponents are expected to be represented by legal counsel, although other representations will usually be heard.

In order for an appeal to proceed, a number of specific steps must be taken. First, no appeal can be made until the bylaw approving the plan, zoning change, and so on, has been passed by the local government body. Second, there is only a limited period of time after approval of the bylaw—30 days is common—in which an appeal can be lodged. Third, the appeal body or the minister in question, depending upon the province, will decide whether the objection is trivial, in which case a hearing would prove dilatory to the planning process and the appeal is not heard.

In many respects, hearings of provincial appeal boards tend to become hearings *de novo* (as lawyers call them), or brand-new considerations, of the planning pros and cons. This not only is time-consuming and costly to all participants, but also may bring in planning evidence and arguments not heretofore considered by the community and its council and planning bodies. In recent years, limitations have been placed on some aspects of appeal-body powers. Still, in the provinces where they are used, provincial appeal boards create a significant and additional avenue through which planning decisions may be made, one that is likely to be developed with its own rationale and criteria for its decisions. This means it has the potential of becoming planning *for* a community rather than planning *by* a community. This is one of the major dilemmas of the legalistic style of planning, for it must honour judicial concepts, including the right to appeal to a third party. Legislation was introduced in Ontario in 2005 to deal with such issues by confirming the ultimate role of a local council to determine land use matters and to restrict the admission of new information into OMB appeals.

Not all provinces use a provincial appeal body with broad-based powers of intervention. Saskatchewan, for example, has two levels of appeal on planning matters. Each municipality with a zoning bylaw is required to appoint its own Development Appeal Board to deal with appeals on plan amendments, rezoning applications, minor variances, development permits, and subdivision plans (where the local council has approval authority). Appeals of the decisions of the local appeal board may be made in many instances to the Planning Appeals Committee of the Saskatchewan Municipal Board. This committee must hold a public hearing on appeals made to it. Similar arrangements also exist for subdivision and development permit appeals in Alberta municipalities. The exception to local appeals in Alberta is when it is determined that the application has a provincial interest (e.g., within specified distances to provincial highways and water bodies). In this instance, the appeal goes to the Municipal Government Board.[29] Ontario introduced mediation in some cases to reduce appeals to the Ontario Municipal Board. The right of appeal to the courts on any planning matter also exists, as is the route in British Columbia but usually only if there have been procedural irregularities or disputes on points of law in previous hearings.

The Community Plan as a Legal Document

Plans for Canadian communities prepared under provincial legislation are legal documents. They require formal council endorsement and usually approval by the province. (Contrast this to the system in the United States, where community plans were until recently considered local policy initiatives and their existence a matter of local prerogative.) However, the strength of the plan as a basis for public decisions, especially for regulating private land development, was not much tested until four or five decades ago. Provincial planning legislation has tended to be permissive, e.g., "A municipality *may* prepare a plan for…." But as land use controls became more prevalent, the courts have been resorted to in order to challenge the community's right to place constraints on the development of private land. Since land use controls are almost inevitably enacted to achieve some intended form for the built environment, it has become necessary to provide the courts and others with the policy rationale—the plan—on which these are based. The plan performs a function similar to that of a national constitution; indeed, some observers have referred to the community plan as having a "constitutive" function.[30]

Another important aspect of this shift in approach is the introduction of flexible land use control practices and instruments to implement an urban community plan. These techniques are discussed in detail in Chapters 16 and 17.

Plans as Community Images

Lastly, plans are more than words. Plans have the ability to convey images in graphic terms of visions of a community's future that other instruments of public policy lack.[31] Plans help connect people to places, and

when a plan's concepts can be conveyed in graphic terms, it can enhance the plan's capacity to promote consensus. The influential European planner Andreas Faludi argues strongly for a plan to have a "spatial organization principle," a graphic image that will "stick" in people's minds if it is to be a politically viable and physically attainable plan.[32] A striking Canadian example of such a spatial principle is the "greenbelt" contained in Jacques Gréber's 1950 plan for the Ottawa region (Figure 6.5, page 156). That concept has become a firmly entrenched reality 50 years later.[33] The designation of a greenbelt around Toronto and Greater Vancouver's Green Zones could play a similar role, as could urban growth boundaries.

This graphic aspect of a community plan, though somewhat sidetracked in the planning literature during the 1990s, has venerable roots. The two-dimensional diagrams and three-dimensional models made by those such as Ebenezer Howard and Le Corbusier, which were examined in earlier chapters, are its forebears. More recently, the Copenhagen "finger plan" (Figure 6.7, page 157) or Washington's 1961 corridor plan (Figure 9.9) have provided strong graphic images that can communicate the spatial essence of a large-scale plan.

Figure 9.9	Graphic Representation of 1961 Corridor Plan for the Washington, D.C., Region

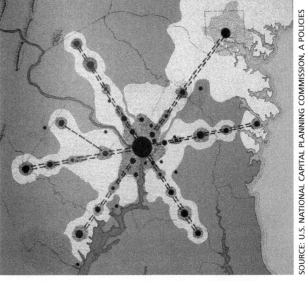

SOURCE: U.S. NATIONAL CAPITAL PLANNING COMMISSION, A POLICIES PLAN FOR THE YEAR 2000 (WASHINGTON, D.C.: NCPC, 1961).

The rail corridors never extended as far into the country as planned, but this plan did accommodate the new towns of Reston, Virginia, and Columbia, Maryland—a new international airport to the south and a stronger connection to Baltimore in the northeast.

The negative urban image of "mindless sprawl" that spurs many of the New Urbanism and Smart Growth efforts shows how evocative a planning image can be, but the photographs of good planning precedents found in many community plans can be even more powerful. We have come to expect in the process of plan-making to find out the "what," "when," and "how" of a community's future; the plan should also tell us "where." Community plans, after all, deal with real geographical spaces and humanly defined places (see also Chapter 13).

Reflections

Recent practices in plan-making encourage diversity and innovation in development from New Urbanism to Smart Growth, mixed land use, brownfield development, and environmental restoration. While there is much to commend in each of these initiatives and in others, it is important to recognize that the more diverse our approaches, the more the need that we proceed with them in an integral way. Without a common plan-making perspective, there are bound to be problems associated with coordinating decisions, not to mention the risk of arbitrariness in such decisions. This perspective is provided by the community plan, and it comes to assume a more vital role as a backdrop against which diverse development concepts and decisions can be assessed. The question raised in one of the references in this chapter, "Does planning need the plan?" deserves a resounding "yes."[34]

How community plans are initiated is yet another question to be debated. The issue is whether a plan imposed by a higher level of government can be as meaningful as one generated by local needs and experience. Certainly, community plans produced to comply with provincial legislation are often complex and ponderous in language in an attempt to forestall legal challenges. There are, however, examples of plans for communities large and small that fulfill the legal requirements yet offer a vigorous rendering of community aspirations. The crafting of a community plan demands skill and sensitivity on the part of plan-makers.

Up to this point, the primacy of the community plan in the planning activity of an urban community has been emphasized. Now, it is necessary to put the community plan into a larger perspective that is both deeper and broader. On the one hand, a plan exists to be implemented and, thus, requires an array of regulatory tool and policy instruments to realize its goals and objectives. The plan's perspective deepens when it is seen as encompassing these means for plan effectuation (discussed in Chapters 13 and 14). On the other hand, a plan's perspective must also be broadened to encompass the region within which it exists. For each community fits within its region and is subject to the growth dynamics of that region, as well as to the plans made for that region. In the next chapter, as the regional planning perspective is discussed, it will be helpful to consider these questions:

- *Which features in a community's land use may have implications for the larger region?*
- *How can community plans and regional plans be mutually supportive?*

Reference Notes

1. For more on the debate on the components that make a "good plan" see Philip Berke and David Godshalk, "Searching for the Good Plan: A Meta-analysis of Plan Quality Studies," *Journal of Planning Literature* 23:3 (2009), 227–240; William Baer, "General Plan Evaluation Criteria: An Approach to Making Better Plans," *Journal of the American Planning Association* 63:3,(1997), 329–344; and Gene Bunnell and Edward Jepson Jr., "The Effect of Mandated Planning on Plan Quality," *Journal of the American Planning Association* 77:4 (2011), 338–353.

2. Cf. Andres Duany and Elizabeth Plater-Zyberk, "Neighbourhoods and Suburbs," *Design Quarterly* 164 (Spring 1995),10–23.

3. T.J. Kent Jr., *The Urban General Plan* (San Francisco: Chandler, 1964), 99. Much of the discussion in this section is based on the concept of a community plan posited by Kent. This influential text was reprinted in 1991 (Chicago: Planners Press, American Planning Association).

4. Provincial planning legislation in British Columbia requires Official Community Plans to include a statement of housing policy, especially regarding affordable housing (BC Municipal Act, Sec. 945, 2.1).

5. Canada West Foundation, "Lines in the Sand: Are Urban Growth Boundaries Effective?" *Western Cities Project Update, June 2004*; see also Smart Growth BC at www.smartgrowth.bc.ca

6. Jeremy Black, *Maps and History: Constructing Images of the Past* (New Haven: Yale University Press, 1997).

7. Michael Neuman, "Does Planning Need the Plan?" *Journal of the American Planning Association* 64:2 (Spring 1998), 208–220.

8. For example, see Vanmap, available online at www.city.vancouver.bc.ca/vanmap/setup/index.htm

9. Nancy Nishikawa, "Survey Methods for Planners," in Hemalata Dandekar, ed., *The Planner's Use of Information* (Chicago: APA Planners Press, 2003), 49–78.

10. Britton Harris and Michael Batty, "Locational Models, Geographic Information and Planning Support Systems," *Journal of Planning Education and Research* 12:3 (1993), 184–198.

11. Robert E. Kent and Richard. E. Klosterman, "GIS and Mapping: Pitfalls for Planning," *Journal of the American Planning Association* 66:2 (Spring 2000), 189–198.

12. Richard Forman, *Land Mosaics: The Ecology of Landscapes and Regions* (New York: Cambridge University Press,1995); and *Urban Regions: Ecology and Planning Beyond the City* (New York: Cambridge University Press, 2008).

13. Ken Tamminga, "Restoring Biodiversity in the Urbanizing Region: Towards Pre-emptive Ecosystems Planning," *Plan Canada* 36:4 (July 1996), 10–15; and Charles

Hostovsky, David Miller, and Cathy Keddy, "The Natural Environment Systems Strategy: Protecting Ottawa-Carleton's Ecological Areas," *Plan Canada* 35:6 (1995).

14. Gerald Hodge, *The Geography of Aging: Preparing Communities for the Surge in Seniors* (Montréal: McGill–Queens University Press, 2008), 169–188.

15. H. Craig Davis, *Demographic Projection Techniques for Regions and Smaller Areas* (Vancouver: UBC Press, 1995).

16. A. Skaburskis and M. Moos, "The Economics of Urban Land," in Filion, Bunting, and Walker, eds. *Canadian Cities in Transition*, 4th ed. (Toronto: Oxford University Press, 2010), 225–247.

17. The foundation for this approach is found in Charles Tiebout, *The Community Economic Base (New York: Committee for Economic Development*, 1962); for a Canadian example, see Craig Davis, "Assessing the Impact of a Firm on a Small-Scale Regional Economy," *Plan Canada* 16 (1976), 171–176.

18. Michael Porter, "The Competitive Advantage of the Inner City," *Harvard Business Review* (May–June 1995), 55–71; Location, Competition and Economic Development: Local Clusters in a Global Economy," *Economic Development Quarterly* 14:1 (2000),15–34; Betsy Donald, "Economic Competitiveness and Quality of Life in City Regions: Compatible Concepts?" *Canadian Journal of Urban Research* 10:2 (2001), 259–274; City of Ottawa, *Ottawa 20/20 Economic Strategy* (April 2003); Nick Novakowski and Remy Tremblay, eds., *Perspectives on Ottawa's High-Tech Sector* (Brussels: Peter Lang, 2007); and Thomas Hutton, *The New Economy of the Inner City: Restructuring, Regeneration, and Dislocation in the Twenty-First-Century Metropolis* (New York: Routledge, 2008).

19. Jane Jacobs, *The Economy of Cities* (New York: Random House, 1969); and her *Cities and the Wealth of Nations* (Toronto: Random House, 1984); Richard Florida,*The Rise of the Creative Class Revisited* (Toronto: Basic Books, 2012); Mario Polèse, "The Arts and Local Economic Development: Can a Strong Arts Presence Uplift Local Economies? A Study of 135 Canadian Cities," *Urban Studies* 49:8 (June 2012), 1811–1835; Timothy Edensor, Deborah Leslie, Steve Millington, and Norma Rantisi, eds., *Spaces of Vernacular Creativity: Rethinking the Cultural Economy* (London: Routledge Press, 2009); Jill Grant, J. Haggett, and J. Morton, "Planning for the Creative Economy: The live Music Scene in Halifax," *Plan Canada* (Summer 2010), 34–37; Alexandra McDonough and Gerda Wekerle, "Integrating Cultural Planning and Urban Planning: The Challenges of Implementation," *Canadian Journal of Urban Research* 20:1 (2011), 27–51; and Nathaniel Lewis and Betsy Donald, "A New Rubric for 'Creative City' Potential in Canada's Smaller Cities," *Urban Studies* 47:1 (2010), 29–54.

20. Deborah Leslie and Norma Rantisi, "Creativity and Place in the Evolution of a Cultural Industry: The Case of Cirque du Soleil," *Urban Studies* 48:9 (2011), 1771–1787; and Carine Discazeaux and Mario Polèse, "Comment Expliquer le Déclin de Montréal comme Centre de Transports Aériens: Une Question de Géographie Economique?" *The Canadian Geographer* 51:1 (2007), 22–42.

21. Philip Berke, D. Godschalk, and E. Kaiser, *Urban Land Use Planning*, 5th ed. (Chicago: University of Illinois Press, 2006).

22. Robert W. McCabe, *Planning Applications of Retail Models* (Toronto: Ontario Ministry of Treasury, Economics and Intergovernmental Affairs, 1974); and François Des Rosiers, Marius Thériault, and Catherine Lavoie, "Retail Concentration and Shopping Center Rents: A Comparison of Two Cities," *Journal of Real Estate Research* 31:2 (2008),165–207.

23. Michael Iacono, David Levinson, and Admed El-Geneidy, "Models of Transportation and Land Use Change: A Guide to the Territory," *Journal of Planning Literature* 22:4 (2008), 323–340; Ahmed El-Geneidy, Assumpta Cerdá, Raphaël Fischler, and Nik Luka, "Evaluating the Impacts of Transportation Plans Using Accessibility Measures: A Test Case in Montréal," *Canadian Journal of Urban Research: Canadian Planning and Policy* 20:1 (Supplement 2011), 81–104; and Patrick Condon and Kari Dow, "A Cost Comparison of Transportation Modes," *Transportation* 7:7 (2008).

24. Madhav Badami, "Urban Transport Policy as if People and the Environment Mattered: Pedestrian Accessibility the First Step," *Economic and Political Weekly* XLIV:33 (2009), 43–51; Ugo Lachapelle and Lawrence Frank, "Transit and Health: Mode of Transport, Employer-Sponsored Public Transit Pass Programs, and Physical Activity," *Journal of Public Health Policy* 30 (January 2009), S73–S94; and Preston Schiller, Eric Bruun, and Jeffrey R. Kenworthy, *An Introduction to Sustainable Transportation: Policy, Planning and Implementation* (London: Earthscan, 2010).

25. Kent, *Urban General Plan,* especially 119–123.

26. Alberta Municipal Affairs, *The Legislative Framework for Municipal Planning, Subdivision and Development Control* (March 2002), 2.

27. Ontario, Commission on Development Reform and Planning in Ontario, *New Planning in Ontario, Final Report* (Toronto, 1993); and Stan Clinton, "Changing Times: Newfoundland's Municipal Planning and Implementation Systems," *Plan Canada* 37:2 (March 1997), 18–20.

28. Cf. Bruce Krushelnicki, *A Practical Guide to the Ontario Municipal Board* (Toronto: LexisNexis Butterworths, 2003).

29. Cf. Frederick A. Laux, *Planning Law and Practice in Alberta,* 3rd ed. (Edmonton: Juriliber, 2002).

30. Stephen Griffin, "Constitutionalism in the United States: From Theory to Politics," in Sanford Levinson, ed., *Responding to Imperfection* (Princeton, NJ: Princeton University Press, 1995).

31. Neuman, "Does Planning Need the Plan?"

32. Andreas Faludi, "European Planning Doctrine: A Bridge Too Far?" *Journal of Planning Education and Research* 16:1 (Spring 1996), 41–50.

33. Richard Scott, "Canada's Capital Greenbelt: Reinventing a 1950s Plan," *Plan Canada,* 36:5 (November 1996), 19–21; and David Gordon, "Weaving a Modern Plan for Canada's Capital: Jacques Gréber and the 1950 Plan for the National Capital Region," *Urban History Review* 29:2 (March 2001), 43–61.

34. Neuman, "Does Planning Need the Plan?"

Internet Resources

Chapter-Relevant Sites

Planning Canadian Communities
www.planningcanadiancommunities.ca

Vancouver neighbourhood plans
www.vancouver.ca/home-property-development/neighbourhood-planning-projects.asp

Coquitlam, B.C., Corporate Strategic Plan
www.coquitlam.ca/city-hall/plans/strategic-plan.aspx

Winnipeg plan
www.speakupwinnipeg.com/ourwinnipeg/

York Region Official Plan
www.york.ca/Departments/Planning+and+Development/Long+Range+Planning/ROP.htm

Greater Sudbury Planning Services
www.planningsudbury.com

Ottawa Official Plan
www.ottawa.ca/en/official-plan-0

Ville de Montréal Master Plan
www.ville.montreal.qc.ca/plan-urbanisme

City of Fredericton Municipal Plan
www.fredericton.ca/en/citygovernment/MunicipalPlan.asp

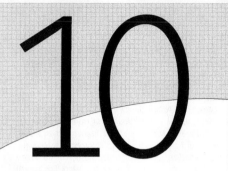

10

Chapter Ten

Planning Small Towns in Rural and Northern Regions

Planning becomes (n)either easier (n)or more difficult in the small community.... Conditions are simply different and demand different approaches, not big-city hand-me-downs.

James Wilson, 1961

Planning practice in Canada and elsewhere has grown mainly out of concerns over the problems that *cities* experience. But there is another type of Canadian community, actually the oldest and most prevalent type, that has its own special planning considerations. These are the small towns and other communities in rural regions and the North; there are over 9000 such places in Canada. They range from good-sized towns of up to 10 000 population (such as Smith's Falls, Ontario, and Estevan, Saskatchewan) down through small towns (such as Clark's Harbour, Nova Scotia, and Luceville, Québec), small villages and hamlets, outports, crossroads clusters, and nearly 3000 First Nations' Reserves and their communities. By contrast, there are only 33 metropolitan areas and 150 small and medium-size cities, all of which began as small towns. Close to seven million people resided in these rural communities in 2011, or about one-fifth of Canada's population.

Smaller communities, too, have problems of land use, housing, transportation, public facilities, and population growth (or lack thereof). But because of their small size, the planning problems of towns and villages manifest themselves in ways different from those of cities. Further, the land use dynamics and development tendencies that are assumed by the land use regulations found in most provincial planning acts seldom fit the mould of most small towns upon which they are imposed. The planning problems of small towns differ in scale, intensity, and pace of change from those of larger centres. In addition, they frequently experience planning problems that do not usually occur in cities. Besides the rural–urban planning differences, there is great diversity among and within the rural regions of the country, which must be taken into account in planning their communities (see also Chapter 8). Recognizing the differences in the planning of small towns is the concern of this chapter and obliges consideration of the following questions:

- *What distinguishes the planning needs of small communities from those of cities?*
- *In which ways does the regional setting affect the planning of its small towns?*

The Regional Context for Planning Small Towns

Non-urban, or rural, Canada is comprised of a large number of regions, some quite vast and each distinctive in the setting of its small towns and for their planning. These different rural situations present planners with a variety of planning needs, circumstances, and problems. An early observer posited the notion of "a continuum" of rural situations from the "completely rural" to the "nearly urban."[1] This approach helps keep us from considering all non-urban areas as being simply *rural*, but needs to go further and point up the diversity of "completely rural" areas. In Canada, they range over the grain-growing Prairies, the apple-growing Annapolis Valley in Nova Scotia, the forestry regions of British Columbia and northwestern Ontario, ore-rich northern Québec, and the Inuit Métis tundra landscapes of Nunavut and Northwest Territories, right down to the farmlands adjacent to our biggest cities. Indeed, what emerges are several rural Canadas.[2]

Types of Rural Regions and Their Communities

Planning in rural regions is linked closely linked with the type and viability of the economic activities practised in the countryside. Whether it be logging, mining, farming, fishing, or trapping, these activities affect the kind, stability, and survival of the communities that comprise them, not least their planning needs and problems. Looking broadly at rural Canada, five types of rural regions can be identified. Each is discussed below with its distinctive planning issues for its small towns and other living areas:

- Rural resource regions
- The city's countryside
- Rural recreation regions
- Northern peripheral resource regions
- Aboriginal peoples rural regions

Before proceeding, it is important to note that these rural regions are seldom spatially separate entities. There is often overlap among them or a combination of the activities that characterize them.

Rural resource regions in Canada are largely devoted to natural resources development and/or harvesting. They have been long-settled and are characteristically served by a broad settlement pattern of small towns and villages and, occasionally, a small city. Probably the easiest to recall are towns situated in agricultural regions (like Cabri, Saskatchewan, St. Mary's, Ontario, or Wolfeville, Nova Scotia). Other rural resource regions, such as those settled for fishing and forestry, also have numerous small communities (like Fogo Island, Newfoundland, and Port Hardy, British Columbia). The primary economic function of small communities in such regions is to provide services to those involved in the prevailing resource development. The universal planning problem for this type of town is the provision of health, transportation, and recreation services for their own population and for those living in the surrounding countryside. In forestry, fishing, and farming regions, many communities tend to have few alternative housing choices, limited job opportunities, and aging populations as young people leave. Those developed over a long time often face chronic unemployment and degraded natural environments.

The city's countryside encompasses those areas and communities within commuting range upwards of 45–50 minutes) of a city. Its small communities tend to be caught up in urban expansion the closer they are to the city. They are frequently transformed from their original rural function as service centres into "dormitory" towns.[3] Among them are municipally incorporated places such as Manotick, Ontario, and Cochrane, Alberta, which find themselves confronting pollution, conflicting land uses, displacement of population, and spiraling land costs. Equally impacted, and usually much less equipped to tackle such problems, are the urban fringe areas that are not incorporated. The latter rural–urban fringe areas fall outside recognized municipal jurisdictions and may lack any land use planning capacity.[4]

Rural recreational regions are also resource-dependent, but in this case it is the land and/or water resource(s) that are considered desirable for recreation and tourism, such as the Laurentides in Québec, the Bay of Fundy in New Brunswick, and the Whistler area in British Columbia. Communities in these regions, many often long-lived and founded to exploit other resources, find themselves coping with vast changes that enlarge their populations, escalate housing prices, transform employment structures, and create social cleavages.

Northern peripheral resource regions lie north of the rural regions identified above and they are often called simply "The North." They are the northern parts of all provinces (except the Maritimes) as well as the northern territories and Nunavut. Resource development dominates the economy (most recently, diamonds and nickel), but their settlements, as well as being small, are very widely dispersed and often not interconnected, with resulting problems for communications, difficulties in supplying public services, and boom-and-bust economies. Noteworthy about these towns is that many were built as "new towns" to facilitate resource exploitation—for example, Schefferville in Québec, Leaf Rapids in Manitoba, and Kitimat in British Columbia. There are only a few sizable centres, such as Yellowknife, Whitehorse, and Iqaluit, but by far the majority of the communities in these regions are small and their populations mostly, if not entirely, composed of Aboriginal peoples.

Aboriginal people's rural regions are located within the northern milieu just described, but also in southern rural resource regions such as northern Ontario and coastal British Columbia and Labrador. Again, the communities are small, with few reaching 1000 in population, and usually widely separated, with community members employed either in traditional activities and/or local commercial and resource development. There is, notably, in these communities a special relationship between the Aboriginal residents and the land, water, air, and animal and fish life.[5] Community conditions often feature extreme poverty, isolation, poor housing, and lack of services, which, given their inhabitants' generally holistic concept of "natural resources," means that special planning approaches are called for with these communities, several of which are described in a later section.

Development Characteristics of Small Communities

Although there is great diversity and individuality among small communities given their regional milieux, there are commonalities that are important for planners to grasp. The discussion below focuses on those places with populations of 300–400, of which there are several thousand in Canada. At this level, it is appropriate to call them "towns" because they begin to develop a distinctive street pattern and distribution of land uses,

and selected planning processes and tools become pertinent to employ.

Land Use Patterns

Small towns differ from one another, as any resident or observer can tell you, but in their physical development there are a number of common characteristics that distinguish them from large communities and affect their planning. These relate to their size or area, density, and land use patterns.

Size It may seem self-evident to say that small towns occupy very little land area. It is worth noting, however, because this dimension is related to such issues as the provision of streets and public utilities, as well as to the accessibility of different land uses to their users. Even the largest small towns, those having 10 000 or so in population, occupy less than five square kilometres of land. All the land uses would be within 1300 metres of the centre of such a community. The typical small town of 500–1000 population occupies less than 1.5 square kilometres and has only 150–300 houses.

Density Despite their small size, small towns are usually not very compact. Development is often spread out at gross densities of two to five dwellings per hectare. Only when the population of a small town approaches 5000 is it likely to have a density near that found in city suburbs of 10–15 dwellings per hectare. Up to that size population, individual residences typically are responsible for their own water supply and sewerage.

Vacant Land A factor that contributes noticeably to the low density is the large amount of vacant, undeveloped land found in most small towns. It is not uncommon to find as much as one-third of the land to be vacant, and not just on the fringes of the town. This is a reflection of the generally non-competitive land market. There is, indeed, plenty of land for all potential uses.

Commercial Development The land use pattern characteristic of most (non-Aboriginal) small towns is one of residential areas concentrically arranged around a single commercial area. "Main Street" is both a retail and social focus for the town. The number of establishments is relatively small and, not infrequently, there are vacant buildings that attest to a slow-growing local market, a declining population, and/or the competition of urban shopping centres within reasonable driving distance. There is, however, evidence of stabilization, and even some growth, in the commercial base of remote towns and villages. And, of course, those within the orbit of a metropolis tend to show major expansion of shopping facilities.

Land Use Diversity A mixture of diverse land uses characterizes all but the largest small towns. It is not uncommon to find juxtaposed on the principal commercial street stores, houses, service stations, churches, and other uses. Even in residential areas, there is a diversity of uses. Yet these land use patterns seem to function satisfactorily, suggesting that a high degree of tolerance or accommodation is possible among land uses when the intensity of development is relatively low and residents are familiar with one another.

Built Environment Issues

To plan effectively for small towns one must recognize the issues that arise from their characteristics of small-scale, small-growth, and diverse land use situations. In cities, planners are mostly concerned with broad problem areas—such matters as traffic congestion, rezoning for high-rise development, and the stability of residential areas. People in towns and villages tend to see their development issues in terms of a number of *specific problems*.

The following list, compiled from various small town planning studies, illustrates the types of problems with which their planners are often confronted:

- There is not an adequate water supply.
- There is no sanitary sewer system.
- Much of the land in the community is not suitable to build upon.
- Existing development is very scattered.
- The railway crossing is dangerous.
- There are many vacant buildings in the town centre.
- The sidewalks need repair.
- No suitable means of garbage disposal exists.
- The cemetery has become overgrown.

City-oriented planners might tend to dismiss these issues as being trivial, and, certainly, there is little place for them in conventional municipal plans. However, they are significant for small communities, especially in rural regions remote from the city. As a Newfoundland report on the topic several decades ago noted, "If the day-to-day problems can be solved with the aid of a plan then ... the value of planning is established."[6]

Water Supply One often finds, for example, that communities with 500 or fewer residents have no community-wide water-supply system or sewage system. These services are usually provided by individual households and firms through individual wells and septic fields. In very small communities outdoor toilets may still be used. Even though most such places have low-density development, pollution problems may arise; thus, the common planning approach of increasing the density by in-filling on vacant lots either exacerbates these problems or necessitates costly utility systems. A related problem in providing basic water and sewer service is that dwellings are, very often, situated in areas of unsuitable building land (steep slopes, rocky, or swampy). Even larger towns with their own waterworks may be at risk of pollution of their water aquifers from surrounding agricultural or industrial uses, as was seen with the E. coli tragedy at Walkerton, Ontario, in 2000.[7] The numerous media stories since then remind us of the vulnerability of the water supplies in smaller communities. Even those communities close to cities such as Central Saanich on Victoria's outskirts may experience such difficulties.[8] The forced evacuation of the Aboriginal communities on James Bay—Kasechewan in 2005 and Attawapiskat in 2011— are the most recent reminders of this critical factor in rural community life.[9]

Traffic and Roads Small towns have their own forms of traffic and road problems. Within the community, both the unsuitable land and scattered residential development may lead to excessive and costly road building and maintenance. Traffic congestion may also occur in the business district because of the lack of adequate parking space. Inconvenient access for the community to a major highway nearby or the hazards of the highway running right through the community are two other burdens many small towns face. Other small communities sometimes find themselves becoming recreational destinations in addition to their traditional natural resource roles, and this often results in seasonal traffic congestion and parking dilemmas.[10]

Care of the Environment There are frequent complaints about the lack of care regarding the physical environment of a small town. The disposal of waste materials— household garbage, worn-out vehicles, etc.—can pose problems for both the maintenance and the location of dumps. Unkempt cemeteries and playgrounds and derelict buildings are other common problems affecting the environment in a small community. That they often defy solution is due as much as anything to the community's meagre resources. However, not uncommon are community-based initiatives for environmental protection as, for example, the award-winning Recycling Depot

| Figure 10.1 | Rural Community Recycling Initiative, Hornby Island B.C., 2006 |

SOURCE: GERALD HODGE

Opened in 1978, the Hornby Island Recycling Depot has been in operation for more than 30 years recycling and reusing more than 70 percent of this 1000-population community's waste stream.

on Hornby Island, British Columbia (2011 population 958) see Figure 10.1.[11]

Social Development Issues

There are several demographic aspects of small towns that have implications for planning their physical development. The first—the aging population—is more general and affects almost all small towns. The second concerns population cleavages in towns, particularly in the rural–urban fringe. A third issue revolves around lack of population growth and, frequently, the loss of population with the out-migration of younger people. A brief description of these situations will quickly reveal some of the land use and development impacts associated with them.

Population Aging Whereas two decades ago people living in small towns often bemoaned the fact that they had little choice but to move to the city when they retired, today they are staying on and other elderly people from the city may be moving there too. Smaller communities in all provinces, and in all locations except northern resource regions, tend to have considerably higher proportions of the elderly (those 65 and older) than do most cities.[12] Moreover, this tendency has been increasing so much that many rural communities have population concentrations of the elderly of 25 percent or more (as compared to 14 percent for Canada as a whole). Among British Columbia's small towns, there have appeared two distinct types of retirement communities. One can be called **indeigenous** retirement

towns, where the retired population is composed mostly of those who have remained living in the community after retirement, a tendency called aging-in-place.[13] The other may be referred to as **itinerant** retirement towns because most of the retirees have migrated there. The latter towns tend to be in regions with high quality natural amenities such as Prince Edward County in Ontario and the Okanagan Valley of British Columbia. The influx of retirees or near-retirees can be a boon to a community's economy.[14]

Regardless of the source of retirees, most small towns present some immediate problems in meeting the needs of older people. Whether it be health care, home-support services, or transportation, there are usually few such services in rural areas and considerable distances to reach those that do exist.[15] Housing accommodation can also be problematic for the elderly living in small towns, mainly because of the lack of variety in housing types. Added to these, the local governments have very limited resources to provide the services and facilities needed by their elderly. Also to be noted in regard to a town's population aging is that this often occurs in conjunction with the out-migration of younger people, which can exacerbate problems of providing public services.

Population Cleavages often occur in the wake of population growth in towns in the rural–urban fringe of cities (and towns in rural recreational regions). The expansion of cities into the countryside often has the result of displacing the rural population that has, sometimes, lived there for generations. The pre-existing social networks of, for example, farmers and traditional service people are changed by new arrivals (e.g., exurbanites, retirees, and "back-to-the-landers").[16] These newcomers, in turn, affect the political dynamics of the community and how it responds to development pressures and the need for additional services.[17] In some cases, as more newcomers settle in earlier arrivals become the vanguard of resistance to further change. Therefore, one cannot overlook the social dimensions of what may seem to the outsider to be a relatively small change in the community environment.

Population Stability, Decline, and Migration The majority of communities in rural regions register little, if any, growth in population from census to census. Just keeping a stable population level is seen as a favourable result by some while others suffer decline and only a relative few see an influx of new households. The primary reason is simply that there are few economic reasons for people to stay in these communities, especially younger people, and they migrate to larger centres.[18] The resulting population is often older and poorer and housing stock tends not to be replenished, much less creating new housing. Services and facilities for social and health care are usually minimal, if they exist at all. Thus, there is often little basis for long-range planning and development, and other ameliorative solutions must be sought.

Economic Development Issues

There is not a rural community whose economy is not tied intimately to its natural environment. Each is surrounded by natural resources that contribute to all or part of the economic base of the community: the farmland around a prairie town; the forest that surrounds a town in Northern Ontario; the ocean on which a Newfoundland outport is situated; the northern river basin that provides the territory for trappers and hunters, to name a few. Despite these being their founding resource bases, almost all rural communities today are experiencing dramatic changes in their relationship to the surrounding natural environment. Some resources have been depleted (e.g., fish stocks, timber, minerals), and others are being exploited differently due to market and/or technological changes.

Agricultural communities, for example, have been affected by increasing industrialization of farming with operations becoming larger and more specialized. The tendency to large-scale, mechanized operations in livestock production, notably hog raising across the Prairie provinces, has led to community planning conflicts over odours and water quality.[19] This situation is reflected in the issues being confronted in Newdale, Manitoba, as described in Planning Issue 10.1. As with other sectors of our economy, agricultural production has become more complex and subject to a variety of pressures (e.g., globalization and urbanization) and uncertainties (e.g., climate change).[20] These, in turn, lead to new demands on planners to be aware of the local and global realities affecting modern agriculture and finding the "right mix" of agriculture and other uses (see Figure 10.2).

Still other communities are coping with new demands on their resources (e.g., new mines, new recreational uses), globalized markets, and increased productivity. Each of these issues makes demands on housing stocks and local services. Not least are the impacts on those communities in the city's countryside, which, in the face of urban expansion, seek ways to retain traditional agricultural uses.[21]

In short, economic factors that are largely out of their control confront rural communities with significant

| Figure 10.2 | The Relationship between Agriculture and Planning |

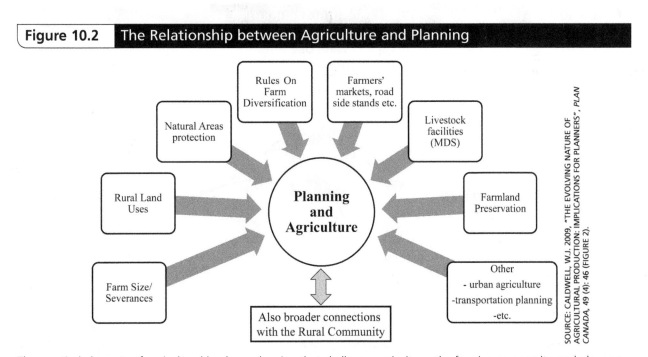

SOURCE: CALDWELL, W.J. 2009, "THE EVOLVING NATURE OF AGRICULTURAL PRODUCTION: IMPLICATIONS FOR PLANNERS", *PLAN CANADA*, 49 (4): 46 (FIGURE 2).

The practical elements of agricultural land use planning that challenge agriculture, the farming community, and planners.

change: employment losses, shifts in demand for labour skills, household income disruptions, business income uncertainty, and inability of communities to fund needed new services and facilities. A recent external trend affecting small communities is restructuring in the retail sector, which has led to a retail geography consisting of fewer and larger stores.[22] Given the much smaller scale of rural communities, these changes loom larger not just in terms of development but often also in terms of survival. Planners working with these communities cannot long ignore economic and natural resource issues.

Scope of Rural Community Planning

Rural community planning obliges planners to respond to a wide range of issues, as the above discussion indicates. Canadian rural planner Wayne Caldwell puts it this way:

> While rural planners focus on traditional land use issues, they also concern themselves with the local economy, labour and employment, demographics, resource management and environmental protection.[23]

Figure 10.3 shows the "diversity of issues, strategies and approaches" that defines the scope of the rural planner's task. Clearly, a scope as broad as this calls for a range of skills well beyond that of most planners. Rural community planners, thus, frequently depend on consultants for the specialty knowledge needed in their work and may utilize them to conduct public meetings dealing with their particular technical area.[24] Nonetheless, planners working with rural communities must be generalists who appreciate the wide array of factors that impinge on rural areas (see Figure 10.3).

Planning Parameters for Small Communities

Dimensions of Physical Development

It is vital to grasp two things about small communities: first, they are not just scaled-down versions of cities; and, second, their development proceeds in distinctive ways from that of cities. Therefore, planners need to have an appropriate perspective from which to assess their development. Four useful dimensions of physical development are:[25]

- *Scale* of development
- *Range* of types of development
- *Intensity* of development
- *Pace* of development

Figure 10.3 The Scope of Planning for Rural Communities

SOURCE: CALDWELL, W.J. 2005, "RURAL PLANNING IN CANADA," PLAN CANADA 45(3) 26.

Rural planning is very broad in scope and the planner must take all these facets into account when preparing a plan for a rural community.

And, for towns with adjacent farmlands, we need to add the dimension of *agricultural land* development. A brief elaboration of each will illustrate the nature of the process of development in most small communities.

Scale "Smallness" is an important dimension of several aspects of rural community development. The level of density is low and the scale of population and of the built-up area is small in towns and villages. So, too, is the scale of change. The additions to a town's housing stock, for example, are likely to be relatively few in number, even though proportionately large for the community. A centre of 500 population experiencing a growth of 40 percent in dwelling units, as many did in the 1970s and 1980s, would have added only 50–60 new houses and required, say, eight hectares of land. This means that the scope of planning problems is usually small and their solutions should be scaled appropriately. The scale issue is at the crux of controversy in Manitoba and Alberta over the use of "big barns" for raising hogs (see Planning Issue 10.1). This is the small town's counterpart to the urban dilemma over "big-box" retail stores, both of which promise local tax revenue and jobs, but at the cost of community transformation.

Range of Types Almost all small towns have only a small array of different activities and structures. From place to place, the range may vary according to the economic base of the community (i.e., a certain industry may predominate), the climate of the region, or the building materials available. There is seldom, however, a large variety in a town's residential, commercial, industrial, or public land use areas. One recurrent issue is the lack of alternative forms of housing available. The single-family dwelling is often the only type of housing available, a situation that precludes those needing to rent an apartment such as seniors wishing to leave their homes or younger residents not willing or able to purchase a home. And, typically, when new economic development occurs, it tends to bring the same kinds of activities and structures as have existed to that point. Thus, the planning implications of most new development have ready precedents. But as we see with the "big barns" mentioned above, the effect of globalization on agricultural communities can have physical as well as economic impacts.

Intensity Unlike the extensive areas of development of a city, a small town does not have either large areas covered with the same kind of development (such as residential suburbs) or highly concentrated activities (such as a cluster of apartment buildings). In most small centres, the development tends to be in discrete units in a more scattered fashion. Exceptions would be the mill, mine, cannery, transportation terminal, or other industrial enterprise in "single-industry" towns, the new shopping centre in a region-serving town, or the condo complex in a recreation town. The value of this dimension is in determining the effect that new physical development has on a community, such as in the traffic generated, the utilities needed, and the schools and parks required.

Pace There are two important facets of this dimension in regard to small towns. First, it can be misleading to view the pace of development in terms of percentage rates of growth. It is usually better with towns and villages to look at the actual amount of new development, or **absolute growth**. In the example used above of a town experiencing a 40 percent expansion in housing in a decade, not only was the number of houses built not very large (50–60), but also this was taking place over a ten-year span. The second facet is that the amount of change is *seldom spread evenly* over time. Because a continuous amount or level of growth cannot be expected, planning around each project must be on a more or less ad hoc basis.

The process of small-scale, scattered, uneven development described above pertains to most, but not all, small towns. There are some that are affected by rapid growth, a high demand for land, and major changes to their character. Resource towns like Fort McMurray, Alberta, come readily to mind, as do towns on the outskirts of metropolitan centres, such as Markham, near Toronto, and towns in recreation regions like Pemberton near Whistler. But this type of town and village development is an exception and probably affects no more than a few hundred of the several thousand small centres in the country.

Agricultural Land Although more of a contextual dimension than those above, the presence of agricultural land in a small town's setting can be a significant factor in its physical development and, thus, its planning. In several provinces, notably Québec and British Columbia, stringent limits are placed on the conversion of agricultural land to non-agricultural purposes, especially for residential development. In these two provinces, application must be made to a provincial commission for permission to further subdivide "protected agricultural areas," as they are called in Québec, and "agricultural land reserves," as they are called in British Columbia.[26] Two major thrusts of this type of intervention are those aimed at (1) assuring current and future supplies of farm products and (2) preserving rural landscapes that symbolize rural ways of life.[27] Other measures to restrain town expansion onto farmland are generally weaker, such as the "urban-containment boundaries" in Ontario.[28] Small towns in the rural-urban fringe are usually the ones most affected by such regulation because of the urban development pressures on them.

| Planning Issue 10.1 | The Side Effects of Estevan's Remarkable Growth Spurt |

The Globe and Mail
July 4, 2012

The Side Effects of Estevan's Remarkable Growth Spurt

Kim Mackrael

Housing shortage, increase in crime cloud sunny outlook for community that sits on top of giant Bakken oil patch

When Jimi Akinsete first visited Estevan, Sask. last January, he wondered if someone had made a mistake. The 48-year-old physician was being wooed by the local health committee, whose members hoped he would move to the rairie city from Manchester and help alleviate a chronic shortage of local doctors.

"Having lived in South Africa and the U.K. for some years, I thought, 'I know what a city is,'" he recalled. And Estevan's population, a mere 11,000 according to the last census, seemed too insignificant to merit the status.

"But when I came back to settle in and work I realized, though it looks small, there's a lot going on," he said.

A dusty two-hour drive southeast of Regina, Estevan is on the cusp of a resource-fuelled growth spurt that's attracting newcomers from across the country and around the world. Added revenue from oil exploration in the area helped the health committee offer generous incentive packages to new doctors, including a $10,000 signing bonus along with housing and a rental car during their first several months in the city.

Dr. Akinsete said he feels welcome in Estevan: He found a church community and is looking forward to giving his kids an opportunity to grow up with more open space.

"I'm happy with the city," he said. "There's fresh air, the space is there for your children to play around. I think Estevan is a very nice place."

But sitting in his office one Friday afternoon, Dr. Akinsete admitted he's worried about where his family will live when they join him later this summer and the housing stipend he's living on runs out.

Houses in Estevan sell for much more than they would in other, similar-sized cities, with an average three-bedroom bungalow going for about $350,000 – and not many available at that. The city also has the second-lowest vacancy rates in the province, after Regina, with tenants in the city paying the highest average rent in Saskatchewan.

Estevan has access to a vast reserve of light crude and there are major upgrades either planned or in progress at two nearby coal-fired power plants. The rapid economic development is expected to boost the city's population significantly over the coming years, adding more pressure to a tight housing market and transforming the demographics of the city.

Already, nine out of 10 doctors in Estevan were trained in another country, about half of its construction workers hail from out of province, and everyone who works at the local Dairy Queen is Filipino.

"The biggest hurdle that people have come across in terms of trying to hire has been the lack of housing. We just simply don't have rental accommodation available," says

Michel Cyrenne, who runs the city's chamber of commerce.

"Some people bring a trailer, winterize and stay in that, a lot of people are just staying with friends or relatives if they've been able to find a bed or couch or what have you."

Accommodation is so scarce that the province's trade union distributed flyers throughout Estevan last fall asking people if they'd consider renting a room or a basement to a construction worker. Some oil companies have bought up entire blocks in hotels, and about 200 workers are housed in a "man camp" – a cluster of well-furnished trailers in the city's southeast end.

But Mayor Gary St. Onge said the city is adopting a cautious approach to housing, adding he's taken some lessons from Fort McMurray – the community at the epicentre of Alberta's lucrative oil sands.

"They put up all sorts of places where people could stay," he said. "You know, they've had kind of a nightmare [with high-density housing]. And they said if you go slower it's better."

The rapid growth has sparked other concerns, as well. Mr. St. Onge said the city has seen an increase in crime, including a spike in the number of bar fights and a growing presence of drugs. And cocaine has become the drug of choice for many oil workers who are flush with cash from the job, he said. "There's no doubt, along with everything good there's usually something bad," Mr. St. Onge said.

The police department recently hired a full-time traffic officer to patrol Estevan's increasingly busy roads. And RCMP officers work with border agents and American law-enforcement agencies to keep an eye on cross-border drug trafficking.

The community sits on top of the giant Bakken oil patch, which the U.S. Geological Survey estimates contains as many as 4.3-billion barrels of oil. Although geologists discovered the oil in the 1950s, it's only in recent years that new, horizontal drilling and hydraulic fracturing

technology have allowed companies to extract the crude more easily from between layers of shale rock. Since then, it's been a boon to the economy in southeast Saskatchewan and neighbouring North Dakota and Montana.

"The opportunity is phenomenal," said Martin Heitkoetter, an oil and gas contractor from British Columbia. "When I first came here, one of the first things that popped in my head was, 'I have never seen a greater diamond in the rough.'"

As locals snap up the highest-paying oil and construction jobs, employers in the service industry say it's increasingly difficult to find anyone from Estevan who's willing to flip burgers or sling beers. Temporary workers from Eastern Europe and the Philippines now staff Estevan's restaurants, bars and fast-food outlets, brought in to fill positions locals in the area declined to take.

"I think that the fast foods got hit first, because everybody kind of went into the construction and the oil fields," said Denise Vandenhurk, who owns the Dairy Queen with her sisters. "We used to have a stack of [local] résumés, but since 2007, that was the big year of dry. Nothing."

Agnes Tolda, 29, was among the first Filipinos Ms. Vandenhurk hired and is now a permanent resident in Canada. In addition to her full-time hours at Dairy Queen, she works two part-time jobs – at a law firm and a motel – and rents a room with a Filipino family.

Since she came here more than three years ago, she's managed to put her younger brother through school and bought a house for her family in Manila. She's paying for two cousins to go to college now.

"I feel proud of myself," she said quietly, looking up from the table at the restaurant. "That's the main goal for us in coming here. We don't just help our family members, we also help our extended family members."

Saskatchewan Economy Minister Bill Boyd said the southeast region, which includes

CONTINUED

Estevan and the neighbouring city of Weyburn, is a significant contributor to the province's revenue base. "It's driving a good portion of our economy right now," he said.

Mr. St. Onge, who was born and raised in southeast Saskatchewan, said this isn't the first time Estevan has experienced a spike in economic development.

"The oil rush basically began in Estevan in 1957," he said. "Of course, oil has a history of going up and down, in the price, and Estevan's population did that as well over the years."

But, he added, "this seems to be a longer-type boom."

Planning Supports for Small Communities

There are two types of supportive frameworks that many small towns may call upon in their planning. Provincial ministries throughout Canada have a variety of measures to assist small communities. In addition, many rural regions have formal frameworks for regional government or regional planning. There is a great variety in these undertakings, but a brief sampling will indicate some of the sources of planning support to which small towns may turn.

Provincial Level

Provincial ministries may offer technical assistance for planning in small towns and rural areas. This can take the form of providing professional planning services directly to communities, financial assistance to obtain outside advisors, or technical assistance in the form of publications on relevant planning topics. The actual forms and the combinations available differ from province to province. For example, Manitoba has operated community-planning field offices in several regional centres from which staff planners could assist small communities in preparing local planning instruments and acting as advocates at formal hearings. Land Use Service Centres fulfill much the same role for Prince Edward Island towns, while in New Brunswick planners are assigned from the ministry to assist designated rural areas and, sometimes, to become the resident staff in regional planning commissions.

Another form of planning assistance that many provinces provide is financial support to promote the preparation of general planning instruments and plans for specific kinds of projects. Several provinces have, for example, a program of "community-planning study grants," which are available only to smaller municipalities. Such programs allow them to obtain the services of consultants to conduct planning studies and to prepare community plans, zoning bylaws, and so on. Aid is also available in most provinces for studies and plans for such specific kinds of projects as business area revitalization, seasonal cottage areas, and housing needs statements. Saskatchewan's Main Street Development Program was designed specifically to assist small towns and is typical of these kinds of programs. Most planning assistance involving provincial grants is in the form of a shared-cost program, in which the province contributes the major portion of the costs and the municipality the remainder. Provincial shares usually range from 50 to 80 percent.

Self-help planning manuals are often available from provincial ministries to provide assistance in a wide range of planning needs. Many are designed specifically to help small communities or those that seldom become involved in planning more than a subdivision. The manuals tend to avoid jargon and provide brief, coherent models for planning reports that are well within the capabilities of small towns and townships.

Technical-assistance programs and services such as those described above may play an invaluable role in planning small towns where resources are meagre. Their success, however, depends upon two factors. First, the provincial programs themselves must have continuity and the ability to integrate the various elements of planning a community. This stems from the fact that the planning process for any size of community involves a long-term commitment on the part of the town the adoption of a community plan is, for example, just the beginning of the next stage of implementing it. In Manitoba, provincial planners are cognizant of pressures on rural communities for "sustainable development" and nowadays urge them to go beyond traditional land use planning to consider "community facilitation, community economic development, and co-management" of rural resources.[29]

The second factor, and probably the most vital one, is having the capability of accessing provincial programs. A small town with few resources often lacks skilled personnel able to recognize the value of the programs that are offered; it may lack the funds needed even to participate in shared-cost programs, and its lack of municipal organization and other community institutions might make it incapable of sustained long-term planning. Well-intentioned programs tend to assume that all communities have similar needs and also capabilities. This can result in two problems: communities may not "fit" programs, and many communities may fail to seek solutions out of lack of awareness of how to adapt to the program.

Regional Level

Planning support programs and services at the regional level are the best arrangement for providing assistance to small towns. County planning departments—such as in Ontario and Nova Scotia—and regional district planning departments—such as in British Columbia— comprise all the communities in a defined area. Such agencies can provide continuous planning staff support for individual communities, as well as for the interrelated services and facilities of the region. Importantly, this type of arrangement makes available to small towns their "own" staff planner, thus approximating the level of staff support needed to nurture a continuous community planning process.

For rural communities in Alberta there are several mechanisms available that allow planning on an extra-municipal basis. Intermunicipal Committees (IMC) may be formed between neighbouring local governments to find ways to deal with land use and infrastructure issues arising in boundary areas.[30] Intermunicipal Development Plans (IDP) are also possible to deal with such issues as urban development in one municipality affecting non-urban areas in an adjacent municipality. IDPs are an important way in which neighbouring communities may be informed of each other's plans and projects, and joint cooperation fostered between the staffs and Councils.

Planning Tools for Small Towns and Rural Communities

The essential point to be made in planning for small town and rural communities is that all planning approaches should be suited to them, be *small-community* approaches. Most of our planning tools are more

suitable for large communities than for small ones. Planners of small towns should consider whether the tools they propose to use are appropriate to the problems and capabilities of small communities. The planning situation usually features a distinctive set of easily identifiable problems that call for seemingly mundane solutions, rather than an abstract arrangement of land uses. Moreover, plans and other planning instruments need to match the resources and the capabilities of a few hard-pressed and often inexperienced municipal officials.

In small towns, planning approaches can be simplified yet be appropriate to the situation; small-town residents often recognize this faster than the city-trained planners who try to help them. There is, fortunately, an increasing amount of experience in small-town planning from which examples of appropriate planning tools can be drawn. Experience shows that the community planning process is essentially the same as for larger communities (as described in Chapter 6), but differs in the tools that are needed to make it effective. Thus, the community plan is a vital component, as are the tools for analysis and implementation. The difference can perhaps be grasped as that between a large and a small wrench in a mechanic's toolbox; each is peculiarly suited to its task. The planner's toolbox in the small-town setting need not contain as many or as wide a range of tools as for city planning situations. But given the uniqueness of each town and village, care must be taken in their application.

The Community Plan

The community plan for a small town deals with land uses, circulation, recreation facilities, and parks, just as a plan for a large city does, but it can be simpler and more direct both in content and style. Its objectives can address the problems residents would like to solve; it needs fewer analyses and fewer land use categories; and it can be concise and brief. Experience in Newfoundland demonstrates such principles of appropriateness. As long ago as 1968, the Newfoundland and Labrador government explored the special planning needs of small communities, using Clarenville (population about 2800) for a prototype plan. The accompanying report advocated that such plans start with a focus on a statement of community problems and possible solutions, noting that "if day-to-day problems can be solved with the aid of a plan then, even if they are of minor importance in themselves, the value of planning is established ... and there will also be an immediately beneficial effect on the physical environment."[31] The land use planning solutions suggested in the plan thereby had a clear connection with the felt needs of community members; they were not as abstract as the solutions in many conventional municipal plans.

This concern over the style of presentation is not misplaced, for it is through its presentation that a plan achieves relevance for community members. A community plan is a way of demonstrating consensus, and a small town plan should heed this fact. Residents of small towns are usually intimately aware of land-ownership patterns and the issues with which the town is concerned, and they will want to see these accurately portrayed. Moreover, there are likely to be few professional planning, administrative, and public-media skills and resources available to interpret the plan if issues arise later. The danger in a poorly presented plan is that it may prove frustrating to officials and citizens; they may either ignore it or only pay lip service to it. A plan for High River, Alberta, in the mid-1970s (population 4800 at the time) is exemplary in its presentation style.[32] Vivid graphic techniques show new facilities, and the five major districts of the town are listed on the town map with their main problems and solutions.

Ucluelet on British **Columbia's** Pacific Coast reiterated the importance of its Official Community Plan (OCP) in a 1998 update because of the loss of traditional fishing and logging industries and the impact of the increasingly popular Pacific Rim National Park just to the north. To quote the planner guiding the OCP process,

> The OCP resembled nothing of its predecessor and included nine new Development Permit Areas establishing policies ranging from environmental protection to design guidelines ... [and] involved the entire community as well as a substantial steering committee which fueled its momentum.[33]

Likewise, the rural Alberta County of Rocky View, northwest of Calgary, in its uses easily grasped illustrations of its planning policy guidelines (see Figure 10.4). These are also available online to residents and developers.[34]

Because planning practice in Canada is conducted within an elaborate statutory framework, this seems to have fostered the lengthy municipal plans one commonly finds. It is rarely apparent that these cumbersome, repetitive plans, so often given to legalistic language and jargon, are inappropriate for any size of community, let alone small towns and rural municipalities. This conventional approach has produced a 50-page plan for a town of 400 people in New Brunswick and a 90-page plan for a community of 1000 persons in Ontario, to cite just two examples. One has to wonder who besides the planners, will read and use them.

Saskatchewan's Planning and Development Act has a special approach to small town plans. That province now acknowledges that not all municipalities may require a comprehensive municipal plan. Those communities that are very small or have a very low level of development activity may prepare a Basic Planning Statement. These are envisioned as short statements of municipal planning policy that would be sufficient to guide the local council in its (probably infrequent) deliberations over development proposals. The statements would play a role similar to that of a municipal plan in that they are a prerequisite to any intended zoning bylaw.

The plans referred to above are for incorporated small towns, which still leaves to be considered the planning situation of the more than three-quarters of small communities that are not municipalities. These places would, at best, be included within the plans of rural municipalities, townships, or counties. Given that the towns, villages, and hamlets are usually the most important centres in the rural locale, attention should be paid to them within the larger plan such as preparing supplementary plans for unincorporated towns, much as one makes special-area plans for downtown districts, historic neighbourhoods, and parks in large city plans. The County of Huron in Ontario has done this as has the county of Rocky View, Alberta.

Analytical Tools

With respect to the type of analytical tools that are required, the same general principles apply as for community plans: that is, planners should strive for simple, direct methods of providing the base of knowledge needed for the plan's preparation. Many tools developed for city planning are simply not needed, given the small size of towns and villages. For example, elaborate studies of land use and economic base will probably be irrelevant; similarly, statistical analyses involving correlations and sampling cannot provide reliable results because of the small size of the population. However, a concomitant of the small size that favours thorough understanding of the community is that the amount of data that is usually required can be readily obtained from field surveys and direct interviews. Information about housing, land use, jobs, age structure, and so forth will not be voluminous, and the direct contact can help elicit richer

SOURCE: McCARDLE. K. 2009, "'RURAL' PLANNING IN AN URBANIZING REGION", *PLAN CANADA* 49 (4): 19 (FIGURE 1).

Figure 10.4 | Illustrating Rural Development Policy

Planning Policy Framework

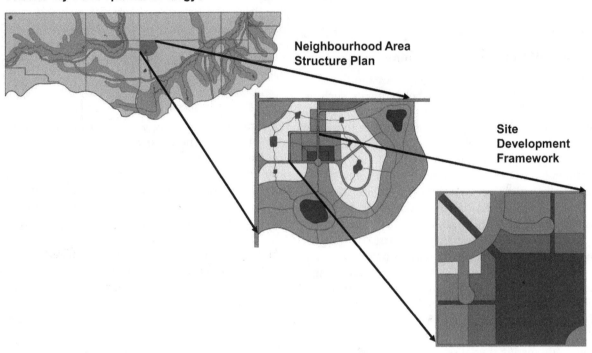

Community Development Strategy

Neighbourhood Area Structure Plan

Site Development Framework

Rocky View County in Alberta plans at the three levels: (1) a Community Development Strategy describes the places to be created; (2) the Neighbourhood Area Structure Plan defines the arrangement of land uses; and (3) the Site Development Framework defines what the built environment will look like.

local information than is generally available to city planners. Moreover, many of the necessary studies may be conducted by community members, thus facilitating the task and engaging community interest in the plan-making process.

Community Profiles and Participation

This tool, as the name suggests, gathers together various data in a single document describing the community's present status, recent trends in population growth and age composition, the environment, the local and regional economy, transportation, recreation, and so on. Residents of small places have a fairly unified view of their community; the profile makes use of this view, instead of fragmenting it with a series of separate studies. Furthermore, the community profile lends itself to use as a community self-survey tool. People of all ages, from children in schools to adults in service clubs, can participate in gathering the necessary data. It is helpful for the planner to incorporate issues into the profile that assist residents in identifying community problems and aspirations. Also worth incorporating is a historical overview of the community that provides both a sense of place and the factors that are important to the town's heritage. Historical photographs and maps may be used to advantage in conjunction with those of contemporary situations.

Citizen participation in planning matters may be more important in rural areas because of the small numbers of people and their familiar circumstances.

A method used to garner participation of community members over planning issues in rural Ontario is a useful tool. Water quality along the Lake Huron shoreline became a concern dividing lakeshore residents and farmers and led to Huron County planners to bring together small groups from the two sides of the dispute tell "their stories." They used a consensus-building method called the "Circle Process" in which those involved could "build relationships of understanding and trust," a process well-suited to small communities.[35]

Analyses of Housing and Population

The planner also needs to make analyses and forecasts beyond those that citizens can help provide such as the trends in the size, composition, and location of the community's housing stock and population base. An accurate survey of all households is the only sure way to acquire these data in a reliable form for analysis, although Statistics Canada now provides some small-area data from the census. The best analyses and forecasts use the simplest methods. It has been found that forecasts for small towns that use linear extrapolation—the projection of absolute increments in past change—are the most accurate. Because changes in population and housing can vary dramatically from year to year, projections based on percentage changes can be misleading. Special attention needs to be paid to the age structure of the population given that small communities tend to have higher-than-average elderly populations; conditions could merit a special section on policies regarding seniors in the community plan.

Economic Analyses

Two kinds of economic analysis can prove useful in planning small communities. One is a **locational analysis** of the residents' places of employment and shopping. People in small communities tend to interact over extensive areas, because they can seldom find a full range of employment and shopping opportunities right in their own communities. A knowledge of the extent to which residents commute to work in other places and shop in other centres will indicate the ways in which the town's economy is entwined with that of other communities. Such information could be helpful in forecasting the impact of changes occurring in the region surrounding the town—for example, the opening or closing of a large plant or new shopping centre nearby. Residents' linkages may be gathered by a local survey that asks about trip purposes, mode of travel,

distance, and frequency and then the results mapped and tabulated.

Another useful tool is called **threshold analysis**. Retail and other commercial firms are the economic backbone of most small centres because they provide basic goods and services and are major sources of employment. This tool calculates the population required in the town and its trade area to support additional retail and service firms. It can be used to identify those types of firms that have good prospects and those that have poor prospects. The Province of Ontario provides an online sample of threshold analysis in its report, *Marketing Your Downtown*,[36] and Statistics Canada publishes a regular Retail Store Survey.[37]

Implementation Tools

As with other planning tools used in small community planning, one must consider the problems that implementation tools are intended to solve. How, for example, will zoning work in the small community context of low density and diverse land use patterns, given that it "grew up" in the city, where there are large common-use districts and competition among land uses? In light of the meagre resources in small communities for administering any kind of regulations, it is important to avoid implementation tools that require continual and demanding administration. If one were to specify the needed characteristics of plan-implementation tools that would be most fitting for small towns, two of the most important would be *flexibility* and *adaptability*. Planners need to assess whether these qualities can be achieved in the tools they consider applying.

Making Zoning Appropriate

Zoning as commonly employed derives its usefulness from its ability to parallel the development patterns of cities, where land uses tend to sort themselves into districts of similar uses and types of structures. Only when its population exceeds 2500 does a small town's development pattern begin to show evidence of homogeneous districts of different land uses. Even then, these districts are not large (perhaps less than 40–80 hectares), and there are likely to be only a few of them (such as one each for the business area, the residential area, and the industrial area). Moreover, they will each probably accommodate a variety of uses. A general or comprehensive zoning bylaw would be too cumbersome in this kind of situation. However, it may be pertinent to frame regulations for any special district where land development is more volatile and subject to conflicts with adjoining areas. There is often a need in small towns to control development along highways, watercourses, or in the business district.

Performance Zoning

The diverse and sporadic development process in small towns tends to accommodate diverse uses adjacent, or in close proximity, to one another that might be considered problematic in urban situations. Conventional zoning tries to anticipate the activity effects of various classes of land uses, thereby predetermining proximate allowable uses. But, in small towns, it is possible, and indeed commendable, to use a more flexible case-by-case approach that deals with the *effects*, or impact, of a proposed land use rather than with its *functional use*. For example, it is probably more important to know whether the proposed use will generate a lot of traffic, have abnormal hours of operation, create extensive noise or odours, make abnormal demands on water supplies, or produce dangerous effluents than to understand the use itself. A type of zoning originally used in industrial districts in cities, performance zoning is widely recommended for use in small communities either independently or along with conventional land use zoning.[38] This tool, sometimes referred to as "flexible zoning," works by establishing performance standards against which proposed uses and their location are judged. Performance standards can include traffic generation, noise, lighting levels, stormwater runoff, loss of wildlife or vegetation, or even architectural style, according to one manual.[39]

Development Control

Development control, in which each proposal for a new or changed land use within a specified area (e.g., a business district or historic zone) must receive permission to proceed, is analogous to performance zoning. That is, a **development permit** must be obtained showing that specified planning criteria have been met. These criteria may, and often do, include protection of the environment and certain design specifications, as well as normal zoning limits on height, coverage, parking, and other details. Again referring to Ucluelet, British Columbia, its new zoning bylaw includes nine Development Permit areas and the bylaw allows for various land uses "to coexist" that assure the continuation of the coastal community's marine atmosphere.[40] Provision is also made for receiving development proposals that are pre-planned using the **comprehensive development zoning** approach (see Chapter 16).

Cluster Zoning

A fairly recent planning tool for rural areas, especially in the rural–urban fringe, is one that blends both zoning regulation and subdivision control. Since expansion of many towns often means impinging on adjacent agricultural land, it is vital to try to reduce the impact that such expansion could bring through normal large-lot subdivision. The technique of cluster zoning, or open-space zoning as it is sometimes called, congregates the new development on a part of the property while the remainder is left for farming or other open use.[41] The "cluster" notion comes from the concept of grouping together new development on several adjacent parcels. This technique leaves larger blocks of open space, thereby maintaining a rural character to the landscape and also making farms more viable.[42] The Township of Langley in British Columbia's fertile Fraser Valley uses a reverse approach by designating lands only available for agriculture (see Figure 10.5).

Land Subdivision

The subdivision of vacant land for new building lots and structures can pose special technical and resource questions for a small community. What may appear to be a boon in terms of new development and an expanded tax base may turn out to be a drain on financial resources and cause future problems for the community if not considered thoroughly at the start. All too often, the sites chosen for houses are on lands with poor buildability—steep slopes, floodplains, poor drainage, or subject to erosion. If the community is called upon later to provide adequate road access, public utilities, and proper drainage, the costs may be very high. Thus, subdivision proposals should be scrutinized for their relation to the development pattern envisioned in the community plan, for the provision of roads, parks, and utilities, and for the treatment of unique and hazardous topography. In farming communities, the clustering of new residential lots is used to prevent the fracturing of farmland and strip development along country roads

Many technical and engineering questions arise in regard to subdivisions, and a small community may not have sufficient expertise on its own staff to deal with them. In many provinces, the final authority for approving subdivisions rests with the province or with the regional government, and advice will usually be available from these upper levels. However, it is still advisable for the town to be involved in reviewing such plans as thoroughly as possible. It may well be able to convene a review committee

Figure 10.5 Rural Land Use Concept Plan, Langley, British Columbia, 2006

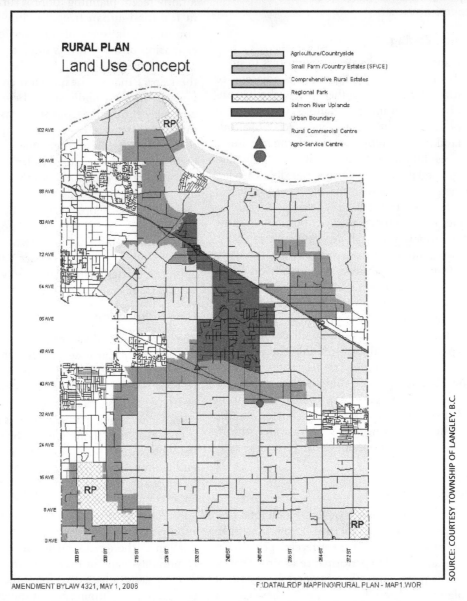

RURAL PLAN
Land Use Concept

Agriculture/Countryside
Small Farm /Country Estates (SF\CE)
Comprehensive Rural Estates
Regional Park
Salmon River Uplands
Urban Boundary
Rural Commercial Centre
Agro-Service Centre

AMENDMENT BYLAW 4321, MAY 1, 2006

F:\DATA\LRDP MAPPING\RURAL PLAN - MAP1.WOR

SOURCE: COURTESY TOWNSHIP OF LANGLEY, B.C.

By explicitly designating areas for farming in community plans, rural communities in urbanizing regions can sustain their agricultural resources.

from among knowledgeable citizens. Such a group, or the council, could make good use of available provincial handbooks on the principles of good subdivision design when assessing proposals.

Lastly, a variant on regulating land subdivision in agricultural areas is using a pre-emptive strategy of financial incentives for breaking up parcels of land for housing and so on. In areas where maintaining viable agriculture is an important consideration, a process of **purchasing the development rights** of farmland can be used. In the especially valuable tender fruit belt of the Niagara Peninsula, for example, the Ontario government established a program to induce farmers to place a covenant on their land which restricts the land from being used other than for fruit growing in return for a stipulated cash payment from the province and the regional municipality.[43] In other words, the farmer still owns the land and can continue to farm it but the right of the property owner to otherwise develop cannot be exercised. An easement, as it is properly called, preventing non-agricultural development has been purchased. Private land trusts often use this kind of device to protect scenic and historic resources. In British Columbia and Québec essentially the same thing occurred when agricultural land reserves were established by government fiat; in these instances no compensation was paid because it was considered in the larger public interest not to do so.

Planning and Governing Small Towns and Rural Communities

Community planning, regardless of the size of the community, is an integral part of the way a community governs itself and takes responsibility for its future built and natural environments. In the Canadian social and political milieu, local (municipal) government is the cornerstone of such community undertakings. All provinces have legislation that enables a municipality to be formed, make plans, regulate land uses, and make expenditures regarding future development. However, this provincial legislation is, by its very nature, meant to apply universally to all municipalities in the province, regardless of size, location, or resources, a situation often unfavourable to small communities, as has been the case several times.

Local Government Structures and Resources

Small towns exist within governmental milieux that put special constraints on their performance of the community planning activity. An essential planning concern in rural regions is how to allocate resources and governmental authority in areas where people live in widely separated centres and in low-density settings in the countryside. The issues are those of determining at what population a centre will be able to govern itself effectively and over what area the governmental jurisdiction should prevail.

Rural Municipalities

Each province has provisions for granting municipal status to towns and villages, usually based on population. Thus, some small places may be **incorporated**, and others not. In Saskatchewan, the incidence of incorporation is very high among towns and villages, including hamlets, whereas in New Brunswick and Nova Scotia, only the larger towns are incorporated. To provide government for dispersed rural populations, all provinces (except the Atlantic Provinces) have **area municipalities**, known variously as townships, rural municipalities, and district municipalities, where settlement is widespread. These latter units often include smaller towns and villages that are not incorporated. They tend to have a common size, for example, and in Ontario, Québec, and the Prairie provinces, they encompass an area of about 260 square kilometres.

Both incorporated centres and area municipalities are local, self-governing units with structures analogous to those of larger communities: that is, each would have its own council and constituent committees and boards, perhaps reduced in scale but with the same powers as city councils to raise taxes, make expenditures, pass land use regulations, and make plans for future development. The crucial difference is the much-reduced scale and quality of resources, both financial and human, that these small municipalities have available to them. Comprising, as they do, only a few hundred or a few thousand persons, their tax base is small, especially when monies are needed for new or renewed physical facilities and infrastructure. As well, they tend to have only a few technical and administrative persons on staff to carry out the regulatory and planning tasks the community might wish to undertake. In the case of the small town that is unincorporated, both the financial and staff resources are at the discretion of the council of the township or rural municipality in which they are located (which is usually also small in size and resources).

It is only partly true, it may be argued, that small towns and townships require much less in the way of resources and administrative structures because their needs are likely to be fewer. There often are fixed costs in providing such town facilities as a water or sewer system, streetlights, or sidewalks, and the modest local resources may not allow the community even to begin development of this kind. Increasingly, the province assigns to municipalities such technical tasks as planning, or environmental protection, or energy conservation, which are administratively infeasible in small towns and townships. In these situations, either the task does not get done or the small community must rely on outside help from consultants, a regional government, the province, or all three. Rural local governments, generally, are in a dependent position in regard to achieving their own goals for planning and development.

Regional Government

Another structural form for providing governmental needs to rural regions is a regional government. The county (in eastern Canada, except Newfoundland) and the regional district or county (in western Canada) are the various provincial counterparts. They may provide services and facilities—hospitals, waste disposal, parks, planning—directly to all communities because of the costs involved or the overriding regional need. They may, and often do, provide technical assistance to constituent communities; this is usually the case in planning. It should be noted that for most small communities the regional or county planning agency is not an alternative. The regional districts in British Columbia may provide planning services to constituent communities, but in provinces to the east there is no consistent system of county or regional planning, and most small towns must rely on their own resources.

Planning Resources

It is assumed in all provincial planning acts that all (incorporated) communities are capable of establishing and maintaining a workable planning function. But, as already indicated, the job of making community plans and land use regulations and enforcing them in a small town falls to a small group of people. Typically, towns with populations below 2000 people have fewer than five employees, and it is on them that the burden falls to make technical and administrative planning judgments. The key personnel on a small town staff are the town clerk, building inspector, and roads superintendent. Seldom does a town below 5000 population have a municipal engineer, much less its own professional staff planner, although many employ consultants on an ongoing basis.

To sum up, in the majority of small towns, human and financial resources are simply too meagre to permit a satisfactory planning process. Nevertheless, just as with large communities, provincial planning legislation requires both the plan-making and the plan-implementation phases be undertaken. Some mechanisms exist to assist small communities to make plans and land use regulations; these mechanisms include grants, which can be used to hire consultants, and technical assistance programs from provincial ministries and regional governments. But the job of plan implementation almost always falls to the community alone. This includes both the enforcement of land use regulations and the programming of capital expenditures. Meanwhile, the intricacies of planning are increasing. Not only do provincial planning regulations and programs undergo frequent change but also new forms of legislation emerge periodically. For example, such planning interests as environmental assessment, farmland preservation, stream protection, and coastal zone management now require local planning responses. The small communities that exist within these dependent situations are often left to seek out their own means to fulfill such obligations.

Planning Aboriginal Rural and Northern Communities

Among the most encouraging situations arising in Canadian community planning over the past decade or so are the advances being made in planning Aboriginal communities. (In Canada, the term Aboriginal is used to refer to anyone of indigenous ancestry and may include status Indians, non-status Indians, Metis and Inuit.) These advances are encouraging for two reasons: one is the recognition of the often-dire needs in these communities that are beginning to be tackled; the other is the recognition by planners of the need to seek and use planning approaches that are appropriate to Aboriginal communities, not least that they are community-driven.[44] The concept of integrated community-based planning for Aboriginal communities emerged in the 1980s. It replaced the previous top-down master plan program administered for Native communities by the federal Department of Indian Affairs and Northern Development (now Indian and Northern Affairs Canada—INAC). The new planning approach, called Comprehensive Community Planning (CCP), seeks to consider "all aspects of life and livelihood and their interrelationships in the community."[45] Evidence of these efforts is seen in Nunavut, the Northwest Territories, British Columbia, Saskatchewan, Newfoundland and Labrador, and the Maritime provinces.[46]

One such project is the planning and building of Natuashish in Labrador to replace the older Davis Inlet (Utshimassits), which had come to national attention after a series of tragic events. In 1997, the people of the community, the Mishuau Innu, began a process of designing and building themselves a new community.[47] The approach gave the Innu control of every aspect of the plan (Figure 10.6). Planners visited elders in their homes, travelled to outpost camps, and asked children

SOURCE: STEVEN FICK, "SOCIAL DISREPAIR IN NATUASHISH," *CANADIAN GEOGRAPHIC*, JANUARY/FEBRUARY 2003.

Figure 10.6	Natuashish Plan

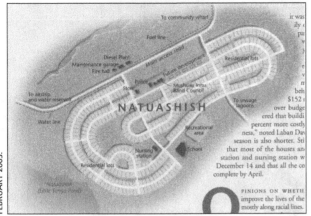

in school for their ideas. Family trees were drawn up to determine family relationships that would guide the location of extended-family groupings of housing which the community wanted. Community members were trained in electrical wiring, plumbing, and carpentry so they could assist in the building. Everyone was consulted, in their own language if wanted, about the location of the school (at the foot of a hill for sledding, but not near the commercial area), about the type of housing (typical clapboard style with a basement), and so forth.[48] Regional approaches covering several communities and the development of their resource base using similar approaches has occurred in the Gwich'in Settlement Area in the Northwest Territories. Here the land use planning is for separate communities and the areas between them with the aim of developing a framework of "co-management" of resources—shared resource decision-making among the communities and the territorial government.[49]

Beyond these earlier northern initiatives Aboriginal community planning has broadened both spatially and conceptually. On the ground, so to speak, there is increasing experience with planning of Aboriginal lands adjoining urban municipalities. This has brought forward the need for "intergovernmental" planning to coordinate land use development in boundary areas and share services such as water, waste management, and transportation as exemplified in the 2003 "Community Accord" between the Sliammon First Nation and the City of Powell River on the British Columbia coast.[50] This has provided important lessons for Aboriginal planning there and elsewhere. Not least

was that the Sliammon First Nation was accorded equal governmental status in the planning process, thereby acknowledging their sovereign rights over their lands as well as cultural sites, in short their ability to speak for themselves and plan the way they wanted. A set of "best practices" for planning by both Aboriginal and non-Aboriginal planners were also derived from this experience:

1. Build a genuine relationship and mutual trust and respect.
2. Establish and maintain regular meetings.
3. Involve and inform the public.
4. Establishing guiding principles or "ground rules" may be helpful in developing an atmosphere of respect and trust.
5. Establish joint committees to enable each party to participate equally and meaningfully in numerous planning processes.
6. Celebrate successes with the community.
7. Negotiate a fair process for the delivery and payment for services.
8. First Nations and local governments have equal jurisdictional limits.
9. Write reciprocal letters of support for various initiatives.
10. Agreeing to disagree helps to avoid a potential conflict and buys time until an agreement can be reached.[51]

The close relationship that evolved is captured in the intergovernmental logo that is now being used on the cover of the City of Powell River Official Community Plan (see Figure 10.7).

The instances of fruitful Aboriginal planning experiences continue to grow across the country from the Lil'wat Nation in British Columbia, through the Standing Buffalo Dakota Nation in Saskatchewan, to the Wagmatcook First Nation in Cape Breton.[52] These and other efforts have pointed to much more developed approaches to Aboriginal planning as well as continuing obstacles in its path. Among the latter are federal government bureaucratic requirements that are time-consuming and costly for a First Nation often with few staff or other resources.[53] Sandercock, among others, notes abiding frustrations of Indigenous peoples in other countries with the planning profession including the latter's frequent assumptions that community and regional planning is a 20th century practice, or that planning processes with Aboriginal peoples need to become more participatory, neither of which is valid.[54]

Figure 10.7 | Logo for Intergovernmental Aboriginal Planning (B.C.), 2008

SOURCE: GALLAGHER, S. 2008, "INTERGOVERNMENTAL COMMUNITY PLANNING: SLIAMMON FIRST NATION AND CITY OF POWELL RIVER EXPERIENCE", *PLAN CANADA* 48 (2): 35.

Out of the intergovernmental planning of the Sliammon First Nation and the City of Powell River this logo of a raven carrying the Pearl of the Sunshine Coast in its beak was developed. It may be interpreted broadly as "the Raven is a messenger bridging the old and the new, it carries news as it travels."

Or as a Canadian planner with First Nations experience, Christine Calihoo, puts it, for "professional planners to lay down their assumptions prior to entering the Nation's territory and prepare to learn and adapt their professional tools according to the Nation's priorities and protocols."[55] Her last point is in regard to planners tending to apply a non-Aboriginal planning template in much of their First Nations work.

Planners need to learn that each Aboriginal community has its own local perspective and this must be understood and acknowledged (a lesson also appropriate in non-Aboriginal communities).[56] It also means that ingrained habits of "time and efficiency … of being direct, getting quickly to the point, being detached" might not be the appropriate way to operate in Aboriginal communities.[57] As Sandercock further asks, "How might planning processes be made more amenable to the Storytelling mode?" Or, indeed, how might the talking circle be incorporated?[58] In short, Aboriginal planning should not simply echo mainstream practice but be a reformulated process "that incorporates 'traditional' knowledge and culture …

[be an] acknowledgement of an Indigenous [peoples] world-view"[59]

Some strides toward these ideals are being made as with the planning for Iqaluit, the new capital of Nunavut. Although a much larger place (6000 population) than those discussed above, the planners found the need to adapt planning principles from "the South" to northern needs.[60] Faced with goals of "protecting the Arctic way of life and reflecting the Inuit cultural heritage" meant, among other things, permitting shacks on the beach to store equipment, and providing snowmobile trails, safe places for sled dogs, and working areas for drying skins. The response of these planners to the ongoing realities of Inuit life goes far to acknowledging and reinforcing the meaning of *place* in the eyes of the residents.[61] Other planners, at Dalhousie University, have fashioned a "First Nations Community Planning Model" and worked with several communities in the Atlantic Provinces in preparing community plans.[62] A step-by-step planning *Workbook* was prepared to assist Aboriginal communities like Pictou Landing, Nova Scotia, Abegweit,

SOURCE: MANNELL, L. & TERNOWAY, H. 2008, "THE NEED TO DO MORE: ADVANCING PLANNING WITH FIRST NATIONS COMMUNITIES", *PLAN CANADA* 48 (2): 22.

Figure 10.8	The Process of Aboriginal Community Planning

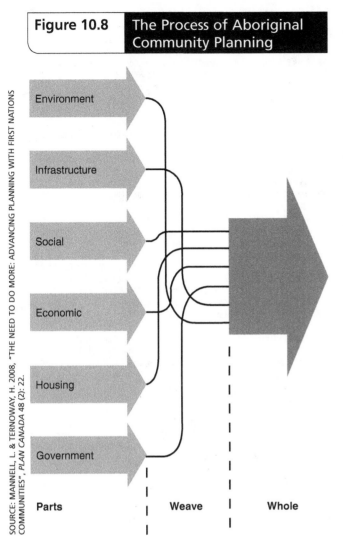

The process of building a community plan by seeing things as a whole.

Prince Edward Island, and Metepenagiag, New Brunswick in creating their own plans (see Figure 10.8) that encapsulate this approach. Finally, planning for northern communities must acknowledge the climate. Simply providing basic services can be difficult in the Arctic, sometimes requiring special systems like the above-ground "utilidors" in Inuvik. Careful community design can help create "livable winter cities"— providing shelter from winds, trapping sunlight, and avoiding snow drifts.[63]

Reflections

Despite their small size, the planning for small communities, both Aboriginal and non-Aboriginal, demands a broader range of concerns be part of the planning process than does the planning for cities. Urban community planning focuses on the use of land and its regulation, but planners for smaller communities seldom have that as a primary concern: the economic viability of the natural resource base, environmental issues, and the cultural milieu are apt to be as important or more so. In addition, what has begun to be achieved in small community planning over the past two decades is an approach that recognizes the crucial connection between the land base and the people of the community.[64] This has led directly to involving the citizens of small towns, from Tofino to Iqaluit, in debating and deciding the merits of planning issues. In Huron County, in southwestern Ontario, the integrated approach has guided planners of small communities to go beyond traditional physical planning and function more as an "informed facilitator and community enabler," with the objective "to empower the local community with additional responsibility for its own future."[65] This principle and the ones cited above suggest a planning style that is less about the technical aspects of planning or about a received methodology than about developing a *relationship* with people in the community.

One cannot help but be struck by the vitality embodied in much of the planning with Aboriginal communities; it's so much a reflection of early planning ideas. It seeks to integrate people *and* place, as Geddes intoned, the very principle that attracted many to planning in the first place. Could it be that Aboriginal peoples have something to teach us about community planning that we have become indifferent to? This principle could, and should, apply just as well to urban community planning.

As we move now to planning for people and places within urban communities it will be helpful to reflect on two questions:

- *How does the scope of planning for rural agricultural communities compare to that of planning for urban places?*
- *What can one learn from planning with Aboriginal communities that would be of benefit in the planning of other communities?*

Reference Notes

1. Alan J. Hahn, "Planning in Rural Areas," *Journal of the American Institute of Planners* 36 (January 1970), 44–49.
2. Gerald Hodge and Ira M. Robinson, *Planning Canadian Regions* (Vancouver: UBC Press, 2001), 139–160.
3. C.R. Bryant, L.H. Russwurm, and A.G. McLellan, *The City's Countryside: Land and Its Management in the Rural–Urban Fringe* (New York: Longmans, 1982).
4. John F. Meligrama, "Developing a Planning Strategy and Vision for Rural–Urban Fringe Areas: A Case Study of British Columbia," *Canadian Journal of Urban Research* 12:1 (2003), 119–141.
5. Jackie Wolfe, "The Native Canadian Experience with Integrated Community Planning: Promise and Problems," in F. Dykeman, ed., *Integrated Rural Planning and Development* (Sackville, NB: Mount Allison University Small Town and Rural Research Program, 1988), 213–234.
6. Newfoundland, Department of Municipal Affairs, *Planning for Smaller Towns* (St. John's: Project Planning Associates, 1968), 23.
7. Dennis O'Connor, *Report of the Walkerton Inquiry* (Toronto: Ontario Ministry of the Attorney General, 2002).
8. Victoria Times Colonist, "Medical Officer Seeks Further Test of Wells," July 20, 2001, B1.
9. CBC News, "Water Treatment Plant Too Small," October 27, 2005; see also CTV News, "Water Crisis in Attawapiskat," November 30, 2011.
10. Kevin S. Hanna, "Planning for Sustainability: Experience in Two Contrasting Communities," *Journal of the American Planning Association* 71:1 (Winter 2005), 27–40
11. www.hirra.ca/recycle
12. Gerald Hodge, *The Elderly in Canada's Small Towns* (Vancouver: University of British Columbia Centre for Human Settlements, 1987), Occasional Paper 43, 14; these tendencies are confirmed in Gerald Hodge, *The Geography of Aging: Preparing Communities for the Surge in Seniors* (Montreal: McGill–Queens University Press, 2008), 88–93.
13. Gerald Hodge, *Seniors in Small Town British Columbia: Demographic Tendencies and Trends, 1961–1986* (Vancouver: Simon Fraser University Gerontology Research Centre and University of British Columbia Centre for Human Settlements, 1991), 10.
14. Raymond Chipeniuk, "Planning for Rural Amenity Migration," *Plan Canada* 45:1 (Spring 2005), 15–17.
15. Gerald Hodge, *Managing an Aging Population in Rural Canada: The Role and Response of Local Government* (Toronto: ICURR Press, 1993).
16. Gerald Walker, "Networks and Politics in the Fringe," in Michael Bunce and Michael Troughton, eds., *The Pressures of Change in Rural Canada,* Geographical Monograph No. 14 (Toronto: York University Department of Geography, 1984), 202–214.
17. Greg Halseth, "Community and Land Use Planning Debate: An Example from Rural British Columbia," *Environment and Planning A* 28 (1996), 1279–1298.
18. Neil Rothwell, Ray D. Bollman, et al., *Migration to and from Rural and Small Town Canada* (Ottawa: Statistics Canada, March 2002), Rural and Small Town Analysis Bulletin 3:6, Cat. No. 21-006-XIE.
19. Wayne J. Caldwell and Michael Toombs, "Rural Planning, the Community and Large Livestock Facilities," *Plan Canada,* 39:5 (November 1999), 27–29.
20. Wayne J. Caldwell, "The Evolving Nature of Agricultural Production: Implications for Planners," *Plan Canada* 49:4 (Winter 2009), 43–47.
21. Paul Crawford, "Preserving Rural Character in an Urban Region: Rural Planning in the Township of Langley," *Plan Canada* 33:2 (March 1993), 16–23.
22. Alexander C. Vias, "Bigger Stores, More Stores, or No Stores: Paths of Retail Restructuring in Rural America," *Journal of Rural Studies* 20:3 (July 2004), 303–318.
23. Wayne J. Caldwell, "Rural Planning in Canada," *Plan Canada* 45:3 (Autumn 2005), 25–28.
24. Hanna, "Planning for Sustainability."
25. Gerald Hodge, *Planning for Small Communities, A Report to the Ontario Planning Act Review Committee* (Toronto, 1978), Background Paper No. 5.
26. Wayne J. Caldwell and Claire Dodds-Weir, "Canadian Approaches to the Preservation of Farmland," *Plan Canada* 49:2 (Summer 2009), 17–20.
27. Barry E. Smith and Susan Hald, "The Rural–Urban Connection: Growing Together in Greater Vancouver," *Plan Canada* 44:1 (Spring 2004), 36–39.
28. Hugh J. Gayler, "Planning Reform in Ontario and Its Implications for Urban Containment and Agricultural Land Use," *Small Town* 26:4 (January–February 1996), 4–13.
29. Peter Mah, "Changing the Dynamics of Rural Planning: A Rural Manitoba Planning Perspective," *Plan Canada* 38:2 (March 1998), 25–29.
30. Kyra McCardle, "'Rural' Planning in an Urbanizing Region," *Plan Canada* (49:4 (Winter 2009), 18–21.
31. Newfoundland, Department of Municipal Affairs, *Planning for Smaller Towns* (St. John's: Project Planning Associates, 1968), 26.
32. Alberta, Task Force on Urbanization and the Future, *High River,* Alberta (Edmonton, 1973).
33. Felice Mazzoni, "Ucluelet: The Little Town That Could," PIBC News 43:2 (April 2001), 12–13.
34. McCardle, "'Rural' Planning in an Urbanizing Region."
35. Jennifer Ball, Wayne Caldwell, and Kay Pranis, "Using Circles to Build Communication in Planning," *Plan Canada* 47:1 (Spring 2007), 17–19.
36. www.reddi.gov.on.ca
37. Statistics Canada, *Retail Store Survey* (Annual), Cat. No. 63F0022XIE.
38. Judith Getzels and Charles Thurow, eds., *Rural and Small Town Planning* (Chicago: American Planning Association, 1979), 89–95; and Lane Kendig, *Performance Zoning* (Chicago: Planners Press, 1980).
39. Urban Land Institute, *Flexible Zoning: How It Works* (Washington, 1988).
40. "Ucluelet ... ," PIBC News.
41. Thomas L. Daniels, "Where Does Cluster Zoning Fit in Farmland Protection?" *Journal of the American Planning Association* 63:1 (Winter 1997), 129–133.
42. Randall Arendt, *Rural by Design* (Chicago: American Planning Association, 1994).
43. Corwin Cambray and Laurie McNab, "Agricultural Easements and the Niagara Tender Fruit Belt," *Plan Canada,* 35:2 (March 1995), 37.
44. Donald Aubrey, "Principles for Successful Community Planning in Northern Native Communities," *Plan Canada* 39:3 (July/August 1999), 12–15.
45. Peter Boothroyd, "To Set Their Own Course: Indian Band Planning and Indian Affairs," Paper Prepared for the BC Region, Indian and Inuit Affairs Canada, 1984; and Margaret Jones, *The Community is Quite Capable* (Guelph, ON: University of Guelph School of Rural Planning and Development, 1985).
46. Cf. Jeffrey Cook, "Building on the Traditions of the Past: The Rise and Resurgence of First Nations CCP," *Plan Canada* 48:2 (Summer 2008), 13–16; and Laura Mannell and Heather Ternoway, "The Need to do More: Advancing Planning with First Nation Communities," *Plan Canada* 48:2 (Summer 2008), 21–23
47. K. Rich et al., "Location Vocation, Natuashish: Planning a New Aboriginal Community, *Plan Canada* 37:6 (December 1997), 16–17.
48. This story is told compellingly by Margo Pfeiff, "Out of Davis Inlet," *Canadian Geographic* 123:1 (January 2003), 43–48.
49. Hillarie Greening and Neida Gonzales, "From Theory to Practice: Land Use Planning in the Gwich'in Settlement Area," *Plan Canada* 39:3 (July–August 1999), 16–18; and David Witty, "The Practice behind the Theory: Co-management as a Community Development Tool," *Plan Canada* 34:1 (January 1994), 22–27.
50. Stephen Gallagher, "Intergovernmental Community Planning: Sliammon First Nation and City of Powell River Experience," *Plan Canada* 48:2 (Summer 2008), 35–38.
51. Gallager, "Intergovernmental Community Planning."
52. Rahul Ray and David Harper, "The Path Forward: First Nations Land Use Planning as a Unifying Community Proceess," *Plan Canada* 48:2 (Summer 2008), 43–45; and *Standing Buffalo Dakota Nation Community Plan* (Halifax: Cities & Environment Unit Dalhousie University, 2011); and www.ceunit.dal.ca
53. Christine Calihoo, "The First Nations Comprehensive Community Plan Process: Potential Impediments to Success," *Plan Canada* 48:2 (Summer 2008), 1–3
54. Leonie Sandercock, "Interface: Planning and Indigenous Communities," *Planning Theory and Practice* 5:1 (March 2004), 94–97.
55. Christine Calihoo, personal communication, August 16, 2012.
56. Laura Mannell and Heather Ternoway, "The Need to Do More."
57. Leonie Sandercock, "Commentary: Indigenous Planning and the Burden of Colonialism," *Planning Theory and Practice* 5:1 (March 2004), 118–124.

Reference Notes (continued)

58. Fyre Jane Graveline, *Circle Works: Transforming Eurocentric Consciousness* (Halifax: Fernwood, 1998).
59. Ted Jojola, "Indigenous Planning an Emerging Context," *Canadian Journal of Urban Research* 17:1 Supplement (2008), 37–47.
60. Pamela Sweet, "Sustainable Development in Northern Urban Areas," *Plan Canada* 44:4 (Winter 2004), 41–43.
61. Erik Borre Nilsen, "Rethinking Place in Planning: Opportunities in Northern and Aboriginal Planning in Nunavut, Canada," *Canadian Journal of Urban Research* 14:1 (2005), 22–38; and John Peters, "Aboriginal Perspectives on Planning in Canada Decolonizing the Process: A Discussion with Four Aboriginal Practitioners," *Plan Canada* 43:2 (Summer 2003), 39–41.
62. Cities and Environment Unit, Faculty of Architecture and Planning, Dalhousie University, *First Nations Community Planning Model*, 2nd edn., Halifax (2003), www.ceunit.dal.ca
63. Norman Pressman, *Shaping Cities for Winter: Climatic Comfort and Sustainable Design* (Prince George, BC: Winter Cities Association, 2004).
64. Floyd Dykeman, "A Return to the Past for a Rural Community-Based Planning and Action Program for the Future: A Challenge for Planners," in F. Dykeman, ed., *Integrated Rural Planning and Development* (Sackville, NB: Mount Allison University Small Town and Rural Research Program, 1988), 147–166.
65. Wayne J. Caldwell, "Rural Canada: Designing a Desirable Future," *Plan Canada* 32:4 (September 1992), 24–29.

Internet Resources

Chapter-Relevant Sites

Planning Canadian Communities
www.planningcanadiancommunities.ca

Ontario Ministry of Agriculture local economic analysis tools
www.reddi.gov.on.ca

Municipal District (County) of Rocky View, Alberta
www.gov.mdrockyview.ab.ca

Rural Cape Breton: Eastern District Planning Commission
www.edpc.ca/

Newfoundland and Labrador, Department of Rural Development
www.ibrd.gov.nl.ca/

First Nations Planning: Dalhousie University
www.ceunit.dal.ca

First Nations Comprehensive Community Planning (CCP) Handbook
www.aadnc-aandc.gc.ca/eng/1100100021972/1100100022090

Planning for People and Places in the Community

Introduction

The broad land use categories and transportation components shown on a community plan map are, in effect, a graphic representation of community life. In the map spaces they each occupy, a multitude of human activities is expected to take place: shopping, driving automobiles, attending school, living in dwellings, playing in a park, waiting for a bus, working, walking, hanging out, and so on. They are beyond classification and many are layered one on another. In other words, these map spaces are meant to accommodate the everyday life of the community's citizens and visitors. Who are, of course, diverse in so many ways: some are young, some speak another language, some are frail, some are women, some have secure housing, some are fearful. In turn, the people and their activities make use of various portions of community space to which they are attached by associations through need, familiarity, and memories. These are "places" in people's lives; one's local neighbourhood is the iconic situation for most. Some of these places are pleasant and exciting while others may be fearsome or out of bounds physically and socially.

The community plan that encompasses the entire community is seldom able to do more than allude to the spatial and human nuances of its residents and their myriad activities. In order to bridge localized spatial situations and needs with community planning goals and objectives, planners may undertake three kinds of planning: (1) Secondary plans are prepared for individual neighbourhoods, special districts (e.g., downtown, heritage areas, waterfronts), land use corridors, and important transportation nodes. Chapter 11 describes such plans. (2) Plans for various infrastructures that gird the community and enable places within it to function are discussed in Chapter 12. And (3) plans made in response to the needs of specific populations such as youth and older adults and are found in Chapter 13; this chapter also examines the place needs of other human groups that are not yet being formally addressed in plans.

The image above is from the Toronto Avenues and Mid-Rise Buildings Study. These corridors are good locations for intensification at a scale set so that buildings should be no higher than the width of the street. The City of Toronto's plan won 2011 urban design awards from the CIP and the Royal Architectural Institute of Canada.

Source: Brook McIlroy (www.brookmcilroy.com)

Chapter Eleven

Planning for Special Places: Neighbourhood and District Plans

In the large-scale task of putting cities together in which we all live and work, we have not yet stretched our abilities.

Humphrey Carver, 1955

It is rare that a comprehensive land use plan can cover all the development issues of a community other than that for the smallest village or town. So, special plans at several different scales will be required for most communities' natural and built environments. For larger communities, a regional plan for the area may serve as the prime contextual plan for all constituent communities (see Chapter 8). The urban community plan (Chapter 9) typically provides the context and policy framework for all other plans for the municipality.

A community plan, if it is to be **comprehensive** and **long range**, will of necessity be a **general** plan. It will be a plan that deals with all the essential physical developments in the community environment but usually not in detail. It is not intended to be a blueprint document but one that presents the major proposals for the community's future physical development in general terms. Thus, it uses a limited number of very broad land use categories, shows only major transportation routes and public facilities, and provides only a general picture of the locations and sizes of major facilities and districts in the city or town. The aim is to provide a guide—both graphically and verbally—to all the major elements in the community built environment and the desired relationships between them. The general plan map for ville de Montréal illustrates the approach described here (Figure 11.1).

Thus, the focus of the community plan for a larger city is on the **main issues** in physical development and the **major proposals** for future development. This is primarily to help direct discussion and debate in the community so as to arrive at agreement

| Figure 11.1 | Comprehensive Land Use Plan Map: Montréal, 2004 |

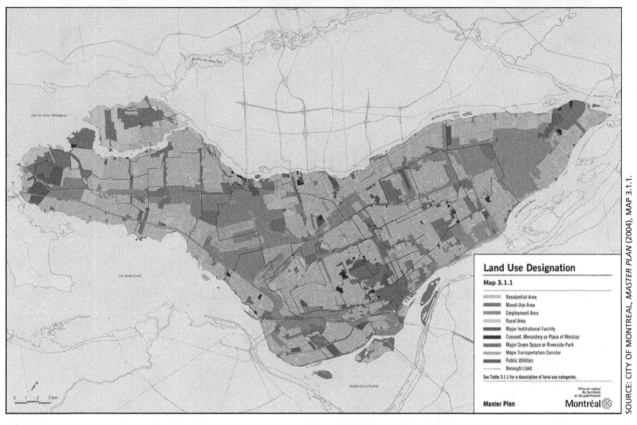

Land Use Designation

Map 3.1.1

- Residential Area
- Mixed-Use Area
- Employment Area
- Rural Area
- Major Institutional Facility
- Convent, Monastery or Place of Worship
- Major Green Space or Riverside Park
- Major Transportation Corridor
- Public Utilities
- Borough Limit

See Table 3.1.1 for a description of land use categories.

Mise en valeur du territoire et du patrimoine

Master Plan   Montréal

The main land uses for Montréal are shown in this map from the 2004 Master Plan, which won a Canadian Institute of Planners' (CIP) National Award of Distinction. The plan serves as a policy framework for the entire island. The detailed policies and proposals for individual neighbourhoods and special districts are found in plans prepared by the boroughs.

on policies and proposals that affect not only the overall functioning of the community but also provide the context for plans that address specific areas and projects.

Every community plan is also a mixture of the general and the specific. Some elements in a community are so prominent—a civic centre, the main thoroughfares, a large institution, the downtown, historic neighbourhoods—that they cannot and should not be cloaked in generalities. What the plan will probably highlight is their relationship with other parts of the community. Some elements may be areas of special importance to the community's future form and character, such as a waterfront area, a district of historic buildings, special vistas, or a greenbelt. The community plan may contain distinct sections devoted to these special areas, but more often it

serves as a general framework for specific area plans that are developed later.

Secondary plans are often prepared for individual neighbourhoods, special districts (such as the downtown), land use corridors, and important nodes in the transportation system. These plans can be for the redevelopment of existing built-up areas or for undeveloped land, using subdivisions or site plans, each of which is discussed below. The special functional plans for community-wide infrastructure such as greenways, transportation, or social programs are discussed in Chapter 12. For the discussion here, consider these questions:

- *Why is it necessary to have secondary plans within a community?*
- *How does the overall community plan influence each secondary plan in a community?*

Neighbourhood/Secondary Plans

Great neighbourhoods such as Winnipeg's Osborne Village (Figure 11.2) evolve over time to acquire characteristics that are much loved by the residents, such as walkable streets, local shopping, and a mix of housing and community institutions.[1] A neighbourhood plan can help enhance or protect these characteristics, especially once a neighbourhood becomes so popular that redevelopment is proposed for many properties. The 2006 Osborne Village Neighbourhood Plan includes policies intended to maintain its long-standing urban character.

Neighbourhoods that are stable and have few new development proposals are often simply guided by the general residential policies of a community plan. Many Canadian cities make separate plans for existing neighbourhoods that are expanding or under development pressure, like Calgary's Glenbrook Glamorgan plan (Figure 11.3). These plans are usually prepared by city staff, with much participation of the neighbourhood stakeholders.[2] A municipality may also prepare redevelopment plans for neighbourhoods that are in decline.

SOURCE: CHRISTOPHER BAKER/CITY OF WINNIPEG.

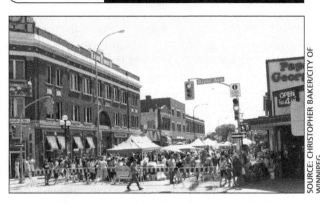

Figure 11.2	Neighbourhood Planning: Osborne Village, Winnipeg, 2012

A street festival in Winnipeg's Osborne Village, which was voted "Canada's Great Neighbourhood" in the 2012 Great Places in Canada competition.

These are called Area Redevelopment Plans in Alberta or Community Improvement Plans in Ontario. They are often used to target special policies and funding to

Figure 11.3	Special-Area Plan for a Residential District, Calgary

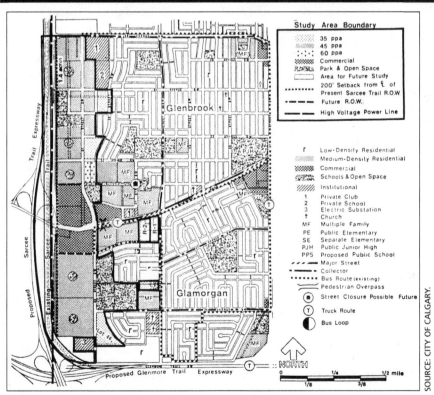

SOURCE: CITY OF CALGARY.

In order to provide a more detailed view of land uses, traffic, and facilities in different districts, special-area (or secondary) plans are prepared. This one is for several Calgary neighbourhoods.

improve social conditions, clean up polluted lands, and update housing and infrastructure (see Chapter 17).

Many Canadian cities also require that secondary plans be prepared for new neighbourhoods on the urban fringe, rather than proceeding with piecemeal subdivision of every farm or rural property. These plans, often at the scale of a section of land (260 hectares, or 640 acres), are usually prepared by planning consultants who are retained by a consortium of landowners. These secondary plans typically protect environmentally sensitive areas, designate general land uses, locate the major roads, and identify sites for community institutions, as shown in the Cornell secondary plan (Figure 5.16, page 120). They must conform to the municipality's community plan, development standards, and design guidelines. Secondary plans are usually reviewed by municipal staff, revised, and then adopted by the local government as a framework for development of the lands. The developers typically subdivide their lands in accordance with the secondary plan in many phases over a decade or more.

Since there are often few adjacent residents near "greenfield" sites, there may not be much public participation in the generation of secondary plans for new neighbourhoods on the urban fringe, other than the statutory hearings for their rezoning from rural to suburban uses. This trend has begun to change with the advent of design charettes for new communities. The Cornell plan (Figure 5.16, page 120) was developed in a week-long exercise that involved hundreds of local stakeholders. The charette plans gave detailed ideas of the future form of the new neighbourhoods and were later simplified to be adopted as a Markham secondary plan.

Special District Plans

Residential areas comprise the largest land use in Canadian cities, so it is not surprising that neighbourhood plans are the most common secondary plans. In addition, the larger cities may have special district plans for their downtown, institutional precincts, medical centres, cultural districts, or airports.

Downtown Plans

The Central Business District (CBD) is the area most commonly singled out for special planning consideration in most communities, because the downtown is usually the key to a community's cultural and economic vitality. The CBD often provides residents and visitors with the strongest visual image of a community; it represents the most dominant concentration of land values and investment in property, and also provides

a locus for social transactions. If the downtown shopfronts are vacant and the sidewalks are empty, the community appears to be in decline, even if there is plenty of retail space in suburban big-box stores. As such, the CBD needs to be continually maintained and renovated in order to function effectively. It is also a complex area requiring detailed planning analysis and design.[3]

CBD plans tend to focus on three aspects of the downtown area. The first is the functional arrangement of land use, because most downtowns accommodate several functions: retail shopping, financial and business services, entertainment, and government institutions. In larger communities, these functions may occupy discrete, but often overlapping, parts of downtown. The second aspect is transportation and parking, for the downtown tends to contain those functions to which the entire community needs access. The third is the three-dimensional character—the urban design—of downtown. CBD plans often address the heights of buildings, prominent views, walkway systems, squares and open space, mall boulevards, and street furnishings (Figure 11.4).[4]

Concerns over community design and architecture are usually greater in CBD plans than in any other physical plan. The best downtown planning also aspires to create good public spaces to improve the quality of life of the entire community.[5] Copenhagen's Jan Gehl and New York's William Whyte conducted extensive research into public space design that improves community life.[6] A recent plan for Saskatoon's public spaces (Figure 11.5) built upon these ideas, using extensive fieldwork by University of Saskatchewan geography and planning students.

| Figure 11.4 | Elgin Street in the Downtown Sudbury Master Plan, 2011, 2012 |

This image illustrates changed land uses and public space improvements proposed for Elgin Street in downtown Sudbury. Note the green street components and mixed-use buildings on the right, with improved sidewalks and pedestrian-oriented shops. The plan won an honourable mention for neighbourhood planning in the CIP's 2012 awards program.

Figure 11.5 | Activity and Urban Form in Saskatoon Public Spaces, 2012

SOURCE: CITY OF SASKATOON & CO. ARCHITECTURE.

This image for an improved public realm in downtown Saskatoon was based upon extensive research and surveys of how the city's public spaces were being used by its citizens. The plan won a 2012 CIP New Planning Initiative Award.

Institutional District Plans

Many government agencies and public institutions prepare long-range plans, since public agencies are among the largest managers of land and buildings,[7] especially in capital cities. Public institutions such as hospitals, colleges, and universities also have complex long-range plans for their lands.

Capital Cities and Civic Centres

Capital cities usually contain unique elements associated with their status as a seat of government, such as a legislative building, departmental offices, cultural facilities, and appeal courts. Capital cities may also have particular planning issues associated with official residences, memorials and monuments, and political relations between the local, provincial, and federal governments.[8] The federal government's National Capital Commission (NCC) has prepared regional and institutional plans for the Ottawa area for over a century,[9] and provincial capital plans have been prepared for Regina's Wascana Centre, Yellowknife, and la ville de Québec, among others. In contrast, Toronto's status as the capital of Ontario barely affects

its community planning; the municipal government was not even willing to protect the grand vista up University Avenue to Queen's Park from new buildings towering over the provincial legislature.[10]

Some capital cities have a "capital complex"—a planned precinct that includes the legislature and other important institutional buildings, such as a courthouse or museum.[11] This idea was extended to municipalities in the City Beautiful period, when community plans often included a civic centre containing a monumental city hall, a courthouse, and cultural facilities. The planned civic centre continues today in the precincts near the city halls of Edmonton and Mississauga.

University and College Plans

Most colleges and universities have a master plan for development of their institutions. Almost all universities were initially built on the edge of their host communities, but many of the older institutions (Dalhousie, UNB, McGill, Montréal, Ottawa, Queen's, and Toronto) have been surrounded by urban growth and are now located in the inner city. These institutions must now plan for urban infill development and expect town-gown conflict as they expand into long-established residential neighbourhoods.

The provincial universities of the early 20th century (UBC, Alberta, Saskatchewan, Manitoba, and Memorial) were granted large land parcels on the edge of their host communities. The initial campus plans for these institutions were based on public transit and had to adapt to the change to automobile access after 1950. In contrast, most of the baby boom universities were planned for automobility from the beginning, with a ring road that separated free parking in large lots on the outside and a pedestrian precinct forming the inside of the superblock. These institutions were usually located in the outer suburbs and one was built on a mountaintop (Simon Fraser). Some universities and colleges from this era experimented with the Modern architectural concept of mega-structures, interconnecting many buildings into one large complex, using tunnels or above-grade pedestrian bridges. The current challenge for these institutions is to further intensify and urbanize their campus settings and to add high-capacity public transit. For example, York University is re-urbanizing its campus to focus on new subway stations, while other universities are adding high-capacity bus routes, sometimes combined with transit passes.

Some community colleges, polytechnics, and CEGEPs were built on greenfield suburban sites, but many cities also built a downtown college. These institutions now have the same infill planning challenges as the older universities, but many seem to have embraced their urban setting from the beginning. Planning researchers began to notice that the few successful downtown districts in medium-sized cities (Halifax, Kingston, Victoria) were enlivened by downtown universities and colleges.[12] This observation became an urban renewal trend early in the 21st century as cities deliberately courted satellite campuses of colleges and universities to their downtowns (see Planning Issue 11.1). Fortunately, students are one of the few groups that consider living over a pub to be a locational advantage, so many new 24-hour residents have followed the new institutions into the downtown.

Meanwhile, the suburban universities with large land banks have also been catalysts for other forms of development. Most universities are building more student housing on campus, while UBC and Simon Fraser are developing large mixed-use communities with a strong emphasis on high-quality, environmentally friendly design (see Figure 1.1 , page 5). Victoria, Waterloo, and McMaster are developing technology parks to foster spinoff companies from their research activities, and many suburban universities have established a downtown campus for continuing education, especially in business. Other suburban institutions have moved some programs downtown to connect to a livelier cultural community, such as UBC in Robson Square, Simon Fraser's new arts campus in the Woodwards building[13] and Laval, which returned its architecture program to its original building within the walls of historic Québec.

| **Planning Issue 11.1** | **Students Bring New Vitality to Brantford's Core** |

Special to The Globe and Mail
Published Monday, Jun. 04 2012

Students Bring New Vitality to Brantford's Core

Jennifer Lewington

As an 11-year old growing up in Brantford, Ont., Peter Vicano delivered the local newspaper, the Expositor, which operated from a 1850s-era downtown landmark.

Today, the 61-year-old developer is converting the red stone building (the newspaper relocated in 2010) into 65 apartment units of student housing leased to the satellite campus here of Wilfrid Laurier University in nearby Waterloo. The $11-million project is one example of how post-secondary institutions are renewing mid-size Ontario cities, anxious to reinvent themselves as 21st century destinations for high-value jobs and investment. In Brantford, higher education is an undeniable catalyst but, alone, cannot complete the rejuvenation.

"The second shoe is going to have to fall in Brantford," says Rick Haldenby, director of the school of architecture at the University of Waterloo. "The postsecondary institutions are there and now the question is 'what private enterprise are you going to be able to add to that mix?' "

Back in the mid-1990s, teaming up with a university was the key for an industrial city situated high above the Grand River known for its famous sons, Alexander Graham Bell and Wayne Gretzky. Hammered by the bankruptcies of Massey Ferguson and other farm equipment manufacturers in the previous decade, Brantford suffered a steep decline with a city centre of vacant buildings, strip clubs and crime.

The city of 93,000 has now become a satellite for three universities and three colleges. A $58.4-million YMCA facility (with Laurier and three levels of government), is planned for the edge of downtown where the city got a black eye in 2010 for demolishing 41 pre-Confederation buildings. The proposed modern Y—a pencil box on stilts that drops three storeys to a lower street—presents a dramatic contrast to the 19th century commercial buildings dotted through downtown.

Over the past dozen years, institutions have invested $130-million downtown, including $21-million from the city.

In 1999, the city invested $1.4-million to renovate the former Carnegie Library, turning over the elegant domed facility to Laurier for $1. From 39 students, Laurier Brantford has grown to 2,700 students in buildings that it owns or leases, with more expansion in the works.

Prior to Laurier's arrival, Mohawk College operated a campus from a south-end industrial area. After failing to move its satellite downtown, Mohawk dispersed students to other campuses in the region, but leased a former movie theatre in Brantford's core "academic district" for some classes. "Great downtowns are great people places and so why not move your people there," says Mohawk president Robert MacIsaac. Ontario colleges have a mandate to promote economic development, but Mohawk eyed downtown for its attractive learning environment. "It is about student life and having students in places that are interesting," Mr. MacIsaac says.

As students and faculty breathe life into the core—the city also built Harmony Square on a main street as a public space for summer concerts and ice skating—local businesses report a pick-up in activity.

Several factors still weigh against a fast infusion of private investment, seen by Mr. Haldenby as vital to robust renewal. For one, postsecondary programs run only eight months of the year. Moreover, the former Massey Ferguson site, on 52 acres of contaminated land about one kilometre from downtown, awaits a clean-up effort with no obvious buyer.

Still, newcomers are bullish on Brantford.

In 2009, architect Paul Sapounzi, president of Ventin Group Architects, moved his company headquarters to a former bank building just opposite the Expositor.

The postsecondary presence, the new Y and talk of performing arts centre are essential first steps to remaking Brantford, he says. "Commercial vibrancy in a downtown is the very last thing and it is not something you can create without the fundamental machinery that is being installed right now."

As Mr. Vicano readies the former newspaper building for occupancy this fall, he is cautiously optimistic. "Brantford isn't where it should be and has to go," he says. "We still have not reached the critical mass of an economy, but we are going to get there."

Source: © JENNIFER LEWINGTON

Hospital and Medical Centre Plans

Many large hospitals have been consolidating into large health centres consisting of interconnected structures. These medical centres exhibit the most advanced form of megastructure planning, with bridges and tunnels linking buildings to ensure that patients and staff can remain within the controlled environment. These health centres are large employers and require good public transit access and large parking structures if they are in suburban locations.[14]

Hospital consolidation and closure of older facilities create opportunities for urban redevelopment. Controversial proposals for redevelopment of former hospital sites in New Westminster (the Woodlands project; see page 1), Toronto (Queen Street), and Calgary have recently won awards for good planning practice. The City of Calgary managed the planning and redevelopment of its former General Hospital site into a model Transit-Oriented Development (Figure 11.6).

Cultural District Plans

Many cities are planning to reinforce their cultural activities as part of community economic development strategies focused on tourism and the creative economy (see Chapters 7 and 13).[15] These plans sometimes include a new precinct for cultural activities, often in the

| Figure 11.6 | The Bridges: Redevelopment Plan for the Calgary General Hospital Site, 2005 |

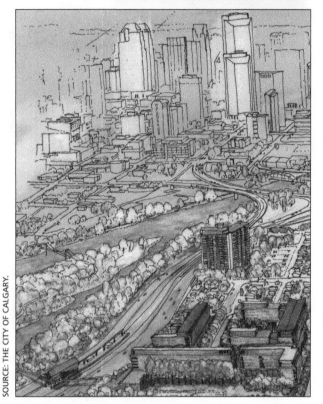

The hospital was served by the Bridgeland LRT station. The redevelopment plan creates a mixed-use neighbourhood with high-density, medium-rise buildings surrounding a large central park and community centre. Street-level shops transformed the struggling retail on 1st Avenue, on the right of the image. The Bridges plan won a 2005 National Urban Design Award.

downtown. Some of these cultural district plans recall the civic centres of the City Beautiful era, minus the imposing city hall. The mid-20th century version of these cultural districts was influenced by New York's Lincoln Centre, an urban renewal project with an opera house, theatre, and music hall executed in high Modern style, but with a site plan influenced by classical precedents from Rome. The French national government adopted a different strategy, building new cultural institutions (*les grand projets*) carefully located across Paris to reinforce that city's claim to be the world capital of culture.[16]

The most interesting Canadian example of cultural district planning can be found in Montréal. The municipal and provincial governments initially embarked on a Modern downtown urban renewal project in the style of Lincoln Centre, producing the monumental Place des Arts complex near the edges of its rather seedy warehouse and adult entertainment districts. The 1960s urban renewal programs left many other vacant lots and parking lots, while the departure of industry left empty multi-level factories and warehouses. Montréal began to program these vacant outdoor spaces for cultural events in the late 20th century, initially as summer festivals (Just for Laughs, Festival International de Jazz) and then year-round, as creative activities began to fill the empty warehouses. The municipal government collaborated with the cultural industries on a plan to attract a critical mass of activities into the district, inter-connected with purpose-built streets and plazas that can accommodate large crowds for festivals (Figure 11.7). The entrances for the many theatres, galleries, schools, and cabarets scattered across the district are cleverly marked by clusters of red lights that shine down onto the sidewalk—an example of an urban design intervention that is uniquely appropriate for its use and location, since it functions better at night and best in winter, when the sidewalks are dusted with snow.

Airport Planning

Airports have replaced harbours and railway stations as the most important transportation gateways to most Canadian communities. Planning for large airports was

| Figure 11.7 | Le Quartier des Spectacles, Montréal, 2007 |

Crowds throng Montréal's entertainment district, le Quartier des Spectacles, all summer long. This image shows spectators and pedestrians at the Festival International de Jazz de Montréal.

the responsibility of the federal government until the late 20th century, when many facilities were passed on to local airport authorities. The airports are so important to the local economy that the larger cities have established independent airport authorities with the mandate to plan, build, and operate not just an airport but also a surrounding industrial and commercial district sometimes called an "aerotropolis."[17] These special authorities have the ability to borrow capital funds and repay them through airport user fees, similar to other implementation agencies (see Chapter 17). An airport authority will also plan and finance the extensive infrastructure required to connect to the local network.

Airports require enormous areas of level land, and must be surrounded by land uses with low buildings and occupants that are not affected by the noise of frequent jet aircraft. Sites adjacent to water bodies and industrial districts are ideal for airports. In contrast, building new residential areas nearby is a mistake, both for safety reasons and since noise complaints can severely restrict airport operations. So airports must be planned perhaps fifty years in advance to ensure that suitable sites are available before the expanding metropolis swallows them. This is not an easy task and sometimes results in a "planning disaster," as in London's search for a site for a third airport.[18] In the 1970s, the federal government acquired new sites for second airports for Montréal and Toronto. The Mirabel airport was a premature white elephant and construction of the Pickering airport was stopped by citizen protests.[19] However, the airport authorities have held onto the sites for decades, because both Trudeau and Pearson airports are now completely surrounded by urban development and face difficulties for future expansion, as air traffic continues to grow. Even if regular passenger traffic remains concentrated at the older facilities, air cargo, military, charter, and general aviation are all being displaced to alternate locations.

Some cities concluded that their older airports could never be properly expanded, and have developed completely new facilities further out on the urban fringe. Abandoned airport sites within the built-up area of a community present opportunities for large-scale urban redevelopment. The Bombardier airfield in the St. Laurent district of Montréal has been redeveloped into the new Bois Franc community, while Downsview Park is being built on the site of the former Canadian Forces Base Downsview in Toronto, following an international design competition.[20] Closing a larger urban facility such as Denver's Stapleton Field or Edmonton's City Centre Airport can create a rare opportunity to plan a large-scale expansion to the metropolitan area that is not on the urban fringe. The City of Edmonton has launched a major public consultation and planning exercise for the redevelopment of the former airport into a series of high-density, medium-rise, mixed-use neighbourhoods, interspersed with a new college campus and other employment lands (see Figure 11.8).

Heritage District Plans

Many Canadian cities have some heritage-protection policies for older downtown districts, such as Halifax's Historical Properties, Vieux Montréal, Ottawa's ByWard Market, or Vancouver's Gastown. In recent years, heritage-conservation areas have spread outside the downtown to coherent residential neighbourhoods and former industrial districts such as Vancouver's Granville Island, Montréal's Lachine Canal, and Toronto's Distillery District.[21] These heritage plans typically call for preservation of important historical buildings and create design guidelines to encourage new infill development that is complementary in scale and materials.[22] The objective is not to freeze an area in a particular period of the past, but to keep the district economically viable while allowing new buildings that are appropriate and not just imitations of past styles. This strategy is particularly necessary in places like downtown St. John's, where large areas of the city are composed of historic buildings (Figure 11.9). Outstanding heritage areas such as ville de Québec's Historic District and Old Town Lunenburg are UNESCO World Heritage sites, with even more complex policy controls.[23]

| Figure 11.8 | Edmonton City Centre Airport Redevelopment Plan, 2012 |

SOURCE: TRANSFORMING EDMONTON: BRINGING OUR CITY VISION TO LIFE, BLATCHFORD REDEVELOPMENT, CITY OF EDMONTON.

Preliminary images for the sustainable redevelopment of the former Edmonton City Centre Airport site.

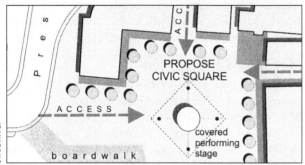

SOURCE: DOWNTOWN ST. JOHN'S STRATEGY FOR ECONOMIC DEVELOPMENT AND HERITAGE PRESERVATION, CITY OF ST. JOHN'S.

Figure 11.9 Heritage Strategy for Downtown St. John's, Newfoundland, 2002

Most blocks of downtown St. John's contain historic buildings, so the city had to develop a combined strategy for both economic development and heritage preservation. The plan has guided the city's actions for over a decade and won a 2002 CIP implementation award.

Residential neighbourhoods with large concentrations of older homes are also being protected because of the cultural heritage value of their streetscapes and collections of buildings from a particular era. The planning for these heritage conservation districts usually begins with an inventory of the buildings and landscapes in the neighbourhood, followed by an analysis of their cultural heritage properties and identifying characteristics that contribute to that value. These characteristics are typically protected by design guidelines that municipal planners will consult when considering redevelopment proposals. Property owners often have concerns about restrictions on the repair or value of their buildings in the beginning of the planning process, but evaluation of the impact of heritage conservation districts has shown generally positive results over time.[24]

Corridor Plans

Corridors connect neighbourhoods and districts within the urban fabric or connect patches in the landscape matrix. Some street and river corridors are so important that specific plans are prepared to protect their special features and guide any future development.

River Corridor Plans

River and stream corridors can be important components of environmental planning using the principles of landscape ecology (Chapter 7), and also can be links in a greenway system for recreational planning (Chapter 12). In natural systems planning, a valley can be a corridor connecting important habitat patches, such as an upstream marsh and a river delta. Environmental planning to protect these corridors might focus on improving water quality and reducing the impact of physical infrastructures that cross the corridor. The plans for river corridors often use the watershed's topographical boundaries to define the study area and require complex ecological analysis to restore a river's health. The restoration of Toronto's Don River (Figure 12.3, page 288) is an example of a long-term plan to rehabilitate a valley that had been severely degraded by a 6–8 lane expressway, railways, diversion of the river into a concrete channel, and the filling of the marsh at its mouth. Michael Hough's plan focused on improving natural processes in the river valley, but it also allowed for better recreational use through such services as a bicycle path and pedestrian trail.[25] Other river corridor plans may have a stronger recreational and open-space focus, such as the Red Deer River Valley and Tributaries plan (Figure 12.1, page 288). If the corridor is wide enough, relatively low-impact recreational uses may coexist with the natural function of the valley. The necessary width of a green corridor requires careful analysis of local conditions; no single standard is appropriate.

There will always be strong pressures for human use of these green corridors in a metropolitan region, either as important components of a parks system or as infrastructure corridors. Frederick Law Olmsted showed, in 1890, how one corridor could serve multiple purposes in his plans for the Muddy River in Boston's Emerald Necklace parks system.[26] Unfortunately, these green seams often appeared to be the least expensive route for major infrastructure corridors such as railways in the 19th century and expressways in the 20th. The damage to the corridors was often gradual, as in Boston's Storrow Drive, or Chicago's Lakeshore Drive, where parkways changed from a pleasure drive for a horse and carriage to wide expressways one lane at a time, over a period of 50 years. Similarly, the mouth of Olmsted's Muddy River is now an off-ramp for the Interstate 95 highway and the Don Valley "Parkway" has destroyed any semblance of a park in most of its valley. The first objective of river valley corridor plans must be to protect these natural resources for future generations.

Street Corridor Plans

Many Canadian community plans call for intensification along major streets, especially if there is a transit line in the corridor. Unfortunately, as a general policy this has little effect, because the small parcels along the streets make it difficult to assemble property, and residents in the adjacent neighbourhoods object to many of the projects proposed. Toronto has proposed mid-rise development along its streetcar avenues for over twenty years, with results awaited.

Redevelopment along a street corridor often requires a specific plan for the corridor, negotiated with the adjacent neighbourhoods. The scale of the proposed redevelopment and transition to the adjacent single-family homes are usually major issues that must be addressed with design guidelines. The planners must also consult with the development industry, since the five- or six-floor mixed-use structure that is often proposed in these schemes (see Figure 11.10(b)) is difficult to build economically under many current building codes.[27] Corridor redevelopment is difficult, even when the conditions appear almost perfect, such as

Vancouver's Cambie Street (Figure 11.10(a)). This corridor has a wide street with low-rise structures and the new Canada Line transit running beneath it, yet there is still considerable community resistance to redevelopment in the area.

The easiest parts of corridors to redevelop are probably greyfield sites such as the declining strip malls and former automobile commercial properties along some suburban avenues (see Figure 11.14).

Planning For Nodes

Another popular place for intensification plans are the nodes created at the intersection of two corridors. These intersections may be planned as mobility hubs or as Transit-Oriented Development (TOD).

Mobility Hubs

Mobility hubs are created at the intersection of two major transportation corridors (Figure 11.11). These hubs must be carefully planned when they are intermodal transfer sites between two or more transportation systems, such as the intersection of Bloor and Dundas Streets in Toronto, where subway, commuter rail, streetcar, and local bus routes connect. Typical concerns for a mobility hub plan include:

- Providing seamless transfers at stations
- Sustainable station access, including walking, cycling, transit priority, and kiss-and-ride facilities
- Mode share and performance targets
- Complete and safe streets, including goods movement strategies
- Strategic parking management, including commuter parking and area-wide strategies
- Phasing strategies to coordinate development with transportation infrastructure improvements[28]

Many mobility hubs also make excellent sites for TODs, while others are so congested with infrastructure that redevelopment is difficult and expensive—a wasted opportunity that might be avoided by good planning.

Transit-Oriented Development

Transit-Oriented Development was initially a planning strategy for Light Rail Transit stations, and was later extended as a central tenant of New Urbanism.[29] Most Canadian cities with rapid transit systems have had general policies in their community plans for decades to encourage development around transit stations, with limited results outside the downtowns. There was some

| Figure 11.10 | Cambie Corridor Plan, Vancouver, 2011 |

The Cambie Corridor Plan existing conditions (top) and proposals for intensification at King Edward Av. (bottom). The plan won the CIP's Sustainable Mobility Award in 2012, but has been intensely controversial. Even though there is a new rapid transit line running underneath Cambie Street, residents in the single detached homes in the adjacent blocks object to the scale of development proposed.

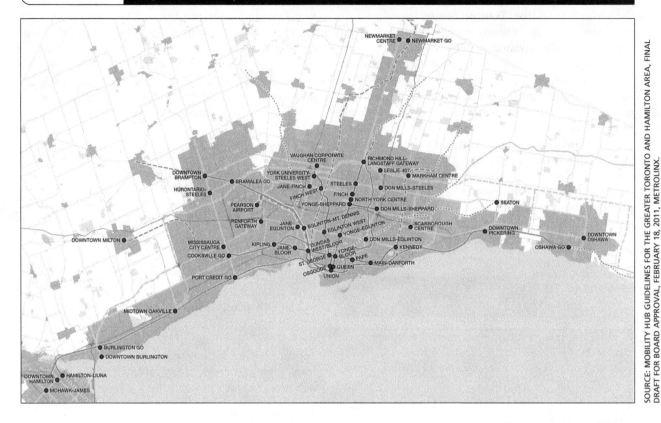

redevelopment around stations on Toronto's Yonge subway line, and at Burnaby's Metrotown, or Vancouver's Collingwood SkyTrain stations. The construction of l'Université du Québec à Montréal (UQAM) at the intersection of two Montréal subway lines could also be considered an inspired example of TOD at a mobility hub. But all too often, the suburban transit stations were surrounded by parking lots and infrastructure.[30]

TOD plans provide guidance for the redevelopment of the area around a station. They typically suggest policies such as:

- High-density development with a mixture of land uses within a five- to ten-minute walk of the transit station
- Layout of small blocks and a hierarchy of streets to allow for efficient movement of all modes of transportation
- Built form with the highest densities located closest to the station and along arterial roads
- Pedestrian and cycling environment with continuous and accessible sidewalks, traffic calming measures, street furniture, and cycling lanes
- Public amenities to promote a sense of place

- Efficient connections between different modes of transportation and public transit
- Environmental integrity and promotion of active recreational activities and passive leisure
- Parking requirements relaxed to increase emphasis on transit and active transportation[31]

Some Canadian TOD success stories are finally emerging, including TOD near an LRT station (Bridges, Calgary, Figure 11.6), commuter rail (Port Credit Village; Village de la Gare, Mont-Saint-Hilaire), bus rapid transit (Metropole, Ottawa), and a SeaBus terminal (North Vancouver).[32]

Redevelopment Plans

In most Canadian communities, districts develop in a consistent, amenable way: buildings and uses are compatible, street patterns are regular, and the renewal of properties follows acceptable community norms. But there are two typical instances where this fails to happen: one is in older areas of a community that deteriorate without benefit of rejuvenation; the other is when inadequate or incompatible development takes place in the fringe areas of communities, despite zoning regulations.

There have been many versions of city-rebuilding programs, from the urban renewal of the 1950s to the neighbourhood-improvement programs of the 1970s. The latter were federally financed programs and, although such programs no longer exist, the planning for redevelopment continues with public–private partnerships (see Figure 5.5, page 113). Provincial policies for redevelopment plans vary across the provinces. For example, in Ontario a redevelopment plan is called a community improvement plan, while in Alberta it is called an area redevelopment plan (see Figure 9.8, page 230). The statutory and fiscal policies to implement these plans are discussed in Chapter 18.

One latter-day example of redevelopment planning is that for post–World War II public-housing sites such as Regent Park in Toronto (Figure 1.2, page 6) or Benny Farm in Montréal (Figure 5.13, page 118).[33] Another is the Woodward's project in a distressed downtown area in Vancouver, in which a former department store and adjacent buildings were redeveloped for market housing (condos), social housing, shops, educational faculties, and public spaces.[34]

On a larger scale, the CBD plans discussed above always contain some redevelopment components. Redevelopment plans are also used to guide the regeneration of neighbourhoods, brownfields (polluted land), waterfronts, suburbs, greyfields (dead malls), and military bases. These types of redevelopment plans are considered below.

Neighbourhood Redevelopment Plans

The future of inner-city neighbourhoods may stimulate special-area planning, as the example from Calgary shows (Figure 11.3). Again, as with CBD plans, these special-area plans are normally framed within the context of the comprehensive plan, and they, too, pay particular attention to detailed functional arrangements of land use, transportation, and visual design.

Redevelopment plans are usually thought of in relation to older, blighted, high-density ("slum-type") neighbourhoods in large cities, but smaller cities may also have areas that require redevelopment. Cornwall, Ontario, faced such a situation when a once thriving neighbourhood went into decline with the closure of a large factory. Urban design teams from McGill University were called in to prepare strategies for urban and architectural rehabilitation to preserve the "Le Village" neighbourhood.[35]

Two other redevelopment situations frequently occur in cities. One is on the fringe of a community that may have a combination of scattered country residential acreages, junkyards, and strips of drive-in services of various kinds. The aim of a redevelopment plan would be to achieve more intensive development that is more efficient for providing public utilities and roads, or for aesthetic reasons, or both.

Brownfield Plans

Another situation for redevelopment occurs with the decline of manufacturing industries or closure of gas stations, whose polluted and abandoned sites, called "brownfields," may have potential to accommodate other uses. The Canadian definition of a brownfield is "abandoned, idle or underutilized commercial or industrial properties where past actions have caused known or suspected environmental contamination, but where there is an active potential for redevelopment."[36]

These sites are often large, easily cleared, and strategically located on a water body or edge of downtown. Their principal disadvantage is site contamination by the previous activity. Well-known examples of this situation include False Creek in Vancouver, LeBreton Flats in Ottawa, and the area of the tar ponds associated with the former iron and steel mill in Sydney, Nova Scotia.[37] Many of these sites languished for years until environmental remediation regulations were revised and new public funding was allocated for cleanup.

Brownfield plans start with historical research and environmental testing to determine the sources and extent of the land pollution.[38] The plans usually include a remediation strategy to clean up the land, a planning and urban design analysis of the future development potential of the site, and a financial analysis of the proposals. Private developers typically cannot tolerate the risks and costs associated with brownfield remediation, so most abandoned sites are cleaned up by a public agency and placed on the market one parcel at a time, as the NCC has done in LeBreton Flats and Waterfront Toronto for the West Don Lands (Figure 11.12). The approval and clean-up phases take a long time, but the central location of many brownfields makes them excellent opportunities for sustainable development—environmentally degraded land is replaced by high-density mixed-use neighbourhoods with good potential for transit and active transportation.[39] There are still thousands of brownfield sites in Canada, but we now have many examples of successful redevelopment, including Brandt's Creek in Kelowna (former rail yard), Oliver Village (Edmonton rail yard), Wellington

Figure 11.12 | Brownfield Redevelopment: West Don Lands, Toronto

SOURCE: WATERFRONT TORONTO.

Existing conditions in the West Don Lands couldn't be much worse: flooding, adjacent expressway and rail corridors, serious soil contamination from former coal gasification, and paint and rendering plants. Redevelopment began after a false start in the 1990s caused by regulatory problems and a recession.

SOURCE: WATERFRONT TORONTO.

The redevelopment plan by Urban Design Associates includes a new park that will connect to the remediated Don River but also act as a flood barrier. The first buildings completed were the affordable housing on the extreme right edge of the image. The mixed-use buildings in the centre of the drawing will be the athletes' village for the 2015 Pan-Am Games.

Square (Cambridge, Ontario, foundry), Spencer Creek Village (Dundas, Ontario, foundry), and Quai des Éclusiers (Lachine Canal, Montréal).[40]

Waterfront Redevelopment Plans

Most Canadian cities have a waterfront on a lake, river, or ocean, and these communities realize its importance to both their heritage and their economy. Prince Rupert, Vancouver, Montréal, Saint John, Halifax, and St. John's still have active commercial ports, but almost every other Canadian waterfront is engaged in a special form of brownfield redevelopment that is part of a worldwide restructuring of transportation methods. Containers and bulk terminals made the traditional inner-city harbours obsolete, and communities have been redeveloping their waterfronts for over 30 years.[41]

Planning for waterfront redevelopment has occurred in Montréal and Windsor, in Nelson, B.C., and in Halifax (Figure 11.13), among others. It has often been used to reclaim a neglected industrial and port area and make it functional once again for business, residence, and recreation. The three basic planning strategies used

Figure 11.13 | Halifax: Waterfront Redevelopment on a Brownfield Site, 2010

SOURCE: HRM BY DESIGN, HALIFAX REGIONAL MUNICIPALITY.

The Downtown Halifax Plan calls for redevelopment of this waterfront parking lot that was a brownfield site (top). The demonstration plan (bottom) illustrates excellent waterfront design: complete public access to the water's edge; shops, restaurants, and other public uses at grade; employment and housing in mid-rise buildings with comfortable scale at the boardwalk; and one point tower that allows views to the harbour from the building behind. The Downtown Halifax Plan won a 2010 CIP urban design award by illustrating the potential for good urbanism at a variety of downtown sites.

in waterfront areas are: 1) securing public access to the water's edge; 2) adaptive reuse of industrial buildings, and 3) enhancing unique water-related uses such as marinas, fishing piers, and ferry terminals.[42]

For many cities, the waterfront is where the community began, and there is frequently a stock of older historic buildings that are worth conserving and adapting. For both an older port area (e.g., Saint John) and a riverfront scenic area (e.g., Saskatoon), public access is crucial. It is not uncommon for these areas to be cut off from the city by railway lines or highways, and public initiatives can be used to link the area to existing streets and create such things as water's edge promenades and parks. The most successful waterfront projects focus on the quality of the public spaces in the project area.[43] In other words, public-policy initiatives, by way of heritage legislation and capital expenditures on streets and parks, are crucial for waterfront enhancement. These improvements are often carried out by a special purpose agency such as Halifax's Waterfront Development Corporation or Société du Havre de Montréal (see Chapter 17).

Sprawl Repair in the Suburbs

The suburbs are home to about two-thirds of Canadians, and they comprise an even larger proportion of the area of our metropolitan regions (see Chapter 5).[44] These vast tracts of low-density uses have some potential for redevelopment, sometimes known as "sprawl repair."[45] Some opportunities for suburban intensification appear to be

- Suburban districts: dead malls (greyfields—see below), college campuses, employment lands, office parks;[46]
- Suburban corridors: commuter rail stations, LRT stations, strip malls, utility corridors, automobile commercial strips (Figure 11.14);[47]
- Suburban neighbourhoods: apartment "towers in the park(ing lot)," secondary suites.[48]

The declining inner suburbs may present good intensification opportunities as the trend to big-box retail and enormous parking lots has made many of the older retail strip mall sites obsolete, while the inexpensive, first-generation single-story suburban commercial buildings have reached the end of their useful lives and mortgages. Suburban intensification plans also make use of the large areas devoted to surface parking and building setbacks in conventional suburban development. The plans are usually based on careful urban design and financial analysis.

Figure 11.14	Retrofitting Suburbia— Revitalizing a Commercial Arterial Strip

SOURCE: PLACES TO GROW GROWTH PLAN FOR THE GREATER GOLDEN HORSESHOE, 2006, OFFICE CONSOLIDATION, JANUARY 2012, ONTARIO GROWTH SECRETARIAT, MINISTRY OF INFRASTRUCTURE. © QUEEN'S PRINTER FOR ONTARIO, 2012.

Hypothetical intensification and revitalization of an arterial road, showing starting conditions that might be found in any Canadian suburb (top): a wide road right-of-way; parking out front; scattered commercial buildings; and miserable conditions for pedestrians, cyclists, and transit riders. The lower image illustrates typical sprawl repair techniques: a "complete street" that maintains the four traffic lanes, but adds transit priority, cycle lanes, sidewalks, and street trees. Buildings are moved up to the street line and made with continuous frontage, a mix of uses, retail at grade, and some parking along the street. This computer visualization illustrated the intensification principles for the Growth Plan for the Greater Golden Horseshoe, which won the 2007 CIP National Planning Award and Daniel Burnham Award from the American Planning Association.

Greyfield Plans

Older commercial districts including shopping malls, strip malls, or retail plazas present opportunities for intensifying and revitalizing Canadian communities (Figure 11.15). These "greyfields" are composed of failing or failed retail uses ("dead malls") and their associated parking lots. Greyfield redevelopment projects are often found in suburban settings such as North Hill (Calgary) or Olde Thornhill Village (Markham). They can also be found in the central business district, as seen in Lakeshore Village (Oakville).[49]

Many conventional suburban developments from the 1950s through the 1970s included a community shopping centre, apartments, and high school near the intersection of four neighbourhood units, following the Don Mills model (Figure 5.15, page 119). These community shopping centres were positioned

Figure 11.15	Retrofitting Suburbia—Greyfield Plan for a Community Shopping Centre

Hypothetical intensification and revitalization of a dying suburban community shopping centre (top): note the huge and almost empty parking lot, the apartments within walking distance, and no facilities for pedestrians, cyclists, or transit riders.

The lower image illustrates typical greyfield intensification techniques: buildings are moved closer to the street line and made with continuous frontage, a mix of uses, retail at grade, and some residential and offices above. Note the big-box grocery store with pedestrian frontage, bus shelter, cycle racks, pedestrian plaza sidewalks, and street trees. This image is another computer visualization illustrating intensification principles from the award-winning Growth Plan for the Greater Golden Horseshoe.

within a 10-minute *walk* of their suburban customers and anchored by a small supermarket, drugstore, and junior department store. They have almost all been made obsolete by big-box supermarkets and drugstores within a 10-minute *drive* of the customers.[50] As a result, many suburban Canadian high schools have a dead or dying mall across the street. Sadly, the default redevelopment scenario seems to be a big-box power centre, if no better plans are in place. A better greyfield plan will typically encourage the subdivision of the mall's site into regular streets and blocks and construction of apartments over retail space.[51]

Military Base Redevelopment Plans

The Department of National Defence is one of Canada's largest landowners and implements plans for its military bases and adjacent residential areas, such as the 1950s new town in Oromocto, New Brunswick. Military bases were built all across Canada during World War II, when the nation had over one million people in uniform. Most of these bases were still in federal ownership towards the end of the 20th century, when the Canadian Forces were only 5 percent the size of the World War II establishment. The Royal Canadian Navy's principal bases in Halifax and Esquimalt will remain core components of the waterfronts of these cities, but the main operational bases for the army and the air force are now located in rural areas, because training with live ammunition is a truly incompatible land use. So the remaining under-utilized military bases in urban areas are prime redevelopment sites, since they were located at the edge of the metropolitan area in 1918 or 1945 on lands that are usually inner suburbs today.

Military base redevelopment is a specialized planning activity. Retired military bases have components of brownfield planning, infrastructure is often antiquated, there may be some heritage buildings (often industrial buildings such as airplane hangars), and there are always significant cultural heritage issues to honour those who trained at the bases and did not return.[52]

Redevelopment of a military facility in a rural area is always a controversial action, since the jobs on the base are often a key component of the local economy and difficult to replace. Urban base redevelopment usually has controversies over First Nations' land claims and alternative uses of the sites. Surplus federal properties are now redeveloped by the Canada Lands Company (CLC), a federal crown corporation that specializes in brownfield cleanup, public engagement, and planning and disposition of land to the private sector (see Planning Issue 17.1, page 423).[53] The CLC closes the bases, cleans up the lands, and negotiates a new plan with local stakeholders using local consultants. The CLC uses a wide variety of community engagement techniques to reach agreement on a plan, which may take several years. After the plan has been approved, the corporation rebuilds the infrastructure, constructs new public spaces, and seeks private developers to build the individual projects through open Requests for Proposals (RFPs) that typically contain urban design guidelines to implement the plan. Redevelopment of a large base would proceed in several phases and take over a decade to complete.

In recent years, surplus military bases in urban areas have begun redevelopment into new neighbourhoods

Figure 11.16	Military Base Redevelopment, Currie Barracks, Calgary

SOURCE: CANADA LANDS COMPANY.

The redevelopment of the third and last phase for the former CFB Calgary is the 81-hectare Currie Barracks site in Calgary's inner suburbs. The first two phases, Garrison Woods and Garrison Green, won several awards for their planning and urban design. Currie Barracks was the first project in Canada to earn gold certification for its plan from the LEED for Neighborhood Development program.

The image shows the proposed design for the Parade Square, the central public space of the Currie Barracks, and Alberta's largest heritage precinct.

such as Garrison Crossing in Chilliwack, B.C., Griesbach Village in Edmonton, Garrison Woods in Calgary (see Figure 11.16), Downsview Park in Toronto, and Pleasantville in St. John's. These projects are distinguished by excellent urban design, mixed uses (but with little social housing), public spaces that commemorate their military history, and a high level of environmental sustainability, often exceeding LEED (Leadership in Energy and Environmental Design) Gold certification.[54]

Land Development Plans

Planners prepare or evaluate two types of plans dealing with new development of the ground space of a community. One is the **subdivision plan**, which involves dividing a large parcel of usually vacant land into numerous building lots. This is most commonly done for residential development, but may also be used in industrial and commercial development. The other is the **site plan**, which involves development on a single parcel of land that is usually either vacant or about to be made vacant by the razing of existing structures.

Subdivision Design

According to an Ontario review of subdivision experience, "Much contemporary subdivision design is still poor to mediocre in quality" and there is a "pervasive utilitarianism" about most subdivision planning.[55] There are two reasons for much of the lacklustre design. The first is that, as with other aspects of civic design, subdivision plans call for special design skills and an awareness of what constitutes a good residential environment. Such skills are unfortunately not plentiful among many surveyors, engineers, and planners who lay out subdivisions; thus the need for guidelines and manuals. The second reason is the tendency of many subdividers to concentrate on the yield of lots from the site, often without regard for the natural topography, amenities, and the need for a rational circulation system. By the 1990s, many municipalities were working with developers to increase the gross density of conventional suburban development by reducing lot sizes and street widths and increasing the mix of townhouses and apartments. More compact development assisted in achieving many objectives for Smart Growth and sustainable development.

The conventional design of subdivisions over the past four to five decades has tended toward curvilinear streets and culs-de-sac bounded by arterial roads. Although efficient in terms of land use and infrastructure, they have not been as successful at providing connectivity to the larger road network, allowing easy orientation, or mixing of uses.[56] **New Urbanism** challenged conventional subdivision design, beginning in the 1990s, to revert to a modified, traditional gridiron of streets, to mix housing types, and to produce more compact, less land-consuming residential areas.[57] Many municipalities, from Abbotsford to Winnipeg to Montréal, have changed their development policies to permit New Urbanism, or **Traditional Neighbourhood Design** (TND) as it is sometimes called.[58] Although the results have been mixed in achieving some New Urbanist principles, more compact, walkable development has ensued and, presumably, better connectivity.[59]

Another approach to subdivision design being considered by other Canadian communities seeks a variation on the classic gridiron, TND, and cul-de-sac suburban models. It is known as the **Fused Grid** and was developed by Canada Mortgage and Housing Corporation.[60] The goals, according to its designers, are to provide a balance between pedestrian and automobile movement and to create "safe, sociable streets and easy connectivity to community facilities." This policy option has been tested in Stratford, Ontario, and in Winnipeg.[61]

Increasingly, municipalities are being faced with proposals to develop subdivisions that are designed to have access limited to persons living there and with their own internal roads. Commonly referred to as **gated communities**, they may range in size from a handful to several hundred homes.[62] Studies indicate that well over 300 gated projects exist across the country. The key land use features of these projects are that their standards for roads, sidewalks, street lighting, and setbacks of houses are unique to the project, and frequently differ from those normally applied in the community.[63] The gated feature prohibits use of the local roads to reach other areas, which results in some traffic calming for the residents. These conditions are sanctioned by the use of legal instruments such as property covenants that regulate relations with the municipality and activities of residents (i.e., as in a mini-zoning bylaw).

Gated communities are popular alternatives with some segments of the population and deliver built environments that residents find quiet, friendly, and safe.[64] As a policy option it means the municipality must vary standards of development for a specific group of residents that apply universally to all other citizens. There are both advantages and disadvantages for the community. On the positive side for the municipality is the fact that care and maintenance of the street system is the responsibility of project residents (often a condominium association), and property taxes still accrue to the municipality. It also helps to know that those community residents who live in the project enjoy calm, safe streets. On the negative side, issues may arise, such as access for emergency vehicles, or reduced connectivity for pedestrians and automobiles to public sites such as parks and education facilities.

Any of the above-mentioned approaches to subdivision design may also come into play at the stage of reviewing subdivision plans, as discussed in Chapter 16. An example of the value of striving for good subdivision design can be seen in a typical situation illustrated for a 4.23-hectare site in Surrey, British Columbia. Figure 11.17(c) shows the design of a similar-sized conventional suburban subdivision in an adjacent area. From the developer's perspective, the second plan, Figure 11.17(d), has a higher yield of units and lower costs per unit for utilities. These factors should compensate for the lower number of big-lot single homes, which would sell quickly. From a sustainable development perspective, the second plan is much better. It provides a greater variety of unit types, higher gross density (26 versus 10 units per hectare), and the same proportion of impervious surfaces. Further analysis indicates building the entire East Clayton neighbourhood according to these standards should also reduce greenhouse gas emissions due to lower car ownership and more walking and cycling for non-work trips.[65]

Other factors that will be taken into account in appraising a subdivision plan include concerns over energy conservation, access for pedestrians, and availability of public transit. Subdivision design can, for example, provide layouts that allow homes to be positioned to maximize transit use[66] and employ natural features and vegetation to reduce the effects of adverse climatic conditions. London, Ontario, requires non-light-polluting, low-energy streetlights in new subdivisions, for example. Good subdivision design also stresses the provision of good quality routes for pedestrians and cyclists. There should be direct and safe connections between dwellings and local activity centres (school, stores, park, library, church), and recreation areas and public transit stops. And wherever possible, pathways should have only moderate grades, so that they can be used by the elderly and those in wheelchairs. The latter criteria reflect planners' concerns that were first articulated in Perry's Neighbourhood Unit of the 1920s (see Chapter 2) and more recently reiterated by advocates of New Urbanism and Smart Growth (see Chapter 5).

Subdivision Plan

A subdivision plan is a legal drawing used to implement the division of land into lots. It is a precise drawing, in contrast to the general land use plans referred to in Chapter 9. A draft subdivision plan must show exactly the proposed property lines, street system, water and sewer lines, and topographic changes to the site. The proposed Ontario subdivision in Figure 11.18 illustrates such a plan. The reason for the detail is that, upon completion, the municipality assumes responsibility for the subdivision as an additional part of the community. Thus, careful scrutiny is given to subdivision plans so as to avoid such problems as those identified below by the Ontario government in alerting its municipalities:

Water pipes, sewers, and roads might have to be run through vacant land to reach scattered subdivisions, thus increasing their length and the cost of services to the public. Subdivisions laid out on

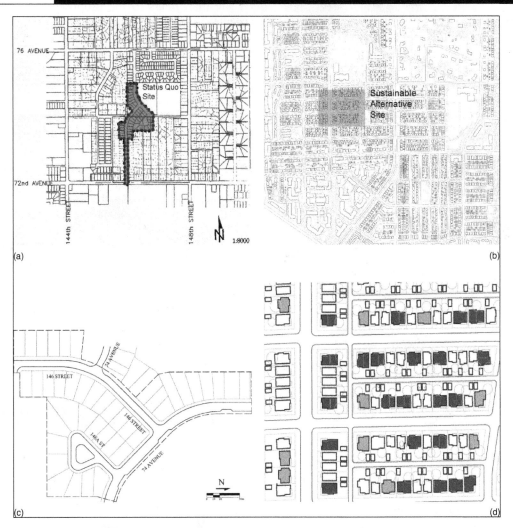

These plans compare the subdivision of two similar sites in Surrey, British Columbia. Site (a) is designed with conventional suburban development principles, resulting in the lot pattern shown in (c); Site (b) uses Vancouver's traditional street, block, and lot structure to generate the pattern shown in (d). The pre-1945 pattern facilitates more than double the gross residential density at half the infrastructure cost per unit, with the same permeability.

	CONVENTIONAL	SUSTAINABLE
Site Area	4.27 ha	4.23 ha
Total Dwelling Units	41	111
Gross Density	9.6 d.u./ha	26.2 d.u./ha
Site Permeability	50%	49.7%
Total Infrastructure Cost	$23 521 per unit	$11 005 per unit

Source: Patrick Condon, "Case Study: Status Quo Standards versus an Alternative Standard, East Clayton," *Technical Bulletin* December 2, 2000, University of British Columbia. Reprinted with permission from the author.

SOURCE: CANADA MORTGAGE AND HOUSING CORPORATION, *RESIDENTIAL SITE DEVELOPMENT ADVISORY DOCUMENT* (1981), 24.

Figure 11.18	Draft Plan of a Subdivision, Ontario

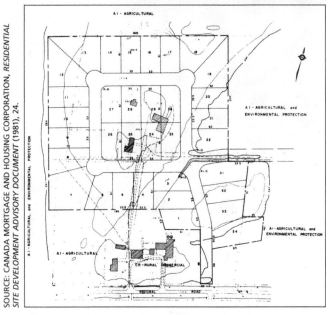

Before land can be subdivided and built upon, a plan must be submitted and approved showing the arrangement of lots, the alignment of streets, and the uses of land. This farm is subdivided into large parcels for 34 big houses on private services. A small rural village might be planned on a similar area, with better results.[68]

hilly ground could have street patterns that ignore the slopes. This also increases costs, makes them difficult to maintain, and more hazardous in cold weather. Others, laid out in poorly drained soil and provided with septic tanks and well water, become health hazards when the septic tanks pollute the wells or when the septic tank beds are subject to flooding.[67]

Subdivision plans must also indicate areas set aside for parks, schools, and any other public facilities, such as walkways, churches, and shopping areas. In a number of provinces, it is required that the subdivider deed 5 percent of the subdivision to the municipality for park use. However, before all these details are considered, the subdivision plan is examined for its conformity with the aims of the comprehensive plan, the requirements of the zoning regulations for the area in question, street alignments and intersections with streets in adjacent subdivisions, and provincial policies.

Site Plan

A site plan refers to the proposed land use arrangements, normally for a single parcel of land. It is usually prepared by the proponent of a development (not necessarily the owner of the property) for one or more new buildings or for making substantial changes to existing buildings. A site plan is a precise, blueprint-type plan that is concerned with the placement of buildings and the connections linking the site to the street system and to public services.[69] All non-building types of facilities such as parking lots, recreation areas, and interior roads must also be included on a site plan, as must any topographic aspects that might affect drainage. Figure 11.19 illustrates a typical site plan.

Increasingly, site plans are required to be submitted so that they can be scrutinized for their consistency with community objectives. Aesthetic and functional considerations are also taken into account in this nearly final phase of land use planning. In Ontario, this process is called "site-plan control"; elsewhere the term "development control" is often used to refer to the same local vetting of developers' site plans (see Chapter 16).

Figure 11.19	Site Plan for an Affordable Housing Project, Montréal

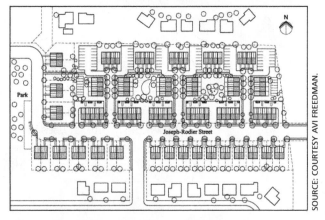

SOURCE: COURTESY AVI FREEDMAN.

The precise location of buildings and arrangement of open space are shown on a site plan for a housing project, like this one for Cité Jardin Fontenaux, a "Grow Home" community in Montréal, designed by Groupe Cardinal Hardy. Such plans are often required when building permits and development-control agreements are being sought.

Reflections

It is a sign of the increasing maturity of the field that community planning in Canada has moved well beyond reliance on a single overall plan. For no community, even the smallest, is a complex of spaces each with its own social and physical characteristics as well as close links to adjoining spaces. The key to successful district planning is the community plan itself and the guidance it provides regarding community goals and objectives, but also for the social values it embodies. The secondary plan should, at a minimum, reflect those same qualities. In other words, plans for neighbourhoods, or waterfronts, or brownfield sites are not primarily about these spaces but rather about completing the plan's desired social, economic, and functional mosaic of the entire community. Failing to do this could result in a patchwork of community spaces disjointed, say, in transportation linkages.

A cautionary note is also due concerning secondary plans in regard to two aspects. One is about the degree to which the individual areas are linked to one another. It is important that there be *room* in secondary plans,

indeed including the community plan, for unintended and unexpected changes in land uses, transportation, and even social connections to occur and be accommodated. It is the social connectedness of people to community spaces, to their neighbourhoods, parks, and shopping areas that, increasingly, planners are called upon to recognize and respond to. Even a greyfield site like a neglected strip mall, which may seem to be uneconomic to external viewers, may still provide some needs to nearby residents and/or carry cherished memories for them. These spaces in current terminology are frequently called "places" in people's minds. This subject is in taken up in the next chapter. The following two questions are aimed at linking the discussion of this chapter to that of the following one:

- *Thinking of a city you know, cite a heritage area for which you think a secondary plan is merited, and discuss the factors that need to be taken into account in the plan?*
- *What are the social factors a planner needs to incorporate into a secondary plan?*

Reference Notes

1. Winnipeg's Osborne Village was voted "Canada's Great Neighbourhood" in the 2012 Great Places in Canada competition; see http://www.cip-icu.ca/greatplaces/en/place.asp?id=6053
2. Wendelyn Martz, *Neighborhood-Based Planning* (Chicago: American Planning Association, 1995), Planning Advisory Service Report No. 455.
3. Pierre Filion, "The Importance of Downtown," *Plan Canada* 46:1 (Spring 2006), 31–33; Charles Bohl, *Place Making: Developing Town Centers, Main Streets and Urban Villages* (Washington, DC: Urban Land Institute, 2002); and Pierre Filion and Heidi Hoernig, "Downtown Past, Downtown Present, Downtown Yet to Come: Decline and Revival in Middle-Size Urban Areas," *Plan Canada* 43:1 (January 2003), 31–34.
4. Bohl, *Place Making*; and Philip Walker, *Downtown Planning for Smaller and Midsized Communities* (Chicago: APA Planners Press, 2009).
5. Beth Moore Milroy, *Thinking Planning and Urbanism* (Vancouver, BC: UBC Press, 2009).
6. Jan Gehl, *Cities for People* (Washington, DC: Island Press, 2010); and William H. Whyte, *City: Rediscovering the Center* (Philadelphia: University of Pennsylvania Press, 2009). Whyte founded the Project for Public Spaces, which carries on his work at www.pps.org
7. Olga Kaganova and James McKellar, eds., *Managing Government Property Assets: International Experiences* (Washington, DC: Urban Institute, 2006).
8. Lawrence Vale, *Architecture, Power and National Identity* (London: Routledge, 2008); David Gordon, "Culture and Capital Cities" in Javier Monclús, ed., *Culture, Urbanism and Planning* (London: Ashgate, 2007); and Rupak Chattopadhyay and Gilles Paquet, eds., *The Unimagined Canadian Capital: Challenges for the Federal Capital Region* (Ottawa: Invenire Press, 2011).
9. David Gordon, ed., *Planning Twentieth Century Capital Cities* (New York: Routledge, 2006), Chapter 11.
10. Pierre Dubé and D. Gordon, "Special Issue: Capital Cities: Perspective and Convergence," *Plan Canada* 40:3 (May 2000).
11. Vale, *Architecture, Power and National Identity*.
12. Pierre Filion, H. Hoernig, T. Bunting, and G. Sands, "The Successful Few: Healthy Core Areas of Small Metropolitan Regions," *Journal of the American Planning Association* 70 (2004), 328–343.
13. Robert Enright, ed., *Body Heat: The Story of the Woodward's Redevelopment* (Vancouver: Blueimprint, 2010).
14. Richard Miller and Earl Swensson, *Hospital and Healthcare Facility Design* (New York, Norton, 2002); and Michelle Gregory, "Planning and Zoning for Medical Districts," *Zoning News* (Chicago: American Planning Association, March 1994).
15. Richard Florida, *The Rise of the Creative Class Revisited* (Toronto: Basic Books, 2012); and Dialog Design, *Saskatoon Culture Plan* (City of Saskatoon, 2012), which received a CIP Social Planning honourable mention 2012.
16. Eugenie Birch, "New York City: Super-Capital—Not by Government Alone"; and Paul White, "Paris: From the Legacy of Haussmann to the Pursuit of Cultural Supremacy," in Gordon, *Planning Twentieth Century Capital Cities*, chapters 18 and 4.
17. John Kasarda, *Aerotropolis: The Way We'll Live Next* (New York: Farrar, Straus, and Giroux, 2011); Alexander Wells, *Airport Planning and Management* (New York: McGraw Hill, 2004); and CMHC, *New Housing and Airport Noise Handbook* (Ottawa: CMHC, NHA 5185 81/05).
18. See Peter Hall's description of London's search for a third airport in *Great Planning Disasters* (University of California Press, 1982).
19. Sandra Budden and Joseph Ernst, *The Movable Airport: The Politics of Government Planning* (Toronto: Hakkert, 1973).
20. Sauer, Louis, "Creating a 'Signature' Town: The Urban Design of Bois Franc," *Plan Canada* 34:5 (September 1994), 22–27; Ray Tomalty and Murtaza Haider, *Comparing New Urbanist and Conventional Suburban Developments in Canada* (Ottawa: CMHC, 2010); and Julia Czerniak, *CASE—Downsview Park*, Toronto (Munich: Prestel, 2001).
21. Desmond Bliek and Pierre Gauthier, "Mobilising Urban Heritage to Counter the Commodification of Brownfield Landscapes: Lessons from Montréal's Lachine Canal,"

Reference Notes (continued)

Canadian Journal of Urban Research: Canadian Planning and Policy 16:1 (Supplement 2007), 1–20.

22. Steven Bell, "Prime Impacts: Putting Urban Design to Work for Changing Heritage Environments," *Plan Canada* 47:1 (2007) 23–26; Christiane Lefebvre and Eve Wertheimer, "An Indispensable Reference for Heritage Conservation," *Plan Canada* 46:1 (Spring 2006), 41–43; and Robert Shipley and Robert Feick, "A Practical Approach for Evaluating Cultural Heritage Landscapes: Lessons from Rural Ontario," *Planning, Practice & Research* 24:4 (November 2009), 455–469.

23. Heather-Anne Risser Getson, "Lunenburg, Nova Scotia, World Heritage Site—Would We Do It Again?" *Plan Canada* 43:2 (2003), 26–28.

24. Robert Shipley, Kayla Jones, and Jason F. Kovacs, "Heritage Conservation Districts Work: Evidence from the Province of Ontario," *Urban Affairs Review* 47:5 (2011), 611–641; Isabelle Laterreur and Marlène Schwartz, "Le Plateau-Mont-Royal: Une approche paysagère du patrimoine urbain," *Urbanité* (June 2008), 38–39; and Jean-Claude Marsan, "Arrondissement historique et naturel du Mont-Royal: Le déni de l'appropriation populaire," *Urbanité* (Winter 2011), 48.

25. Michael Hough, *Cities and Natural Process* (New York: Routledge, 2004).

26. Cynthia Zaitzevsky, *Frederick Law Olmsted and the Boston Park System* (Cambridge, MA: Harvard University Press, 1982).

27. Brook McIlroy and City of Toronto Planning Dept., *Avenues and Mid-Rise Buildings Study* (City of Toronto, 2011).

28. Metrolinx and IBI Group, *Mobility Hub Guidelines* (Toronto: Metrolinx, 2011).

29. Peter Calthorpe, *The Next American Metropolis* (New York: Princeton Architectural Press, 1993); and *Congress of the New Urbanism, Charter of the New Urbanism* (New York: McGraw Hill, 2000).

30. Charlotte Horny, "Les débuts d'une mutation? Le métro à Laval," *Urbanité* (Spring 2010), 10–11.

31. See Hank Dittmar and Gloria Ohland, "The New Transit Town: Best Practices" in *Transit-Oriented Development* (Washington, DC: Island Press; 2004); R.T. Dunphy, et al. *Developing Around Transit: Strategies and Solutions That Work* (Washington, DC: Urban Land Institute, 2004); and Michael Bernick and Robert Cervero, *Transit Villages in the 21st Century* (New York: McGraw-Hill, 1997); this list was developed by Queen's University graduate students in the 2011 SURP 826 Hurdman Station project.

32. CMHC, "The Bridges, Calgary"; "Village de la Gare, Mont-Saint-Hilaire, Québec"; "Metropole, Ottawa"; "Time, North Vancouver, British Columbia," *Transit Oriented Development: Case Studies* (Ottawa: CMHC, 2010).

33. Mary Lamey, "Vision for Future Pays Off," *The Gazette* (Montréal, October 15, 2005); www.clc.ca/success-story/benny-farm

34. Helena Grdadolnik, "Woodward's Take Shape: 'Nothing Like it in North America,'" April 4, 2006, available at www.thetyee.ca; Robert Enright, ed., *Body Heat: The Story of the Woodward's Redevelopment* (Vancouver: Blueimprint, 2010); and Nathan Edelson, "Inclusivity as an Olympic Event at the 2010 Vancouver Winter Games," *Urban Geography* 32:6 (2011), 804–822.

35. Avi Friedman and David Krawitz, "Retooling the Historic Neighbourhood of Le Village," *Plan Canada* 42:1 (January–March 2002), 24–26; and Avi Friedman and David Krawitz, "The Development Process of Urban and Architectural Guidelines for the Rehabilitation of an Inner-City Neighbourhood: Le Village, Cornwall, Ontario, Canada," *Journal of Urban Design* 7:1, 5–34, 2002.

36. National Round Table on the Environment and the Economy, cited in David Adams, Christopher De Sousa, and Steven Tiesdell, "Brownfield Development: A Comparison of North American and British Practices," *Urban Studies* 47:1 (January 2010), 75–104.

37. Michael Hayek, Godwin Arku, and Jason Gilliland, "Assessing London, Ontario's Brownfield Redevelopment Effort to Promote Urban Intensification," *Local Environment* 15:4 (April 2010), 389–402; Pamela Welbourn, H. Cleghorn, J. Davis, and S. Rose, *The Story of Brownfields & Smart Growth in Kingston Ontario: From Contamination to Revitalization* (San Diego, CA: Classroom Complete Press, 2009); and Tera Camus, "Sydney's Toxic Woes Widespread," *Halifax Herald* (August 6, 2001).

38. M. Hayek, M. Novak, G. Arku, and J. Gilliland, "Mapping Industrial Legacies: Building a Comprehensive Brownfield Database in Geographic Information Systems," *Planning Practice and Research*, 25:4 (August 2010), 461–475.

39. Christopher De Sousa, *Brownfields Redevelopment and the Quest for Sustainability* (London: Emerald Group Publishing, 2008); and "Brownfield Redevelopment versus Greenfield Development: A Private Sector Perspective on the Costs and Risks Associated with Brownfield Redevelopment in the Greater Toronto Area," *Journal of Environmental Planning and Management* 43, 831–853.

40. CMHC, "Brandt's Creek Crossing"; "Oliver Village"; "Wellington Square"; "Spencer Creek Village"; "Quai des Éclusiers," *Brownfield Redevelopment for Housing: Case Studies* (Ottawa: CMHC, 2006).

41. Jill L. Grant, Robyn Holme, and Aaron Pettman, "Global Theory and Local Practice in Planning in Halifax: The Seaport Redevelopment," *Planning, Practice & Research* 23:4 (November 2008), 517–532; and Ann Breen and Dick Rigby, *The New Waterfront: A Worldwide Urban Success Story* (New York: McGraw Hill, 1996).

42. David L.A. Gordon, "Implementing Urban Waterfront Redevelopment," *Remaking the Urban Waterfront* (Washington, DC: Urban Land Institute, 2004), 80–99.

43. David L.A. Gordon, "Planning, Design and Managing Change in Urban Waterfront Redevelopment," *Town Planning Review* 67:3 (1996), 261–290.

44. Pierre Filion, Trudi Bunting, Dejan Pavlic, and Paul Langlois, "Intensification and Sprawl: Residential Density Trajectories in Canada's Largest Metropolitan Regions," *Urban Geography* 31:4 (2010), 541–569; and David Gordon and Mark Janzen, "Suburban Nation? Estimating the Size of Canada's Suburban Population," ACUPP/Canadian Association of Geographers conference, Calgary, 2011.

45. Galina Tachieva, *The Sprawl Repair Manual* (Washington, DC: Island Press, 2010); and Ellen Dunham-Jones and June Williamson, *Retrofitting Suburbia: Urban Design Solutions for Redesigning Suburbs* (New York: Wiley, 2011).

46. CMHC, "The Renaissance at North Hill, Calgary," *Residential Intensification—Case Studies* (Ottawa: CMHC, 2006).

47. CMHC, "Harmony, Toronto," *Residential Intensification—Case Studies* (Ottawa: CMHC, 2006).

48. City of Toronto Planning Department; CMHC, "Accessory-Apartments-Policy, Guelph," *Residential Intensification—Case Studies* (Ottawa: CMHC, 2006).

49. CMHC, "The Renaissance at North Hill, Calgary," *Residential Intensification—Case Studies* (Ottawa: CMHC, 2006); CMHC, "Olde Thornhill Village, Markham"; and "Lakeshore Village, Oakville," *Greyfield Redevelopment for Housing in Canada—Case Studies* (Ottawa: CMHC, 2011).

50. PricewaterhouseCoopers, *Greyfields into Goldfields: Dead Malls Become Living Neighborhoods* (San Francisco, Congress for New Urbanism, 2002).

51. Tachieva, *Sprawl Repair Manual*; Dunham-Jones and Williamson, *Retrofitting Suburbia*; and Congress for New Urbanism, *Malls into Mainstreets* (San Francisco: CNU, 2005).

52. US Environmental Protection Agency, *Turning Bases into Great Places: New Life for Closed Military Facilities* (Washington, DC: EPA, 2006); and Bernard Frieden and Christie Baxter, *From Barracks to Business: The MIT Report on Base Redevelopment* (Washington, DC: US Department of Commerce, 2000).

53. www.clc.ca

54. Tomalty and Haider, *Comparing New Urbanist and Conventional Suburban Developments*; David Couroux, Noel Keough, Byron Miller, and Jesse Row, *Toward Smart Growth in Calgary: Overcoming Barriers to Sustainable Urban Development* (Calgary: Sustainable Calgary, 2006); CMHC, "Garrison Woods, Calgary," *Residential Intensification—Case Studies* (Ottawa: CMHC, 2006); and Czerniak, *CASE—Downsview Park*.

55. Ontario Economic Council, *Subject to Approval* (Toronto, 1973), 65–66.

56. Jill Grant, *Planning the Good Community: New Urbanism in Theory and Practice* (New York: Routledge, 2006); David Gordon and Shayne Vipond, "Gross Density and New Urbanism: Comparing Conventional and New Urbanist Suburbs in Markham, Ontario," *Journal of the American Planning Association* 71:2 (Winter 2005), 41–54; and Ian Wight, "New Urbanism versus Conventional Suburbanism," *Plan Canada* 35:5 (1995), 3–4.

57. Jill Grant, "The Ironies of New Urbanism," *Canadian Journal of Urban Research* 15:2 (Winter 2006), 158–174; and Andres Duany and Elizabeth Plater-Zyberk, "The Second Coming of the American Small Town," *Plan Canada* 32:3 (1992), 6–13.

58. Jill L. Grant and Stephanie Bohdanow, "New Urbanism Developments in Canada: A Survey," *Journal of Urbanism* 1:2 (July 2008), 109–127; and Jill L. Grant, "Theory and Practice in Planning the Suburbs: Challenges to Implementing New Urbanism, Smart Growth, and Sustainability Principles," *Planning Theory & Practice* 10:1 (March 2009), 11–33.

59. Tomalty and Haider, *Comparing New Urbanist and Conventional Suburban Developments*; Jill Grant and Katherine Perrott, "Where is the Café? The Challenge Of Making Retail Uses Viable In Mixed-Use Suburban Developments," *Urban Studies* 48:1 (January 2011), 177–195; Jill Grant and Katherine Perrott, Producing Diversity in a New Urbanism Community: Policy And Practice, *Town Planning Review* 80:3 (2009), 267–289: and Paul Hess, "Fronts and Backs: The Use Of Streets, Yards And Alleys In Toronto Area New Urbanist Neighbourhoods," *Journal of Planning Education and Research* (Winter 2008), 28:2, 196–212.

60. Fanis Grammenos, Barry Craig, Douglas Pollard, and Carla Guerrera, "Hippodamus Rides to Radburn: A New Model for the 21st Century," *Journal of Urban Design* 13:2 (2008), 163–176; and Canada Mortgage and Housing Corporation, "Applying Fused-Grid Planning in Stratford, Ontario," *Research Highlights* (Ottawa, November 2004), Socio-economic Series 04-038.

61. Fanis Grammenos, "Stratford Leads the Way to a New Model of Suburban Development," *Plan Canada* 45:1 (Spring 2005), 20–22; and Canada Mortgage and Housing Corporation, "Evaluating Arterial Road Configuration Options for a New Community," *Research Highlights* (Ottawa, March 2005), Socio-economic Series 05-008.

62. Jill Grant, "An American Effect: Contextualizing Gated Communities in Canadian Planning Practice," *Canadian Journal of Urban Research* 16:1 (2007), Supplement 1–19; Jill Grant and Andrew Curran, "Privatized Suburbia: The Planning Implications of Private Roads," *Environment and Planning B: Planning and Design* 34 (2007), 740–754; and Jill Grant et al., "The Planning and Policy Implications of Gated Communities," *Canadian Journal of Urban Research* 13:1 (Summer 2004), 70–89.

63. Andrew Curran and Jill Grant, "Private Streets: A Survey of Policy and Practice," *Canadian Journal of Urban Research* 15:1 (2006), Supplement 62–78.

64. Katherine A. Greene and D. Kirsten Maxwell, "Taking Matters into Their Own Hands: Traffic Control in Canadian Gated Communities," *Plan Canada* 44:2 (Summer 2004), 45–47.

65. Patrick Condon, "The Headwaters Project—East Clayton Neighbourhood Concept Plan," *Research Highlights* 62488 (Ottawa: CMHC, 2001); and Geoff Gilliard, "Surrey Shifts Sustainability Status Quo with Neighbourhood Concept Plan," *Plan Canada* 43:1 (January 2003), 13–16.

66. Urban Strategies, *Transit-Supportive Guidelines* (Toronto: Ontario Ministry of Transportation, 2011).

67. Ontario, Department of Municipal Affairs, *Three Steps to Tomorrow* (Toronto, 1972), 44.

68. Randall Arendt, *Rural by Design: Maintaining Small Town Character* (Chicago: APA Planners Press, 1994).

69. Kevin Lynch and Gary Hack, *Site Planning*, 3rd ed. (Cambridge, MA: MIT Press, 1984).

Internet Resources

Chapter-Relevant Sites

Planning Canadian Communities
www.planningcanadiancommunities.ca

Project for Public Spaces
www.pps.org

CMHC (Canada Mortgage and Housing Corporation) case studies—greyfield, brownfield, and TOD
www.cmhc-schl.gc.ca/en/inpr/su/sucopl/

Sprawl Repair
www.sprawlrepair.com

Canada Lands Company
www.clc.ca

Winnipeg's Osborne Village
www.cip-icu.ca/greatplaces/en/place.asp?id=6053

12

Chapter Twelve

Planning Infrastructure Systems to Connect Communities

We look for tools to allow us to shape our own future and to make all of our settlements strong and beautiful.

Jill Grant, 2008

Except for perhaps the roads they drive on, the public transit they ride, and the parks they enjoy walking in, most residents are largely unaware of the infrastructure that enables their community to function. Moreover, few of them grasp the networks that each involves and the planning needed to try to ensure its reliability. Indeed, much of the infrastructure isn't visible to citizens, such as supplying water and dealing with sewage, or, when visible, as with electricity supply, largely goes unnoticed. The community plan includes all the necessary infrastructure of a city or town, explicitly in the case of roads, parks, and public facilities, and implicitly in the case of underground services.

A community plan often aims to improve specific functions within a community. Increased traffic may need to be accommodated, sewage systems may need to be upgraded, and affordable housing may be in short supply. Such needs often occupy large portions of land and/or demand considerable public investment. They usually require a separate functional plan showing location, land acquisition, and the disposition of capital expenditures, as well as other expected outcomes of the project. The following are typical of such projects:

- Rapid-transit systems that aim to relieve current traffic congestion in the downtown area, as with the systems in Montréal, Ottawa, Toronto, Calgary, Edmonton, and Vancouver;
- Social-housing projects that provide affordable housing for the elderly and other low-income groups not normally able to compete in the economic marketplace;[1] and

- Regional parks developments that aim to improve recreational opportunities and protect natural environments.

To this list could be added improvements to an airport, a new convention centre, college, or health-care facility, or an expanded freeway system. A demonstration of this is the approach used by the City of Calgary in planning its future transportation system. The Calgary *Go-Plan* was aimed at guiding capital expenditures on transportation over the next 30 years; the planning process itself is costing several millions of dollars.[2] Often, one of the outcomes from such a functional-planning exercise is to bring into sharper focus the larger questions about the community's future shape. This happened when Calgary proposed transportation corridors that provoked considerable public debate over the urban form, the ecological consequences, and the balance between public transit and automobile transportation, and led to improvements in the plan.

The planning and programming of public projects is undertaken for three main reasons: (1) to benefit present residents; (2) to direct new development in a growing community; and (3) to attract development to a stagnant community. Typically, some combination of these reasons comes into play. A new rapid-transit system, for example, may both relieve downtown auto traffic congestion and direct new development to locales adjacent to new stations that now have improved accessibility; similarly, a new college could both benefit local residents and attract new residents and businesses. Before proceeding further with this chapter, consider the following questions:

- *What are four major types of community infrastructure that require planning? Why is it important that their planning be linked?*
- *What are the main reasons for planning public infrastructure?*

Green Infrastructure

Many community plans include separate maps showing the existing and proposed environmental systems. The natural systems in a community are ecological infrastructure that can be divided into two major categories: "green infrastructure" and "blue infrastructure" (streams, rivers, lakes, and waterfronts). The green networks include the community's parks system and its interconnected greenways.[3] The largest communities often have separate plans for each of these green networks.

Parks and Open-Space Systems

An interconnected parks system has been an important component of community plans since the late 19th century Parks Movement (Chapter 3), with Frederick Law Olmsted's Emerald Necklace in Boston as the leading example. Olmsted brilliantly connected natural features such as ponds and marshes with new parks and parkways. Frederick Todd's 1902 park system plan for the Ottawa region is a leading Canadian example of this method.[4]

During the mid-20th century, parks system planning took a quantitative turn, with standard provision of each type of park (such as five acres of neighbourhood parks per 1000 people) or a regulation that 5–10 percent of land in a subdivision be given to the local government for parks.[5] Many municipalities still have quantitative parks standards written into their community plans, which provide a steady stream of new suburban parkland in a growing community. However, these regulations often had little or nothing to say about the quality or design of the parkland. Developers typically gave the worst, most unbuildable 5 percent of their land to the local government. As a result, many neighbourhood parks were isolated and barely used.[6]

In the 21st century, more emphasis was placed on the quality of public space, especially in downtown or inner-city locations (Chapter 11). A small, well-designed square in the right place may attract far more public use than a windswept peripheral green field.[7] Interconnected green spaces are greatly valued by the public, with the ability to go for a long, uninterrupted walk or bicycle ride highly prized in a larger city. Parks planning began to return to its Olmstedian roots, with more emphasis on parks systems, natural features, and greenways, in places like Red Deer, Alberta (Figure 12.1).

Greenways

The return to planning interconnected parks systems in the late-20th century fit well with the rise in environmental planning during that period. Landscape ecologists pointed out the critical role that hedgerows and valleys play in connecting key habitat patches (Chapter 7). The desire to protect, rehabilitate, and enhance these green corridors fit with the expanding interest in creating interconnected trail systems in urban areas. As a result, the ecological analysis that is the first task of many community plans often identifies key greenway connections to be acquired for natural systems and human use.

Many plans create a "greenprint" of patches and corridors to acquire (Figure 12.2), and a greenways plan to connect them. Other, more urban communities, such as

Figure 12.1 | Parks Systems Planning in Red Deer, Alberta, 2010

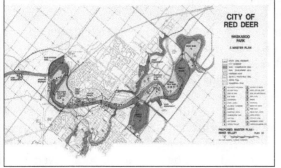

SOURCE: RIVER VALLEY + TRIBUTARIES PARK CONCEPT PLAN, COURTESY OF PARKLAND COMMUNITY PLANNING SERVICES.

Parks systems planning in Red Deer considers the entire river valley. The plan received the 2011 CIP Recreation Planning Award.

Vancouver, B.C., and Portland, Oregon, designate some existing road corridors as greenways and reconstruct them to add street trees, pedestrian paths, and bike paths.[8]

Blue Infrastructure

The natural infrastructure in green corridors and parks systems is matched by a community plan's "blueprint" for its streams, rivers, lakes, and waterfronts. These features are also key components for ecological planning and should be planned as a system at a regional scale.[9] Some blue planning

Figure 12.2 | Green and Blue Links in the 1999 Ottawa-Carleton Regional Plan

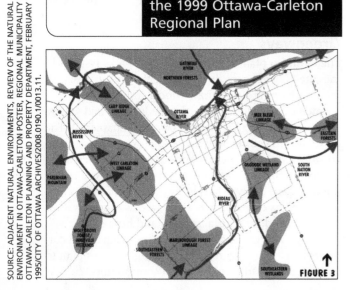

SOURCE: ADJACENT NATURAL ENVIRONMENTS, REVIEW OF THE NATURAL ENVIRONMENT IN OTTAWA-CARLETON POSTER, REGIONAL MUNICIPALITY OF OTTAWA-CARLETON PLANNING AND PROPERTY DEPARTMENT, FEBRUARY 1995/CITY OF OTTAWA ARCHIVES/2008.0190.1/0013.11.

occurs on a very large scale, such as the International Joint Commission (IJC), a bi-national (Canada and the U.S.) special purpose authority that governs trans-border water quality issues and flood control, including the Great Lakes and part of the St. Lawrence River.[10] Other blue infrastructure planning takes place at scales that intersect with community planning more directly, such as the river basins, lakes, and waterfronts discussed below.

River Basin Planning

Planning for rivers and streams should be done on a watershed basis to capture impacts on important natural

Figure 12.3 | Don River Valley Rehabilitation Strategy, Toronto, 1991

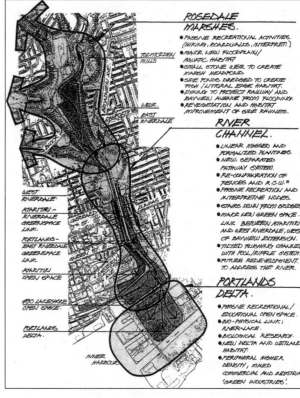

SOURCE: BRINGING BACK THE DON, HOUGH STANSBURY WOODLAND, LTD. DRAWING BY KEN TAMMINGA.

This strategy to clean up the lower Don River proposed creating new marshes and habitat (upper portion of the drawing), increasing public access along the channel (middle), and re-naturalizing the mouth of the river (lower). The plan won the 1992 CIP National Award of Excellence, and the first two phases were extensively implemented with the leadership of a citizens' advocacy group, the Task Force to Bring Back the Don. Rehabilitating the mouth of the river may take another 20 years.

processes, especially for water quality issues and stormwater flows (Chapter 7). Watershed planning agencies, such as Ontario's Conservation Authorities or Québec's river basin agencies (*organismes de bassins versants*) started by addressing flood control to protect human life and property. They develop and maintain sophisticated engineering models to predict stormwater flows, but the standard civil engineering works such as dams, dykes, and levees are rarely adequate to protect a metropolitan region from flooding without a broader strategy to manage infiltration and runoff throughout the watershed.[11] Similarly, water quality issues can rarely be dealt with by improvements at the mouth of a river; they must be addressed throughout the entire watershed.[12]

Degraded urban rivers, such as the Don in Toronto, can be particularly difficult to rehabilitate, since so much of their watershed is paved or developed (Figure 12.3). A more comprehensive effort to protect the adjacent Rouge River may prove more successful in the long-term, since the health of the river has been considered on a watershed basis. The watershed will host a significant human population, but key ecological patches have been preserved, and urban development practices have been modified to reduce stormwater runoff and improve water quality.[13]

Planning Issue 12.1   Don River's Gritty Past Stands It in Good Stead

The Globe and Mail
July 15, 2011

Don River's Gritty Past Stands It in Good Stead

Ian Merringer

Biking down the Don River Trail, John Wilson rarely has two hands on the handlebars. The 16-year veteran and former chair of the Task Force to Bring Back the Don is pointing left and right at dozens of naturalization projects the group has spearheaded since 1989.

But Mr. Wilson is no longer in a good position to lobby city hall for trail improvements. He is the task force's former chair because the body no longer exists. Even though the volunteer members funded themselves through donations and only asked the city for some staff support and an occasional empty meeting room, Toronto Mayor Rob Ford declined to re-establish it this year.

The Don's past is as gritty as any other urban river. After being used by industrialists who saw it as a resource, it was ignored by politicians who considered it a civic liability. Despite winning dubious honours for its levels of pollution, the Don has shown itself to be resilient. And, with an engaged public, it is among those urban rivers turning the corner.

Looking back on 22 years of rehabilitating the Don, Mr. Wilson calls the task force a "wonderful success story." But the ending has yet to be written. Ontario's Ministry of the Environment is reviewing an environmental assessment for a Waterfront Toronto proposal that would re-naturalize the mouth of the Don through a redeveloped western Portlands. The plan is ambitious, and would mark the river's ultimate redemption, but if a volunteer task force is too much for city hall to get behind, what chance does a transformative redevelopment have?

Just south of the viaduct, Mr. Wilson points out Chester Springs Marsh, a three-hectare site the task force created in 1996. The site was once one of the Don Valley's countless garbage dumps, and then a parking lot for utility trucks. Four years after excavation and planting, an Environment Canada survey found the wetland had more nesting marsh birds than the Great Lakes' average.

But if nature is going to bounce back fully, it has a long way to go.

Dr. Henry Scadding, who was the first student enrolled at Upper Canada College before becoming a folklorist and clergyman, wrote about catching 20 salmon in one hour at his farm in what is now Riverdale Park in the 1830s.

Effluent from the many slaughterhouses, tanneries and soap factories turned the

CONTINUED

CONTINUED

Ashbridges Bay estuary, one of the largest wetlands on the Great Lakes, into a potential source of typhus and cholera, historian Dr.Jennifer Bonnell says. It had to go, and in 1912, it was filled in to create the Portlands. The Don was forced into a right-angle turn to enter Lake Ontario through the concrete Keating Channel.

By the 1950s, shipping and economic forces were moving heavier industry off the Lower Don. Then came the Don Valley Parkway.

"Twenty-five years ago you had to climb fences to get here," says Mr. Wilson, pointing to the hard-won public river access the task force gained between Lake Ontario and Pottery Road.

Mr. Wilson bikes past the staircases the task force lobbied for at Riverdale Park and Queen Street, arriving at a pedestrian wormhole under the railway that will link the river to the new Don River Park, a sculpted flood barrier that now protects the West Donlands precinct that Waterfront Toronto is building around the Distillery District.

Carp push around plastic water bottles behind booms that keep a city's flotsam out of the lake, while Mr. Wilson looks south from the channel and imagines a new mouth for the Don. The river would cut through 125 hectares of urban renewal, including 53 hectares of parks and public spaces among mixed-use neighbourhoods for 25,000 people.

"How is it possible that such a spectacular moment in such a spectacular city even exists?" asks project architect Michael Van Valkenburgh, arguing that the views, green space, and proximity to the lake will make for some of the most valuable commercial and residential real estate in the city.

Before that value is unlocked, there has to be billions in public and private investment to open the flood-friendly mouthHowever, there is increasing force pushing the Don out of its industrial confines.

"Every community meeting on the proposal had 200 people come out," says Mr. Van Valkenburgh. "It was exciting to work with people who were so passionate."

Source: © Ian Merringer

Lake Planning

The ecosystems in freshwater lakes near Canadian communities can be damaged by human activity such as the use of fertilizers, sewage disposal, clearing forests, and introducing alien species. Lakes are also damaged by acid rain, mercury pollution, and climate change.[14] The results can include reduction of aquatic species, declines in water quality, and algae blooms that reduce a lake's recreational potential. More serious pollution may cause the water to become dangerous for fish and humans. Ecological analysis for a lake plan would typically examine the bedrock geology, soils, groundwater vegetation, wildlife, rare species, fish, and aquatic habitat in the watershed (see Figure 12.4). This background inventory would be used to make estimates about the carrying capacity or "build-out" of the ecosystem, the appropriate locations for human activity, and their potential environmental impacts.[15] The plan recommendations are typically implemented with standard land use planning tools (Chapter 16), although

| Figure 12.4 | North Pigeon Lake Area Structure Plan, Leduc County, Alberta, 2011 |

SOURCE: NORTH PIGEON LAKE AREA STRUCTURE PLAN, LEDUC COUNTY, © BRUCE THOMPSON AND ASSOCIATES.

This image shows the vegetation patches in the immediate drainage area of North Pigeon Lake. Leduc County's Area Structure Plan manages growth and land uses around the north side of this lake, based upon ecological planning principles. The plan received an honourable mention for environmental planning in the 2011 CIP Awards.

special programs such as the Lake of Bays Waterfront Development Permit zone and community monitoring may be needed.[16]

Planning for the Water's Edge

The places where land and water meet are among the most ecologically significant zones in a region. These littoral zones often need careful planning to protect their environmental integrity, especially for sensitive areas such as coastal dunes and estuaries. Coastal zones, lake shores, and riverfronts are also some of the most popular recreational areas, so the landscapes must be carefully analyzed and any development planned using ecological planning techniques, such as those pioneered by Ian McHarg for coastal dunes. The other major planning principle is to maximize public access and minimize private ownership of the water's edge.[17]

The urban waterfront is typically only a small proportion of regional coastal zones, but one with intense redevelopment pressures and special planning techniques (see Chapter 11).[18] Urban design joins ecological analysis as important elements for the planning of these water's edge environments (Figure 12.5), often producing popular public places such as the Vancouver Seawall or Québec's new walkway along the St. Lawrence River, le Promenade Samuel de Champlain.

Figure 12.5	Waterfront Planning: Les Bassins du Nouveau Havre, Montréal, 2009

SOURCE: CANADA LANDS COMPANY.

Les Bassins du Nouveau Havre are a redevelopment of former industrial waterfront lands adjacent to Montréal's Lachine Canal. Cardinal Hardy's plan received a 2009 award for urban design from the CIP.

Grey Infrastructure: Transportation Plans

Urban transportation planning begins with land use forecasts of population and employment for each neighbourhood (traffic zone) in a metropolitan area. The planning process then typically follows a classic four-step model:

1. *Trip generation* estimates origins and destinations from each zone based on land use planning;
2. *Trip distribution* matches origins and destinations;
3. *Mode choice* distributes trips to various transportation modes; and
4. *Route assignment* allocates trips between origins and destinations to routes.

Complex computer models are used for the planning and cost-benefit analysis to set investment priorities in transportation infrastructure.[19]

For most of the 20th century, *mode choice* in transportation planning meant expanding the road system to facilitate freight delivery by trucks and personal travel by automobiles, which make up the majority of work trips in Canada's suburban society. Community planners must understand transportation planning for roads, but there has been greater emphasis on more sustainable modes of transportation in the 21st century.[20] Infrastructure planning for pedestrians, cycling, and transit has received increasing attention since judgments about the quality of life in a community are affected by the ability of non-drivers to get around safely and conveniently. Gil Penalosa calls this the "8–80 principle": if the infrastructure works for a child (aged 8) or a grandparent (aged 80), then the rest of the community will benefit. Sustainable transportation also has a social equity component, since it is expensive to own and operate an automobile. If a car is needed to access most jobs, then it is more difficult for low-income households to participate in the economy.[21]

Planning for Pedestrians

Most journeys begin and end with a pedestrian trip, even if it is just from a parking lot to the destination. Encouraging travellers to choose to walk or cycle for entire trips requires that the safety, comfort, and convenience of these modes of travel be addressed in transportation planning. Safety and comfort are particularly important for children, women, and the elderly (see Chapter 13).[22] The distance that people are willing to walk depends on their perception of the distance and the quality of the walking

Figure 12.6 Improving Pedestrian and Cycling Infrastructure

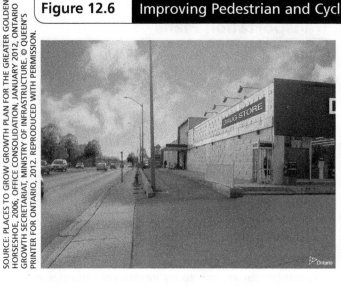

The left image is a typical arterial road that could be found in any Canadian suburb. Unsurprisingly, there is not a cyclist in sight—the wide lanes of fast-moving traffic would feel quite unsafe to most riders. One lonely pedestrian can be seen by the loading dock—since walking along the parking lot would be safer than the unprotected sidewalk at the edge of the high-speed road. A transit rider waiting at the pole would feel completely exposed to the traffic and the elements.

The right image demonstrates potential design improvements to the streetscape of this road to make it more pedestrian, transit, and bicycle-friendly. The buildings have been oriented to the street and their loading bays moved to the rear. The parking lot at the front has been replaced with street trees and a row of parallel parking along the street edge, with a bus shelter and pedestrian bulb-out at the corner. Gaps in the frontage have been infilled with new buildings that face the street. The sidewalk has been moved away from the curb, and is now protected from traffic by a row of parked cars and the transit shelter. All these changes greatly improve the environment for pedestrians. Finally, auto traffic lanes have been narrowed slightly and a diamond lane created for buses and bicycles. Many arterial road rights-of-way are wide enough that these changes can be made with minimal loss of traffic lanes.

This image is a computer-generated visualization of sprawl repair, which received 2007 CIP and American Planning Association awards.

environment. People who will walk many blocks in a vibrant downtown will drive to another store in a "power centre" rather than navigate the parking lot on foot. Similarly, some neighbourhoods need to be retrofitted to remove barriers to pedestrians, especially apartment tower complexes within inner-suburbs such as Toronto.[23]

Good pedestrian planning begins with an interconnected network of safe and comfortable routes. Sidewalks and pedestrian walkways should be at least 1.9 metres (5–6 feet) wide to allow two people to walk together. They need to be wider along blank walls and at least 4–5 metres (12–15 feet) along commercial streets to provide space for seating and displays. Sidewalks should rarely be placed at the curb of a busy street, since the pedestrians will be at risk from moving cars and the walking surface will be blocked by plowed snow. A buffer strip with street trees, parking, and street furniture reduces the fear of walking for pedestrians of all ages (Figure 12.6). Street crossings can be made safer by breaking the journey with a median and narrowing the gap with bulb-outs (curb extensions) and tighter corner radii.

Cycling Plans

"Bicycles are fast, efficient, small, low-profile, non-polluting, and take up little space. Bicycles easily rival the car and public transit for speed for short- and medium-haul trips," according to *Reinvent Montréal*, that city's 2008 transportation plan.[24] Although cycling accounts for less than 2 percent of Canadian work trips, recent transportation plans pay more attention to this sustainable transportation mode. Planning for bicycles (and pedestrians) starts with engaging the community; collecting and analyzing data; conducting field audits of existing infrastructure conditions; identifying, mapping, and analyzing problems; designing alternative solutions (new cycle routes); ranking and phasing new infrastructure projects; and encouraging elected officials to adopt and implement the plan.[25]

Cycling facility design has improved in the 21st century, adapting some advanced European features for North American conditions. On-street bikeway design now provides separate bike lanes in urban areas and paved shoulder bikeways in rural areas. Intersection improvements such as "bike boxes" in front of stop lines and bicycle signals improve safety at these dangerous locations. In communities such as Portland, Oregon, and Vancouver, B.C., some local streets have been converted to bicycle boulevards to safely carry cycle traffic long distances in parallel to auto arterials.[26]

Canadians cycle to work at three times the rate of Americans.[27] A hardy band of Canadians will cycle, even in winter weather, provided that the civic infrastructure supports this environmentally friendly travel mode. For example, chilly Ottawa has one of the nation's highest proportions of people cycling to work because the National Capital Commission developed an excellent long-distance bicycle network along its parkways and through its open-space system. The City of Ottawa now routinely includes bike lanes in its suburban roads and has opened a downtown route with a separated bikeway. Montréal has declared that it wants to be North America's most bike-friendly city and has planned a 63-kilometre Reseau Blanc ("white network") of separated urban routes that are plowed in winter. Its Bixi public bike rental system has over 5000 bicycles available in central Montréal, and the system has also been adopted in Boston, New York, London, Minneapolis, Chicago, Ottawa, and Toronto.[28] So if Montréal and Ottawa can influence people to choose cycling trips, this sustainable transport mode has the potential to absorb more short-range trips in other urban cores, despite Canada's winter.

Transit System Planning

Public transit is a bus system in most Canadian cities and towns, but there is a range of urban transit options for larger communities. These include (in approximate increasing order of capacity):

- Local buses (almost every transit system; powered by various fuels)
- Express buses (pioneered in Ottawa, now in several larger cities)
- Streetcars (Toronto; called trams in Europe)
- Bus rapid transit (BRT, in Ottawa)
- Light rail transit (LRT, in Toronto, Calgary, Edmonton, Vancouver)

- Heavy rail (Toronto's subway, Montréal's Metro)
- Commuter rail (Toronto, Montréal, Vancouver)

Other components of a local transit system might include taxis, ferries (such as Vancouver's SeaBus or Halifax's Harbour Ferry), and local circulators such as public escalators or the funicular railway that climbs Québec's escarpment.

Ottawa's Transitway BRT is North America's leading high-capacity bus system and much studied for adoption in other medium-sized communities, such as Gatineau and York Region. Larger cities (Montréal, Toronto, Vancouver) are considering BRT as part of expanded, multi-modal transit systems for routes that cannot be served by heavy rail or LRT. Economists and transit planners appreciate BRT because local and express buses can join the BRT and also run on the street network.[29]

An LRT system has streetcar trains running on separate rights-of-way in the street (Toronto's Spadina and Harbourfront lines) or elevated on a viaduct (Vancouver's Skytrains, Scarborough RT). Some LRT systems run partially underground (Vancouver's Canada Line, Toronto's new Eglinton line) and begin to approach the characteristics of heavy rail systems, but without the higher capacity from their larger trains. Transit riders prefer subways and light rail to buses, but the land uses in most suburban areas do not have the corridor densities to economically support the higher-level services.[30]

Ottawa, Montréal, Toronto, Hamilton, York, Mississauga, and Kitchener-Waterloo are planning to convert parts of their bus systems to LRT, but there has been community resistance and constant controversy for every system. Some of the opposition to LRT is that the capital costs are so much higher than bus service. Car drivers on congested arterial streets also are unwilling to give up road lanes, even if an LRT line carries 5–10 times the volume of travellers of a traffic lane in the same space. Clever re-designs of wide suburban road corridors can sometimes accommodate better transit and cycling without reducing road capacity (Figure 12.6), but in more urban locations, the roads have usually been widened to the maximum, even removing street trees, lawns, and wider sidewalks to provide the maximum space to cars in rush hour. New public policies should give priority to higher-capacity and more sustainable transportation modes, but there is political resistance to change since a large majority of trips are made by automobile drivers.

Transit systems planning is a component of the larger transportation planning process described above. Although LRT and subway planning are highly specialized fields, many community planners can implement land use policies that support better transit at the local level. Simple policies such as designing neighbourhoods and districts to place higher density uses close to transit stops (Figure 12.7) and spacing collector roads at distances that leave most homes within a 400-metre walk, both of which will improve the quality of bus service in any community.[31]

Road System Planning

The automobile was perhaps the most important appliance that reached wide consumer distribution in the first half of the 20th century. When combined with good roads, this machine radically increased the mobility of middle-class households and restructured North American metropolitan areas. The car permits personal, private, rapid, and direct journeys and is the preferred method of urban travel for most middle-class families. Unfortunately, almost a century of experience indicates that major cities cannot rely entirely upon the automobile for the daily journey to work, despite the vigorous efforts of cities such as Los Angeles, Atlanta, Montréal, and Toronto to build regional expressway systems to support it in the 1960s and 1970s. However, the advantages of car ownership are so valued by many citizens that community planners should expect many middle-class families may continue to own a vehicle, even if it is not used for the daily journey to work.

The automobile presents several challenges for transportation planners. First, not everyone can afford to own and operate a car—the elderly, children, and the poor are not served well. Second, the automobile enables very low-density suburban and exurban development that is difficult to serve by other, more sustainable forms of transportation. Third, most cars are powered by non-renewable hydrocarbon fuels and pollute the air. Finally, automobiles require a lot of pavement to carry few people, since most automobiles have only one passenger and must be stored at either end of a trip. While the last two problems may be ameliorated by electric vehicles, car-sharing, and road-pricing, community planners are still left to struggle with equity and built form problems.

The challenge is not to create a car-free city but to plan communities where car ownership is not a requirement for everyday life. For example, Los Angeles is now building one of North America's largest public transit systems despite its strong car culture.[32] Transportation planning for sustainable development should focus first on providing excellent pedestrian, cycling, and public transit to all citizens, second on economic distribution of goods, and third on automobility. Good public streets are required for all three tasks.

Hierarchy of Streets and Roads

Streets should be designed differently, depending on their function. Transportation engineers use a standard hierarchy of streets:

- Expressways or freeways (high volume, high-speed travel; no property access)
- Arterials (continuous streets, high-traffic volumes, little access)
- Collectors (connect locals with arterials, some access)
- Local streets (low speed, continuous property access)

The local loops, culs-de-sac, and crescents make up 90 percent of a conventional road network but carry only 10 percent of the vehicle-kilometres travelled. The arterials are the long, continuous streets that cross an urban area. They are the backbone of the system, typically carrying 50 percent of the traffic.

SOURCE: MINISTRY OF TRANSPORTATION, TRANSIT-SUPPORTIVE GUIDELINES, P. 14. © QUEEN'S PRINTER FOR ONTARIO, 2012. REPRODUCED WITH PERMISSION.

Figure 12.7 Transit-Supportive Planning Guidelines

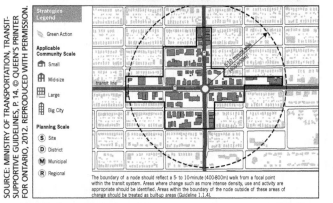

Land use planning and urban design can support public transit. This design guideline recommends that higher-intensity uses should be places within a 5–10 minute walk (400–800 metres) of a transit stop. The limit for local bus service is about 400 metres; people will walk further for higher-quality service, or if the walk is interesting and safe.

Guidelines of this type are best presented with graphics, supported by text. This set of guidelines won a 2012 CIP publication award.

The street hierarchy was demonstrated most clearly in modern suburbs such as Don Mills (Figure 5.15, page 119) and Radburn (Figure 4.18, page 82). These rigid hierarchies are now criticised because there is often only one or two possible routes for a trip. There is practically no traffic on a cul-de-sac, but almost every trip ends up on the collector and arterial roads. Suburban arterial congestion is becoming a major problem in the suburbs of several Canadian cities and one that cannot easily be solved by building more road lanes. As a result, the connectivity of street networks now receives more attention—an interconnected web of streets provides more options for pedestrians, cyclists, and transit than the standard street hierarchy.[33]

Urban designers regard streets as public places that also carry traffic. They have a larger typology of streets and more precise ideas about how they fit in urban and suburban communities (Figure 12.8).

For example, boulevards are long-distance, free-movement thoroughfares traversing an urbanized area. Unlike most arterial roads, a boulevard is flanked by parking, sidewalks, and planters buffering the buildings along the sides. Boulevards similar to those in Paris and Barcelona have been constructed as replacements for an elevated expressway in San Francisco, Seattle, and Portland, Oregon.[34] Montréal has begun a similar effort to replace the crumbling Bonaventure Expressway entering its downtown (Figure 12.9). The conversion of the Montréal expressways into boulevards[35] is a large-scale, downtown example of the

movement to build "complete streets" throughout an urban region. Complete streets carry automobile and service traffic, but they are designed to create good environments for pedestrians, cycling, and transit. New development standards for road infrastructure have been collaboratively designed by civil engineers and urban designers in several jurisdictions. These context-sensitive design solutions (Figure 12.6) are a significant improvement over the conventional road standards from the mid-20th century. They are being implemented in many Canadian communities, from Vancouver's local "skinny streets" to new road designs in Halifax.[36]

Traffic Calming

A traditional grid of streets is wonderful for walking and cycling, but older neighbourhoods can be inundated with through traffic if the adjacent arterial roads are overloaded. Similarly, suburban collector streets are often lined with homes whose residents are unhappy about the high volumes and speed of traffic whizzing past their driveways. At the behest of neighbourhood groups, many municipalities have made a policy decision to reduce the amount and speed of automobile traffic in local areas through the use of various pavement and signage devices, and thereby achieve **traffic calming.** This approach got its start in Europe (Germany, the Netherlands, Denmark) in the 1970s and later in Australia.[37] Three basic principles motivate traffic-calming approaches:

Figure 12.8	Conventional Street Hierarchy Compared to Traditional Street Types

CONVENTIONAL STREET HIERARCHY	TRADITIONAL STREET TYPES	
	MORE URBAN TYPES	MORE SUBURBAN TYPES
Expressway	Highway	Highway
Arterial	Boulevard, Main Street	Boulevard, Drive
Collector	Avenue	Connector
Local	Street	Road
Cul-de-sac	Stub	Close
Driveway	Back alley	Rear lane
Walkway	Passage	Path

Source: Adapted from Marshall Macklin Monaghan and Berridge Lewinberg Greenberg, *Making Choices: Alternative Development Standards* (Toronto: Ontario Ministry of Housing and Ontario Ministry of Municipal Affairs, 1994); and Duany & Plater-Zyberk Town Planners, *A Lexicon of the New Urbanism v.3.2* (Miami, Florida: DPZ, 2012).

Chapter 12 Planning Infrastructure Systems to Connect Communities

Figure 12.9	Transformation of Montréal's Bonaventure Expressway into an Urban Boulevard

The elevated Bonaventure Expressway was a major barrier in Montréal's Downtown Gateway in 2007 (top).

1. The function of streets is not to act just as a corridor for automobiles.
2. People have a right to a quality of life not spoiled by undue traffic caused by automobile use.
3. Trips are a means of accessing some desirable land use or activity, not an end in themselves.[38]

The thrust of these principles contrasts with the traditional planning principle of separating various forms of traffic (autos, cyclists, pedestrians) from one another. Traffic calming invokes public policy in regard to one of the fundamental public responsibilities in a community environment—creating and maintaining public rights-of-way. Various methods are used in traffic calming, including raising the surface of streets at intersections (traffic "bumps"), narrowing streets with trees, building traffic circles, and looping streets.[39] Usually, traffic calming is undertaken on a neighbourhood-by-neighbourhood basis upon the request of the residents.

The Land Use/Transportation Connection

Land use has an important and strong connection to transportation demand. Land use variables such as district population and employment are the first inputs to the traditional transportation planning process, and there are reliable, accurate, and detailed models for trip generation for a wide variety of land uses.[40] Some community planners and urban designers would like to push the land use/transportation relationship further, suggesting that built form can directly affect travel behaviour. Advocates of Smart Growth and the New Urbanism have asserted that compact, mixed-use communities and transit-oriented development can reduce the demand for automobile travel.[41]

The idea that modifying the built environment can reduce automobile trips and increase the demand for sustainable transportation (walking, cycling, and transit) is quite appealing to planners and policymakers. Unfortunately the evidence is far from clear on this topic. Concentrating development close to rapid transit stations may increase ridership on these lines, but

An ambitious plan to replace the expressway with an urban boulevard contributes to the city's urban revitalization, freeing up land for development (bottom). This conceptual design focuses on office, hotel, and residential uses. The central city blocks, municipally owned, could accommodate nearly 600 residential units, plus shops and office space.

overall connections between built form and automobile travel demand are notoriously difficult to analyze. For example, a more connected street network not only shortens trips for pedestrians and cyclists but it also makes auto trips shorter. Despite two decades of debate and research, there is still no conclusive evidence that good urban design can change people's travel behaviour.[42] Progress in Transit-Oriented Development has been slow and the policy tools that economists judge to be most effective in changing behaviour (congestion charges in road tolls and higher parking prices) are seen as politically impractical.[43]

Planners prefer to reframe the issue to one of choice: we should promote better community planning because bad urban design makes walking, cycling, and public transit almost impossible, even for those who might wish to use more sustainable transportation. Transportation planner Susan Handy has identified twelve strategies that North American cities have adopted that can improve the population's mobility without promoting more driving:

1. Improve transit service information—web and smartphone apps for bus schedules
2. Encourage targeted transit—express buses, hospital and university shuttles
3. Improve walkability
4. Improve cyclability
5. Facilitate car-sharing
6. Encourage flex-work and telecommuting
7. Market directly to individual consumers
8. Impose congestion pricing on toll roads and bridges
9. Abolish minimum parking requirements and free parking
10. Improve connectivity for pedestrians and cyclists (new bridges)
11. Design complete streets
12. Coordinate land use and transportation planning.[44]

These strategies are the beginnings of a toolkit for sustainable transportation.

Grey Infrastructure: Utility Plans

Utility systems are the other major component of "grey infrastructure." The concrete pipes and poles that make up water, sanitary, stormwater, power, heat, and telecom systems are essential for urban life. Most of these systems are buried underground and we often ignore them

unless they fail. Most communities have functional plans for potable water, sanitary, stormwater, power, heat, and telecom systems, and the best-planned communities have integrated the planning of infrastructure and land use.

Water System Plans

An adequate supply of clean fresh water is an absolute requirement for human settlement, the urban economy, and public health—communities disappear if their potable water supply fails. Most Canadian cities are lucky, since they were originally sited beside enormous natural supplies of fresh water, which we continue to use in large quantities and discard. We take our water systems for granted until they stop working, often with serious public health consequences.

Planning for potable water, sanitary sewage, and stormwater systems was done separately for most of the 20th century. The three systems must be considered together as cities expand into metropolitan regions, especially in the Prairies, where Calgary, Edmonton, Lethbridge, Red Deer, Prince Albert, and Saskatoon are all dependent upon water flows in branches of the Saskatchewan River.[45] For many cities, water should be considered as a resource that flows into and through their region, to be used downstream by the next community.

Potable Water

The potable water system collects, stores, disinfects, and distributes this resource in pressurized pipes. This technology was developed in the 19th century and has proved quite successful in delivering clean drinking water to residents of most Canadian communities at a remarkably low cost. And when a resource is free or underpriced, it is often abused. Citizens of the many water-starved nations are astonished that Canadians use drinking water for industrial use, firefighting, or to flush toilets and water lawns.

The crucial planning decision for water systems is to select and protect a source of pure fresh water that is well *upstream* of the point where treated sanitary sewage is deposited. Disaster ensues when either selecting or protecting is forgotten. For example, Ottawa had two typhoid epidemics in 1911–12 because its water intake was downstream from a suburb that dumped raw sewage into the river, while the water supply in Walkerton, Ontario, was polluted in 2000 by farm runoff into an adjacent well.[46] Both these tragedies illustrate the importance of source water protection on a watershed basis, especially when the supply is from a river or groundwater.[47]

Water is cleaned and disinfected at a central plant in most cities. Distribution is relatively routine in most communities (Figure 12.10), since elevated reservoirs and electric pumps can push the water through a grid network of pressurized pipes to almost any urban location. Providing power to the community water systems pumps is therefore one of the most important considerations in disaster planning.

Sustainable water supply practices include reducing demand by using more water-efficient appliances such as low-flow shower heads and toilets, fixing leaks, and charging fees for water use. Domestic and industrial users may also be encouraged to recycle some of their less-polluted wastewater for tasks that do not require potable water, such as irrigation, toilets, and cooling.

Sanitary Sewage

The hydraulic system for removing wastewater used in Canadian communities is based upon engineering methods dating from the Roman era. Large amounts of fresh water are used to move small amounts of waste down oversized pipes using gravity flow. The sanitary sewage pipe network is therefore fundamentally different from the water supply grid. Sewer pipes run downhill in a branched network that follows the topography of a sub-watershed. The first sanitary sewers simply ran downhill under the streets and dumped their waste into the nearest creek or river. Some combined sewers also carried the runoff from paved streets. The next step was to build large interceptor sewers along the rivers or waterfront to collect the waste and carry it to an outlet pipe, downstream from the community.[48]

Most Canadian cities now treat their sanitary sewage because the cities grew so large that the human waste would destroy life in the receiving waters (see Figure 12.11). Primary and secondary plants were built at the end of the interceptor sewers. Primary treatment removes solids, while secondary treatment cleans the water to remove biological and chemical pollution. Some Canadian cities also have tertiary treatment, where advanced methods are used to clean and "polish" the effluent from the plant.

The Prairie cities on low-flow rivers had to lead the way, establishing secondary treatment plants prior to World War II. Ontario and Québec followed

Figure 12.10	Main Water Supply System in Winnipeg's New Plan, 2011

SOURCE: AECOM, "REGIONAL WATER SUPPLY AND FEEDERMAIN SYSTEM", IN SUSTAINABLE WATER AND WASTE DIRECTION STRATEGY, *OUR WINNIPEG* (2011), CITY OF WINNIPEG, PAGE 16.

Winnipeg's 2011 community plan is somewhat unusual, since it includes detailed discussions of the plans for its piped infrastructure, tying its comprehensive land use plan to its capital budget.

Figure 12.11	Green's Creek Water Pollution Control Plant, Ottawa

SOURCE: LIBRARY AND ARCHIVES CANADA E010775276/CANADA MORTGAGE AND HOUSING CORPORATION (CMHC).

This secondary treatment plant was built at the downstream edge of Ottawa's greenbelt. Raw sewage from 400 000 people was dumped into the Ottawa River before this plant was opened in the early 1960s.

in the 1950s and 1960s, but many coastal cities continued to dump their waste down a big pipe into the ocean until the late 20th century. Victoria still dumped raw sewage into the Juan de Fuca Straight in 2012, while Vancouver and Montréal discharge large quantities of waste that have only had primary treatment.[49]

One community planning implication of sanitary sewerage networks is that it is expensive and inefficient to locate a new neighbourhood downhill from the sewage treatment plant, since all the waste from this development must be pumped back uphill to the plant. A second implication is that if all the sanitary sewer pipes in a region flow downhill towards one point, then the treatment plant at that location must have plenty of room for expansion to meet the population growth of the region.

More sustainable practices for domestic wastewater are to disconnect combined sewers and reduce overall water consumption as described above. The "greywater" from showers, sinks, and washing machines might be recycled and used for irrigation and to run toilets, using slightly more complex plumbing and some on-site treatment.

Stormwater Planning

While water and sanitary sewage are still using collection and treatment systems from the 19th century, stormwater systems are changing drastically. Ditches, culverts, and storm sewers are still used to remove stormwater runoff, but more sustainable practice now focuses on managing the stormwater rather than diverting it as quickly as possible to the nearest stream. As land is developed for urban uses, the area of impervious surfaces increases, infiltration and evapotranspiration decrease, and stormwater runoff increases in volume and pollution loads. Installing bigger storm sewer pipes puts a larger pollutant load into the receiving waters and causes downstream flooding faster.[50]

More sustainable practice is to design new neighbourhoods, districts, and corridors to maximize infiltration and hold more water on site for longer, as recommended by Michael Hough and Ann Spirn.[51] This strategy may involve infiltration beds (see Figure 12.12), disconnecting roof drains, green roofs, swales, grass channels, and stormwater retention ponds. The objective is to have the new districts mimic healthy local watersheds in terms of the quality and quantity of stormwater flow. This involves designing new buildings,

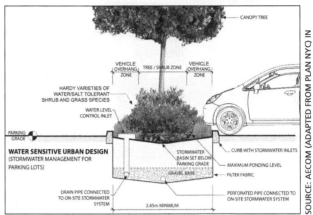

Figure 12.12 Stormwater Mitigation: Winnipeg Green Parking Lot Design, 2011

SOURCE: AECOM (ADAPTED FROM PLAN NYC) IN SUSTAINABLE WATER AND WASTE DIRECTION STRATEGY, *OUR WINNIPEG* (2011) CITY OF WINNIPEG, PAGE 42.

Winnipeg's 2011 community plan advocates water-sensitive urban design such as this stormwater management scheme for a parking lot. Water would be held in the planted areas and treated on site, rather than being piped to the nearest creek. This reduces peak flows in the creek and reduces pollution from the salts and oils and gasoline in most parking lot runoff.

streets, parks, and parking lots to conserve water and reduce flooding.[52]

Energy Systems Plans

Energy infrastructure is planned and managed by municipal utilities departments or special commissions in many Canadian communities. Every community has an electrical distribution system, and some larger cities also distribute natural gas in pressurized pipes. District heating systems pipe steam from a central boiler plant on the campuses of universities and hospitals and in some downtowns. Some sustainable new communities also include district heating. These are usually located in central urban sites, as Toronto's Regent Park, but master-planned new communities may also include district heating (Figure 12.13).

Residential and commercial space heating may also be fueled by oil or propane distributed by truck. High-efficiency wood stoves may be a sustainable fuel supply for domestic heating, especially in energy-efficient rural homes. Energy-efficient buildings use special design and construction techniques to reduce the fuel used in heating and air conditioning. CMHC offers much guidance on energy-efficient homes, while the Leadership in Energy

Figure 12.13	District Heating Proposal: New Monaco, British Columbia, 2011

District heating proposal for a small new community in New Monaco, Peachland, B.C.

The secondary plan for the community received the 2011 CIP Award for Rural/Small Town Planning.

and Environmental Design Canada (LEED Canada) ranking system from the Canada Green Buildings Council is now widely used to evaluate and compare the energy efficiency of commercial and institutional buildings.[53]

The **energy-efficient community** was an idea that came into prominence during the energy crisis of the 1980s and prompted the examination of built environments for opportunities to conserve energy.[54] It involves reducing the amount of travel by residents (especially by automobile), clustering land uses, and orienting buildings to take advantage of solar-heating possibilities. More recently, this concept is enfolded within Smart Growth and New Urbanism initiatives, especially with the LEED Neighbourhood Development (LEED-ND) initiative. The Bridges (Calgary), UniverCity (Burnaby), Vancouver's Village at False Creek, Upper Richmond Village (London), Montréal's Les Bassins du Nouveau Havre, and Pleasantville (St. John's) are examples of neighbourhoods planned with LEED-ND principles.

Planning Social Infrastructure

In well-managed communities, the physical infrastructure systems for social services have functional plans that are integrated with land use and transportation plans. Schools, libraries, recreation, and health care are examples of social infrastructure for which functional plans are prepared. The social infrastructure planning process is surprisingly similar to other plans: existing facilities are evaluated, historical and current demand is analyzed, future demand is forecast, and alternative

plans are evaluated and turned into a ranked set of capital projects.[55]

Unfortunately, infrastructure for social services is typically planned by separate functional boards, often with little coordination among them or with the land use planners. For example, an under-enrolled high school that is a vital community institution in north Kingston was threatened with closure in 2012, while adjacent properties held a library in need of repair and a community health clinic renting space in a strip mall. However, when these agencies planned collaboratively, their facilities were successfully combined in schools that became community hubs. Similarly, public and Catholic school boards in Kingston were carrying out separate system reviews in which all the downtown elementary and high schools were threatened with closure, while the municipality's land use and transportation plans called for residential intensification in the downtown area.[56]

School System Planning

Schools are a responsibility of Canadian provincial governments, with the services delivered by regional school boards or districts. There are three major types of schools, with the grade division varying across the provinces:

- Elementary schools (Kindergarten through Grades 5 or 6)
- Middle schools (Grades 6–9)
- Secondary/high schools (Grades 9–12; Grades 7–11 in Québec)

In addition, cities and larger towns could have a community college (CEGEP in Québec) and metropolitan areas have universities. College and university campuses are planned as separate districts (Chapter 11), while schools are typically planned as part of a community-wide system.

School system planning is loosely coordinated with neighbourhood planning in most Canadian communities. The neighbourhood unit principle (Chapter 4) recommends an elementary school at the centre of each neighbourhood, so that the children may walk to school. This is still considered the ideal in most communities, but in provinces with multiple school boards (Public/Catholic/English/French), new elementary schools may have to be placed in a campus at the edge of two or three neighbourhoods because there are not enough children from each school board within walking distance. As a result, the number of Canadian children walking to school is falling rapidly, with serious public health consequences.[57]

There are standard site sizes and land use planning locational criteria for schools in many communities: A new suburban elementary school site is typically about 4–5 hectares (10–12 acres) and located in the middle of a residential community, next to a neighbourhood park. A new middle school often has a 10-hectare site at the intersection of four neighbourhoods, and a high school is typically 15 hectares and adjacent to a district park, library, and other community facilities. School sites are usually identified in secondary plans and donated by the land developer to the school board. Good planning practice is for the municipal government and school boards to share parks and for school boards to share school facilities (gyms, libraries, cafeterias) so that one building complex may serve a neighbourhood within walking distance. Clustering of community facilities such as daycare centres, libraries, seniors' centres, health clinics, and recreational facilities can turn a school into a valuable community hub.[58]

School boards also use planning techniques for the operation of their facilities. Most boards have planning staff who are expert at predicting and tracking the generation of school children from various residential building types. Other school board planners use GIS technology to plot the bus routes that service most schools.

Recreation Planning

Recreation facilities planning has been similar to parks infrastructure planning discussed above. Municipal departments inventory the recreation facilities in their neighbourhoods, forecast demand, and prepare capital plans for more swimming pools, arenas, playing fields, and community centres. These facilities needs studies are sometimes based upon recreational planning standards (e.g., one 50-metre swimming pool per every 20 000 population) but are better forecast by detailed community needs studies.[59] Parks and recreation planning is typically supplemented by analysis of facility service areas using GIS to identify neighbourhoods that have little access.

Existing local taxpayers are usually unwilling to pay for new recreational facilities to serve future residents, so the capital expenditure program in a recreation facilities plan is sometimes used to justify a development charge for new homes and commercial buildings (Chapter 17). The operating expenses for some recreational facilities, such as arenas, may be recovered through user fees.

Recreation facilities are increasing in size and detaching themselves from neighbourhoods in many Canadian communities. There may still be a softball diamond in the neighbourhood park, but the trend is to create regional recreation centres with multiple sports fields, multi-pad arenas, and big parking lots. These facilities command higher rents and can be supervised by fewer staff, but few neighbourhoods want the ensuing traffic. Like big-box stores, these facilities are sometimes located in industrial districts where land is cheap, roads are wide, and there are few residents to complain about the evening and weekend parking (see Figure 12.14). Unfortunately, these facilities are then only useable by families with cars, since there is likely no evening or weekend transit service in the employment lands.

Health Systems Infrastructure Planning

A community's health system includes hospitals, speciality care facilities, medical offices, and seniors' care facilities. All these facilities may be combined in a medical district or suburban medical campus (Chapter 11). General hospitals are major building complexes that

Figure 12.14	Muskoseepi Park Plan, Grand Prairie, Alberta, 2009

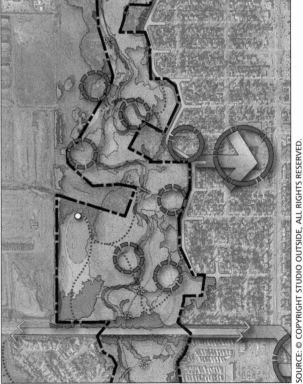

Recreation projects for the Bear Creek Corridor of the Muskoseepi Park.

require special access for emergency care and room for expansion and change. Teaching hospitals are associated with university medical schools and typically have significant research functions. They may be the centre of a biomedical research cluster that is a significant local new business generator, such as the MaRS Discovery District in downtown Toronto, or the two new super-hospital clusters under construction in Montréal.[60]

Speciality care facilities include rehabilitation clinics, psychiatric centres, and hospices for terminally ill patients. These are often located away from the hospitals in more quiet sites. Medical offices are distributed across a community to serve residents. The traditional neighbourhood doctor's office clinic in a home is almost extinct, as family care physicians are collaborating in group practices to share patients, nurse practitioners, and better facilities. These group practices may co-locate with a pharmacy or some specialists in a community medical office building. Other specialists may share medical office buildings co-located with a hospital campus.[61]

Senior living and care facilities will become more important community facilities in the decades ahead as the baby boomers age into retirement (see Chapter 13). There are several types of these facilities—traditional nursing homes with long-term skilled care, assisted living, and independent living facilities. An **independent living complex** looks like an apartment building but has more common facilities, usually including dining rooms. Sometimes these three levels of services are combined in a single complex and form a **continuing-care retirement community** that allows seniors to add services as needed. Some seniors' facilities may be located at or near a medical campus with others distributed throughout the city or town.[62]

Many other important medical services are delivered in free-standing clinics or directly to patients in their homes. Overall medical systems planning for a community is sometimes coordinated by a provincial or regional agency, such as Ontario's Local Health Integration Networks (LHINs). Typically, there is not much interaction between health policy planners and community planners about medical systems infrastructure outside the usual institutional land use planning process. Notably the City of Mississauga has taken steps to link its (CIP award-winning) Older Adult Plan with the "nodes" policy in its official plan.[63] Its goal is to concentrate vital services for elders in "nodes or pockets across the City" including medical clinics, pharmacies, and libraries.

| Figure 12.15 | Infrastructure as Public Art |

Infrastructure as Public Art: Charles River Bridge, Prague.

Infrastructure as Public Art: Millennium Bridge, London. Pedestrian bridge designed by Arup Foster.

Infrastructure as Public Art: Peace Bridge, Calgary. Pedestrian and cycling bridge designed by Santiago Calatrava.

Public health officials across Canada, by comparison, have been linking with community planners on various preventative medicine strategies, collectively known as Healthy Communities. These initiatives are explored in Chapter 13 along with discussion of planning for the needs of special population groups.

Reflections

The mundane world of community infrastructure is an aspect of development that many, including some planners, tend to take for granted. We may notice recurrent traffic snarls on a favourite work route or the lack of nearby schools, parks, and libraries in a home neighbourhood but seldom think that solutions to such problems are often interconnected. A community's land and water base are in many respects a "platform" for development, and the infrastructure provides the necessary linkages that allow for its beneficial functioning. Hence, the need for planning its many components.

Infrastructure planning is therefore essential for each of its separate parts and, not least, for those areas where they link and/or overlap with other infrastructure such as schools and parks or seniors' housing and sidewalks.

These practical connections, though difficult sometimes to ensure, may be the least difficult planning challenge. That may lie in the organizational landscape that deals with the various infrastructure components. It is seldom that all the components of a community's infrastructure lie within the realm of a single agency or department, much less that of the local planning department. The classic example of a "company town" would be one of the few exceptions, but even this community would be subject to connection with provincial infrastructure like highways and telecommunications systems. What planners must ultimately face up to is working with and obtaining cooperation among a number of agencies and departments over which there is nothing but a general obligation for them do so. This continues to be a recurring dilemma in much community planning.

- **Which types of infrastructure should be planned jointly and what would be the implications if not?**

- **Which types of infrastructure should be planned taking into account population groups in the community?**

Reference Notes

1. An amendment to B.C.'s planning legislation in the early 1990s requires every local government to include a policy statement on affordable housing in its official community plans.

2. Barton Reid, "Go-Plan Looking into the Future," *City Magazine* 16:1 (Spring 1995), 8–10.

3. Mark Benedict and Edward McMahon, *Green Infrastructure: Linking Landscapes and Communities* (Washington, DC: Island Press, 2006); and Michael Hough, *Cities and Natural Process: A Basis for Sustainability* (New York: Routledge, 2004).

4. Cynthia Zaitzevsky, *Frederick Law Olmsted and the Boston Park System* (Cambridge, MA: Harvard University Press, 1982); Frederick Todd, *Preliminary Report to the Ottawa Improvement Commission* (Ottawa: OIC, 1903); and David Gordon, "Frederick G. Todd and the Origins of the Park System in Canada's Capital," *Journal of Planning History* 1: 1 (March 2002), 29–57.

5. Hok-Lin Leung *Land Use Planning Made Plain,* 2nd ed. (Toronto: University of Toronto Press, 2003).

6. Paul Wilkinson, "The Golden Fleece: The Search for Standards," *Leisure Studies* 4:2 (1985), 189–203; and Seymour Gold, "Non-use of Neighbourhood Parks," *Journal of the American Institute of Planners* 38:6 (1972), 369–386.

7. Jan Gehl, *Cities for People* (Washington, DC: Island Press, 2010); William H. Whyte, *City: Rediscovering the Center* (Philadelphia: University of Pennsylvania Press, 2009); and Clare Cooper Marcus and Carolyn Francis, *People Places: Design Guidelines for Urban Open Space* (New York: Wiley, 1998).

8. Cynthia Girling and Ron Kellett, *Skinny Streets and Green Neighborhoods: Design for Environment and Community* (Washington, DC: Island Press, 2005), Chapter 6, "Green Fabric".

9. Tom Daniels and Katherine Daniels, *The Environmental Planning Handbook for Sustainable Communities and Regions* (Chicago: APA Planners Press, 2003); and Thomas Dunne and Luna Leopold, *Water in Environmental Planning* (New York: Freeman, 1978).

10. Barry Sandler, "Shared Resources, Common Future: Sustainable Management of Canada–United States Border Waters," *Natural Resources Journal* 33:2 (1993).

11. B. Stone, "Paving over Paradise: How Land Use Regulations Promote Residential Imperviousness," *Landscape and Urban Planning* 69 (2004),101–113.

12. Thomas Schueler and Heather Holland, *The Practice of Watershed Protection: Techniques for Protecting and Restoring Urban Watersheds* (Washington, DC: Center for Watershed Protection, 2000); and C.L. Arnold and J. Gibbons, "Impervious Surface Coverage: The Emergence of a Key Environmental Indicator," *Journal of the American Planning Association* 62:2 (1996), 243–259.

13. Rouge Watershed Task Force, *Rouge River Watershed Plan* (Toronto, ON: Toronto Region Conservation Authority, 2007); Ontario Ministry of Environment & Energy/ Ontario Ministry of Natural Resources, *Subwatershed Planning* (1993); and Hough Stansbury Woodland, *Bringing Back the Don* (City of Toronto,1991).

14. John P. Smol, *Pollution of Lakes and Streams: A Paleoenvironmental Perspective,* 2nd ed. (Cambridge, MA: Blackwell, 2008).

15. J. Durley, "Linking Integrated Sustainability Planning and Watershed Planning in Ontario, Canada," *Environments* 35:1 (2007), 57–76; David Godschalk, "Build-Out Analysis: A Valuable Planning and Hazard Mitigation Tool," *Zoning Practice* (2006), 3; and Queen's School of Urban and Regional Planning, *Lake and Watershed Planning in the Cataraqui Region: Challenges, Tools & Innovation* (Kingston, ON: Cataraqui Region Conservation Authority, 2008), www.cataraquiregion. on.ca/management/lakeplanning.htm

16. Township of Lake of Bays, ON, *Development Permit Bylaw 04-180*, March 2007; and R.M. Pollock and Graham Whitelaw, "Community-Based Monitoring in Support of Local Sustainability," *Local Environment* 10:3 (2005), 211–228.

17. Ian McHarg, *Design with Nature* (New York Doubleday, 1969), chapter 3; Timothy Beatley, David Brower, and Anna Schwab, *An Introduction to Coastal Zone Management* (Washington, DC: Island Press, 2002); and Betsy Otto, Kathleen

McCormack, and Michael Leccese, *Ecological Riverfront Design: Restoring Rivers, Connecting Communities* (Chicago: American Planning Association, 2004), PAS report 518/519.

18. Urban Land Institute, *Remaking the Urban Waterfront* (Washington, DC: ULI, 2004).

19. Michael Meyer and Eric Miller, *Urban Transportation Planning,* 2nd ed. (New York: McGraw Hill, 2001).

20. Preston Schiller, Eric Bruun, and Jeffrey R. Kenworthy, *An Introduction to Sustainable Transportation: Policy, Planning and Implementation* (London: Earthscan, 2010); and Madhav Badami, "Urban Transport Policy as if People and the Environment Mattered: Pedestrian Accessibility the First Step," *Economic and Political Weekly*, XLIV:33 (2009), 43–51.

21. Charles Montgomery, "Life Cycles," *Canadian Geographic* 129:2 (April 2009), 17; Evelyn Blumenberg, "En-gendering Effective Planning: Spatial Mismatch, Low-Income Women, and Transportation Policy,". *Journal of the American Planning Association*, 70:3 (2004), 69–281; and Devaiyoti Deka, "Social and Environmental Justice Issues in Urban Transportation," in Susan Hanson and Genevieve Giuliano, eds., *The Geography of Urban Transportation* (New York, Guilford Press, 2004).

22. Raktim Mitra, Ron Buliung, and Matthew Roorda, "The Built Environment and School Travel Mode Choice in Toronto, Canada," *Transportation Research Record* 2156 (2010), 2150–2159; Ruben Mercado and Antonio Páez, "Determinants of Distance Travelled with a Focus on the Elderly: A Multilevel Analysis in the Hamilton CMA, Canada," *Journal of Transport Geography* 17:1 (2009), 65–76; and Xinyu Cao, Patricia Mokhtarian, and Susan Handy, "Neighborhood Design and the Accessibility of the Elderly: An Empirical Analysis in Northern California," *International Journal of Sustainable Transportation* 4:6 (2010), 347–371.

23. Paul Hess and Jane Farrow, "Walkability in Toronto's High-Rise Neighbourhoods," (University of Toronto, 2011); Asha Weinstein, Marc Schlossberg, and Katja Irvin, "How Far, by Which Route and Why? A Spatial Analysis of Pedestrian Preference," *Journal of Urban Design* 13:1 (2008), 81–98; and Peter Bosselmann, *Urban Transformation: Understanding City Design and Form* (Washington, DC: Island Press, 2008).

24. *Ville de Montréal, Reinvent Montréal: Transportation Plan,* 2008, 54.

25. Bruce Appleyard, "Bicycle and Pedestrian Planning," in Gary Hack, Eugénie Birch, Paul Sedway, and Mitchell Silver, eds., *Local Planning: Contemporary Principles and Practice* (Washington, DC: ICMA, 2009), 366–374.

26. Mia Berk, "On-Street Bikeways," in Frederick Steiner and Kent Butler, eds., *Planning and Urban Design Standards: Student Edition* (New York: Wiley, 2007); and Girling and Kellett, *Skinny Streets*, chapter 4.

27. John Pucher and Ralph Buehler, "Cycling in Canada and the United States: Why Canada is So Far Ahead," *Plan Canada* (Spring 2007), 13–17.

28. Ville de *Montréal, Reinvent Montréal*, Section 3-A; and Jacob Larsen and Ahmed El-Geneidy, "A Travel Behavior Analysis of Urban Cycling Facilities in Montréal Canada," *Transportation Research Part D: Transport and Environment,* 16:2 (2011), 172–177.

29. Transportation Research Board (TRB), *Bus Rapid Transit* (Washington, DC: TRB, 2004), TCRP Report 90.

30. Transportation Research Board (TRB), *Light Rail Transit: Planning, Design and Implementation* (Washington, DC: TRB), TRB Special Report 195.

31. Ontario Ministry of Transportation and Urban Strategies, *Transit-Supportive Guidelines* (2011); Pierre Filion, K. McSpurren, and B. Appleby, "Wasted Density? The impact of Toronto's Residential-Density-Distribution Policies on Public-Transit Use and Walking," *Environment and Planning A* 38 (2006),1367–1392; and Ajay Agarwal and Genevieve Giuliano, "Public Transit as a Metropolitan Growth and Development Strategy, in H. Wolman, N. Pindus, and H. Wial, eds., *Urban and Regional Policy and Its Effects, Vol. 3* (Washington, DC: Brookings Institution, 2010).

32. John Lorinc, "While Toronto Feuded, Los Angeles Built," *The Globe and Mail* (April 2, 2012).

33. Susan Handy, Kent Butler, and Robert Paterson, *Planning for Street Connectivity* (Chicago: American Planning Association, 2003), PAS Report 515; the Fused Grid is an attempt to combine a road hierarchy similar to Radburn with a pedestrian and cycling path grid as seen in Fanis Grammenos, Barry Craig, Douglas Pollard, and

Carla Guerrera, "Hippodamus Rides to Radburn: A New Model for the 21st Century," *Journal of Urban Design* 13:2 (2008), 163–176; and Fanis Grammenos, "Stratford Leads the Way to a New Model of Suburban Development," *Plan Canada* 45:1 (Spring 2005), 20–22.

34. Alan Jacobs, Elizabeth Macdonald, and Yodan Rofé, *The Boulevard Book: History, Evolution and Design of Multiway Boulevards* (Cambridge, MA: The MIT Press, 2002); and Alan Jacobs, *Great Streets* (Cambridge, MA: The MIT Press, 1993).

35. Raphaël Fischler, "What Sort of Problem is the Replanning of the Turcot Interchange?" in Pierre Gauthier, Jochen Jaeger, and Jason Prince, eds., *Montréal at the Crossroads: Superhighways, the Turcot and the Environment* (Montréal: Black Rose Books, 2009), 79–89.

36. Marshall Macklin Monaghan and Berridge Lewinberg Greenberg, *Making Choices: Alternative Development Standards* (Toronto: Ontario Ministry of Housing and Ontario Ministry of Municipal Affairs, 1994); and Institute of Transportation Engineers, *Designing Walkable Urban Thoroughfares: A Context Sensitive Approach* (Washington, DC: ITE, 2010); Girling and Kellett, *Skinny* Streets, Chapter 4.

37. A good example from Australia is Citizens Advocating Responsible Transportation, *Traffic Calming: The Solution to Urban Traffic and a New Vision of Neighbourhood Livability* (Angrove Q., Australia, 1989).

38. Citizens Advocating Responsible Transportation, 18–19; see also Donald Appleyard, *Livable Streets*, (Berkeley, CA: University of California Press, 1981).

39. J.P. Braaksma & Associates, "Reclaiming the Streets: Setting the Stage for a Traffic Calming Policy in Ottawa" (City of Ottawa, 1995); Cynthia Hoyle, *Traffic Calming* (Chicago: American Planning Association), PAS Report 456; and Reid Ewing, *Traffic Calming: State of the Practice* (Washington, DC: Institute of Transportation Engineers, 1999).

40. Meyer and Miller, *Urban Transportation Planning;* Institute of Transportation Engineers, *Trip Generation Manual,* 9th ed. (Washington, DC: ITE, 2012); Michael Iacono, David Levinson, and Ahmed El-Geneidy, "Models of Transportation and Land Use Change: A Guide to the Territory," *Journal of Planning Literature* 22:4 (2008), 323–340.

41. Ray Tomalty and Murtaza Haider, *Comparing New Urbanist & Conventional Suburban Developments in Canada* (Ottawa: CMHC, 2010); Andres Duany, Elizabeth Plater-Zyberk, and Jeff Speck, *Suburban Nation: The Rise of Sprawl and the Decline of the American Dream* (New York: North Point Press, 2001); and Congress of the New Urbanism, *Charter of the New Urbanism* (New York: McGraw Hill, 2000).

42. Marlon Boarnet and Randy Crane, *Travel by Design: The Influence of Urban Form on Travel* (New York: Oxford University Press, 2001); Reid Ewing and Robert Cervero, "Travel and the Built Environment: A Meta-analysis," *Journal of the American Planning Association* 76:3 (2010), 1–30; Pierre Filion, "The Mixed Success of Nodes as a Smart Growth Planning Policy," *Environment and Planning B: Planning and Design*, 36 (2009), 505–521; and Pierre Filion and Kathleen McSpurren, "Smart Growth and Development Reality: The Difficult Coordination of Land Use and Transport Objectives," *Urban Studies* 44:3 (March 2007).

43. Ahmed El-Geneidy, Assumpta Cerdá, Raphaël Fischler and Nik Luka, "Evaluating the Impacts of Transportation Plans Using Accessibility Measures: A Test Case in Montréal," *Canadian Journal of Urban Research: Canadian Planning and Policy* 20:1 (Supplement 2011), 81–104; Pierre Filion, "The Mixed Success of Nodes as a Smart Growth Planning Policy," *Environment and Planning B: Planning and Design* 36 (2009), 505–521; Anthony Downs, *Still Stuck in Traffic: Coping with Peak-Hour Traffic Congestion* (Washington, DC: Brookings Institution, 2004); and Donald Shoup, *The High Cost of Free Parking* (Chicago: American Planning Association, 2005).

44. Susan Handy, "Twelve Ideas for Improving Mobility," in Hack et al., *Local Planning* 364–366.

45. www.albertawatersmart.com

46. Dennis O'Connor, *Report of the Walkerton Commission of Inquiry* (Toronto: Publications Ontario, 2002). Part 2 has a good discussion of water system issues across Ontario and the background papers address national trends.

47. Daniels and Daniels, *Environmental Planning Handbook*.

48. Metcalf and Eddy, *Wastewater Engineering Treatment and Re-use* (New York: McGraw Hill, 2003).

49. Jamie Benedickson, *Water Supply and Sewage Infrastructure in Ontario, 1880–1990s* (Toronto: Queen's Printer, 2002); Sierra Legal Defense Fund, *The National Sewage Report Card: Grading the Sewage Treatment of 22 Canadian Cities* (Vancouver: SLDF, 2004); Victoria may finally have secondary treatment by 2017; and Cindy Harnett, "Three Governments Announce Deal for Greater Victoria Sewage Plant," *Victoria Times Colonist* (July 16, 2012).

50. Schueler and Holland, *Practice of Watershed Protection*.

51. Hough, *Cities and Natural Process*; and Anne Whiston Spirn, *The Granite Garden; Urban Nature and Human Design* (New York: Basic Books, 1984).

52. Girling and Kellett, *Skinny Streets*, chapter 7.

53. See CMHC's Equilibrium Housing at www.cmhc-schl.gc.ca; Canada Green Building Council, www.cagbc.org

54. Hans Blumenfeld, "Some Simple Thoughts on the 'Energy Crisis,'" *Plan Canada* 20:3 (September 1980), 145–153.

55. Paul Brown, "Infrastructure Planning," in Hack et al., *Local Planning* 356–359.

56. David Clandfield and George Martell, eds., *The School as Community Hub: Beyond Education's Iron Cage* (Toronto: The Canadian Centre for Policy Alternatives, 2010); and David Gordon, "'School Desert' Would Doom Inner City," *Kingston Whig Standard* (May 10, 2012).

57. Juan Torres, Yves Bussière, and Paul Lewis, "Schools Territorial Policy and Active Commuting: Institutional Influences in Montréal and Trois Rivières," *Journal of Urban Planning and Development* 136:4 (2010), 287–293; and G.E.J. Faulkner, R.N. Buliung, P.K. Flora, and C. Fusco, "Active School Transport, Physical Activity Levels and Body Weight of Children and Youth: A Systematic Review," *Preventive Medicine* 48 (2009), 3–8.

58. Hok-Lin Leung, *Land Use Planning Made Plain* (Toronto: University of Toronto Press, 2003), chapter 5; and "Minister Applauds Boards for Joint School," *Brantford Expositor* May 11, 2012).

59. Leung, *Land Use Planning*, Table 5-2; and Wilkinson, "The Golden Fleece."

60. Hannah Hoag, "Ontario: Messages from MaRS," *Nature* 434:7033 (2005), 676–677; and Chee Chan, "A Comparative Analysis of The McGill University Health Centre Glen Campus and the Proposed Université de Montréal Campus Developments," McGill University CURA Working Paper WP08-02E, May 2008.

61. Richard Herring, "Medical Facilities," in Steiner and Butler, *Planning and Urban Design Standards*, 138–141.

62. Bradford Perkins, *Building Type Basics for Senior Living* (New York: Wiley, 2004); and Jacqueline Kerr et al., "Assessing Health-Related Resources in Senior Living Residences," *Journal of Aging Studies* 25:3 (August 2011), 206–214.

63. City of Mississauga, *Older Adult Plan* (2008), www.mississauga.ca/file/COM/Older_Adult_Plan

Internet Resources

Chapter-Relevant Sites

Planning Canadian Communities
www.planningcanadiancommunities.ca

Canada Walks
www.canadawalks.ca

13

Chapter Thirteen

Planning for Diverse and Healthy Communities

...to be able to carry out life's activities within a normal community setting, to be able to make choices about these activities, and to have a degree of control over one's life.

Blossom Wigdor and Louise Plouffe, 1992

The epigraph that heads this chapter was composed originally to highlight the strongly held desire of elderly people to continue to participate in the life of their communities, to retain their independence.[1] It is about a goal of reducing barriers to participation while still maintaining individual autonomy and choice. This goal pertains just as readily to other population groups in a community as it does to older people. For example, think of women, youth, cultural groups, persons with disabilities, Aboriginal peoples, single parents, and the homeless. They, too, frequently face barriers, physical and otherwise, to active participation in their cities and towns. The hurdles may differ among groups, as will the means for overcoming them but not the overall end. These groups, and others, comprise the "diversity" proclaimed so frequently about our communities and which planners are urged to heed in their practice. As Healey notes, "Traditionally, planners assumed that people were more or less the same—a standardized unit."[2] As planners came to know early on from the popular reactions to freeways and urban renewal, differences among the people of a community are abiding components. These differences are both social and personal, but they are also often closely linked to a city or town's space, to the "places" in which the residents live, shop, work, recreate.

Planners have come to recognize that the diversity in a community they're urged to take into account can be extremely variegated and pose problems regular planning and policy models do not allow for. In this chapter, the spatial aspects of community diversity are explored along with their implications for planning and planners. As discussion proceeds two questions should be considered:

- *What are three traits that link different human groups in a community?*
- *What distinguishes "place" among a community's human groups?*

Planning Theory: Planning for Diversity on the Ground

The notion that diversity in a community's population is important for planners entered planning discourse two or more decades ago. It was associated with the recognition of distinct ethnocultural neighbourhoods, notably, in large cities.[3] Paralleling this was the emergence of concerns over women, the poor, blacks, gays, Aboriginal peoples, and ethnic groups excluded from planning thinking and practice as well as feeling excluded from using city spaces.[4] Well before that, public protests over freeway building and urban redevelopment, plus numerous NIMBY (Not In My Backyard) reactions, had shown that community interests and values were far from homogenous. Indeed, Davidoff's 1965 notion of "advocacy planning" on behalf of districts within a city is a benchmark in urging the recognition of diversity among people and neighbourhoods as an important objective of planning.[5]

The extensive history of street and theoretical protests confirms that not all citizens of a city or town can be expected to view planned land use changes in the same way. However, beyond this broad recognition of diversity the planner needs to grasp the spatial basis of concerns that may be raised. For what is frequently at the heart of expressed differences over community environments is twofold. On the one hand, it is about *"disturbing"* the land uses, structures, and/or natural features in localities that people know well and strongly value. Neighbourhoods are a good example of such spaces in a community; residents experience them physically and personally. They become, often in a very short time, more than a set of land uses and buildings; they become "places" to which residents are attached through memories, needs, and associations.[6] Strong attachments to other places in a community are also not uncommon, such as parks, special shopping

areas, and waterfront sites. On the other hand, concerns about plans for developing these familiar "places" may arise from a sense of being *excluded* from the decision making—from the planning—that could change them.[7]

Places are not finite geographical spaces; for example, they would not usually fit the areal divisions of a zoning map. A place is, at root, an "interpretation" of the qualities, the meaning, of the particular space given to it by people, by users and visitors.[8] Further, a characterization by one resident (or shopper or employee or visitor) may not be shared by all who cohabit or frequent the area. Two examples of place attachment, one about older people and another concerning people in an ethnic enclave, can help understand the repercussions planners could face with initiatives for change:

- Senior citizens have a strong tendency to reside for a long period of time in the same dwelling and in that way accumulate a strong attachment to their home and neighbourhood. This results from the familiarity with their locale and routinely traversing its space, socializing with neighbours and shopkeepers, visiting the local park, and attending church or library, places that impart to them a sense of identity and stability. Changes in transportation, gentrification, and commercial redevelopment are three "disturbances" that may be unsettling for seniors' lives.[9]
- The residents of a Chinese neighbourhood in Ottawa learned that an application had been made to build a funeral home in the area. Since the presence of the dead near their homes and businesses is anathema in Chinese culture, they protested this move. Despite this, funeral homes were a legitimate land use in the zoning bylaw.[10]

Whether the situations are highly localized (e.g., funeral homes) or more generalized (e.g., older residents), they each emphasize the diversity of needs and values of people in the community. And because of this, a planner's typical notion of the city as an integrated system of land uses and functions linked by transportation is disrupted.[11] This paradigm needs to be reshaped to include the multiple conceptions of community space. Alongside, planning practice needs to be recast to "hear" better the "voices" of these places. Communicative planning approaches that emphasize dialogue when contesting views need to be resolved are suggested to help frame the dialogue and thereby articulate the place itself.[12] That is, by using an inclusive, empowering approach to widen discussions, planners and residents are better able to understand each other's interpretation of the space/place in question (see also Chapters 6 and 15). Critics of this approach note that communicative theory does not provide for a system of reasoning to handle conflicting rationales among participants, or difference in institutionalized power (as we shall see below with Aboriginal peoples).[13]

When planners deal with diversity "on the ground," so to speak, what appears on the typical community plan as a two-dimensional city or town is now is no longer "flat" or the land uses universal.[14] It has topography, what might be called a "social landscape," something standard planning instruments generally are not able to capture adequately. There are, however, two avenues open for planners to consider. The first is a variation on sub-community or district plans (see Chapter 11), such as those currently being prepared for the elderly in a community. Among the latter are Older Adult Plans; there are already several notable ones in Canada.[15] Their focus is on older *people* and is not geographical but applicable to the entire community space. The aim of district plans is to respond to the needs and concerns of particular human groups (e.g., youth, women, ethnic populations, the homeless, Aboriginal peoples, persons with disabilities) and may appropriately be called *Human Services Plans*. Such plans, both in their preparation and implementation, allow "voices" from within the community's diverse components to be heard.

The second tack arises when responding to diversity situations featuring differing land use interpretations as with the funeral home example cited above. The approach now widely used is to respond to each situation on a case-by-case basis in the context of land use regulations and to seek a solution within their allowable limits. That is, "embedding [it] within the existing planning system," which characterizes the current practice in much multicultural planning both in Canada and the United States[16] The approach is called "reasonable accommodation" and is very much akin to the long-standing planning practice of granting a *variance* to a zoning designation (see Chapter 16). Both approaches will be found in the various sections that follow.

Older Adult Planning

Planning for seniors, or any of the other groups of a community's citizens discussed in this chapter, takes planners beyond the scope of the built and natural environments. The actual *users* of those environments become an active ingredient in making planning policy; they become more than a demographic category, an age group, or a social class "to take into account." Planning practice has only relatively recently taken up the challenges implicit in seniors' planning, and valuable experience is accumulating which can be drawn upon. There are as yet no agreed upon models and most of what can be said is at the guideline and checklist stage. However, two basic building blocks are required: (1) a demographic portrait of the community's elderly to show both their extent and diversity; and (2) an understanding of key attributes of aging and of older people's perspective on community life.

Demographic Perspectives

The 2011 Canada Census confirmed the long-forecasted surge in the county's seniors' population. With only a small fraction of the post-war baby boom's survivors counted, the share of those aged 65 and older rose to 14.8 percent, up from 13.7 percent in 2006, to a total of just under five million. Statistics Canada projections indicate that numbers of seniors will continue to grow even more until they double and account for more than one-quarter of the population at 2031.[17] And over the same period, most communities will also see a doubling of their seniors' population[18] (see Figure 13.1).

| Figure 13.1 | Impending Surge in the Seniors' Population |

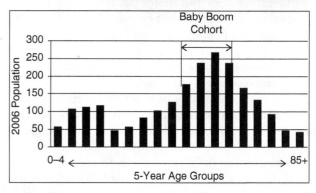

Typical community age profile for 2006 showing the surge of baby boom cohorts (45–64) who will become seniors in 2011.

Note: The term "seniors" is used in this and the following discussion to refer to those persons aged 65 and older. This is the standard term used in gerontology research in North America and is associated with assumed retirement from outside employment and pension entitlement. Other terms such as "the elderly" and "elders" are also used occasionally in referring to the same 65+ group. In planning and social service circles, the term "older adults" has come to be used and includes those older people who are not yet 65 and who may have similar needs for service.

In responding to this trend community planning will be affected in two ways: first, it will need to balance a "people" orientation with its normal built and natural environment orientation, that is, to focus on "users"; this will lead to the second effect of the need to engage a wide array of public and private agencies in the planning process, as the City of Regina found.[19]

Numbers alone are not what make the surge in seniors' population relevant for planners. For one, the surge of the baby boom cohorts into the ranks of the elderly will greatly diversify an already diverse seniors' population. To those who grew up in the 1920s and 1930s will be added those who grew up in the 1950s and 1960s. The "new" seniors' cohort will bring different social and economic experiences, as well as different perspectives on growing old compared to their older peers. The seniors' cohort that is emerging will include many foreign-born seniors, especially from Asian immigration since the 1970s. These visible minority seniors will age along with the Canadian-born boomers, but at a faster rate. Even faster will be the rate of increase in the number of Aboriginal elders in the population in the same period.[20]

For another, the age structure of the older population will have to be considered. The accepted way of describing the elderly is by a series of age groups as follows: those aged 65–74 (the old), those aged 75–84 (the old-old), and those aged 85 and older (the very old). Those approaching senior status, aged 55–64, are termed the young-old. Recognizing the seniors' age structure is vital for planning because of the differences in personal capacity and outlook that occur as a person ages. Generally, the older the age group, the greater the need for a variety of supports from those in the design of the home to low-floor buses in the transit system. Particular attention needs to be paid to the old-old and very old comprising the seniors' population (see Figure 13.3). As the baby boom cohort reach and pass age 65, the numbers and proportions in each age group will change. The most noticeable change in the first decade will be the dramatic expansion of the young-old group. It is important in this transition not to overlook the continued aging of existing seniors, especially the very old.

Parameters of Aging

Beyond gaining a picture of demographic dynamics associated with the current surge in seniors is the need to acquire an appreciation of several factors central to an aging and aged population:

- *Seniors' Independence (SI):* This goal, which opened this chapter, is cited perennially by seniors. It is a broad concept in which seniors are able to remain active in their community and choose the form that might take.[21] British Columbia seniors, when asked what needed to be in place to assure their independence, cited first the need for security of *health* and security of *income*.[22] Canadian seniors enjoy a great deal of such security through federal and provincial programs. Three other factors were identified as needed to offer independence in the communities where they lived: security in each of *housing, transportation,* and *community support*. These are functions that occur primarily at the community level and involve local and regional governments, service agencies, and the voluntary sector. These factors clearly impinge on the domain of the planner. As shown in Figure 13.2 these factors are closely associated with one another and should be dealt with at the same time.[23] Further, to the formal terms of housing, transportation, and support have been added commonplace words to indicate their place within a senior's everyday world.

- *Diversity:* Whatever term used to identify them, "seniors," "older adults," or "65+," they are not a homogenous group. They differ by gender, age, income, ethnicity, and living arrangements, among other attributes. Planners are urged to assemble a knowledge base of these data at a minimum in order to understand better the seniors in their community, preferably at the census tract level (see Figure 13.4). In addition, interrelationships need to be observed such as between income and gender (women seniors are less affluent, especially those who live alone) and

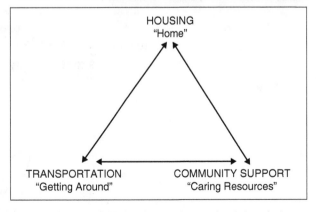

Figure 13.2 **Community Factors in Seniors' Independence**

All three factors are central to seniors maintaining their active participation in the community. Importantly, each factor is closely linked to each of the other two.

Chapter 13 Planning for Diverse and Healthy Communities

age and gender (women are more numerous in older age groups).[24] As noted above, our communities frequently house seniors from various ethnocultural backgrounds. Regrettably, most gerontological research has been "colour blind" and little is known about whether our knowledge base of such as seniors' living arrangements, family support, and daily activities fit those of visible minority seniors.[25] Thus, planners are urged to note such gaps when encountering situations in which ethnic elders' needs are prominent.

- *Aging:* Diversity among seniors changes with time. Entire age cohorts change over time as do individuals within them. Some will retain the ability to carry out a wide variety of activities well into later life while some will not (e.g., driving a car or climbing stairs). Frailty differs among seniors by degree, the age it occurs, and the kind of frailty. Thus, planning decisions based on age alone, or any other single characteristic, are seldom wisely taken (see Figure 13.3).
- *Aging in Place:* This now-commonplace term in matters dealing with the elderly means the tendency of

Figure 13.3	Characteristics of Older Adult Age Groups, Richmond, British Columbia

OLDER ADULT AGE GROUPS	EXPECTED BC % INCREASE 2007–2032	GENERALIZED CHARACTERISTICS	PROGRAM IMPLICATIONS
55 to 59 Young Old	38%	• working adults, early retirees, starting to caregive for parents, while looking after teens • generally healthy and pursing self-health management • knowledgeable about needs, informed consumers • financially stable • want control and involvement in planning and implementation • competing priorities (work, life, caregiving, roles) • had more opportunities to choose and participate in leisure over lifetime • advanced retirement planning, especially for men, appears to be the key element in regards to retirement planning	• one off and short term • active, non-traditional (yoga, pilates) • social and learning opportunities • choice of activity and timing (evenings) • open to explore alternative wellness options • expect knowledgeable instructors and quality environments/equipment • retirement exploration/ planning leisure education
60 to 64	82%	• retired or retiring, working part time or volunteering • healthy, beginning to experience some declines in strength and stamina • knowledgeable about needs, informed consumers • interested in learning how to protect against decline in their own health • may have limitations due to chronic conditions	• adaptive programs (e.g. Better Backs & Balance) • flexible schedules • variety & outrips • learning component • need some introductory level services with leisure education and counseling • 3rd age specific instructors

Age	%	Characteristics	Program/Service Considerations
65 to 75 Middle Old	137%	• as above • newly retired • caregiver role for children diminishing, increasing spousal and friend role • declining social and family connections • more tied to cultural roots, less flexible to adapt • engages in some physical activity and can perform activities of daily living, but may have functional limitations • may have medical conditions or chronic conditions	• opportunities for social connection • seniors centers, club membership, groups • well paced health promotion • flexible scheduling • culturally appropriate programming • need some introductory level services with leisure education and counseling • 3rd age specific instructors and programs • caregiver respite and shared leisure programs • translated program information
75 to 84	133%	• experiencing general age related decline – physical, sensory changes • variable cognitive decline • decreasing social connections, and opportunities • more diverse than other groups • engage in limited physical activity • may have medical conditions or movement limitations and increased likelihood of chronic conditions • elder women 'tribes' experiencing leisure together	• intergenerational opportunities to teach and understand youth • more traditional leisure pursuits like bridge, bingo, seasonal events • exercise to improve strength, range of motion, balance and coordination • caregiver respite and shared leisure programs • supported entry options for 1:1 or groups
85+ Oldest Old	131%	• frail elderly often experience physical or mental disabilities that may interfere with the ability to independently perform activities of daily living • experience of loneliness found to increase with age, leveling at age 90 • decreased mobility and increased use of public or group transportation	• movement that helps maintain or improve physical function for basic self-care • opportunities for social connection • more traditional leisure pursuits • supportive environments and programs with skilled staff/care including food • increased transportation

Developmental Goals in Later Adulthood

Middle-Age Adult – Generativity versus Stagnation. Seeks satisfaction through productivity in career, family, and civic interests.

Older Adult – Integrity versus Despair. Reviews life accomplishments, deals with loss and preparation for death.

SOURCE: OLDER ADULT SERVICES PLAN, PAGE 12, 2008, CITY OF RICHMOND, BC.

Differences in age structure must be taken into account when planning programs and services for seniors.

them wanting to remain in their current dwelling as they grow older. There is considerable research to show that seniors' mobility decreases noticeably with age, both locally and beyond the community.[26] Objective measures, however, capture only a small portion of the significance of this concept for seniors and their planning. There is embedded in it, for one, seniors' attachment to their own homes because of the security it represents, the memories it holds, and its location in relation to friends, familiar neighbourhoods, and their services.[27] "Home," thus, comes to mean more than mere shelter; it embodies a substantial relationship—transactions between seniors and their residential environments, including "getting around" in it and being able to obtain "support" (see Figure 13.2). It follows that these accumulated layers of meaning about home and neighbourhood comprise a "place" for a senior. These valued spaces in a seniors' community should be reflected and their "voice" allowed for in its planning as discussed at the outset of the chapter.

Approaches to Seniors' Planning

There is no single precept on which to construct a seniors' plan. Given the limited and variable experience to this point, several approaches suggest themselves and are explored below. They range from a generic seniors' plan, an accommodation to accepted plan modes, and a human services plan devoted to seniors and other older adults. A further option to be briefly discussed flows from the Age-Friendly model of the World Health Organization (WHO).[28]

Generic Seniors' Planning

The making of a seniors' plan, whether free-standing or a constituent of a larger plan, would follow the process used in other community planning efforts. It would follow a process that is essentially linear and has ample opportunity for review of decisions and choices at the various steps and for reiteration of all or part of the process, as discussed in Chapter 6 and shown in Figure 6.1, page 145. Putting this process into more formal terms, seniors' planning should comprise five stages:[29]

1. *Seniors' Plan Steering Committee:* Assemble a panel of seniors and empower them to guide the conduct of plan-making, to make recommendations on its implementation, and to continue to monitor its progress. The aim is to ensure a seniors' imprint on the plan.

2. *Seniors' Plan Assessment:* There are two phases to this stage: (1) to determine the preferences and needs of community seniors, perhaps through visioning exercises, surveys, and group discussions as noted in Chapter 15; and (2) to acquire demographic and other relevant data about seniors (e.g., neighbourhood safety audits) as indicated in Figure 13.4.

3. *Seniors' Plan Development:* This is the process of establishing goals and developing an action plan to implement them. Two sample goals are (1) to ensure that all seniors in the community are adequately housed and have transportation to all necessary facilities and services; and (2) to assure that seniors from all cultures will be able to obtain information about community transportation, services, and resources.

4. *Seniors' Plan Implementation:* Take the necessary policy and regulatory steps to carry out the plan. It is central to seniors' planning that seniors be involved not only in formulating the plan but also in implementing it, and the latter role could fall to the Steering Committee.

5. *Seniors' Plan Review:* The plan and its outcomes should be reviewed regularly as should the demographic picture (e.g., census updates) and other contextual variables (e.g., accident and safety data).

The process just described, while generally applicable, needs to be fine-tuned for each community to take into account differences in location, land use structure, community resources, housing stock, etc.

Planning communities that enable seniors to express their independence and enjoy a high quality of life goes well beyond the location and types of housing, the provision of transportation, and the availability of support resources, although these are major elements, and involves concerns about 'belonging" and "making life meaningful" and safety.[30] Not least, there has also to be a concern over details in the environment such as sidewalk surfaces, the placement of benches, well-lit transit stops, legible signs, and snow clearance.[31]

Seniors' Planning within Official Plans

A second approach is to explicitly incorporate planning for the seniors' population and their needs into the overall community plan. At this time, there is limited experience of Canadian communities making use of this approach. Nonetheless, some brief conjecture on the scope of what this would entail is possible. Given seniors' expressed desire for independence (SI) and the important

Figure 13.4   Preparing for Seniors' Planning: A Checklist

Where Do Seniors Live?

- ❏ Identify community neighbourhoods
- ❏ Identify neighbourhood shopping facilities
- ❏ Determine public transit services
- ❏ Assess sidewalk quality/coverage
- ❏ Identify different housing types

Who are the Neighbourhood Seniors?

- ❏ Numbers
- ❏ Age composition
- ❏ Gender composition
- ❏ Living arrangements
- ❏ Income levels
- ❏ Ethnic/cultural composition

How to Communicate with Seniors?

- ❏ Establish a Seniors' Committee
- ❏ Identify seniors' meeting places
- ❏ Identify neighbourhood meeting venues
- ❏ Inform by appropriate media

Who Should be Involved in Seniors' Planning?

- ❏ Seniors and families
- ❏ Municipal departments
- ❏ Provincial agencies
- ❏ Health care sector
- ❏ Community support groups

SOURCE: ADAPTED FROM GERALD HODGE, *THE GEOGRAPHY OF AGING: PREPARING COMMUNITIES FOR THE SURGE IN SENIORS* (MONTREAL: McGILL-QUEEN'S UNIVERSITY PRESS, 2008), FIGURE 8.2, P. 241.

A minimum set of information to be gathered at the outset of seniors' community planning.

factors linked to it, the community's plan should, at a minimum, include goals and objectives that recognize seniors' needs in the areas of *housing* and *transportation*. Two helpful housing examples follow; first is an objective in the Housing and Neighbourhoods section of the Richmond, British Columbia, Official Community Plan:

- Encourage a broad variety of housing types, universally designed dwelling units, tenures, and price ranges suitable to meet the needs of everyone in the community, including families, singles, couples, people with disabilities, and seniors.[32]

And, second, the following policy is included in the City of Kitchener, Ontario, Draft Official Plan:

- The City will support developments that allow seniors to age in place.[33]

These are, admittedly, minimal gestures toward addressing the surge in the seniors' population that each plan acknowledges is an important contextual area for

planning. They are, however, indicative of what a community plan could contain if a more extensive review of seniors' needs took place.

Regarding housing, seniors require a variety of options that take into account changing circumstances of physical ability, household composition, and income to be able to continue to make choices about their residence. Most communities see the introduction of new types of housing and their plans usually provide guidelines for their development; New Urbanism–designed homes are one of the styles often proposed. Following the second example above, it is good to remember that any new housing could be places where seniors might reside—to age in place, if they choose. Of each proposal, the question needs to be asked: *are they suitable for seniors as they age?* For example, an assessment of New Urbanist housing was conducted with that question at the forefront and it was found wanting in some respects as suitable for seniors—front porches with steps do not make an accessible entrance.[34]

Collective transportation is also an essential element in most community plans. It is especially important regarding seniors being able to participate in their neighbourhoods and communities where one-quarter or more are unlikely to have the ability or desire to drive.[35] For elders continuing to drive strategies may be needed to eliminate safety and mobility barriers such as providing a network of lower-speed roads and enhancing the connectivity of local street networks.[36] Neighbourhood shopping, banking, and restaurant facilities should also be easily accessible by foot (preferably within 400–600 metres).[37] These types of issues could well be in the official plan of a community desiring to include, not merely acknowledge, the needs of seniors in their planning. Each of the two cities noted above have prepared a separate Older Adults Plan, as have a number of others, that covers many of the broader seniors' planning issues cited; that approach is discussed next.

Older Adult Planning

The past decade has seen the emergence of a new approach to planning for older people in Canadian communities. The plans are being called Older Adult Plans or Older Adult Strategies in the several recent and noteworthy instances. These plans have expanded the demographic focus from "seniors," those aged 65 and older, to "older adults" who are 55 and older (50 and older in some cases). Their substantive focus, currently, varies, with some being concerned with social and recreational services, some taking a more comprehensive planning approach, and some following the Age-Friendly mode promoted by the WHO. An example of each is described below.

Of special note regarding the development of Older Adult Plans is that the expanded age cohort, say 55+, falls outside normal gerontological parameters. Thus, there is no research base to fall back on for important characteristics such as living arrangements and family structure and their implications that is already in place for seniors (65+). Following from this is the matter of blending the data on the young-old, who are largely still employed and may still have children at home, with the extensive seniors' data and theoretical concepts which is currently available.

Older Adult Human Services Plan The City of Richmond, British Columbia, developed a well-regarded plan for its 55+ population.[38] The plan builds on the responsibility of local governments to provide community facilities (e.g., parks, libraries, recreation centres)

and social supports. It is grounded in a set of principles that include ensuring accessibility and intercultural and intergenerational interaction, coordinating services, and creating comfortable, safe, and empowering environments. A set of strategic directions point to needed initiatives, and the plan is reviewed and its progress evaluated. Notably, the plan recognizes the range of ages involved and the implications of that for program planning (see Figure 13.3), the cultural diversity of the community's older adults, and the income disparities that accompany old age and gender. Richmond's plan deals with neither housing nor transportation needs of its older adults. There is also no stated connection with these policies included in the City's Official Community Plan such as encouraging suitable housing types for seniors as noted above. It does, however, take up strongly the third SI factor of community support (see page 367) for the array of services under local control.

Older Adult Comprehensive Plans The Ontario City of Mississauga's approach is wide-ranging and deals with several matters beyond those found in human services plans for the older population.[39] Two goals in the plan include access to transportation and better information services in various media and languages. There are two other noteworthy goals in the plan: the first is to concentrate vital services for elders in "nodes or pockets across the City." The services considered vital to cluster include medical practitioners, pharmacies, groceries, community organizations, libraries, and leisure programs and services. Further, the clusters will be encouraged on established transit routes in accessible locations. Notable too, this goal in the Older Adult Plan is explicitly linked to the "Nodes "policies in the City's Official Plan, although the reverse is not the case. The second goal of note promotes the use of *universal design principles* in developing public facilities and outdoor environments. The expanded scope of the Mississauga plan brings it much closer to integrating the needs of older adults with those of the broader community and, thus, to the sphere of community planning.

Age-Friendly Community Planning A third variation being used in planning for a community's older population derives from the initiative of WHO in 2007 promoting Age-Friendly Cities.[40] Many Canadian communities, large and small, have employed this model. Its central premise is the need for a community's policies, services, settings, and structures to enable people (of all ages) to age comfortably, safely, and actively. Its *Global Age Friendly Cities: A Guide* focuses on a checklist of eight age-friendly urban features of a community (see Figure 13.5):[41]

- Outdoor spaces and building
- Transportation
- Housing
- Social participation
- Respect and social inclusion
- Civic participation and employment
- Communication and information
- Community support and health services

These are at the heart of the City of Ottawa Older Adult Plan[42] and that of several dozen Age-Friendly plans for smaller communities in Western Canada, notably in Manitoba and British Columbia.[43]

Multicultural Planning

New immigrants are reshaping the cultural identities of many Canadian communities. Although most communities have faced this change more than once in the past, Canada's recent immigrants come with a wider array of ethnic backgrounds, languages, religious perspectives, and cultural traditions. Since the 1970s, Canadian immigration policy has been aimed at attracting people from non-European countries with the result that today's immigrant stream comprises mostly (70 percent) visible minorities from a wide variety of Asian, African, and Latin American countries.[44] Moreover, most recent immigrants (over 90 percent) go to live in the country's 33 metropolitan areas; and of these, over three-quarters go to Toronto (Figure 13.6), Vancouver, and Montréal, where they have formed "visible minority neighborhoods," or "ethnic enclaves."[45] The scale of these changes should not be underestimated, since Canada's three largest cities are now among the world's most multicultural communities.

This raises new challenges for planners in Canada to broaden their own social perceptions. And new and old citizens alike are challenged to consider the emerging cultural landscape and its implications for planning. The planning issues that emerge with expanding cultural diversity cover the spectrum from housing and transportation to employment, commercial development, institutions, and community services. In other words, it is a planning agenda much the same as for other members of the community. However, there is an important facet of the "diversity" agenda not frequently enough discussed, that is, fairness or equity in "the provision of public policies, programs, and services and equal access to the planning decision-making processes."[46] Add to this that the understanding—the meaning—of land use terminology, planning concepts, and participation processes may differ significantly from one ethnic community to another.[47]

As well, incomes of residents in ethnic enclaves may differ, as may national origin, language, religion, family composition, class divisions, housing customs, shopping habits, and mobility.[48] The concept of "neighbourhood," for example, may have different connotations and spatial dimensions and land use composition than that implied in planners' traditional norms and terminology. The tragedy of Africville in Nova Scotia (see Chapter 5) should remain a constant reminder to planners that they need to recognize the "cultural assumptions" embedded in their current planning practice when dealing with "land use," "activities," and "functions." Indeed, seemingly technical issues can become "cultural issues," and this has been nowhere more obvious than in zoning applications for places of worship.[49] For example, plans and zoning bylaws that have typically allowed for "churches" as a land use and regulated their height limits and parking requirements now face applications for mosques and other places of

SOURCE: WORLD HEALTH ORGANIZATION, GLOBAL AGE-FRIENDLY CITIES: A GUIDE, (GENEVA, 2007), FIGURE 6, P. 9.

| Figure 13.5 | Age-Friendly Topics |

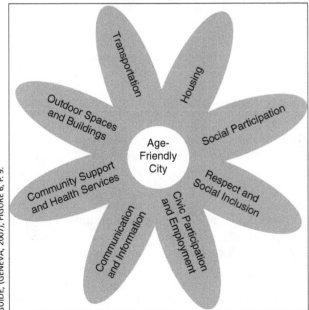

Eight topics guide Age-Friendly planning initiatives by the World Health Organization.

SOURCE: MOHAMMAD QADEER, SANDEEP K. AGRAWAL AND ALEXANDER LOVELL. "EVOLUTION OF ETHNIC ENCLAVES IN THE TORONTO METROPOLITAN AREA, 2001-2006" JOURNAL OF INTERNATIONAL MIGRATION AND INTEGRATION, (2010) 11:326, FIGURE 2. WITH KIND PERMISSION FROM SPRINGER SCIENCE AND BUSINESS MEDIA.

Figure 13.6 Ethnic Enclaves in the Toronto CMA, 2006

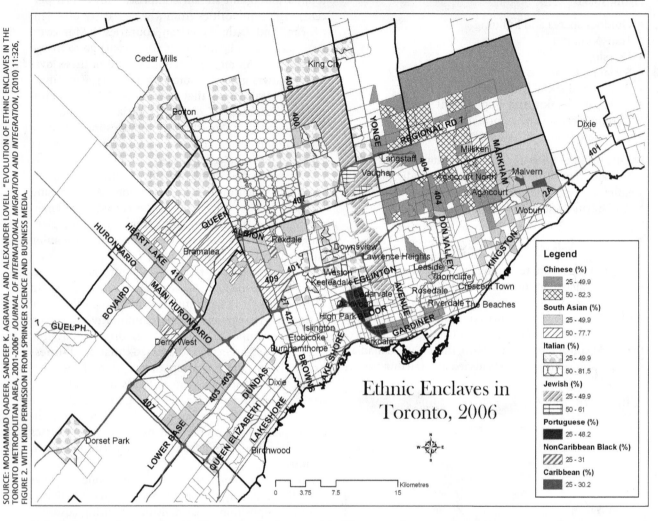

Note the many ethnic enclaves in Toronto's suburban municipalities.

worship whose minarets and temple domes often don't conform to the same standards. Or another case, that of responding to an apparently simple rezoning application to allow a funeral home in a residential area of Ottawa—was met with a storm of protest from citizens in the neighbourhood with Chinese backgrounds.[50] It is easy to say that planners need to be able to cross cultural boundaries in such situations, but, as a study of applications for minority places of worship in Montréal shows, it is neighbourhood social and political dynamics that are often central in resolving locational issues.[51]

A distinguishing feature of these enclaves is the complex of malls, stores, restaurants, movie houses, places of worship, and professional offices, with their distinctive signage that serves the nearby ethnic population as well as those living farther afield.[52] The addition of these enclaves to the urban fabric generates two types of community planning issues that will increasingly require attention. The first is the social dimension of providing social and economic opportunities, services, and infrastructure for their residences and businesses. The latter task needs to be done in such a way as to balance the reality of diversity with the promotion of unity.[53] Canadian planner Mohammad Qadeer argues for providing infrastructure and local services that are tailored to these neighbourhoods and yet are equitable with other neighbourhoods. This would involve linguistically and culturally accessible public schools, community centres, health services, facilities for the elderly, and so on.[54]

The second issue concerns both the procedural and physical aspects of planning practice. On the one hand, cultural and religious dimensions may arise in the administration of simple matters such as zoning, variances, and development permits. The need is to review current planning policies from a multicultural perspective and, if necessary, revise zoning bylaws and development standards accordingly. The physical design side of ethnic enclaves, especially their commercial districts, offers a number of challenges and opportunities. Again, in regard to the cultural character of an enclave, planners have the opportunity to enhance the diversity of a business area through urban-design approaches to street signage, sidewalk designs, and murals, for example.[55]

Nevertheless, these types of challenges, occasioned by the increasing diversity of cultures, provide an opportunity to broaden planning processes, as well as heighten planners' cultural sensitivity and refine their practice. Information can be translated into the language of the neighbourhood, as is already done in several cities. Planning staffs can be augmented to include people who understand ethnic-community concerns and languages. And the mode of public consultation may have to be adapted to the means of communication and the settings with which the local community is most comfortable in articulating its aspirations. For example, Vancouver's CityPlan process made a special effort to involve ethno-cultural groups in its visioning process, with some success.[56] One of the foremost observers of this facet of planning, Canadian planner Mohammad Qadeer, notes that while such procedural modifications to practice are important, the aim should be to develop visions of community plans and programs that reflect the inclusion of multicultural realities. He describes this goal as being attained through a series of steps, a "ladder of planning principles supporting multiculturalism (see Figure 13.7)."[57]

In Qadeer's view, many Canadian planners have reached level 3; that is, generally, being sensitive to cultural differences on a case-by-case basis, accommodating matters within current legislation and practice. Some cities such as Vancouver and Toronto now work at higher levels (4–5) as, for example, in Leonie Sandercock's research on Vancouver's Collingwood Neighbourhood House.[58] The aim, in his trenchant phrase, is to go "beyond sensitivity" to specific group and project needs and enfold a true pluralism in our community planning that would "explicitly recognize

Figure 13.7 | **A Ladder of Planning Principles Supporting Multiculturalism**

7 — A multicultural vision of the development strategy for a city or region

6 — Cultural and racial differences reflected in planning policies and acknowledged as bases for equitable treatment

5 — Provision of specific public facilities and services for ethnic communities

4 — Special District designation for ethnic neighbourhoods and business enclaves

3 — Accommodation of diverse needs through amendments and exceptions, case-by-case

2 — Inclusionary Planning Process—participation by and representation of multicultural groups on planning committees

1 — Facilitation access by diverse communities to the planning department

SOURCE: ADAPTED FROM MOHAMMAD A QADEER, "PLURALISTIC PLANNING FOR MULTICULTURAL CITIES: THE CANADIAN PRACTICE", *JOURNAL OF THE AMERICAN PLANNING ASSOCIATION*, 63:4 (AUTUMN 1997), 481-494. FIGURE 1. USED WITH PERMISSION OF TAYLOR & FRANCIS LTD. WWW.INFORMAWORLD.COM

Planning responses to multiculturalism can range over seven levels, from adapting administrative procedures to redefining goals that inform plans, policies, and programs.

promotion of community cultures, religious freedoms and human rights" in community plans.[59]

Moving in this direction carries with it substantial challenges for planners, for land use planning and regulation. Types of community services (e.g., spiritual institutions), housing (e.g., family and household size), and neighbourhood arrangements (e.g., the mix of commercial firms) required by ethnic minorities may diverge from community norms. Conflicts may then arise over land use and confront a key premise that planning (and zoning) should be based on use and function and not on people.[60] To respond appropriately will necessitate understanding the basic factors at work in the formation of these new patterns of residence.[61] The prevailing planning approach is one of "reasonable accommodation," that is, being reasonable about finding a solution within the bounds of the common good.[62] Fortuitously, this principle has been embedded in planning practice

Chapter 13 Planning for Diverse and Healthy Communities

concerned with zoning over the history of this implementation tool, or nearly a century, through the allowance of a variance. Because zoning regulations cannot cover the situation of each property, owners are able to apply to *vary* the regulations on their property within limits of creating only minimal effects on surrounding properties and not conveying any special advantage for the applicant (see Chapter 16). The variance is, therefore, a valid precedent in approaching contentious multicultural planning situations. It remains then to articulate and make explicit such accommodations in community policies, not least in the community plan, and move ongoing planning practice further up the ladder.

Urban Aboriginal Planning

More than half of Canada's Aboriginal population currently lives in cities, large and small. In Saskatoon, Prince George, Thunder Bay, and Vancouver their numbers are substantial.[63] Over 70 000 call Winnipeg home, 10 percent of the city's population. Frequently, the neighbourhoods they live in are in need of physical and economic improvement and social support.[64] These neighbourhoods tend to be in the inner city and other low-income areas, which they now share with newer immigrant groups of visible minorities. These communities may seem akin to the multicultural neighbourhoods just discussed; however, the Aboriginal people's component must alert planners otherwise. For Aboriginal people— First Nations, Métis, Inuit—are citizens of Canada and in the case of First Nations' people are also citizens of their own (First) nations and have sovereignty and special rights. Their ancestors probably occupied for several thousand years the very same lands these urban neighbourhoods now sit upon. Indeed, almost all the places European colonists chose for their settlements, at river mouths and river junctions, which would later become cities and towns, were locations where Aboriginal peoples also congregated over the centuries, and to which in many cases their names came to be attached.

The importance of this background to planners is threefold. First, it signals a special jurisdictional milieu for local planning and programming because of federal and provincial legislation and its application to Aboriginal peoples living on and off-reserve. Second, it raises the importance of "land" in the traditions of Aboriginal cultures[65] and its role in neighbourhood planning. And, third, because of the constitutional sovereignty of Aboriginal peoples, the notion of self-determination must be accorded them in the

development of plans and programs. All three of these factors must be considered in regard to planning urban Aboriginal situations as the experience in Canada, although still limited, confirms.[66]

Two types of situations have been broached: Aboriginal city neighbourhoods and "urban reserves"; some guidance is emerging for both.

Aboriginal City Neighbourhoods Aboriginal peoples have, for decades, migrated from their reserves and outlying communities to cities in Canada, especially in Western Canada. They have tended to live in clusters, some of which are long-lived as in Winnipeg, in neighbourhoods where the poor live. Where once they might have been a majority, today Aboriginal citizens live in the same neighbourhoods in which other less affluent migrants also cluster. In short, urban Aboriginal peoples nowadays live in mixed neighbourhoods along with numerous visible minority groups. However, the needs of Aboriginal peoples cannot be addressed as if this were simply a typically under-served inner-city neighbourhood or as a multicultural one because of their distinctive Canadian citizenship. Experience is currently limited in how best to approach the design and delivery of needed services and the alleviation of hardships within the urban Aboriginal population.

Two priority areas have, however, been identified for approaching the development of needed resources.[67] The first is to develop viable means for engaging Aboriginal peoples in reliable and ongoing efforts to improve their circumstances. The second is to foster working relationships between municipalities and Aboriginal peoples so that mutual consultation and decision-making can occur. Aboriginal advisory bodies have been established in several municipalities toward this end. A number of cautions have been raised regarding such entities including the importance of letting Aboriginal community members select their own representatives, ensuring gender and age in the representation, and including all Aboriginal (First Nations' peoples, Métis, and Inuit) communities as needed. Many Aboriginal neighbourhoods thus comprise a mixture of persons from each of these groups. When it comes to the arrangements for securing engagement of Aboriginal peoples it is important that they be "people-centred." In preparing the 2011 Downtown Sudbury Plan, the planners engaged Aboriginal youth to express their concerns and preferences at the N'Swakamok Native Friendship Centre. The use of the neighbourhood for organizing citizen efforts, which municipalities and their planners tend to prefer, may not be amenable to Aboriginal peoples who may prefer a cultural, educational, or other local organization to carry forth joint efforts. Or they may wish to establish their own community-based organization for the purpose.

A strong case can be made for an Aboriginal organization to take on the tasks of design and delivery of needed resources. This approach is called "co-production," and by sharing responsibility for formulating issues and priorities and developing the means of delivery of resources, both the sovereignty and right to self-determination of Aboriginal peoples is recognized.[68] Indeed, the very act of Aboriginal self-planning is considered "transformative" in restoring self-esteem and strengthening sovereignty.[69] Another avenue of engagement is through the introduction of Aboriginal culture and history in a variety of ways into the planning of the larger community, of recognizing it as a "municipal asset."[70] Public art, monuments, and street and park naming are ways of acknowledging, indeed celebrating, Aboriginal presence in the larger civic history as well as stimulating consciousness-raising among the citizenry. Whistler, B.C., streets and its new Aboriginal museum are a testament to that approach, which was developed in preparation for the 2010 Winter Olympics in cooperation with the Lil'wat First Nation, the region's original settlers, and grew out of their own Land Use Plan.[71]

Unfortunately, the pursuit of safe, affordable, and appropriate housing for Aboriginal peoples can't be similarly admired. The policy realm of this resource is complex, being shared among federal, provincial, and municipal governments, which proponents sometimes find "confounding" and feel responsibility is just being "passed from one to the other."[72] These particular references are from a study about providing housing for elderly Aboriginal peoples in Canadian cities, the fastest-growing cohort of the elderly in Canada.[73] The governmental difficulties are frequently further reinforced by the neoliberal business climate which tends to shun collective solutions in housing investment.

Urban Reserves Two other venues for linking municipal and Aboriginal planning are (1) urban reserves inside municipal boundaries and (2) relationships between First Nations' reserves and neighbouring municipalities. The first of these is now a prevalent situation in Saskatchewan and Manitoba and begins with the acquisition of land, and sometimes buildings, by First Nations governments within urban municipalities to further their economic development or other

goals.[74] The First Nation then makes application to the federal government to have these lands designated as a "reserve" under the *Additions to Reserves* policy. This process involves removal of land from municipal status and raises two issues: the loss of property tax revenue for the municipality and the need for municipal services by the First Nation owner. Contracts need to be negotiated covering these issues and any other relevant matters such as the application of planning, fire, and building regulations by the new owner. Several dozen urban reserves have been created in Saskatchewan in municipalities of all sizes, including two in downtown Saskatoon with office buildings. The potential for urban reserves exists for cities throughout Canada, and they can be of benefit to both local and First Nation governments. Observers urge the adoption of effective approaches to negotiations including the setting of clear goals, flexible arrangements, patience, and avoidance of politicizing the process.

The second of these venues is the situation of a First Nation with reserve land adjacent or nearby to a city or town; such situations can generate difficulties for one or both of them. On the one hand, new housing and population on the reserve may increase its demand for water and sewerage and the need for servicing from the municipality. On the other hand, the city or town may need to expand its urban area in the direction of reserve lands and seek compatible arrangements for servicing and planning. The City of Powell River on B.C.'s southwest coast and its neighbour, the Sliammon First Nation, provide a good example of such a situation (see Chapter 10).[75] In order to coordinate planning efforts since each community has a comprehensive plan, the two governments formed an Intergovernmental Community Planning Technical Committee. This Committee promotes more integrated and mutually supported outcomes as in coordinating land use and infrastructure planning. It also establishes a means of communications between the two governments that is important, not least, in identifying and protecting Aboriginal cultural sites within the City.

A concluding note: though much of the above discussion seems to focus on governing and planning formal undertakings, it is vital one not forget that these various successes and failures with Aboriginal peoples are as much about "place" as anything, their place in our and their communities. For planners this means recognizing the spatial experience of Aboriginal peoples, which in some cases may mean working with them in spaces their ancestors lived and worked.[76]

Planning Women In

Women are central to the planning of a community's built and natural environments. They are, as one-half of the population, major users of urban space in residential areas, employment places, shopping areas, and leisure environments. However, our planning needs to heed the evidence of the past two or so decades—and the experience of two millennia—that women experience cities and city-spaces in different ways from men.[77] The conventional suburban planning approach of separating land use areas into different spheres and linking them with transportation systems fragments aspects of everyday life for women. Their caregiving roles, work–home relationships, economic opportunities, and personal safety are all affected, and not always positively.[78] Planning for urban space, for all types of settlement, needs to include a woman's perspective and women's participation in developing its plan.

To make planning "gender-inclusive," as is increasingly urged, requires at the start that the full scope of the notion of the female gender be an integral part of any proposal. That is, women in our communities live in a wide array of family and household situations and are affected in various, and sometimes distinctive, ways by planning and policy decisions. Initially, the general category should be broadened to *women and girls* so that pre-teenagers (ages 10–14) and their space needs are recognized. For adult women the perspective should include at a minimum women in nuclear families, women as heads of single-parent families, women living alone, women of colour, elderly women, women with disabilities, women in lesbian and transgendered relationships, as well as the various possible combinations of these situations. Add to this mix the dimensions of age, race, and income. Women from these various sets and others not listed are all users of community space and their voices should be heard.[79] (A similar set of these facets may, of course, be attributed to men in the community.) Indeed, planning practice that is sensitive to gender differences enables planners to make informed choices regarding the way urban space is being used and not assume, as do many planning practices, that "one-size-fits-all."[80]

Barriers to Access and Use

Four elements of city development and functioning impinge on women's use and comfort in urban surroundings: housing, transportation, employment, and safety and security. Each of these are known to present barriers to women that can disrupt their everyday lives such as in caregiving, maintaining employment, and enjoying leisure opportunities. In the discussion of each below it will be seen that there is considerable overlap and interdependency as there is for everyone in the city, town, or neighbourhood. Further, of the myriad effects on women's activities in regard to these elements only a few are noted here.

Housing and Home

Home is an important "place" in everyone's life and for women home is associated, by herself and others, with the almost-inherent roles of caregiving and domestic maintenance. This is especially so when the household milieu includes children, the elderly, or other dependent person(s). Home is also a type of housing and part of a neighbourhood; it has a location in the urban space relative to all other land use locations. Thus, if her home is in a low-density suburb, almost all outside activities, from local shopping to school drop-offs and medical appointments, would require the use of an automobile; so, too, if her employment were not home-based. The situation where a woman's home and work are significantly separated can create family tensions if work hours need to be interrupted by her caregiving responsibilities. Workplace tensions could also arise and compromise the stability of her employment and the portion of family income it represents. This is also true for the other parent if working outside home, but tends to fall disproportionately on the woman to respond to the care of children and the elderly and is the situation most cited regarding women's urban inequality.[81]

If we replace this household situation with one that is less affluent and is dependent upon public transportation to get around, the work–family demands on a woman would lead to family tensions perhaps more intense than for the suburban woman. Substitute the situation of the single-mom household, with or without a car, and consider the dilemmas that may arise in balancing childcare or other caregiving and employment. Any of these typical situations have broad implications. On the one hand, they work to constrain a woman's ability to seek and to sustain stable employment, thereby limiting her personal level of economic development. On the other hand, they also limit her opportunities to participate in civic and other public life.

The human circumstances just described are in large part consequences of planning and policy decisions regarding the location of housing, workplaces, and shopping areas, and not least of the quality of those when developed. Housing density is one of these decisions and the mix of uses is another. They require women to accommodate their activities to these realities and in the process their "place" is compromised. One might say these planning consequences were unanticipated, or even unintended. In either case, they reveal a "gender-blindness" in planning thinking. Ironically, the above typical suburban situation for younger women is coming full circle as suburbs and their residents have aged and now being experienced by further generations of women. Now, analogous constraints face elderly women in the suburbs regarding shopping and getting around, many of whom live alone and do not drive and require a younger caregiver who, most often, is a daughter, granddaughter, or niece.[82]

Transportation: Access and Safety

Transportation is a key to urban living, not least for women. Roads, public transit, and walkways allow them to connect to healthcare, social networks, and employment, as well as to numerous neighbourhood destinations associated with shopping, childcare, other caregiving, and recreation. But how well do our transportation systems meet women's needs for getting around? Not well, according to many reports.[83] Women who are automobile-dependent for employment are challenged, as discussed, to access both employment places and near-home destinations. For those dependent upon public transit, such problems are magnified and, moreover, many local destinations (e.g., healthcare, shopping, children's activities) are not readily accessed. Further, both modes can pose challenges regarding safety for women (and men), not only at transit stops and within vehicles but also getting to and from buses, streetcars, and subways, which always involves some walking. Parking structures are considered unsafe points in a journey for women driving, as well as park-and-ride lots for those combining auto and transit, and transit stops generally, which have been called "hot spots of crime"[84] for all women using public transit. Women perceive these dangers to be multiplied when their trips need to be made during darkness (see Figure 13.8).

Studies from various parts of the world, for more than two decades, find a majority of women are fearful of becoming victims of violence in public spaces generally.[85] Those spaces associated with transportation consistently prove to be challenging for women, both those with a car and without and for both young and old. However, those women entirely dependent on public transport are likely to be more fearful, especially when travelling with children, as are many of the very old who no longer drive.

Variables closely correlated with public transit unease among women are their income, age, race, and sexual preferences; this says, among other things, that planners should not consider women a homogenous group. Other feared transit settings besides those mentioned are unstaffed transit stations and ticket booths, bus shelters without lighting, bus stops in "dark, desolate, or confined spaces," streets without sidewalks, and subway escalators.[86]

Faced with these potentially disquieting situations, women adjust their travel behaviour and take other precautions. These include not walking alone, avoiding bus stops in desolate and unlighted areas, not travelling at night, or not using public transit at all. Take, for example, the insights gained in regard to travel adjustments made by elderly women in Winnipeg.[87] Many made trips to fulfill *social obligations*, other than "ordinary" trips for shopping, doctor's appointments, the library, or recreation. These trips had special meanings in their lives such as visiting spouses or friends in nursing homes, or attending weddings and funerals. Being able to make such trips underlined their sense of independence and autonomy. However, these trips could not always be made because of two types of risks these women perceived about travel around the city. On the one hand were continuous and familiar risks like their own personal fears and conditions in their neighbourhood such as unsafe sidewalks and street crossings. Then there were unpredictable risks such as weather changes, the time of day of scheduled visits, and things to confront at the destination such as strangers and parking. These women developed various coping strategies which could include using a different mode of travel such as a taxi, travelling with a friend, taking a different route, or cancelling the trip (see Figure 13.9).

Women in the Solutions

The threshold step for any planning of the issues discussed above, be it by urban planners or transit planners, is to incorporate women directly into the planning process, as members of the planning team as well as consultants on implementation measures and the evaluation of outcomes. Women's voices through surveys and safety audits need to become a basic component in planning for gender-sensitive transport systems. Establishing a Women's Advisory Committee that would work jointly with transit operators and the city planners is one way to ensure this. A Safe City policy such as in Montréal or Toronto would lend support to transportation and mobility planning oriented to women.[88]

Other more targeted planning measures will also be needed. The use of **Women's Safety Audits** (WSA) is

Figure 13.8

Gender Differences Regarding Safety in Transportation Settings after Dark

WOMEN	MEN
Walking in multi-story parking structure (62%)	Waiting on underground station platforms (32%)
Waiting on underground station platforms (61%)	Travel on the underground (32%)
Waiting on train platforms (60%)	Walking in multi-story parking structure (31%)
Travel on the underground (60%)	Waiting on train platforms (25%)
Walking from bus stop or station (59%)	Walking from bus stop or station (25%)
Travel on train (51%)	Walking in surface parking lot (21%)
Walking in surface parking lot (51%)	Walking to bus stop or station (20%)
Waiting at bus stop (49%)	Waiting at bus stop (20%)
Walking to bus stop or station (48%)	Travel on train (20%)
Travel on bus (40%)	Travel on bus (18%)

Source: Anastasia Loukaitou-Sideris, Amanda Bornstein et al, *How to Ease Women's Fear of Transportation Environments: Case Studies and Best Practices*, (Mineta Transportation Institute: San Jose CA, 2009), p. 10 Table 1; also available at www.transweb.sjsu.edu/project/2611.

Both women and men feel unsafe in transportation settings, but to different degrees and in different settings. ("The underground" refers to an electric train running below the ground, or "subway" in North American jargon.)

Figure 13.9   Travel Coping Strategies of Elderly Women

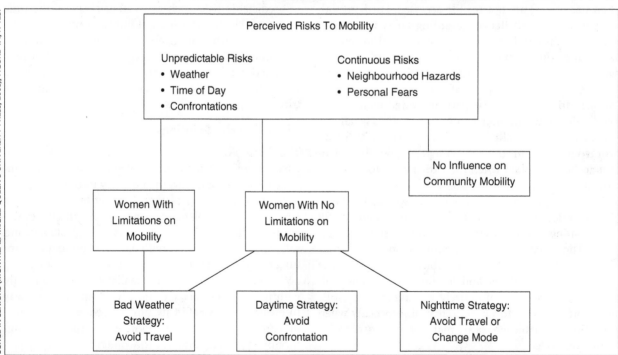

SOURCE: GERALD HODGE, *THE GEOGRAPHY OF AGING: PREPARING COMMUNITIES FOR THE SURGE IN SENIORS* (MONTREAL: McGILL-QUEEN'S UNIVERSITY PRESS, 2008), FIGURE 4.4, P. 123.

Elderly women develop coping strategies either to minimize perceived risks of travel or to avoid them all together.

an approach that is both practical and participative.[89] WSAs involve a group of 6–8 women walking around an area (streets, bus stops, markets, parks) to observe, consider, and record views about safety-related issues and to develop proposals for action by transit operators and/or the community's planners. WSAs should involve women from diverse groups and they should be encouraged to speak to people such as shopkeepers, residents, or shoppers during their walks. Among the external factors they consider are lighting; escape routes and signage; the presence of crowds, vendors, or drug dealers; and the presence or lack of police and transit staff. Walks need to be undertaken in each area during the day and after dark. They are also an effective means of empowering "ordinary" women in planning their communities (see also Chapter 15).

Several cities have found it helpful to develop partnerships with community-based **Mediating Organizations** to provide a bridge between city policymakers and planners and the transit operators. In Toronto a nonprofit group METRAC (Metropolitan Action Committee on Violence Against Women and Children) has worked with the Toronto Transit Commission since the 1980s and has helped achieve improvements such as Designated Waiting Areas and the Request Stop Program for women and other vulnerable riders.[90] METRAC invented the Safety Audit process in 1989 and the idea is now used internationally. A comparable organization, RightRides, offers women, transgender, and gender queer individuals, who may, for example, have late shifts, free rides home on Saturday nights and early Sunday morning in 45 New York City neighbourhoods.[91] Its program, Right Rides for Women's Safety, uses volunteer drivers and donated vehicles.

Every trip a woman takes involves her traversing a number of different spaces, each with potential risks to her safety: for example, to and from or within or a parking structure, to and from a bus stop, or within a transit vehicle. These components comprise the **whole journey** and each part needs to be considered if communities and their policymakers, planners, transit operators, and police desire women to be safe everywhere, to ensure they have a right to the city.[92]

Planning and Children and Youth

In 1997, the declaration of the Second United Nations Conference on Human Settlements states in its preamble:

> The needs of children and youth, particularly with regard to their living environment, have to be

taken fully into account. Special attention needs to be paid to the participatory processes dealing with the shaping of cities, towns, and neighbourhoods; this is in order to secure the living conditions of children and youth and to make use of their insight, creativity, and thoughts on the environment.[93]

This robust statement is the outgrowth of an initiative taken by MIT planner the late Kevin Lynch in 1970 and resulted in two international projects in 1970 and 1997, both called *Growing Up In Cities* (also the title of Lynch's influential book).[94] Both projects, undertaken in cities and rural areas around the world, had as their aim to assemble information on local environmental features, on how children used community space, and from children (boys and girls) on how they perceived their surroundings and needs for improvement.[95]

The results of these studies showed similarities in the ways young people evaluated their communities and the social and physical attributes they valued in their lives:[96]

- *Social integration*—how welcome youth feel in their communities. Communities that possess social integration are ones in which young people are able to interact with other age groups in public places and have a sense of belonging and of being valued.
- *Variety of interesting settings*—a community in which young people have access to a range of places where they can meet with friends, play sports, join in community work, shop and run errands, be away from adult supervision, and observe action on the street.
- *Safety and freedom of movement*—a general sense of safety occurs when young people are familiar with the community, feel comfortable being there, and have the ability to move about freely and easily reach their destinations.
- *Peer meeting places*—niches in the community that youth can claim as their own places in which to socialize, such as plazas, empty lots, street corners, coffee shops, and community centres.
- *Cohesive community identity*—meaning that a place has clear geographic boundaries, that residents take pride in the history and culture of the place, and that a positive identity is expressed through festivals and art.
- *Green Areas*—these consist of some sort of vegetation that is accessible to young people, from flat grass playing fields to tree-shaded parks and wild, overgrown landscapes.

Although this framework is generally applicable, planners need to note that the degree of importance of each factor or criterion may differ from community to community.[97] For example, though an isolated suburb may be safe for children and youth, it may be difficult for them to get around; or a city neighbourhood with mixed uses may offer places for them to "hang out" but may not be safe because of heavy traffic. These factors, it also needs to be noted, are about both *social* and *physical* qualities of community spaces, and there can be both negative and positive perceptions about each one depending upon children's and youth's experience. For example, as Figure 13.11 shows, even a community with positive physical features for them may not meet their needs if there are policies and restrictions on their activities that prevent, say, "loitering" or skateboard use, or impose curfews. A planner would do well to use this diagram as a "map" when seeking the opinions of children and youth for their particular neighbourhoods *and* requesting their suggestions for improvement. Indeed, planners are part of a community's "adult" world that often seems to children and youth to be ready to thwart their desire to be listened to and have their views taken seriously.

Numerous efforts have been made in the academic and research realms to promote youth participation in planning decisions. Five useful lessons for effective participation have emerged: (1) *Give youth responsibility and voice*; (2) *Build youth capacity*; (3) *Encourage youthful styles of working*; (4) *Involve adults throughout the process*; and (5) *Adapt the sociopolitical context to be welcoming*.[98] A Vancouver-based study of youth participation in four non-governmental organizations concurs with the lessons above, not least in how youth themselves structured their participation.[99] They favoured shared leadership, regular check-ins, and "team-based" structures. A project in Memphis, Tennessee, involved youths in evaluating the development in two city neighbourhoods and included digital technology to heighten their interest.[100] Using GIS, ArcReader, hand-held computers, and Flickr, the young participants created images of life in the neighbourhoods, which, along with personal blogs, they shared online.

Two British Columbia cities, Victoria and Vancouver, followed these lessons framing their community plans. Victoria's 2012 Official Community Plan (OCP) explicitly engaged youth in its preparation using several different formats.[101] At Victoria High School students

| Figure 13.10 | Indicators of Environmental Quality for Children and Youth |

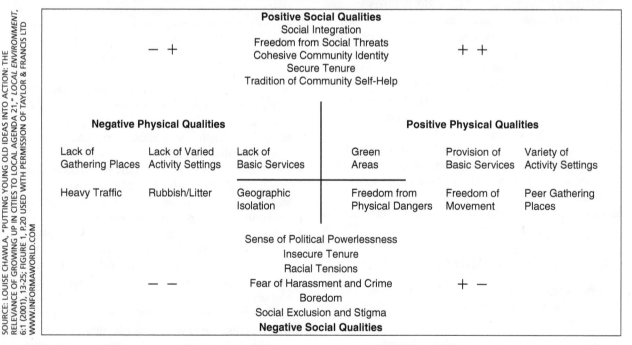

SOURCE: LOUISE CHAWLA, "PUTTING YOUNG OLD IDEAS INTO ACTION: THE RELEVANCE OF GROWING UP IN CITIES TO LOCAL AGENDA 21," *LOCAL ENVIRONMENT*, 6:1 (2001), 13–25; FIGURE 1, P.20 USED WITH PERMISSION OF TAYLOR & FRANCIS LTD WWW.INFORMAWORLD.COM

Whether community spaces work well for children and youth must be considered in terms of both their social and physical qualities. This chart shows indicators of environmental quality based upon the evaluations of 10 to 15-year-olds.

Figure 13.11   "Got Questions or Ideas?"

SOURCE: CITY CENTRE NEIGHBOURHOOD PLAN, NOVEMBER 14, 2011, P. 4. CITY OF VERNON, B.C.

Vernon (B.C.) youth involved in a city planning exercise were asked for their input.

completed a survey on priorities for the city at electronic kiosks set up at the school. The Victoria Youth Council participated in a workshop with city planners to explore goals and strategies for Victoria's OCP. City staff also held a Community Café with young people to talk about Victoria and what matters to them for the city's future; the youth attendees created community maps and shared ideas. And, in addition to the traditional modes of communication, social media—including Facebook and Twitter—were used to promote OCP events.

Vancouver places much importance in engaging children and youth in its ongoing planning activities and developed a special youth website to promote this.[102] For example, in 2011, staff held workshops with students at elementary and secondary schools in downtown Vancouver to help plan the Comox-Helmcken Greenway, a proposed active transportation route across downtown, and are using the students' drawing, writing, mapping, questions, and comments in its design. In planning the Mount Pleasant Community in 2008, planners gave local youth disposable cameras and asked them to visually document their lived experience of the Mount Pleasant commercial area. From these images the participants set forth a series of vision statements and developed photo collages to represent these visions, which were then presented to policymakers and at a community forum.

Municipal Youth Services Plans

Another type of municipal plan that addresses youth needs is a Youth Services Plan. Many cities across Canada have prepared such plans, which aim primarily at (1) developing facilities and services for youth, and (2) creating programs to encourage youth involvement, learning, and confidence. These plans are usually made in conjunction with community parks and recreation departments, library boards, and school boards. Most of these plans are *for* youth rather than made *with* them. Some communities involve their youth in preparing these plans through surveys, focus groups, and advisory committees—the City of Mississauga, Ontario's 2009 Youth Plan is exemplary in this respect.[103] Both its logo and slogan ("Our Future to Hold") were designed by city youths. This is a full-fledged plan with a vision statement, guiding values, and a set of five principles, two of which are noteworthy here. Principle number one states *Public transit is an essential service for youth;* it then offers several initiatives to realize its outcome. Principle number three states *The contribution of young people in community decision-making, program development, and public policy is valued and reflective of the diverse youth population* and, again, suggests means of implementation. The plan does take into account the diversity of the city's youth population (e.g., household and personal income, cultural differences, and gender differences). Moreover, its implementation is guided by Youth Advisory Teams. This plan, its substance and presentation, and its approach toward youth involvement offer much to emulate.

Planning and the Frail and People with Disabilities

As with children and youth, there is international concern for the people in our communities who are frail or have disabilities in the form of the (2006) UN Convention on the Rights of Persons with Disabilities. It stresses that people with disabilities should have access to the physical environment, to transportation, and to other facilities and services open or provided to the public. This follows from the widespread recognition that the design of many urban environments includes barriers that exclude people with disabilities from the use and enjoyment of community spaces and activities.[104] Or put another way, when they encounter barriers instead of being enabled they become *dis*abled from using a desired space.[105]

Barriers that may constrain, or even preclude, the simple activity of walking include steep steps, poor lighting, slippery surfaces, uneven and cracked sidewalks, and unsafe road crossings.[106] For the elderly, who make up a large proportion of people with disabilities, such barriers frequently lead to falls, the leading cause of injury among Canadian seniors and reason for their admission to hospital.[107] However, what is a barrier to one person is not necessarily a barrier to others. Planners will need to learn more about the urban barriers encountered by people with disabilities. They cannot assume that architects, engineers, landscape architects, and urban designers appreciate the constraints with which people with disabilities often have to contend.

The Disabilities of People

There are many types of disability as well as many combinations and degrees of impairment within each. In order to plan for a barrier-free community it is vital to grasp what "disability" means for it covers a number of conditions that can affect people's ability to get around in, use, and benefit from community spaces. Below is a basic list of disabling conditions:

1. Physical disability or impairment (e.g., broken limb, blindness, deafness);
2. Physical illness (e.g., pulmonary disease, multiple sclerosis);
3. Psychiatric illness (e.g., dementia);
4. Intellectual or psychological disability or impairment (e.g., chronic pain syndrome);
5. Any other loss or abnormality of psychological, physiological, or anatomical structure or function; and
6. Reliance on a guide dog, wheelchair, or other remedial means.

Each of these conditions may be present to a different degree depending upon the individual; for example, a blind person may have complete lack of vision or peripheral vision. In addition, a person may experience a combination of the above conditions such as being deaf and also relying on a wheelchair.

An immediate caution is due here. The attributes of disability listed above are medically oriented conditions, conditions of the body. Yet it is *people* who suffer these conditions, that is, people of different ages, gender, income, ethnicity, sexual orientation, and so forth. These disabling conditions affect their social status, their view of the community and community's view of them, and their access to community life. Consider briefly the situations that might be faced by a middle-aged woman with a red and white cane seeking to cross a street or by a young Aboriginal man on crutches facing the entry stairs

to a building.[108] There is always a social and an interpersonal side to the disability situation being faced. As with the other human groups discussed in this chapter, people with disabilities are not homogenous, and may differ within the socioeconomic categories also used to describe them. In fact, the incidence of disability has been found to differ in each of these categories, e.g., the elderly are more prone as are women and the poor.[109]

Barriered and Bounded Spaces

Planners call them land uses but each of them has an aspect of social division and difference. Each component is a city space and each is bounded legally and physically by neighbouring properties and/or public infrastructure. These limits, be they curbs without slopes or a public library without a ramp or a park without wheelchair-accessible toilets, may be barriers to people with disabilities who may, in a sense, be excluded from full citizenship. These barriers are present in numerous ways the able-bodied may not perceive: in access to public transport vehicles with high steps, in transit stations only accessed by escalators, in street signage without a Braille component.

People with disabilities daily face the boundaries and barriers to any need or desire that requires a trip or journey outside their dwelling. Some of them may be due to the nature of their disability: going to lunch or using a restroom, which involves short trips for the ambulatory, may be time consuming for those with a disability.[110] Some of them may be due to the architecture or engineering design at their destination, as already noted. Some of them may be due to the sociopolitical context in the community such as hours of access to public facilities, curfews on youth, and security concerns in the private domain. And some may be due to the unique situation of the person and with the frequency of specific activities: for example, an older person may have to visit the doctor often, or a younger person attends school frequently. Of course, some people may face barriers for all of these reasons.

Facets of Accessibility

An accessible journey is one when a desired destination can be attained within some defined time or distance range. For the ambulatory person there may be several travel and route options to accomplish the trip while for the person with a disability the same trip may have many fewer options and take longer. In other words, accessibility on each trip is a *relative* condition with one outcome for the ambulatory and one for people with disabilities. An example offered by Church and Marston is to consider the same geographic space with the same starting point (an office), the same destination (a coffee cart), and two persons (one ambulatory and one who uses a wheelchair).[111] The physical configuration of the space and the routes of both persons are shown in Figure 13.12. The coffee cart is *absolutely* accessible to both persons. However, the person with a disability because of a substantially greater distance to travel and much more time needed to complete the journey has only *relative* accessibility.

All steps in the accessible journey are interlinked and are of equal importance. Thus, in the above example, the journey of the person using a wheelchair has additional links as compared to the other person; e.g., getting to the elevator, waiting for the elevator, riding the elevator. This is typical of most journeys taken by people with disabilities. A further aspect to look at when considering accessibility is the range of activities taken in a journey because people, whether with a disability or not, tend to combine several destinations in a single trip (e.g., shop, visit a doctor, and go to the library) or in a single location (e.g., use the telephone, go to drinking fountain, and visit toilet facility). Recognition that journeys are multi-faceted has led to the "whole journey" approach when seeking to improve accessibility for people with disabilities. Its use involves GIS-participation techniques with affected persons, mapping their routes and neighbourhoods.[112]

Two approaches are available to planners seeking better urban environments for people with disabilities. One that is just emerging is called "social topography" by its Canadian proponent and invokes the image of journeys consisting of *nodes* (a restaurant, a park bench) and *links* (sidewalks, public transit) both comprising a community network.[113] Another is the widely adopted practice of employing the Principles for Universal Design in the design of public and private facilities and spaces (see Figure 13.13). Briefly, these principles are:[114]

1. Equitable Use—Places are accessible to all users and provide the same means for all users;
2. Flexibility in Use—Places accommodate a wide range of individual preferences and abilities and provide choice for all;
3. Simple and Intuitive—Understanding a site and context should be easy, regardless of experience, knowledge, language, or skill;
4. Perceptible Information—Information is communicated effectively to users regardless of ambient conditions or the user's sensory abilities;
5. Tolerance for Error—Hazards and the adverse consequences of accidents are minimized;
6. Low Physical Effort—The space can be used efficiently and comfortably with a minimum of fatigue; and
7. Size and Space for Approach and Use—Appropriate size and space is provided for approach, reach, and manipulation, regardless of user's body size, posture, or mobility.

Figure 13.13	Accessibility and Universal Design in Winnipeg

SOURCE: WINNIPEG RIVER WALKWAY. *OUR WINNIPEG,* (2011) CITY OF WINNIPEG, PAGE 78.

The principles of Universal Design were used in building this Winnipeg river walkway making it accessible to all citizens. Our Winnipeg/Speakup Winnipeg won the CIP 2011 Award for City Planning.

SOURCE: RICHARD L. CHURCH AND JAMES R. MARSTON, "MEASURING ACCESSIBILITY FOR PEOPLE WITH A DISABILITY." *GEOGRAPHICAL ANALYSIS* 35:1 (JANUARY 2003) P. 91, LOWER HALF OF FIG.1. REPRODUCED WITH PERMISSION.

Figure 13.12	Relative Differences in Accessibility

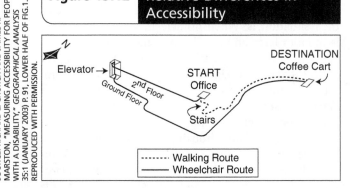

The routes of two people, one ambulatory and one using a wheelchair, seeking a coffee break.

Chapter 13 Planning for Diverse and Healthy Communities

Planning and the Homeless

Homelessness, no stranger to cities, especially larger ones, became increasingly evident in the 1990s and is now evident across the country in communities small and large. Not only have the numbers of homeless increased, but they now comprise youth, women, seniors, and even children. The numbers comprising the homeless are always difficult to determine, but a 2006 report suggests upwards of 300 000 live either on the streets or in shelters in Canada.[115] Homelessness statistics typically include those living in emergency shelters and transition houses for women, children fleeing abuse, youth living in safe houses, and others living in related facilities, as well as those living on the streets or in parks or other outdoor locations.

In the Vancouver metropolitan area, where statistics have been kept regularly since 2002, the number of homeless has increased approximately 1.5 times from 1100 to over 2660 in the most recent count in 2011.[116] However, the Vancouver figures are useful for more than their numbers (indeed some levelling-off has occurred there since 2008) but for what they tell about the big-city homeless. For one, homelessness is occurring in all municipalities, inner city as well as suburbs, and Aboriginal people, notably women, are over-represented. For another, the proportion of homeless youth has increased such that average age among the urban homeless has declined from about 50 to the low 30s. The proportion of women and of seniors has also grown. Nearly three-quarters of all the homeless have substantial health problems including addiction, medical conditions, mental illness, and physical disability. Overall, the homeless as a proportion of the total population is slightly less than 2 percent, a typical level for large cities. Low income and high rent were most frequently cited reasons for continuing homelessness by Vancouver's homeless.

Homelessness is being seen in smaller centres as well; a telling example is Brandon, Manitoba. In 2007, the Brandon Homelessness Steering Committee (BHSC) estimated there was a need to house as many as 1400 homeless comprising individuals living in shelters, hotels/motels, or "couch surfing" with family and friends.[117] Homelessness in Brandon was found mainly as a result of family and relationship breakdowns, newcomers who lacked housing, and evictions from previous housing; less than 10 percent was accounted for by transiency and addictions. The BHSC addressed their homelessness through the "Housing First" approach used in the United States, which, simply put, says to cure homelessness start by providing housing and ally it very closely with health and social services.[118] They then developed a community plan for homelessness which included acquiring an old four-storey building in the downtown area for conversion to housing of several different types: emergency shelter units, rental units, and some that could be purchased. This allowed the homeless a choice of housing to suit their wishes. A Health Access Centre was developed in an adjacent location to provide a range of services to homeless residents and the larger community including support in several languages. A distinguishing feature of the Brandon solution is the array of partnerships entered into with, among others, the Regional Health Authority, the Aboriginal Friendship Centre, and the local Habitat for Humanity.

Housing the "hidden homeless" is how Brandon termed it and the same phrase has also been used in Iqaluit.[119] Following Nunavut's 1999 launch into self-government, the new capital strained to keep up with the influx of people imported from the south to help run the new territory and Northerners who have moved here from other parts of the Arctic. In 2003, it was estimated that 1000 of Iqaluit's 6500 residents were without adequate shelter of their own. A similar picture of homelessness and overcrowding exists in Inuit, Dene, Innu, Cree, and Inuvialuit communities across the North. These are not the southern homeless on display on sidewalks and alleyways, but people who live in cars, sleep on couches, or crash in porches, church basements, and, in Nunavut, the Arctic College cafeteria. For a graphic illustration of the extent of the "hidden homeless" in Canada see Figure 13.14.

What do all of these examples have in common? First it is important to go beyond the images of homelessness often portrayed on TV or in newspapers, for it is a much more comprehensive problem than affecting individuals on the street or in shelters, as desperate as their situation is. When homelessness is tackled, as it is in cities large and small across the country, what is revealed is the general lack of affordable housing for many citizens (see Figure 13.14). Take just two community plans for homelessness—London, Ontario and Greater Vancouver—which both concluded that there will not be success "without an increase in the amount of stable affordable housing."[120] As Jeanne Wolfe pointed out more than a decade ago, federal government housing policy has shifted away from the provision of social housing and moved strongly towards market approaches to housing.[121] The gap has not been

Figure 13.14 The Homeless Housing Iceberg

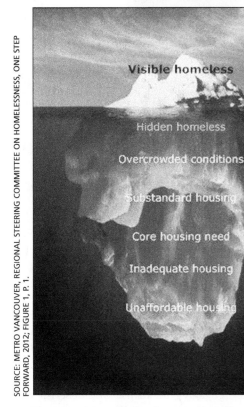

The persons counted as homeless, on the street and in shelters, are above the waterline. There remains an even greater number who are potentially homeless, the "hidden homeless."

filled by the provinces and territories to which this policy area has been passed. In short, for those at the bottom of the housing ladder there are literally no lower rungs for them to begin to step up. Municipalities have been left with this problem and many have responded well. Brandon saw the importance of providing a set of transitional housing types instead of, as is the common response, concentrating on emergency shelters. This provided their homeless with steps upward they could take—their own choices—to obtain better housing. As vital as are emergency shelters in responding to homelessness, they are the minimum social response, the lowest rung, toward anyone's housing needs.

What, then, of the planner's role in countering homelessness? Homelessness is not marginal to planning in that it concerns one of the fundamental human needs that the earliest planners addressed: *housing!* Planners are

at the nexus of decisions about what housing is produced and where in the community. It's what has enabled them, in Vancouver and elsewhere, to advocate the inclusion of "social housing" as a portion of large private sector housing projects, often a highly contested position for them to take. Housing changes at a more modest scale, such as gentrification of single housing units and transformation of apartment buildings to condominiums, are also on planners' agendas. In their incremental way, these processes often displace lower-income people from their homes; while this may not lead them to homelessness, it does reduce affordable housing choices for those below them. Regarding emergency shelters, for which municipalities have to take responsibility, planners could take on ensuring decent and consistent living standards for those who have no other housing options.[122] Success in countering homelessness ultimately comes down to there being a community vision, a plan, for the shelter and well-being of all segments of the population—of all citizens. A crucial question for the planner is, where does he/she stand on this matter?

Planning and LGBTQ Communities

The LGBTQ (lesbian, gay, bisexual, transgender, and queer) community is a layer, a slice, of a city's population that includes all ages, genders, incomes, races, and ethnicities. In other words, it is a human group of a city's citizens with the right to the use of city space, facilities, and services.[123] In a city's population they may comprise 4–6 percent of the total, and their neighbourhoods often encompass distinctive arrays of businesses catering to its LGBTQ or gay residents. (Henceforth, gay is used interchangeably with LGBTQ.) Not infrequently, gays have been responsible for revitalizing previously seedy neighbourhoods, as with one in Ottawa.[124] Typically, clusters of gay residents and businesses have been located in the inner city, but recently have become visible in smaller cities and the suburbs. In general, gay residential enclaves serve a number of purposes, not the least for their residents being the security and acceptance of a community of others who have experienced discrimination in housing and harassment in public places.

The people living in gay enclaves, it must be emphasized, are not homogenous, including in their sexual orientations and perceptions of the community. In objective terms, they can be described by age, income, gender, ethnicity, location, religion, living arrangements, and family status. Regarding the latter characteristic, think of same-sex couples, some married, some not, some with children and some without; these groups underline the diversity of gay neighbourhoods. Add to this mix the fact that many are homeless and often poor. LGBTQ clusters are, thus, home to many vulnerable citizens. Understanding this diversity is an important first step for planners, one that will ultimately test their core values on such issues as the integration or assimilation of gays in the larger society. A not-to-be-overlooked planning issue arises with living arrangements in the LGBTQ population. Typical are groups of unrelated persons living together, or at least wishing to do so. Zoning has always had a preoccupation with families and often labelled its housing types as "single-family," "multi-family," etc. This has caused instances of blocking gays' access to housing and may be ameliorated in some respects by using terms in zoning bylaws such as "detached housing" and "apartments."[125]

Situations also likely to test the planner in regard to gay neighbourhoods will come with the ongoing development of the urban environment and its inexorable competition for space. That is, when others seek the space gays live, work, and play in. Because gay neighbourhoods tend to be in areas with lower-cost housing they can and have been targeted for gentrification.[126] Pressures may also come from public redevelopment efforts and large-scale private commercial and housing projects. No matter the reason, what is often put in jeopardy is dispersal of a coherent set of residents, their housing, and the businesses and institutions that support them. Especially important in the mix of a gay neighbourhood are the businesses such as bars, bookstores, and restaurants, which provide community meeting places and, in the process, establish a sense of community. Of course, it should also be noted that they represent legitimate business investments. Indeed, some cities have recognized the commercial importance of these districts in their larger economy for such as gay and lesbian tourism.[127] Gay Pride events have become prominent in the economies of Canadian cities such as Vancouver, Windsor, and Toronto. For example, the week-long 2009 Toronto event attracted over 100 000 tourists and its economic impact was estimated at over $40 million.[128]

The special events and their economic aspects are noteworthy for more than the dollars they earn. They demonstrate the existence of real communities of people with needs and concerns who also desire to be included in the larger community. To repeat, gays are not homogenous in how they see their "places" evolving, as shown in the views of many lesbian communities like Montréal's Boulevard St-Laurent neighbourhood where the preference is for a heterogeneous situation, a "place of differences."[129] Population enclaves of ethnic groups are now commonly mentioned in planning documents but gay enclaves have mostly been ignored. When planners are not responsive to LGBTQ communities they may appear to be engaging in, to use one observer's words, "discrimination by omission."[130]

| Planning Issue 13.1 | Can a Locavore Dream of Public Produce Come True? |

Globe and Mail (BC Edition)
July 7, 2012

Can a Locavore Dream of Public Produce Come True?

Sarah Elton

In downtown Kamloops, B.C., on a narrow patch of land near the hospital thrift shop and a tanning salon, there's a vegetable garden. Its raised beds are planted with kale, peas and squash—a whole variety of produce, growing in the open, with no fences to keep out passersby.

Which is exactly the point. The garden is called the Public Produce Project and has an official open-picking policy: Anybody is invited to come in and harvest food for free. There are signs instructing people what to take, when and how.

Chelsea Bailey, who runs the nearby restaurant The Ploughman's Lunch with her family, took advantage of it on her breaks last summer, as a refuge from her busy job. "I would go to the garden, pick a couple pieces of lettuce and sit on a bench and eat them," she says. "It was so freeing. You could just go outside and eat something."

There were always a lot of people coming, particularly children and university students, as well as the homeless. And the garden had a lasting influence on Ms. Bailey's own diet: "Since then, I have eaten more fresh foods, because I realized how lovely they are."

The Kamloops garden was launched on land donated by people in the community after the municipal government saw the garden's impact, it was quick to join in, opening two more this summer, including a raised bed at City Hall with strawberries and pumpkins for all to harvest.

Elaine Sedgman, who is with the local chapter of Master Gardeners, an organization that teaches gardening to the public, saw how quickly people took to the idea. "There were ladies across the street who worked at the hospital thrift store who would pick. There would be homeless people and business people who picked the produce. ... Whenever I went to work there, there wasn't anything ripe because it was so well-picked."

The garden in Kamloops is part of a growing movement. It advocates using public lands for food instead of flowers—creating spaces in cities for vegetable beds and fruit trees rather than lawns and dog walking. While the work may be done by volunteers, it requires the support of the community at large.

Growing food on public ground has roots in history. It recalls the "commons" that people who lived in rural communities shared for agriculture. Before the Industrial Revolution in England, villagers grazed their animals in public fields, until they were taken over by private landowners.

Not everyone likes the idea of food being produced in their urban neighbourhoods. In Toronto, there was acrimony in the Eglinton West neighbourhood near Ben Nobleman Park when the idea of launching a public orchard was first proposed. Some tried to stop it, fearing that the fruit trees would be neglected and attract bees that could sting children.

"It was tense and it was uncomfortable," says Susan Poizner, one of the founders. Nevertheless, the orchard of 14 trees was planted and the community has seen a transformation. "Suddenly, Ben Nobleman Park is a destination. It's not a just a park you walk through."

Certainly in Kamloops, there has been no opposition, according to city councillor Donovan Cavers. "There is definitely strong support," he says. "The symbolism is caring for your neighbour and pulling a few weeds for their benefit. It's a small idea, but the concept behind it is pretty profound." Inspired by the Kamloops example, Cranbrook, B.C., started its own public produce garden this year.

Source: © Sarah Elton

Planning for Healthy Communities

For each of the groups discussed in this chapter their healthfulness is a central feature in enabling them to access, use, and appreciate their community. The *Housing First* approach to homelessness used in Brandon insists on locating health and support services adjacent to housing for the homeless. Mississauga's Older Adult Plan recognizes a need for its elderly citizens to have ready access to "nodes" of health and social services such as doctors' offices, pharmacies, libraries, and recreation facilities. Children and youth, too, are the subject of much discussion about obesity and their physical activity in urban settings.[131]

One could say the notion of a healthy community goes back to the planning of Roman aqueducts and Parisian sewers. It was a central idea in the minds of planners of the model industrial towns of the 19th century and in the minds of Patrick Geddes and Ebenezer Howard. It was certainly a major concern of Dr. Charles Hodgetts in 1909 when the Commission of Conservation appointed him as Advisor on Public Health (see Chapters 2 and 4). It became a more formal planning approach at the urging of the WHO in 1988 and entered Canadian practice shortly thereafter, led by Dr. Trevor Hancock.[132] The Canadian Institute of Planners strongly embraced the notion and, together with the Federation of Canadian Municipalities and the Canadian Public Health Association, initiated the Canadian Healthy Community Project (CHCP) and managed it for three years. It focused on all aspects of health (physical, mental, emotional, and economic well-being) and led to initiatives in environmental cleanup, reduced pesticide use, and community recreation that emphasized cycling and walking.[133] Its overall goal was to enable people to support each other more effectively and achieve a better overall quality of life.[134]

The **Healthy Community** concept has re-entered the purview of planners, again at the behest of the WHO in 2005.[135] The qualities of a healthy community are:[136]

- A clean, safe physical environment of a high quality (including housing quality);
- An ecosystem that is stable now and sustainable in the long term;
- A strong mutually supportive and non-exploitative community;
- A high degree of participation in and control by the citizens over the decisions affecting their lives, health and well-being;
- Meeting basic needs (food, water, shelter, income, safety and work) for all the city's people;
- Access by the people to a wide variety of experiences and resources, with the chance for a wide variety of contact, interaction, and communication;
- A diverse, vital, and innovative economy;
- The encouragement of connectedness with the past, with the cultural and biological heritage of city dwellers, and with other groups and individuals;
- A form that is compatible with and enhances the preceding characteristics;
- An optimum level of appropriate public health and sickness care services, accessible to all; and
- High levels of positive health and low levels of disease.

Clearly, the condition of the built environment impinges on all these aspects. Whether it is fear of crime, homelessness, environmental degradation, respecting cultural differences, or providing walking milieus for seniors, all relate to community health and involve the choices community planners make and/or facilitate regarding the built environment. This is, of course, a stupendous task to be undertaking and one not easily achieved. For it invokes the need for integration

and coordination of many policy areas, government departments, levels of government, and the private and nonprofit sectors. The CIP and OPPI have made a start on this task with guidelines for planning healthy communities (Figure 13.15).[137]

The current trend towards evidence-based decisions and practice is a contrast to the Healthy Communities movement from the 1980s. Public health advocates now have a solid foundation of medical research on which to base their proposed changes in the way our cities are planned.[138] This research interest in community environments and health and well-being is stimulated by widespread concerns over obesity and lack of physical activity in the population, especially among children and youth.[139] Current interest focuses on how urban form, especially street patterns and their walkability, affects physical activity patterns and, thence, better overall health.[140] Evidence has been accumulating that residents walk more in areas with land use patterns that have more street intersections and shorter blocks, patterns not commonly found in the suburbs.[141] This, in turn, has led to concerns about suburban sprawl and its preponderance of low-density, single-use areas with disconnected street networks, and its role in discouraging active community environments.[142] As one might have expected, the research has led to a broader view of walking behaviour related not only to street patterns but also to safety and fear of crime and, further, to

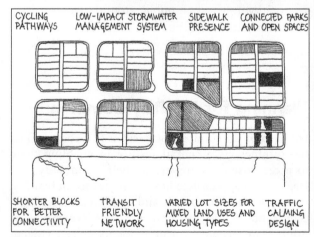

Figure 13.15 Healthy Community Subdivision Guidelines

CYCLING PATHWAYS LOW-IMPACT STORMWATER MANAGEMENT SYSTEM SIDEWALK PRESENCE CONNECTED PARKS AND OPEN SPACES

SHORTER BLOCKS FOR BETTER CONNECTIVITY TRANSIT FRIENDLY NETWORK VARIED LOT SIZES FOR MIXED LAND USES AND HOUSING TYPES TRAFFIC CALMING DESIGN

SOURCE: ONTARIO MINISTRY OF MUNICIPAL AFFAIRS AND HOUSING AND THE ONTARIO PROFESSIONAL PLANNERS INSTITUTE, PLANNING BY DESIGN: A HEALTHY COMMUNITIES HANDBOOK, (2009) P.20, © QUEEN'S PRINTER FOR ONTARIO, 2009. REPRODUCED WITH PERMISSION.

This diagram shows several healthy community practices that can be implemented during the subdivision stage of land use planning.

gender and age.[143] And it has also led to a more nuanced view of community health wherein all the elements—the built and natural environments, the social environments, and individual and collective health—interact with each other in complex and adaptive ways.[144] In this same mould is the Healthy Built Environment Alliance in British Columbia begun in 2007. It consists of more than two dozen organizations across the province working in conjunction with the Provincial Health Services Authority to better connect planning and health professionals.[145] One of its first projects was to develop a training module that would build a common language between planning and health, called Health 201, to provide health professionals with some of the knowledge and tools to become more involved in land use planning. In the end, achieving healthy communities will be bound up with planners in healthy alliances (Figure 13.16).

SOURCE: HEALTHY COMMUNITIES PRACTICE GUIDE, OTTAWA, 2012, FIGURE 1, P. 6. CANADIAN INSTITUTE OF PLANNERS.

Figure 13.16 | Healthy Communities: Key Issues and Possible Alliances

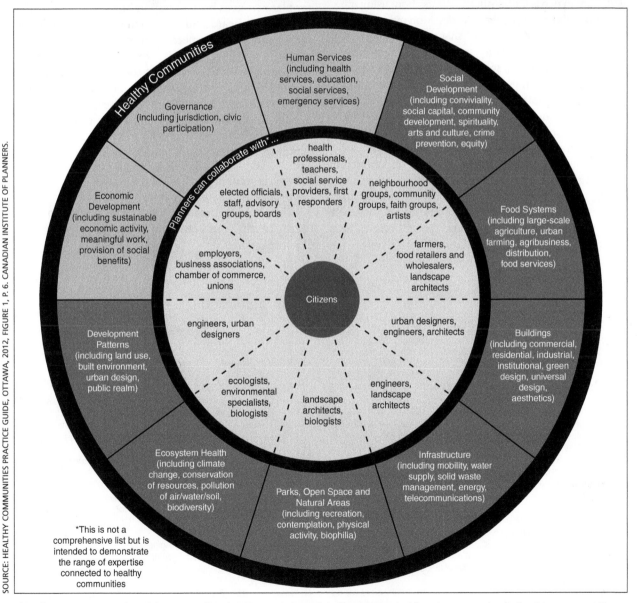

This diagram presents the wide range of topic areas and potential alliances needed for planners to create healthy communities.

Reflections

Planners frequently scan variables like gender, age, living arrangements, and ethnicity when planning for housing and transportation. At a glance such statistics seem to have no substance; although they refer to characteristics of human beings who are living in their communities, do the planners see real people? The purpose of this chapter has been to break out of the bind Healey identified early in this chapter of assuming "people were more or less the same—a standardized unit." If this aim has been met, the reader may be surprised to find that it is aggregates of human beings with human needs for housing and fears about using transportation who comprise the statistics. Moreover, they have personal perceptions of "place" that they consider important but also know how its use and enjoyment may be constrained by physical, social, and regulatory barriers and boundaries. Further, even public space may not welcome these various "publics," these *citizens*.

Exploring the *diverse* who comprise the *diversity* at the ground level, even in the limited way done here, reveals some telling aspects of our communities, some dark, some light and gratifying. For one, obtaining and retaining satisfactory housing is a problem for all: old, young, Aboriginal, gay, and the poor. So, too, mobility is a problem for those in each of the sectors that were explored: for women and their perceptions of fear in "public" transportation settings, for people with disabilities and the frail elderly, and for children and youth. When the diverse have been accommodated by planners and policymakers, our urban environments have been immensely enriched for shopping, eating, and playing. Nonetheless, much remains to be done to ensure that planning practices are fair and just for every minority seeking to be heard regarding the future of their "places."

Canadian planners have responded strongly and thoughtfully to many of the needs and concerns that were identified: in Richmond with the elderly, in Brandon with the homeless, in Mississauga and Vancouver with youth, and in Sudbury with Aboriginal peoples. The challenge for planners goes beyond responding to each group that wants to be heard and recognizing the intersection of these various human needs and concerns within a community's citizenry. That is, there is value in looking both intensely and broadly at the spectrum of people enmeshed in a planning situation and then utilizing this composite view for the benefit of those directly involved *and* for others who might be similarly affected.

The following questions go toward a better understanding and planning of people and places:

- *Why is housing a central feature of "place" for different community populations?*
- *Why is it important for planners not to regard different community populations as homogenous?*

Reference Notes

1. Blossom T. Wigdor and Louise Plouffe, *Seniors' Independence: Whose Responsibility?* (Ottawa: National Advisory Council on Aging, 1992), 8.
2. Patsy Healey, *Collaborative Planning: Shaping Places in Fragmented Society* (UBC Press: Vancouver, 1997), 99.
3. Feng Hou and Garnett Picot, "Visible Minority Neighbourhoods in Toronto, Montréal, and Vancouver," *Canadian Social Trends* 72 (2004), 8–13; and Mohammad Qadeer, "Pluralistic Planning for Multicultural Cities: The Canadian Practice," *Journal of the American Planning Association* 63:4 (December 1997), 481–494.
4. Cf. Leonie Sandercock and Ann Forsyth, "A Gender Agenda: New Directions for Planning Theory," *Journal of the American Planning Association* 58:1 (Winter 1922), 49–59; and H. Thomas and V. Krishnaraya, *Race Equality and Planning: Policies and Procedures* (Aldershot: Ashgate, 1994).
5. Paul Davidoff, "Pluralism and Advocacy Planning," *Journal of the American Institute of Planners* 319 (November 1965), 331–338.
6. The classic treatise on "place" is Y.F. Yuan, *Space and Place* (Minneapolis: University of Minnesota Press, 1977).
7. Patsy Healey, "Institutionalist Analysis, Communicative Planning, and Shaping Places," *Journal of Planning Education and Research* 19:2 (December 1999), 11–121.
8. Eric Borre Nilsen, "Rethinking Places in Planning: Opportunities in Northern and Aboriginal Planning in Nunavut Canada," *Canadian Journal of Urban Research* 14:1 Supplement (2005), 22–37.
9. Gerald Hodge, *The Geography of Aging: Preparing Communities for the Surge in Seniors* (Montréal, McGill-Queens University Press, 2008), 123–124.
10. Nancy Smith, "Diversity: The Challenge for Land Use Planning," *Plan Canada* 40:4 (July–September 2000), 27–28.
11. Stephen Graham and Patsy Healey, "Relational Concepts of Space and Place: Issues for Planning Theory and Practice," *European Planning Studies* 7:5 (1999), 623–647.
12. Patsy Healey, "Institutionalist Analysis."
13. H. Campbell and R. Marshall, "Utilitarianism's Bad Breath? A Re-evaluation of the Public Interest Justification of Planning," *Planning Theory* 1:2 (2002), 464–478.
14. Barbara Rahder and Richard Milgrom, "The Uncertain City: Making Space(s) for Difference," *Canadian Journal of Urban Research* 13:1 Supplement (2004), 27–45.
15. Of special note is City of Richmond, *Parks, Recreation & Cultural Services Older Adults Services Plan* (City of Richmond, BC, 2008).
16. M.A. Qadeer and S.K. Agrawal, "The Practice of Multicultural Planning in American and Canadian Cities," *Canadian Journal of Urban Research* 20:1 (2011), 132–156.
17. Statistics Canada, *Population Projections for Canada, Provinces and Territories 2005–2031* (Ottawa, 2005) Cat. No. 91-520-XIE. Scenario No. 2 is used here.
18. Gerald Hodge, *The Geography of Aging*, 183–187.
19. Regina and District Seniors' Action Plan Steering Committee, *Seniors' Action Plan Report* (Regina: City of Regina, 2000).
20. Gerald Hodge, 179–183.
21. Jenny Secker, Robert Hill et al., "Promoting Independence: But Promoting What and How?" *Ageing & Society* 23 (2003), 375–391.

22. British Columbia Task Force on Issues of Concern to Seniors, *Toward a Better Age*, Victoria, 1990.

23. Larry Orr, "An Aging Society: A Municipal Social Planning Perspective," *Plan Canada* 30:4 (July 1990), 42–45.

24. Deborah Howe et al., *Planning for an Aging Society*, Planning Advisory Service Report No. 451 (Chicago: American Planning Association, 1994), 4ff.

25. Gerald Hodge, "Whither Ethnic Elders? Looming Needs in Community Research and Design," Paper presented at the Environmental Design and Research Association Conference, Vancouver, 2005.

26. Cf. Eric G. Moore and Mark W. Rosenberg, *Growing Old in Canada: Demographic and Geographic Perspectives* (Toronto: Nelson Canada and Statistics Canada,1997), 205.

27. G.D. Rowles and H. Ravdal, "Aging, Place, and Meaning in the Face of Changing Circumstances," in Robert Weiss and Scott Bass, eds., *Challenges of the Third Age: Meaning and Purpose in Later Life* (New York: Oxford University Press, 2002), 81–114.

28. World Health Organization, *Global Age-Friendly Cities Project*, Geneva, 2007, www.who.int/ageing/projects.age_friendly_cities/en

29. Gerald Hodge, 243–271.

30. City of Regina (2000). Seniors and Safety Working Paper, Regina and District Seniors' Action Plan Steering Committee, 4ff.

31. Gerald Hodge, "The Seniors' Surge: Why Planners Should Care," *Plan Canada* 30:4 (July 1990), 5–12.

32. City of Richmond, *Official Community Plan*, 1999, 3–23.

33. City of Kitchener, *Draft Official Plan*, 2011,139.

34. Mary Catherine Mehak, "New Urbanism and Aging in Place," *Plan Canada* 42:1 (Jan.–Mar. 2002), 21–23.

35. David R. Ragland, William A. Satariano, and Kara E. MacLeod, "Reasons Given by Older People for Limitation or Avoidance of Driving," *The Gerontologist* 44:2 (2004), 237–244.

36. Eric Dumbaugh, "Designing Communities to Enhance the Safety and Mobility of Older Adults," *Journal of Planning Literature* 23:1 (August 2008), 17–36.

37. James Wilson, "Assessing the Walking Environment of the Elderly," *Plan Canada* 21:4 (1982), 117–121.

38. City of Richmond, *Parks, Recreation & Cultural Service Plan*, 2008, www.richmond.ca/services/Sustainable/social/policies/olderadult

39. City of Mississauga, *Older Adult Plan*, 2008, www.mississauga.ca/file/COM/ Older_Adult_Plan.pdf

40. World Health Organization, *Global Age-Friendly Cities Project*; Ontario Professional Planners Institute, *Planning for Age-Friendly Communities: A Call to Action* (Toronto: OPPI, June 2009).

41. World Health Organization, *Global Age-Friendly Cities: A Guide* (Geneva, 2007), 9ff, www.who.int/ageing/projects.age_friendly_cities/en

42. City of Ottawa, *Older Adult Plan*, 2011, ottawa.ca/en/social_com/seniors/ consultation

43. umanitoba.ca/centres/aging/cura/coa_cura_communities

44. Statistics Canada, *Canada's Ethnocultural Portrait: The Changing Mosaic*, 2001 Census Analysis Series, (Ottawa, 2003), Cat. No. 96F0030XIE2001008, 39.

45. Feng Hou and Garent Picot, "Visible Minority Neighbourhoods in Toronto, Montreal, and Vancouver," *Canadian Social Trends* 72 (2004), 8–13.

46. M.A. Qadeer and S.K. Agrawal, "The Practice of Multicultural Planning."

47. Sylvie Grenier, "Urban Planning in a Multicultural Society," *Plan Canada* 41:3 (July–Sept. 2001), 31.

48. Mohammad Qadeer & Sandeep Kumar, "Ethnic Enclaves and Social Cohesion," *Canadian Journal of Urban Research* 15:2 (Summer Supplement 2006), 1–17.

49. Marcia Wallace and Beth Moore Milroy, "Ethno Racial Diversity and Planning Practices in the Greater Toronto Area," *Plan Canada* 41:3 (July–Sept. 2001), 31–34.

50. Nancy Smith, "Diversity: The Challenge for Land Use Planning," *Plan Canada* 40:4 (July–August–September 2000), 27–28.

51. Annick Germain and Julie Elizabeth Gagnon, "Minority Places of Worship and Zoning Dilemmas in Montreal," *Planning Theory & Practice* 4:3 (September 2003), 295–318; and Sandeep Kumar Agrawal, "New Ethnic Places of Worship and Planning Challenges," *Plan Canada* 49 (2009, Special Edition), 64–67.

52. Sandeep Kumar and Bonica Leung, "Formation of an Ethnic Enclave: Process and Motivations, *Plan Canada* 45:2 (Summer 2005), 43–45; and Heidi Hoernig, "Planning amidst Cultural Diversity: Lessons from Religious Development," *Plan Canada* 49 (2009, Special Edition), 55–59.

53. Mohammad Qadeer and Sandeep Kumar, "Ethnic Enclaves and Social Cohesion," *Canadian Journal of Urban Research* (May 2006), 1–17; and Mohammad Qadeer, "Dealing with Ethnic Enclaves Demands Sensitivity and Pragmatism," *The Ontario Planning Journal* 20:1 (2005), 10–11.

54. Mohammad Qadeer, "Ethnic Segregation in Toronto and the New Multiculturalism" (University of Toronto, Centre for Urban and Community Studies, March 2003), Research Bulletin No. 12.

55. Sandeep Kumar and George Martin, "A Case for Culturally Responsive Urban Design," *The Ontario Planning Journal* 19:5 (2004), 5–7; and Celia Zhang, "Ethnic Retailing and Implications for Multicultural Communities," *Plan Canada* 49 (2009, Special Edition), 79–82.

56. Joyce Lee Uyesugi and Robert Shipley, "Visioning Diversity: Planning Vancouver's Multicultural Communities," *International Planning Studies* 10:3,4 (August– November 2005), 305–322.

57. Mohammad Qadeer, "Pluralistic Planning for Multicultural Cities: The Canadian Practice," *Journal of the American Planning Association*, 63:4 (Autumn 1997), 481–494.

58. Leonie Sandercock, "From Nation to Neighbourhood: Integrating Immigrants through Community Development," *Plan Canada* 49 (2009, Special Edition), 6–9; and Sandercock and G. Attili, *Where Strangers Become Neighbours: Integrating Immigrants in Vancouver, Canada* (Heidelberg: Springer, 2009).

59. Mohammad Qadeer, "Dealing with Ethnic Enclaves Demands Sensitivity and Pragmatism," *The Ontario Planning Journal* 20:1 (Jan.–Feb. 2005), 10–11.

60. Nancy Smith, "Diversity: The Challenge for Land Use Planning."

61. Sandeep Kumar and Bonica Leung, "Formation of an Ethnic Enclave: Process and Motivations," *Plan Canada* 45:2 (2005), 43–45.

62. M.A. Qadeer and S.K. Agrawal, "The Practice of Multicultural Planning."

63. Annie Baker, "Recognizing Urban Aboriginal Populations in Canadian Cities," *Plan Canada* 48:2 (Summer 2008), 53.

64. Ryan C. Walker, "Improving the Interface Between Urban Municipalities and Aboriginal Communities, *Canadian Journal of Urban Research* 17:1 Supplement (2008), 20–36.

65. Leonie Sandercock, "Interface: Planning and Indigenous Communities," *Planning Theory and Practice* 5:1 (March 2004), 95–97.

66. Yale Belanger and Ryan Walker, "Interest Convergence and Co-Production: An Examination of Winnipeg's 'Urban Pathways,'" *Canadian Journal of Urban Research* 18:1 (2009), 118–139.

67. Ryan C. Walker, "Improving the Interface between Urban Municipalities and Aboriginal Communities."

68. Yale Belanger and Ryan Walker, "Interest Convergence and Co-Production."

69. Marcus B. Land and Michael Hibbard, "Doing It for Themselves: Transformative Planning by Indigenous Peoples," *Journal of Planning Education and Research* 25 (2005), 172–184.

70. Ryan C. Walker, "Improving the Interface...."

71. Rahul Day and David Harper, "The Path Forward: Land Use Planning as a Unifying Community Process," *Plan Canada* 48:2 (Summer 2008), 43–45.

72. Lauren Lange, Ian Skelton, and Thelma Meade, "'I Want to See These Words Turned Into Action': Neoliberalism and Urban Housing for Elderly People of Aboriginal Origin," *Canadian Journal of Urban Research* 19:1 (2010), 71–88.

73. Gerald Hodge, *The Geography of Aging*, 182–183.

74. Lorne Scully, Livia Kellett, and Ryan Walker, "First Nations Urban Reserves: Partnerships for Positive Development," *Plan Canada* 48:2 (Summer 2008), 39–42.

75. Stephen Gallagher, "Intergovernmental Community Planning: The Sliammon First Nation and the City of Powell River Experience," *Plan Canada* 48:2 (Summer 2008), 35–38.

76. Barbara Rahder and Richard Milgrom, "The Uncertain City: Making Space(s) for Difference."

77. Cf. Clara Greed, Women and Planning: Creating Gendered Realities (London: Routledge, 1994).

78. Monika Jaeckel and Marieke Geldermalson, "Gender Equality and Urban Development: Building Better Communities for All," *Global Urban Development Magazine* 2:1 (March 2006), www.globalurban.org

79. H. Lefebvre, *The Production of Space* (Oxford: Blackwell, 1991).

80. Commonwealth Secretariat, *Gender in Planning and Urban Development*, Discussion Paper 7, London (December 2009), www.thecommonwealth.org; Sue Hendler and Julia Markovich, "Beyond 'Soccer Moms': Feminist and New Urbanist Critical Approaches to Suburbs," *Journal of Planning Education and Research* 25 (2006), 410–427.

81. Katherine B. Silbaugh, "Women's Place: Urban Planning, Housing Design, and Work-Family Balance," *Fordham Law Review* 76 (December 2007), 1797–1852.

82. Gerald Hodge, *The Geography of Aging*, 210–211.

83. Cf. Katherine B. Silbaugh, "Women's Place"; and "Women, Transit and the Perception of Safety" (February 2010), www.planitzen.com/node/42878

84. Anastasia Loukaitou-Sideris, "Hot Spots of Bus Stop Crime: The Importance of Environmental Attributes," *Journal of the American Planning Association* 65:4 (Autumn 1999), 395–408.

85. G. Lynch and S. Atkins, "The Influence of Safety Fears on Women's Travel Patterns," *Transportation* 15 (1988), 257–277 and Women's Planning Network, *Women's Transport Needs* (Victoria, Australia, 1995), www.wpn.org.au

86. Anastasia Loukaitou-Sideris, Amanda Bornstein, et al., *How to Ease Women's Fear of Transportation Environments: Case Studies and Best Practices* (Mineta Transportation Institute: San Jose CA, 2009), 13–18, www.transweb.sjsu.edu/project/2611.html

87. M. Finlayson and J. Kaufert, "Older Women's Community Mobility: A Qualitative Exploration," *Canadian Journal on Aging* 21:1 (2002), 75–84.

88. City of Montréal, *The Montréal Declaration on Women's Safety, 2002*, www.villemontréal.qc.ca and www.femmesetvilles.org; Gerda Wekerle and Carolyn Whitzman, *Safe Cities: Guidelines for Planning, Design, and Management* (New York: Van Nostrand Reinhold, 1995).

89. Women in Cities International, *Learning from Women to Create Gender Inclusive Cities* (Montréal, 2010), 19–20, www.femmesetvilles.org

90. METRAC programs can be viewed at www.metrac.org

91. RightRides for Women's Safety at www.rightrides.org

92. Anastasia Loukaitou-Sideris, Amanda Bornstein et al., *How to Ease Women's Fear of Transportation Environments.*

93. United Nations Centre for Human Settlements, *The Istanbul Declaration and the Habitat Agenda* (Nairobi: 1997).

94. Kevin Lynch, *Growing Up in Cities* (Cambrige, MA: MIT Press, 1977).

95. Louise Chawla, "Putting Young Old Ideas into Action: The Relevance of Growing Up in Cities to Local Agenda 21," *Local Environment* 6:1 (2001), 13–25.

96. Camille Passon, Daniel Levi, and Vicente del Rio, "Implications of Adolescents' Perceptions and Values for Planning and Design," *Journal of Planning Education and Research* 28:1 (September 2008), 73–85.

97. Ontario Professional Planners Institute, *Plan for the Needs of Children and Youth: A Call to Action* (Toronto: OPPI, February 2009).

98. Kathryn L. Frank, "The Potential of Youth Participation in Planning," *Journal of Planning Literature* 20:4 (May 2006), 351–371.

99. Penny Gurstein, Chris Lovato, and Sally Ross, "Youth Participation in Planning: Strategies for Social Action," *Canadian Journal of Urban Research* 12:2 (2003), 49–274.

100. Charles A. Santo, Nathan Ferguson, and Andrew Trippel, "Encouraging Urban Youth through Technology: The Youth Neighbourhood Mapping Initiative," *Journal of Planning Education and Research* 30:1 (September 2010), 52–65.

101. City of Victoria, *Official Community Plan*, 2012, http://www.shapeyourfuturevictoria.ca/get-involved/

102. See "Children, Youth & City Planning," www.vancouveryouth.ca

103. City of Mississauga, *Mississauga Youth Plan!* (May 2009), www.mississauga.ca

104. Rob Imrie, "Barriered and Bounded Places and the Spatialities of the Disabled," *Urban Studies* 38:2 (2001), 231–237.

105. Here we are following the distinction made between *impairment*, when a person has a defective limb or organ, and *disability*, and when an impaired person is excluded ("disabled") from public space by barriers of various kinds. Cf. Brendon Gleeson, *Geographies of Disability* (London: Routledge, 1999), 25.

106. Anastasia Loukaitou-Sideris, "Is It Safe to Walk? Neighbourhood Security Considerations and Their Effect on Walking, *Journal of Planning Literature* 20:3 (February 2006), 219–232.

107. Paula C. Fletcher and John P. Hirdes, "Risk Factors for Serious Falls among Community-Based Seniors: Results from the National Population Health Survey," *Canadian Journal on Aging* 21:1 (2002), 103–116.

108. National Network on Environments and Women's Health, "Women with Disabilities in the Urban Environment," Toronto (2005), 7; and Douglas Durst, Shelly M. South,

and Mary Bluechardt, "Urban First Nations People with Disabilities Speak Out," *Journal of Aboriginal Health* 3:1 (September 2006), 34–43.

109. Statistics Canada, *A Profile of Disability in Canada* 2001 (Ottawa, 2002), Cat. No. 89-579-XIE.

110. Richard L. Church and James R. Marston, "Measuring Accessibility for People with a Disability," *Geographical Analysis* 35:1 (January 2003), 83–96.

111. Richard L. Church and James R. Marston, "Measuring Accessibility."

112. Graeme Evans, "Accessibility, Urban Design, and the Whole Journey Environment," *Built Environment* 35:3 (September 2009), 366–385.

113. Mike Prescott, "A Very Brief Introduction to Social Topography—A Model for Advancing Accessibility and Inclusion," *Sitelines* (Vancouver, August 2012), 16.

114. Adapted from North Carolina State University, The Center for Universal Design, www.ncsu.edu/project/design-projects/udi/; see also Wolfgang Preiser and Korydon H. Smith, *Universal Design Handbook*, 2nd ed. (New York: McGraw-Hill Ryerson, 2010).

115. "Homelessness," *The Globe and Mail*, June 12, 2006.

116. Metro Vancouver, Regional Steering Committee on Homelessness, *One Step Forward*, Vancouver, 2012, www.metrovancouver.org/planning/homelessness/Homelessness%20Docs/FinalPlanUpdateReport.pdf

117. Brandon Homelessness Committee, Community Plan, 2007, www.brandonhomelessness.ca as reported in Vince Barletta, "Hidden Homeless in Brandon Manitoba: Seeking Solutions through Community Partnerships," *Plan Canada* 50:1 (Spring 2010), 24–26.

118. S.Tsemberis, L.Gulcur, and M.Nakae, "Housing First, Consumer Choice, and Harm Reduction for Homeless Individuals With a Dual Diagnosis," *American Journal of Public Health* 94 (2004), 4651–4656.

119. This paragraph draws from Gordon Laird, *Shelter: Homelessness in a Growth Economy: Canada's 21st Century Paradox,* A Report to the Sheldon Chumir Foundation for Ethics in Leadership, Calgary, 2007, 18ff.

120. Ginsler & Associates, *Community Plan on Homelessness in London*, October 2001.

121. Jeanne M. Wolfe, "Canadian Housing Policy in the Nineties," *Housing Studies* 13:1 (1998), 121–133.

122. Suzanne Gessler, "Where the Other Half Lives: A Call for Emergency Homeless Shelter Standards," *Plan Canada* 50:1 (Spring 2010), 20–23.

123. Ann Forsyth, "Sexuality and Space: Nonconformist Populations and Planning Practice," *Journal of Planning Literature* 15:3 (February 2001), 339–358.

124. Randy Boswell, "The Village People: Gay Community Breathes New Life Into Seedy Section of Centretown," *Ottawa Citizen* (November 3, 1996), A1.

125. Ann Forsyth, "Sexuality and Space."

126. Petra L. Doan and Harrison Higgins, "The Demise of Queer Space? Resurgent Gentrification and the Assimilation of LGBT Neighborhoods," *Journal of Planning Education and Research* 31:1 (March 2011), 6–25.

127. Michael Frisch, "Planning as a Heterosexist Project," *Journal of Planning Education and Research* 21:3 (March 2002), 254–266.

128. Paul Gallant, "Study Shows Pride is an 'Economic Powerhouse,'" *Toronto Star*, June 23, 2010.

129. Julie A Podmore, "Lesbians in the Crowd: Gender, Sexuality, and Visibility Along Montréal's Boul. St-Laurent," *Gender Place and Culture* 8:4 (2001), 333–355.

130. Petra L. Doan and Harrison Higgins, "The Demise of Queer Space?"

131. Cf. Joshua van Loon and Lawrence Frank, "Urban Form Relationships with Youth Physical Activity: Implications for Research and Practice," *Journal of Planning Literature* 26:3 (2011), 280–308.

132. Trevor Hancock and Leonard Duhl, *Promoting Health in the Urban Context* (World Health Organization: Copenhagen, 1988).

133. David R. Witty, "Healthy Communities: What have We Learned?" *Plan Canada*, 42:4 (Oct.–Dec. 2002), 9–10.

134. Cf. Brijesh Mathur, "Community Planning and the New Public Health," *Plan Canada* 29:4 (July 1989), 35–44.

135. World Health Organization, *Healthy Cities and Urban Governance: Introduction to Healthy Cities* (Geneva, 2005), www.euro.who.int/healthy-cities/introducing/20050202_1

136. Victoria Barr and Jodi Mucha, "Healthy Cities/Communities: An Enduring Approach to Linking Urban Planning and Citizen Health," *Plan Canada* 49:4 (Winter 2009), 38–42.

137. Canadian Institute of Planners, *Healthy Communities Practice Guide* (Ottawa: CIP 2012); Hazel Christy, David Harrison, et al., "Our 21st Century Challenge: Healthier Communities" *Plan Canada*, Spring 2012, 53–55; Ontario Ministry of Municipal Affairs and Housing and the Ontario Professional Planners Institute, *Planning by Design: A Healthy Communities Handbook* (Toronto: OMMAH, 2009); and Ontario Professional Planners Institute, *Healthy Communities; Sustainable Communities* (Toronto: OPPI, 2007).

138. Andrew Dannenberg, Howard Frumkin, and Richard Jackson, *Making Healthy Places; Designing and Building for Health, Well-Being and Sustainability* (Washington, DC: Island Press, 2012).

139. Brian Saelens, James Sallis, Lawrence Frank, et al., "Obesogenic Neighborhood Environments, Child and Parent Obesity: The Neighborhood Impact on Kids Study," *American Journal of Preventative Medicine* 42:5 (May 2012), e57–e6; Ester Cerin, Lawrence Frank, James Sallis, Brian Saelens, Terry Conway, James Chapman, and Karen Glanz, "From Neighborhood Design and Food Options to Residents' Weight Status," *Appetite* 56:3 (June 2011), 693–703; Abby King, James Sallis, Lawrence Frank, et al., "Aging in Neighborhoods Differing in Walkability and Incomes: Associations with Physical Activity and Obesity in Older Adults," *Social Science & Medicine* 73:10 (November 2011), 1525–1533; and Lawrence Frank, Jacqueline Kerr, James Sallis, et al., "A Hierarchy of Sociodemographic and Environmental Correlates of Walking and Obesity," *Preventative Medicine* 47:2 (August 2008), 172–178.

140. Lawrence Frank, Peter O. Engelke, and Thomas L. Schmid, *Health and Community Design: The Impact Of The Built Environment On Physical Activity* (Washington, DC: Island Press, 2003).

141. Cf. Lisa Wood, Lawrence Frank, and Billie Giles-Corti, "Sense of Community and Its Relationship with Walking and Neighborhood Design," *Social Science & Medicine* 70:9 (May 2010), 1381–1390; and B. Giles-Corti and R. Donovan, "Relative Influences of Individual, Social Environmental, and Physical Environmental Correlates of Walking," *American Journal of Public Health*, 93:9 (2003), 1583–1589.

142. David Charles Sloane, "From Congestion to Sprawl: Planning and Health in Historical Context," *Journal of the American Planning Association*, 72:1 (Winter 2006), 10–18.

143. Scott Doyle et al., "Active Community Environments and Health: The Relationship of Walkable and Safe Communities to Individual Health," *Journal of the American Planning Association* 72:1 (Winter 2006), 19–31; and Loukaitou-Sideris, "Is It Safe to Walk?"

144. Sholom Glouberman et al., "A Framework for Improving Health in Cities: A Discussion Paper," *Journal of Urban Health* 83:2 (2006), 325–338.

145. Health 201 is available at www.phac-aspc.gc.ca/publicat/2009/be-eb/bc-cb-eng.php

Internet Resources

Chapter-Relevant Sites

Ontario Healthy Communities Handbook
www.mah.gov.on.ca

World Health Organization, Global Age-Friendly Cities Project
www.who.int/ageing/projects.age_friendly_cities/en

City of Mississauga, *Older Adult Plan*, 2008
www.mississauga.ca/file/COM/Older_Adult_Plan.pdf

Commonwealth Secretariat, *Gender in Planning*
www.thecommonwealth.org

Mineta Transportation Institute: *How to Ease Women's Fear of Transportation Environments*
www.transweb.sjsu.edu/project/2611.html

Montréal Declaration on Women's Safety, 2002
www.femmesetvilles.org

Vancouver Youth and Planning
www.vancouveryouth.ca

The Center for Universal Design
www.ncsu.edu/project/design-projects/udi/

Metro Vancouver, Regional Homelessness Plan, 2003
www.metrovancouver.org/planning/homelessness/Homlessness%20Docs/FinalPlanUpdateReport.pdf

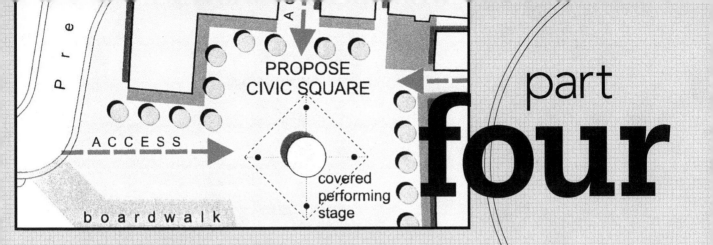

Participants and Participation in Community Plan-Making

Introduction

Probably no other instance of a community's decision-making involves so many and such a wide array of citizens as does community planning. Making community plans demands democratic participation before, during, and after the plan is made. This can, and should, involve a wide range of participants, from ordinary citizens to planners, politicians, developers, interest groups, and associated professionals. There are formal structures that provide opportunities for involvement in various phases of making and reviewing plans. But there is as much or more participation that occurs in informal settings, which contributes to community plan-making and amending.

In the end, participation is about community members communicating with one another about what should be included in a plan so that it will best enable the community to reach its goals. The effectiveness of a community's plan is more a function of the participation that occurs in planning decisions than of any other factor. Planning acts may prescribe a planning process, but it is people, individually and in groups, who make it a reality and who give it texture. This requires blending the myriad values of participants and integrating the numerous roles they play in this extensive community dialogue.

The image above is from the project Downtown St. John's Strategy for Economic Development and Heritage Preservation, St. John's, Newfoundland and Labrador, which received the Canadian Institute of Planners' Award for Planning Excellence, Category of Implementation, 2002.

Source: Downtown St. John's Strategy for Economic Development and Heritage Preservation, City of St. John's.

Chapter Fourteen

Deciding Upon the Community's Plan

Effective planning of human settlements ... will come to depend more on human relations in the process of arriving at decisions than it will on the planner's science and art of preparing plans.

Harry Lash, 1976

Community planning has been referred to as a social activity many times in preceding chapters, for it is the process a community of people follows when deciding upon its future built and natural environment. Community planning is not just a matter of planning *for* a community; it is equally a matter of planning *by* and *with* a community. Thus, community planning is a process orchestrated around the aspirations, contributions, and needs of a diverse array of people—citizens, firms, groups, institutions, developers, politicians, planners, the fortunate and the less fortunate, landowners, tenants, long-time residents and newcomers, and others—who make up the community.

It is now time to consider *who* participates in plan-making as well as *when* and *how* they make decisions concerning the form and substance of the plan and its various tools of implementation. That is the purpose of this chapter and the next. The focus here is on the decisions made in the course of making and adopting a community plan and the complementary processes of implementing the plan and amending it. The principal participants in these various phases are arrayed; the technical and procedural steps that need be taken are also indicated. In the next chapter the dynamics and texture of participation are examined. As this exploration of how the process of community planning unfolds, consider these questions:

- *What is the purpose of the formal steps required of a municipality when making a plan?*
- *How is the process of community planning affected by the amount and type of public participation?*

The Decision Sequence in Municipal Plan-Making

When a community sets out to make a plan for its future built and natural environment (or renew or amend the plan and many of its associated tools), it initiates a decision-making *process* (see also Chapter 6). Further, it is a process consisting of two roughly parallel sets of actions, each with its own logic. One is highly structured and has specific steps that are spelled out in provincial legislation which must be followed. These are the *formal* or *required* steps and they are considered first. The other set of steps in the planning process is concerned with rendering the *substance* or content of the plan and develops out of community interests and conventions as well as from professional planning practice. These are the *informal* steps, and they are considered second.

The Formal Required Steps

Community planning in Canada occurs within a framework prescribed by the province or territory in which the community is located. A provincial/territorial planning act sets out for all its incorporated communities a number of specific steps that must be taken when planning; as well, it identifies the participants and their responsibilities at these required steps. The formal plan-making process does not contain all the steps in the model plan-making process described in Chapter 6. However, it contains the steps that a municipality must follow in making a plan (see Figure 14.1).

The formal, municipal planning process is concerned with defining the roles of public and private interests in the community with regard to the ownership and development of land. As such it specifies participants, specific decisions, and legal requirements and responsibilities. When the built environment might be changed either by private initiative or government action, many interests become involved besides the interests of those who directly initiate change. The interests of other landowners, neighbourhood residents, other public agencies, and of the community as a whole must be taken into account. Thus, decisions must be specified so that all interested parties (i.e., stakeholders) will be aware of their rights and responsibilities. Further, the formal process is concerned with establishing the balance between provincial and municipal authority in regard to private property rights. Since responsibility for these rights, when they are delegated to a municipality (as they are under the planning act), rests ultimately with the province, this shift in responsibility must be speci-fied. The municipal plan-making process as shown is a composite of steps found in various planning acts; actual steps may differ from province to province.[1] (See also Figure 9.8, page 230, for comparative terminology among provinces and territories.) However slight these differences they only heighten the concern over specifying steps and responsibilities. The seven main steps in the formal process are described below in terms of the decisions that are made, the interests involved, and the planning objectives of the decision.

1. Decide to Prepare a Plan (or Amend It)

Since a municipality's (or other local body's) plan becomes an official statement of policy, an explicit decision by the local council is required to initiate plan-making, usually through passing a bylaw. Thereby all interests in the community, and those with an interest in the development of land in the community, are informed that the process is to begin. Such a decision to prepare a plan may arise from a sense in the community that development problems exist and/or that initiatives for major new projects are underway and that these should be dealt with in a more comprehensive, long-term, framework. The municipal council may have been prompted in this decision, by planning staff, other public officials, an advisory planning body, developers, and/or public interest groups. Important decisions about content of the proposed plan and the process of its preparation are often taken at this stage. These may include the problems the plan will focus on and the ways in which the public may participate.

2. Solicit Concerns and Suggestions of the Community

Recognizing that there will be diverse opinions in the community concerning its future built and natural environment, most provinces mandate public participation at this step so that these views can be solicited. The object is to acknowledge the right of involvement of community members in the identification of planning goals for future development. The formal requirements for community input usually specify that it be obtained through one or a few **public meetings**. In practice other informal public consultations occur, including open houses, visioning processes, design charettes, and Internet surveys; these are discussed further later in the chapter.[2] No official decision is forthcoming from these formal and informal consultations, but the conclusions drawn from them become important input for planning staff and

Figure 14.1 | The Formal (Municipal) Planning Process

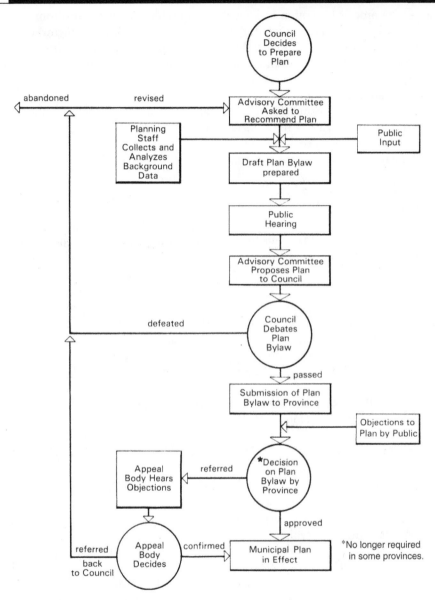

The municipal process of plan-making explicitly takes into account the roles of public and private interests that participate in the development of the community's land base.

other officials drafting the substance of the plan. These consultations are usually conducted by the community's planners and/or the local planning advisory committee.

3. Present the Draft Plan

A draft of a proposed plan is submitted by the professional staff and/or advisory planning body to the council, along with a draft of the bylaw that would officially sanction the plan. Public hearings are then authorized to be held by the council (or its advisory body) as required by provincial legislation. This provides community members with an opportunity to evaluate the plan's proposals. Typically, only one version of s plan is presented. In most provinces, provincial ministries such as transportation, environment, and housing; federal agencies; and other public bodies with an interest in the plan's outcome are also given the opportunity to evaluate the draft plan. The local council makes the decision to set this part of the process in motion by giving first reading to a bylaw that incorporates the draft plan and allows it to go forward for debate and formal public input. Presentations by citizens, developers, and other groups, and submissions by provincial agencies can then be made at public hearings. These are documented and become official input into subsequent deliberations before staff or the planning advisory body recommend the draft plan to the council. It should also be noted that such formal hearings are usually late in the process and can often become adversarial, be dominated by private property interests and their legal representatives, and result in little real consultation. Except in environmental assessment, planning legislation does not encourage the development and evaluation of alternative plans in the manner proposed by the model planning process.

4. Decide on the Plan Bylaw

The local council adopts a community plan by approving a bylaw that makes the plan an official statement of policy about the community's built and natural environment. This is a formal, legislative procedure requiring a formal vote by councillors on the second and third readings of the bylaw. In this way, the plan becomes "official" and legally binding on the council and all parties with interests in land development.

5. Province Approves the Plan

Most provinces require that a community plan be submitted for review and approval to the provincial government department responsible for local planning matters. The plan is checked for the adequacy of its planning approach and its consistency with provincial government policies. The plan is usually not considered official, or the bylaw in effect, until it has been approved and signed by the minister. In several provinces this step is a formality.

6. Implement the Plan Using Various Tools

The passage of a zoning bylaw, the acceptance of a subdivision plan proposal, and the renewal or amendment of the community plan tend to follow a set of required steps similar to the process for adoption of a first-time plan. Each initiative of this sort is regarded as a supplementary process of plan-making, in which the aims of the plan are reaffirmed, refined, and possibly revised. Indeed, provinces normally require that implementation tools conform to the community plan. Initiatives

for amendments often originate with private land-development interests, individual landowners, or corporations, but may also come from public agencies outside the community (e.g., for highways, waste disposal, etc.). Vetting of such proposals involves planning staff, the planning advisory body, and, sometimes, provincial agencies (especially in land subdivisions that impinge on provincial highways). Again, they are approved by a vote of the local council on an enacting bylaw (see Chapters 16 and 17).

7. Review the Plan

It has become standard practice for provinces to require that each municipality (or similar jurisdiction) review its community plan on a regular basis, commonly every five years. The stated purpose is to update the plan with relation to demographic, economic, and physical changes in the community and revise policies where needed. Left unstated is the simple need for the local council and its citizens to re-acquaint themselves with this key document and reaffirm its policies. Review of the plan entails the same steps as in the creation of the original plan. The process involves public consultations and formal public hearings and, lastly, approval of an enacting bylaw by the local council. Concomitantly, implementation tools, such as a zoning bylaw, that are based upon the community plan are required to be revised accordingly following the plan review.

Overview of the Formal Process

This set of formal steps is what gives structure to the planning process in a Canadian community. It acts to ensure that the rights of property owners are properly considered, the right of community members to participate is respected, and the community plan achieves legal, binding status. It also prescribes who may participate at each step and their responsibilities vis-à-vis the decision to be made. There are, essentially, only three sets of participants in the formal process:

- Members of the municipal council;
- Members of the general public; and
- Provincial government officials.

Of these three, only the councillors and the provincial officials are charged with making binding decisions, of giving final approval to the plan or zoning bylaw. Although the citizenry participate, their role is only advisory.

These steps are key decision points in the total planning process. They are the points of convergence of the various technical (e.g., of the planners) and consultative (e.g., of the citizens) activities that also comprise necessary parts of plan-making. These decision-making steps each consume a relatively small amount of time. For example, there is the time taken by the council to debate the bylaw that enacts the plan, the time for one or a few public information meetings, the time for official public hearings, and the time for provincial review of the plan. These steps, at which official decisions need to be taken, are the *visible* steps in the process; they deal with procedures, authority, and responsibilities of participants. Essentially, they are about getting the plan to the stage where it can be formally adopted. All together, they may take up to three months of what is typically found to be two or more years of plan-making. However, much still needs to be done to put *substance* into the plan, and this occurs in the interstices of these formal procedures. The activities and participants in this facet of plan-making are discussed below.

Phases in Developing the Substance of the Plan

In getting a community plan ready for adoption, important steps are necessary to develop the *substance* or content of the plan. These steps, or phases, run all the way from drafting the plan's goals so they are consistent with citizen participants' aims to drafting land use regulations that are consistent with the plan's intent. These phases are technical, consultative, and/or deliberative in nature and consume the most time in the entire plan-making process. However, much of what occurs in these phases is not visible to those outside the local government's planning apparatus. They have been referred to as being "*obscure*" because many of the decisions occur in planning offices as planners gather and analyze data, in meeting rooms negotiating with developers and citizen groups, in meetings with local and provincial officials, and so on.[3] Also, the phases do not necessarily occur in sequence and differences encountered in one phase may upset the flow of the overall process of plan-making. These interlocking steps confirm the complexity of the planning process.

Who Gets Involved: How and When?

It should be clear by this point that community plan-making is not a monolithic process, but rather several sub-processes, each concerned with different phases of developing the plan and its implementation modes. Each of these phases has its own distinctive set of participants; some involve large numbers as in community visioning while others involve relatively small numbers as in actually writing the plan. Just who participates may be better appreciated by considering the main phases that go into developing the content and style of the community plan. The following phases parallel the steps in the general model of community plan-making discussed in Chapter 6 and shown in Figure 6.1, page 145):

1. Determining community preferences;
2. Articulating goals and objectives;
3. Plan writing;
4. Implementing the plan; and
5. Clarifying the plan.

Phases and Their Participants

Determining Community Preferences The process of developing a plan's substance usually begins by consulting citizens about their views on the future development of the community's built and natural environment. Citizens understand most aspects of it because the consultation process is intended to involve them. This phase officially follows the decision of the local council to make a plan, but discussions among the community's planners, councillors, and other officials about the timing, venues, and format for citizen involvement may have already taken place. Indeed, the stimulus for a new plan may arise from the public and be endorsed or even encouraged by the planners employed by the community. Further, once this phase has begun, both community members and staff planners (including consultants) become highly dependent on one another.

A few other points about the participants in this phase are important to note. First, the "*public*" participants usually comprise many elements or stakeholders—individuals and organized groups within the community, those representing their personal interests, and those espousing community interests. Second, other officials of the local government are likely to be involved along with the planners in organizing the public engagement process such as the city's administrative officer, engineer, solicitor, parks director, and traffic engineer. The latter participants can affect the form and content of the means for obtaining the public's planning ideas (see Figure 14.2).[4]

The key facet of this phase is that current best practice is to open it up and both engage larger numbers and include a greater diversity of citizens. Canadian planners now use an array of techniques to obtain public input to try to ensure the participation of people who do not usually participate.[5] Stronger and more broadly acceptable plans emerge when such initiatives are taken early,

Figure 14.2 Key Participants in the Phases of Community Planning

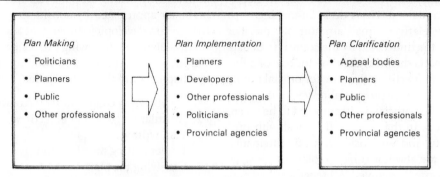

Plan Making
- Politicians
- Planners
- Public
- Other professionals

Plan Implementation
- Planners
- Developers
- Other professionals
- Politicians
- Provincial agencies

Plan Clarification
- Appeal bodies
- Planners
- Public
- Other professionals
- Provincial agencies

Each of the three phases of community planning has its own distinct set of participants, although some are involved in more than one phase. Within each phase, there is considerable interdependency among participants in their aims and decisions.

when a wide array of different people are involved, and when several different techniques are employed to engage the citizenry.[6] Among the techniques commonly used at the outset of this phase are public meetings, open houses, questionnaires, charettes, videos, and visioning exercises; the use of the Internet and social media have recently also become standard public engagement tools. Staff planners are usually assigned the task of formulating, coordinating, and facilitating the approaches to be used; specialist consultants may be employed to conduct the engagement processes. (See Chapter 15 for a further discussion of public engagement techniques.)

Visioning has become one of the most widely used techniques in this initial phase of developing the community plan's substance.[7] Its aim is, literally, to seek answers from citizens to the following type of question: "How would you like this community to be, look like, and function in the future?" As practised, a multiplicity of modes is frequently used to conduct such a "community dialogue." Saskatoon, in its 2011 visioning project, *Saskatoon Speaks*, used at least fifteen different formats to elicit community values and preferences, many of them numerous times (see Figure 14.3).[8] The entire process took one year and was iterative in several segments, which afforded participants the opportunity to determine if draft visions prepared by staff planners reflected citizens' original intent when elicited through community and youth "voice" sessions, questionnaires, and social media. Over the course of the project in Saskatoon between 7000 and 10 000 were involved in the dialogue, a significant portion of the population, which was 222 189 in 2011.

The document that emanated from the Saskatoon project contained for each of eight themes (from social well-being to the environment) a Community Vision statement; a list of Signs of Success, which would indicate achievement of the vision; and a What We Can Do list of potential strategies for achieving the vision. With these latter indicators of methods and outcomes of implementation, the visioning document became a major input into the City's Strategic Plan.

This phase of substantive planning, whether through visioning, crowd-sourcing, or other means of public engagement, involves the largest number of participants that is ever involved in community plan-making.

Figure 14.3 Public Engagement Techniques for Saskatoon Speaks, 2011

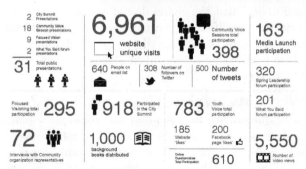

Array of modes of public engagement used in the visioning project by the City of Saskatoon, 2011.

Indeed, one might think of the plan-making process as funnel-like, involving fewer and fewer participants as it unfolds. An important implication of this is that the responsibility for distilling the input of a phase, in this case from many citizens, for use in a subsequent phase, flows to a relatively small number of persons, usually city staff and/or consultants in this case. The latter are, thus, responsible for distilling the citizen input so that it reflects true community preferences. If there is dissatisfaction with that rendering, which can occur because, among other reasons, some actors have tacitly different goals, the plan-making process may be interrupted, called by some a "disconnect."[9] It is important to note similar interruptions may occur in all phases of making the community plan (see Figure 14.4).

Articulating Goals and Objectives The multi-layered and voluminous information about community values, preferences, and aspirations emerging from the foregoing phase must be distilled into a set of planning goals and *actionable* objectives.[10] This task normally falls to the planning staff who may be organized, along with other key community administrative staff, into what is frequently called a Technical Planning Committee. This group will have in hand information from the public engagement phase as well as information provided by individual specialists, public agencies, and development interests. Further information will also be provided by staff planners from their technical studies of population trends, economic tendencies, housing, traffic, etc.

The use of this wide array of information requires a high degree of cooperation among the participants when compounding it into workable planning propositions. Moreover, each participant in this essentially technical–professional phase brings to it his or her own values, knowledge, and motivations, as well as hopes, fears, and criteria for judgment. These perspectives may be personal, professional, or group views, or some combination of the three. Suffice to say, at this point the planner needs to have an acute awareness of the social relations inherent in his or her local planning process, as well as a personal frame of reference regarding the social *intervention* that plan-making constitutes for the various participants. And while cooperation is necessary for community goal setting, the task will not be completed, or if completed will not be fully accepted, unless there is agreement among participants about the goals and objectives of the plan. For example, goals may conflict with each other, not be consistent with community values, or not be politically acceptable. Some communities require the use of formal consensus methods to attain agreement in such situations.[11] Lack of agreement would represent another possible "disconnect" in the overall process (see Figure 14.4). Further discussion on consensus building is found in the next chapter.

Plan Writing The casting of the plan's goals and objectives into text, diagrams, and maps gives the community plan its basic direction. The next task for the community's planners is to render the content of the plan so that its proposals for the built and natural environments affirm the goals and objectives that make them actionable. That is, to "write" the plan so that it leads to the realization of its goals and objectives, in spatial, functional, and policy terms. It will harken back to the question posed for citizens at the outset and in written and graphical forms will show what the community will be like and look like, and how it will function in the future. Generally, it is the community's planning staff (and/or consultants) who are the primary participants in carrying out this phase

The plan, at this stage, should also contain specific steps needed to be taken toward its implementation. These may include proposals for setting up development districts for downtown, designating heritage areas and special environmental features, as well as indicating regulatory provisions and principles for zoning. Good practice suggests the importance of also identifying those responsible for carrying forth the proposals, such as the city council, business groups, the zoning bodies, provincial departments, and other agencies. Not least,

SOURCE: CAROLYN G. LOH, "FOUR POTENTIAL DISCONNECTS IN THE COMMUNITY PLANNING PROCESS," JOURNAL OF PLANNING EDUCATION AND RESEARCH 32:1 (MARCH 2012), 33–47. FIGURE 1, THE FOUR POTENTIAL DISCONNECTS..., P36. REPRINTED BY PERMISSION OF SAGE PUBLICATIONS.

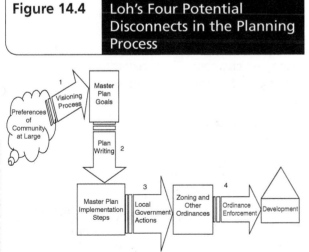

| **Figure 14.4** | Loh's Four Potential Disconnects in the Planning Process |

Four potential disconnects in the planning process. Each dashed arrow represents a decision point where the planning process could break down.

proposed implementation initiatives must be within the community's financial and resource capability and its jurisdictional abilities. This is often undertaken with the development of a Strategic Plan.

Prior to the completion of plan-writing, the draft document will normally be submitted to provincial ministries for review (e.g., ministries of highways, environment, and municipal affairs). This involves participants outside the community vetting the plan for conformity with provincial legislation and jurisdiction; possibly revisions will be required. The plan finally submitted to council for their approval and adoption, thus, has gone through several iterations, each with different sets of participants.

Implementing the Plan After council adopts the community plan it is implemented utilizing a wide range of tools (see Chapter 16). The land use provisions are implemented primarily through a zoning bylaw. Sometimes called a zoning map or plan because it encompasses the same spatial extent as the community plan, its purpose is to regulate the uses of land throughout the community. Since, in effect, it is a new plan it must go through a similar process of formulation, public scrutiny, debate, and adoption by council as its counterpart. The community's planners (including consultants) usually develop the zoning plan and its regulations; public engagement occurs through information meetings and public hearings. It's worth noting that each of the two plans comprises the same community space but each through a different descriptive language: one of general policy and the other of legal specifications. If the zoning bylaw (or any other ordinance for implementation) is seen to be inconsistent with the community plan's intentions, a "disconnect" could occur affecting the entire planning process. The same can be said about the later phase of actually enforcing the regulations, not least because zoning deals with the issue-laden area of the disposition of private property.

Planning Issue 14.1	Marpole Looks Back to Its Future

Vancouver Sun
May 12, 2012

Marpole Looks Back to Its Future
Jeff Lee

Residents are divided over the best ways to grow, as the city develops a new community plan

Gudrun Langolf and Claudia Laroye have two different visions of what their Marpole neighbourhood should look like 20 years from now. Laroye favours denser development, with residential towers along arterial roads. Langolf wants a much lighter touch, with a slower rate of change. But they share a common view that this southern corner of Vancouver has suffered from considerable neglect by city hall and as a result is now under considerable pressure from development.

Over the next 21 months, the city will develop a new community plan for the district between Angus Drive and Ontario Street, and from 57th Avenue south to the Fraser River.

One of the city's oldest communities, Marpole has long been a mix of low-, medium-and high-income neighbourhoods, all anchored along the Fraser River with one of the city's oldest continuous industrial districts. But Marpole has also undergone a transformation of late and is under considerable scrutiny by developers.
The new Canada Line under Cambie Street prompted city council's decision to densify the entire corridor from 25th Avenue to Marine Drive.

No Consensus
Laroye, the executive director of the Marpole Business Improvement Association, says the community of nearly 24,000 is ready for development, including higher towers along the most southern reaches of Granville Street and 70th Avenue.

Langolf, who is president of the Marpole Oakridge Area Council Society that operates Marpole Place Neighbourhood House, says minor densification in the form of row houses, duplexes and three-storey walk-ups is great - but the 16-and 20-plus storey towers that now threaten to puncture the skyline along Granville and the foot of Cambie "are not conducive to community living." It irks her that PCI's Cambie development and Westbank's three-tower plan for the old Safeway store site on Granville were approved in advance of the new Marpole community plan.

Differences aside, Laroye and Langolf both say the city failed to address significant problems that have afflicted Marpole for more than half a century, starting with the opening of the Oak Street Bridge to Richmond in 1957.

"It might as well be our Berlin Wall," Langolf says of Oak Street. "I don't know of a lot of people who live on one side who dare to cross to the other side, and that has had a huge impact on the cohesiveness of our community."

Angst Triggered New Plan

Neighbourhood angst caused the city to develop its first community plan in 1979 to try to mitigate the significant impacts. "The 1979 plan was supposed to do two things. One was to deal as best we could with the traffic impacts of the new bridges and the widening of Oak Street, and the second was to try to support the viability of a new or enhanced retail area on Granville Street," according to

Matt Shillito, the city's assistant director of community planning.

Trust Tough to Come By

City council's recent decision to approve the Rize Alliance tower at Broadway and Kingsway in Mount Pleasant and the dense development along the Cambie corridor has also given some people in Marpole reason to distrust the new community plan process, Langolf says.

"At the moment I believe that the trust between the city and neighbour-hood is at very rock bottom. I don't want to say it's the lowest it's ever been, but it feels like it," she says.

"We've got people who went to those [Cambie and Rize] public meetings and expressed concerns and then found out the politicians won't do any-thing ... because the bylaws that regulate growth and business in the city have really not been written for the benefit of citizens, they've been written to facilitate development."

The city has broken the planning process into four chunks, Shillito says. Planners sought public opinion last week. They will come back to the community this fall with policy options based on those submissions, with a draft plan to follow a year later. The final plan will be taken to council in the winter of 2013.

Clarifying the Plan The community plan is conceived with the idea of dealing with future change in its built and natural environment by providing a preferred perspective and guideline for development. Of course, very little of the future can be known and more so knowing the almost infinite instances of possible development of properties in the community. Thus, the intent of the plan or the provisions of the zoning bylaw may need to be clarified periodically. One instance is the simple case of a variance desired to allow a taller building; another could be the more complex situation where a developer feels a (major) project should be allowed within the plan and the council disagrees. Appeal and amendment processes

clarify the current thinking with regard to planning in the community. The appeal bodies are a focal point for participation in this phase, and their legally based procedures define the participants. With simple variances participants usually are closely associated with the property, such as the property owner, owners of neighbouring properties, or other neighbourhood residents. Appeals of council decisions involve a wider array of participants. In both types of appeals it is important to the integrity of the plan and the entire process that decisions are consistent with the plan's intent, indeed of the original citizen input. Again, see Chapters 16 and 17 in Part Four for detailed discussions of implementation tools.

The Milieu of Roles

Knowing *who* is involved in the various phases of planning is one side—the objective side—of decision making. The other side is qualitative, that is, *how* the various participants respond, react, behave, perform, and so forth in the actual decision making. (The cartoon below reflects on this qualitative side of participation.) The quality of the involvement in the planning process is affected by the nature and extent of the participation of those involved. The *formal* agents (councillors, planning advisory committee members, and provincial officials) have defined places and functions in plan-making: they *have to* participate. Others act in an *individual* capacity (professional planners, other professionals, private developers, members of the public) and *choose* to participate. And some act in *both* capacities, in particular the politicians and professional planners, especially when the latter are on the staff of the local government. With this mixture of participants we can expect that the people involved will act from a variety of personal and professional backgrounds and possibly have different perceptions of the aims of planning.

Each participant plays one or several roles and while some are prescribed by planning statute or regulation, many are not (see Figure 14.5). Further, each participant plays at least one formal and one informal role. The formal roles come from legal and institutional definitions of the participant, while informal roles arise from cultural norms of the situation, as well as from the personality and behaviour of the participant.

A public-participation program over the development of an important site in the heart of Winnipeg was examined for the roles assumed by various participants and provides a useful example of such situations.[12] In this case the public-participation process had become as much an issue as the proposed development. It was found that participants played varying roles ranging from "proponents" (who supported the process) to "challengers" (who felt the process was manipulative). Between these extremes were roles such as "positive explainers" (who supported the project but not always the process), "negative explainers" (who felt the need for changes in the process), and "observers" (who did not take a position about the process). Proponents included consultants to the agency charged with the development, agency board members, provincial officials, and local politicians. Challengers were mostly activists and one local politician—individuals essentially outside the decision-making arena. The study concluded that public-participation programs are "primarily shaped by the values of the power holders."

Each participant also "acts out" informal roles. Municipal councillors may, for example, champion development interests in debates because the district they represent is populated by voters known to profess this orientation. A thoughtful self-evaluation by a city councillor in a fractious planning situation in a Midwest American city allows a rare view "behind the scenes" of how personal predispositions affect participants:[13]

> The most emotionally intense experiences I had … occurred in those situations where people felt that their worries, fears, hope, dreams, or visions were cavalierly disregarded … Whenever I saw, heard, or read such intemperate dismissals, I could feel my blood boil and my own anger beginning to build.

There are, of course, parallels for citizens and planners who also have their roles shaped by personal factors.

Figure 14.5	"Theory" and "Practice"

SOURCE: HELLMAN CARTOON FROM BUILT ENVIRONMENT 22, NO. 4 (1996), "THEORY AND PRACTICE IN URBAN DESIGN," REPRODUCED BY PERMISSION OF LOUIS HELLMAN AND ALEXANDRINE PRESS.

A citizen participant with the professional qualifications of, say, a lawyer is likely to pursue things differently from a retired schoolteacher or blue-collar worker. And, more pointedly for planners, if they are personally convinced of the need for citizen participation in planning, they could respond differently from planners who see their role as strictly technical and neutral. Regardless, planners may find it difficult to play the role of being both the proponent of change (in, say, density) and the facilitator of public debate over the matter. In one reported case, in Tofino, British Columbia, the planner who also lived in this small community proposed the use of consultants to carry out the public-participation program for this very reason.[14] This is a clear illustration of an ethical dilemma often faced by planners in purveying information that they themselves have produced in plan-making. Or, as Forester would characterize it, the planner took steps to avoid being a possible source of "misinformation" to fellow community members.[15] Local contexts differ but general and professional ethical principles help resolve such dilemmas (see Chapter 15 for an extended discussion).

Some of these less visible facets of the planning process have been made intentionally more visible in practice by the use of, for example, public participation programs, advisory groups, focus groups, and panel discussions. Alternately, some are made more visible through street demonstrations (see Figure 6.3, page 150). Regardless of mode, the informal "steps" discussed in this section are crucial to the planning process; for it is through them the plan is actually formulated, its substance attained.

Making Supplementary Plans

Community planning does not stop with the formulation of the overall community plan. Its completion is usually followed immediately by a number of supplementary plans to bring the community plan to fruition. Besides the zoning plan larger cities may also prepare secondary plans to institute detailed land use policies for the downtown, districts of special note, and individual neighbourhoods (see Chapter 11). The city-wide plan thereby becomes a *policy* framework for environmental, transportation, and open-space systems with the details being in the secondary plans (see Chapters 12 and 13).[16]

Supplementary planning efforts refine the community plan's goals and policies. They are usually required by the provincial planning act to conform to the overall plan. Further, the decision-making sequence is formal and very similar to that for making the overall plan.

Public information meetings are held to solicit views about the draft plan; a planning advisory committee deliberates on the planning proposals, taking into account the views of the public, and makes a recommendation to the municipal council; the council debates the proposal in the form of implementing a bylaw; and, lastly, provincial approval is sought. The array of participants is also much the same as in general plan-making.

A major exception in the array of participants occurs in planning for specific projects, as with a secondary plan for a large suburban greenfield site, a new subdivision, an application for rezoning, or a development permit. In these cases, the draft plan is usually prepared by consultants and put forward by the individuals wishing to modify the sites. The proponents in these instances are commonly referred to as "developers," and they play a prominent role in advocating the merits of the plan. This type of planning situation is one that is most likely to create controversy and conflict and elicit opponents to the project including nearby landowners, neighbourhood groups, environmental groups, or other public agencies.

Responding to Development Initiatives

The community-planning process must be responsive to ongoing initiatives for urban development in addition to promoting long-range goals. These initiatives that could result in new buildings or redeveloped older buildings on private land—the bulk of all community land—may come from a wide range of sources. And it is often only in the course of responding to these many private decisions that the vagaries of land development become apparent and the community (or supplementary) plan gets tested.

Three facets of land development affect the process of plan-making or call for modification of the plan's policies and also affect who participates in these decisions:

1. Inherent differences among pieces of property that could affect the type of development;
2. The ways different developers view the potential for land development on specific sites; and
3. The different ways other landowners or the public view development initiatives.

None of these conditions can be ignored. To do so would be not only unrealistic but could also deny "natural justice" to participants. Formal planning frameworks thus provide the means by which these differences can be reconciled.

Differences in Developability

Zoning bylaws treat each property within a zone as equally developable. However, occasionally one or a few properties may differ from their neighbours in terms of their topography, size, shape, or location, such that the property cannot be developed as required by the zoning bylaw without causing their owners hardship. For such cases, provision is made to vary, or adjust, the zoning regulations; this is called a **variance** (see Chapter 16). A landowner who feels that her or his property requires a variance may make an appeal to a special committee established for this purpose. In some provinces, these committees are called a **Committee of Adjustment**; in others, a **Zoning Appeal Board**. They are appointed by the municipal council, and are usually composed of three citizen or council members.

A hearing (which has legal standing in many provinces) is held, and the committee can decide to allow or disallow the application. The committee's decision can usually be appealed to a provincial planning appeal body.

Differences in Developers' Perceptions

The land use designations in a community plan and zoning bylaw are the planners' *estimate* of the development potential of properties at particular locations. But not until a developer takes the initiative to build a new building or refurbish an old one on a site can the accuracy of that estimate be determined. It is difficult to imagine all the uses that could be appropriate for a given site: for example, properties that adjoin an intersection may appear to be appropriate for retail commercial uses. However, the same properties may appeal to a developer as a good location for a motel or an office building. Another example could be a site that the plan envisions and the zoning allows to be developed for residential use, and a developer submits a proposal for a shopping centre. In order to accommodate these sorts of possibilities, planning regulations provide for applications to amend the zoning bylaw and, possibly, the community plan. The proponent of the project, the developer, usually initiates this process and remains a key participant throughout.

Proposed development projects requiring amendments to existing planning policy usually receive (1) technical scrutiny by the planning staff and other officials, (2) a formal public hearing to receive citizen comments, (3) debate by the municipal council, and (4) final approval by the province.

In these situations the planner is expected to act in the public interest and not on behalf of the developer or any other interests. This calls for considerable skill in designing processes that involve all affected interests effectively and justly in the decision making and do not inhibit investment. Many communities require developers to discuss their project with affected groups and seek their support before initiating a re-zoning. The same applies in many places regarding applications for development permits.

Different Reactions to Development

An essential feature of community planning is the consideration given to whether, and in which way(s), development on one site might affect surrounding properties as well as the community as a whole (especially if the project is large). It is something of a truism in planning that reactions to planning decisions become more intense the closer a proposal for development appears about to become an actual project. Thus, taking an example from the preceding section where a developer proposes a project that differs from what is allowed under the plan and bylaw, we have one of the classic situations in which strong reaction emerges in the planning process (see Chapter 15). Our planning statutes allow for these reactions to be channelled formally into the plan-making process through three formal avenues: public information meetings, public hearings, and the filing of formal appeals.

Dispute Resolution

Frequently, planners find themselves having to balance competing demands of politicians, other municipal departments, developers, and public-advocacy groups. Sometimes, these demands are not readily reconcilable through technical or design analyses, and even political bodies may be stymied. Usually, this is because the demands are rooted in differences in basic attitudes and values. Dispute-resolution methods are increasingly being used by planners to reach constructive solutions without going to costly litigation or to appeal tribunals.[17] Two such methods being used are **negotiation** (where advocates for each side seek a mutual solution) and **mediation** (where a neutral third party assists each side in finding an acceptable solution). Planners trained in these methods find that they can help solve problems, enhance mutual understanding, and strengthen the planning process. Outside professionals may also be utilized by the planners to facilitate problem solving between stakeholders.[18]

A number of cities in Canada employ mediation mechanisms for resolving difficult planning problems, notably Kitchener-Waterloo, Ontario, and Kamloops, B.C.[19] The City of Calgary, which has been operating a planning-mediation program since 1998, provides a good example of how this mode works. It is important to understand that mediation is used to resolve disputes between applicants for planning department approvals (say, a developer) and opposing parties (often nearby residents) to a project, and not between the planning department and applicants. A successful outcome would be a development application that could then proceed through the approval process. Mediators contracted by the city's Planning Mediation Program work to help the parties to achieve their different goals, not to determine who is "right" or "wrong." The program has resolved conflicts over bylaw enforcement, design issues, conflicting land uses, group homes, restaurant noise, and neighbourhood industrial uses.[20] Mediation does not always succeed in resolving all planning disputes and courts may have to be involved. However, it is an approach along with other non-confrontational techniques that cultivates consensus building around planning issues as we see in the next chapter.

Community Planning versus Corporate Planning

It should be evident by now in our discussion of community plan-making that there is *no single entity or person in control* of the decision-making process. The local council has a central role in making planning decisions, but it depends upon advice from others and reactions from still others and its decisions are subject to appeal. The planner is involved in almost all phases of plan-making, but is not in a position to direct the process of carrying out the plan.

One observer calls this diffuse undertaking of community planning a process in "social cooperation."[21] This is an apt term for this diffuse community activity of community planning involves the processing of information, ideas, and reactions among a diverse group of participants who, it is likely, do not fully share each other's values about the development of the community. In community planning there must be a sharing of information and the opportunity to refine proposals and bring new alternatives into the discussion. It has an essential need for a large measure of feedback so that goals and courses of action may be re-examined and, where necessary, modified. In short, community planning is an ungainly process and one that has been the subject, not infrequently, of suggestions that it be

"streamlined" using corporate planning as its model. Others suggest modifying the community planning process so that it is seen as one of political choice. Both these perspectives deserve examination in order to better understand community plan-making.

The Limits of the Corporate Planning Model

For many decades, going back to the 1920s and earlier, there has been considerable pressure to model community planning decision-making after the process followed in private business firms, for community planning "to become more business-like." In the early decades of community planning, there were frequent initiatives from commercial groups seeking to "keep politics out of planning" and to "get on with making decisions." More recent initiatives, recognizing that community planning is, essentially, a process of political choice, seek rather to improve the information on which councillors base their choices and to organize the communication in the process of implementing decisions.

Much of this latter effort focuses on improving budgeting and financial planning. Various new approaches to budgeting have been introduced into local government decision-making with the aim to improve the link between the services and programs that are being provided and the goals of the political decision-makers. Performance budgeting (which looks at the output obtained by expenditures), program budgeting (which looks at the output of groupings of expenditures), and zero-base budgeting (which requires all operating units annually to justify expenditures against community goals) have added significantly to the effectiveness of local governments.[22] It is through the local budget that actions of officials are controlled to achieve policy objectives.

Some proponents of improving local government performance and planning advocate the use of corporate planning models, which aim at a rational selection of effective means to obtain predetermined ends. Plunkett and Betts, for example, propound a four-stage model: (1) *policy planning*, for the purpose of defining priorities and selecting objectives; (2) *action planning*, for the purpose of establishing program alternatives and budgets; (3) *operations*, which involves carrying out program activities; and (4) *feedback and review*, which involves assessing program impacts.[23] At first glance, this paradigm seems to mirror the rational–comprehensive model of community planning. However, almost all corporate models start with the assumption that the ends (goals) are given and that the need is to activate an administrative structure to achieve these designated ends. They further assume that the tasks of the organization can be subdivided and delegated to facilitate their implementation.

A typical corporate planning model is that offered by Redman, illustrated in Figure 14.6.[24] It is a four-stage model that includes a feedback loop for plan modification and relates the tasks of the chief executive officer(s), the managers, and the department heads. This model puts into operation the sequence of decision making implied in the typical organization charts made for firms and governments: from chief executive to staff officers to line departments. It is a *hierarchical* model in which administrative responsibilities may be specified progressively from the highest to the lowest levels of the organization. It further assumes that problems or tasks may be handled simultaneously and independently from each other.

There are, however, several important ways in which the corporate model is not consonant with physical planning for a community: (1) The time horizon of corporate planning is much shorter (3–4 years) than that of most community-planning activities (10–20 or more years). (2) Corporate planning assumes that the goals will be established by the top executive of the organization and these will be agreeable to all other participants. In community planning, by contrast, goals are a product of extensive deliberation at all levels, as well as subject to debate between levels. (3) Corporate planning assumes a hierarchy of responsibilities between participants, but such a division of labour does not exist within community planning. (4) The corporate model assumes that tasks can be divided in such a way as to allow participants to act independently. Further, it is clear that the aims of both the ongoing activities and the planning procedures in the two realms are fundamentally different. The planning objectives in the private sector are

Figure 14.6 Model of the Planning Process Used in Corporations

PHASE	FUNCTION	RESPONSIBILITY	TIME HORIZON
1. Strategic planning	Establishes objectives, strategies, goals, and policies to govern acquisitions, use, and disposition of resources, and provides resources to business units.	Executive management	Long-term—4+ years
2. Management control	Establishes objectives and strategies relating to implementation of strategic plan, and allocates resources.	Managers	Long- and short-term—1 month to 3 years
3. Operational control	Develops programs to utilize resources effectively and efficiently.	Department heads	Short-term—1 month to 1 year
4. Plan modification	Assesses performance of resource use.	Executive management	Short-term

SOURCE: ADAPTED AND EXPANDED BY GERALD HODGE FROM MATERIAL IN LOUIS N. REDMAN, "THE PLANNING PROCESS," *MANAGERIAL PLANNING* 31:6 (MAY–JUNE 1983), 24–25.

This model is essentially hierarchical and allows responsibilities for achieving objectives to be specified from the highest to the lowest levels of the organization. Such a division of labour does not usually exist within community planning.

concerned with, to quote Seasons, "efficiency, concern with competitive position, and profit or product maximization," while those in the public sector are developed in organizations that "function within complex, multilateral power, influence bargaining, voting, and exchange relationships."[25]

Nonetheless, some facets of local government operations can and are being adapted from that part of the corporate planning model called *strategic* planning. Many larger Canadian communities, such as Edmonton, Saskatoon, and Ottawa, are employing it at the broad, city-wide level.[26] The municipality in these cases is referred to as "the corporation," and the work of the planning department is expected to help fulfill the entire municipal corporate plan (see Figure 8.3, page 189).

Community Planning and Political Choices

One main reason community-planning decision making is not easily adaptable to corporate or other organizational planning models is its inherent involvement with *plural* political choices, with politics.[27] Or, put another way, community planning is a mode of decision-making peculiar to the needs of diverse peoples and interests to decide upon their community's future. There is, therefore, a multiplicity of goals representing a plurality of interests to be reconciled. There is no single hierarchical structure for channelling initiatives or commands. What regularity there is comes from legislative processes prescribing when the municipal council or other body has the authority to make a decision, and this occurs among the ever-present competition between economic and social interests in the community.

The Local Political Economy

Before the advent of community-planning institutions early in the 20th century, decisions about the future development of a community's built and natural environment were resolved by one or both of two mechanisms: the **economic marketplace** or the **political arena**. These mechanisms still exist, of course, and play a prominent role, but are now mediated by the approach of community planning. It will help in understanding the special character of decision-making in community planning to look at these counterpart mechanisms and their relationship to planning as shown in Figure 14.4. There it can be seen that (1) the scope of both the political arena and the economic marketplace overlap;

(2) the planning realm must accommodate the pressures of the other two realms; and (3) planning directly affects only a relatively small proportion of all community decision-making.

Marketplace Decisions and Neoliberalism The built and natural environment of a community is the outcome of choices made by private landowners and project developers, as well as by public agencies. The former build the homes, apartment buildings, shopping centres, and factories, while the latter build the roads, schools, parks, utility lines, and other public buildings and facilities. In some instances they may combine their initiatives. The decisions of private developers are largely motivated by economic considerations: How much will a home cost? How much profit can be realized by erecting an office building? Such decisions are articulated by mechanisms of the economic marketplace such as the residential real estate market or the commercial and industrial land markets. The decisions by public agencies to construct buildings or other facilities are made and adjudicated mainly in the political arena.

The marketplace in Canadian society is not controlled by any central mechanism but is open to the participation of all who have the financial resources and the will to risk them. Decisions are made on the basis of financial resources that are bid for houses, properties, and so forth, and on the asking price for them. Transactions of this sort are made all the time in the typical Canadian community, the outcomes of which determine much of the character of the built and natural environment— its appearance, location, and stability. The essence of the marketplace mechanism is the contention that the development of a community's land is most likely to occur, and in the best fashion, through the efforts of buyers and sellers who most fully appreciate their own interests—this is the so-called neoclassical economic model. A contemporary variation is called the neoliberal model, which promotes even more strongly the economic arena over the political arena in mediating development decisions.[28]

At its extreme, neoliberalism ideology contends that *only* through the marketplace can the community's best development be achieved—a contention not without its critics.[29] Its advocates tend to discourage regulations on development and spending on social projects like affordable housing, as one observer perceived of Vancouver's development priorities in hosting the 2010 Winter Olympics.[30] Other visible evidence of the influence of neoliberalism on current urban development includes the naming, or renaming, of sports venues and theatres after a corporation, the increasing privatization of various public services and utilities, and public–private partnerships such as the Highway 407 toll road in Ontario. Some critics refer to such instances as "the privatization of public space."[31] These highly capitalistic tendencies suggest the need for revising Figure 14.7, that is, enlarging the marketplace circle and reducing that of the political arena with the consequent reduction of the overall role and possible influence of community planning.

Political Arena Decisions The political arena exists to make those decisions about the development of the community that affect the entire populace. On the one hand are those decisions about facilities and services whose provision is the responsibility of the community, such as the street system and public utilities. On the other hand are those decisions about steps that are taken to protect the interests of all citizens, such as building and traffic regulations, and waste-disposal services. Provincial statutes provide local councils with the authority to raise money through various taxes to pay for facilities and services and to pass regulations in the general interest of the community. Further, the council's decisions frequently affect development in the private

sector, such as decisions about the basic infrastructure and regulations that might constrain the quality, location, and/or pace of development.

There are inherent differences in the form and basis of decision making in the political arena and in the marketplace. Both, it might be said, involve *voting*. In the council's milieu, the voting is done by a group of people that must publicly declare its position. Councillors are elected to represent the values and interests of the community, so that when they decide upon matters affecting physical development, their vote is expected to be for the general good. In the economic marketplace, the voting is done with money and the transactions are conducted in private, with only the interests of the participants at stake. In both arenas, the decisions are similar in that they tend to concentrate on short-term considerations: concluding a deal, passing the annual budget, establishing a regulation.

We call this overall community milieu, using the older tradition of the social sciences, a **political economy**. The decisions of local councillors are seldom made without either explicit or implicit reference to economic consequences: What will be the impact on jobs with or without this new project? Will we drive investors away if we don't approve this project? Concomitantly, those involved in developing land and trading real estate have, since the beginnings of formal community planning, taken an explicit interest in the workings of local government—running for council and getting appointed to planning boards, not to mention lobbying. Indeed, some politicians may have an inherent interest in furthering marketplace solutions when confronted by community planning issues to resolve. Conversely, many councillors have been elected in recent years on "reform" platforms that espouse more social content in decisions—for example, housing programs for the homeless and poor and protection of the natural environment. Sitting astride both of these realms as it does, community planning thus becomes the primary governmental activity that attempts this reconciliation, which, in turn, imparts special pressures and tensions to those engaged in the practice of planning.

| Figure 14.7 | The Place of Planning in Community Decision Making |

COMMUNITY PLANNING

THE POLITICAL ARENA

THE ECONOMIC MARKET PLACE

Community planning plays a limited role in reconciling political and economic interests affecting the development of the built and natural environment in the interest of the community as a whole.

Planning, Politics, and Power

Community planning grew up and persists as a distinct mode of public decision-making because neither of the two traditional modes deals effectively with all the concerns that arise when deciding upon the future built and natural environment. Developers usually have their eyes on short-term economic gains from a particular project.

And politicians often have their eyes on an upcoming election. The approach of community planning is to employ a more pervasive socially and spatially based long term where community-wide interests are at stake. But planning becomes subject to the vagaries of political power and choices when pursuing this course.[32] Planners thus come to play a political role, an attribute that planners themselves have often had difficulty accepting. For many planners "politics has meant conflict," to quote Forester, "and conflict has meant irrationality … [and] loss of control."[33] In actuality, it is virtually impossible for planners, or any others who become involved in planning decisions (e.g., citizens, businesspeople) to avoid the politics that is entwined with community planning. Quoting Forester again,

> We often have to interpret what a goal, policy, regulation or bylaw means. Once we do that, knowing that multiple and conflicting interpretations are always possible (some favouring some people, others favouring others) we're right back to politics.

This is most evident in recent environmental issues. Whether it concerns protecting the water supply in Wawa, Ontario, or ridding Sydney, Nova Scotia, of pollutants, these issues are highly politicized. Friedmann has said in this regard, "No matter what position planners take in an argument concerning environmental policy they are certain to antagonize important segments of the population."[34] Hence, as both Forester and Friedmann conclude, planners must establish *relationships* with key participants in order to function effectively. This is due to the fact that working in a political milieu means coming to terms with power—the power of others as well as one's own power. Planners in Canada have little political power in the conventional sense (i.e., they are able only to give advice) and cannot control political outcomes. But planners are able to wield considerable influence on those who can (the politicians) and those who try to influence politicians (developers, citizens, business interests, and others).[35] An example of influencing the mode of development is the *Urban Design Manual* published recently by the Town of Collingwood, Ontario which establishes guidelines for all developers of property.[36] Much more is said about the roles of planners and other participants in the next chapter.

Community planning, seen this way, does not operate independently of either economic or political modes or their criteria because planning does not entirely replace either of the modes and must draw upon them both.

Those involved in community planning cannot help but bring their own biases and interests into the process. Some would argue, since not all segments of the community are likely to be able to participate, that planning outcomes tend to favour the interests of the more powerful over those of the weak and disadvantaged.[37] Plans, therefore, are not just neutral technical solutions for when planners advocate a planning solution they are in effect *taking a political* stand that will affect different groups in different ways.

The potential for planning decisions to be discriminatory is very real. When a stable neighbourhood is divided by an urban expressway, or tenants with low incomes have their rooming houses demolished for high-rise apartments, or small businesses on downtown streets are forced to compete with large shopping malls or "big-box" stores, it is clear that there are always *some who gain* and *some who lose* from a planning decision. These sorts of situations create tensions in the planning process and affect the behaviour of participants. The long-standing utilitarian ethic of planners—to produce the greatest good for the greatest number—cannot, it seems, ever be fully met.

A graphic illustration of this kind of planner's dilemma is found in the situation that faced the Victoria Park neighbourhood on the southeast edge of downtown Calgary. In 1992, the Calgary Stampede Board proposed an expansion of the Stampede Grounds over the entire 32 hectares of Victoria Park, wiping out a 1000-person older community that had undergone some gentrification. The main justification offered by the board was the need to sustain the economic contribution of the Stampede to the local economy, reputed to make up about 20 percent of all tourist revenues.[38] The city's planners supported the board's plan and, further, argued that the community was marginal and not entitled to protection, even though their previous redevelopment plan had tried to protect it. They chose to support the position of the "developer" (albeit a public developer in this case), weighing the whole city's presumed economic gain against the needs of the citizens of Victoria Park, who would lose their homes and community. Most residential structures have been levelled for some years (Figure 14.8), but the Stampede expansion project is only now, two decades later, coming to fruition. The reconciliation of such positions in the realm of community planning is never easy. Thus, the milieu in which planners find themselves working frequently has a *moral* as well as a *political* side to it.

Figure 14.8	Demolition of Calgary's East Victoria Park Neighbourhood, 2006

SOURCE: © JEREMY HOOD.

Reflections

Although we establish structures that offer opportunities for involvement—such as consultation, debate, deliberation, and appeal—in planning matters, we cannot know the nature and extent of that involvement. For, at its best, community planning is a process in social cooperation. It requires the involvement of many participants of many different kinds, and demands their interaction with one another to make, implement, and clarify plans. It will always be somewhat ungainly, time-consuming, and unpredictable, not least because some participants have formal roles they are required to play according to provincial legislation, while many other roles emerge and are played out in the myriad off-the-record deliberations that comprise community plan-making and amending. The latter are the invisible or obscure phases of plan-making that Paul Cloke has shrewdly noted.[39]

Other than the official steps required to bring a plan to adoption, the involvement of others than the planner(s) in plan-making will differ from one community to another, both in quantity and quality. This arises from the simple fact that the composition of persons and groups and the cultural norms of the community determine who becomes involved in plan-making in any of its phases. The presence (or absence) of persons with certain skills or of specific interest groups can affect the quality of involvement in community planning. As well, each community may differ in its inclination to become involved in planning issues and in the intensity of that involvement. Beyond these "chance" factors are the personal and professional preferences of the plan-makers themselves (both planners and politicians) toward the kind and amount of involvement they wish to encourage. The numbers, composition, and performance of participants, as well as the effectiveness of their participation, may be enhanced or dampened by the access that is afforded to citizens and other stakeholders and by the processes employed, as recent research has shown.[40]

The search for more effective and inclusive processes in planning has become more energetic in the past decade, along with pressure not to judge the level of citizen participation by numbers alone, but also by the diversity, and the inclusiveness, of participants.[41] As the next chapter discusses in detail, modes of participation can be expected to be further adapted and expanded in the future, and the pressure on planners and others who are responsible for making this happen will continue. In anticipation of this discussion, consider:

- *How do the formal and the informal steps of plan-making differ?*
- *How are planning choices seen by participants in the economic marketplace as compared to participants in the political arena?*

Reference Notes

1. A useful review of the formal processes in use in each province is found in R. Audet and A. Lettenaff, *Land Planning Framework of Canada: An Overview,* Working Paper No. 28 (Ottawa: Lands Directorate, Environment Canada, September 1983).
2. For a description of one of the most comprehensive public consultation processes see Ann McAfee, "Vancouver CityPlan: People Participating in Planning," *Plan Canada* 35:3 (May 1995), 15–16.
3. Paul J. Cloke, *An Introduction to Rural Settlement Planning* (London: Methuen, 1983), 3.
4. John Forester, "Politics, Power, Ethics and Practice: Abiding Problems for the Future of Planning," *Plan Canada* 26:9 (December 1986), 224–227.
5. Note the Vancouver experience in McAfee, "Vancouver CityPlan."
6. Raymond J. Burby, "Making Plans That Matter: Citizen Involvement and Government Action," *Journal of the American Planning Association* 69:1 (Winter 2003), 33–49.
7. Robert Shipley, "Visioning in Planning: Is the Practice Based on Sound Theory?" *Environment and Planning A* 34:1 (2002), 7–22.
8. City of Saskatoon, *Community Vision: Saskatoon Speaks,* Saskatoon, June 2011.
9. Carolyn G. Loh, "Four Potential Disconnects in the Community Planning Process," *Journal of Planning Education and Research* 32:1 (March 2012), 33–47.

10. See Virginia W. MacLaren, "Urban Sustainability Reporting," *Journal of the American Planning Association* 62:2 (Spring 1996), 184–202.

11. Judith E. Innes, "Planning through Consensus Building," *Journal of the American Planning Association* 62:4 (Autumn 1996), 460–472; and Patsy Healey, *Collaborative Planning: Shaping Places in Fragmented Societies* (Vancouver: UBC Press, 1997).

12. Beth Sanders, "A View from the Forks: Coming to Terms with Perceptions of Public Participation," *Plan Canada* 38:2 (March 1998), 30–32.

13. J.A. Throgmorton, "On the Virtues of Skillful Meandering: Acting as a Skilled-Voice-in-the-Flow of Persuasive Argumentation," *Journal of the American Planning Association* 66:4 (Autumn 2000), 367–383.

14. Kevin S. Hanna, "Planning for Sustainability: Experience in Two Contrasting Communities," *Journal of the American Planning Association* 71:1 (Winter 2005), 27–40.

15. John Forester, "Politics, Power, Ethics and Practice: Abiding Problems for the Future of Planning" and "Planning in the Face of Power," *Journal of the American Planning Association* 48 (1982), 67–80.

16. Recent comprehensive land use plans for Saskatoon (2012), Winnipeg (2011), Montréal (2005), Toronto (2003), Ottawa (2003), and Edmonton (2000) have taken this general approach.

17. Richard B. McLagan, "Custom Negotiation and Mediation: Updating Our Planning Toolkit," *Plan Canada* 36:4 (July 1996), 26–27.

18. Philip Dack, "Mediation for Land Use Decision-Making," *Plan Canada* 41:1 (March 2001), 10–12.

19. Randy Diehl, "Resolving Community Development Disputes: The Kamloops Experience," *Plan Canada* 35:5 (September 1995), 30–34.

20. Dack, "Mediation."

21. Rolf-Richard Grauhan, "Notes on the Structure of Planning Administration," in Andreas Faludi, ed., *A Reader in Planning Theory* (Oxford: Pergamon Press, 1973), 297–316.

22. Cf. T.J. Plunkett and G.M. Betts, *The Management of Canadian Urban Government* (Queen's University Institute of Local Government Kingston:, 1978), 230–249; and C.R. Tindal and S.N. Tindal, *Local Government in Canada*, 2nd ed. (Toronto: McGraw-Hill Ryerson, 1984), 207–224.

23. Plunkett and Betts, *Management of Canadian Urban Government*, 247.

24. Louis N. Redman, "The Planning Process," *Managerial Planning* 31:6 (May–June 1983), 24–40.

25. Mark Seasons, "Strategic Planning in the Public Sector Environment: Addressing the Realities," *Plan Canada* 29:6 (November 1989), 19–27.

26. Gord Jackson and Mary Ann McConnell-Boehm, "Plan Edmonton: A Plan and a Process," *Plan Canada* 39:5 (November 1999), 17–19.

27. Art Cowie, "Politics and Planning: Ten Lessons from an Old Campaigner," *Plan Canada* 43:3 (Autumn 2003), 18–20.

28. David Harvey, *A Brief History of Neoliberalism* (London: Oxford University Press, 2005).

29. Jason Hackworth, *The Neoliberal City: Governance, Ideology, and Development in American Urbanism,* (Ithaca, NY: Cornell University Press, 2006).

30. Mark Stevens, "Exploring Vancouverism: The Political Culture of Canada's Lotus Land," *Canadian Journal of Urban Research* 19:1 (2010 supplement), 143–145.

31. Cf. Peggy Kohn, *Brave New Neighborhoods* (New York: Routledge, 2004).

32. Ian Wight, "Mediating the Politics of Place: Negotiating Our Professional and Personal Selves," *Plan Canada* 43:3 (Autumn 2003), 21–23.

33. Forester, "Politics, Power, Ethics and Practice: Abiding Problems for the Future of Planning."

34. John Friedmann, "Planning, Politics, and the Environment," *Journal of the American Planning Association* 59:3 (Summer 1989), 334–338.

35. Jana Carp, "Wit, Style, and Substance: How Planners Shape Public Participation," *Journal of Planning Education and Research* 23:3 (2004), 242–254.

36. Robert Voigt, "Creative, Communicative, and Progressive: Developing the Collingwood Urban Design Manual," *Plan Canada* 51:3 (Fall 2011), 45–49.

37. Two Canadian planners noted this issue three decades ago: Matthew Kiernan, "Ideology and the Precarious Future of the Canadian Planning Profession," *Plan Canada* 22:1 (March 1982), 14–24; and T.I. Gunton, "The Role of the Professional Planner," *Canadian Public Administration* 27:3 (Fall 1984), 399–417.

38. Barton Reid, "The Death of Victoria Park Neighbourhood, the State of Urban Reform and the Battle of Mythologies in Calgary," *City Magazine* 13:1 (Winter 1991–1992), 36–42; and Max Foran, "Coalitions and Demolitions: The Destruction of Calgary's East Victoria Park, 1960–1998," *Prairie Forum* 32:1 (Spring 2007), 17–45.

39. Cloke, *Introduction to Rural Settlement Planning.*

40. Samuel D. Brody, David R. Godschalk, and Raymond J. Burby, "Mandating Citizen Participation in Plan Making: Six Strategic Planning Choices," *Journal of the American Planning Association* 69:3 (Winter 2003), 245–264.

41. Two examples are Beth Moore Milroy, "Some Thoughts about Difference and Pluralism," *Planning Theory* 7–8 (1992), 33–38; and Peter Marris, "Planning and Civil Society in the Twenty-First Century," in Mike Douglass and John Friedmann, eds., *Cities for Citizens* (New York: Wiley, 1998), 9–17.

Internet Resources

Chapter-Relevant Sites

Planning Canadian Communities
www.planningcanadiancommunities.ca

City and Town Official website
www.citytown.info/Canada

Community Visions Program, Vancouver
www.vancouver.ca/docs/planning/sunset-community-vision-full-report.pdf

Edmonton City Vision
www.edmonton.ca/city_government/city_vision_and_strategic_plan/city-vision.aspx

Public Participation, City of Toronto
www.toronto.ca/civic-engagement/pdf/engagement_meta_data_march_2012.pdf

Regional Plan Process, Halifax
www.halifax.ca/regionalplanning

Urban Design Standards Manual, Collingwood, Ontario
www.town.collingwood.on.ca/node/3354

Visioning Process, Saskatoon
www.saskatoonspeaks.com

Visioning Process, Vernon, B.C.
www.vernon.ca/services/pde/citycentre/citycentre.html

Chapter Fifteen

The Texture of Participation in Community Planning

Challenging public decisions could be viewed as a form of Kafkaesque baseball. Citizen groups are always the visiting team in their own home town.

Linda Christianson-Ruffman, 1977

The participation of citizens in community planning in Canada was not always as common as it is today. It has gone through several stages and continues to change. In the decades leading up to World War I, the impetus for planning frequently arose from elite community groups, such as boards of trade and arts organizations (see Chapter 4). In the 1920s, using the provisions of new planning acts many municipalities established advisory "town-planning" commissions whose members were frequently selected from the real estate and construction industries or other lines of commerce. The Community Planning Association of Canada (CPAC) was established in the mid-1940s with the support of Central (now Canada) Mortgage and Housing Corporation and functioned as a broad-based citizen pressure group outside government. Its aim was to promote the advantages of planning with citizens, local and senior governments, and the business community. By the 1960s and into the 1970s, proposals by planners began to be questioned, often vociferously, by ordinary citizens and neighbourhood groups. Terms such as "citizen activism," "participatory democracy," and "advocacy planning" were coined and participation was demanded by citizens. This marked a major shift in the evolution of community participation in planning towards more openness and inclusion in actual plan-making.

It now goes without much saying that a well-designed plan and a thoughtfully drafted zoning bylaw must be deliberated and communicated among community members and planning officials of the community. The process they engage in amounts to a "flow of argumentation," in which the various participants attempt to persuade others of the merits or otherwise of the proposed plan, project, or regulation.[1] Mirroring the significant shift in the thinking about planning practice in recent years, Judith Innes says bluntly, "What planners do most of the time is talk and interact."[2] This observation applies equally to *all* participants in community planning: their participation carries with it the need, indeed the demand, to communicate, to become involved in *dialogues* with other participants.

This chapter examines the texture of participation in community plan-making including who participates and the shape, rhythm, and pace of their involvement. This means moving beyond the various formats for participation, especially those that are prescribed, and considering its style and quality, that is, considering the nature and quality of "the dialogue." In this examination of the place of politicians, professional planners, the public, and developers in community plan-making, the following questions are the focus for this chapter:

- *Who are the key participants in community planning and why?*
- *In what ways does citizen participation affect the outcome of a community's plan?*

Planning Theory: Linking the Public, Politicians, and Planners

Within the varied milieu of decision making for community planning there are several community participants whose behaviour is crucial for an effective planning process. Politicians, the public (citizens), professional planners, professionals in public agencies, and developers are the primary participants, and significant relationships exist among them, as we shall see. But, first, the key interrelationship between the citizens of the community, the members of the local governing body, and the professional planners is explored.

The effectiveness with which this particular triad—public, politician, and planner—works together largely determines the success of the planning process in a community.[3] Their situation is not unlike that of the distinctive Russian sleigh that is pulled by three horses (*troika*) whose energies must be balanced to achieve both forward motion and the desired direction of the sleigh. So, too, the citizenry and the municipal planners and councillors are dependent upon one another in the process to attain a plan that embodies an acceptable direction

for the future of the community. The perspective within planning practice and theory of how to achieve a harmonious and productive blend of these participants has undergone considerable change, especially in the past few decades. Prior to 1960, for example, community planning was a relatively sedate activity. Politicians received and accepted the "expert" advice of the planners, while the public seemed willing to let their elected representatives judge the appropriateness of planning proposals. However, the disruptions to neighbourhoods caused by the planning responses to, especially, urban renewal schemes and expressway projects changed the way these relationships worked. Citizens confronted politicians over proposed projects and rezonings, and politicians sought more workable solutions from the planners.[4] By the 1990s, many of these kinds of confrontations, and newer variations on them, continued. Although most Canadian communities have extended their public-participation efforts, more still needs to be done to attain fully effective participation.[5]

Two lessons for planning emerge from this experience. The first is that community planning is a *political* activity that makes choices among values held by community members. This then affects each of the three key participants—public, politician, and planner—in different ways. The second is that participation in planning decisions is not just a one-way process of communication. There needs to be a *dialogue* among all three interests. In some communities, planners and politicians have begun to learn these lessons. Where they have been absorbed, the planning process features a high degree of interaction between the public, the politician, and the planner—a "six-sided triangle" of communication, as Harry Lash called it. The six-sided triangle refers to the six interdependent links of communication in community planning. Thus, each interest must have the potential of dialogue with each of the other two. Anything less and the effectiveness of the planning process is diminished (see Figure 15.1). Harry Lash and his staff at the Greater Vancouver Regional District in the 1970s developed this innovative perspective foreshadowing today's shift toward decision-making through consensus building, or what is now called the communicative approach to plan-making.[6]

But achieving a good working relationship among all three sets of participants is not a simple matter. Personal and professional expectations, mutual trust, and communications skills and preferences are at the heart of making the six-sided triangle work effectively.[7] Planners must consider what their role is to be: a neutral technical

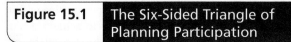
Figure 15.1 The Six-Sided Triangle of Planning Participation

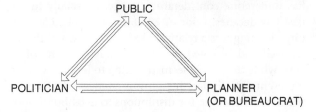

The effectiveness of the community-planning process is largely determined by the degree to which this triad—public, politician, and planner—can work together. It requires a good deal of what may be called *social cooperation*.

advisor to the politician, an advocate of particular positions held within the community, a mediator between the politician and the public, or a public educator of best planning practice. (These roles and their challenges are discussed in the next section.) Politicians must consider whether, how, and when to invite citizens into the decision-making process, that is, to share some of their *power*. And citizens must consider how to work in a constructive way with planners and politicians in the planning process. These are the main threads that weave the texture in this important part of the planning process.

Linking Politicians and Planners

The relationship between the politician and the professional planner is complex and, in some ways, paradoxical. It has several aspects, one of which is that of employer (politician) and employee (planner), because the planner is either on the staff hired directly by the local governing body or is hired as a consultant to the council. Another aspect is that of expert (planner) and client (politician), because the planner comes to the situation with certain socially sanctioned skills from his or her education and professional experience. In the planning process, however, they are each dependent upon the other—indeed, interdependent—since both seek the similar end of coordinating diverse interests in the community and achieving a good quality of environment generally.[8] Yet in this relationship tensions exist, and politicians and planners may find themselves in conflict over who should give leadership in plan-making.

The Politician The job of the politician is not well understood. Nominally, elected officials are there to represent the interests of the people in the community.

But those interests are diverse and often compete with one another. Thus, the job of "representing" becomes one of reconciling and integrating the many competing demands that citizens, groups, firms, and other officials place on the local councillor. This role of the politician has been called that of "broker-mediator."[9] The politician also has to provide leadership as to what direction the community's development should be taking, so that the competing private and public interests are merged into a general, community-wide, common interest.

The politician's job of providing leadership and resolving conflicts has some incompatible aspects. If there is conflict around an issue—for example, the closing of a neighbourhood school or allowing a group home—the politician must try to hear as many of the competing views as possible and not make up her or his mind too early. This uncommitted stance may be scorned as failing to show leadership. But when the politician decides on a possible solution to an issue too early in the process, he or she may then be rebuked for being biased toward one interest. A planner who was active in local environmental matters and then elected as a city councillor in an American city has recounted that he was portrayed as having "an underlying agenda" reflecting that of a special interest group.[10] As Lash similarly observed about politicians faced with the same dilemma:

> On any given issue in the community, he/she cannot *lead* unless he/she is *committed* to a solution, but if there is serious conflict around an issue, he/she cannot *resolve* it if he/she is *committed*.[11]

A related dilemma for the politician revolves around sharing his or her power to make decisions with others in the process, or what might be perceived as "giving up" power to others.

The politician generally tries to bring together two sets of interests. One set comprises the views held by members of the community, including developers. The other comprises the advice given by the community's planners and other technical advisors both inside and outside of local government (which is taken up more fully below). But first it is important to point out a distinctive facet of community interests that the politician is obliged to respect, and incorporate into her or his understanding and deliberations—the perspective of the developer.[12] Those individuals and firms involved in promoting land and property development are usually also members of the community. They include, as well as the landowner(s), local builders, architects, appraisers, lawyers, engineers, realtors, and bankers (see Figure 15.2). In a largely capitalist economy such as ours these latter "citizens" represent a legitimate view about their projects being in the community's interest. Not infrequently it is found to be a view contrary to that held by other citizens and, thus, adds to the work of the politician.

The Planner In reconciling the diverse interests in the community, the politician is very dependent upon the local planning staff. The issues often require an almost immediate appreciation of technical matters, and it is the duty of the planner to present all the relevant information and analyses to the politician. Yet even exercising such seemingly straightforward tasks involves the planner in the political realm by virtue of the choices about the type and quality of information to present, thereby complicating the interdependence of the two.[13] And when it comes to making a recommendation of one or another course of action, the planner then becomes a competitor for the politician's attention, indeed a stakeholder in the planning process.[14] This situation raises at least two ethical dilemmas for the planner regarding the planning option he or she advocates in the political debate. On the one hand, if the planner's position seems to support that of the politician, then citizens may lose confidence in the planner's impartiality. On the other hand, too-vociferous support for citizens' positions on an issue may be seen by the politician as being at odds with those of the planner's "employer." And to the politician is left the difficult task of bringing together the judgment of the "expert" and the "will of the people."

At some point in the process, the relationship between the politician and the planner may shift from employer–employee to client–expert. The ease with which this shift of roles occurs depends a great deal upon the planner's concept of leadership in community planning. The planner's essential contribution to the planning process is to be able to prepare a plan for a physical development situation that integrates a multitude of public and private interests and concerns. Through training and experience, the planner is in a position of "intellectual leadership" in plan-making.[15] Yet conflict can arise between the planner and the politician if the planner thinks herself or himself best fit to serve the community needs and assumes a measure of political leadership by acting strategically. But the planner's training seldom equips her or him for political leadership, a factor that is increasingly stressed as planning processes become more interactive.[16]

Tensions between planners and politicians are correlated with the relationship that each has with the other set of participants—the public. In playing out their respective roles, the politician and the planner have both an obligation and a need to involve the larger public in order that each can say they hold planning positions reflecting the community at large. Just as with the politician, the planner has close contact with developer–members of the public, including involvement in a process of mutual learning, as we saw in Chapter 6, about policies, regulations, economic realities, and so on. The competition for the public's attention again indicates the high degree of interdependence of the three sets of participants. Despite this, there are few formal specifications for making these relationships work.

Linking with the Public

There is a long democratic tradition of a community making plans for its own future through its locally elected councillors. There is likewise a tradition of public participation where public-spirited citizens and groups advocate the need for a community plan (see Chapter 4). However, neither of these traditions provide for the direct participation of the public in actually making a plan.[17] When the public is *included* in making decisions about the plan for the future community environment (as is the expectation nowadays), the relationships among all three sets of participants are affected. Both the politician and the planner must redefine their roles. With direct citizen involvement, the politician may no longer assume that he or she provides the best reflection of the views of the public in the planning process; the planner may no longer assume that he or she serves the public by serving only the politician.

Involving citizens in plan-making constitutes a sharing of power over the content and implementation of the plan as well as over the process of getting to the plan. There have been available, for some time, mandated, formal avenues of communication between the public and local government officials, such as public meetings and hearings (see Figure 15.2). These venues permit citizens to be heard, but not necessarily in a comprehensive or continuing way or with any guarantee that their concerns are being taken into account. They do not constitute a dialogue. Effective participation implies some direct citizen input into decisions that could influence subsequent developments in the plan. This often leads to the apprehension among citizens that they will be used for the politicians' own ends if they participate.

Figure 15.2   Typical Public Meeting

Public meetings are often mandated parts of the planning process, but an auditorium, a stage, and microphones are usually evidence that communication is rather limited and there is not a lot of mutual learning going on.

For example, the Canada Lands Company organized a broad, inclusive, and creative process to develop an innovative and sustainable plan for the Benny Farm veterans' housing project in Montréal's Notre-Dame-de-Grâce community. The planning process used many techniques beyond public hearings, including charettes, design competitions, working committees, and open houses.

As for planners, citizens often feel "talked down to," or ignored by them, or hampered in obtaining information. Many citizens may feel they are not listened to at all, as numerous feminist critics have pointed out with respect to the participation of women and of persons from marginal groups in planning processes.[18] (A later section discusses this more fully, along with some of the new approaches for enhancing public participation and inclusiveness.) These tensions are an inevitable part of any political process in which those with power are being asked to share it. Further, the legislated planning processes do not assign power to citizens, only the right to be consulted. Even though provision may be made for including citizens in plan-making decisions, the final responsibility rests with the politicians and planners to see that the participation occurs.

Despite the conflicts and difficulties, the relationships between citizens, politicians, and planners are essential to the planning process. The reasons are quite simple. The citizens are a primary source of information about the problems that are being experienced by the community, about the impacts of proposed solutions, and about the values and aspirations of community members. The politicians and planners, on the other hand, know the resources that are available to solve problems, the limits of knowledge about project impacts, and the institutional and legislated procedural avenues that must be observed.

The politician is the key actor in determining the form participation will take and whether it will be positive, for it is the politician's ultimate decision-making prerogative, with regard to the issues and options, that would be opened up to scrutiny. The politician must come to believe that public participation will enhance his or her ability to resolve conflict and provide leadership; in other words, to know the community better. When the public is included, there are sometimes risks for the planners: "expert" opinions may have to be justified to "non-expert" citizens, uncertainties may have to be acknowledged, and information may have to be shared. And, while the politician may make the ultimate decision about participation, it is the planner who shapes the participation process and controls much of the flow of information.[19]

In short, another party is brought into the decision-making, and this always complicates the resolution of issues. As the six-sided triangle shows, there are *three times* as many interactions to consider if citizens participate than if the planner and politician are the only participants. The triangle of public–politician–planner can lead, as does any three-sided relationship, to unequal coalitions and resulting stress. If the politicians come to rely more on the citizens' views than on those of the planner, the latter may feel that his or her technical competence is being devalued.[20] Politicians may come to distrust their staff planners, fearing that they will cater to citizen groups espousing different political ideas. Citizens, for their part, often learn that they cannot expect their recommendations always to be accepted by politicians and planners. Indeed, each of the participants has much to learn, not only about the others but also about the planning process and its possible outcomes when seen through others' eyes. The latter point is often referred to as *social learning* and reflects both the need for broad learning to occur and the acceptance of the mutual obligations (i.e., "to attend, share, listen, initiate creative contributions, and identify and mediate problems") among all participants in the process.[21]

Roles of the Planner

In many ways, the community-planning process centres upon the professional planner. Although not necessarily the one to initiate the process, the planner soon becomes responsible for sustaining it, for shaping it so that plans, policies, and programs emerge to guide future physical development. It can be said that it is in the planner's own interest to carry out the task. Nevertheless, it is a demanding task, involving interaction with all the other participants in the planning process. The planner, it must be emphasized, plays a multi-faceted role in a political milieu, a role that is gaining even more facets as the milieu itself shifts. Early on, the basic scope of the planner's task was identified as involving four basic roles:

1. The planner as leader (or representative) of the planning agency,
2. The planner as technical advisor,
3. The planner as political innovator, and
4. The planner as citizen educator.[22]

The past two decades have revealed additional roles and elaborations of these four roles as planning theory and ideology have evolved, but the four basic roles listed above are a good starting point. It needs to be noted that each of the roles may be played differently depending upon the individual planner's personal disposition, the community setting, and the stage in the planning process. Different community institutional and environmental situations may call for the emphasis to be placed more on one role rather than another, and in some cases require other participants to substitute for the planner.

As Planning Agency Leader/Member The planner must be concerned with the organizational base from which he or she operates. This involves the agency's status and relationships with the local governing body, community groups, other governmental organizations, and developers as well as with its own staffing and morale. The planning agency must be accepted as an essential part of the community's governmental machinery if the goals of planning are to be achieved. Thus, the planner must develop the confidence of elected and appointed officials, developers, and the public about the necessity of planning.[23] This means developing relationships of trust, cooperation, and encouragement with each of these groups and, just as important, cultivating channels of communication through which to obtain and disseminate information.[24]

The effectiveness of the planner is closely linked with the credibility of the planning agency and whether and to what degree it is either welcomed or excluded in promoting planning solutions with politicians, developers, other agencies, or the public. This must be perceived and nurtured by the planner as a routine part of the task. Allies as well as enemies, and cooperators as well as antagonists, must be identified. Planners thus need skills that go beyond the technical knowledge of planning; that is, the need "to go beyond technical expertise to organizational and political savvy."[25] Planners need to be able to work with others and develop trust and support for the agency and its views especially when the agency's development proposals will not be carried out by them but by others (e.g., engineers, lawyers, architects, building inspectors). And in multicultural community situations planners must become more sensitive to ethnic group needs and also consider issues of inclusiveness and the norms of practice.[26]

Not to be overlooked is the bureaucratic milieu in which the staff planner works. Municipalities and other forms of government that employ planners have hierarchical structures that assure that strategic decisions are taken by elected officials and tactical decisions by planning department heads. But, as Filion notes, this hierarchical form of decision-making "slows the planning process and reduces planners' capacity to make commitments."[27] So, being a "leader" for some significant planning or development reform may be a challenge for the planner.

As Technical Advisor The planner brings to the community-planning job the values and standards of the planning profession by virtue of education and experience. The community looks to the planner to provide these skills and experience to organize the particular planning task. In doing so, the planner employs approaches that are consistent with the outlook and practice of the planning profession, and this requires both a continual monitoring of these mores (from professional literature and conferences, for example) and the ability for self-reflection about his or her practice.

It will be recalled that planning practice involves both technical and social-organizing skills, which both contain a political component. On the one hand, the planner uses accepted technical skills in research and design. Although apparently neutral, decisions about what data to gather, which analytical model to use, which design precedent to draw upon, and what information to make public involve a judgment about what is most likely to further plan-making. Thus, even in carrying out technical tasks, as Sandercock says, "there is no way to avoid being political."[28] On the other hand, the planner must also organize the process that will be followed, including who will participate, when, and to what extent. In this case, the planner generally will invoke the prevailing and professionally accepted values of governmental responsibility, good design, environmental sustainability, democratic planning, public participation, and so forth. Given that planners nowadays generally advocate widespread public participation may, for example, draw objections from politicians who would like a narrower context for planning decisions. It is a delicate task for the planner to balance the value of being a neutral technical advisor with the social values of the profession.[29]

As Political Innovator All planning activity involves changes in the community, either in the short or long run, and requires approval by the governing body. Even where the changes are slight, there may be some political pressure to resist or delay the change. Affected landowners may protest; politicians may be reluctant to commit capital expenditures; other department heads may have competing proposals. Getting planning proposals accepted often means changing the political climate in the community toward new ideas. The planner, therefore, is frequently called upon to promote proposals in such a way as to bring about political innovation.

In general, in every community there is a reasonably well-defined group whose support is crucial to those political innovations that would interest the planner. They are sometimes referred to as the "influentials," and may comprise elected politicians and appointed officials as well as others outside the local government whose views are often sought. These may include chambers of commerce, real estate interests, environmental organizations, and property owners and tenant associations. The planner will usually try to identify all stakeholders with a specific interest in a proposal and predict their reaction to it. Then the planner will have to consider what steps to take to improve the chances that the plan or other proposals will be accepted. These steps may include the timing of proposals, the structure of participation, the use of outside advisors, the establishment of advisory committees (elite or otherwise), selected pre-release consultations, and even overt political pressure. For example, the evolution of Vancouver's innovative development-approval and design-review systems required two decades of

effort by the planning commissioners to negotiate the roles of politicians, the public, outside advisors, and professional staff.[30] This innovator role implies a possible need for the planner to adapt to political realities. There are limits to this adaptation, however, as modifications to plans may begin to conflict with the planner's professional standards or may threaten the integrity of the planning agency.

One dominant and long-lasting view of the planning profession is that the planner's primary obligation is to serve the public interest.[31] This is related to the notion that community members share certain underlying personal and group interests with regard to the subjects that planning deals with, as well as the way it deals with them. For example, it may be argued that it is in the interest of the whole community to acquire parkland today to ensure that it is available for future generations and, similarly, that means of public participation are in everyone's interests to ensure that issues are properly aired. Planners have adopted this stance in order to fulfill the mandate of serving all the community and not only the interests of one group. But it is not an easy stance to defend because it depends upon deciding *who defines the public interest*.[32] It has been found that many planners tend to choose only from a limited array of possible participants, even when public participation is mandated. They have tended to favour business groups, elected officials, development groups, and local government departments, and far less frequently target groups representing disadvantaged people, ethnic minorities, or the elderly.[33] Politicians often argue that voters have sanctioned them and their views of the public interest; many individual citizens and groups argue that their grassroots views truly reflect the public interest; and planners are known to argue that their comprehensive view of the community provides the basis for such a definition. Clearly, there is ample room for conflict among participants in whichever definition the planner adopts. Quite simply, there is no ready mechanism for determining the public interest or, as some claim, can there ever be. Probably most important in this frequently contentious situation is that planners not argue for their own purposes but for openness in hearing all interests and facing all issues.[34]

As Citizen Educator The planner seeks to affect the basic attitudes and values of the community at large regarding the benefits and consequences of planning. The planner is obliged to do this, given his or her commitment to the broader community interest. The extent to which planning is undertaken will depend upon the degree of tolerance for new ideas in the community, but this will vary depending upon citizens' previous experience with planning and development, their cultural milieu, and their perception of the resources that might be needed. The planner needs, therefore, to be aware of the factors affecting attitudes toward planning and also of the avenues available to enlarge the area of acceptance in the particular community.

This is doubly important, for example, in planning with Indigenous communities (as discussed in Chapters 10 and 13).[35] Much the same can be said regarding planning for multicultural communities. The planner needs, therefore, to be aware of the factors affecting attitudes toward planning and also of the avenues available to enlarge the area of acceptance in the particular community and its neighbourhoods.

Enhanced Planners' Roles The four roles discussed above provide only the broad institutional parameters of the planner's participation in the planning process. Within this institutional context, there are a number of specific roles that a planner might play. In a planning agency requiring several planners, some will function as plan-makers and others as researchers, regulators, or managers. The scope of a planner's contacts with those within the agency and with other participants outside the agency will differ, and so too the possible perceptions of the outcome of the process. Some will come in contact more with the public, with developers, with elected officials, or with other agencies. Increasingly, it has been noted that planners practise in relation to a variety of special-interest groups, settings, and regulatory systems, and may be seen as technical staff, evaluators, and advocates.[36] Or, as Canadian planner Tom Gunton observed, planners may, and may need to, modify their role such that it becomes "social reformer," "advocate," "referee," or "social learner, or all four," and possibly also Guttenberg's suggested role of "social inventor."[37]

Each planner brings to the particular role individual differences in outlook that affect the way in which he or she plays out the role. Research into planning practice indicates that individual planners tend to fashion their own concept of how the role should be played.[38] Planners thus "frame their role" according to their personal views of the problem at hand and their preferred courses of action in solving problems, especially when in conjunction with others. Planning practice is still evolving, both in relation to changes in the role that planning plays in our society and in relation to planners' own understanding of planning processes. The most recent shift involves the elaboration of participatory processes in plan-making from the formal consultation approach, sometimes referred to as "notice and hearing," to more open collaborative relationships among plan-makers.[39]

The planner has a key role in the latter approach in identifying stakeholders, choosing venues for deliberations, and providing information for discussion. This requires the planner to develop skills in facilitation because collaborative processes depend upon using processes of consensus rather than formal hierarchical authority.[40] Implicit in this role, as one observer notes, is the need "to learn to listen and how to communicate in ways that allow others to hear and enable others to speak for themselves."[41] The import of these suggestions is to indicate that the traditional perspective on what a planner does, or could do, is clearly too limited.

Involving the Community in Planning

There are two basic dimensions for assessing public participation in community planning. The first deals with the *depth* of participation, which is the degree to which members of the public are enabled to share the power to make decisions regarding approval of plans. The second deals with the *breadth* of participation, or the extent to which the citizenry is involved in plan-making. A discussion of each follows.

Degrees of Participation

Citizen participation is not a unitary concept; that is, power may be shared with citizens to different degrees.[42] It may vary according to the legislative needs of the decision situation as well as the disposition of those in control of making decisions. In its most modest form, the "notice and hearing" format noted earlier, citizens are informed of planning proposals by a formal notice and told of a public hearing in which they may attend and participate. Additional power is shared when, for example, citizen advisory committees are employed in the planning process. Still greater power is shared when citizens are *included* in the making of plans. Again, institutional roles and practical considerations may constrain the sharing of planning power.

The different degrees, or depth, of citizen participation are readily discerned in Sherry Arnstein's classic "ladder of citizen participation," with each higher rung corresponding to a greater degree to which citizens could share power in planning decisions (see Figure 15.3).[43] There are eight rungs on the ladder in three broad categories: (1) **"Contrived Participation"** concerns ways of avoiding sharing any direct planning power; (2) **"Token Participation"** concerns ways of sharing a bare minimum of power with citizens; and (3) **"Power Sharing"** where citizens share increasingly greater degrees of power with planners and politicians. In other words, the greater the depth (or height on the ladder) of participation, the more citizens share in the power to make decisions about the direction and content of plans.

Figure 15.3 | Ladder of Citizen Participation

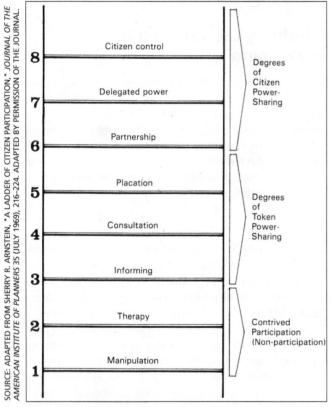

SOURCE: ADAPTED FROM SHERRY R. ARNSTEIN, "A LADDER OF CITIZEN PARTICIPATION," *JOURNAL OF THE AMERICAN INSTITUTE OF PLANNERS* 35 (JULY 1969), 216–224. ADAPTED BY PERMISSION OF THE JOURNAL.

Citizen participation involves the sharing of power over planning decisions with members of the community. This may vary according to the needs of the decision situation and the disposition of those in control of planning decisions to share their power.

Contrived Participation

1. **Manipulation** may be practised when participation is organized to "educate" and persuade citizens to support already-decided-upon plans and programs. One example would be citizen committees with no mandate, even to give advice, or broad city information websites may simply act as "public-relations" vehicles for plans and planners.

2. **Therapy** refers to the practice of engaging citizens in diversionary activities that will "cure" them of their concerns over basic flaws and injustices. This rung is seldom encountered in community planning in full-blown form. There may, however, be gradations of it in "workshops" provided for citizen members of planning committees and, more recently, in the use of digital media (e.g., videos, websites) in disseminating planning materials.[44]

Token Participation

3. **Informing** is the first level at which the planning process is opened up to citizens. Information is supplied to them on the nature of the planning task, its schedule, and the role of citizens. At its best, a full description is provided to each household in timely and easily understood ways, and responses of citizens are sought and facilitated. Social media such as official Facebook pages used in Toronto's Jarvis Streetscape project are increasingly employed for disseminating information and collecting comments from citizens.[45] At its worst, this stage will feature only one-way communication, such as by the use of only printed or news media formats, combined with legalistic and technical jargon, and will not recognize language differences in the community.

4. **Consultation** occurs when explicit means are used to obtain the views of citizens, such as through attitude surveys and public meetings. While at this level citizens are given the opportunity to be heard, they are not assured of being adequately understood or responded to. The design of survey questionnaires and online surveys and their interpretation by recipients may require some forms of feedback and additional dialogue with citizens. An encouraging example on this level is the "Picket Fence Project" of departments of parks and recreation in three

municipalities in Vancouver's eastern suburbs to survey the sense of community held by residents.[46]

5. **Placation** refers to forms of participation in which citizens are given the opportunity to be heard, say, on advisory committees or planning websites requesting input but with no certainty their advice will be heeded. One such effort at this level of participation was the system of nine citizen policy committees used to advise the governing board of the Greater Vancouver Regional District in the preparation of its 1970s metropolitan planning policies. Staff planners provided committees with technical assistance; but, in the end, the politicians only "received" their reports and did not debate them, thereby relegating the citizens to a token advisory role.[47]

Citizen Power Sharing

6. **Partnership** involves an agreement to share responsibilities for planning through joint policy boards or committees. Often used to resolve impasses over a specific project, such mechanisms allow citizens to influence the outcome of the plan by their votes (on preliminary if not final versions). Partnerships may also be used on a broad community plan such as occurred with the development of Vancouver's City-Plan, where citizens made choices all the way to the draft plan presented to city council.[48] Similarly, the City of Red Deer, Alberta, in 1998, fostered an extensive partnering for revitalization of its Riverside Meadows neighbourhood.[49]

7. **Delegated power** gives citizens dominant decision-making responsibility over a plan or program, usually from the outset. The traditional planning board or commission, with a majority of appointed citizen members and legislative authority to prepare the community plan, is an ideal example of this level of participation. Some communities have delegated to neighbourhood committees the task of making neighbourhood plans and provided them with a professional planner to assist them (as with several neighbourhoods in Vancouver).

8. **Citizen control** is a level at which citizens govern a program or project in all its policy and managerial aspects. Although this is not likely in regard to preparing a community-wide plan, instances of citizen control are found in cooperative and other citizen nonprofit

housing developments throughout the country. Community groups that obtain grants from senior governments for recreation facilities also operate at this level, as did a group in Kingston, Ontario, which designed and constructed a public waterfront walkway. It should be noted that the City of Kingston will retain ultimate control of it because of its responsibility for public safety. A variation of this level of participation occurred in Calgary, where a citizen's organization took the initiative of developing community-sustainability indicators and preparing a "State of Our City" report analyzing 36 indicators.[50]

Broadening Participation

It is commonplace, today, to talk about involving the *diversity* of a community's population in planning activities. Many differences exist among any community's citizenry with age, gender, income level, literacy, and cultural background being the most obvious factors. Yet public-participation programs in community plan-making seldom broach these differences. Even though the depth of public participation has increased to higher rungs on Arnstein's ladder in many places, the same progress cannot be said for increasing its breadth. While more attention is now paid to neighbourhood differences, differences between "neighbours" are not often considered. To be sure, the public *is* being involved in these programs and in greater numbers. But, too frequently, the public is seen as an undifferentiated human category both in the city-wide sense and its separate "publics" (e.g., the elderly, youth, and women).

When any part of the public is not included, intentionally or otherwise, the effect is to deny their citizenship in their own community and their right to engage in its planning and development. Research and critiques have been emerging for some time that point toward the failure both to acknowledge differences among citizens and to engage those excluded in plan-making.[51] To rectify this situation is, of course, no small task for, as Sandercock says, the public is a very diverse collectivity comprising "multiple publics."[52] The excluded and undifferentiated "publics" that have received the most attention are women, youth, the elderly, persons with disabilities, and those from culturally different backgrounds.

Women One of the groups most excluded from public participation processes are women, as feminist critics have frequently noted.[53] This exclusion can come from at least two sides. First, it may happen because the process is not made physically accessible to women (the time of day of meetings, the need for child care,[54] the availability of transportation, etc.). Second, the planning process may also fail to take into account women's knowledge of the city, or their experience from their daily lives.[55] Planners have tended to rely on expert, technical data about land use. Thus, the knowledge that comes from the personal experience of women—such as safety on the streets, difficulties with mass transit, or scarcity of affordable housing for a single-parent family—has had little or no place in the planning process. In the eyes of some observers, the knowledge that planners do use, therefore, has a male/professional bias.[56] Including women's perspectives in planning calls for dealing with **aspatial** concerns, those human things that one can't always put on a typical planning map. A Vancouver project that involved women in the planning of their own neighbourhood alerted planners about the need for things such as crosswalks, street lighting, community meeting spaces, "latch-key" programs, recycling, and a crisis centre.[57]

Youth Also not included in most definitions of "the public" are young people who are, indeed, the inheritors of the community form and character that is decided in plan-making. Again, as with women, there is extensive research on the ways that children and older youth experience the city and engage with it to define place.[58] But to attract youth participants requires programs that are aimed at them and that give them decision-making power along with adults (see Figure 15.4). Planners can benefit from working with and through organizations that have youth components, such as community centres and schools.[59] For example, during recent community visioning sessions for a downtown plan for the small interior–British Columbia city, Vernon, one of the stakeholder groups involved was students from the city's two high schools who were interviewed and videotaped (see also Chapter 13).[60]

The Elderly Now, more than six decades after the beginning of the baby boom of 1946–65, a major surge in the seniors' populations (those aged 65 and older) of most communities has begun.[61] Yet the community needs of this "public" are only starting to be acknowledged by planners and the elderly invited into public-participation programs. A national study

| Figure 15.4 | Children Involved in a Safety Audit in Winnipeg |

SOURCE: *OUR WINNIPEG*, (2011) CITY OF WINNIPEG, PAGE 41.

As part of the citizen engagement process for SpeakUp Winnipeg, these children walked their neighbourhood with local police officers, describing areas that felt unsafe to them. The safety audit is a Crime Prevention through Environmental Design (CPTED) tool originally developed to engage citizens on women's safety issues, and it is still used for this purpose in many areas.

by Health Canada in 2000 on the quality of life in Canadian cities heard seniors lament their "sense of powerlessness in influencing decisions."[62] When they are encouraged to participate it is necessary to recognize that they, too, have gender differences, and are diverse, with a range of incomes, skills, and physical impairments. Not least, they have age differences that span one-third of a century. To include seniors in plan-making planners may need to accommodate them by holding meetings in neighbourhood settings, during daylight hours, and in venues that are easily accessible and have adequate acoustics; as well they may possibly provide special transportation for seniors with disabilities. And when graphic, printed, and video materials are used, planners should ensure that they can be easily grasped by older people with diminished vision and hearing. And elders who are accustomed to other languages and symbols, including Aboriginal elders, should be similarly accommodated (see also Chapter 13).[63]

Persons with Disabilities Over 12 percent of Canadians experience some form of physical impairment that limits their participation in daily activities.[64] The result, as several social geographers have pointed out, is to significantly affect the way people with such limitations experience and navigate built environments to the extent of often being excluded from the activities of other citizens.[65] To be included in public-participation efforts will demand that planners convene these activities so that they are accessible to people with physical disabilities, visual impairments, hearing loss, and developmental disabilities. Again, it is important that these "publics" not be seen as homogeneous by age, gender, income, mobility, etc. (see also Chapter 13).[66]

Ethnic Populations Canada is a country built on immigration. However, recent trends have changed the composition of the immigrant stream. Seventy percent of all new immigrants are "visible minorities," with the bulk of new immigrants, both visible minorities and others, destined for the cities.[67] Since the 1990s, over 90 percent of immigrants have gone to live in the country's 27 metropolitan areas. Of these, over three-quarters now reside in just three census metropolitan areas: Toronto, Vancouver, and Montréal. One result of such flows is the emergence of numerous "visible minority neighbourhoods," or "ethnic enclaves," in these cities.[68] Further, these enclaves are frequently not ethnically homogenous but home to several cultural minority populations. Thus, planners are confronted with the challenge of working with people who may see the world from quite different perspectives, and need to adapt their participatory planning practice.[69] Among the responses open to planners are to translate information into the language(s) of the neighbourhood, as is already done in many cities, to augment planning staffs with people who understand ethnic-community concerns and languages, and to use modes of public consultation with which the community is most able to articulate its aspirations.[70]

Sexual Orientation An instance of the value of broadening of participatory categories is seen is in the unintended effects of policies toward gentrification that have displaced established LGBTQ (lesbian, gay, bisexual, transgendered, and queer) neighbourhoods in one U.S. city.[71] Such enclaves (sometimes referred to as queer spaces) are common in most large cities and provide a measure of safety and tolerance for residents and their accompanying social and business infrastructure (see Chapter 13). Again, cases like these underline the importance of accommodating a broader, less routine, more subjective approach in planning practice.

Overview Immediate reflection suggests many interconnections among these members of the population, such as elderly women, youth with disabilities, and elderly male immigrants, to name a few. This, in turn, indicates the need to expand public-participation programs so that they recognize the implicit breadth of the citizenry and use categories that are porous. Further, there are a number of cogent issues regarding community planning that arise from this critique. A primary one is to expand the perspective on the substance of planning from mainly land use and spatial relations to include social and personal relations, that is, to consider relations that come out a perspective of "home" and its role in people's lives, rather than just the physical attribute of "housing"; relations that come out of a "community" perspective, rather than just a physical "neighbourhood" perspective. Fainstein is particularly forceful in arguing for including "groupings according to gender, race, sexual orientation, and immigrant status" when considering the scope of public participation programs.[72] It also means accommodating, *including*, all citizens in the heart of planning decision-making.

Participation, Inclusion, and Empowerment

The engagement of citizens in the planning of their communities nowadays takes diverse forms. They range from city-wide visioning exercises directly involving numerous participants to web-based approaches involving unseen single participants. A broad menu of participatory approaches is appropriate in that there cannot be a one-size-fits-all given differences among communities as well as their various needs for civic engagement. However, such approaches do not all achieve the same ends and obliges planners and to consider three dimensions when choosing methods to involve the public.

Participation This term, so long argued for and now so widespread in its use, has come to refer to almost any of the different forms that public engagement can take. Essentially, *participation* is about ways of "increasing input" in plan-making both in the number of people involved and the array of viewpoints.[73]

Or, as referred to above, it is about "broadening participation" by making the involvement of the public both representative of the citizenry and accessible to them. However, accomplishing greater breadth in the process is, frequently and mistakenly, referred to as being "inclusive" when what has been achieved is the valuable attribute of greater "openness" to diverse participants.

Inclusion This dimension of public engagement goes more to the depth of participation and is about practices in which community members are involved in *"co-producing processes, policies, and programs"* related to plan-making.[74] It may be likened to achieving the higher rungs on Arnstein's ladder where power is shared with the public in plan-making. In other words, it transcends just "being there"; it's about "taking part," playing an acknowledged role in the actual decision making. Moreover, being included in this way allows for the opportunity of continuing connections to be made among various participants about pertinent issues. In practice, inclusion can be fostered in a variety of ways from large-scale participatory processes that encourage comments and provide feedback to the use of social media to engage individuals in an iterative "discussion" of issues.

Empowerment Various types of power are embodied in both participation and inclusion dimensions of civic engagement. Arnstein's ladder, for example, reflects gradations of the success citizens might attain in sharing decision-making power.[75] However, its concern is with one type of power: the ability to affect the behaviour of others, in our case the plan-making authorities. Empowerment is about the manifestation of different types of power and who experiences them and how they are experienced.[76] In other words, empowerment may occur from the individual involved in participatory planning activities to the larger community's involvement.

Rocha offers a Ladder of Empowerment that embodies several forms of empowerment from that of the individual to that of the community (see Figure 15.5). In comparison, Arnstein's top rungs of sharing power with the community are similar to the top two rungs of Rocha's ladder; they both concern empowering the community. A major difference between the two is that individual citizens may be empowered when engaging in those public planning exercises that are assigned to lower rungs on the participation ladder as "therapy" and "informing." For

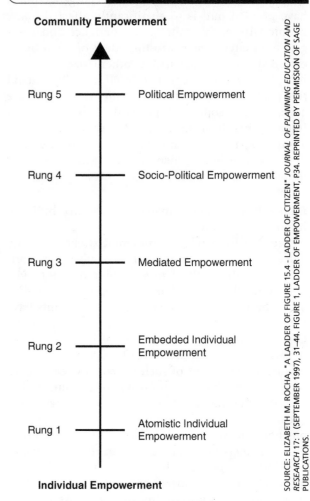

Figure 15.5   Ladder of Empowerment

Community Empowerment

Rung 5 — Political Empowerment

Rung 4 — Socio-Political Empowerment

Rung 3 — Mediated Empowerment

Rung 2 — Embedded Individual Empowerment

Rung 1 — Atomistic Individual Empowerment

Individual Empowerment

SOURCE: ELIZABETH M. ROCHA, "A LADDER OF EMPOWERMENT," *JOURNAL OF PLANNING EDUCATION AND RESEARCH* 17: 1 (SEPTEMBER 1997), 31–44. FIGURE 1, LADDER OF EMPOWERMENT, P34. REPRINTED BY PERMISSION OF SAGE PUBLICATIONS.

Empowerment is about the manifestation of different types of power in participatory planning activities and who experiences them and how they are experienced. Empowerment may occur for the individual citizen as well as for the larger community when engaged in participatory planning.

example, being invited to complete a survey about different planning options, in person or online, can be empowering to the individual citizen by virtue of being invited to participate, at rung two on the empowerment ladder. Or when community stakeholders were asked, "Did we get it right?" by Vernon, Downtown Neighbourhood planners regarding their Draft Plan synthesis of suggestions made earlier in the visioning process (Figure 15.6), empowerment is occurring there at the fourth rung.[77]

Figure 15.6 — Vernon, B.C., Community Visioning Results, 2011

Residents were asked, "What do you like about the draft plan?" and a simple computer program generated this "wordle" (or "word cloud") that increased the size of the most frequently used word combinations.

Using Public Input Effectively

The importance to citizens of planning their community almost guarantees they will want to participate in it. And, so much so, if they are not accorded a viable role, they may unceremoniously insist upon it, because people nowadays are reluctant to give up control over their local environments. Nevertheless, how best to include citizens effectively is another question. It is a process that involves a good deal of mutual trust and confidence among all participants, characteristics that cannot be legislated or easily institutionalized. Further, there are a number of aspects about citizen involvement that are frequently raised that can prove to be contentious, if not disruptive. The following aspects need to be identified and better understood:

Representativeness About those citizens who participate in the name of a larger citizen constituency, in person or on a committee, it is often asked: "Who and how many do they represent?"

Experience shows that the citizens who actively participate are bound to be relatively small in number and proportion of the population. But counting heads will not ascertain whether they are a good cross-section of the public. Regardless of whom or how many they represent, those who do get involved bring the views of truly interested citizens, and these views are valid in and of themselves. The issue of representativeness is possibly more crucial when it comes to selecting a small number of citizens to sit on advisory committees, choosing stakeholders, or targeting groups to be involved. For those making the appointments, there will be questions of the completeness of the representation; for those appointed, there is the matter of to whom they are accountable.

Accountability To whom are citizen participants accountable? This question often arises because citizens cannot be held legislatively, professionally, or legally responsible for their decisions.

This should not, however, be invoked to restrict public participation, since final authority in municipal matters always rests with the elected council. It may simply require a limitation to participation no higher than the partnership level on the participation ladder. Regardless, it should be axiomatic when involving citizens in plan-making to be clear at the outset "about who is making what decisions."[78]

Responsibility Citizens have a duty to act responsibly when they become involved. Despite that principle, instances of neighbourhood "protectionism," often broadly referred to as NIMBY or "not-in-my-backyard", occur to distort responsible discussion. It is known that citizen participants are able and willing to consider the broader needs of the community when they are accorded a meaningful role in the planning process; that is, actually helping to make the decisions. NIMBY-ism is frequently a sign of citizens taking responsibility for their own neighbourhood when it may seem that such a voice has not been allowed for. This can also indicate that more active, inclusive participatory methods, such as consensus building, are required (see below).

Access Who may participate in the planning process? This question is related to one of the fundamentals of democracy (i.e., that all citizens have access to the processes of governing and planning their communities).

Related to this issue is whether there are barriers that prevent any citizens from participating either from the procedures being used or out of neglect to include them, or both. Clearly, the public cannot be involved in all levels of planning decisions, so the nature of public access must be made clear (and unfettered where it can occur). One unfortunate instance of exclusion was the Alberta Energy Board's use of a hall for a public hearing in Calgary (in 2001) that had capacity for less than half of the 300 people who wished to attend, and the hearing had to be called off. Although rescheduled for the next day, this probably meant that some people who had taken time off work might not have been able to attend at the new time.[79]

Transparency How are planning decisions being made, and who is making them? It is also a vital facet of democracy that the processes of decision-making not be obscured from the public—even those processes that cannot be shared with them. (This could be said to be the citizens' right to accountability from their government.)

Further, citizen participants will want to be assured that any limits placed on their role are not just a form of co-optation, an attempt to make the participation appear to be broad-based.

Dialogue Who is communicating with whom in plan-making? If planners are merely providing information *to* public participants, the communication is a one-way process, not a dialogue, not real participation much less inclusion.

Public participation must be set up in such a way as to ensure that the viewpoints of the various publics in a community have an equal chance of being heard, as well as safeguarding their right to receive relevant information and to be able to collaborate in the planning.[80] In short, participation has the most chance of being effective in the public's eyes if there is both the appearance and experience that citizens have been listened to and have had the potential to influence planning decisions.

To make the participation of citizens more effective and empowering, planners have, for almost two decades, been employing a host of techniques. At the basic level of publications about planning most now include translation into various local languages. Other means include disseminating information through city-wide media, personal contacts by the planning staff, speeches, public meetings, neighbourhood drop-in centres, and provision of planning services and information directly to citizen groups. Vancouver's planners, for example, when preparing CityPlan, created the opportunity for small groups of people to discuss planning issues. Each group, called a CityCircle, was supplied information kits and a facilitator and the language of the community was used when requested. Over 200 such groups formed and they made submissions that were put into an "Ideas Book," which was then used in a city-wide Ideas Fair. It is estimated that 20 000 citizens (out of a population of 400 000) took part in this process. Calgary followed a similar process in its GoPlan transportation planning.[81] More recently, social media and other digital technologies have been used to broaden the engagement of citizens in their community's planning including Facebook, Twitter, and Wikimedia.[82]

Planning and Consensus-Building

A much more aware citizenry regarding planning matters, as is the case now in most communities, can be a blessing to plan-makers if the citizenry is able to participate actively, or can be a burden if not. Many a plan remains on the shelf because key interests in the community did not have a direct role in framing it and will not support it. The need to confront these unsettling conditions, fortuitously, has spawned a variety of ways to address complex and controversial public issues that involve multiple interests. Methods of negotiation and mediation referred to in earlier chapters grew out of the need to resolve disputes that occurred during implementation of a community plan or other public policy projects that can cause a "disconnect" in the planning process (see also Chapter 6).[83] Refinements to these methods have led to broader, more democratic approaches to achieve agreement and support among the diverse interests one finds in a community.

In general, these are called **consensual**, or **consensus-building**, approaches and fall under the rubric "communicative" planning processes. They aim to reach mutually beneficial agreements among participants about planning issues.[84] Most of these methods have two essential features. The first concerns process; the second concerns the array of participants. The consensus-building process works *horizontally*, using the consensus mode of deliberation with discussion, not votes, on principles and criteria that would provide a framework for reaching agreement on solutions to issues. This contrasts with the usual, formal, vertical approach in which, typically, "solutions" (i.e., motions) are debated using parliamentary procedures. The latter approach generates and heightens differences among participants and does not ensure that all viewpoints will be expressed and explored. The former, consensus building, provides for knowledge, experience, ideas, and concerns to be shared among equal participants and accumulated as part of the solution. A consensus is thus achieved in which all participants have been partners and share a concern over the solution—say, the community plan—and its future disposition.[85]

The second major feature of the consensus-building approach is the extensive array of participants who are involved, most often referred to as **stakeholders**. Indeed, consensual approaches are assumed to work best when the discourse is broad and not limited by professional rank or social or electoral status. So, if all groups or individuals "with something significant to gain or lose by the deliberation" are included as stakeholders, the process has the highest chance of success. Notwithstanding, the use of consensus-based participation is constrained by the number of stakeholders able to be involved: not all citizens can participate directly in this format. The consensus approach in community planning will work best when all the stakeholders can meet in a situation where they can interact (i.e., carry on a dialogue). This can be achieved utilizing representatives of stakeholder groups, especially in instances where many citizens may wish to be involved. The experiences of Burnaby, British Columbia. (Figure 15.7), and Port Colborne, Ontario, are instructive in this regard.

In the early 1990s, Port Colborne, Ontario (population about 18 000), undertook a planning process to create a community-wide plan. It ensured its citizenry that anyone who was interested could become "a fully-participating member of the planning process."[86] This planning exercise was not accomplished by one single body of the public but rather evolved from a partnership of groups in the community. The result, in their words, was a process that "enhances communications and mutual awareness among its stakeholders." Another outcome of this consensus-building approach was that the process permitted both more difficult issues (such as the allocation of scarce budgetary and space resources) and a wider range of issues to be addressed than is typical in a plan for the built environment of a community. The Port Colborne plan came to encompass areas such as economic development, physical infrastructure, social development, and commercial revitalization.

Another, more recent, Canadian example involves using a collaborative approach to resolve issues of water quality along the Lake Huron Shoreline between lakeshore residents and farmers.[87] Called the "Circle Process" it brought together small groups from the two sides of the dispute to "tell their stories" and "build relationships of understanding and trust" using the consensus method. A distinctive feature of this approach is dividing the time of a meeting equally, 50 percent for building relationships and 50 percent for dealing with issues and solutions (see Figure 15.8).

The need for consensus building and other communicative approaches is often based on many less-than-salutary instances of planning dialogue. However, these processes are about more than the mitigation of problems or failings of participation. They represent a fundamental shift toward a more democratic, pluralist,

| Figure 15.7 | Consensus-Building around a Table in Burnaby, 2012 |

SOURCE: BURNABY SOCIAL SUSTAINABILITY STRATEGY REPORT; CITY OF BURNABY.

The City of Burnaby, B.C., engaged a broad range of stakeholders to build consensus for its social sustainability strategy. The project received the CIP 2012 Social Planning Award.

| Figure 15.8 | Components of the Circle Process |

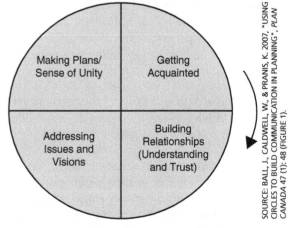

SOURCE: BALL, J., CALDWELL, W., & PRANIS, K. 2007, "USING CIRCLES TO BUILD COMMUNICATION IN PLANNING", *PLAN CANADA* 47 (1): 48 (FIGURE 1).

A fundamental principle of the Circle model is that each activity is of equal importance and therefore receives an equal amount of time.

and inclusive approach to public participation in community planning.

NIMBY and Participation

A public meeting in Vancouver in the 1990s heard objections from residents of the city's East End to city council's plans to locate a plant for recovering recyclable materials from city garbage *in their neighbourhood*. This is not an untypical situation encountered in civic engagement regarding the siting of public and social facilities and other land uses. It would also not be unfamiliar to find skeptics at city hall, in the media, and in other neighbourhoods probably classing this as just another case of NIMBY.

Community objections to planning decisions that are perceived as damaging neighbourhood quality (through noise, traffic congestion, and decreased property values), which are frequently heard today, are not new. In the early 1950s, Meyerson and Banfield found them in their pioneering study of planning for public housing in Chicago.[88] Chicagoans, in general, favoured the establishment of housing projects for low-income people, but the Housing Authority was rebuffed by many neighbourhoods in its search for sites. Such a reaction recalls, in many ways, demands by affluent property owners in the early decades of the 20th century for zoning regulations to protect their properties and businesses. The contemporary parallel is the desire of some for "exclusive" zoning. The term NIMBY came into use in the early 1980s to characterize these often frustrating events for planners, politicians, and developers, and other citizens.

The NIMBY response is frequently blamed for costly delays in formulating plans and bylaws, and for holding up construction projects. While this may be true when viewed from the level of city authorities, private developers, or public agencies proposing social facilities, from the neighbourhood perspective it is the *residents* who have to live with the outcome of the decision. Projects visualized in plans become actual buildings, traffic, and so forth in someone's neighbourhood. The need for, say, a recycling plant or group home may be accepted by the whole community as meeting its value for a better environment. And the affected neighbourhood may even share this value, but it may also have other values that are unique and just as important to its residents. Additional acronyms have come into use to denote these situations such as LULU (locally-undesirable-land-uses; see sidebar). At the heart, both NIMBY and LULU are names for some of the basic tensions in the planning process (see Chapter 6) between neighbourhood and city values (see also Planning Issue 15.1).

Why NIMBY? Implicit in NIMBY is the desire to alert planners and politicians to local concerns and values, and to bring local knowledge, which is often invaluable, into the process. On some occasions, NIMBY is the reaction of a neighbourhood or a community to not having been informed, or only at the last minute, about a planning proposal affecting it. To long-time Vancouver civic activist, the late Jim Green, "NIMBY-ism arises from a perceived feeling of powerlessness. It is often the result of the failure of those in power to allow a democratic planning process."[89] Politicians may make hasty decisions about a project (for or against the neighbourhood) or make none at all. Or they may plan a new round of meetings, which further protracts a process that may already be perceived to accord citizens only a token role.

NIMBY and LULU are complex phenomena and no two instances are the same. Each involves the individual motivations, values, and perceptions of participants, both pro and con. The complexity is also based in the various types of facilities proposed, variations in impacts of different facilities and land uses, and various ways in which NIMBY is characterized.[90] It is important for planners to understand what has stimulated a NIMBY reaction. It may arise from varying perceptions of the impacts of the proposed facility or land use change (e.g., environmental impacts, health impacts, effects on property values); indeed, there is likely to be a wide array of perceived impacts and perceived risks needing to be grasped.[91] In addition, it may be unrelated to the risks assessed by experts for proponents of the project. NIMBY participants may also vary in their perceptions of other participants (e.g., promoters of the project, local authorities, and expert evaluators); literally, what is the level of trust among participants? Then there are perceptions about the siting process: Has it been fair? Has it been open to residents from the outset? Have community preferences been included in the planning process?[92]

The motivations for NIMBY reactions are diverse: sometimes altruistic (e.g., about the environment) and sometimes ill-informed and selfish (e.g., about lifestyle). Examples of the latter include the tribulations of a Winnipeg clergyman who tried for four years to find a site for a seminary to train Aboriginal people. Urban and rural municipalities alike refused the necessary land use permission, citing increased traffic and lowered property values.[93] Paradoxically, the opposite situation can occur,

Macleans
January 4, 2012

Enough with the NIMBY Neighbours in Guelph

Josh Dehaas

A developer hoping to provide students with much-needed housing directly across from the entrance to the University of Guelph got tired of waiting for the city to decide on its proposal. Abode Varsity Living was so tired it appealed to the Ontario Municipal Board to make the decision, reports the *Guelph Mercury*.

Good for the developer, I say. The site at the corner of Gordon St. and Stone Rd., a five minute walk to the University Centre, couldn't be a better place to build a large student housing complex. High-density housing near campus is much better for students than low-density suburbia, which is the increasingly common option in Guelph. Besides, the needs of 20,000 students should trump the demands of roughly 20 NIMBY neighbours.

The City has taken more than a year to make its recommendations for the project, in part because 20 residents of the Mayfield Park neighbourhood across from campus registered their opposition last January. The up-to 16-story development housing 1,600 students is simply too big, they said.

In response to the opposition, the City hired a facilitator to bring the two sides together. According to the Mayfield Park Community Association's Kate MacDonald, the developer was willing to decrease the buildings' height and lower the occupancy 18.75 per cent, from 1,600 to 1,300.

"But that's still not acceptable," MacDonald told *The Mercury*.

Personally, I think it's unacceptable that other parts of Guelph will suffer more urban sprawl and clogged roads if developers can't build dense housing close to campus. Personally, I think it's unacceptable that many of the 1,300 students who might live at Gordon and Stone will endure longer commutes and more crowded buses if they're forced to live on the suburban periphery.

Guelph has 20,000 students and counting. There was a 10 per cent increase in first-year students in 2011 alone. Those students need somewhere to live. Across from campus is the best option.

I know the options well. In my five years at Guelph between 2003 and 2008, I watched the campus population leak farther and farther into the city's low-density south. In my final year, I moved into one of the south's single-family homes and realized just how badly the neighbourhood works for students. The low-density makes buses few and far between. It makes the grocery stores difficult to reach by walking. There's little recreation nearby. It's OK if you have a car, but most students don't.

If I'd lived closer to the school, I would have had a higher quality of life in that final year, plus less time spent on buses, which I could have used to study, work or volunteer. In other words, I would have had a better experience in Guelph. Permanent residents of Guelph should care about that. The university is undoubtedly one of the reasons its unemployment rate remains one of the lowest in North America—4.1 per cent—at a time when similar cities without universities, like Barrie, Ont., have seen their unemployment float up to 11 per cent.

If residents near the university want low-density neighbourhoods they should consider moving south. The land beside the university is the best place for students—and the best thing for Guelph.

Source: © Josh Dehaas

as in an old downtown neighbourhood in Toronto that attracted middle-class residents wanting to gentrify the area. Several drop-in agencies for many of the city's destitute, which had already existed in the neighbourhood, found themselves and their homeless clients subject to a campaign to shut them down.[94] Both cases illustrate competing claims on neighbourhood land, each from different value perspectives.

Responding to NIMBY On one level, NIMBY protests are a form of public participation, and public participation satisfies one of planning's primary values—**democratic participation**. That these protests have grown more prominent is, no doubt, a reflection of the more open planning processes of the past two decades. It is also an indication of a further "feedback loop," where many citizens, experiencing the constraints on public participation when they do get involved, opt for direct ways to be better heard. On another level, NIMBY may be the result of the expectations of planners and other proponents of projects about local responses to their proposals. For example, planners should not assume that everyone protesting in the locality prefers not to have the project in their backyard, or what is often called NIABY (not-in-anyone's-backyard). Among those protesting there will be many different motives for resisting a project, including those who agree with its need. NIMBY is truly expressed when those opposed also agree with the need for the type of project—but not here.[95] NIMBY may be responded to in a number of ways including reducing opposition by modifying the siting process, and improving the project proposal. Beyond these approaches, compensation-type methods have been used to reimburse affected parties for potential losses (e.g., property tax credits, contributions to neighbourhood needs such as parks). Finding more effective ways to communicate with those affected about the impacts provides them with opportunities to learn about the project so as to increase citizens' trust and credibility of the planners and developers. Extending this approach would empower those affected (e.g., by becoming members of an advisory committee, by allowing them to use alternate experts). Further, there is some evidence that consensus building and other informal processes are effective in resolving NIMBY concerns.[96] Lastly, the institutional structures that are used to address concerns of affected citizens, such as rezoning hearings, should be examined for their potential to be more open, inclusive, and consistent and reduce political uncertainty.

The Developer as Participant

As discussed in the previous chapter, a very large part of community planning is involved with anticipating and responding to initiatives generated in the so-called private sector to develop land. The proponents of these initiatives are referred to generically as **developers**. The term refers broadly to individuals, corporations, and other commercial groups who make decisions to convert raw land to urban use and/or to convert an already existing use to a different use (called redevelopment). The developer's role generally is to satisfy the demand for new space for such establishments as shopping centres, condos, factories, and office buildings. Private developers play a key role in the process of creating the overall built environment, and are thus an integral part of the activity of community-building.

Playing a similar development role in the community are "institutional developers" such as school boards and churches and other public and semi-public bodies. Their projects may cover group homes, homeless shelters, as well as energy facilities, and waste transfer stations proposed by senior and regional government agencies. Most of the discussion in this section applies also to these groups.

The developer's initiative to turn a parcel of land into usable space engages him or her in a complex process involving a number of persons and firms. Included are land assemblers, architects, builders, site planners, mortgage lenders, and realtors as well as public officials and approval bodies. However, it is the developer (an individual, firm, or public agency) who makes the decisions about whether a project will go ahead and when. The process of development occurs in a series of four discernible stages, each of which comprises its own set of participants: (1) land acquisition, (2) site preparation, (3) project production, and (4) project marketing (see Figure 15.9).[97]

Figure 15.9	Participants in the Development of an Urban Project

STEPS TAKEN BY DEVELOPER	PARTICIPANTS				
	(A) ACTIVE	(B) PASSIVE	(C) CONSULTANTS	(D) INTERMEDIARIES	(E) REGULATORS
1. Land acquisition	–landowner(s) –land developer	–lenders	–appraisers –lawyers	–realtors –lawyers –assembly agents	
2. Site preparation	–land developer	–landowner(s) –lenders	–planners –engineers –architects –lawyers		–planning board –council –ministry –appeal body
3. Project production	–builder	–land developer –mortgage lender –mortgage lender	–architects	–mortgage brokers	–building inspectors
4. Project marketing	–builder –consumer	–mortgage lender	–lawyers	–realtors –lawyers	

Many different individuals, groups, and professions participate in bringing a project to fruition, and their roles differ according to the stage of development: (A) active participants have a financial interest in the land and are directly involved in improving its value; (B) passive participants also have a financial interest in the land and/or improvements, but are not actively involved in the development; (C) consultants are called in by active participants to advise on technical and legal aspects; (D) intermediaries act as a liaison between active and passive participants; and (E) regulators represent the public's interests, and their approval is required for the project to go ahead.

When the project centres on the creation of a sizable new use for a site such as an apartment complex, shopping mall, or industry, the stage at which a developer becomes involved in the planning process may be as early as **land acquisition**—that is, when it has been decided to proceed with a project to build anew or renew. The next steps will usually require some physical and legal changes to the parcel of land. Physically, the developer may need to demolish existing buildings, undertake excavations, and arrange for provision of roads, sewers, and water supply. Legal changes are often needed in the form of official approvals for amending the community plan, subdividing the land, rezoning the site, and building construction. Municipalities may also exercise various kinds of development control as well as require financial contracts to provide basic utilities, for which they may make development charges (see Chapter 17).

Each application for approval by the developer involves personal interaction with public officials, especially planners. What ensues is a complex **negotiation–bargaining** situation. The developer seeks approvals that will keep the project plans intact. The municipality seeks, where necessary, to modify any aspects of a project that

will require undue expenditures of public funds and/or prevent infringement on public rights of access. The planners may also try to persuade the developer to include more amenities in the project for the occupants and the public, such as more open space. In large cities and in large projects in particular, the bargaining between developers and planners has become very complex, with various trade-offs being made.[98] Planners may offer bonuses, such as additional height on office building projects, in return for the provision of a public plaza; or land may be given by the developer in return for closing a public right-of-way; or a heritage building may be retained in return for other concessions. Even citizens' groups may become involved in such bargaining, as when a large office project in Toronto was stalled in order to obtain money from the developer for low-income housing.[99] In the case of large-scale housing projects a common approach used by municipalities is to require that the developer devote a certain proportion of units, often 10–15 percent, to low-income housing.

The often-intense negotiations between developers and planners in the site-preparation stage indicate the strong mutuality of the two participants. One observer has termed it a "symbiotic interrelationship" in which the following occurs:

1. Planners prepare plans basically intended to modify and build upon, what developers already do; and
2. Developers make their development decisions based on their interactions with planners and their knowledge of what planners will accept.[100]

In situations involving the development of raw land, most of the bargaining will be done by the developer and the planner, along with other municipal officials.[101]

As concerns over environmental matters and sustainability have come to the fore in urban development, developers have frequently initiated discussions with planners about making their projects "greener."[102] Instances such as these should put somewhat to rest the long-held myth that all developers are uncaring about the community. The prolongation of such ideas is often due to wariness by citizens about the openness, the "transparency," of development planning processes, much of which take place out of public scrutiny, an issue raised above regarding NIMBY.

In redevelopment situations where the local populace has a strong interest in maintaining the status quo, a good deal of the bargaining may be subject to public scrutiny and public input as well. Indeed, many local governments require that developers discuss their plans with neighbourhood residents and neighbourhood organizations and attempt to reach consensus on their projects before initiating formal proceedings for rezoning, development control, or subdivision approval.

Reflections

As desirable and necessary as it may be, public participation may not occur in the scope and form hoped for; in fact, it may not happen at all. Participation is a voluntary act; it can be promoted but not guaranteed. Given their experience, the poor and cultural or ethnic minorities may feel powerless to influence decisions. Middle-class citizens may choose not to participate out of cynicism or apathy. Deliberate efforts to promote participation have had only limited success when no plans are in the offing. People respond much more readily to changes in their immediate environment than to large, remote projects or abstract plans. Moreover, organized groups of citizens, it has been known for some time, tend to avoid devoting much time to pre-planning exercises, preferring to save their resources for more immediate decision-making stages.[103] The vagaries of citizen participation reflect the complexity of the actual choices to be made in planning for the future built environment of a community. Irksome though it may sometimes be to other participants, the advent of direct involvement of citizens has revealed the poverty of the notion of one correct plan and the suppression of relevant value positions that often accompanies it. At the same time, it helps reveal the wider range of possibilities for action that exist in reality, thereby enriching the substantive side of planning as well. Probably most important, many community members are involved in decisions about their environment. Notably, this includes women, who provide much of the initiative and leadership in citizen-participation efforts. Through citizen participation, planning our cities and towns becomes much more a *community* planning process, and raises these questions:

- *How can we continue to expand participation in planning, and what modifications might be needed to the roles of various participants?*

- *Which forms of public participation engage citizens most deeply?*

Reference Notes

1. J.A. Throgmorton, "On the Virtues of Skillful Meandering: Acting as a Skilled-Voice-in-the-Flow of Persuasive Argumentation," *Journal of the American Planning Association* 66:4 (Autumn 2000), 367–383.
2. Judith E. Innes, "Information in Communicative Planning," *Journal of the American Planning Association* 64:1 (Winter 1998), 52–63.
3. Harry Lash, *Planning in a Human Way*, Cat. no. SU32-3 (Ottawa: Ministry of State for Urban Affairs and Macmillan Canada, 1976), 9–13.
4. Among others: Paul Davidoff, "Advocacy and Pluralism in Planning," *Journal of the American Institute of Planners* 31:4 (December 1965), 331–338; and Nancy Marshall and Richard Roberts, "That Thing Called Public Involvement," *Plan Canada* 37:3 (1997), 8–11.
5. Andrei Nicoli, "The Twenty-First Century is Here: Is Anybody Home? Community Participation and the Role of Local Government," *Plan Canada* 41:1 (January–February–March 2001), 21–23.
6. Patsy Healey, "The Communicative Turn in Planning Theory and Its Implications for Spatial Strategy Formation," *Environment and Planning B: Planning and Design* 23:2 (1996) 217–234.
7. Recognizing this interdependence is crucial according to David E. Booher and Judith E. Innes, "Network Power in Collaborative Planning," *Journal of Planning Education and Research* 21:3 (March 2002), 221–236.
8. Booher and Innes, "Network Power in Collaborative Planning."

9. Norman Beckman, "The Planner as Bureaucrat," *Journal of the American Institute of Planners* 30:4 (November 1964), 323–327.

10. Throgmorton, "On the Virtues of Skillful Meandering."

11. Lash, *Planning in a Human Way,* 75.

12. Larry Diamond, "The Developer as a Partner in Change: Defying Popular Myths," *Plan Canada* 50:1 (Spring 2010), 42–47.

13. Leonie Sandercock, "Towards a Planning Imagination for the 21st Century," *Journal of the American Planning Association* 70:2 (Spring 2004), 133–141; and John Forester, "Planning in the Face of Power," *Journal of the American Planning Association* 48 (Winter 1982), 67–80.

14. Cf. Patsy Healey, *Collaborative Planning: Shaping Places I Fragmented Societies* (Vancouver: UBC Press, 1997), 59.

15. Melvin M. Webber, "Comprehensive Planning and Social Responsibility," *Journal of the American Institute of Planners* 29 (November 1963), 267–273.

16. Karen S. Christensen, "Teaching Savvy," *Journal of Planning Education and Research,* 12:3 (April 1993), 202–212.

17. Kathryn S. Quick and Martha S. Feldman, "Distinguishing Participation and Inclusion," *Journal of Planning Education and Research* 31:3 (September 2011), 272–290.

18. Cf. Susan Fainstein, "Planning in a Different Voice," *Planning Theory* 7:8 (1992), 27–31; and Penelope Gurstein, "Gender Sensitive Community Planning: A Case Study of the Planning Ourselves In Project," *Canadian Journal of Urban Research* 5:2 (December 1996), 199–219.

19. Jana Carp, "Wit, Style, and Substance: How Planners Shape Public Participation," *Journal of Planning Education and Research* 23:3 (March 2004), 242–254.

20. Michael Seelig and Julie Seelig, "CityPlan: Participation or Abdication?" *Plan Canada* 37:3 (May 1997), 18–22.

21. Carp, "Wit, Style, and Substance."

22. These basic categories derive from Robert T. Daland and John A. Parker, "Roles of the Planner in Urban Development," in F. Stuart Chapin Jr. and Shirley Weiss, eds., *Urban Growth Dynamics* (New York: Krieger Publishing, 1962), esp. 190–196.

23. John Forester, "Know Your Organizations: Planning and the Reproduction of Social and Political Relations," *Plan Canada* 22:1 (March 1982), 3–13.

24. Kevin S. Hanna, "The Paradox of Participation and the Hidden Role of Information," *Journal of the American Planning Association* 66:4 (Autumn 2000), 398–410.

25. Christensen, "Teaching Savvy."

26. Mohammad Qadeer, What is This Thing Called Multicultural Planning?" *Plan Canada*, Special Edition (2009), 10–13.

27. Pierre Filion, "The Weight of the System," *Plan Canada* 37:1 (January 1997), 11–18.

28. Sandercock, "Towards a Planning Imagination for the 21st Century."

29. Ian Wight, "Valuing Planning: An Ethic/Ethos in the Making," *Plan Canada* 51:1 (Spring 2011), 36–39.

30. John Punter, *The Vancouver Achievement: Urban Planning and Design* (Vancouver: UBC Press, 2003), Chapters 8 and 9.

31. The extent to which this value pervades the Canadian planning profession may be seen in the survey results of John Page and Reg Lang, *Canadian Planners in Profile* (Toronto: York University Faculty of Environmental Studies, 1977), a report to the Canadian Institute of Planners.

32. Jill Grant, "Rethinking the Public Interest as a Planning Concept," *Plan Canada* 45:2 (Summer 2005), 48–50.

33. Samuel D. Brody et al., "Mandating Citizen Participation in Plan Making: Six Strategic Planning Choices," *Journal of the American Planning Association* 69:3 (Winter 2003), 245–264.

34. Matthew Kiernan, "Ideology and the Precarious Future of the Canadian Planning Profession," *Plan Canada* 22:1 (March 1982), 14–24.

35. Laura Mannell and Heather Turnoway, "The Need to Do More: Advancing Planning with First Nations Communities," *Plan Canada* 48:2 (Summer 2008), 21–23.

36. Donald A. Schon, "Some of What a Planner Knows," *Journal of the American Planning Association* 48 (Summer 1982), 351–364.

37. Thomas Gunton, "The Role of the Professional Planner," *Canadian Public Administration* 27:3 (Fall 1984), 399–417; and Albert Z. Guttenberg, *The Language of Planning* (Urbana and Chicago: University of Illinois Press, 1993), xiv.

38. Schon, "Some of What a Planner Knows."

39. Cf. Richard D. Margerum, "Collaborative Planning: Building Consensus and Building a Distinct Model for Practice," *Journal of Planning Education and Research* 21:3 (March 2002), 237–253; and Patsy Healey, *Collaborative Planning.*

40. Richard D. Margerum, "Evaluating Collaborative Planning: Implications from an Empirical Analysis of Growth Management," *Journal of the American Planning Association* 68:2 (Spring 2002), 179–193.

41. Booher and Innes, "Network Power in Collaborative Planning."

42. Quick and Feldman, "Distinguishing Participation and Inclusion."

43. Sherry R. Arnstein, "A Ladder of Citizen Participation," *Journal of the American Institute of Planners* 35:3 (July 1969), 216–224.

44. Lynn Mandarano, Mahbubur Meenar, and Christopher Steins, "Building Social Capital in the Age of Civic Engagement," *Journal of Planning Literature* 25:2 (November 2010),123–135.

45. http://www.facebook.com/group?gid=6949283325

46. Cherie Enns and Jennifer Wilson, "The Picket Fence Project," *Plan Canada* 39:4 (September–October 1999), 12–15.

47. Lash, *Planning in a Human Way,* 35.

48. McAfee, "Vancouver CityPlan."

49. Neale Smith and Nancy Hackett, "Partnering for Neighbourhood Revitalization: Riverside Meadows, Red Deer," *Plan Canada* 41:1 (January–February–March 2001), 13–15.

50. Noel Keough, "Calgary's Citizen-Led Community Sustainability Indicators Project," *Plan Canada* 43:1 (Spring 2003), 35–36.

51. Ananya Roy, "A 'Public' Muse: On Planning Convictions and Feminist Contentions," *Journal of Planning Education and Research* 21:2 (December 2001), 109–126.

52. Leonie Sandercock, *Towards Cosmopolis: Planning for Multicultural Cities* (New York: Wiley, 1998).

53. One of the earliest critiques is J. Leavitt, "Feminist Advocacy Planning in the 1980s," in Barry Checkoway, ed., *Strategic Perspective in Planning Practice* (Lexington, MA: Lexington Books, 1986); two later valuable sources are Leonie Sandercock and Ann Forsyth, "Gender: A New Agenda for Planning Theory," *Journal of the American Planning Association* 58:1 (1992), 49–59; and Clara Greed, *Women and Planning: Creating Gendered Realities* (London: Routledge, 1994).

54. Susan Prentice, "Childcare, Justice and the City: A Case Study of Planning Failure in Wiinnipeg," *Canadian Journal of Urban Research*, 16:1 (Winter 2007), 92–108.

55. Fainstein, "Planning in a Different Voice"; and Mary Gail Snyder, "Feminist Theory and Planning Theory," *Berkeley Planning Journal* 10 (1995), 91–106.

56. Sue Hendler (with Helen Harrison), "Theorizing Canadian Planning History: Women, Gender, and Feminist Perspectives," in Kristine B. Miranne and Alma H. Young, eds., *Gendering the City: Women, Boundaries and Visions of Urban Life* (Lanham, UK: Rowan & Littlefield, 2000), 139–156.

57. Karen Hemmingson and Leslie Kemp, "Planning Ourselves In: Exploring Women's Involvement in the Community Planning Process," *City Magazine* 14:4/15:1 (Fall–Winter 1993), 14–17.

58. Cf. the review in Rae Bridgman, "Criteria for Best Practices in Building Child-Friendly Cities: Involving Young People in Urban Planning and Design," *Canadian Journal of Urban Research* 13:2 (Winter 2004), 337–346.

59. Penelope Gurstein et al., "Youth Participation in Planning: Strategies for Social Action," *Canadian Journal of Urban Research* 12:2 (Winter 2003), 249–274.

60. City of Vernon, *City Centre Neighbourhood Plan*, September 2011, 4–5.

61. Gerald Hodge, *The Geography of Aging: Preparing Communities for the Surge in Seniors* (Montréal: McGill-Queens University Press, 2008), 169–190.

62. Canada, Centre for Health Promotion, *A City for All Ages* (Ottawa, 2000), 89.

63. Deborah A. Howe et al., *Planning for an Aging Society*, Planning Advisory Service Report No. 451 (Chicago: American Planning Association, 1994), 47–50.

64. Statistics Canada, *A Profile of Disability in Canada, 2001,* Cat. no. 89-577-XIE (Ottawa: Statistics Canada, 2002), Table 2.

65. David Sibley, *Geographies of Exclusion* (London: Routledge, 1995); Brendon Gleeson, *Geographies of Disability* (London: Routledge, 1999); and Hester Parr and Ruth Butler, "New Geographies of Illness, Impairment and Disability," in H. Parr and R. Butler, eds., *Mind and Body Spaces* (London: Routledge, 1999), 1–24.

66. Rebecca Schi, Jeannette Waegemakers Schi, and Barbara Schneider, "Housing for the Disabled Mentally Ill: Beyond Homogeneity," *Canadian Journal of Urban Research*, 19:2 (Winter 2010), 108–128.

67. Statistics Canada, *Canada's Ethnocultural Portrait: The Changing Mosaic, 2001,* Census Analysis Series, Cat. no. 96F0030XIE2001008 (Ottawa: Statistics Canada, 2003), 39.

68. Feng Hou and Garnet Picot, "Visible Minority Neighbourhoods in Toronto, Montréal, and Vancouver," *Canadian Social Trends* 72 (2004), 8–13.

69. Karen Umemoto, "Walking in Another's Shoes: Epistemological Challenges in Participatory Planning," *Journal of Planning Education and Research* 21:1 (2001), 17–31.

70. Mohammad Qadeer, "What is This Thing Called Multicultural Planning," *Plan Canada,* 2009 Special Edition, 10–13.

71. Petra L. Doan and Harrison Higgins, "The Demise of Queer Space? Resurgent Gentrification and the Assimilation of LGBT Neighborhoods," *Journal of Planning Education and Research* 31:1 (March 2011), 6–25.

72. Susan S. Fainstein, "New Directions in Planning Theory," *Urban Affairs Review* 35:4 (March 2000), 451–478.

73. Quick and Feldman, "Distinguishing Participation and Inclusion."

74. Quick and Feldman, "Distinguishing Participation and Inclusion" (emphasis added).

75. Arnstein, "A Ladder of Citizen Participation."

76. Elizabeth M. Rocha, "A Ladder of Empowerment," *Journal of Planning Education and Research* 17:1 (September 1997), 31–44.

77. City of Vernon, 4.

78. Michael Hibbard and Susan Lurie, "Saving Land but Losing Ground: Challenges to Community Planning in the Era of Participation," *Journal of Planning Education and Research* 20 (Winter 2000), 187–195.

79. Maria Canton, "Energy Board Halts Power Plant Hearing," *Calgary Herald,* August 14, 2001.

80. Ann McAfee, "Vancouver CityPlan: People Participating in Planning," *Plan Canada* 35:3 (May 1995), 15–16.

81. Calgary, City Planning Department, *Public Participation in the Planning Process* (Calgary, 1993).

82. Lynn Mandarano, Mahbubur Meenar, and Christopher Steins, "Building Social Capital in the Age of Civic Engagement."

83. Carolyn G. Loh, "Four Potential Disconnects in the Community Planning Process," *Journal of Planning Education and Research* 32:1 (February 2012), 33–47.

84. An excellent overview is provided in Judith Innes, "Planning through Consensus Building: A New View of the Comprehensive Planning Ideal," *Journal of the American Planning Association* 62:4 (Autumn 1996), 460–472.

85. The consensus method is also laid out in L. Susskind et al., *Consensus Building Handbook* (Thousand Oaks, CA: Sage, 1999).

86. Manfred Fast, "Communities Can Make It Happen: Forging the Port Colborne, Ontario Strategic Plan," *Small Town* 26:1 (July–August 1995), 10–15.

87. Jennifer Ball, Wayne Caldwell, and Kay Pranis, "Using Circles to Build ommuni-cation in Planning," *Plan Canada* 47:1(Spring 2007), 17–19; and Jennifer Ball, Wayne Caldwell, and Kay Pranis, *Doing Democracy with Circles: Engaging Communities in Public Planning* (St. Paul, MN, Living Justice Press, 2010).

88. Martin Meyerson and Edward C. Banfield, *Politics, Planning and the Public Interest* (Glencoe, IL: Free Press, 1955).

89. Jim Green, "Regional Government, Revolution, and NIMBY-ism," *City Magazine* 13:2 (Spring 1992), 29.

90. Carissa Schivley, "Understanding the NIMBY and LULU Phenomena," *Journal of Planning Literature* 21:3 (February 2007), 255–266.

91. Lois M. Takahashi and Michael J. Dear, "The Changing Dynamics of Community Opposition to Human Service Facilities," *Journal of the American Planning Association* 63:1 (Winter 1997), 79–93.

92. Bruno S. Frey and Felix Oberholzer-Gee, "Fair Siting Procedures: An Empirical Analysis of Their Importance and Characteristics," *Journal of Policy and Management* 15:3 (June 1996), 358–376.

93. Geoffrey York, "Native Seminary Meets Only Rejection," *The Globe and Mail,* Toronto, January 29, 1990, A1.

94. Margaret Philip, "Toronto's Destitute Wear Out Welcome, *The Globe and Mail,* July 18, 1997, A6.

95. Maarten Wolsink, "Entanglement of Interests and Motives: Assumptions behind the NIMBY-Theory on Facility Siting," *Urban Studies* 31:6 (June 1994), 851–867; and John Andrew, "Examining the Claims of Environmental ADR: Evidence From Waste Management Conflicts in Ontario and Massachusetts," *Journal of Planning Education and Research* 21:2 (2001), 166–183.

96. Carissa Schivley, "Understanding the NIMBY and LULU Phenomena."

97. This classification is derived from two sources: Simon B. Chamberlain, *Aspects of Developer Behaviour in the Land Development Process,* Research Paper No. 56 (Toronto: University of Toronto Centre for Urban and Community Studies, 1972); and Urban Land Institute, *Residential Development Handbook* (Washington, 1978).

98. A penetrating review of such negotiations and their consequences for city development is found in James Lorimer, *The Developers* (Toronto: James Lorimer, 1978).

99. The validity of this tactic is questioned in Stanley Makuch, "Planning or Blackmail?" *Plan Canada* 25:1 (March 1985), 8–9.

100. Chamberlain, *Aspects of Developer Behaviour,* 45.

101. An excellent description of bargaining between developers and municipal planners in Scarborough, Ontario, is given in Hok-Lin Leung, "Mutual Learning in Developmental Control," *Plan Canada* 27:2 (April 1987), 44–55.

102. Larry Diamond, "The Developer as a Partner in Change: Defying Popular Myths."

103. Gerald Hodge and Patricia Hodge, "Citizen Participation in Environmental Planning in Eastern Ontario," *Plan Canada* 19:2 (March 1979), 22–29.

Internet Resources

Chapter-Relevant Sites

Planning Canadian Communities
www.planningcanadiancommunities.ca

CMHC Gateway for Housing Professionals and Community Groups
www.cmhc.ca/en/inpr

The Citizen's Handbook: A guide to building community
www.vcn.bc.ca/citizens-handbook

Georgia Strait Alliance: Caring for our Coastal Waters
www.georgiastrait.org

Metro Vancouver Homelessness Plan
www.metrovancouver.org/planning/homelessness/

Joint Centre of Excellence for Research on Immigration and Settlement
www.ceris.metropolis.net

Metropolitan Action Committee on Violence Against Women and Children
www.metrac.org

National Charrette Institute
www.charretteinstitute.org

Implementing Community Plans

Introduction

Turning the aspirations of a community plan into reality requires tools that can guide the many decision makers with an interest in the outcome of the community's built environment. These tools are more than just complementary to the community plan; they are an integral part of the planning process of attaining the community's goals. In essence, a plan without tools for implementation is probably destined to gather dust on the shelf. The tools of planning—zoning, subdivision control, capital budgets, and so on—are very familiar. People encounter the effects of these tools more often than they come in contact with the plan itself. Indeed, they sometimes have negative connotations in people's minds because they can be used to restrict development or change on privately owned property.

Achieving the aims of a community plan is a matter of combining land use regulations and public policy instruments to influence the decisions of private developers and other public agencies. They are complementary: the former are reactive to development initiatives, constraining the choices of land developers, while the latter can be proactive in influencing the decisions of private developers and public agencies alike. Thus, the adoption of a community plan is the beginning, not the end, of the need for choices about community-building.

The image above is from the Woodlands Rezoning project, New Westminster, British Columbia, which received the Canadian Institute of Planners' Award for Planning Excellence, Category of Implementation, 2004.

Source: Woodlands Rezoning project, New Westminster, British Columbia.

Chapter Sixteen

Land Use Regulation Tools for Plan Implementation

Discretion is an essential element of planning. Somebody has to say yes or no to a request for permission to develop land at a certain time and in a certain way.

Anthony Adamson, 1956

For a community to prepare a plan is commendable, indeed essential, in order to set about attaining the built environment to which it aspires to. But turning those aspirations into reality requires tools that can guide the many decision-makers with an interest in the outcome of the community's space. The planner's tools are more than just complementary to the community plan; they are an integral part of the planning process of attaining the plan's goals. The "archway" of planning shown in Figure 16.1 could not exist without both plan and tools. In short, a plan without tools for implementation is probably destined to gather dust on the shelf, and planning tools without a plan add up to meaningless or even arbitrary regulation.

This chapter and the next examine the tools and approaches used in implementing the community plan. In many ways, the tools of planning—zoning, subdivision control, capital budgets, and so on—are very familiar. People encounter the effects of these tools more often than they come in contact with the plan itself. Not infrequently, the planning tools are seen as the end product of planning rather than its means. And where planning tools are also land use regulations, they often have negative connotations in people's minds because they can be used to restrict development or change on privately owned property. Sometimes they are believed to have more power over the plan's implementation than they actually carry. It is important, therefore, to grasp the nature and capabilities of each of these planning tools.

The planning tools we examine in this chapter are those that are used to guide development on private land. That is, they are the planner's traditional tools for

Figure 16.1	Key Role of the Community Plan in Land Use Control

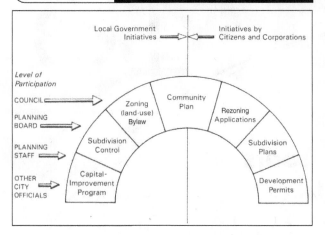

The community plan has the same position as that of this keystone in the arch. The sections ahead will follow the tools down this arch, from plan through to implementation. Zoning, subdivision control, and development permits will be examined from the perspective of the local government (left) and private stakeholders (right). The arch diagram will be repeated for each major section, to guide the reader.

regulating land use. These tools each have a specific role and capacity in implementing a community plan. Thus, as they are reviewed here, two overriding questions should be kept in mind:

- *What potential do the planning tools have to implement a community plan and what are their limitations?*
- *What are the differences between planning tools used in regard to developed lands and those used with undeveloped lands?*

The Main Tasks of Plan Implementation

The ultimate aim of plan-makers is to establish the conditions that will attain the goals of the plan. Those conditions derive from a combination of policy directives, legal instruments, administrative practices, and means of promoting community participation in planning. Implementing a community plan is, thus, accomplished using a variety of tools and approaches. While making a community plan concludes at a particular point in time (at least until it needs to be amended), plan implementation is a *continuous* process. Since the

tools of planning deal with a continuous, functioning community, they must be able to respond to the type and character of present-day development initiatives and to the decisions that will be made as the future unfolds.

Planning tools act as an *interface* between the policies of the plan and the aims of those who make decisions that transform the physical environment. The latter include all those who own some land within the community—the average residential homeowner, who may have no plans for developing his or her property, as well as those who are in the business of land and building development. Also included are the staffs in public agencies who make decisions to invest public funds and construct roads, schools, parks, parking garages, and so on. All have the potential for making decisions that could affect the future built environment. Considering this array of participants involved in land use decisions, two basic needs, or dimensions, of plan implementation emerge. The need to:

1. **Guide development on private land.** This, in turn, breaks down into two sub-dimensions:
   a. Presently developed areas, and
   b. Vacant or undeveloped areas.
2. **Coordinate public development efforts.** This applies especially to capital investments.

Around these two dimensions have developed the best-known and most refined planning tools, such as **zoning**, or "districting," as it used to be called, and **development control** or site-plan control; these are used to guide development on presently developed private land. **Subdivision control**, another traditional tool, is used to guide development on large parcels of vacant land. These familiar tools are designed for the *direct* guidance of the individual, group, business, or public agency that wishes to make decisions about the use of land in the community. This guidance is aimed at encouraging certain land use to occur in particular locations while constraining or limiting that development. To do this, the tools are usually backed by statutory powers vested in the municipality by the province.

There are also tools that work to influence development decisions *indirectly*. Indeed, a good deal of planning implementation is involved with more than regulating land use. Considerable attention and time must be devoted, for example, to guiding persons who are considering development of their land and who look to officials in other municipal departments and agencies to explain planning policies. Promoting citizen participation is also important to test public acceptance of plans and policies. These latter tasks have not generated formal, institutionalized tools. Certain implementation *approaches* have emerged to obtain public input and use alternative organizational arrangements for municipal planning operations. The approaches often differ in form from community to community (with the exception of provincially prescribed public hearings). Thus, communities develop individual planning styles with which to achieve the goals of the community plan. For example, Vancouver's approach to downtown development is quite different from that used in Toronto or Montréal, incorporating extensive design review and staff approval delegated by City Council.[1]

One final point about plan implementation and the tools associated with it concerns the outcome—the physical result—of decisions taken in the name of planning. The community plan is intended to encompass *all* community land use decisions, present and future, in order to achieve some envisioned built environment. In a planned new town, the physical results may approximate the design promoted in the overall plan. But in the typical Canadian city or town, change in the existing environment is not subject to such direct design. The regulations for guiding development on private land are usually invoked only when the persons or groups with interests in the land signal their intention to develop or redevelop their properties.

Planning Tools for Already-Developed Lands

Planning tools that are typically used in the developed portion of a community include **zoning**, **development control** (site-plan control); and **redevelopment plans**. The developed part of a community is the portion that, in general, comprises relatively small parcels of land that are already built upon or could be developed. There are usually a few large parcels of land occupied by such institutions as hospitals, factories, or parks. These are part of the developed area, too. But large parcels of land in use as farms or for other resource extraction, or those that are simply vacant and not divided into small parcels are not considered developed land. The latter types are usually found on the fringe of the community and may, indeed, become developed in the future, but their future use is still to be determined at the time of its subdivision into smaller parcels. Here again is another distinction that should be kept in mind when considering such planning tools as zoning: these tools are designed for land for which the intended use has already been determined.

Zoning
Origins and Nature

Zoning (land use) Bylaw

Zoning grew out of the early observation about city development that similar uses tend to congregate in areas separate from other uses. Further, when congregated in their distinctive areas, the land uses and activities—industry, commerce, residences—seem to perform their respective functions more effectively than when intermingled. German town planners in the latter half of the 19th century employed these observations to devise ways of organizing the growth of industrial cities to ensure efficiency for the factories and amenable workers' housing.[2] Municipalities in all countries experiencing industrialization in this period, including Canada, sought to regulate the siting of buildings and the provision of basic services for safety and health reasons. The German approach was, however, to differentiate the regulations according to the needs of the uses located in (or planned for) their respective *districts*. The practice became known as "districting" and, later, as "zoning," especially in North America.

Besides observing the functional differences in land use (e.g., many industries have noxious effluents, commercial areas generate a lot of traffic), early planners also perceived aesthetic differences among land use districts: the height of buildings, the space between them, their setback from the road, and the road pattern that best suited the use. Not least, early planners noted that differences between land uses reflected differences in *density* of land use. In residential districts, there were differences, for example, in the number of dwellings on each parcel of land, as reflected in the height and bulk of buildings, the size of dwelling units, and the amount of open space around them. Analogous observations were made in regard to industrial and commercial land uses and their structures. In short, districting principles lent themselves to consideration of the physical design of communities to achieve the arrangements and densities of land uses a community might prefer.

Zoning can be applied simultaneously to individual properties or large areas, which may account for its longevity among planning tools. When zoning was established, it was a major departure in the exercise of statutory powers by municipalities. Previously, municipalities had used powers for enforcing safety, health, and structural standards on an individual property basis.[3] But since land use occurs on a spatial basis, it was necessary to apply the same regulations to all the properties in a similar area. With this sort of tool, planners were more likely to achieve consistency in the types of uses and structures that constituted the physical environment of the distinctive zones or districts of development.

In North America, the first comprehensive zoning bylaw was enacted by the City of New York in 1916. The first such Canadian zoning bylaw was enacted in 1924 for Kitchener, Ontario, and was formulated by planners Thomas Adams and Horace Seymour (see Figure 4.26, page 97).[4] A comprehensive zoning bylaw established districts for the entire community. Prior to the above dates there were districting bylaws in some communities that dealt selectively with heights of buildings and the location of noxious uses.[5] For example, in 1904, Ontario cities had the right to control the location, erection, and use of buildings for laundries, butcher shops, stores, and "manufactories."[6] And there were instances of bylaws designed in a discriminatory fashion to limit the residency of specific minority groups to certain areas of the city.[7] As zoning came more widely into practice in the 1920s, it had to meet the test of court challenges, especially with regard to the principle that it must apply *universally* and *uniformly* to all properties within the areas in question. Earlier exclusionary tendencies gave way to a more general rationale of the protection from dramatic shifts in property values due to the mixing of incompatible land uses.

Zoning practice developed along the same general lines in Canada and the United States, although there are significant constitutional differences between the two countries that affect zoning. The basic difference lies in the fact that the U.S. Constitution spells out personal property rights, whereas the Canadian Charter of Rights and Freedoms does not (nor did the British North America [BNA] Act). In the United States, the validity (constitutionality) of zoning bylaws was not confirmed as a power available to municipalities until it had been tested by the U.S. Supreme Court.[8] In Canada, municipalities were deemed, under powers granted to the provinces under the BNA Act and British Common Law, to have the statutory power to regulate land use.[9] The usual concern over zoning practice in the United States is whether the bylaw involves a "taking away" of property rights granted to property owners. The concern in Canada is more general—that is, whether the bylaw is discriminatory in pursuing the public interest. Thus, zoning bylaws in Canada can have much broader scope than those in the United States. This constitutional difference has given rise in Canada to the complementary practices of development control and site-plan control, which allow a municipality to specify certain land use regulations on a property-by-property basis. More will be said about these later in the chapter.

Substantive Focus

Zoning has a very precise focus. It provides a set of standards regarding

1. the *use* to which a parcel of land may be put, and
2. the *size, type,* and *placement* of buildings on that parcel.

These standards are made explicit in the text of the zoning bylaw, according to the districts in the community to which they apply. An accompanying **map**, or **zoning plan**, as it is sometimes called, specifies the boundaries of each zone and, thus, the properties affected by the different district regulations (Figure 16.2). The zoning plan is the second most important planning instrument in the community next to the overall plan.

The zoning bylaw may also regulate the density of population from district to district by specifying the number of dwelling units allowed per building and/or the number of individuals that may occupy a dwelling unit. Most zoning bylaws contain provisions covering the external effects of activities carried on in buildings such as through requirements for off-street parking and loading areas, size and placement of signs, and accessory uses and home occupations. There may be the need or desire in a community to specify land use districts that contain distinctive local features for functional, historical, environmental, or aesthetic reasons, in which case the zoning bylaw may contain provisions covering a number of special districts.

Land Use Types and Districts Three basic land use categories are usually identified in zoning bylaws: residential, commercial, and industrial. In each of these categories, there may be a series of zones, depending upon the nature of the activities, the type of building, the density of development, or the lot size. A variety of residential zones may be distinguished, for example, by the number of dwelling units permitted on the lots that are typical of the zone. If large apartment buildings and large tracts of land are being developed, the zone may be defined by the number of dwelling units per hectare. Among commercial zones, the distinctions may be in terms of the service needs of people: central business, neighbourhood commercial, highway-oriented commercial, or shopping centre. For industrial zones, the differences in standards

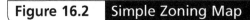

Figure 16.2 Simple Zoning Map

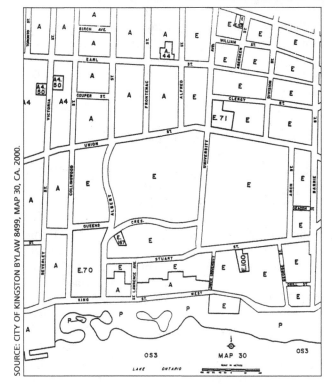

SOURCE: CITY OF KINGSTON BYLAW 8499, MAP 30, CA. 2000.

Zoning maps are precise drawings based on property boundaries, as illustrated in this simple zoning bylaw diagram from a medium-sized city. Note the way that the boundary of the "A" zone (low-density residential use) meets the "E" zone (institutional use). This was intended to be the boundary between a university and the adjacent neighbourhood. However, in practice, many adjacent homes were converted to student housing. The buildings are still in residential use, but the policy intent of the community plan has been subverted.

usually reflect the characteristics of the processes carried on by the firms. For example, industries using heavy machinery or emitting considerable smoke, noise, or odours would usually be in a zone separate from those whose processes had much less external impact. Similarly, those engaged in mostly the shipping, storing, and transfer of goods would likely warrant a separate zone. Figure 16.3 illustrates a typical listing of zones found in the zoning bylaws of a medium-sized city.

For each land use zone, it is common practice to specify the uses that are *permitted* to locate there. This may necessitate a long list of valid uses in order to include all likely and desirable types. The following list shows the establishments permitted in the Neighbourhood Commercial Zone of the City of Kingston, Ontario:

- Retail stores
- Neighbourhood stores
- Offices for or in connection with a business or profession
- Banks or financial institutions
- Restaurants
- One-family dwellings and two-family dwellings, provided that such dwellings are located within a commercial structure
- Libraries, art galleries, or museums
- Shopping centres

A brief look at the uses permitted in the above commercial zone indicates how, even in this rather ordinary bylaw, an interesting mixture of land uses might be accommodated: dwelling places, offices, restaurants, and stores. Yet, in recent times, the result is a strip mall. Other communities, especially larger ones such as Toronto, Montréal, and Vancouver, have developed zoning provisions that encourage special combinations of mixed uses, thereby considerably blunting the criticism that zoning prevents mixing.[10]

Figure 16.3 Land Use Districts in Typical Zoning Bylaw for a Medium-Sized City

ZONE	PREDOMINANT LAND USE
R1	Single-family residential
R2	One- and two-family residential
R3	Apartment residential (medium density)
R4	High-density residential
C1	Downtown commercial
C2	Neighbourhood commercial
C3	Automobile-oriented commercial
M1	Light industrial
M2	Wholesale and transportation
M3	Heavy industrial
P	Public use (health, education, religious, administration)
R	Rural and agriculture
EN	Environmentally sensitive area

Zoning bylaws must conform to legal standards and must, therefore, be specific in their language. In the listing above, the specified uses are the only ones permitted and any other uses are thereby excluded from being located within the zone. Occasionally, excluded uses may be specified in order to prevent any ambiguity in interpretation. Unspecified uses already present in the zone before the bylaw was enacted are usually "excepted" (or "grandfathered") from the provisions. The list of permitted uses in each zone is thus distinctive, although a small amount of overlap will undoubtedly occur between the lists of permitted uses within the sets of zones in each of the basic residential, commercial, and industrial categories. Banks and restaurants will generally be permitted in all commercial zones, for example.

The land use zones, and the lists of permitted uses associated with each, in most instances, reflect the types of uses already existing in the community. Where residential neighbourhoods, commercial areas, and industrial districts already exist and are in stable condition, the zoning regulations are formulated so as to continue those uses in their respective areas. This is the basis for the concern of some people that zoning is essentially *protective* of existing uses and *restrictive* of new uses. But zoning may also be used to specify building types in areas that are in the process of new growth or redevelopment from earlier uses. A new and dramatic example of this strategy is the initiative being taken in Toronto to revitalize two old industrial districts close to downtown. The land use provisions of the zoning regulations were eliminated, leaving only specifications for building height and performance standards, all with the aim of attracting alternative activities to the districts.[11] In this sense, zoning may also be used in a *prospective* way.

In Burnaby, an older inner suburb of Vancouver, there is a similar provision in the land use regulations to accommodate new development, but using a different approach. Planners in Burnaby employ a regulatory device called Comprehensive Development Zoning, or CD zoning, that, in effect, creates a unique zoning district for the site of a project. In order for the developer of the site to obtain a CD zone classification, a Comprehensive Development Plan of the given site must support the application.[12] The CD plan is usually accompanied by architectural, landscape, and engineering drawings, illustrations of the proposed project, and more. As with other proposed zoning changes, CD plans are required to go through public hearings and thereby allow public scrutiny; it is also mandatory in

most provinces that the resulting zoning be consistent with the municipality's overall community plan.

Building Height, Bulk, and Placement Just as important as land use in zoning is the resulting effect of the size of buildings constructed on parcels of land, along with the placement of the buildings on the parcels. For example, **height** controls often existed in cities long before comprehensive zoning was accepted (including in ancient Rome). Controls regulating how close buildings could be placed to the street (now called the **setback**) were also long-lived concerns in cities. Zoning bylaws gathered together these various concerns over the built environment and refined and articulated them in conjunction with the aims for land use districts to further the community environment.

In a typical zoning bylaw, one will find that each land use zone includes specifications for the maximum height of buildings and the proportion of the parcel of land that may be built upon. From these two dimensions—height and building area—the potential **bulk** of a building may be ascertained. If there are requirements for leaving space around the building, specified as setbacks from the boundary lines of the property, then the exact space within which the building may be sited on the property is identified. This exact space on the parcel combined with the allowed bulk of building defines what is called the **building envelope** (see Figure 16.4).

In each zone there is a distinctive building envelope within which property owners may build. If the building being built on a parcel of land completely filled the building envelope, this would be the most intense development that could occur in the zone. In practice, for a number of reasons, this intensity does not always result: for example, owners may not wish their buildings to be as tall as allowed, or may want more space around them, or may not be able to afford to build such a bulky building, or the shape of the building may be different than the building envelope (as with peaked-roof houses in residential zones). Custom is also important in influencing the bulk of buildings. An owner may want his or her building to be in keeping with the bulk of buildings already existing in the district. And existing norms for building bulk, it should be noted, may be a function of long-standing zoning standards.

Figure 16.5 codifies the requirements for building height, lot coverage, and setbacks for a typical set of residential zones in a city. If one were to visit the actual districts in which they apply, it would probably be obvious that the requirements reflect the norm of existing

<table>
<tr><td>**Figure 16.4**</td><td>Basic Dimensions for the Placement, Coverage, and Height of Structures on Building Lots (the "Building Envelope")</td></tr>
</table>

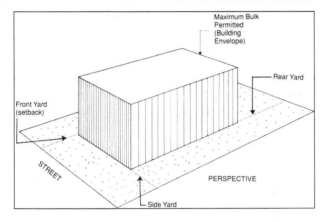

These dimensions determine a "building envelope" and govern the bulk of building allowed on a site.

conditions in those districts of the city. For example, older residential districts may have smaller or more variable yard or height situations than newer, more uniform suburban districts. Often, more affluent residential areas will be found to have requirements for large lots and setbacks commensurate with their more spacious character. Until recently, the regulation of building bulk was confined to areas where large office or apartment buildings could be built. But nowadays, in many cities, bulk regulations are being added to zoning bylaws concerned with one- and two-family residential areas. The trend to "mega homes" (sometimes called "monster homes" or "McMansions") caused consternation in many communities because neighbours felt that the new, large houses changed the neighbourhood character. In effect, what was happening was that builders were now using most, if not all, of the allowable building envelope under the zoning regulations, thereby permitting monster homes to dominate the streetscape (see Figure 16.6). Municipalities in the suburbs of Vancouver have revised residential-area zoning regulations by reducing the size of the building envelope and applying a FAR, usually

Figure 16.5	Typical Building Envelope Standards for Residential Buildings in a Larger City

RESIDENTIAL ZONE	MIN. LOT AREA m²	MIN. LOT WIDTH m	MAX. LOT COVERAGE	FRONT YARD m	SIDE YARD m	REAR YARD m	FLOOR AREA RATIO %	MAX. HEIGHT m	STOREYS
R1	1000	22.5	35	10.5	4.5	9.0	—	10.5	3
R2	500	15.0	30	7.5	3.0	7.5	—	10.5	3
R3	330	9.0	40	4.5	2.5	7.5	—	10.5	3
R4	200	7.5	50	4.5	1.5	4.5	—	10.5	3
R5	1000	15.0	50	6.0	✓	4.5	1.0	12.5	✓
R6	1500	15.0	50	4.5	✓	✓	1.5	25.0	8
R7	1500	15.0	70	4.5	✓	✓	3.0	✓	✓
R8	4000	25.0	100	✓	✓	✓	5.0	✓	✓

✓ Indicates variable standard to suit project.

A zoning bylaw specifies the maximum or minimum measurements for the placement, coverage, and height of buildings in each district. In an older city, it is usually necessary to accept the smaller dimensions of lots plotted before the bylaw (e.g., R3 and R4). In larger cities, provision must be made for tall structures (e.g., R7 and R8), with no height limit but constrained in their bulk. New "monster homes" may require Floor Area Ratios in zones R1 to R4.

Figure 16.6	The Increasing Bulk of Recent Dwellings

SOURCE: GERALD HODGE.

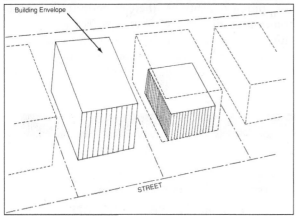

New "monster homes" often dwarf older neighbouring dwellings (top), even though they are built within the same zone regulations. The new houses take advantage of the entire building envelope (bottom).

around 0.3, which would limit the bulk of new dwellings. The Floor Area Ratio, sometimes called the Floor Space Index, was discussed in Chapter 7.

In central commercial areas, it is common to permit building on 100 percent of the lot area in recognition of owners' need to extract maximum use from the higher value land. Larger lot coverage is usually allowed in areas where tall apartment and office buildings are located, also because of the higher value of land and buildings. However, in recent decades, in order to reduce the bulk of such buildings and to provide usable open space for residents of apartments or for office employees, provisions are included in zoning bylaws to require more open space at ground level for every increase in height.

As well, the overall height of tall buildings may be regulated according to the total area of all floors expressed as a ratio of lot area—that is, according to the Floor Area Ratio (FAR) of the building. Thus, referring to Figure 16.5, a FAR of 1.0 in an R5 zone that limits lot coverage to 50 percent means that the owner could build a building of two storeys equal in floor area to the lot size, or else build a taller building, also equal in floor area to the lot size, but covering less than 50 percent of the lot.

Since cities are always changing in their physical form, it is not uncommon to see a conventional urban activity change in its physical characteristics. Such is the case with retailing, an almost inherent urban activity. In the past decade or so, new retailing "formats," as they are called, have appeared in the form of bulky, warehouse-type establishments that dwarf existing retail operations. The advent of these so-called big-box retailers has led many municipalities to revise their zoning regulations and community plans to accommodate a wider mix of retail building types. The town of Markham, Ontario, for example, has added a "retail-warehouse" designation to its zoning provisions.[13]

Density The intensity with which the community's land is used is a basic planning factor because it relates to the issue of congestion in the use of public infrastructure such as water and sewer lines, streets, parks, and so on. Although land uses and building bulk on a parcel of land may be specified, this does not deal with the number of users of the land and buildings. This is especially crucial in residential areas where multiple-family accommodation is provided to ensure that overcrowding does not occur, whether inside or outside of dwellings.

Most zoning bylaws where multiple-family dwellings are common now include specific density regulations. In the community plan, density may be calculated by the number of people per unit of land area. However, the zoning bylaw must be specific enough to relate to individual parcels and buildings. Density specifications in zoning bylaws may take one of two forms, or a combination of both. The first, and most common, is to *specify the maximum number of dwelling units per unit of land area (hectare)*. Various multiple-residence zones may then be created that correspond to existing development patterns or follow new styles and trends in the housing market. At the lower-density end of the scale, zones corresponding to three- and four-storey walk-up apartments may limit development to 25–50 units per hectare, for example. Medium densities (100–200 units per hectare) are usually related to areas in which the buildings would be taller and have elevators, but probably not exceed 10 storeys. High-density zones would be for much taller buildings with densities of 240 units per hectare and more. Of course, what is considered a "high" density or a "low" density is related to local conditions and tastes. (It may help to refer to Figure 7.8, page 177.)

The second method of specifying residential density is according to the *amount of floor area* included in a project site (net density) or in the neighbourhood (gross density). This is sometimes stated as a minimum area (in square metres) in order to ensure that adequate-size apartments are built. Such a regulation is often required in older parts of communities, either where conversion of existing buildings to apartments is likely to occur or where original lot sizes were small. In many urban areas, the bulk of apartment buildings is controlled by a floor area ratio (FAR), which eliminates variations caused by the size of residential units. Such a regulation is usually combined with a limitation placed on the height of buildings.

Other Concerns of Zoning

Parking/Loading Minimum requirements for off-street parking and loading are common in zoning bylaws. Again, the main objective is to minimize possible congestion in the public streets in the vicinity of a property that might be used more intensively, such as for multiple residences or commercial purposes. Parking standards have been developed through planning experience with various land uses. In residential areas, at least one parking space per dwelling unit is usually needed. However, in higher-density areas this may need to be higher in order to accommodate parking by residents and visitors. In commercial and manufacturing areas, the standards are usually set in terms of the gross floor area (or sometimes by the number of employees) on the assumption of providing space for those who drive their cars to work. Loading facilities located off the street are a common requirement in commercial, manufacturing, and institutional zones, with standards usually set in terms of the number of square metres of the establishment.

Signs Most zoning bylaws deal with the size, height, and location of signs on a building or property. Signs tend to be discouraged altogether in residential areas; in commercial areas the signs may be regulated to reduce "sign competition" and produce a particular character for the area (see Figure 16.7). The specifications for signs vary from one community to another as a result of local tastes and preferences. Signs that overhang public streets are regulated as well for safety purposes.

Accessory Buildings Most land uses require, in addition to the principal structure, structures for parking or storage. A garage on the same lot as a single-family house is an accessory use, as is a storage shed on a commercial property and a security guards' building at a manufacturing plant. These are usually quite closely defined in the regulations for each particular zone, including their size and location. The implication is that these uses and structures would not normally be permitted in the zone without the principal use to which they are appendages.

Home Occupations From zoning's earliest days, communities sought to limit commercial activities in residential areas, while usually allowing individuals such as music teachers, insurance agents, doctors, accountants, and hairdressers to offer services from their homes. Traffic, safety, and noise were the concerns with respect to some "home occupations," as they are usually called in zoning bylaws. Until the late 20th century, few people carried on business from their homes, but this has now dramatically changed. Both economic pressures and the potential of computers and other telecommunications have promoted many new home occupations right across the country, in large cities and small. For example, it was estimated that one-third of Toronto's dwellings in 1993 housed some form of business activity or home occupation.[14] This stimulated the city to amend its zoning bylaw to allow a wide range of "new" home occupations. Changes to the exterior would not be allowed, nor would exterior signs advertising the business be allowed; there are similar provisions in other cities.

Aesthetics Although zoning usually strives for compatibility of uses within a zone, many communities also attempt to encourage compatible scale and massing for buildings.[15] However, few explicit specifications of building appearance have been included in zoning bylaws, save those governing the height of buildings. This is largely because zoning grew out of a notion that public intervention in private property should occur only to protect health, safety, and the general welfare of a community.

The regulation of architectural qualities of structures means, of course, being able to define aesthetic norms

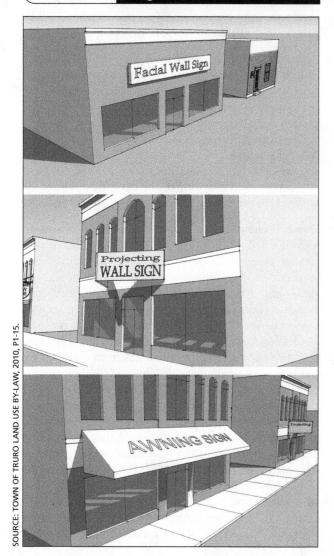

SOURCE: TOWN OF TRURO LAND USE BY-LAW, 2010, P1-15.

These images from the zoning bylaw of Truro N.S., demonstrate how a small town controls signs along its main commercial street. The top image is for a wall sign attached to the façade of the building. The middle image illustrates a projecting wall sign, while the bottom image demonstrates a sign printed on an awning. The bylaw mandates the size and location of each type of sign. This bylaw's illustrated approach helped Truro win a CIP 2011 award for small town planning.

in legally defensible terms, something not easy to do in such a subjective area. A compromise position used in a number of cities is the designation of particular zones in which the architectural plans of structures are reviewed because the areas are considered of major importance in the "civic design" of the community. One such zone was established for Toronto's University Avenue in the 1920s in the hope of achieving a monumental character to this street leading to the provincial legislative buildings. In the 1950s, Vancouver enacted similar regulations for new structures on its West Georgia Street. These two approaches act as a separate "zone" superimposed on the bylaw's district regulations.

Comprehensive Development Zoning, discussed above, does allow design criteria to be applied to new projects. The increased power of computer aided design (CAD) software allows more detailed review of design issues in special control districts such as the area around the Parliament Buildings in Ottawa. These tools are now routinely used to create visualizations of future development, so that the height, bulk, and shadow effects for intensification can be examined at the time of a rezoning. These visualizations have the advantage that they can create images and animated walk-through tours from the viewpoint of a pedestrian, rather than the bird's-eye view created by most traditional architectural models (Figure 16.8).

The difficulty of formulating aesthetic regulations on a comprehensive basis in zoning bylaws has led to several new variations. Within the jurisdiction given by development-control procedures to municipalities, it is possible to request modifications to façades and exterior materials used on buildings. Because of concern over historically important districts, many provinces have enacted legislation allowing the architectural quality to be closely regulated in such districts. Zoning also can aid in this, as the "heritage main street" district in Markham, Ontario, demonstrates.[16] Both these approaches serve to guide private development on a building-by-building basis, in contrast to zoning bylaws, which strive to develop regulations that apply generally to all buildings and properties. It is because the ideal of comprehensive regulations has significant limits that such supplementary tools have come into existence.

Cultural Diversity The increasing cultural diversity of Canadian communities has begun to affect land use planning in general and zoning in particular. New immigrant populations with their different cultural perspectives have frequently encountered difficulty in three facets of the built environment: places of worship, ethnic business enclaves, and housing types.[17] The traditional notion that it is *land use*, not *people*, that is the subject of community planning practice creates an obstacle to changing policies and tools. "People planning" was, with good cause, seen as allowing for human discriminatory practices under the guise of planning, as some early zoning bylaws revealed. This dilemma has been confronted in a number of rezoning applications; a recent Ontario court decision has noted that "land use practices are made by human beings, by people … and, therefore, that social and cultural matters are valid planning and zoning concerns."[18] This is an area of concern that will continue to evolve (see previous discussion in Chapter 13).

Recent Zoning Perspectives

It should come as no surprise that a planning tool that has been around for three or four generations would acquire some critics and require some changes. Indeed, zoning has been blamed for many planning ills over the years that were due more to its misapplication than to inherent flaws. But, like all the planning tools described here, zoning has considerable flexibility and has been applied in a variety of ways to suit local conditions and local preferences. Still, zoning is a simplified view of city development that envisions activities located in discrete districts, housed in distinctive types of structures. It generalizes the pattern of development and then categorizes the activities that take place there in terms of discrete physical forms. This has the result in many communities, especially larger ones, of reducing the diversity of activities that exist in the real world to a limited number of technical categories. The very mixture of activities that gives character to older neighbourhoods may be obscured in the zoning of new residential areas. This is a valid complaint of proponents of **New Urbanism** and **Traditional Neighbourhood Design** (TND).[19] There are now a number of examples across Canada of recent zoning bylaws that promote an approach to neighbourhood planning of a mix of housing types and other uses.[20] Indeed, revisions to zoning bylaws to allow for a **mixture of land uses**, such as retail, housing, office, and home occupations, has now become common across the country to revitalize old commercial and industrial districts.[21] Downtown mixed-use zoning is commonly implemented with a FAR with sliding scale for residential and commercial uses. For example, a downtown zone might permit a maximum FAR of 12.0, with commercial maximum of 8.0 and a residential maximum of 7.0. This would allow a range of uses from 8.0 commercial/4.0 residential to 5.0 commercial/7.0 residential. Some recent mixed-use bylaws are even more flexible, permitting a maximum total number of employees and residents, comprised of any combination of the two.[22]

Mixed-use districts are one response to changing neighbourhood activities or the increased accessibility caused by public transit stations (Figure 16.8). New uses may be accommodated in structures not originally meant for them (such as professional offices in old warehouses or the many new home occupations made possible through telecommuting). Or completely new formats may emerge for an old activity (such as the advent of "big-box" retailing and "ethnic" shopping malls). Planners now allow distinctive land use demands in zoning regulations to "customize regulations" for individual sites, especially in dealing with large, complex developments as with **Comprehensive Development Zoning** described above.

Form-Based Codes

Traditional zoning relies on words, numbers, and maps to control built form and separate land uses. This implementation tool is quite effective at separating

Figure 16.8 Visualization of a Proposed Mixed-Use Centre at a Rapid Transit Station

Before and after images for proposed mixed-use redevelopment of a commuter rail transit station in the GTA (greater Toronto area) in 3-D visualization. Station intensification is encouraged by provincial guidelines that specify a minimum density for each transit node and corridor.

Chapter 16 Land Use Regulation Tools for Plan Implementation land uses, but this objective has become much less important in most Canadian communities in the 21st century, following the decline of noxious heavy industry, increase in mixed uses, and rise of service and creative industries. However, traditional zoning has been much less effective in controlling built form. Residential densities based on units per net hectare allow wildly different building mass depending on whether the units are 40-square-metre bachelor apartments or 400-square-metre luxury suites. Similarly, most zoning bylaws consider a 20-storey apartment tower on 5 percent of the lot as essentially the same as two-storey townhouses covering 50 percent of the lot, except for the height (Figure 7.9, page 179). The tower and the townhouses are both residential land uses at a net FAR of 1.0, yet the former would be unacceptable intensification adjacent to single-family homes in most Canadian communities.

Most intensification battles are caused by similar conflicts over **building types**, rather than over **land uses**. A tower is not appropriate adjacent to single homes, regardless of its use or density. Similarly, a single storey commercial building with a drive-through and a parking lot out front will destroy the integrity of a main street, regardless of whether its use or density conforms to a zoning bylaw. Unfortunately, the words and numbers in traditional zoning bylaws are not very good at managing building-type conflicts, specifying how buildings relate to the public realm, or creating worthy places.

Visual codes that rely mainly on drawings appear to be more effective for place-making.[23] They can specify building types, accommodate mixed uses, and guide urban design issues. For politicians and the general public they also have the advantage of being easier to interpret than the dense legal zoning texts. These form-based codes emerged from suburban mixed-use projects and have recently been adopted to control development in major American cities such as Austin, Texas and Miami, Florida. In Canada, they have been adopted to control the design of several new suburban neighbourhoods and the entire City of Revelstoke, British Columbia (See Figure 16.9).[24]

Rezoning and Plan Amendments

The outright revision of a zoning bylaw, or of a community plan, for that matter, can be seen as a means of adjusting to special

Rezoning Applications

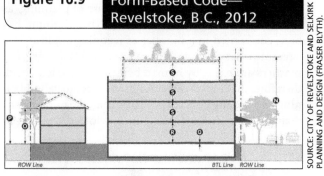

Figure 16.9 Form-Based Code—Revelstoke, B.C., 2012

This diagram from Revelstoke's Unified Development Code shows how the techniques of form-based coding can be deployed to control mixed-use building types in a small city. Clear graphics illustrate the heights of the main structure and outbuildings (N & P), the location for retail (R), and the build-to-line (BTL) that ensures a continuous street-wall on a main street.

needs and changes in the community environment. The reason for not considering revision sooner in this discussion of the myriad of adjustment tools is that it represents a more far-reaching step, involving a broader public interest. In the opinion most people involved in conceiving and administering plans, this is a step that should not be taken lightly. Provincial legislatures require formal steps to be taken for an amendment, steps that are much the same as those for the original enactment of a zoning bylaw or community plan.

The extra statutory hurdles in the amending process, as compared to the other forms of adjustment, reflect the need to provide security in the continuance of major commitments to planning decisions. In the case of zoning bylaws, particularly those of long standing, property owners come to rely on the district standards and have a right to expect their continuance unless a major change can be justified on planning grounds. (Indeed, it is not unreasonable to call amendments "major variances.") For the community plan, the rationale for amendment should be more substantive, such as a major change in growth patterns, the introduction of new forms of transportation such as a rapid transit line, the establishment of large, new land uses, or the disposition of the community to alter its course of development. A change in a community plan often necessitates an amendment to the community's zoning bylaw, and a proposed bylaw amendment may signal the need to consider a plan change. Good planning practice makes these two initiatives interdependent, and some provinces require that the implications for each be considered simultaneously. Amendments of bylaws and plan changes should be possible when the planning considerations are substantial and the community as a whole is in agreement with making the change.

Planning Tools for Vacant and Undeveloped Lands

A characteristic of the built environment of cities and towns is that its development usually takes place on individual parcels of land. These parcels are created by splitting up large tracts of land through a formal process known as **land subdivision**. The process is formal because of the need to register and certify land ownership with respect to these parcels. But the process is also part of a larger process of the economic land market—supplying developable parcels of land to the community. In the latter case, land subdivision is a competitive process by which each subdivider aims to attract development to his or her new parcels of land. It should be noted that land subdivision might also occur on those sites approved for redevelopment (as described above) and not just on vacant land.

One of the earliest difficulties confronted by community planners was achieving satisfactory town extensions as cities and towns expanded. Canada's first planning acts recognized that the creation of new parcels of land could have adverse effects on both the nature and direction of the future development of the community. There was experience with subdivisions in which individual parcels had inadequate access from adjoining streets, streets that did not align with or match the size of, and building lots that were not drained properly or were not even of sufficient size and shape to create a pleasant, much less efficient, built environment. Since the community has the responsibility to provide public services and street access to all parcels of land, it has a direct financial interest in the proper subdivision of land for future development. It was the early planning acts that established this community interest to maintain consistent standards among competing land subdividers, and to create the kind of environment that was compatible with the community's aims and within the community's economic capability to maintain. Thus, emphasis was put on the cost and quality of the subdivision, as Canada Mortgage and Housing Corporation noted, three decades ago.[25] A contemporary version of these dilemmas occurs with the establishment of gated communities, wherein private subdivisions are closed off to public access and local street patterns are disrupted.[26] This and other issues of gated communities are discussed in the next chapter.

Subdivision Control

Subdivision Control

The tool developed by planners in response to the above need is known generally as **subdivision control**. In essence, it consists of the authority of the community to approve any plans for splitting up land for development to ensure that such plans meet local standards for health, safety, and convenience. In subdivision control, community approval is tied to the province's power over registration and certification of valid parcels of land for future sale. This enables planning authorities to exercise a high degree of control over the manner in which land can be used for residential building or other purposes, as well as the timing of development.

Provincial planning legislation vests subdivision-control powers in provincial or local authorities, and sometimes in both. The municipality gives "draft" approval and the province grants "final" approval to the registered plan of a subdivision. There is usually a provision stating that registered plans are not required where only one or two small parcels are being created, or where the new parcels are too large to be sold as building lots. Provisions of the latter kind are known as "consents to a land severance" and constitute a special (and not insignificant) form of land subdivision regulation, which will be dealt with in a later section.

Subdivision control has two basic components, one substantive and the other procedural. On the substantive side, this tool attempts to obtain high-quality built environments. It does this by subjecting plans that propose the subdivision of land to an appraisal of their content, according to planning and engineering standards. On the procedural side, subdivision control operates as a monitoring process, with prescribed steps and with respect to all those public bodies having an interest in the outcome of the proposed land subdivision and subsequent development. The procedural, formal side is necessary because of the constraints that this scrutiny places on the ownership rights of those proposing the subdivision and of the ultimate owners of the subdivided parcels alike.

It can be seen that subdivision control is a *process* type of planning tool (in contrast to zoning, which is legislative). Subdivision-control processes differ in detail from community to community and from province to province, with respect to both provincial planning institutions and concepts of subdivision standards. On the general level, the substantive and procedural components of all the provinces have much in common. We deal now with each of these components briefly, concentrating on residential subdivisions, which constitute the bulk of subdivision activities in most communities.

Subdivision Standards

Central to subdivision control is the examination of the actual design of the proposed subdivision and an appraisal of the standards and dimensions used in its layout. A subdivision plan, as a Newfoundland planning manual states, "is in itself a small planning scheme."[27] It is thus scrutinized according to planning criteria pertaining to the form and density of housing, street systems, open space, and essential community services. Since a subdivision is likely to involve modification of the land surface, various engineering criteria pertaining to drainage, road construction, and the installation of public utilities are also invoked in appraising a plan of subdivision.

Most provinces, in their planning legislation, establish the general factors that a proposed plan must take into consideration. In the Ontario Planning Act, a plan of subdivision must indicate the legal boundaries of all parcels, the location and widths of streets, the intended use of parcels, natural features of the site, physical features such as railways and highways, and the availability of water supplies and other municipal services. Such a plan, obviously, contains a good deal of detail and must be accurately drawn; subdivision plans are usually required to be certified by a licensed land surveyor as to the boundaries of the overall site and the individual parcels. This is called the **draft plan**, since it may still undergo revisions before final approval is given. The draft plan is also required to consider subdivisions, streets, and land uses on adjoining lands, as well as any zoning or other land use controls pertaining to the site.

In addition to these basic formal requirements of the planning legislation, most provinces and many communities have manuals or handbooks that set forth design standards for subdivisions. They are part of a continuing effort to promote good quality subdivision design, an outcome that is easier to advocate than to achieve, as seen in Chapter 11. There are clearly many factors that contribute to the ultimate quality of the residential environment that will result from a subdivision plan. No simple list can possibly encompass all of them; however, a set of questions that planners use in reviewing residential proposals will provide a basic overview of

concerns (see Figure 16.10). Before leaving this discussion, the reader should note that where a subdivision plan is intended to accommodate commercial or industrial uses, analogous subdivision standards are applied in appraising it.

Subdivision Application Procedures

Subdivision Plans

Subdivision control is a system that prescribes the way the subdivider applies for a permit that allows a tract of land to be split up and parcels sold off. Because of legal constraints, the province defines a procedure to be followed in applying for approval of the plan for a subdivision, as well as the prerequisites for such approval. Procedures differ among provinces, largely as a result of where the final authority for approving a plan is lodged. Some have reserved this power for the provincial minister in charge or for appointed officials. Others have delegated subdivision-approval powers to municipalities; still others involve such intermediate-level bodies as regional planning commissions or metropolitan governments. There are, however, five features common to all subdivision control procedures:

1. **Specified process.** In order to protect the rights of owners to subdivide their land, the process of applying for approval is specified. It indicates the form the application must take, the steps the plan's review will follow, and often the maximum amount of time the process will take.

2. **Plan circulation.** Since a proposed subdivision of land may affect the interests and activities of a wide array of agencies, a draft plan is circulated broadly for comment and recommendations. Typically, all provincial government departments with an interest (such as transportation, housing, energy, agriculture, health, and environment) are asked to review a plan. Also, public and private utilities, transportation companies, and special-purpose bodies are included in the review process, along with various departments of the local government.

3. **Conditions for approval.** The subdivider is considered responsible for the provision of the roads, parks, and public utilities necessary to serve the subdivision. Since they ultimately come under community ownership (except in gated communities), it is necessary to specify how they shall be paid for and the standards to which they will be built.

4. **Subdivision agreement.** In order to ensure that the basic services are provided for the subdivision, a contract or subdivision agreement must usually be signed between the subdivider and the municipality, and is often registered against the deed to the property. These agreements cover such matters as staging of development, provision of services, road standards, minimum construction and mate-

rial standards, conveyance of lands for parks, and demolition and removal of existing buildings.

5. **Final plan.** The plan of subdivision is not operative until it has received final approval. Such approval is given only after any conditions imposed on the draft plan from the review process have been fulfilled and a subdivision agreement exists to secure the necessary services and stan-

---

Figure 16.10 Planning Checklist for Proposed Residential Subdivisions

REVIEW EACH SUBDIVISION PLAN WITH THESE QUESTIONS IN MIND:

Community Context
❏ Does the street layout conform to the existing street pattern?
❏ Does the plan relate well to existing community facilities?
❏ Does the plan conform to the policies of the community plan?
❏ Does the plan provide adequately for the education, recreation, and shopping needs of residents?

Residential Needs
❏ Do the proposed dwelling types suit community needs?
❏ Do dwelling arrangements ensure privacy?
❏ Will dwellings be affected by excessive noise, dust, or fumes?
❏ Is the size of lots adequate for the dwellings?

Streets and Parking
❏ Are the grades, widths, and intersections of streets adequate?
❏ Are parking provisions adequate?
❏ Is pedestrian access separated from the street?

Public Services and Utilities
❏ Has drainage been carefully considered?
❏ Are water and sewage facilities adequate and conveniently located?
❏ Is street lighting adequate?

Environmental Considerations
❏ Does the arrangement of lots and dwellings make the best use of the climate?
❏ Have trees been left to stabilize the soil?
❏ Has provision been made so that stormwater runoff does not pollute other water bodies?
❏ Has the amount of paved area been minimized?

Aesthetic Considerations
❏ Do dwelling arrangements result in attractive streetscapes?
❏ Will street furniture be provided?
❏ Are natural features of the site incorporated in the design?

dards. At this point, the plan may be registered and will be binding on all future landowners. No additional demands can be made on the developer of the land.

The subdivision plan-review process is the community's opportunity to have a direct effect on the outcome of the development of a portion of its built environment. There are, as well, two vital elements the community should be looking for in reviewing plans of subdivision, regardless of whether it is the final approving authority. The first is to determine the proposal's *compatibility* with the aims and design envisioned for the area in the community's overall plan. In conjunction with this, the community reviews the plan's compliance with zoning regulations that already apply to the area, as well as the possibility that amendments to both the zoning bylaw and community plan may be required to accommodate the subdivision. The second facet that the community will need to be concerned with is whether the subdivision is *premature* or not. An approved subdivision makes demands on the community's resources, in that services must be provided, roads and parks maintained, and so on, whenever the land is built upon and people come to live there. It is therefore in the community's interest to know the timing or staging of the actual development. In most provinces, a community can establish conditions regarding the staging of development on the site to coincide with its own plans for investments in services as well as with its desires to achieve a particular spatial pattern of development. For example, where urban growth boundaries are in effect, the subdivision's conformance with them will need to be checked.[28] In the larger sense, subdivision control becomes part of an integrated planning process, rather than being an isolated act affecting only one proponent and one area.

Consents and Severances

A special form of land subdivision, particularly for rural areas, is the severing of one or two small parcels of land from a large tract such as a farm. A subdivision plan is normally not required for this purpose, but since it is necessary to register the new parcel and convey title properly, a formal process is required. It is known as **granting consent to the land severance**, or, in popular terms, simply as a "consent" or "severance."

This process was, until recent decades, mostly used to allow farmers to create a homestead site for themselves or for a close relative also involved in the farming or other rural activity, and to create occasional lots for summer cottages. However, with the increased demand

for year-round country residences and cottages after 1950, obtaining a consent became source of income to rural landowners. It also became a source of problems for rural communities by creating scattered and ribbon development that consumed agricultural land with additional difficulties and costs of providing services and road maintenance (Figure 16.11). In recreational regions, increased numbers of severances for cottages often led to the pollution of lakes. Indeed, the ills associated with excessive use of rural severances led to the popularization of the term "sprawl" to characterize development in fringe areas of cities and in rural areas and, more recently, to efforts to promote Smart Growth (which will be discussed in the next chapter).

Consents must be formally approved, often by the same approving body that processes subdivision plans. A consent is usually required to meet the same conditions as a subdivision plan with regard to dedicating land for streets, road widening, and parks. However, beyond these basic requirements, provincial planning legislation is noticeably silent on the planning criteria that should be considered. Some efforts were made by local approving authorities in Ontario in the 1970s to establish criteria for consents—for example, conformity to community plans, maintaining integrity of high-grade agricultural lands, and adequacy of waste disposal to prevent pollution of nearby bodies of water. The results can be characterized as inconsistent, even in these areas.

| Figure 16.11 | Rural Consents on Prime Agricultural Land |

SOURCE: THE FARMLAND PRESERVATION RESEARCH PROJECT AT THE UNIVERSITY OF GUELPH.

Too many adjacent residential lots on prime agricultural land may compromise the effectiveness of this farm community near Guelph, Ontario.

An Ontario report calls consents "the Achilles' heel of planning."[29] And a probe of the issue in New Brunswick cites the lack of a planning system that could provide for "suitable consideration of the overall implications" of individual land-severance proposals.[30] While individual applications for a consent may be justified, it is the accumulation of consent decisions that needs to be considered. Two provinces, Québec and British Columbia, appear to have made some headway in reducing rural consents, especially where agricultural land is concerned. British Columbia established its Agricultural Land Reserves in 1973, and Québec established its "protected areas" under its Commission de protection du territoire agricole in 1978. Although there has not been a halt to the subdivision of agricultural land as was intended by these government interventions, it is clear that it has been greatly reduced.[31]

Replotting Schemes

A special form of subdivision planning that has received much attention from planners in western Canada has to do with salvaging subdivisions that attracted little or no development. The practice is called **replotting**, because it involves redesigning the street system, the pattern of building lots, and the open space of a pre-existing legal subdivision. In many communities in the past, the promise of rapid growth often led to considerable subdivision of land in excess of actual growth (see Chapter 4). These subdivisions usually predated planning and subdivision-control practices and, not infrequently, were inefficient and unimaginative gridiron designs bearing little relation to topographic features or existing community patterns. Many of these older, undeveloped subdivisions were in fringe areas, and, as communities expanded, especially after World War II, they were found to be incompatible with present-day planning and subdivision standards.

Provisions were incorporated into planning legislation to allow communities to, in effect, redesign these old subdivisions. A replotting scheme in Alberta involves three steps.[32] First, the existing subdivision must be cancelled and all parcels consolidated. Second, a new design is formulated by the community and registered. Third, the newly subdivided land is redistributed among affected landowners. Replotting offers a number of advantages to a community: more efficient street patterns and utility service, more pleasing residential settings, and higher tax returns from land that was previously underutilized.

Condominium Subdivisions

A type of subdivision of property that is relatively new in the realm of planning is that of condominium ownership, or "strata-title," as it is called in some provinces. Essentially, it denotes conveying ownership to a housing unit without conveying title to the land on which it sits. The latter, the site, is held in common by the owners of all the dwelling units sharing the site. The typical forms of **condominiums** are row housing and apartment buildings, although this also occurs in commercial and industrial development projects. The main advantages are the sharing of common community facilities and having no responsibilities for site maintenance, which is provided by a corporation formed by the owners.

Because creating a condominium project results in splitting up a larger piece of property among several owners, most provinces have developed means to ensure property rights and consideration of planning standards. Condominium legislation has been developed to cope with the special features of ownership, and existing subdivision-control legislation and regulations are used to allow examination of the planning implications of the project (Figure 16.12).

Condominium development may take the form of either a brand new building(s) or transference of the single ownership of an existing building to shared

| Figure 16.12 | Condominium Plan for an Apartment Building |

SOURCE: YORK REGION STANDARD CONDOMINIUM PLAN 1134, REGISTERED 14TH NOVEMBER 2008. © MMM GROUP LIMITED.

This drawing shows the floor plan (right) and section (left) of an apartment building, creating a condominium plan. A draft version of this drawing was circulated for comments and approval in a process similar to a subdivision; except that condominium plans have three dimensions.

ownership. The latter approach, **condominium conversion** of existing multiple-unit rental buildings, has received special attention from planners because it neither creates any additional dwelling units nor assures present residents of the continuation of their housing. While conversion is popular with owners of older apartment buildings, it has frequently proved contentious when tenants are forced to move as buildings are upgraded to attract higher-income purchasers. Elderly and/or low-income tenants are often caught in such conversions and must try to find accommodation in a rental housing market that, in many cases, is already tight. Since condominium conversion may actually reduce the stock of rental units in a community, many cities have enacted conversion policies that limit conversions where the rental vacancy rate is abnormally low and where present tenants are not going to be the subsequent condominium purchasers in the project. The experience in Montréal is a good example of the difficulties that surround this issue.[33] With over three-quarters of city households being renters, it searched for 20 years for a solution. "Benchmark" rents were finally established in 1993 so that conversions could not occur in apartment buildings with rents below this level, the purpose being to protect low-income tenants, including university and college students. Even this can produce a dilemma for municipalities that often enjoy higher tax returns from the refurbished apartments.

Development Control

Development Permits

Development control was an important addition to the planner's kit of implementation tools during the 1950s. It is an extension of municipal power to undertake zoning and gives them the right to review proposed plans for new development in already built-up areas. Under normal zoning regulations, there is no stipulation that developers reveal their plans for a vacant or redeveloped site, as long as they adhere to the provisions for land use, height, and lot coverage (and all building regulations). Thus, whether a building will "fit" into an area in terms of its scale, its appearance, and its effect on traffic may often not be known until the building is completed. In rapidly growing downtown areas in the 1950s, this caused planners many problems. They therefore adopted the largely British method of requiring development plans to be submitted for scrutiny before construction could begin, even though they were in compliance with zoning

provisions. In this way, not only might the community be saved trouble but also the developer might be alerted to more attractive alternatives.

Origins and Nature

Until the 1950s, Canadian planning practice closely followed the primary mode of land use control in the United States—zoning. However, in Canada, neither the old BNA Act nor the more recent Charter of Rights and Freedoms entrenches property rights, as does the U.S. Constitution. Thus, for zoning in Canada there is no legal basis to limit land use regulation.[34] Development-control approaches entered Canadian planning practice largely through the efforts of British and British-trained planners who emigrated to Canada after World War II. British planning practice never embraced zoning, preferring to leave responsibility for plan implementation in the hands of local administrators. Development control was considered particularly useful for the period during which a formal community plan was being prepared, especially in fast-growing cities. Each proposal for new development, buildings, or subdivisions thus could be reviewed to ensure consistency with the aims of the emerging plan, and a development permit was issued as warranted. The system was widely used in western Canada from the mid-1950s, but did not enter regular planning practice in Ontario until 1970. While it began as an interim measure to be used during plan preparation, development control has become part of the routine of planning practice, in conjunction with zoning.

Substantive Focus

Development control is known by various names among the provinces (see Figure 9.7, page 228): in Alberta, the term is **development permit**, while in Ontario, the term used for basic review is **site-plan control**, but municipalities have the option of deploying a more comprehensive development permit system. The approach is, however, similar in most jurisdictions. Development-control regulation is invoked at the actual time a proposal is made to erect a new building or to significantly expand an existing one, usually within predetermined areas of the community (such as a waterfront area, business district, or heritage zone). Importantly, the focus is on the building, rather than its use. Since development control works within the context of zoning, it starts with the premise that the zoning regulations as to the use of the site and the allowable building envelope provide the basic frame of reference. The latter are usually not negotiable at this stage of regulation.

Development control is concerned with the actual placement of the building on the site (within the building envelope), the massing of the building, its relation to surrounding buildings and areas, its relation to streets, and, in some provinces, its appearance (Figure 16.13). The following extract from the Ontario Planning Act illustrates the scope of the approach one generally finds in development control. The person or group proposing the development must provide the municipality with the following:

1. Plans showing the location of all buildings and structures to be erected and showing the location of all facilities and works (e.g., swimming pools, fences and walls, landscaping, walkways, outside lighting, parking areas); and

2. Drawings showing plan, elevation, and cross-section views for each building ... sufficient to display:
   a. the massing and conceptual design of the proposed building;
   b. the relationship of the proposed building to adjacent buildings, streets, and exterior areas to which members of the public have access; and
   c. the provision of interior walkways, stairs, elevators, and escalators to which members of the public have access from streets, open spaces, and interior walkways in adjacent buildings.[35]

A development-control bylaw usually requires proponents of a project, which occurs in a specified development-control district, to submit their application and plans for review, especially for commercial, industrial, and apartment projects. Many places have specified their entire community as subject to development control. The applications may be reviewed by a committee or a designated official on whose recommendation a development agreement or contract is drawn up, specifying the conditions that the developer is legally bound to fulfill in the actual construction process.

The original purpose for which development control was introduced into Canadian planning—the bridging of plan-making and zoning—still exists in most provinces. In specific areas, it may be necessary or desirable to reconsider present zoning and planning policies. Development control can be invoked on a limited-term basis under what are often called "interim control bylaws" or, more commonly, "holding bylaws." This tool, a hybrid of zoning and development control, must specify the area, the duration of time for which the bylaw applies, and the types of changes that will be allowed in that period. Usually only minor changes will be allowed, according to existing zoning regulations.

The availability of development-control powers opened up avenues of plan implementation beyond those envisioned for it originally. The technique enables a community's plan-makers to deal with developers and their projects on a *case-by-case* basis, rather than on the uniform basis found in zoning. Development control, then, means that a community can enter into *negotiations* with regard to each project and impose individualized conditions for it within the limits of the existing zoning. This approach "provides and encourages flexibility and variety in development that zoning would not allow," says planning lawyer Stanley Makuch, because "different developments create different demands."[36] The advantage of planners being able to directly influence a project's outcome is very attractive. At the same time, it underlines the role of the community plan in providing guidelines for such negotiations. Many larger communities have established site-plan control guidelines to suggest local norms and establish a framework for staff review. This discretionary approach is prominent in much of community planning today.

A number of other new tools for plan implementation were developed over the past few decades that expanded the approach of development control. One might call them "hands-on" approaches, and they are now a distinguishing feature of Canadian planning practice. Bonus zoning was introduced as incentives to developers in order to attain the kind of development desired in the

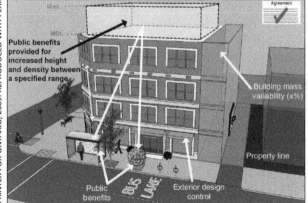

Figure 16.13 Development Permit System

Most development permit systems allow for approval of height, massing, siting, and landscaping. Ontario's system also considers bonus zoning for public benefits.

Chapter 16 Land Use Regulation Tools for Plan Implementation location desired (Figure 16.14). Other municipalities used Comprehensive Development Zoning and Planned Unit Development techniques in order to be able to work with developers before a project is fully designed. This kind of planning has become increasingly common as planners seek ways to obtain better-quality physical surroundings.[37]

Transfer of Development Rights

As noted earlier in this chapter, zoning defines for each property a building envelope in which the owner has a right to develop a structure of a specified volume or envelope—that is, there are "development rights" for each property. Several decades ago some communities began to allow an owner to sell the development rights on one property to someone who owned land located in an area where the community wished to encourage development, such as in an urban redevelopment area. This policy of Transfer of Development Rights (TDR) is now widely practised in large cities (see also Chapter 7).

TDR basically shifts density potential from one area to another. It aims at benefiting three interests. One is the owner, who can sell the development rights on a parcel on which he or she cannot or does not wish to use all of a building envelope, perhaps because there is already a satisfactory building on it. Another is the purchaser, or transferee, of the development rights who may benefit by obtaining sufficient additional density to make a project economically feasible. And the community could also benefit, sometimes doubly, by achieving development where it had been planned, and by limiting development at the location from which the development rights were transferred. For example, in some cities TDR has saved historically important buildings from demolition and replacement. However, this planning power can also be abused. For example in the 1980s, a Toronto developer had mixed-use zoning on two parcels, one at King and Bay Streets and the other on the waterfront. He abused TDR by moving all the waterfront commercial rights to create a taller office tower at King and Bay and move all the residential development to huge slab buildings on the waterfront, thus perverting the purpose of mixing uses. (This abuse is usually foiled by limits of 100 metres or so to the transfer of density).

The process through which such transfers take place is one of negotiation between property owners and city officials. This and other forms of negotiation in the planning process are discussed in Chapter 15. While TDR can be useful in meeting urban-design objectives in cities, this tool can also be used to implement agricultural or ecological-planning objectives in rural areas. Conservation organizations have purchased the development rights of private wetlands and forests using legal agreements in the past. But municipalities need the power to transfer rights from developable lands to link up green corridors and patches as recommended by the principles of landscape ecology.

SOURCE: BUILDING BLOCKS FOR SUSTAINABLE PLANNING - 5 IN A SERIES OF 12: HEIGHT AND DENSITY BONUSING (S. 37) MINISTRY OF MUNICIPAL AFFAIRS AND HOUSING © QUEEN'S PRINTER FOR ONTARIO, 2008. REPRODUCED WITH PERMISSION.

Figure 16.14	Density Bonusing and Transfer of Development Rights

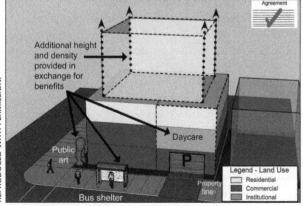

The building in this site plan drawing would receive extra height and a density bonus in exchange for public benefits such as the daycare centre and public art. Transfer of Development Rights (TDR) is another form of reward for a public benefit, such as preserving a heritage building or wetland. The development rights that would normally be associated with the heritage or ecological property would be transferred to an adjacent parcel such as the one in this image.

Building Regulations and Other Permits

Building Permits In general, municipalities in Canada have the power to regulate the construction of buildings within their jurisdiction. The reason for this is to ensure that new buildings and the reconstruction of older buildings will not endanger the health, safety, or general welfare of the public. This power to approve building construction derives from a constitutional power—**police power**, in legal terms— delegated to the municipality by the province. The task of the municipality, in essence, is to enforce the provincial building code that sets basic standards for construction. To accomplish this, the municipality employs building inspectors whose job it is to review plans for buildings and to issue building permits if the plans meet basic standards of the code. Building inspectors also monitor the actual construction to ensure adherence to the agreed upon plans.

The issuance of a building permit represents, in many ways, the final step in developing a building project. It is, therefore, a crucial step for the municipality. It can determine at this point whether the construction plans for the building conform to community-planning expectations of the project. Not infrequently, building plans are found to contravene the setback and height regulations of zoning bylaws. Many communities combine a review of zoning requirements with the building inspector's review of construction plans at this stage. In a related way, the issuance of a building permit is seen as the indication that building on a site is going to proceed shortly thereafter, but there is no guarantee of this. There are usually some sites in a city or town on which development is preferred by the community to occur as soon as possible. Increasingly, communities are tying the approval of zoning amendments and development agreements to either the issuance or the duration of a building permit.

Occupancy permits are often required, especially for residential projects, before use of a building can be allowed. The prime criteria at this stage are usually the meeting of fire and other safety conditions. Since zoning bylaws and/or development agreements may have required the buildings to meet other conditions, such as the provision of open space or walkways, this is another opportunity to ensure that planning conditions have also been met. To some, this may suggest undue constraint on developers and buildings, but it should be remembered that construction requires a legal, contractual arrangement with the municipality in which the steps of issuing building and occupancy permits are specified. There is also the case of development permits that may be needed and their terms satisfied, as discussed in Chapter 13. The municipality should be rigorous in taking these steps and in verifying any related planning provisions, and it need not be dilatory in its procedures.

Fine-Tuning Regulatory Tools

The main tools of land use regulation used by planners—zoning and subdivision control—are founded on the principle of being universally and uniformly applicable in regard to the properties and the landowners in the community. In other words, the regulations that will affect the development of a property apply equally to all similar properties and are known to the owner beforehand. This means that land use regulations are formulated in *general* terms to cover normal configurations of site, location, and property characteristics. But among the numerous parcels of land and kinds of projects to which these must apply, it is evident that not all will have similar characteristics. Moreover, the regulations may cause hardship for some owners, or result in anomalous land use arrangements for the community. Thus, a number of planning tools have been developed to respond to special circumstances of properties and land uses not adequately covered by the general regulations. The most common of these tools for fine-tuning what occurs in the built environment are described briefly below. In effect, they refine the impact of zoning.

Variances

Zoning bylaws cannot cover all the distinctive situations that might affect each of the parcels of land within a zone. There may be unusual conditions of topography, size, shape, and location that adversely affect the development of a parcel in the manner envisioned in the regulations. For example, a parcel with a steep slope may not allow, without undue cost, a building to be sited to meet setback requirements, or the specific land uses applying to a property in a commercial zone may not cover a similar use that is being proposed. To avoid creating situations of special hardship, planning legislation allows adjustments in bylaw provisions to be considered in regard to a *particular parcel* of land. One type of adjustment is called a **variance**, since it allows the provisions of the zoning bylaw to vary from its stated terms. (Versions of this tool have been used extensively when responding to land use situations in multicultural communities where conditions may warrant variations in implementation of regulations; see Chapter 13).

Variances introduce a needed degree of flexibility in the application of a zoning bylaw, which otherwise might require a formal amendment. The variance does, however, operate in a delicate area of judgment, wherein it must be decided whether a *major* hardship or difficulty is created by the regulations and, moreover, whether in relaxing the zoning standards there might be adverse effects on adjoining properties and the community environment. Since the variance that is allowed is expected both to create only minimal effects on surrounding properties and to convey no special advantage for the applicant, it is usually referred to as a "minor variance." Criteria defining what qualifies as minor have never been well established, which has led, at worst, to numerous abuses of the variance and, at best, to controversy over many decisions.

The granting of a variance, because it affects property rights and also involves an appeal from the requirements of legislation, is a formal process spelled out in provincial legislation. It is a process that usually devolves to the municipality in the form of a special appeal body. The names of these appeal bodies differ from province to province. In Manitoba, the appeal body is called the Variation Board; in Saskatchewan, the Board of Zoning Appeal; and in Ontario, the Committee of Adjustment. These bodies are usually required to give notice of the application for a variance to all property owners within the vicinity and to provide reasons for their decision, which is ordinarily final and binding. In some communities, the municipal planning staff coordinates the activities of the appeal body, but in most cases no connection with local planning efforts is attempted or, possibly, even recognized.

Non-Conforming Uses

A zoning bylaw is essentially future-oriented, but in already-developed areas, its standards are not likely to fit all the uses and structures that existed before it came into effect. The concept of *natural justice* prevents the violation of property rights that existed before the bylaw was passed. Thus, there may be uses and structures that do not conform to the standards in the new regulations but that will legally be allowed to continue. It is customary to refer to them as **legal non-conforming uses**. There are actually three forms of pre-existing conditions that may not conform to the current bylaw. One is the *use* to which a property is put, such as a store in a residential neighbourhood; another is a *structure* that may be situated so as to not provide the required yard space; and the last is a *lot* that is smaller than would now be required.

Non-conforming use status copes with anomalies between the standards of earlier development and the standards now favoured by the community in its current bylaw. However, if the community wants to achieve its new standards, then there must be a way of bringing the earlier development into conformity with them. Thus, most zoning bylaws have provisions that prohibit or limit any expansion of the non-conforming structure and limit the non-conforming use to what it was at the time of the new bylaw, as well as provisions for rebuilding in the event of the building's destruction by, say, fire. In this way, the aim of the community to have the non-conforming uses replaced in time is balanced against vested property rights. The record of non-conformities disappearing is not salutary in most cities, and there are many instances of applications to enlarge such uses. An application for a change in a non-conforming use is often handled by the same zoning-appeal body that deals with variances, and the procedures are much the same.

Planned Unit Development

Many communities have included in their zoning bylaws a means by which the requirements of normal zoning districts may be modified and more innovative standards incorporated in the plan for a project. This approach, which is generally called **Planned Unit Development** (PUD), offers the developer an option to build within a set of requirements established especially for the project, rather than in strict conformity with existing regulations. The incentive for the developer in PUD may lie in achieving a few more dwelling units, in being able to mix several kinds of dwelling units and even some retail uses, or in producing a better quality and hence more marketable project. The community, of course, also wants the better design and offers, through PUD, to relax such standards as height, yard size, lot size, and dwelling type in return for working along with the developer to achieve a mutually acceptable project that has been planned as a unit.

The most noticeable result of PUD is that more common open space is available to residents than would occur if normal zoning regulations were followed. This is often obtained by foregoing the requirements for side yards, which are usually underused, reducing the width of lots, and allowing dwellings to be built with no intervening space. This approach is called **zero-lot-line** and offers the opportunity to stagger, cluster, and group dwellings instead of using the traditional form of subdivision with standard setbacks. There may also be noticeable savings in land costs for each dwelling, thereby providing more affordable housing. This, along with efficient use of utilities, increased transit demand, and reduced automobile usage are attributes we now find in the Smart Growth strategy for planning. The Alberta Planning Act of 1977, for example, quite explicitly promoted PUD by permitting municipalities to apply to have an Innovative Residential Developments Area established. The success of PUD depends on negotiations between municipal staff and the developer. The Comprehensive Development Zoning approach used by Burnaby, British Columbia, referred to earlier in the chapter, works essentially the same way as PUD by requiring that a comprehensive plan detailing the project be submitted prior to rezoning.

Community Design Tools

Conventional Canadian planning practice in the 1970s and 1980s focused upon land use and avoided aesthetic issues. But, as we saw in Chapter 5, concern over community appearance revived in the late 20th century with urban design units added to planning departments in most large cities and in some of the leading suburban municipalities. The urban-design toolkit available for planners varies widely from city to city, but some of the more common policies are **design guidelines, view planes, design review,** and **special districts.** In addition, form-based codes have begun to emerge in some districts.

Surprisingly, some of these urban design approaches can be implemented using standard land use planning tools, simply re-calibrated to create alternative built environments. For example, zoning bylaws were used to create the skyscraper canyons along Manhattan's avenues, and also to replicate Don Mill's characteristics across Canadian suburbs. Zoning can also be used to implement mixed-use urban precincts, New Urbanist neighbourhoods, and gated communities. The key point is to develop a strong urban design concept that fits the intended community and then prepare tools to implement it. Mixing and matching guidelines and codes from various cities rarely lead to good results.

Design Guidelines

Design guidelines are a combination of text, graphics, and images that explain an urban-design concept aimed at shaping public space or built form (see Figure 16.15). Typically, they address issues such as the design of public spaces and streets, the limit to the location of buildings, and the exterior design of buildings. While public agencies may prepare guidelines for public spaces and streets, other design guidelines have no legal basis, since most provincial planning acts do not allow municipal governments to regulate the external design of private buildings unless they are within a heritage district. However, some municipalities prepare guidelines as an indication of intent, especially after consensus is reached in a public-participation exercise. Design guidelines are sometimes included in secondary plans or business improvement area plans to indicate the standards that will be used to evaluate requests for a rezoning to increase density or

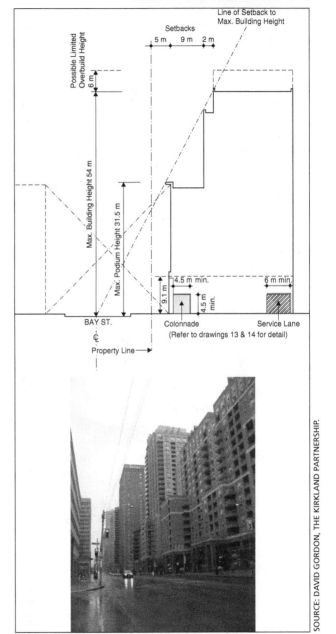

Figure 16.15 **East of Bay (Toronto) Urban Design Guidelines, 1990–2005**

SOURCE: DAVID GORDON, THE KIRKLAND PARTNERSHIP.

These urban design guidelines for the Bay Street canyon in midtown Toronto were consciously modelled on the 60-degree angular plan in the 1916 zoning bylaw that controls building height on the north–south avenues in Manhattan. The image below shows the effect of the guideline on built form, which was completed a decade after the guideline was adopted.

to receive public subsidies for redevelopment. Finally, both public and private landowners may attach design guidelines to requests for proposals (RFPs) to develop their lands, especially if they have special design objectives for the site.

Design guidelines were mainly used for urban areas in the 1970s and 1980s, often for projects in downtown districts. An example is the guidelines used to shape the "canyon" in Toronto's upper Bay Street, which were modelled on Manhattan's 1916 zoning bylaw (Figure 16.15). Other downtown design guidelines included protection of key vistas with view planes (see below) and access to sunlight.[38] Increasing interest in the design of suburban areas during the 1990s led to guidelines such as Calgary's Sustainable Suburb Design Guidelines.[39] Some New Urbanist suburban guidelines established the basis for form-based codes in their secondary plans, starting with a hybrid approach in Markham's Cornell neighbourhood.[40] Smart Growth advocates have also promoted using design guidelines at a regional scale.[41] Design guidelines can also be used to good effect in smaller cities; two examples are Collingwood, Ontario, and Vernon, British Columbia.[42]

View Planes and View Corridors

Throughout the practice of land use regulation there is always the need to consider the balance between the development rights conveyed to a property owner and the rights of the community, which might be impinged upon by the actual development. Sometimes those latter rights may be infringed upon at some distance from the parcel being developed. A common case in point is the obstruction of views, which people in the community have traditionally enjoyed, by new tall or bulky buildings. Planners have become aware that the character of a community is very often grasped by people through the recurring views they have of landmarks, historic and significant structures, and special landscapes, and have developed legal mechanisms that specify the protection of selected views. Thus, communities can enact bylaws that limit building height and bulk in specific "view-plane" or "view-corridor" areas. **View planes** are three-dimensional and govern both height and breadth of view from a specified area. Halifax, for example, protects traditional views of the harbour and old parts of the city from the area of the Citadel that overlooks the harbour. Montréal's plan contains view corridors to protect the vistas of Mount Royal at the end of key streets, and the location and height of tall buildings are controlled to ensure that the mountain has a

clear form on the skyline (Figure 16.16). In Ottawa, the National Capital Commission has regulations governing views of the Peace Tower, but has had only limited success in protecting them. Vancouver's city council decided to allow taller, but not bulkier, buildings in its downtown area in order to maintain existing view corridors to the mountain backdrop.

Design Review

Large public and private land developers sometimes appoint a master architect to review the preliminary designs of structures proposed for individual lots. The results can be commendable, such as the 1950's Modern aesthetic guided by the look of Don Mills (a private development) or the informal industrial look of Vancouver's Granville Island (guided by the Granville Island Trust). Similarly, the National Capital Commission has operated a design review panel since the 1950s for buildings proposed for federal lands in the Ottawa region.

However, few Canadian municipalities engage in a peer review of the detailed design of buildings proposed for private property because provincial planning legislation often does not permit such action. Architects and developers are wary of design review, especially when it is conducted by planners with little design training. The major exception to these trends is Vancouver, where the civic design review panel gradually achieved considerable local support during the 1980s and 1990s. The review panel makes judgments about the quality of proposed building designs and on whether projects meet the guidelines for density bonuses. The panel's members are appointed on recommendation of the design professions, and the planning staff who administer the process are also educated as architects. International observers have praised the results,[43] and similar design review panels were recently established in Calgary, Toronto, and Ottawa.

| **Figure 16.16** | Montréal View Control Diagram, 2003 |

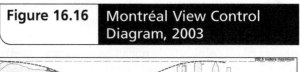

Montréal's Master Plan controls the location and height of tall buildings in the CBD to ensure that Mount Royal has a prominent role on the city's skyline.

Special Districts

Traditionally, zoning took a simple view of city development and district classifications reflected this. Three general categories of land use were used—residential, commercial, and industrial—and within these only limited numbers of subcategories. Each of the districts—whether single-family, two-family, neighbourhood commercial, or light industrial—had standards for bulk, yards, and uses, standards that were the same no matter where in the city the district was located. As well, these standards ignored differences in character between one such district and another in the same category. Zoning practice now recognizes that many neighbourhoods in cities have unique characteristics or problems. Some may be historically important in the community, and some may be stable while others are not.

Special-district designation, which is now a standard part of zoning, is designed to cope with new and special needs in land use. One of the most common is the historic district. Another is the special designation of districts in which large institutional or public uses occur (such as hospitals, universities, and airports). Other zones to protect and encourage waterfront development are also common. One of the most widely used types of special district is that defined for environmentally sensitive areas, such as those subject to flooding or those having special ecological characteristics. Another widely used special district is the Business Improvement Area (BIA), which is used to promote rejuvenation of older commercial areas. The advent of special districts indicates not only that cities are too complex for the range of responses offered by simple land use regulations but also that we may have new perceptions of what is important in land use.

Reflections

Land use regulation definitely falls on the process side of planning. The various statutory controls described above are themselves not plans of desired development but rather the means by which the community's planning objectives are linked to the development process—that is, linked to the aims, inclinations, and decisions of those individuals, firms, and organizations that may wish to develop land. Mostly, land use regulations are intended to shape the plans of prospective developers in the private sector, but they also affect public bodies, including the local government.

In their basic forms, like zoning and subdivision control, land use regulations are negative in their approach. They function, essentially, to establish minimum standards for development. But while they can be effective in preventing development considered undesirable, these regulations are relatively powerless in obtaining desirable development. In other words, they inform the developer of what is minimally acceptable, but the actual decision to develop land at or above these standards remains with the developer. A few new approaches, such as Planned Unit Development, Transfer of Development Rights, Comprehensive Development Zoning, and Design Guides offer *positive* incentives to developers to work with planners in return for relaxing burdensome aspects of the regulations. Development-control approaches are simply tools with which the community's planners can actively work with developers to secure the most amenable projects. The tools do not cause good or bad places—zoning does not cause suburban sprawl, for example. But the implementation tools may be calibrated on a model of urbanism that is no longer relevant to the community. For example, the zoning and development standards in many suburban municipalities are specifically calibrated to produce conventional suburban development based upon Don Mills as a model. If the community wishes to permit other types of urbanism, it must re-calibrate its tools.

Land use regulation is a process in which land developers respond to the standards set by community officials. In this sense, it is a reactive process for the community's planners: they must await the initiatives of the developers. Further, the community's "planners" in this realm are diverse. They include the professional planners on staff (or consultants), members of planning boards, zoning boards of appeal, the local council, regional or district planners, and provincial planning ministries, as well as other government bodies and public utilities. All of these may be "actors" in one area or another of land use regulation, depending upon the prescribed procedures. It is important to appreciate that each actor is able to influence the outcome of the planning goals of the community; in effect, each participates in implementing the community plan. Thus, the need for promoting active roles for participants to secure mutual learning (i.e., mutual respect and appreciation) is self-evident.[44]

Making land use regulation effective in the attainment of a community's planning goals is a complex task. Coordination among the diverse actors is essential to assure that the various tools are used in a consistent fashion. The two main components of this task are (1) the presence of an overall community plan, and (2) an organizational focus for planning within the community. The plan, or at least a clear statement of planning objectives, provides the benchmark against which the various actors can assess the impact of the decisions they must make. But there must also be an explicit commitment within the community to the plan by way of some person or group whose responsibility it is to uphold it. This could be the director of planning, a planning committee, the council, or some combination of all these. The approach that needs to be taken will involve both monitoring all activities in the regulation of land use (such as subdivision proposals, applications for variance, etc.), and influencing the deliberations of various bodies (through representations, analyses, etc.).

Land use regulation, as noted at the outset of this chapter, is only one of the major tasks involved in implementing a community plan. There are other areas in which the community influences the outcome of development in its built environment by policies and programs it institutes such as through the capital investments it makes for roads, and so forth. These policy tools are described in the next chapter and generate consideration of these questions:

- *In which ways can land use regulation tools be coordinated with investment policy and program tools to enhance implementation of the community plan?*
- *In which ways can the tools for implementing plans be made sensitive to the needs of individual property developers?*

Reference Notes

1. John Punter, *The Vancouver Achievement: Urban Planning and Design* (Vancouver: UBC Press, 2003).
2. Thomas H. Logan, "The Americanization of German Zoning," *Journal of the American Institute of Planners* 42 (October 1976), 377–385.
3. Raphael Fischler, "Health, Safety, and the General Welfare—Markets, Politics, and Social Science in Early Land Use Regulation and Community Design," *Journal of Urban History* 24:6 (1998), 675–719.
4. Elizabeth Bloomfield, "Reshaping the Urban Landscape: Town Planning Effects in Kitchener/Waterloo, 1912–1926," in G.A. Stelter and A. Artibise, eds., *Shaping the Urban Landscape* (Ottawa: Carleton University Press, 1982), 256–303.
5. Richard Dennis, "'Zoning' before Zoning: The Regulation of Apartment Housing in Early Twentieth Century Winnipeg and Toronto," *Planning Perspectives* 15:3 (2000), 267–299; and Walter Van Nus, "Towards the City Efficient: The Theory and Practice of Zoning, 1915–1939," in A.F.J. Artibise and G.A. Stelter, eds., *The Useable Urban Past: Planning and Politics in the Modern Canadian City* (Toronto: MacMillian, 1979), 220–246.
6. Ian MacF. Rogers, *Canadian Law of Planning and Zoning* (Toronto: Carswell, 1973), 120.
7. Cf. John C. Weaver, "The Property Industry and Land Use Controls: The Vancouver Experience, 1910–1945," *Plan Canada* 19 (September–December, 1979), 211–225.
8. Cf. Richard F. Babcock, "Zoning," in Frank S. So et al., eds., *The Practice of Local Government Planning* (Washington: International City Managers' Association, 1979), 416–444.
9. Cf. Rogers, *Canadian Law*, 119.
10. A comprehensive review of Canadian experience with mixed-use areas is found in Jill Grant, "Mixed Use in Theory and Practice: Canadian Experience with Implementing a Planning Principle," *Journal of the American Planning Association*, 68:1 (Winter 2002), 71–84.
11. Ken Greenberg and Frank Lewinberg, "Reinventing Planning in Toronto," *Plan Canada* 36:3 (May 1996), 26–27.
12. Kenji Ito, "Comprehensive Development Zoning," *Plan Canada* 37:4 (July 1997), 6–11.
13. Brenton Toderian, "Big-Box Retailing: How Are Municipalities Reacting?" *Plan Canada* 36:6 (November 1996), 25–28.
14. Alan Demb, "No Place Like Home: Legalizing Home Occupations in Toronto," *City Magazine* 14:2 (Spring 1993), 8.
15. Robert Voigt, "Creative, Communicative and Progressive: Developing the Collingwood Urban Design Manual," *Plan Canada* 51:3 (Fall 2011), 45–49.
16. Toderian, "Big-Box Retailing."
17. Mohammad Qadeer, "Planning Approaches to Ethnic Enclaves," *Ontario Planning Journal* 19:6 (2004), 6–7.
18. See Nancy Smith, "Diversity: The Challenge for Land Use Planning," *Plan Canada* 40:4 (July–August–September 2000), 27–28.
19. See such critiques as Andres Duany et al., *Towns and Town-Making Principles* (Cambridge, MA: Harvard University Press, 1991); and James Howard Kunstler, *Home from Nowhere* (New York: Simon and Schuster, 1996).
20. For the experience in Markham, ON, see David Gordon and Shayne Vipond, "Gross Density and New Urbanism: Comparing Conventional and New Urbanist Suburbs in Markham, Ontario," *Journal of the American Planning Association* 71:1 (Winter 2005), 41–54.
21. Cf. Jill Grant, "Mixed Use"; and Andrea Gabor and Frank Lewinberg, "New Urbanism," *Plan Canada* 37:4 (July 1997), 12–17.
22. This approach is championed by Ontario's *Growth Plan for the Greater Golden Horseshoe* (2008) and also the City of Ottawa.
23. Justin Webber, "Manufacturing Genius Loci? Design Codes and the Challenge of Place-Making," *Plan Canada* 52:2 (Summer 2012), 16–20; and Emily Talen, *City Rules: How Regulations Affect Urban Form* (Washington, DC: Island Press, 2011).
24. Andrea Gabor and Frank Lewinberg, "New Urbanism, New Zoning," *Plan Canada* 37:4 (July 1997), 12–17; David Moffat, "New Urbanism's Smart Code," *Places* 16:2 (Spring 2004), 74–77; and Emily Talen and Hazel Borys, *The Codes Project* (Tempe, AZ: Arizona State University, 2012), accessed October 2012 at codesproject.asu.edu.
25. Canada Mortgage and Housing Corporation, *Residential Site Development Advisory Document* (Ottawa, 1981), 2.
26. Jill Grant et al., "The Planning and Policy Implications of Gated Communities," *Canadian Journal of Urban Research* 13:1 (2004), 70–88.
27. Newfoundland, Provincial Planning Office, *Residential Subdivision Design Criteria* (St. John's, 1975), 1.
28. Cf. Sharon Fletcher, "Coping with Growth in the Regional District of Nanaimo," *Plan Canada* 41:4 (Fall 2001), 16–17.
29. Ontario Economic Council, *Subject*, 66.
30. Comay Planning Consultants et al., *A Study of Sprawl in New Brunswick* (Toronto, 1980), 96.

31. Evelyne P. Reid and Maurice Yeates, "Bill 90—An Act to Protect Agricultural Land: An Assessment of Its Success in Laprairie County Quebec," *Urban Geography* 12:4 (1991), 295–309; and Christopher Bryant and Thomas Johnston, *Agriculture in the City's Countryside* (Toronto: University of Toronto Press, 1992), 137–189.

32. Alberta, Municipal Affairs, *Planning in Alberta* (Edmonton, 1978), 25–28.

33. Arnold Bennett, "Montreal Debates Condo Conversion Again," *City Magazine* 14:2 (Spring 1993), 10.

34. Earl Levin, "Zoning in Canada," *Plan Canada* 7 (June 1957), 85–90.

35. *The Planning Act*, R.S.O. 1990, Ch. P.13. But the act specifically forbids the use of site plan control to regulate "the colour, texture and type of materials, window detail, construction details, architectural detail and interior design of buildings," sec. s. 41 (4).

36. Stanley Makuch, "Planning or Blackmail?" *Plan Canada* 25:1 (March 1985), 8–9.

37. Hok-Lin Leung, *Land Use Planning Made Plain,* 2nd ed. (Toronto: University of Toronto Press, 2003), Ch. 7; and R. Fischler, "Linking Planning Theory and History: The Case of Development Control," *Journal of Planning Education and Research* 19:3 (Spring 2000), 233–241.

38. Peter Bossleman, Edward Arens, Klaus Dunker, and Robert Wright, "Urban Form and Climate: Case Study, Toronto," *Journal of the American Planning Association* 61:2 (Spring 1995), 226–239.

39. Robin White, "Designing More Sustainable Suburban Communities: Calgary's Approach," *Plan Canada* (July 1996), 16–19.

40. Andrea Gabor and Frank Lewinberg, "New Urbanism, New Zoning," *Plan Canada* 37:4 (July 1997), 12–17.

41. Brook McIlroy, "Planning and Urban Design," *Model Urban Design Guidelines* (St. Catherines, ON: Regional Municipality of Niagara, April 2005), www.regional.niagara.on.ca/urban-design/pdf/pdfs/1.pdf

42. City of Collingwood, ON, *Urban Design Manual*, www.town.collingwood.on.ca.node/3354; and City of Vernon, BC, *City Centre Neighbourhood Plan,* September 2011.

43. John Punter, "From Design Advice to Peer Review: The Role of the Urban Design Panel in Vancouver," *Journal of Urban Design* 8: 2 (2003), 113–135.

44. Hok-Lin Leung, "Mutual Learning in Development Control," *Plan Canada* 27:2 (April 1987), 44–55.

Internet Resources

Chapter-Relevant Sites

Planning Canadian Communities
www.planningcanadiancommunities.ca

Citizens' Guide to Land Use
http://northstar.sierraclub.org/priorities/land_use_open_space/

Lehmans Zoning Trilogy
www.zoningtrilogy.com

The Codes Project
http://codesproject.asu.edu

Centre for the Study of Commercial Activity
www.csca.ryerson.ca

Canadian Urban Institute
www.canurb.com

17

Chapter Seventeen

Policy Tools for Plan Implementation

Sustainable development is easier to imagine than the political processes required for implementation.

Jeanne Wolfe, 2004

When one examines the built environment of a community it is readily seen that it is a blend of private and public structures, facilities, and spaces. And while private development comprises the largest part of a community's land use, public development may be said to constitute the most strategic part of the land use. The framework of the public roads, utility lines, parks, libraries, fire stations, parking structures, community centres, and so on can be said to articulate the form of the community within which private development takes place. But both are needed to achieve the goals of the community plan.

Achieving the desired blend is a matter of combining land use regulations and various other public policy decisions that can influence the decisions of private developers and other public agencies. The previous chapter discussed the planning tools that establish the basic "ground rules" for the development of the properties of private landowners. Those regulatory tools influence and/or constrain the choices that landowners have when they choose to develop or redevelop land. However, neither the effectiveness of the tool nor the nature of the development is apparent until such choices are exercised—that is, until an application for zoning or a subdivision plan is made, and until physical development actually takes place. As important as those regulatory tools are, they are essentially reactive in nature. A community (with municipal status) can, however, be proactive in implementing its planning goals. On the one hand, it can strategically use decisions about the nature, location, and timing of its own development efforts. And, on the other, it has means by which it can influence the decisions of private developers and other public agencies such as school boards, public utilities, and senior levels of government. In short, a local government can strategically use its policy-making powers to achieve its planning goals. Thus, when implementing a community plan the following questions need to be considered:

- *In what ways can a community use its public-policy prerogatives to influence and guide private and public action to bring its planning aims to fruition?*
- *Which policy tools allow planners to more closely link a plan's goals to action?*

On Guiding a Plan Toward Implementation

A community that makes a decision to plan cannot count on the necessary action being taken by landowners, or the local government itself, to make the plan come to fruition within any explicit time frame. While plan-making is aimed at stimulating and guiding the actions of both public and private decision-makers, *planning* and *action* are distinctive activities. In logical terms, planning is necessary but not sufficient to obtain the actions needed for a planned outcome. This dilemma has been recognized for many decades, but probably no more incisively than by American planner Martin Meyerson in his concept of the "middle-range bridge" for planning.[1] He perceived the dilemma that is posed because of the long-range aims of the community plan and the short-range perspective of most private development actions and public-action programs. To solve this, he advocated various planning tools to link the two. These tools would include, in particular, the budgeting and programming of the community's capital investment in facilities and land, as well as public incentive and support programs to stimulate private action and detailed plans for improving specific areas. His challenge has been taken up in many Canadian communities to develop a number of middle-range planning tools that can allow a community's planners to take the initiative to bring planning, policy, and action closer together.

It is clear by Meyerson's challenge that a community, having prepared a long-range plan, needs to move into a mode of short-range planning and action. Moreover, local governments have a considerable array of tools at their disposal. On the one hand, there are the various land use regulations, as described in the last chapter, which can be designed to render land use decisions consistent with the plan. And on the other hand, there is the ability to make and carry out policies toward the built environment both within the local government itself and toward the broader community. Two middle-range approaches—strategic planning and capital improvements programming—are key to strengthening a community's capacity to link long-range planning with short-range action. Each is a further planning endeavour by the community to ensure progress toward implementation of the community plan and is described below.

Managing Regional Growth

Two salient characteristics of most larger communities in recent decades are growth in the number of both people and dwellings, and expansion in area. The rapidity as well as the scale of much urban growth has often led to egregious amounts of land being consumed, not infrequently at very low density in a "leapfrog" manner, and environmentally sensitive areas converted to urban uses. These changes, in turn, lead both to escalating infrastructure costs and uncoordinated patterns of development, not to mention traffic congestion, pollution problems, and a failure to redevelop old neighbourhoods.[2] Responses to these undesirable features have centred on **growth management**—that is, methods to limit and/or direct new growth.

New growth occurring outside a community's boundaries, perhaps in an adjacent community, or simply well beyond existing built-up areas in a large municipality, requires an area-wide or regional perspective to manage it. The basic policy choice that needs to be made is to decide *where* urban development should and should not occur. The latter concern should be prompted by a study of the natural features and an analysis of the landscape that should be conserved and/or reclaimed.[3] With that policy parameter in place, there still remains the matter of where and how much land is needed by ongoing and projected growth and how to contain such growth. **Urban containment boundaries**, which fix the limits on a map, are a widely used approach to this issue. Sufficient land must be provided within these boundaries for continuing as well as expected new development in order to keep land prices stable. In Calgary, a 30-year supply of developable land is allowed for.[4] In addition, the city's policy requires that new growth be contiguous with existing built-up areas. It also tracks the absorption of land being developed and aims to have a three- to five-year supply of land available with municipal infrastructure. York Region in Ontario follows a similar path with a commitment to "firm urban boundaries" and also uses a rigorous system of monitoring regional conditions every three years.[5] In British Columbia, regional districts with growth and expansion problems among their communities may invoke the use of a Regional Growth Strategy. Within this arrangement, all constituent municipalities agree upon the urban containment boundary, and a further formal agreement binds each of them and their community plans to it.[6] Alberta communities are strongly encouraged to prepare and adopt inter-municipal development plans with adjoining municipalities for fringe areas lying astride their boundaries that are critical for growth and/or conservation.[7]

A more nuanced approach than simply "containing" growth is encompassed by the notion of **Smart Growth**, which combines urban and suburban planning at the regional scale. Its urban principles include raising residential densities, emphasizing public transit, providing for mixed land uses, revitalizing old neighbourhoods, and allowing for more diverse layouts and street designs.[8] This broad menu of policies is often associated with the movement among planners, politicians, environmental groups, and others to "control sprawl" and develop more compact communities.[9] The concern over the form and quality of suburban development covers a number of issues including prohibiting low-density growth at the suburban margin. Communities are urged to embrace Smart Growth ideas and enact policies to promote them. According to critics, this may be more difficult to achieve than it appears because it requires a coordinated approach both within and between communities and with higher levels of government.[10] Further discussion of the issues embedded in efforts to control sprawl follow in the next chapter.

Community Strategic Planning

Community Plan

One of the newer middle-range planning tools that many communities now employ is called Community Strategic Planning. Strategic-planning processes, long used in business planning, have been adapted for community use. A strategic plan differs from the overall community plan in several ways: for one, it is cast in a shorter time frame; for another, it is aimed much more at implementing specific objectives; and for yet another, it is more closely oriented to changes in the community's context, or functioning environment.[11] Local government strategic plans typically have a five-year perspective and are reviewed and updated every year so that there is always a five-year planning perspective in place. Strategic plans are usually undertaken in conjunction with a community's overall plan and, thus, provide for a set of actions that comprise a multi-year portion

of the long-range plan. Importantly, the community's strategic plan is attuned to changes in social, political, demographic, economic, and natural factors that could affect the plan's attainment and attempts to allow for responses to such changes.

A resource manual for Nova Scotia communities describes a strategic plan as answering the following questions:[12]

- Where are we right now?
- Where do we want to be in the future?
- What strategies will we need to implement to get there?
- What internal and external forces are operating that will hinder or help us achieve our long-term goals?

Strategic planning, as with long-range community planning, involves establishing goals and objectives, and this is frequently done on a broad community basis, as was done in the newly amalgamated City of Kingston, Ontario in 2000.[13] The small city of Port Colborne, Ontario, conducted a similar process and, according to this community, its strategic plan "has made the journey ahead much clearer."[14] Strategic planning processes often entail highly collaborative processes involving a wide array of community stakeholders from both inside and outside the local government.[15] In the Nova Scotia approach, a Strategic Planning Team, which needs to include a very broad base of stakeholders, is formed to prepare the strategic plan. Suggested contributors are local elected officials, managers of civic departments, managers of other public agencies (school boards, utilities, transportation, etc.), and representatives of the public, the business community, public interest groups, civic employees, unions, and provincial and federal governments. It is important that all interests that play a significant role in the community are at the table as, for example, a university or major hospital. Such an array respects the fact that many stakeholders outside of the planning department of the community (including those in other local government departments) not only have the means but often also their own plans for utilizing their resources. It can also be appreciated that involving such a variety of people will complicate decision making on the plan, and consensus-building approaches will work best in the give-and-take that is necessary to reach a common ground (see also Chapter 12).

The City of Edmonton has practised strategic planning for several years as a way of implementing its overall plan, Plan Edmonton.[16] The general flow of decision-making in Edmonton is shown in Figure 17.1.

Figure 17.1 — A Guide to Municipal Decision-Making, Edmonton

A Guide to Municipal Decision-Making

A community plan, such as Plan Edmonton, has a strategic role to play in the development and refinement of other planning instruments required by the municipality.

A particular aspect of Edmonton's strategic planning is the preparation of a Servicing Concept Design Brief (SCDB). The SCDB is prepared by the civic planners and establishes "a general framework for municipal infrastructure, servicing, planning, and environmental requirements."[17] The SCDB is prepared for specified areas of the city as designated by the city council to define municipal servicing requirements in advance of new development or renewal. In this way, not only are landowners and developers informed of the city's intent but also the brief identifies capital projects for the municipality's Capital Priorities Plan. A strategic-planning process is a valuable supplement to preparing the overall community plan and has been taken up in communities from Coquitlam, British Columbia, to Thunder Bay, Ontario.

Linking Capital Spending to Local Planning

Capital-Improvement Program

Each year, local public officials, both elected ones and their staffs, are in the position of making decisions about expenditures that may contribute significantly to the implementation of their community's plan. The most important of these are capital expenditures for physical facilities, for development incentives, and for special-project-area development. Most of these are part of the local government's annual budget and, thus, within the control of a municipal council to directly influence the outcome of much of its own plan. The local council usually sees the annual budgetary process as the most important activity it performs because its choices allocate the community's normally limited financial resources among various activities, programs, and facilities. However, planning and budgeting are not synonymous and, unless a deliberate effort is made to link the two activities, a

lack of coordination in the use of resources can hinder the plan. There is a need to develop procedures that keep the objectives of the plan, and the efforts of planners to implement it, tied to the budgetary process, an approach that is exemplified by the planners, politicians, and civic managers in Edmonton alluded to above.

Coordinating Capital Improvements

There is always a financial cost to a community in achieving its overall development plan. Even in a community that decides its future lies in maintaining the status quo, there will be upkeep and maintenance costs as facilities and streets wear out. In communities that choose to improve their built environments, city facilities will always need to be built, renewed, or upgraded to some degree. Communities that accept the growth of new subdivisions, office complexes, and other developments are destined to expand community facilities at some substantial cost to the local treasury. In each case, the question is not *whether* these sorts of costs will be incurred, but *when*.

The community plan, by projecting the best possible arrangement for development, determines what kind of improvements, or investments, are needed. The plan is, however, only a general guide. Development projects differ as to when they will happen, if private, and as to when they are needed, if public; the plan is not able to anticipate precisely the timing of development. Moreover, the availability of funds for public facilities and projects will determine when the community can afford to make the capital investment. Thus, as the community sets about implementing its plan, it is faced with choices as to which investments it will make from its always limited capital resources, and when it will make them.

This kind of activity, which arranges the expenditures for projects according to a time schedule, is called "capital programming." A form of programming in use for over a half a century in community planning is **Capital Improvements Programming** (CIP). Specifically, CIP is a means of linking physical planning with its long-term perspective and the budgeting of community expenditures with its annual perspective. The basis of CIP is the expenditure of funds for such physical facilities as roads, sewer lines, parking garages, and community centres (Figure 17.2). These sorts of projects are relatively costly as well as long lasting. Because their financing is often subject to borrowing funds with long periods of amortization, the community must decide on the level of debt that it can support each year. Further, because physical facilities are not easily changed once constructed, it

Figure 17.2	Winnipeg Capital Budget and the Growing Infrastructure Deficit

SOURCE: A SUSTAINABLE WINNIPEG DIRECTION STRATEGY, OURWINNIPEG (2011), CITY OF WINNIPEG, PAGE 13

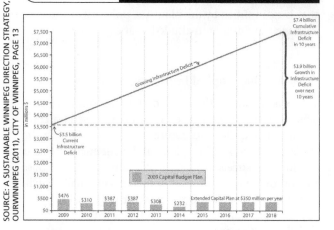

Winnipeg's comprehensive land use plan directly addresses the city's growing deficit in maintaining its infrastructure.

is necessary to consider both the expenditure and the planning ramifications of each project.

Three basic definitions will help provide a context for CIP:[18]

- **Capital Improvements:** new or expanded physical facilities that are relatively large, expensive, and permanent, such as streets, libraries, fire halls, and water mains.
- **Capital Improvements Budget:** the expenditures for physical facilities to which the community is committed in the next fiscal year. This annual budget usually comprises the first year of the multi-year CIP.
- **Capital Improvements Program:** a schedule of proposed expenditures for public physical facilities covering a period of several years into the future, usually five years.

The primary objective of CIP is "to determine that set of projects for each time period which if carried out would provide the greatest 'product' over all future time periods."[19] In order to achieve this objective, CIP involves several important sub-tasks that must be blended together into a viable program to guide capital expenditures. In many respects, preparing the CIP is a process, like that of preparing the overall community plan. Although it deals with more details of development and its time frame is shorter, the CIP must reconcile competing ends into a composite "middle-range" plan of facilities. The cost of the proposed facilities must be within reach of the

community's financial resources, and the facilities must contribute toward implementing the overall plan.[20]

The facilities and projects that the CIP will need to consider arise out of the activities of various functional departments and agencies of the community government—the roads department, the parks department, the library board, and others. Each group will have its own set of projects that it believes will enhance the development of the community. Rarely will the community be able to afford all projects at once. Moreover, it is likely that some facilities will need to be constructed before others (e.g., roads will precede a community centre). This leads to two basic decisions about each proposed project:

- What is its importance relative to other projects?
- What is its desirable sequence relative to other projects?

Steps in the CIP Process

The CIP process involves a number of formal steps conducted by a specified office or department of the local government. Often it is the planning department that is assigned the role of soliciting proposals for capital improvement projects and assigning the priorities for construction. Typically, the CIP process is conducted on two different levels: a five-year program is prepared every four years, with the first year comprising the expenditures in the upcoming budget year (i.e., the capital improvements budget). Then the capital improvements program is reviewed annually to adjust the sequence of projects should major changes occur in financial resources or community needs in the projected time period of the program.

All communities conduct the CIP process according to their own organizational arrangements. The order of steps may not exactly parallel those listed below, but at some point each step will be taken in each community:

1. **Analysis of financial resources.** Projects in the CIP must be financed out of the community's available resources. Thus, projections of revenues and/or expenditures must determine how much money will be available in the current and subsequent years. The community will have expenditures for projects already built or authorized, usually in the form of bonds that have been issued. New projects requiring the community to borrow funds (issue new bonds) may have to wait until previous projects have been partially or completely paid for. And the operating costs of new and proposed projects after they are built can

affect the allocation of revenues between operating and capital budgets in the future.

2. **Requests for Proposed Projects.** Each department involved in making capital expenditures in the local government submits proposals for the projects that they hope to undertake over the coming five years. Proposals must usually conform to a format that provides the planning department (or other CIP agency) with all the necessary information, enabling it to compare the merits of each project. The basic information to be supplied includes:

   - a description of the project, its location, and when it is required;
   - the expected cost of the project and when these costs would likely be incurred (possibly over several years if the project is large);
   - the justification for the project and its relation to other projects in the same and/or other departments;
   - the status of ongoing projects;
   - the sources of funding in cases where other-than-local sources might be available; and
   - the priority rating in comparison to other departmental projects.

3. **Choices Among Functional Groups.** The essential aim of CIP is to complete the development envisioned in the community plan for a given capital outlay. There is, however, no analytic system that allows direct choices among separate projects emanating from different departments, as, say, between a new sewer, playground, or fire hall. Also difficult is deciding on the projects according to specific years. It is usually recommended, first of all, to conceive of the five-year CIP as a whole and decide on those functional groups of projects that would best achieve the plan's objectives.[21] For example, projects may be grouped into such categories as transportation, residential development, industrial renewal, health care, recreation, protective choices, or whatever is appropriate for the particular plan and the planning period. Thus, some sewers or streets might be important for industrial renewal areas and others for new subdivisions.

4. **Determining the Sequence of Projects.** The timing of projects is central to CIP if the community's development sequence is to be both efficient and generally acceptable. Initially, when considering the sequence of projects, it is necessary to exclude those for whose services there will not be a demand until after the five-year CIP period. Then, the projects of each functional group are organized in terms of the order in which they need to be built. At this point, only a sequence of construction, without specific dates, is shown. Some projects need to be built early because (a) they will increase the service performed by existing facilities (e.g., additional sewage-treatment capacity); (b) they could cost much more if delayed (e.g., the acquisition of park space), and (c) they are strategic in influencing the form and pace of private development (e.g., the extension of water mains and arterial roads). There is, as well, the need to consider the advantage of linking such projects as sewer and street construction to avoid repeated road disruptions.

5. **Setting the Priority of Projects.** Choosing the projects to be built and those that will not be built in the time period is the most crucial step in the CIP process. To determine the priority of projects, it is necessary to go beyond their sequence and rate them according to their relative importance in the community's development. The first criterion is whether they can be achieved within the given capital budget. A second criterion is whether the project is specifically identified in either the comprehensive plan or some functional plan adopted by the community. Beyond these two criteria, the setting of priorities is difficult, because of local preferences and political considerations. Various ranking schemes have been developed to derive a measure of the relative importance of projects.[22] The final determination of which projects should be included combines their sequence and importance positions and, starting from the most important and progressing to the least, they are placed in time sequence until all the capital resources available for the five years are exhausted.

As with all planning decisions, capital improvement programming has a *technical* and a *policy* side. The process described above pertains mostly to the technical side—that is, the process undertaken by the community's staff of planners in analyzing capital needs and formulating a program. Both elected and appointed officials will use their political roles to influence the CIP. Department heads tend to favour projects in their own departmental area more than city-wide issues. Elected officials often desire projects that favour particular areas or groups in the community. And often elected officials wish to keep capital commitments vague so as to be able to change their minds and respond to new needs. The relatively rational CIP process, therefore, cannot be considered apart from its political aspects, which, at their best, enhance the technical judgments and make the CIP more pertinent to community needs and goals.

Beyond these tensions, capital improvements programming has three major advantages:[23]

- It provides a link to the long-range plan by focusing attention on community goals, needs, and financial capacity when considering whether new infrastructure should be constructed and existing infrastructure should be replaced.
- It improves cooperation and communication among operating departments within the local government.
- It clearly indicates the community's investment intentions for several years ahead, so that private developers and other government agencies may better program their investments.

The City of Vancouver calls its CIP a Capital Plan, which it puts forward every three years in a public plebiscite.[24] The City of Edmonton calls its CIP a Capital Priorities Plan. In both instances, as with other communities that prepare a CIP, the process is closely linked to its strategic planning.

Policy Tools for Influencing Development

A local governing body has the special prerogative of making its voice known, and listened to, about how a community's growth and development should proceed. It does this by the *policies* it espouses. A policy decision is like saying "this is the route we should be taking and this is how we should travel it." The decision to make a community plan is a policy choice to improve the built environment using a planning approach rather than leaving future development to chance. Thus, a community plan, upon adoption, is a major statement of policy. And that policy document requires, in turn, further policy choices that reflect preferred actions to achieve its objectives.

Strategic plans and capital improvements programs further refine policy initiatives by pursuing particular objectives, facilities, and programs, or favouring particular areas. Through the latter tools a community may, for example, decide to use its resources to create low-cost housing or refurbish a historic district or attract private investment to an abandoned industrial area that the community plan has recommended. The policies it

chooses to pursue also contain the means by which to achieve them. Broadly speaking, a community's policy choices revolve around the use of its resources. A community's resources cover its land resources, financial capacity, and its ability to use statutory instruments; any or all may be strategically important to achieve goals for the built environment. Using these resources may be limited by the provincial government (e.g., by prohibiting lower tax rates to attract business) and sometimes encouraged when the province (or federal government with provincial approval) wishes to achieve results through local government actions, such as area-wide transportation planning.

Financial Development Incentives and Tools

Communities often make financial resources available to influence decisions by private landowners and builders. This is done by providing financial incentives through grants and/or low-interest loans to encourage participation in a program favoured by the community. As an example, one of the most widely used incentive programs was the Neighbourhood Improvement Program (NIP) of the mid-1970s. Under NIP, homeowners and communities could receive federal funds in areas that were identified as needing upgrading in housing and community facilities. Homeowners could receive grants and loans to repair and improve their dwellings in such areas. The community could receive grants to assist in acquiring parkland, in improving streets and sewer lines, and in carrying out other activities that would promote residential renewal (see also Chapter 5).

Other similar programs include those to promote the development of low-income housing through municipal nonprofit housing corporations, to rehabilitate unused upper storeys of downtown commercial buildings for apartments, and to renovate disused industrial buildings for commercial or residential uses. These programs vary in the way the resources are made available. In some cases, the municipality may offer the incentives directly, while in others the community may be asked to approve the award of funds by a senior government to ensure that the use conforms to local planning objectives.

Financial incentive programs may be strategically important to stimulating private development in previously uneconomic types of uses and in parts of the city avoided by developers. For example, older, often-blighted industrial areas, called brownfields, may be desirable to keep as employment areas in factories or offices. Toronto has such a policy and has developed a program of financial incentives for office and industrial developers that are willing to invest in designated brownfield areas. The program utilizes a **tax-increment financing** (TIF) approach in which the property owner and the city share, over a 10-year period, the increase in property taxes brought about by the new investment.[25] Further, the city's share of the tax increment is earmarked for public projects (such as parking, roads, landscaping) in the designated area. Other financial incentives for brownfields, or other areas requiring redevelopment, could include property tax reductions, tax freezes, or cancellation of tax arrears.[26] These tools help bring more certainty in regard to private development and investment that are relatively uncontrollable. Incentive programs may also be linked with capital investments by the community itself for a more concerted effort at rejuvenating the physical environment.

Development Charges and Property Taxes

Municipalities have two fiscal tools for influencing development of private lands. One is the charge applied to the development of a site to provide public infrastructure, called "development-cost charges." The other is the rate of property taxation applied to the land and buildings of a site. Both of these devices impose a cost on landowners and developers that must be included in calculating the cost of a proposed land development project. In general, private land interests will want these costs minimized while the municipality will want to make sure that its initial and ongoing service costs are met. It follows, therefore, that the size of these costs may affect decisions about the scale and type of project, or even whether it goes ahead at all.[27] Planners also need to be aware of the costs of urban growth and of the effects of these and other fees imposed on new development.

Property taxes are the primary source of income for a municipality and, in most provinces, tax rates are based on the current market value of properties. Separate valuations are made for the land portion and the building portion of a property's value. Thus, vacant land is taxed less than land with buildings, which means that if a community wished to see a particular site developed, it could reduce the property tax rate on vacant land. It has been shown in a Canadian study that land developers consider differences in property taxes between adjacent municipalities important when deciding on the location of a project.[28] Similarly, development-cost charges, which enable a municipality to have public services for a project paid for by the developer, are another important factor in deciding which municipality to locate a project

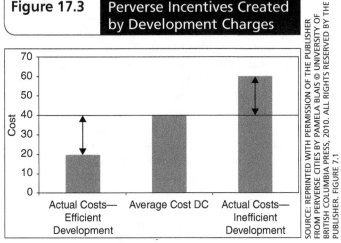

Development charges calculated on an average cost basis across a city can subsidize low-density suburban growth and be a barrier to intensification. This result is the opposite of the policy intent in most Canadian community plans.

in. To work, differences in these fiscal tools must occur in similar economic settings, zoning, and administrative processing practices. Development-cost charges, in particular, may be varied to reflect differences in recouping environmental costs to a community, as well the costs of normal urban infrastructure.

Unfortunately, many of the deeply embedded fiscal tools in many North American cities were developed during the period of rapid suburban expansion in the late 20th century and may be working against attempts to create a more sustainable urban form in our metropolitan areas. For example, Donald Shoup has demonstrated that the large supply of "free" parking required by zoning bylaws and development standards subsidizes automobile drivers and imposes many costs upon municipalities.[29] More recently, Pamela Blais has shown how development charges may have the perverse effect of subsidizing suburban sprawl and penalizing inner-city intensification if they are applied at a uniform rate across a city or region (Figure 17.3).[30]

Public–Private Partnerships

A relatively recent approach to funding urban development projects is for a community to enter into partnerships with private developers. They are called public–private partnerships (P3s) and have emerged to blend private resources and expertise with government policies and need for facilities and services.[31] This approach arose in response, on the one hand, to shrinking public financial resources and, on the other, to political pressures for the privatization of services that governments had previously provided. These partnerships tend to be focused on specific projects rather than on, for example, downtown renewal or neighbourhood traffic calming. One finds them used in the development of toll highways (such as Highway 407, which skirts the Toronto metropolitan area), transit systems (the Canada Line in Vancouver), and waterfront historic areas (such as Historic Properties in Halifax).

The first generation of Canadian urban public–private partnerships focused on redevelopment of publicly owned land, as described in Chapter 5. Projects included Granville Island and the recent Woodwards project in Vancouver, Toronto's Regent Park, and Le Vieux Port in Montréal. The public owner would often solicit private-developer interest with a request for proposals (RFP), usually incorporating planning policies and urban-design guidelines for the site. Private developers would purchase or lease the land and agree to follow the appropriate policies. These RFPs must be carefully structured to share risk among the stakeholders.[32]

Almost any public facility that a government body constructed and has operated—including hospitals, bridges, schools, transit lines, and airports—is now being considered for such partnerships. The essential arrangement is that a private body (a for-profit corporation or nonprofit group) provides the capital to build or buy a facility the governmental body wishes for the community or region, and the governmental body establishes standards for its construction, regulates its operation, and often becomes a tenant. The private partner then gets a return on its investment, usually by charging users, as with tolls for the Confederation Bridge to Prince Edward Island or fares on the Canada Line in Vancouver.

The primary rationale put forward for P3s is that the taxpayers are relieved of a portion of the capital investment costs in the projects. There is still considerable debate over these types of partnerships, however, ranging from concern over their social costs to the failure of governments to maintain existing "free" facilities. Some opponents cite the differential benefits for those citizens able to pay the tolls and those who can't. Others are concerned with the monopoly aspects given to private companies. Yet others claim that the cost of added pollution occasioned by, for example, a toll road is not being recovered by these arrangements.[33] Suffice to say, such project arrangements are often instituted on grounds other than those established in community plans.

Statutory Tools

There are several other means by which communities can influence the quality of the built environment. Two of the most important, expropriation and building regulations, are embedded in legislation codifying the responsibilities of communities to their residents. Communities are assigned roles, as municipalities, to provide a safe and convenient environment for all their citizens. That is, the municipality has a formal (legal) responsibility to act on behalf of the entire community to make sure that the decisions made by individual landowners not only do not impinge on their neighbours but also serve the best interests of the entire community. Building regulations and the power of expropriation stem, respectively, from two constitutional powers that reside in the municipality—the *police power* and the power of *eminent domain*. The police power provides the constitutional framework for the building regulations discussed in Chapter 16.

Expropriation

From another long-lived constitutional power held by Canadian provinces—**eminent domain**—municipalities derive the power to obtain land needed for community purposes. The essence of eminent domain is that the highest property right on the use of land rests ultimately with the Crown, or the municipality in this case. Specifically, if there are public uses of specified parcels of land that would be of more benefit than those proposed by the private owners, then the community may acquire the land. Normally, most municipalities have been delegated this power by their province, as have such other public agencies as school boards, highway departments, and public utilities.

The term used in Canada for this municipal power is **expropriation**. It is probably most often used for road-widening purposes when an existing right-of-way is not sufficient to accommodate an enlarged thoroughfare. Other instances include a community's need for park space in an already built-up area or space to build a public building or an arterial road. When a community designates a property for public use, it must acquire it from the owner by paying a reasonable price. Usually, the price to be paid will be the current market value as judged by an independent land appraiser. Strictly speaking, the power of expropriation is used only when the public agency cannot acquire the needed property through normal purchase procedures; it then has the power to acquire the property regardless of the willingness of the owner to sell. Municipal councils tend to use their power of expropriation sparingly because of the political ramifications of taking away private property; they try instead to negotiate a purchase. Nevertheless, this power of eminent domain has a valuable place among planning tools, as it ensures acquisition of properties that are of strategic importance to the completion of the plan.

Targeting Special Areas and Functions

Beyond incentive programs to entice private investment to occur in response to the community plan, the community may decide to undertake specific development projects on its own. It may target a specific *area*, such as downtown, an industrial area, a waterfront, or an historic district, the improvement of which would benefit the entire community and attain the objectives of the plan (Chapter 11). Or it may target a specific *function*, such as the mass-transit system or hospital services or parks, as a strategic move to achieve the plan (Chapter 12). The essential feature of both types of community initiative is the investment of *public funds*, sometimes in conjunction with outside (private or nonprofit) investors. Often, these are accompanied by special land use regulations devised for the project or area.

Special Area Initiatives

The targeting of special areas for development offers a strategic tool for achieving planning objectives. Such targeting acknowledges two facets of city development. First, there are differences in the pace of development between various areas at different times (e.g., the suburbs growing faster than downtown). And second, public infrastructure expenditures (for roads, parks, etc.) usually precede private investment. Thus, a substantial investment in public funds within a short period of time may be necessary to stimulate new private development or the renewal of existing uses. Five common initiatives—for business areas, heritage districts, waterfronts, institutional areas, and local ecosystems—will demonstrate the issues and the outcomes of this policy approach.

1. Business Improvement Areas (BIAs) Plans and programs for the revitalization of downtown and neighbourhood business areas are the most common special-area initiatives (see Chapter 11). Most of the buildings in these areas, in both large cities and small towns, represent extensive private investment, if not the largest concentration of such capital in the community. So, it is usually in the community's interest to protect this investment and maintain the economic and cultural vitality of these business areas. The approach of the Business Improvement Area was devised in Canada and is used in all provinces. It designates a specific commercial area for which a plan for improvement is made in conjunction with property owners and businesses in the area who form a nonprofit association. These groups are then able to access provincial and local funds to make physical improvements and undertake economic development activities.

BIAs are normally based on a plan that details the objectives for the area. The BIA plan describes the attributes to be achieved (e.g., street patterns, land uses, open spaces, views, streetscape, signage) along with the set of public and private actions that must be taken to attain the plan's objectives. In 2012, there were over 230 BIAs in Ontario, and the province provides a handbook to guide such planning.[34] Other provinces provide similar assistance for all sizes of community from Ladysmith, British Columbia, to Corner Brook, Newfoundland.[35] These programs help underwrite capital investments, such as new sidewalks, sewers, and streetlights, and may also offer incentives to private builders and landowners to participate. The community, in turn, is required to make a commitment in budgeting its capital and organizational resources to provide needed improvements such as parking structures, public open spaces, or a civic building to give impetus to the local development.

On a much larger scale are redevelopment programs for central districts of major cities, such as those for the Winnipeg downtown core, le centreville de Trois-Riviéres, and Market Square in Saint John. In the latter cases, the capital resources of both provincial and federal governments were also required. Their aims may include (as they do in the Winnipeg Core Area Initiative) the development of new housing, heritage conservation, new community facilities, the formation of local economic development corporations, retraining of core-area residents, industrial modernization, and assisting the development of new commercial buildings.[36]

2. Heritage District Implementation Canadian heritage protection policies often began in older downtown districts, such as Halifax's Historical Properties or Vancouver's Gastown. The aims may differ from those found in other core-area programs, but the means for achieving them are much the same, as seen in Chapter 11 above.[37]

3. Redevelopment Plans Redevelopment initiatives are implemented by designating a specific area for redevelopment and preparing a plan for its rejuvenation. There is an essential difference between this type of planning approach and that of zoning, whereby the community can only encourage development on privately owned parcels. Under a **redevelopment plan**, the community can intervene directly in private property and, indeed, take the initiative for improvement away from the landowner by acquiring land and removing or replacing buildings. Provincial planning acts delegate the power to prepare redevelopment plans to municipalities, under the condition that the plans are conceived within the concept and objectives of the overall community plan.

Terminologies differ among planning acts: in Ontario the redevelopment plan is now called a **community improvement plan** (See Figure 17.4), while in Alberta it is called an **Area Redevelopment Plan (ARP)**. The scope of a redevelopment plan is well illustrated in the purposes contained in the City of Edmonton's *Planning and Development Handbook*.[38] An ARP may designate an area for purposes of "preservation or improvement of land and buildings, rehabilitation of buildings, removal of buildings and/or their reconstruction or replacement; and

the relocation and rehabilitation of utilities and services." In Edmonton, to continue the example, an ARP may address such topics as urban design, social and community development, transportation, historic preservation, and environmental protection, as well as conventional planning issues of infrastructure and physical-development patterns. These planning prescriptions are very similar to those found in Canada's earliest planning acts. This no doubt reflects a continuing concern that some physical development may be of poor quality from the outset and/or that the land use is now obsolete and the need for public intervention persists to set it on a proper course.

4. Special Purpose District Agencies Plans for the many types of special districts described in Chapter 11 are sometimes implemented by special purpose agencies specifically chartered for their areas. Most metropolitan areas have an airport authority that operates the facility and implements the redevelopment of its property into an *aerotropolis*. Similarly, the larger coastal cities have federally chartered port authorities. These agencies have the critical ability to borrow capital improvement funds to be repaid from the future operating revenues of the airports and harbours.

Operating agencies are less effective at planning the redevelopment of their facilities for other uses. Harbour commissions are not good at closing port facilities and redeveloping waterfront land for public uses, since the operating authority wants to conserve its land in hopes that the port may re-emerge in the future.[39] Waterfront redevelopment agencies have been set up in Halifax, Québec, Montréal, and Toronto, although the combination of federal, provincial, and municipal oversight varies in each case. Similarly, the City of Edmonton has removed the responsibility for the redevelopment of its former City Centre airport site from the authority that operates the new Edmonton International Airport.

Land redevelopment for specific sites may be implemented by a targeted special purpose agency, such as the Forks North Portage Corporation in Winnipeg. This federal/provincial/municipal agency is responsible for redevelopment of two prominent sites in downtown Winnipeg. However, many municipalities have an urban development agency that manages redevelopment of public lands scattered across their cities. The Canada Lands company performs a similar, nationwide role in redeveloping surplus federal sites such as CFB Calgary (Planning Issue 17.1).

Figure 17.4	Community Improvement Plans

A community improvement plan might combine grant/loan programs for brownfield remediation, public open space, affordable housing, green roofs, and façade improvements with direct municipal initiatives such as street furniture, bike lanes, transit stops, street trees, and bike racks. Combining and targeting these initiatives in priority areas can stimulate redevelopment.

The Globe and Mail
August 23, 2010

Turning Problem Properties into Profit

Steve Ladurantaye

Crown corporation Canada Lands is getting international attention for how it gets maximum value for its properties

The Dominion Building in downtown Charlottetown was every landlord's nightmare when the federal government declared it surplus to its needs.

The feds had built a new home for its employees on the island, leaving the run-down six-storey building without a single tenant to occupy its 176,000 square feet of office space. The 55-year-old property was in need of some major repairs and would be unlikely to fetch much beyond its scrap value on the open market.

There was only one real option: sell the property to Canada Lands, a Crown corporation that has been discreetly disposing of problem properties for 15 years. It was a good call—Canada Lands sold the building last week for $1-million, twice as much as it paid in 2007.

The agency has been working behind the scenes for 15 years, but has suddenly found itself the subject of global interest as governments from around the world send delegations to learn how Canada turns a profit on properties that would be difficult to sell without improvements and updating.

In the past few months it has hosted delegations from China, the United States and Eastern Europe. They are all interested in the same thing—how to redevelop government properties such as abandoned army bases in a way that they earn profits for the taxpayers instead of only the developers.

"We always pay market value when we take over a property and we never sell low because there's no need for us to engage in fire sales," said Gordon McIvor, Canada Lands' vice-president of strategic acquisitions. "We have the luxury of time and remediation. When we sell, we are getting maximum value for those assets."

Foreign governments are interested for one main reason—Canada Lands has never received a cent of federal funding and has paid $370-million in dividends to the state. It has spent about $61-million on environmental improvements to its properties, and every building and piece of land in its sizable portfolio will eventually be sold to the private sector.

Mr. McIvor points to an executive order issued in June by U.S. President Barack Obama in which he called for the government to undertake a review of its properties with an eye of unloading surplus space onto the private sector as a sign the Canadian government has been ahead of the rest of the world in dealing with unwanted properties.

"For decades, the federal government, the largest property owner and energy user in the United States, has managed more real estate than necessary to effectively support its programs and missions," Mr. Obama wrote. "Both taxpayer dollars and energy resources are being wasted to maintain these excess assets."

Here at home, the government's decisions about what is and is not surplus has led to the creation of a quirky portfolio of properties for Canada Lands to deal with. It owns five military bases (it has already redeveloped and sold six others), a trendy housing development in Calgary, a bustling industrial park in Burnaby, B.C., and plots of land in the downtown cores of many of the country's largest cities.

CONTINUED

CONTINUED

In each case, it buys the property and then consults with the local governments about what each site's best use would be. If there are environmental issues - many old military homes are packed with asbestos, for example—it will take care of them before marketing the site to developers.

Its most high profile holdings are in downtown Toronto, where it inherited the CN Tower, the Metro Toronto Convention Centre and the Intercontinental Hotel as a side effect of CN Rail's initial public offering in 1995.

The properties could be sold at any time, at least in theory, but Queen's University real estate professor John Andrew said Canada Lands is a convenient way for the government to park valuable properties it doesn't want to be seen as holding onto as a landlord. But, it also operates in a grey area because its role is to sell unusual properties that aren't easy to slap a value on.

"The role of Canada Lands is a bit odd because on the surface of it their job is to dispose of real estate assets, yet they hold some for a long time and others are really not for sale," he said.

"Some of these are so unusual that it is difficult to determine their fair market value, or for any buyer to offer what they might be worth to the government," he said. "If the asset is of great value to a wide range of potential buyers - an office building with government tenants, for example—one wonders why the government is selling it at all."

Mr. McIvor insists every property is on the table except the CN Tower, which is being held "on behalf of Canadian taxpayers to ensure things like federal visual identity." Everything else in downtown Toronto—the hotel and convention centre as well as an office tower—will make it to market at some point.

"Since the company does not engage in fire sales and because of the serious economic downtown last year, the properties have not yet been put on the market but we intend to do so in the near future," Mr. McIvor said.

That could happen as soon as this fall. The Canadian commercial real estate market rebounded sharply in the first half of the year from the recessionary lows of 2009, up around 60 per cent compared to the year earlier period.

If ever there was a time to sell, he said, this may be it.

"The interesting thing about being a large national organization is we can have a balanced approach to development and hold on to things until the time is right," he said. "You'll see three very big commercial announcements from Canada Lands this fall in three different areas of the country."

5. Implementation Agencies for Functional Plans

While the functional needs of the community may be spelled out in the community plan, the actual functional plan is often prepared by agencies outside the local government that provides the funding. A provincial government department or Crown corporation may be responsible for rapid transit and freeway projects, or a metropolitan government may have responsibility for regional parks, hospitals, and airports. An example of this is the siting of treatment and transfer facilities for hazardous wastes in Manitoba communities. This is handled by the provincially owned Manitoba Hazardous Waste Management Corporation (there are similar agencies in other provinces). Not surprisingly, such projects are often called "difficult-to-site" projects. The Manitoba agency has developed a voluntary process in working with communities to assure greater acceptance of these facilities by sharing power and decision-making responsibility and is achieving considerable success.[40]

Regional public transit agencies are a standard technique for providing service across the territory of multiple municipal governments. In the absence of an effective regional governance or finance, provincial agencies such as Metro Vancouver's Translink or Ontario's Metrolinx may step in to operate transit systems. The Ottawa–Gatineau metropolitan region is a particularly awkward case because the region straddles a provincial border. As a result, there are separate transit operators in the two provinces and little interconnection between the two systems.[41]

Some Implications of Targeting

The great advantage of targeting special areas and functional needs is that it can generate tangible results from the planning process in a relatively short span of time. But it must be remembered that such specific planning has the effect of directing the allocation of public spending (and, if successful, private investment) toward one area or project and away from others. Thus, care must be taken not to starve existing projects of public funds and opportunities for private development. As with other middle-range planning tools, special-area and/or project targeting requires that considerable attention be paid to integrating planning and action.

This need is especially evident in view of the diverse interests involved in realizing a refurbished downtown or rapid transit system. These include departments within a local or regional government, agencies and departments of one or more senior governments, and private development interests. Given the often substantial amounts of resources required, a city may be able to do no more than indicate the desired project or redevelopment in its community plan. The public agency that, for example, can develop a rapid transit system may opt to do the project planning itself. Or the private developer with large and/or strategic land holdings may demand concessions in zoning. In such instances, project developers rather than community planners become the ones controlling public policy on the location of facilities and the bulk of buildings. Not infrequently, special development agencies are formed to push a project ahead, and they may come into competition with the community's planners for funds and political favour. This can cause relationships with the host community to turn sour as projects diverge from local planning norms and objectives. Nowhere was this more evident than in the Harbourfront project in Toronto, which required a federal royal commission to seek a reconciliation of local and agency planning aims.[42]

Reflections

Meyerson's notion of a "middle-range bridge," invoked at the outset of this chapter, has two main supports. The first is the array of land use regulation tools, described in the last chapter, that undergird so much of planning for the built environment that they are seen by many as synonymous with community planning. That is, it is

seen as essentially a regulatory process. As important as regulatory tools and processes are in providing a uniform base for private land use decisions, they are, as was mentioned, primarily *reactive* in nature—they come into play after a proposal has been made to build or rebuild part of the community. The second main support of the middle-range bridge, planning policy tools, described in this chapter, is *proactive* in nature. That is, these tools allow the community to take its own steps to achieve the built environment envisioned in the community plan: making strategic capital investments, targeting areas to be rejuvenated, and managing growth and development. Neither of these arrays of tools is more vital than the other in bringing a community plan to fruition, although they may vary in importance in the course of plan implementation—both are needed to support the middle-range bridge.

The policy tools that communities have available to shape both the form and the pace of community-building have much in common with the current approach of embedding natural ecosystem needs early in the planning process. Policy tools, too, can be *pre-emptive*. They can establish, early on, priorities for the type, location, and timing of private development that are essential for forming and filling out the built environment. They cannot be as precise as are regulatory tools and they involve risks, as with committing public monies for capital investments for facilities and infrastructure. So, policy tools have to be utilized wisely and sensitively with regard to private land and housing markets, and this is best done by encompassing them with in community strategic plans. The planners in Edmonton framed their municipal plan, Plan Edmonton, knowing that it would have to provide not only land use policies but also integrate the "business plans" of the municipal corporation and its departments, including city budgets (see Figure 17.1). The planners for York Region and both Calgary and Ottawa follow a similar planning trajectory. In short, the community plan is just one plan, albeit the lead one, in a chain of plans to achieve a community's goals.

Given their importance, it is surprising that policy tools are not used more widely. They are adaptable to all sizes of community as demonstrated in Nova Scotia. Further, presenting policy options such as those described above to a community's elected leaders engages them more thoroughly in the ongoing decisions required to implement a community plan. The adoption of a community plan is itself a major policy commitment by local councillors, but it is the beginning, not the end, of the need for choices about community building. Moreover, addressing these issues allows for greater awareness and participation in the planning process, thereby enriching the end result. As the discussion moves to consider future prospects and challenges for community planning, the questions below deserve attention:

- *How can communities develop more open, integrated planning processes that will allow them to meet challenges yet to come?*
- *Which aspects of a community's development can benefit most from the use of policy implementation tools?*

Reference Notes

1. Martin Meyerson, "Building the Middle-Range Bridge for Comprehensive Planning," *Journal of the American Institute of Planners* 22 (Spring 1956), 58–64.
2. Anthony Downs, "Smart Growth: Why We Discuss It More Than We Do It," *Journal of the American Planning Association* 71:4 (Autumn 2005), 367–378.
3. Ken Tamminga, "Restoring Biodiversity in the Urbanizing Region: Towards Pre-emptive Ecosystems Planning," *Plan Canada* 36:4 (July 1996), 10–15.
4. Marjorie Young, "Accommodating and Managing Municipal Infrastructure Investments in Calgary," *Plan Canada* 41:4 (Oct.—Dec. 2001), 18–20.
5. Bryan Tuckey, "The Cornerstones of Community-Building," *Plan Canada* 41:4 (Oct.–Dec. 2001), 14–15.
6. Sharon Fletcher and Christine Thomas, "Coping with Growth in the Regional District of Nanaimo, BC," *Plan Canada* 41:4 (Oct.–Dec. 2001), 16–17.
7. Alberta, Municipal Affairs, *Land Use Policies*, September 1996, 4.
8. Downs, "Smart Growth."
9. Ray Tomalty and Don Alexander, *Smart Growth in Canada: A Report Card* (Ottawa: CMHC), Socio-economic Series 05-036, December 2005.
10. Larry S. Bourne, "The Urban Sprawl Debate: Myths, Realities and Hidden Agendas," *Plan Canada* 41:4 (Oct.–Dec. 2001), 26–28.
11. John M. Bryson and William D. Roering, "Applying Private Sector Strategic Planning in the Public Sector," *Journal of the American Planning Association* 53:1 (Winter 1987), 9–22; and Mark Seasons, "Strategic Planning in the Public Sector Environment: Addressing the Realities *Plan Canada*, 29:6 (November 1989), 9–27.
12. Service Nova Scotia and Municipal Relations, *Local Government Resource Handbook* (Halifax: 2000), 7.
13. Called the Focus Community Strategic Plan, it can be viewed at www.cityofkingston.ca/cityhall/strategic/index.asp
14. Manfred Fast, "Community Can Make It Happen: Forging the Port Colborne Ontario Strategic Plan," *Small Town* 26:1 (July–August 1995), 10–15.
15. Richard D. Margerum, "Getting Past Yes: From Capital Creation to Action," *Journal of the American Planning Association* 65:2 (Spring 1999), 181–192.
16. Gord Jackson and Mary Ann McConnell-Boehm, "Plan Edmonton: A Plan and a Process," *Plan Canada* 39:5 (November 1999), 17–19.
17. City of Edmonton, *Planning and Development Handbook* (Edmonton, 2000).
18. Frank S. So and Judith Getzels, eds., *The Practice of Local Government Planning* (Washington: International City Manager's Association, 1988).
19. Robert Coughlin, "The Capital Programming Problem," *Journal of the American Institute of Planners* 26 (February 1960), 39–48.
20. Government Finance Officers Association, *Capital Improvement Programming: A Guide for Smaller Governments* (Chicago: GFOA, 1996).
21. Coughlin, "The Capital Programming Problem."
22. Robert H, Bowyer, *Capital Improvements Programs*, (Chicago: American Planning Association, 1993), Planning Advisory Service Bulletin 442.
23. Service Nova Scotia, *Government Handbook*, Section 6.2.
24. The 2012–14 Vancouver Capital Plan may be viewed at http://vancouver.ca/your-government/capital-plan.aspx
25. Casey Brendon et al., "Urban Innovations: Financial Tools in Brownfield Revitalization," *Plan Canada* 44:4 (Winter 2004), 26–29.
26. Christopher A. De Sousa, Changshan Wu, and Lynne M. Westphal, "Assessing the Effect of Publicly Assisted Brownfield Redevelopment on Surrounding Property Values," *Economic Development Quarterly* 23:2 (May 2009), 95–110; Michael Hayek, Godwin Arku, and Jason Gilliland, "Assessing London, Ontario's Brownfield Redevelopment Effort to Promote Urban Intensification," *Local Environment* 15:4 (April 2010), 389–402.
27. Greg Lampert and Marc Denhez, *Levies, Fees, Charges, Taxes, and Transaction Costs on New Housing* (Ottawa: Canada Mortgage and Housing Corporation, 1997).
28. Andrejs Skaburskis and Ray Tomalty, "Development Charges and City Planning Objectives: The Ontario Disconnect," *Joint Issue Canadian Planning and Policy/Canadian Journal of Urban Research* (2003), 142–161; and Skaburskis and Tomalty, "How Property Taxes and Development Charges Can Be Used to Shape Cities," *Plan Canada* 41:1 (January–February–March 2001), 24–30.
29. Donald Shoup, *The High Cost of Free Parking* (Chicago: Planners Press, 2011).
30. Pamela Blais, *Perverse Cities: Hidden Subsidies, Wonky Policy, and Urban Sprawl* (Vancouver, BC: UBC Press, 2010).
31. Canadian Council for Public–Private Partnerships, *Canadian PPP Project Directory* (Toronto, 2012).
32. James McKellar and David Gordon, *The RFP Process for the Disposition of Publicly Owned Real Estate Assets* (Kingston, ON: National Executive Forum on Public Property, Queen's University, November 2007).
33. Matti Siemiatycki, "Urban Transportation Public–Private Partnerships: Drivers of Uneven Development," *Environment and Planning A* 43 (2011), 1707–1722; Matti Siemiatycki, "Implications of Private–Public Partnerships on the Development of Urban Public Transit Infrastructure: The Case of Vancouver, Canada," *Journal of Planning Education and Research* 26 (2006),137–151; and David Ross, "Le partnering, une méthode de prévention des conflits dans le cadre de projets urbains," *Urbanité* (Winter 2010), 32–33. Canadian Centre for Policy Alternatives, BC Office, *Assessing the Record of Public–Private Partnerships* (Vancouver, 2003).
34. Ontario, Ministry of Municipal Affairs and Housing, *Business Improvement Areas Handbook* (Toronto: Queen's Printer, 2010).
35. Cf. Francois Leblanc, "La renaissance des centre-villes: Le programme Rues princi-pales," *Plan Canada* 29:5 (September 1989), 8–13.
36. Matthew Kiernan, "Intergovernmental Innovation: Winnipeg's Core Area Initiative," *Plan Canada* 27:1 (March 1987), 23–31.
37. Christaine Lefbure and Eve Wertheimer, "An Indispensible Reference for Heritage Conservation," *Plan Canada* 46:1 (Spring 2006), 41–43.
38. City of Edmonton, *Planning and Development Handbook* (Edmonton, 2000).
39. Peter Brown, "America's Waterfront Revival: Port Authorities and Urban Redevelopment (Philadelphia, PA: University of Pennsylvania Press, 2008); and David Gordon, "Managing the Changing Political Environment in Urban Waterfront Redevelopment," *Urban Studies* 34:1 (1997), 61–83.
40. Alan Richards, "Implementing a Voluntary Process for Difficult-to-Site Projects," *Plan Canada* 36:1 (January 1996), 31–32.
41. David Gordon and André Juneau, "Bridging Mechanisms for the Ottawa–Gatineau Region," in R. Chattopadhyay and G. Paquet, eds., *The Unimagined Canadian Capital: Challenges for the Federal Capital Region* (Ottawa: Invenire Press, 2011), 87–104.
42. Barton Reid, "Harbourfront: Aesthetics vs. Dollars," *City Magazine* 8:3,4 (Fall 1986), 9–10; David Crombie, Royal Commission on the Future of the Toronto Waterfront, *Regeneration: Toronto's Waterfront and the Sustainable City, Final Report* (Toronto: Queen's Printer, 1992); and David Gordon, "Managing Change on the Urban Edge: Implementing Urban Waterfront Redevelopment in Toronto," in G. Halseth and H. Nicol, eds., *(Re)Development at the Urban Edge* (Waterloo, ON: University of Waterloo Press, 2000), 175–226.

Internet Resources

Chapter-Relevant Sites

Planning Canadian Communities
www.planningcanadiancommunities.ca

Iqaluit sustainable subdivision
www.city.iqaluit.nu.ca/i18n/english/plateau.html

Vancouver CityPlan Projects
www.vancouver.ca/home-property-development/neighbourhood-planning-projects.aspx

Heritage Planning, City of Windsor
www.citywindsor.ca/residents/planning/planning-policy/heritage-planning/pages/heritage-planning.aspx

Waterfront Toronto
www.waterfrontoronto.ca/

Montréal Harbourfront
www.montrealsnewharbourfront.ca/en/

Nova Scotia Waterfront Development Corporation
www.wdcl.ca

Epilogue

Community Planning in Canada and the Future

"Big plans never stirred women's blood. Women have always been willing to consider little plans."

Jane Jacobs, 1980

The epigraph that opens this concluding discussion is Jane Jacobs's response to major New York developer James Rouse in 1980 when he propounded Daniel Burnham's 1909 dictum: "Make no little plans".[1] It is used here to signal one of many different human perspectives (this between women and men) on how to approach the planning of a community. Today's professional planners in Canada must respond to a diverse future. The voice could just as likely be that of youth, people with disabilities, Aboriginal peoples, recent immigrants, or the elderly (see Chapter 13). It is the latest of the many changes, and one of the most important, that have occurred in planning's ethos in the century since Burnham. Planners must still deal with such basic problems as providing suitable housing, unsnarling traffic congestion, and disposing of human and industrial wastes, but in the form they present today *and* within a diverse social milieu that demands its voice(s) be heard. In the broad sense, it is no more than the fulfillment of democracy's promises and the needed "pooling of intelligence" and "collaboration" Ken Greenberg reminds us is required of successful community-building.[2]

This epilogue discusses a number of salient issues that will challenge Canadian community planning as it moves further into its second century. This will include looking at issues that are still in need of full resolution, such as citizen participation, environmental protection, and the supply of housing. As well, there are the issues that will become even more central in the years ahead such as climate change, urban and rural community differences, and the future of the suburbs. Beyond these substantive issues it will be wise to anticipate the unexpected and unanticipated consequences that arise among the best considered planning decisions. Possibly the most important challenge will be the sociopolitical form that substantive issues present themselves, or are presented, to planners. There will be voices of neoliberalism and citizen activism vying to be heard and terms such as resilience, equity, diversity, and accountability competing with one another. Figure 18.1 from the City of Burnaby's Social Sustainability Strategy captures the ungainly milieu facing planners and their citizens. And echoes of the urgings of Jane Jacobs and John Forrester[3] will resound with reminders to community planners to examine their own premises, presuppositions, and practice, and ask of themselves the following questions:

- *How will planning practice need to be modified to provide guidance appropriate to communities in the coming decades?*
- *What principles will be needed to guide planning decisions so they are fair and equitable?*

Figure 18.1

Burnaby Social Sustainability Strategy Summary, 2011

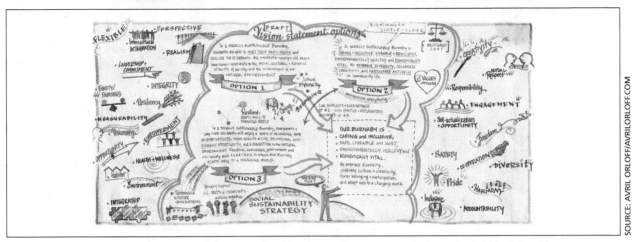

This charming graphic summarizes the main strategies to engage diverse groups in Burnaby, British Columbia.

The Burnaby Social Sustainability Plan received the CIP 2012 Social Planning Award.

Continuing and Emerging Challenges

The future shape of community planning will unfold from its past and also enfold new ingredients. This seemingly obvious statement is indicative of the somewhat paradoxical nature of the activity—it makes plans that promote change in a continually changing world. Present-day problems are, for example, part of the future the planners of two decades ago strove to change. Community changes, planned and emerging, always challenge community planners in terms of both *substance* (the form and content of plans) and *process* (making and implementing plans), and often both at the same time. Although the full array of challenges that will face Canadian planners in the future can never be foreseen, the following are already insistent on being tackled:

- Housing supply
- Citizen participation
- Climate change
- Retrofitting the suburbs
- Sustainability

Continuing to Address Housing

The problem of providing sufficient housing for all the people in a community plagues planners and city councils just as insistently today as it did in the past. Slums, and what to do about them, were central to the concerns of the "utopian" planners of the 19th century and comprised one of the prime issues for the planning profession throughout the 20th century. Why is this problem so resistant to resolution? The answer, in simple terms, is because ensuring the availability of housing is a complex problem. It is what some call a "wicked problem," because dealing with one aspect can unleash a host of other problems, often of a fundamental nature, that we are not either equipped for or prepared to tackle. The issue of housing a community's citizens means going beyond the physical problem of constructing dwellings to encompass both social and economic components, involving as it does the economically and socially vulnerable—the poor, recent immigrants, the elderly, single parents, people with disabilities, and the homeless. Such a situation is vividly revealed in a Toronto study that shows higher-poverty neighbourhoods now predominantly comprise newcomers, visible minorities, and youth.[4] Moreover, this is occurring in the city's older inner suburbs that were not originally endowed with a strong social and economic infrastructure.

Gentrification is one process that transforms existing housing stock and causes lower-income families to seek more affordable housing elsewhere in the city. This process occurs when older neighbourhoods with solid housing close to downtown are sought by higher-income households and speculative renovators with the intention of upgrading the dwellings. The usual outcome includes the loss of rental units, the increase of rents on remaining units, and the displacement of current occupants to other low-cost districts. A recent wide-ranging study by Andrejs Skaburskis examined gentrification over the census tracts of the Toronto Census Metropolitan Area for the period 1971–2001 and its effects on household incomes and characteristics including gender.[5] It confirmed that gentrification occasioned the loss of lower-priced housing stock to households of higher income and education. The lower-income households, especially in inner-city tracts, were not only displaced from their housing but were also faced with housing choices in areas that did not have the formerly easy access to downtown. Only those in social housing were not displaced in these tracts. To the extent that planners and policymakers desire a moderate degree of social mix in a district, the solution lies in non-market housing programs that provide secure tenure for residents.

Conversion to condominiums is another process that can transform the supply of housing. Owners of older apartment buildings and single-room occupancy hotels (Figure 18.2), at times faced with costly renovations, frequently seek either to convert them to condominium ownership or to raze the buildings and erect new condominium apartments. As with gentrification situations, current tenants often have lower incomes (frequently they are also elderly) and are unable to purchase a new unit and are, therefore, displaced. Similarly,

---

Figure 18.3	Site of a Once-Low-Income Neighbourhood, Calgary, 2007

The Victoria Park neighbourhood was razed to provide land to expand the Calgary Stampede Grounds.

conversions usually result in fewer units of higher cost with fewer people being housed.

Redevelopment A residential area may be razed and replaced as a result of physical deterioration of the area, expansion of adjacent land uses, or space needed for public uses (e.g., highways). The area may not be economically competitive with other "higher" land uses, with the result that the current dwellings are completely withdrawn from the housing market. Most frequently, these are areas that consist of lower-income households, who are then displaced. A recent example of this form of displacement in an old lower-income Calgary neighbourhood is vividly shown in Figure 18.3.

Inclusive Zoning is an approach that ties zoning approval for a commercial housing project to the inclusion of a fixed proportion of low-income units within the finished project (see Chapter 17). It has been used by planners and local policymakers, notably in larger centres, to acquire small amounts of affordable housing for their communities. This approach evokes several dilemmas, however. One is that the resulting negotiated units tend to be located where the private developer proposes building and may not be where the planners and others in the community know they might most be needed. Another dilemma is that such units tend to be defined by *income* affordability rather than by the *type* of shelter that may be needed given the family structures and living arrangements of those needing housing. Yet

---

Figure 18.2	Social Housing: Tamura House Hotel Renovation, Vancouver, 2008

This single-room occupancy (SRO) hotel is being renovated to preserve its role as social housing, which is particularly useful for addressing urban homelessness issues.

another is that the new housing project, being a form of gentrification, may lead to displacement of other low-income households and traditional businesses associated with the area. Moreover, this tool is not likely to help in supplying affordable housing in communities in non-metropolitan Canada, the bulk of the country, which tends not to experience the same development pressures of metropolitan centres.

Jeanne Wolfe lamented the retreat of the federal government from social housing and other social programs a decade and a half ago and then the devolution of these programs to the provinces and municipalities.[6] Since then the supply of housing in Canada has been left primarily to the private marketplace. The neoliberal philosophy guiding the marketplace approach contends that free market institutions better allocate economic resources and create the greatest economic return for all. Minimum barriers to the flow of goods, services, and capital are required in turn. Thus, collective social solutions to housing needs by, for example, municipalities, cooperatives, or nonprofit organizations are considered anathema to free market functioning by commercial interests and governments that follow their lead. However, this dependence on the commercial marketplace leaves very few means of supplying sufficient and secure shelter to Canadians in need of housing, who are currently estimated (2010) to comprise upwards of 1.5 million households (see Figure 18.4).[7] For within the neoliberal claim of producing overall economic benefits for Canadian society there is *no room* for considering the specific housing needs of, for instance, those with lesser incomes, physical disabilities, or limited social mobility. These may be supplied, if at all, through a patchwork of programs with less-than-secure funding and zoning initiatives by planners. **The challenge for planners is to strive for social housing policy at the national and/or provincial level.** There need be no other reason than to honour those planners who, long ago, knew how much the availability of safe and secure housing is a key to community resilience.

Fulfilling Citizen Participation

Major strides have been made in the past two decades to engage citizens in the planning of their communities. It has become almost standard practice in large cities and small towns to open plan-making with a visioning project.[8] Indeed, some communities employ a broad array of formats to elicit the values and preferences from their citizens including web-based and social media tools

Figure 18.4	The Scale of Unmet Housing Needs in Canada

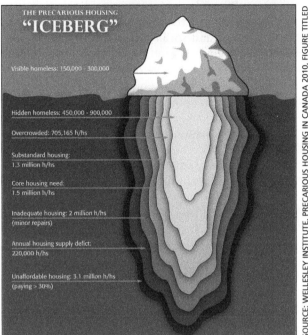

SOURCE: WELLESLEY INSTITUTE, PRECARIOUS HOUSING IN CANADA 2010, FIGURE TITLED "LAYERS OF THE AFFORDABLE HOUSING ICEBERG" P. 32.

Most of the unmet needs for housing are not readily visible, like the underside of an iceberg.

as witness Saskatoon's approach.[9] When supplemented by active participation of citizens on planning advisory committees and boards, it becomes apparent that community planning in Canada has in general reached the middle rungs—*consultation*—on Arnstein's ladder of participation (see Figure 15.4, page 370). However, going further upward into the area of sharing plan-making power with citizens is a rare situation.

Although widespread consultation occurs, this achievement is fragile. Offering the opportunity to citizens to participate does not guarantee that all are able to, even if willing. To be truly inclusive means being aware of possible barriers to participation for some because of language, timing, physical access, or cultural custom. Although many techniques of public engagement are being used, it is important to grasp that each engages citizens in different ways: information meetings seldom involve dialogue with citizens, citizen panels engage only a few, and Internet sites provide one-way engagement. While it is now considered good 21st-century practice to use more and novel techniques of engagement,[10] two cautions are needed. First, there is no known way of summing the citizen input obtained from each engagement tool (e.g., are they of equal importance and by what measure?). Second, there is little knowledge about the effectiveness of web-based approaches in public participation in planning compared to traditional techniques (e.g., are web-based and social media tools more empowering?).[11] Moreover, a good deal of community consultation tends to favour more organized segments of the public and thereby exclude or not provide for an equal voice for those less prepared.

Citizen participation is constrained, not least, by our legislated information meetings and public hearings (see Chapter 14). These remain, essentially, one-way means of communication with no provision either for dialogue or for ensuring citizens that they have been heard. Based as they are on commenting on plans or other proposals already made, there is no role for citizens but to react. They have no entitlement to answers to their questions and assertions. Ideally, it would be preferable if other means of two-way communication were allowed for in legislation. But, in lieu of that, the best course is to determine the public's pulse well before the public hearing and use collaborative means to deal with contentious issues.

Language is one of the confounding issues in citizen participation for both citizens and planners, regardless of the degree of inclusiveness. Words written down or spoken, by professionals or citizens, often convey such different meanings that little meaningful communication actually takes place.[12] As one planner notes:

> The core of planning activity involves bringing the different interests of the private and public sectors into a certain balance and therefore planners need to speak several "languages."[13]

Other uses of language in planning can also be problematic, such as the too-easy use of words such as "activist" and "NIMBY" to dismiss those who persist in making their points, much less listening to them.[14] Furthermore, attitudes frequently change when details of a project become known and/or it is shown that the plans, when compared with local knowledge, are faulty.[15] Lastly, there is the fashionable tendency to refer to citizens as "customers," apparently to parallel the positioning of municipalities as businesses proceeding in a business-like way.[16] Referring to citizens as customers obscures the issue of citizens' rights and reinforces an all-too-frequent "ambivalence" on the part of planners and politicians toward *citizen* participation.[17] Some of this wariness may be attributable to the often high level of

emotions citizens bring to meetings, emotions bred frequently from the intensity of their attachment to their "place," their neighbourhood (see also Chapter 13).[18] The people who do participate, and those who might, are citizens, and they deserve planning processes that give them more than a time and a place to vent their ideas and feelings, to be more than just consulted. **The challenge for planners is to ensure the public participation they engage in is inclusive, evokes trust, and is empowering to citizens.**

A New Environmental Challenge: Addressing Climate Change

Canadian community planning has embraced sustainable development over the past decade, and the natural environment component of sustainability has become a standard element of the planning process, as described in Chapter 7. However, these well-established environmental planning practices are being pushed beyond their roots in landscape ecology to address the growing global climate change agenda (Figure 18.5).[19]

The Canadian Institute of Planners' *Declaration on Climate Change* states:

> Climate change, caused by the excessive consumption of energy derived from hydrocarbons, is a reality. The overwhelming evidence around the world is that human action is driving rapid and unprecedented global climate change.[20]

Figure 18.5	Climate Change in Rankin Inlet, Nunavut

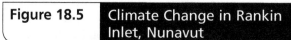

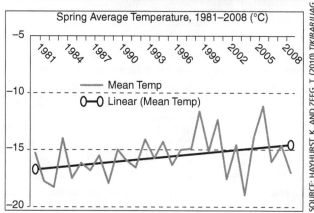

SOURCE: HAYHURST, K. AND ZEEG, T. (2010) TIKIRARJUAG (WHALE COVE) CLIMATE CHANGE ACTION PLAN. PREPARED FOR CANADIAN INSTITUTE OF PLANNERS.

The historical spring temperature in Rankin Inlet, Nunavut, is trending upwards and showing more volatility. This has implications for the sea ice and coastal conditions for this Inuit Arctic community.

To combat this problem, the Canadian planning profession is committed to:

- creating livable, sustainable, healthy, safe, and welcoming places that have a measurable, direct, and significant impact on mitigating climate change;[21]
- the transformation of suburbs into carbon neutral communities;[22]
- human-scale transit that moves high volumes of people in energy-efficient low-carbon modes and supports sufficient transportation of goods;[23]
- the preservation of significant and large natural spaces and maintenance of endemic biodiversity;[24]
- integrated design and planning for community-building that promotes effective and resilient mitigation and adaptation processes;[25] and
- continual exploration of innovative relevant practices that address climate change.[26]

This ambitious agenda will not be easy to move forward, especially in the face of climate change denial from some elements of Canada's political spectrum. One of the first steps will be to move our standard environmental planning practices forward beyond simple ecological planning.

Beyond Ecological Planning

Over the evolution of Canadian community planning, a number of issues have been transformed and become more complex, but none more so than environmental protection. The long-standing planning traditions of conservation, park planning, and open-space preservation began to give way, about three decades ago, to concerns over ecosystems and biodiversity. The planners' response to ecological concerns in many ways has been commendable, among them North Vancouver's Alpine Area Official Community Plan, Markham's Natural Features Study, and greenways planning for pedestrians and bicycles in Kelowna and Windsor. Nevertheless, local land use planning is primarily about improving the built environment and achieving livability of a community; the defence of nature has often been left to regional or provincial initiatives such as the central Ontario Greenbelt or agricultural land preservation in British Columbia and Québec. An inherent difficulty in planning for the two environments—natural and built—is that it raises an underlying conflict, as North Vancouver's and other planners have realized, of "protecting the natural environment vs. land development," or what would come to be called the "property conflict" in debates over sustainable development (see Chapter 7 and Figure 18.6).

To address climate change, we need to move beyond these dilemmas and see ourselves as part of the natural system of the planet and "redesign ourselves into the system of life." Beyond this, planners need to strive for the "ecological restructuring of urban form and the development of ecological efficiencies in urban systems." The concept of compact urban form has received considerable attention as a model for urban environmental planning, especially the forms to reduce sprawl promoted by the New Urbanists (see Chapters 5 and 7). Although there is much to commend these forms for increasing urban density, more important is that development (compact or otherwise) has to be "in the right place, at the right time, in the right form" so as to not disrupt ecological systems. Planners need to incorporate into their plan-making, from the beginning, an appreciation of the integral connection of human communities and natural ecological processes. One of the ways is to foster partnerships between governments and local conservation groups and neighbourhood organizations to acquire sensitive lands and to steward them. More pointedly planners should undertake **to make the human–ecological mutuality a guiding principle for land use planning.**

Community Planning to Address Climate Change and Create Resilient Cities

Several Canadian communities have initiated planning policies to address climate change, developing a selection of tools and strategies.[27] Municipal governments such as Red Deer, Alberta, Prince George, British Columbia, and Toronto have produced climate change action strategies, while others are including the issue in their comprehensive plans.[28]

In addition to planning to reduce the amount of global climate change, Canadian communities must also plan to ameliorate the effects of the rising temperatures, increased weather extremes, and rising sea levels that are already creating problems. For example, Sudbury has developed a hot weather response plan, New Brunswick's Tantramar dykelands must be protected against storm damage, and British Columbia coastal communities such as Gibson's Landing and Vancouver are considering new flood protection.[29]

The general approach is to create communities that are more resilient to disasters and long-term change. Canadian planners must learn from disasters, such as Hurricane Katrina's destruction of New Orleans, that may be useful for minimizing the impacts of extreme events in the future.[30]

Retrofitting the Suburbs: Sprawl Repair?

Canada is a suburban nation. Canadian cities grew at an unprecedented rate after World War II, and most of that growth was in the form of low density, auto-dependent suburbs. As a result, approximately two-thirds of Canadians live in post-1945 suburbs.[31]

The post-war transformation of Canadian communities was extraordinary, not just in numbers of people and houses but also in the spatial dimensions of urban community life. These dramatic changes are often viewed in a pessimistic light, with the suburbs being stereotyped as undifferentiated streetscapes that are inconvenient, energy-inefficient, and promote social anomie and gender discrimination.[32] Other observers are concerned about the inefficiency, ecological impacts, financial burdens, and governance challenges of our expanding metropolitan areas.[33]

Although the decentralization of cities has been apparent throughout history, in the past few decades, this low-density, scattered urban development has been re-coined as "sprawl."[34] Considerable effort has been directed toward eliminating sprawl, most recently under the umbrella of Smart Growth, which argues for more compact (i.e., higher-density) communities with better transportation and protection of natural areas.[35] Debate over sprawl has ensued from its supposed ills to how to measure it and even over whether it really exists. The noted urban geographer Larry Bourne states candidly that "urban Canada has relatively little sprawl if this is thought of as 'haphazard, disorganized, poorly serviced and largely unplanned.'"[36]

These differences in viewpoints about the suburbs are as much about attitude as about substance. "Sprawl" is a pejorative, just as "slum" and "urban blight" were before; it is equally hard to define and fails to recognize that the suburbs are where most *people* currently live. Essentially, people make conscious choices to move into these new communities. As suburbs mature, almost all major land uses start to be found there (or nearby) and so residents can, and do, conduct most of their daily lives within these localized "urban realms."[37] Moreover, planning efforts to redevelop older suburbs to accommodate higher densities often encounter the dilemma that residents want to maintain the existing densities,[38] and these policies were regarded as good planning by most observers in the 1950s and 1960s. Indeed, if sprawl is defined as haphazard and *unplanned* suburban development, as described by Bourne, then Canada must have relatively little sprawl, since almost all suburban development in the past fifty years has been approved through the land use planning systems. If Canada has suburban sprawl, then it is because conventional suburban development was the planning policy of federal, provincial, regional, and local governments for a forty-year period.

At this juncture, there is not much point arguing over labels or playing the blame game. Over the past decade, policymakers at most levels of government have been trying to change the direction of metropolitan growth because of concerns about environmental sustainability, energy efficiency, transportation issues, and a lack of fit between our housing stock and demographic changes that are rushing forward with the aging of the baby boom generation.[39] But the financial and regulatory edifice that underpins conventional suburban development has proven remarkably difficult to modify, and the accumulated momentum of a half-century of suburban development means that most of the building stock that is available for the next generation is already constructed. In nautical terms, we must turn the direction of a large, slow-moving ship using steering gear that is sticky.

There are three aspects of existing suburban development that need particular attention. The first of these is that *a vast amount of housing is already 50 or more years old* and soon may be considered obsolete. Recognizing this dilemma, Montréal architect and planner Avi Friedman and his colleagues have been developing approaches that would allow suburbs to evolve gradually to meet current housing needs and become more complete.[40] A comparable effort aimed at retrofitting ville de Québec post-war suburbs is planned by that city's Inter Disciplinary Research Group on Suburbs.[41] The process in both cases would be resident-motivated and gradual, and the transformations would be small scale; its key is the built-in flexibility to allow each neighbourhood to change in its own way at its own pace. Retrofitting the inner suburbs will be a major challenge in Toronto, where low-income residents have migrated to older rental housing built in the 1960s and 1970s, in neighbourhoods that are difficult to serve by public transit.[42] The older suburban retrofitting process depends upon the availability of compatible land use planning tools and regulations, thus posing the following challenge for planners: To **develop appropriate plans and planning tools that will facilitate the transformation and renewal of older suburbs on the residents' terms.**

The second aspect of suburban areas needing attention reflects *the aging of their population.* The people who moved to the suburbs as young and middle-aged adults have now become seniors, or soon will be; more than half of all urban seniors live in the suburbs. The import of this is that most suburbs were designed for families with children and with access, almost exclusively, by automobile. Housing tends to be uniform, single-family detached types, and commercial and service clusters are widely separated. Seniors, by comparison, are less mobile (as many as one-quarter do not have access to an automobile), subject to more physical impairment, and, with increasing age, often require alternative forms of housing. Given their natural desire to continue living in the neighbourhoods they've become accustomed to, suburban seniors face many constraints: stores and doctors' offices are not usually within walking distance, sidewalks might not exist even where transit stops are relatively near, and options for apartment living are rarely available if a spouse should pass on.

The general solution is to retrofit suburban neighbourhoods to suit the needs of their elderly populations, most of whom will want to continue to live there far into old age. The answers are relatively straightforward (as indicated in Chapter 13): add sidewalks and good street lighting, add other housing types, implant small-scale clusters of health, social service, and commercial facilities, and devise transportation options that are flexible and appropriate.

A final challenge for retrofitting suburbia is *"sprawl repair"*—redeveloping greyfields (dead malls), brownfields (former industrial sites), and auto corridors, as well as intensifying lands near transit stations, institutions, and low-density office parks, using the techniques described in Chapter 11.[43] Intensification on suburban sites is often an easier task from an urban design perspective, but community engagement and opposition can be just as fierce as in inner-city neighbourhoods.[44]

Planning Issue Epilogue	Canadian Cities Trying to Redefine What It Means to Be an Urban Planner

The Globe and Mail
July 6, 2012

Canadian Cities Trying to Redefine What It Means to Be an Urban Planner

John Lorinc and Siri Agrell

Toronto, Vancouver, Calgary and Halifax face towering challenges as they replace and redefine the roles of their chief planners

When Rollin Stanley worked for the City of Toronto, he often joked that he didn't "do suburbs."

Last month, shortly after he started a new job as Calgary's top planning official, a local alderman presented him with a bumper sticker that read, "I do suburbs, and I do them better."

After stints in two U.S. cities, Mr. Stanley has returned to Canada with a mandate to help Calgary build subdivisions that are more compact, higher density, and accessible to transit.

"They know where they want to get to," he said. "My job is to help them understand how they get there, and helping them define what that vision is."

He steps into the job at an interesting time for those tasked with urban design, when economic uncertainty is kneecapping municipal budgets and the pressures of suburban sprawl, downtown development and aging infrastructure are becoming impossible to ignore. And Mr. Stanley is not alone in his challenges: Several major Canadian cities are looking to replace their chief planners, a hiring spree that could significantly change the country's urban landscape.

Toronto's chief planner has retired, while his Halifax counterpart has moved to an academic posting. And Vancouver is looking to replace its director of planning, Brent Toderian, who Mayor Gregor Robertson fired in January, saying he wanted the city to re-focus on housing affordability.

CONTINUED

All the turnover is worrisome, says Joe Berridge, a Toronto planning consultant in the private sector, because of the complex, vital role these bureaucrats play in a city's development.

"There are very few people around in the world who can do it well. It's like being a concert master," he said. "That's why there's such a dearth of candidates for your Vancouvers and Halifaxes and Torontos."

The churn also raises a nagging question about the role of these influential municipal officials: do fast-growing cities need – or indeed, want – visionary chief planners? Or do they actually require can-do administrators who have the contacts and political savvy to deliver change in modern metropolitan areas?

The biggest threat, according to Larry Beasley, Vancouver's former co-planning director, is that the position will be devalued, or submerged in bureaucracy.

Chief planners must be risk takers, he said, and play the role of the "enfant terrible" in municipal governments.

There's little doubt that forward-looking planners have made dramatic differences in places like Copenhagen, New York and Melbourne, bringing life surging back into central areas that had either been choked with cars or semi-abandoned.

And although Canadian cities are largely thriving, that does not mean the next generation will have it easy.

The new challenges revolve around livability and sustainability, especially in cardependent suburbs that aren't well served by transit. Many of today's top planners, including Mr. Stanley and Mr. Toderian, promote similar ideas – green buildings, cycling, pedestrian-friendly streets, accessible waterfronts and transit-oriented development.

Yet much of what they're able to implement will depend on political and regulatory context. In U.S. cities with strong mayors, leaders like New York's Michael Bloomberg can hand-pick top planners to execute their agendas. In Ontario cities, planners' recommendations are routinely vetoed by the Ontario Municipal Board.

Each Canadian city looking to replace its top planner has unique advantages and obstacles.

In Vancouver, Mr. Beasley said he succeeded because the job of planning director was split in two, allowing him to concentrate on large- and small-scale vision while Ann McAfee oversaw the department's administrative responsibilities. But even with that setup, chief planners must sell their ideas to voters, and Mr. Toderian reportedly ran into opposition from ratepayer groups. He's now in private practice.

In Calgary, Mr. Stanley has the benefit of an ambitious master plan and a progressive mayor, Naheed Nenshi. But the city has sprawl issues, and Mr. Nenshi said the priority is to find "sensitive" ways to add density and vitality to the city's older suburbs. "That's why Rollins' job is unbelievably critical," he said.

The 54-year-old barely had time to unpack his suitcase before he began conferring with developers about zoning changes that could foster better suburbs.

"We've already had an impact in the three weeks I've been out here," he said.

In Toronto, a search is under way for a new chief planner, who will have to hustle to keep abreast of an unprecedented high-rise building boom even as the city struggles to find cash to build transit lines, improve public space and accelerate waterfront development before the 2015 PanAm Games.

"The right person could triumph over what are undoubtedly tricky bureaucratic, administrative structures in city hall," Mr. Berridge said.

Toronto chief planner Paul Bedford negotiated similarly stressful times in the mid-1990s, and managed to push through a plan allowing the conversion of old downtown warehouses into offices or condos – a radical move that brought waves of new investment and residents to the core.

He credits advice from his mentor, Jane Jacobs, who told him to be bold and outspoken. "'If you're going to do something,'" she counselled, "don't do it in a half-assed way.'"

Mr. Beasley remains optimistic that Canada's urban visions will be crafted by the right hands. He believes many top planners from U.S. cities will be eager to work north of the border, where budgetary dilemmas look manageable by comparison.

And he says up-and-coming Canadian planners now moving into senior positions have impeccable credentials and a global outlook.

"The new generation, it's their time to take over," he said. "I think you're going to see some wonderful new initiatives across the country over the next few years."

Achieving Sustainability

The broad concerns encompassed by the concept of sustainable development have influenced environmental planning since the 1980s. However, sustainability is turning out to be an extremely complex issue; clearly, it reaches beyond simple questions of ecosystems protection and resource conservation. It involves a concern with three major facets: economic growth, social development, and environmental protection, or the three E's as they have been called—economy, equity, and environment.[45] A quick glance at these facets of sustainability indicates that even though each of them is integral to the planning of cities, towns, and regions, they were central to the work of the World Commission, which defined sustainable development as "development that meets the needs of the present without compromising the ability of future generations to meet their own needs."[46] Yet the building of a community constitutes "development," so can it too be made sustainable?

The nature of sustainable development presents the planner with three broad goals that are integral to one another. In other words, the community plan should promote

- economic growth and efficiency;
- environmental protection (natural and built); and
- social justice and equity.

American planner Scott Campbell suggests that one imagine these as three points of a triangle in which each point, or goal, is linked to the other two.[47] Viewing Figure 18.6 one can quickly grasp that there are inherent conflicts in attaining each individual planning goal, much less all three. Campbell identifies them as

- the **property conflict** between economic growth and social justice;
- the **development conflict** between environmental protection and social justice; and
- the **resource conflict** between economic growth and environmental protection.

Planners have recognized one of these dilemmas, the "property conflict," for some time. It goes back to the earliest days of zoning and other public land use regulation and, more recently, in such interventions as urban renewal and gentrification in established neighbourhoods. It has also been evident (although not in these

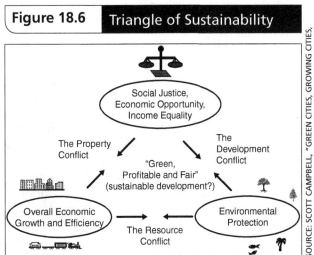

| Figure 18.6 | Triangle of Sustainability |

The triangle of three potentially conflicting goals for planning and associated conflicts.

Planners define their outlook on sustainability on where they stand in the triangle.

SOURCE: SCOTT CAMPBELL, "GREEN CITIES, GROWING CITIES, JUST CITIES?: URBAN PLANNING AND THE CONTRADICTIONS OF SUSTAINABLE DEVELOPMENT," *JOURNAL OF THE AMERICAN PLANNING ASSOCIATION* 62:3 (SUMMER 1996), 296–312. FIGURE 1. TAYLOR AND FRANCIS LTD WWW.INFORMAWORLD.COM

terms) to people in communities suffering the after-math of major industrial development (i.e., economic growth) causing toxic pollution of their backyards many years later (i.e., social equity). From the pollution in Calgary's Lynnview Ridge (due to a former oil refinery), to Wawa in Ontario (due to iron ore processing), and Sydney, Nova Scotia (due to a steel mill), residents have not only sought solutions but have also been frustrated in their attempts to determine who is responsible for undertaking a solution.[48]

The ideal position for the planner, the sustainability position, is at the centre of the triangle balancing off each of the goals. Even this is not a complete answer, as Godschalk has pointed out, for when planners tout "livability" they posit a competing visionary idea.[49] His resolution to this apparent conflict is to reconstruct the sustainability triangle by adding livability and forming a three-dimensional prism, thereby incorporating all the principal values that are needed to broach sustain-ability in human settlement terms. Further refinement is needed in order to recognize, in actual communities, that sustainability will need to be tackled at different scales, from the region to the neighbourhood. For example, the initiatives to design and gather indicators of progress toward sustainability, such as in Hamilton and Calgary,[50] have to recognize that indicators at the regional level will differ from those used at the city-wide and neighbourhood levels. In the same vein, what would constitute sustainable housing is some-thing that becomes apparent at the neighbourhood level, as shown in Vancouver's Village at False Creek (Figure 18.7).

One Canadian study has determined that row housing is the most sustainable[51] and that the "grow home" and "next home" designed by Avi Friedman at McGill University's School of Architecture may be an affordable prototype. But, as Friedman points out, creating energy efficient buildings is not sufficient to create a sustainable community—location and scale make a difference.[52] Thus, regional plans, community plans, and small-area plans will each need to employ different tools and mirror sustainable development needs in different ways, hopefully, as an integrated set, an "ecology" of plans. The Leadership in Energy and Environmental Design- Neighbourhood Development (LEED-ND) rating system is an encouraging attempt to move beyond the individual green building to consider sustainability at the neighbourhood scale.[53]

The challenge for planners is to respond to Robert Gibson's salient question:[54] **"Is a brilliant planning**

| Figure 18.7 | Vancouver's Village at False Creek |

SOURCE: SEFC PROPERTIES LTD.

The Village at False Creek (Olympic Village), Vancouver, winner of the 2010 CIP Award for Neighbourhood Planning, was designed as a model of sustainable devel-opment. It was certified as LEED Platinum—"the greenest community in North America," according to the U.S. Green Building Council. However, its developer ran into difficulties after the 2008 financial market meltdown and had to be bailed out by the City of Vancouver, which preserved the environmental and social housing compo-nents of the project, even as the market housing costs escalated.

initiative [enter your favourite example here] helping us to move closer to a desirable and resilient future or is it just slowing our descent into ever deepening unsustainability?"

The Sufficiency of Practice

The topics in the foregoing section raise a basic ques-tion: **Is planning practice sufficient to meet the kinds of challenges that planners will have to confront?** It can be seen in this array that there are challenges yet to be fully met and those that have only recently emerged within the ever-changing societal milieu and its values. Indeed, one is struck by both the increasing number and diversity of the challenges and, within them, the demands to respond to the needs and capabilities of individuals and groups from diverse parts of the citi-zenry: demands for inclusion and participation in their community's plan-making. Though many would demur, planners are the lead professionals in this facet of public life in a community; they have the power to conduct plan-making processes. Further, these are not just challenges about the content of community plans, programs, and policies: they are, significantly, about the content and conduct of planning practice.

These and other challenges confront planners today with the need to consider their values, their moral positions, and, not least, their concept of the roles they play as professionals. Indeed, the demands of this new milieu for planners could require them to choose between the two contrasting roles, so trenchantly pointed to by Sandercock, of "anti-hero" or "passionate pilgrim."[55] The former refers to the neutral technical advisor role, so common for planners in institutionalized and bureaucratic settings, while the latter refers to playing a proactive advocacy role on behalf of citizens, a not-uncommon stance among planners in the 1930s and the 1960s. The planning profession, in turn, must consider whether and how it could encompass these distinctive perspectives within its activities. How would planning staffs function? Who would take the lead role in plan-making? How would this affect the content of community plans, or even the need for plans? This concluding section considers such questions with the aim of developing a more self-conscious, reflective approach to planning practice.

Whither Planners and Planning?

Accepting to meet even one of the challenges posed in this epilogue will, at a minimum, demand planners appraise both the *substance* and *style* of their current planning practice. The issues, which range across housing, the environment, the elderly and disabled, and multiculturalism, involve not only plans and their making but moral questions as well. There is today far greater community consciousness about both the potential for planning and its limits. This consciousness has given rise to concerns about the livability of communities and, more specifically, about economic opportunities and social justice. These tendencies argue for a planning process that is both more fine-grained and more inclusive. For city-building is a complex project with multiple actors from governments, the private sector, and civil society, "each of whom brings relevant knowledge to the table."[56] The active involvement of more participants will bring into focus the need for planners to work more and more with custom-made plans for particular neighbourhoods, functions, and projects.

Leaders or Followers?

Facing this sort of agenda will require transformations in planners' styles and planning-agency relations. For one, it will demand that planners acknowledge that planning and politics are linked even in the technical work of data gathering and analysis, modelling, forecasting, and so forth. Even there one has to make assumptions about the best course to take and thereby accept only some options with their "political implications and consequences."[57] Beyond this it will demand that planners know how to make their efforts politically effective, including encouraging citizen empowerment.[58] Given the bureaucratic orientation planners have adopted, can such changes be attained? Can (and will) planners share their powers with other participants? Not easily, if some recent reactions of planners are indicative. Many planners are frustrated by ungainly citizen-participation processes and see themselves as becoming subordinated to the lay public, as "abdicating" their role of shaping cities.[59] Planners may not, however, have the luxury of entertaining the issue of leadership in an increasingly complex world that demands a greater variety of expertise and a broader range of involvement. More fruitful would be to assume the role of initiating and guiding the formation of the partnerships among governments, the private sector, and citizen groups that are so necessary to achieving many of today's planning situations. For, as Earl Levin points out, "No single person can master all the disciplines which are required for a comprehensive understanding of the complexities of the contemporary metropolis."[60]

Short Term versus Long Term

A dilemma for many planners is how to achieve timelier and more certain implementation of plans and policies. From within the profession, there are calls to abandon long-term comprehensive planning in favour of a "short-term, problem-oriented" stance. It would probably be relatively easy for planners in bureaucratic settings to shift to such a perspective. While this may result in more rapid implementation of policies, it could lead to a less open planning process at a time when public sentiment is for more, not less, citizen participation. Also it would be contrary to the need for long-term thinking regarding matters of sustainability. An approach such as strategic planning, which deliberately links a plan and the means for its implementation, might offer a way out of the dilemma providing, of course, it allows adequate time for participation and proper consideration of sustainability issues. Moreover, when we consider the need for planning at several scales—neighbourhood, city, region, province—and each addresses different problems within different time frames, which can "only be loosely coordinated," short-term planning would be limited.[61]

If planners gravitate entirely toward short-term planning, long-term planning will be weakened. The major conceptual argument against long-term planning has been its inability to take into account unanticipated changes within its time frame—for example, the failure of projects to materialize, the emergence of new opportunities, and even disasters. However, the solution is not to substitute short-term planning (where vagaries also occur) but to institute *contingency* or *action* planning. To this one might add regular plan reviews, including thoroughgoing evaluations, which planners in many communities today seem to do grudgingly if at all. As well, there are tools such as capital improvement programs that set out realizable steps. Planners need to recognize, as did Harvey Perloff, that in reducing the time frame of a plan it also reduces their "capacity to deal with the future," where the unexpected and unintended seem always to occur.[62] We will only deal with climate change and other environmental consideration by planning half a century ahead, as some communities are already prepared to do.[63]

The short-term perspective suits many developers and builders and, it needs to be added, those who construct regulations to satisfy them. Planning regulations most often are designed to respond to immediate or recent land use concerns and seldom consider whether they will be viable for the community over the longer term.[64] Plans and regulations that abetted low-density suburbs with bigger and bigger houses, regrettably, did not think ahead to the aging of urban population with its much smaller households and citizens with mobility and transportation limitations. This future was predicted more than two decades ago.[65] Mark Seasons wonders, "Who is going to live in these big houses in the future," a future already with us?[66] And of the bigger picture of achieving sustainability for Canada and its cities, Jill Grant puts **the challenge for planners to think long-term, "to acknowledge mortality and avoid complacency.[67]**

How Do We Know What We Know?

Regardless of the level at which they practice, planners are looked to by others (colleagues, politicians, the public) to provide forecasts about future conditions and outcomes. Yet, too often, these forecasts either overstate or understate the situations they seek

to portray.[68] While they tend to fade in prominence, into background studies, forecasts have an impact on the amount and source of resources that are mobilized in implementing a plan. Not only must planners work to improve their means of analysis and forecasting, but they must also be more aware of their use and impact. In a related way, insufficient attention is paid to developing skills in critical appraisal of data and research findings in the training of planners. The dearth of case studies in the planning literature adds further to this and means that there is no easy way for planners to know what works and what doesn't. This is especially important as planning becomes increasingly interactive, involving multiple actors of whom each brings their own rational understanding to the task. These, too, can be knowledge-producing situations, but their value may be diminished unless the planner also has the "organizational and political savvy" to take advantage of them.[69] Another form of savvy is for planners to be aware of the presuppositions that guide much practice. (A few of these are examined in Figure 18.8.)

It is now widely assumed that planners cannot rely only on technically based professional knowledge, which in many ways has become compartmentalized. It will require planners to integrate knowledge from different fields, as Pierre Filion notes (see Figure 18.9).[70] Further, planning is "communicative." It is about having dialogues with others and through such dialogues planners will be introduced other ways of knowing. With demands for greater inclusion of more participants, this new "knowledge" must have an equal role to that of professional knowledge in planning processes.[71] Planners thus have the opportunity to know more about the situations under deliberation, knowledge that does not meet the same criteria as scientific, technical knowledge. It is knowledge that comes from the other participants' own experience, personal stories, the images and representations participants employ in making their points, and from the intuition of participants.[72] As planners collaborate more with others, the richness of knowing a planning problem from many perspectives and, thus, its various possible solutions, will become evident to all participants. Jean Monteith tells planners directly: **"No form of public should be dismissed."[73]**

Professional and Personal Ethics

Planners frequently find themselves facing dilemmas in their professional worlds that impinge on their

Figure 18.8 Ten Things Every Planner Knows ...

Every field of activity is based on *presuppositions*. It is important in reading this book, or any other planning document, to know the presuppositions of planners, to insist that they be articulated. Some of the presuppositions listed below may challenge accepted propositions. The aim is to improve the basis on which we do community planning.

1. To Make a Plan Is to Advocate a Position

A plan constitutes a combination of all the elements of land use in a workable relationship. If it is workable, it is defensible. It constitutes one position regarding how the urban pattern could work. Alternative plans constitute other preferred combinations. One should also ask, can a planner truly recommend more than one plan?

2. Planners Cannot Keep All Their Options Open

In the face of the uncertainties that abound in planning, it is tempting not to make a plan for the future. Some would contend that this allows them to deal with new events and conditions when they arise. This approach means, of course, that at least one major option—making a firm commitment to attain desired future conditions—has been foreclosed.

3. One Rezoning Does Not Lead to Wholesale Rezoning

By convention, rezoning is considered for one project at a time through variances or the recognition of changed conditions affecting viability of a project. Whether other landowners in the same zone will see it as a precedent depends upon their individual aims and available resources. In any case, a precedent only exists if the zoning authority wishes to treat the particular situation that way. If a plethora of other rezoning applications arise, the zoning regulations probably should be changed for all landowners.

4. Zoning is Necessary, but Not Sufficient for Development

Grandiose development schemes and a sense of urgency usually accompany (re)zoning applications. All too often, no construction follows a successful application. Since zoning confers development value on a property, this usually results in large potential profits being made merely by getting zoning approval. That may be as much the aim as actually building something and it is why many communities limit the time available to begin building.

5. Public Approval Processes Do Not Slow Down Development

Government regulations regarding subdivisions and zoning are an easy target for those desiring to expand development. However, studies have failed to confirm that such regulations have been the culprit, to any appreciable degree, in reducing the pace of development. The development process involves many actors, besides planners, who have the ability to slow a process, not least those providing financial backing. Development proponents usually know how long the approval process takes well beforehand.

6. A Shortage of Subdivided Land Does Not Cause the Price of Housing to Rise

The cost of housing is a function of location, cost of commuting, amenities, types of housing, and consumer preferences exercised in many geographic and social submarkets that have few substitutes. It is essentially behavioural. Subdivided land is a physical entity that will create yet another submarket, on the periphery, *if* it gets built upon. Subdivided land is to housing costs what a sperm bank is to the birth rate. They are different logical types, as Bateson would say.

7. The Home-to-Work Journey Seldom Exceeds 40 Minutes

For over a century, through changes in city size and modes of transportation, the vast majority of

CONTINUED

commuters have chosen not to travel more than 40 minutes to or from work. This self-imposed limit is achieved through personal adaptations to the urban environment such as changing residences and/or jobs, modifying working hours, and finding new routes and modes.

8. Things Have to Get Better Before They Get Worse

Hans Blumenfeld many years ago observed that traffic congestion in cities seldom improved for very long by adding more capacity. Cities are self-adjusting systems of land use, and those seeking access to them thereby generate a certain level of congestion. It won't worsen unless steps are taken to reduce it by adding more lanes to the freeway and/or improving public transit, which will make the land use more accessible and more in demand.

9. Rapid Transit Stations Do Not Cause High Density Nodes

Rapid transit stations are located at accessible junctions to serve existing activity centres and/or to link with surface transportation. These are usually traditional nodes that have reached a level of development commensurate with their locale. All a rapid transit line does is bring people to the junction more efficiently so that they may be dispersed more efficiently by bus or car to surrounding areas. Dreams of high-rise development around stations are just that. The political will has to be there, the zoning has to be in place, and the developers have to see the potential. Consider the surroundings of so many stations that never see much change at all.

10. Canadian Regions Will Never Have the Densities of New York and Paris

Toronto, Montréal, and Vancouver are not simply at a lesser "stage of development" than New York or Paris, such that they will eventually have the latters' densities of people and buildings. Population densities of cities and their Floor Space indexes are a product of the local, perhaps even national, cultural norms. In effect, city growth and density do not have a linear relationship over the long run; of course, planners may promote higher density to occur as with recent efforts of intensification.

---

personal beliefs and the standards they apply in their work. Throughout this book, the normative side of community planning has been highlighted, as have the notions of greater inclusiveness and empowerment of all citizens. Implicit in them are value-based choices of the authors that we, in turn, advocate to those involved in community planning, professional planners as well as others. More than this, these choices reflect aspects of planners' work that, increasingly, thrust the "value-laden nature" of the planning profession to the fore.[74] Central to tasks of planners is the distribution of community resources among different groups, and in this planners need to always assess whether their decisions are equitable, whether they foster fairness.[75]

These issues are intended as an invitation to Canadian planners to question their decisions, the directions of their organizations, the tools they use, and the plans they help make in light of the ethical dimensions they employ. For some the question will be the relationship between planning and politics,[76]

| Figure 18.9 | Categories of Knowledge Relevant to Planning |

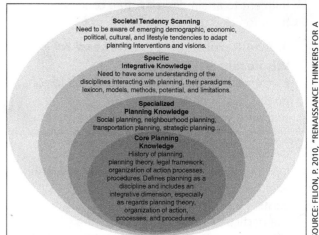

SOURCE: FILION, P. 2010, "RENAISSANCE THINKERS FOR A FRAGMENTED WORLD," PLAN CANADA 50 (3): 40 (FIGURE 1).

Planners cannot rely only on technically based professional knowledge; they must integrate knowledge from different fields.

while for others it will be the question of mediating between "big picture planning" and the "human dignity of individuals."[77] And these are only two ethical issues of many that surround planners' professional lives and invoke responses, knowingly or otherwise, within themselves as individuals acting from within their own belief systems. As Larry Beasley told fellow planners in 2004, "We must face ourselves and know ourselves because what we intend is often just as influential as what we do."[78]

Reflections: A Future of Challenges

Communities and planners face a very different set of conditions today than were encountered in the recent past and, moreover, there can be little doubt that even these conditions will continue to change. We have come to see many issues in their true complexity and have identified more clearly the competing choices, as is the case with the meta-problems of *sustainability* and *climate change*. The active discourse about *gender issues* serves to alert us that other groups and interests need to be included in planning theory *and* practice (see Chapter 13). And while the planning process in most communities tends to involve more people, in most it is still at the middle rung—consultation—of Arnstein's ladder of participation, and hence there is the consequent, and often valid, complaint that the process is not much more than "public nattering."[79] Add to these the globalization of the economy, fiscal constraints, and the rise of civil society, and there is no doubt that planners face a future of challenges. Not least will be the challenge to the ongoing practice of planning in terms of how planners see their role in an increasingly complex and dynamic world. A place to turn for guidance is the new comprehensive community planning being undertaken by our Aboriginal peoples. They are reclaiming not only their planning from established planners but also their own heritage; they are approaching the planning task with an eye on community and its integral connection with the land, to place.[80] The words of several Canadian planners may further help in conveying the shape of the planning task ahead, one that is bound to be ungainly at best:

Jill Grant:

The planner can never be comprehensive in [terms of] technical skills; but must be as comprehensive as possible in understanding the limitations of whatever [those] special skills may be, and of the consequences of [planning] advice when applied to urban problems.[81]

Larry Beasley:

Planners must show real leadership and not just be factotums for politicians or only do background studies. We must inspire, mentor and guide. We must tap interests—not just take positions. We must find solidarity with our citizens.[82]

Mark Seasons:

The big question is this: why do we perpetuate this pattern of land use, urban form, and building design in our cities and communities? If we know better, then why do we persist with this model?[83]

Jean Monteith:

This one thing is true, only solid consensus building results in a Vision and a Plan that the community will buy into and call their own ... only then does it work.[84]

Michael Dudley:

We cannot have absolute certainty about urban outcomes arising from our planning, especially since cities are not merely artifacts but the result of the collective behaviours thousands or millions of ... ultimately unpredictable—people.[85]

Rae Bridgman:

Bring public toilets back to the public agenda ... [they] represent society's aspirations about responsible "civil" behaviour.[86]

François Lapointe:

If Canadians are to continue to be successful as people and as a country, they must conjure up a *"projet de société"* that will enable them to chart a forward course in an increasingly urban world.[87]

In the end, planning will need to adapt itself further if it is to respond effectively to the issues of its second century—not just those described above, but those that are bound to arise as time continues to pass. For change is a "core concept of planning" and, at the very least, something planners need to anticipate.[88] Planners inhabit a milieu of change: there will be those changes they advocate along with those that come unbidden from new societal interests and structures. The essential challenge for planners is **to prepare ourselves to see opportunities for change both in what we know and in what may await us.**

Reference Notes

1. Roberta Brandes Gratz, "Jane Jacobs and the Power of Women Planners," Nov. 16, 2011, www.theatlanticcities.com
2. Ken Greenberg, *Walking Home: The Life and Lessons of a City Builder* (Toronto: Random House, 2011), 11.
3. John Forrester, "Know Your Organizations: Planning and the Reproduction of Social and Political Relations," *Plan Canada* 22:1 (March 1982), 3–13.
4. United Way of Greater Toronto, *Poverty by Postal Code: The Geography of Neighbourhood Poverty,* City of Toronto 1981–2001 (Toronto, 2004), 54.
5. Andrejs Skaburskis, "Gentrification and Toronto's Changing Household Characteristics and Income Distribution," *Journal of Planning Education and Research* 32:2 (2012), 191–203.
6. Jeanne M. Wolfe, "Canadian Housing Policy in the Nineties," *Housing Studies* 13:1 (1998), 121–133.
7. Wellesley Institute, *Precarious Housing in Canada 2010* (Toronto), 32. www.wellesleyinstitute.com/publication/new-report-precarious-housing-in-canada-2010/
8. Dick Ebersohn et al., "ImagineCalgary: A 100-Year Vision for Sustainability," *Plan Canada* 45:4 (Winter 2005), 35–37; and Kevin S. Hanna, "Planning For Sustainability: Experience in Two Contrasting Communities," *Journal for the American Planning Association* 71:1 (Winter 2005), 27–40.
9. City of Saskatoon, *Community Vision: Saskatoon Speaks*, Saskatoon, June 2011.
10. Judith E. Innes and David E. Booher, "Reframing Public Participation: Strategies for the 21st Century," *Planning Theory and Practice* 5:4 (December 2004), 419–436.
11. Eliahu Stern, Ori Gudes, and Tal Svoray, "Web-Based and Traditional Public Participation in Comprehensive Planning: A Comparative Study," *Environment and Planning B: Planning and Design* 36:6 (2009), 1067–1085.
12. Heather Campbell, "Talking the Same Words but Speaking Different Languages: The Need for Meaningful Dialogue," *Planning Theory and Practice* 4:4 (December 2003), 389–392.
13. Marta Doeler, "How to Communicate as a Planner," *Planning Theory and Practice* 3:3 (December 2002), 364–365.
14. Ben Bennett, "An Activist's Experience of the Planning Process," *Plan Canada* 43:3 (Jan–Mar. 2002), 14–16.
15. Maarten Wolsink, "Entanglement of Interests and Motives: Assumptions behind the MINBY-ism Theory on Facility Siting," *Urban Studies* 31:6 (1994), 851–866.
16. Robert Shipley, "The Sinister Implications of Language: The Difference between a Citizen and a Customer," *Plan Canada* 43:1 (Spring 2003) 28–30.
17. Innes and Booher, "Reframing Public Participation: Strategies."
18. Lynne C. Manzo and Douglas D. Perkins, "Finding Common Ground: The Importance of Place Attachment to Community Participation and Planning," *Journal of Planning Literature* 20:4 (May 2006), 335–350.
19. Gregory Richardson, *Adapting to Climate Change: An Introduction for Canadian* Municipalities (Ottawa, ON: Natural Resources Canada, 2010); and Reid Ewing et al., *Growing Cooler: The Evidence on Urban Development and Climate Change* (Washington, DC: Urban Land Institute, 2008).
20. "Declaration on Climate Change and Communities: A Call to Action," *Plan Canada* 50:4 (2010), 16.
21. Patrick Condon, *Seven Rules for Sustainable Communities: Design Strategies for the Post-Carbon World* (Washington, Covelo, London: Island Press, 2008); and Brent Gilmour, Jessica Webster, and Taylor Zeeg, "Planning the Energy Resilient Community," *Plan Canada* 50:4 (2010), 22–25.
22. Elisa Campbell and Jackie Teed, "Getting to Minus 80: Urban Form Strategies for Measurably Achieving Greenhouse Gas Emission Reduction Targets" *Plan Canada* 50:4 (2010),18–21.
23. Peter Calthorpe, *Urbanism in the Age of Climate Change* (Washington, DC: Island Press, 2011), Ch. 6; and Lawrence Frank, Michael Greenwald, Steve Winkelman, James Chapman, and Sarah Kavage, "Carbonless Footprints: Promoting Health and Climate Stabilization through Active Transportation," *Preventative Medicine* 50, Supplement (January 2010), S99–S105.
24. Shannon Hagerman, Hadi Dowlatabadi, Terre Satterfield, and Tim McDaniels, "Expert Views on Biodiversity Conservation in an Era of Climate Change," *Global Environmental Change* 20:1 (February 2010), 192–207.
25. Ellen Pond et al., "Climate Change and a Small Mountain Town: Visualizing a Rural Community's Climate Impacts, Adaptations and Mitigation: City Of Kimberley, KCAP and CALP," *Plan Canada* 50:4 (2010), 32–35; and Calthorpe, *Urbanism in the Age of Climate Change*, Ch. 4.
26. "Declaration on Climate Change," 17; Beate Bowron and Gary Davidson, "Ecological Footprint and Land Use Scenarios: Calgary, Alberta," *Climate Change Planning: Case Studies from Canadian Communities* (Ottawa: Canadian Institute of Planners, March 2012); Joe D'Abramo and Lawson Oates, "Toronto's Climate Change Initiatives: Overview, the Toronto Green Standard and The Green Roof Bylaw," *Plan Canada* 50:4 (2010), 29–31; and Patrick Condon, "Planning for Climate Change," *Land Lines* (Lincoln Institute of Land Policy, January 2008), 1–7.
27. Marni Cappe and David Brown, "Mainstreaming Climate Change Tools for Planners," *Journal of the Alberta Association of the Canadian Institute of Planners* (Winter 2009/2010), 5–7; and Beate Bowron and Gary Davidson, "Waterfront Toronto's Carbon Tool: Toronto, Ontario," *Climate Change Planning: Case Studies from Canadian Communities* (Ottawa: Canadian Institute of Planners, March 2012).
28. Gregory Richardson and Donald Lemmen, "Lessons Learned from Canadian Municipal Climate Change Adaptation Case Studies," *Plan Canada* 50:4 (2010), 26–28; Beate Bowron and Gary Davidson, "Planning for Climate Change Mitigation and Adaptation: Red Deer, Alberta"; "Climate Change Adaptation Strategy: Prince George, British Columbia"; and "Toronto Green Standard," *Climate Change Planning: Case Studies from Canadian Communities* (Ottawa: Canadian Institute of Planners, March 2012).
29. Beate Bowron and Gary Davidson, "Hot Weather Response Plan: Sudbury, Ontario"; "Interim Flood Construction Levels: Vancouver, British Columbia"; and "Gibsons Harbour Area Plan."
30. John Lindsay, "Planning For Equity in Disaster Recovery," *Plan Canada* 51:3 (2011),18–21; Eugenie Birch and Susan Wachter, *Rebuilding Urban Places after Disaster: Lessons from Katrina* (Philadelphia: University of Pennsylvania Press, 2006); and Lawrence Vale and Thomas Campanella, *The Resilient City: How Modern Cities Recover from Disaster* (New York: Oxford UP, 2004).
31. Pierre Filion, et al., "Intensification and Sprawl: Residential Density Trajectories in Canada's Largest Metropolitan Regions," *Urban Geography* 31:4 (2010), 541–569; and David Gordon and Mark Janzen, "Suburban Nation? Estimating the Size of Canada's Suburban Population," ACUPP/Canadian Association of Geographers conference, Calgary, 2011.
32. Laura Taylor, "Green Sprawl," *Plan Canada* 52:3 (2012),16–21; Gerda Wekerle, "Gender and the Neoliberal City: Urban Restructuring, Social Exclusion and Democratic Participation," in H. Hiller, ed., *Urban Sociology in Canada* (Toronto: Oxford University Press, 2009), 210–233; and Charles Raux and Martin Lee-Gosselin,

"Transport, Energy and Greenhouse Gases: Perspectives on Demand Limitation," *Energy Efficiency* 3:2 (2010), 111–113.

33. See John Sewell, *The Shape of the Suburbs: Understanding Toronto's Sprawl* (Toronto: University of Toronto Press, 2009) and *The Shape of the City: Toronto Struggles with Modern Planning* (Toronto: University of Toronto Press, 1993); and Pamela Blais, *Perverse Cities: Hidden Subsidies, Wonky Policy, and Urban Sprawl* (Vancouver, BC: UBC Press, 2010).

34. Robert Bruegmann, *Sprawl: A Compact History*, (Chicago: University of Chicago Press, 2005), 17.

35. Cf. Don Alexander et al., "The Challenges in Implementing a Smart Growth Agenda: The BC Sprawl Report 2004," *Plan Canada* 45:4 (Winter 2005), 23–26.

36. Larry S. Bourne, "The Urban Sprawl Debate: Myths, Realities and Hidden Agendas," *Plan Canada* 41:4 (Oct.–Dec. 2001), 26–28.

37. John Friedmann, "Urban Communes, Self-Management and the Reconstruction of the Local State," *Journal of Planning Education and Research,* 2:1 (Summer 1982), 37–53.

38. Andrejs Skaburskis and Dean Geros, "The Changing Suburb: Burnaby, BC Revisited," *Plan Canada* 37:2 (March 1997), 37–45.

39. Christopher Leinberger, *The Option of Urbanism: Investing in a New American Dream* (Washington, DC: Island Press, 2008).

40. Avi Friedman, *Planning the New Suburbia: Flexibility by Design* (Vancouver: UBC Press, 2001).

41. Genevieve Vachon, et al., "Retrofitting Quebec City's Postwar Suburbs: The Renovation and Densification of Rental Housing Developments," *Plan Canada* 46:1 (Spring 2006), 12–15.

42. David Hulchanski, *The Three Cities Within Toronto: Income Polarization among Toronto's Neighbourhoods, 1970–2005,* University of Toronto Cities Centre, December 2010.

43. Ellen Dunham-Jones and June Williamson, *Retrofitting Suburbia: Urban Design Solutions for Redesigning Suburbs* (New York: Wiley, 2011); Galina Tachieva, *The Sprawl Repair Manual* (Washington, DC: Island Press, 2010); and Patrick Condon, *Seven Rules for Sustainable Communities: Design Strategies for the Post-Carbon World* (Washington, DC: Island Press, 2008).

44. Alain Miguelez, "Infill in Mature Neighbourhoods: New Directions in Ottawa," *Plan Canada* 52:3 (2012), 29–31; and Stephen Davis, "Humber Valley Village Residents Furious over Development Proposal," *The Globe and Mail,* Oct. 19, 2012.

45. Philip R. Berke, "Does Sustainable Development Offer a New Direction for Planning? Challenges for the Twenty-First Century," *Journal of Planning Literature* 17:1 (August 2002), 21–36.

46. World Commission on Environment and Development, *Our Common Ground* (Oxford and New York: Oxford University Press, 1987), 8.

47. Scott Campbell, "Green Cities, Growing Cities, Just Cities? Urban Planning and the Contradictions of Sustainable Development," *Journal of the American Planning Association* 62:3 (Summer 1996), 296–312.

48. Interestingly, three similar pollution situations were reported during August 2001: Kerry Williamson, "Report Warns of 10-Year Cleanup," *Calgary Herald,* August 11, 2001; Bill Schiller, "Town Plagued by Fears over Arsenic," *Toronto Star,* August 26, 2001; and Tera Camus, "Sydney's Toxic Woes Widespread," *Halifax Herald,* August 6, 2001.

49. David R. Godschalk, "Land Use Planning Challenges: Coping with Conflicts in Visions of Sustainable Development and Livable Communities," *Journal of the American Planning Association* 70:1 (Winter 2004), 5–13.

50. Cf. Noel Keough, "Calgary's Citizen-Led Community Sustainability Indicators Project," *Plan Canada* 43:1 (Spring 2003), 36–36.

51. Karen Ramsey, "What is Sustainable Housing?" *Plan Canada* 42:4 (October–December 2002), 25–26.

52. Avi Friedman, *The Grow Home* (Montréal: McGill Queen's University Press, 2001); *Fundamentals of Sustainable Dwellings*, (Washington, DC: Island Press. 2012), Ch. 2.

53. Godschalk, "Land Use Planning Challenges"; and Canada Green Building Council, "LEED 2009 for Neighbourhood Development," www.cgbc.org

54. Robert B. Gibson, "Sustainability and the Greenbelt," *Plan Canada* 51:3 (Fall 2011), 38–40.

55. Leonie Sandercock, "A Portrait of Postmodern Planning: Anti-Hero and/or Passionate Pilgrim," *Plan Canada* 39:3 (May 1999), 12–15.

56. John Friedmann, "Globalization and the Emerging Culture of Planning, *Progress in Planning* 64 (2005), 183–234.

57. Leonie Sandercock, "Toward a Planning Imagination for the 21st Century," *Journal of the American Planning Association* 70:2 (Spring 2004), 133–141.

58. Elizabeth M. Rocha, "A Ladder of Empowerment," *Journal of Planning, Education and Research* 17 (1997), 31–44.

59. Michael and Julie Seelig, "CityPlan: Participation or Abdication?" *Plan Canada* 37:2 (May 1997), 18–22.

60. Earl Levin, "City Planning as Ideology and Practice," *Plan Canada* 51:2 (Summer 2011), 25–27.

61. Friedmann, "Globalization and the Emerging Culture of Planning."

62. Harvey S. Perloff, *Planning the Post-Industrial City* (Washington: American Planning Association,1980), 87.

63. City Of North Vancouver, *North Vancouver Official Community Plan,* 2011 http:// www.cnv.org/CityShaping/index.html

64. Jill Grant, "Planning for the Longer Term: Regulating for Resilience," *Plan Canada* 51:4 (Winter 2011), 23–25.

65. Gerald Hodge, *The Geography of Aging: Preparing Communities for the Seniors' Surge* (Montréal: McGill–Queens University Press, 2008), 170–178.

66. Mark Seasons, "Opinion Piece," *Plan Canada* 50:3 (Fall 2010), 56.

67. Jill Grant, "Planning for the Longer Term."

68. Andrejs Skaburskis and Michael B. Teitz, "Forecasts and Outcomes," *Planning Theory and Practice* 4:4 (December 2003), 429–442.

69. Karen S. Christensen, "Teaching Savvy," *Journal of Planning Education and Research* 12 (1993), 202–212.

70. Pierre Filion, "Renaissance Thinkers for a Fragmented World," *Plan Canada* 50:3 (Fall 2010), 40–43.

71. Karen Umemoto, "Walking in Another's Shoes: Epistemological Challenges in Participatory Planning, *Journal of Planning Education and Research* 21 (2001), 17–31.

72. Judith Innes, "Information in Communicative Planning," *Journal of the American Planning Association* 64:1 (Winter 1998), 52–63.

73. Jean Monteith, "What I Have Learned," *Plan Canada* 51:2 (Summer 2011), 46–47.

74. Sue Hendler, "It's the Right Thing To Do—Or Is It?" *Plan Canada* 42:2 (April–June 2002), 9–11. Many planning professional associations have adopted some form of a code of ethics. See, for example, the CIP Statement of Values and Code of Professional Practice, www.cip-icu.ca/English/members/practice.htm

75. Leela Viswanathan, "Integrated, Equitable, and Transformative: A Hopeful Future for Planning, Plan Canada 5:3 (2010), 33–35; Doug Aberley, "Telling Stories to the Future: Integrative Approaches to Planning," *Plan Canada* 40:1 (Dec.–Jan. 2000), 24–25.

76. Art Cowie, "Politics and Planning: Ten Lessons from an Old Campaigner," *Plan Canada* 43:3 (Autumn 2003), 18–20.

77. Gary Davidson, "Rummaging in the Compost," *Plan Canada* 39:3 (May 1999), 15–16.

78. Larry Beasley, "Moving Forward in Canadian Communities: Soliloquy of an Urbanist," *Plan Canada* 44:4 (Winter 2004), 16–19.

79. John Dakin, "Heading for New Minds," *Plan Canada* 34:2 (July 1994), 93–98.

80. Cf. Ryan Walker, Ted Jojola, and David Natcher, eds., *Reclaiming Indigenous Planning* (Montréal: McGill Queens University Press, forthcoming 2013).

81. Jill Grant, "Planning for the Longer Term."

82. Beasley, "Moving Forward."

83. Mark Seasons, "Opinion Piece."

84. Jean Monteith, "What I Have Learned."

85. Michael Dudley, "Planning Journals Between Orthodoxy and Contrarianism in Challenging Times," *Plan Canada* 52:3 (Fall 2012), 10–12.

86. Rae Bridgman, "Human Dignity on Main Street: Public Toilets," *Plan Canada* 50:1 (Spring 2010), 27–30.

87. François Lapointe, *Cities as Crucibles: Reflections on Canada's Urban Future* (Ottawa, ON: Invenire Press, 2011), xv.

88. Gary Davidson, "Rummaging in the Compost.

Appendix

Highlights of Canadian Community Planning, 1890–2008

Historically, the achievements in Canadian community planning fall into four distinct periods of development. There was, first, a *formative period* in which the perceived problems of cities were allied with planning solutions, and institutional arrangements began to be put in place to facilitate community planning. This period began in the final decade or two of the 19th century and lasted until 1930 in Canada. A second, the *transitional period*, spanning the years from 1930 to 1955, saw steps to build an infrastructure for community planning at the national, provincial, and local levels. The period from 1955 to 1985, the *modern period*, was an era of putting planning ideas into practice on a widespread basis, a period of experimentation and innovation, of trial and error, and, notably, of the acceptance of the approach of community planning. There are indications that community planning has, since the mid-1980s, moved into a new period that could be called the *postmodern period*. Many planning initiatives in this period are moving beyond single-problem formats and linking factors in broader based approaches, as with Healthy Communities, Smart Growth, and sustainable development.

The evolution of community planning in Canada may be seen in the sets of important events constituting each of the four periods shown in the following chronology, with plans that won the CIP's Vision in Planning Award marked.*

The Formative Period, 1890–1930
1896   Herbert Ames's study of Montréal slums.
1903   Frederick Todd's plan for a park system for Ottawa and Hull.
1904   City Beautiful plan for Prince Rupert, British Columbia.
1906   Toronto Civic Guild of Art prepares City Beautiful plan for city.
1908   Garden Suburb plans prepared for Shaughnessy Heights in Vancouver, Mount Royal in Calgary, etc.
1909   Commission of Conservation formed by the federal government.

1911   City Planning Commissions established in Winnipeg and Calgary.
1912   New Brunswick passes first provincial planning act.
1913   Alberta's Town Planning Act allows municipalities to acquire 5 percent of subdivisions for parks.
1914   Thomas Adams appointed Town Planning Advisor to Commission of Conservation.
1914   Sixth National City Planning Conference held in Toronto.
1914   *Conservation of Life* begins publication for seven years (Thomas Adams, ed.).
1915   Local planning boards required in Nova Scotia.
1915   Plan for National Capital area of Ottawa and Hull prepared by Edward Bennett.
1917   Thomas Adams submits plan for rebuilding the Richmond District in Halifax, which was devastated by a wartime explosion.
1917   Garden City plan prepared by Thomas Adams for new resource town (Temiskaming, Québec).
1919   Town Planning Institute of Canada founded with 117 members; publishes its own journal.
1921   Commission of Conservation disbanded.
1923   First zoning bylaw adopted for Kitchener and Waterloo; drafted by Thomas Adams and Horace Seymour.
1929   Harland Bartholomew and Horace Seymour's comprehensive plan for Vancouver.
1929   Provincial Planning Office established in Alberta; Horace Seymour first director.

The Transitional Period, 1930–1955
1935   Prairie Farm Rehabilitation Administration established.
1935   Housing Centre formed at University of Toronto by Humphrey Carver and Harry Cassidy.
1938   National Housing Act passed.
1939   National Housing Conference held in Toronto.
1943   Metropolitan Planning Commission for Greater Winnipeg formed; Eric Thrift is director.
1944   Report of the Advisory Committee on Reconstruction (the "Curtis Committee").

1945 Central (now Canada) Mortgage and Housing Corporation established.

1946 Founding of Community Planning Association of Canada; publishes *Community Planning Review* for the next 25 years.

1946 Ontario Planning and Development Act passed.

1947 McGill University establishes the first Canadian planning program.

1948 Regent Park North slum-clearance project built in Toronto.

1949 Lower Mainland Regional Planning Board formed; James Wilson is director.

1950 Jacques Gréber prepares plan for Ottawa capital region, featuring a greenbelt.*

1951 Plan made for Kitimat, B.C., by Clarence Stein, using the neighbourhood principle.

1951 University of Manitoba establishes first graduate planning degree.

1953 Metropolitan government instituted for the Toronto area and given wide planning powers; Murray Jones is director.

1954 Canada's first subway system opens along Toronto's Yonge Street.

The Modern Period, 1955–1985

1955 Macklin Hancock's plan for Don Mills "New Town" is implemented.

1959 National Capital Commission established to implement Gréber plan and acquire the greenbelt.

1961 "Resources for Tomorrow" Conference held in Montréal.

1961 Agricultural Rehabilitation and Development Act passed.

1964 National Housing Act, 1964, enunciates new housing and urban-renewal policies.

1964 Establishment of le Bureau d'aménagement de l'est du Québec for regional planning in the Gaspé.

1966 Trefann Court urban-renewal citizen protest begins in Toronto.

1966 Plan for the Future of Downtown Calgary.*

1967 Mactaquac Regional Development Plan unveiled in New Brunswick by Leonard Gertler's team.

1967 Habitat '67 model housing exhibit at Montréal's Expo '67, designed by Moshe Safdie.

1968 University of Waterloo establishes the first undergraduate planning program.

1970 Ontario government presents plan for 14 250-square kilometre Toronto-Centred Region.

1971 Spadina Expressway (Toronto) ordered stopped.

1972 Federal government organizes Ministry of State for Urban Affairs, based on recommendations by Prof. Harvey Lithwick in his report, *Urban Problems and Prospects*.

1973 B.C. Agricultural Land Commission established.

1974 Niagara Escarpment (Ontario) Plan initiated.

1975 Greater Vancouver Regional District unveils "Proposals for a Livable Region."*

1976 United Nations' Habitat Conference held in Vancouver.

1978 Québec moves to protect agricultural land with its Loi sur le protection du territoire agricole.

1978 In Toronto, plans for Harbourfront and new inner-city housing in the St. Lawrence precinct.

1978 In Vancouver, False Creek redevelopment, including Granville Island's unique industrial-commercial-artistic mix.

1978 Dartmouth, N.S., Municipal Development Plan.*

1979 Meewasin Valley Authority established to plan and develop 80 kilometres of river banks in the Saskatoon area.

1980 Revitalization plan begun for Market Square in Saint John.

1981 The Core Area Initiative to redevelop downtown Winnipeg agreed to by three levels of government.

1982 Light Rapid Transit systems built in Edmonton and Calgary.

The Postmodern Period, 1985 to the Present

1985 Niagara Escarpment Commission Plan.*

1986 Regional plan for Communauté urbaine de Québec adopted.

1987 Introduction of the City of Sudbury Strategic/Corporate Plan, encompassing physical, economic, human, and organizational development.

1987 The Forks renewal plan in Winnipeg.*

1988 Hans Blumenfeld dies in Toronto at age 96.

1988 Healthy Communities Initiative launched by Canadian Institute of Planners.

1989 Grand Concourse walkway network established in St. John's, Newfoundland.*

1990 Waterfront planning for the Toronto region by the Crombie Commission recommends a bioregional perspective.

1992 Montréal's first downtown plan is adopted.

1993 Highly participative planning process in the preparation of Vancouver's CityPlan and Calgary's GoPlan.

1993 Regional planning commissions are disbanded in Alberta.

1996 New Greenbelt Plan for Ottawa embraces ecosystems approach.

1996 City of Toronto modifies zoning regulations in two "reinvestment areas" to promote diversity and adaptation of uses.

1997 Municipal governments within Metropolitan Toronto amalgamate.

1998 Plan Edmonton breaks new ground in combining strategic and financial planning with physical land use planning.

1998 Town of Banff Community Plan.*

1999 The regional plan for Ottawa-Carleton links its growth-management policies to ecosystems needs for the region.

2000 New Urbanism concepts influence suburban plans from Langley, B.C. (Murray's Corner), Calgary (McKenzie Towne), Markham (Cornell), and Montréal (Bois Franc).

2001 The First Nations Community Planning Model is developed at Dalhousie University.

2002 The (newly amalgamated) City of Ottawa adopts the 2020 Plan, integrating land use, the natural environment, transportation, infrastructure, culture, economic development, and social plans.

2003 Toronto's Regent Park Revitalization Plan adopted after extensive community consultation.

2004 First Master Plan for the entire island of Montréal adopted.

2005 Dockside Green begins sustainable redevelopment of Victoria's inner harbour.

2005 Ontario Government implements a Greenbelt Plan for the area bounded by the Niagara Escarpment and Oak Ridges Moraine.

2006 Planning begins for the Environmental Research Pavilion, Flying Dust First Nation, Meadow Lake, Saskatchewan.

2006 Growth Plan for the Greater Golden Horseshoe.

2006 World Planning Congress and United Nations' World Urban Forum held in Vancouver.

2008 Québec Sustainable Development Strategy.*

Index

Note: Page references in bold type indicate an illustration